"Eve Shapiro, in this important book, has contribu
First, she has relayed the stories of 100 health profes
given us all a framework within which we can make sense of their stories. Second, she has engaged two powerful currents—burnout within healthcare and the worst public health challenge in a century—and has given us a reason for hope. This is a book all health professionals, as well as those in the public who care about their welfare, should read."

John R. Ball, MD, JD, MACP
Executive Vice President, Emeritus, American College of Physicians
Former Chair, Mission Health System, Asheville, NC

"In *Joy in Medicine?*, Eve Shapiro provides unique and valuable insights into understanding the challenge of clinician burnout. We will not fix the myriad problems in healthcare without a deep understanding of what contributes to both joy and burnout. Her in-depth interviews with clinicians provide insights that every healthcare leader needs to understand if they are serious about being part of the solution, rather than part of the problem."

Paul DeChant, MD, MBA
Author, Executive Coach, and Prior CEO, Sutter Gould Medical Foundation

"A growing body of research about the physician/caregiver experience identifies the causes, consequences, and remedies for physician burnout and the factors most highly related to physician joy and fulfillment. While this research is certainly informative, in my view, in *Joy in Medicine? What 100 Healthcare Professionals Have to Say about Job Satisfaction, Dissatisfaction, Burnout, and Joy*, Eve Shapiro's *narrative* approach, using firsthand interviews that illuminate real people in real settings, yields rich, *qualitative* information that has a much greater potential to impact physicians, teams, and organizations.

"Those she interviewed share their stories—about highs and lows in their careers, their frustrations and stresses, their joys and satisfaction—and they offer advice to others who seek fulfillment in the practice of medicine. Stories are like pollen. They engage and persuade. They move people to action. They spark conversations with ourselves and others. The stories shared in Eve's book have that power. Individuals and organizations can use this book to understand and support caregivers and to identify and pursue improvement initiatives in our quest to achieve human-centered care and a gratifying caregiver experience."

Wendy Leebov, Ed.D.
Author, Creator of Language of Caring
www.languageofcaring.org

"Eve's Shapiro's book, *Joy in Medicine?*, is a call to action to save lives: lives of patients and families, and lives of physicians, nurses, and all stakeholders inside (and outside) the traditional healthcare system. Eve interviews 100 men and women who work in the healthcare industry in our country today. She listens to understand, she reflects, and she shares their wisdom and insight (and her own) with the reader.

"*Joy in Medicine?* will teach healthcare leaders, people on the front lines of healthcare, patients and families, and communities what must be done to achieve betterment and bring joy back into medicine."

Thomas H. Dahlborg, MSHSM
President, Dahlborg Healthcare Leadership Group (DHLG)
Director Health Care, Global Listening Centre Board (India)

Joy in Medicine?

Joy in Medicine?

What 100 Healthcare Professionals Have to Say about Job Satisfaction, Dissatisfaction, Burnout, and Joy

Eve Shapiro

Foreword by Gene Lindsey, M.D.

11/2/2020

To Stacie

With my thanks,

Joz

Routledge
Taylor & Francis Group
A PRODUCTIVITY PRESS BOOK

First published 2021
by Routledge
600 Broken Sound Parkway #300, Boca Raton FL, 33487

and by Routledge
2 Park Square, Milton Park, Abingdon, Oxon OX14 4RN

Routledge is an imprint of the Taylor & Francis Group, an informa business

ISBN: 978-1-138-32825-9 (hbk)
ISBN: 978-0-367-61495-9 (pbk)
ISBN: 978-0-429-44875-1 (ebk)

Typeset in Palatino
by Newgen Publishing UK

*Courage is what it takes to stand up and speak; courage
is also what it takes to sit down and listen.*

Winston Churchill

To Lauren, Justin, Brooke, and Lily, the lights of my life.

In memory of my father, Daniel David Nelson,
who always told me to do what I love.

And to Howard, with love, for—literally—everything.

Contents

Foreword

By Gene Lindsey, M.D.

Eve Shapiro's *Joy in Medicine? What 100 Healthcare Professionals Have to Say about Job Satisfaction, Dissatisfaction, Burnout, and Joy* is a remarkable book that is inspiring and thought-provoking as it examines the material and spiritual forces that bear on the lives of those who work in healthcare. It is a "must read" for all of us who care about healthcare and the well-being of those who provide it. It is meant for you if you work in any area of healthcare, and its message is of interest to anyone who receives care.

No matter what place you occupy in the evolving hierarchy of healthcare, this book is for you. If your job entails managing other healthcare professionals, your board or CEO should require you to read this book. If you are the CEO or a senior manager in a system of care, you should read a few pages to orient yourself each time you venture out to speak to the people who look to you for leadership. If you are struggling and can't remember why you ever thought there was a role for you in healthcare, this book has the potential to be a balm for your soul. If you are not a healthcare professional, reading this book will give you an even greater appreciation for the challenges that are part of the world that can at times come between you, your care providers, and our system of care.

Eve tells us in the Preface, much like the Methods section of a paper in a peer-reviewed journal, how she conceived of and conducted this work. We see the long list of open-ended questions that opened the door to reflection, personal revelation, and sometimes to confession. It is clear from the presentation of her process that her intention was not to generate more statistically significant data to add to all the metrics that are easy to find on burnout and employee satisfaction/dissatisfaction, but rather to give us the many complex personal images that the data obscure by averaging out our identities and quantifying our feelings to fit into some graph that could be the basis for a policy or strategy.

As Eve's interviews underscore, the healthcare professionals who provide patient care deserve our collective interest in their humanity. Without some insight into who they are and the forces with which they struggle every day, we cannot fully appreciate the obstacles to providing the care we all want for ourselves and our families—and that can so easily compromise that care. As many of Eve's witnesses told her, providing care can become hard very early on in a career that began with high ideals and expectations of service.

We learn from their stories that organizations' preoccupation with finance and volume have forced more and more professionals, who once took pride in their clinical autonomy, to adopt the status of employees. We must counter by asking ourselves how we can take better care of the caregivers. Any circumstance that compromises their performance threatens us all.

After reading the thoughtful commentary and analysis in the Preface, Introduction, and the focused introductions of each of the four sections, I suggest you savor the story, or portrait, of one professional a day as a reminder of what is important. Eve has carefully crafted the testimony offered in each interview.

Every portrait needs an appropriate frame; it needs to be hung on the wall where it can catch the light that will draw your eye to the intricacies of the story the painter is trying to tell. I do not usually spend much time with prefaces and introductions. The Preface and Introduction to this book, however, serve to frame the portraits, containing information vital to our understanding and appreciation of the concerns expressed in the profiles that follow. When I first read the Introduction I felt that in this era of concern about "burnout" and professional satisfaction, her Introduction would make an excellent article for the "Perspectives" section of *The New England Journal of Medicine*.

I don't think it's disrespectful to say that I have come to think of Eve's profiles of healthcare professionals in much the same way as I've thought of the great AIDS quilt, created to memorialize individual lives of those lost in the protracted AIDS epidemic. Each panel of the quilt represented one person's unique story. Each of the 100 profiles in *Joy in Medicine?* tells one person's unique story, a portrait painted with the words of its subject.

I was delighted to tell my own story to Eve. Of the remaining 99 profiles, I know three of the individuals she interviewed. I can attest to how closely the words I read on the page match the words I have heard them say. That fact alone is remarkable and is a testimony to the respect and care given to each story. I believe that everyone wants to tell his or her story. It is human to want to be "known." We also are intensely curious about other people's stories. The stories of other lives reveal the paradox that although we are unique, we share many thoughts, concerns, challenges, disappointments, and small victories with people we have never met. As I read Eve's words, I found myself saying, "That's what I think, too." At other times I am reassured that the feelings of failure, fatigue, fear, and outrage that have made me ashamed of myself at painful times have also been experienced by many of the 99 professional siblings she introduces to me.

I received the draft of this book to review on March 20, 2020, at about the time when the government in this country started to take the COVID-19 pandemic seriously. We were less than a week into the isolation of social distancing, but it was already clear that medical professionals were going to be stressed far beyond anything they had ever imagined. We had been given a preview of what might lie ahead for us by events in China, Iran, and Italy. By March 20, many were sensing that we had crossed the threshold from a world we had known well, but would never live in again, and were standing for just a little while on the uncomfortable threshold of what we would soon call the "new normal."

Dr. Li Wenliang died of the virus on February 7, a little more than a month after he had tried to warn the world with a post on the Internet on December 30, 2019: "A new coronavirus infection has been confirmed and its type is being identified. Inform all family and relatives to be on guard."

By March 20, we had stories of medical personnel in Italy who had given their lives while providing care. Before I finished reading the manuscript and had begun to write this Foreword, we would read of the first death from the virus of an ER physician in America, Dr. Frank Gabrin, who died on March 31, 2020. Dr. Gabrin was an experienced emergency room physician who worked at East Orange General Hospital in New Jersey and Saint John's Episcopal Hospital in Queens. It was reported that because of a shortage of personal protective equipment (PPE), he had used the same mask for four days. Ironically, he had published a book in 2013 entitled *Back from Burnout: Seven Steps to Healing from Compassion Fatigue and Rediscovering (Y)our Heart of Care*. Soon the nightly news would contain reports of the daily 7:00 p.m. salute to care givers coming from doorways and windows of sequestered New Yorkers.

During the past seven weeks of continuing concern and suffering from the COVID-19 pandemic, as the number of lives lost climbs past 60,000 toward who knows what depressing number, I have found great solace in reading the testimonies that fill the pages of Eve's well written and superbly organized book. They are stories that demonstrate, without a doubt, that although we have had inadequate PPE, too few ventilators, and woefully inadequate testing, we have had an abundant supply of committed people like Dr. Gabrin and hundreds of thousands of other healthcare professionals and other essential public servants like first responders, bus drivers, and grocery store workers who have been prepared and willing to answer the call to serve their communities.

As I read Eve's book, I realized that the interviews she presents are proof positive that we have been blessed with people who are committed to service. The people who told her their stories between 2018 and 2019 would be the same people who would rise in 2020 to close the gap between the lack of preparedness of our government and the challenges of an enemy that we had never seen before.

While reading this book I found myself thinking about three other pieces of medical literature that drew similar feelings from deep down inside me. One is Francis Weld Peabody's famous 1927 paper and lecture "The Care of the Patient." Peabody wrote during a time of transition and tension between "the art" of individual care in the home and office and the increasingly science-based care offered in the hospital:

> Hospitals, like other institutions founded with the highest human ideals, are apt to deteriorate into dehumanized machines, and even the physician who has the patient's welfare most at heart finds that pressure of work forces him to give most of his attention to the critically sick and to those whose diseases are a menace to the public health...there then remains little time in which to cultivate more than a superficial personal contact with the patients. Moreover, the circumstances under which the physician sees the patient are not wholly favorable to the establishment of the intimate personal relationship that exists in private practice...

Peabody concludes with the famous last pronouncement that I hear echoing in the stories Eve gives us: "One of the essential qualities of the clinician is interest in humanity, for the secret of the care of the patient is in caring for the patient."

In the 93 years since Peabody offered us his wisdom, we learn through Eve's witnesses that the tensions he described between art and science, institutional concerns and those of individuals, financial preoccupations and the time needed to see the "whole patient," and the competing concerns of the mind and the soul, are still with us.

Eve's book also calls to mind what I learned from Robert Cole's 1993 book, *The Call of Service: A Witness to Idealism*. As a physician psychoanalyst, Cole presented many of the human responses to the personal sacrifices of caring for people and working in difficult environments, trying to achieve noble objectives that are often ignored or rejected by the status quo. Cole divided his fourth chapter, which he calls "Hazards," into five parts that match nicely with many of the themes that emerge from Eve's witnesses: "Weariness and Resignation," "Cynicism," "Arrogance, Anger, and Bitterness," "Despair," and "Depression ('Burnout')." In this chapter, Coles described the mood of a medical student he knew:

He was edging toward a fuller discussion of weariness, the resignation he sometimes felt as he stood at the nursing station and looked
down a long corridor at all those rooms full of people nearing the
end of their time on earth. He had once thought about all those
people being so grateful for even the smallest gestures, and hence he
was rewarded and even stimulated because he had so many chances
to make them more comfortable. They were glad to engage with
him, talk to him with warmth and appreciation. Now, it seemed, he
was noticing the cranky side of even those people who were usually
cheerful.

Finally, I realized that Eve's book was propelling me back to what I learned about the bidir-
ectional process of care that was driven home for me when my own analyst suggested that
I read Michael Balint's 1957 classic, *The Doctor, His Patient and The Illness.* I had sought help
because early in my practice I was struggling. It occurred to me that although I was in a
group practice, I felt alone and uncertain whether anyone was noticing my efforts, or, more
importantly, was aware of the mistakes I was sure I was making. Going from the intense
and interactive environment of the busy floors of a world-class academic medical center to
the relative isolation of an office was disorienting. Have you heard the description of the
usual group practice, "doctors doing their own thing while sharing a parking lot?"
   I longed for the opportunity to talk with colleagues about the management of the
patients I was seeing but was afraid of revealing my sense of inadequacy. Little did
I know that many of my colleagues were struggling with the same concerns. Fortunately,
my group practice did have a prototypical clinician support group, much like what has
evolved since the 1980s as Balint Groups. In these groups, doctors and nurses met over
sandwiches at noon on Thursdays to discuss our feelings associated with practice. Our
feelings often were an expression of our frustration with management or the loss of professional autonomy. I was heard, but I was also a "hearer." In the group we revealed who we
were and wanted to be in much the same manner as Eve's witnesses present themselves
in this book. That process satisfied our need to tell our own stories, enabling us to make it
through until things might begin to change. It did not occur to me in the moment of those
group encounters that we were calling out concerns and forming relationships that in time
would result in organizational transformation.
   It was clear that, like our patients, we wanted to be known. We wanted to be heard,
but we wanted to be heard by someone who cared enough to want to learn who we were.
Improvement began with wanting to be heard and was sustained by learning that our
problems, worries, and concerns were shared by others. I am certain that reading the testimonies in Eve's book will allow many isolated and disillusioned caregivers to realize
that their own story is unique, but the issues and feelings described are shared by many.
I hope, in time, that shared awareness will foster efforts to further improve the things that
frustrate us all and prevent us from always presenting our best selves to the people who
come to us for help.
   Eve's book offers us a chance to be "hearers," and as we read, we realize that the story
we are reading is also our story. Eve's book reproduces the feeling of that long-ago lunchtime "touchy-feely" group experience for me. That experience is now almost a half-century
behind me, lying halfway in time between Francis Peabody and Eve's book. As I read her
book I was reminded of how the positive expectations that called us to serve others run
into the mundane realities that on some days can defeat us—and that the best defense is to
avoid isolation from our colleagues who are trying to weather the same storm.

I met Eve when she co-authored *The Patient Centered Value System: Transforming Healthcare through Co-Design* with Dr. Anthony DiGioia in 2017. I have known and respected the work of Dr. DiGioia for many years. I was honored and delighted when Dr. DiGioia asked me to write the preface for that book. During that process, Eve and I recognized a "kinship" and continued to correspond after the book was published. She became a faithful reader, and frequent commenter, on the subjects I discussed on my blog, "Strategy Healthcare," where I have frequently written about professional satisfaction, the joys of practice, and burnout.

Along the way we discovered we were "related." We both held the late Dr. Jack Russell in our hearts as the most remarkable teacher we had encountered during our college and graduate school days. I took all of the English literature courses Dr. Russell taught at the University of South Carolina back in the mid-60s. Eve took Dr. Russell's courses at the University of Maryland some decades later. It has been great fun to compare our experiences and to realize that Dr. Russell's life demonstrated that one of the defining qualities of human excellence is the life-long, consistent pursuit of high standards with integrity.

In early 2018, I was delighted when Eve told me she had been inspired by a visit to the annual meeting of the Institute for Healthcare Improvement, where the focus was joy in work, to explore professional satisfaction or joy in medicine in her next book. After the focus on "burnout" that has been such a concern in every organization with which I have had contact, the idea of talking about joy, as much as or more than burnout, seemed like a novel idea to me. I was eager to see what she produced.

As her work evolved, I was a little surprised to hear that the people to whom she spoke were not complaining about burnout, per se. They had no shortage of concerns. They talked about all the things that are mentioned as etiologic factors in the discussion of burnout: the distortions to practice created by the electronic medical record, inadequate time with patients, poor organizational support, demands that negate work–life balance, fear in the workplace, oppressive managers, the widget counting of relative value units, and so forth. But those she interviewed also explained their coping mechanisms; the little moments of satisfaction that sustain them; the choices they've made; the relationships that keep them afloat; and how their careers have evolved in ways they may not have expected, but that have remained consistent with their core values.

Eve recognizes this surprise in her Introduction and raises the question of whether there was a "selection" problem in her interviews. I too was surprised when she told me what she was finding, but as I thought about it, I concluded from my own experience that burnout is not the opposite of joy in medicine, or, if you prefer "professional satisfaction." I remembered my confusion during my time in practice when I discovered that our organization had low rates of physician satisfaction; but when physicians were asked if they were looking to leave, their answer was "No." The rate of turnover in the practice, which was in the low single digits, confirmed that response.

Healthcare professionals can easily articulate what is wrong, and they can also persevere through great personal distress. Training in healthcare is a great process for selecting those who can set aside or delay their gratification for years and years. Eve's interviews confirm that we do have many organizational issues that decrease joy in medicine, but they also reveal a level of commitment that remains the preferred focus of the majority of professionals. This fact is good to remember—that strength can form the foundation of a better "new normal."

I consider Eve Shapiro to be a healthcare professional even though she has no MD, RN, or MPH after her name. She is a writer who focuses on healthcare and is driven to help present our challenges, and what we have learned, in a way that might contribute to the continuous improvement of care.

This jewel of a book—a source of insight, inspiration, and spiritual sustenance—is also a practical guide and reference for the values we should sustain as we move into this uncertain time. This book should motivate us to use all we have learned about the contributors to joy and satisfaction in the "old" world while engineering out the sources of dissatisfaction and burnout as we enter the new one. Healthcare needs all of our awareness and activism if we are to successfully meet the challenge of providing everyone the care that should be their entitlement. I hope this book will provide you some relief and insight as it demonstrates the human qualities upon which we will build a better future.

Preface

"Why are you writing a book about joy in work?" was the question most frequently asked by the healthcare professionals I interviewed for this book. The truth is, I was searching for my own joy after publication of a book in 2017 that took well over five years to write (it was *The Patient Centered Value System*, with co-author Anthony M. DiGioia, MD, published by Taylor & Francis). Its publication left me depressed. I didn't know what I was going to do to fill the void that inevitably follows such a long gestation. Because I have learned that my joy comes from writing books, I knew I had to write another one.

I have been writing about patient safety and patient-centered care for clinicians, as well as patients and families, since 2007. My particular interest had been what happens at the point of contact between patients and clinicians—whether in an office, an exam room, the emergency department, the surgical suite, or the bedside—but always from the patient's point of view.

When I attended the Institute for Healthcare Improvement Annual Forum in December 2017, my perspective pivoted to those on the other side of that "sacred inter-action," as many people interviewed for this book have called it. The theme of the Forum that year was joy in work. The questions and answers posed at that conference left me wondering, is joy in work possible? Is attaining joy in work as straightforward as some speakers made it sound? Was there a roadmap for organizations and clinicians to follow that would inevitably lead to joy? Is the path to joy top down or bottom up? I knew I had to explore the subject by talking to as many types of healthcare professionals as I could. In the words of journalist Pete Hamill, this is "knowledge you can get only from talking to ordinary people, one at a time."

I am grateful to the ordinary people who agreed to talk to me for this book between June 2018 and February 2019. They are primary care doctors, emergency room doctors, pediatricians, obstetricians and gynecologists, radiologists, and specialists; registered nurses, nurse practitioners, nursing directors, and nurse educators; CEOs, medical directors, pharmacy directors, nursing directors, quality managers, and the director of emergency and safety services for a municipality; physical therapists, psychologists, psychiatrists, social workers, and an integrative manual therapist who is better known for starting and spreading dental clinics in Nepal; physician assistants, medical assistants, office managers, emergency medical technicians (EMTs), technologists, and a woman who cleans an operating room; experts in the field of physician burnout; and others. I used an unscientific method for finding my subjects, who, for the most part, I found by word of mouth. They are friends, friends and colleagues of friends, and friends of relatives and their colleagues, with varying degrees of separation, all over the country.

These professionals have in common that they work in healthcare in some capacity: some work for the same hospitals or health systems. They have worked at their jobs for different lengths of time. Some are residents and some are retirees. Many were advised to go into healthcare by people who took an interest in their futures: parents, relatives, neighbors, bosses, and friends who recognized their talents and led them to what would become their life's work. They come from different ethnic backgrounds, are gay and straight, and work in urban, rural, and community settings in the North, South, East, West, Midwest, Southwest, and Puerto Rico. They serve diverse populations of insured, underinsured, and uninsured. They treat those who are wealthy, those who are employed, unemployed, and struggling. They serve the homeless, immigrants, and other vulnerable populations. A number treat the underserved not only domestically but globally. They deliver care in solo, large, and small group practices; hospitals; academic medical centers; federally qualified health centers; and large, small, and medium-sized integrated health systems.

These healthcare professionals shared their enthusiasm, joys, frustrations, disappointments, insights, advice, stories, fears, and pain in conversations lasting any-where from 30 minutes to more than three hours. They explained what it looks and feels like to work in healthcare today no matter who you are, where you work, or what your position is in the organizational hierarchy.

I intended to ask them all the same questions about joy in work (and lack thereof) in the space of a 45-minute telephone (mostly) and in-person (a few) interview. A few were hesitant and had to be coaxed to talk for 30 minutes. Others, given their first chance to talk about what they do and how they feel about it, talked nonstop for more than three hours. Most fell between these two extremes.

What follows are the questions I asked, with some exceptions. I soon realized that asking yes-no questions like, "Is your work environment fair to individuals and groups, regard-less of gender, ethnicity, or professional status?" received such quick "yes" answers—with a few notable exceptions--that eventually I stopped asking. When time was short, I had to choose which of my questions not to ask. When people anticipated my questions, I didn't have to ask them. I modified the questions when interviewing those in organizational lead-ership positions and those in group or solo practices as made sense to me.

- What is your degree and job title?
- Where do you work now, in what capacity? Where else have you worked?
- What does your job entail?
- How long have you done this work?
- When and why did you choose to go into healthcare? This particular area?
- What are your hours?
- How do you define joy in work?
- What diminishes joy in work for you?
- Do you ever feel overloaded by work?
- Do you feel you have control over your time, work environment or workload?
- When something goes wrong, what happens in your organization?
- Do you feel a tension between meeting patients' needs, your own needs, and the needs of your bosses and administrators?
- Is there a relationship between money and joy?
- Do you feel sufficiently rewarded by your administrators, bosses, and colleagues for your work (aside from money—recognition, gratitude, etc.)?
- Is there something the administration could do to enhance your joy in work?
- Do you think there is a connection or a disconnection between what you think of as problems and what the administration thinks?
- If you could change anything about your job (any number of things), what would it be?

- What advice do you have for your bosses? Colleagues?
- What else would you like me to know?
- Do you have any colleagues who might be willing to talk to me?

Was everyone completely honest in answering my questions? Whether the format is survey or interview, who can be sure? People tell you what they want you to know. But asking questions paves the way for more questions and for conversations, which was what most of these interviews turned out to be.

The answers to my questions and others that arose naturally in the course of our conversations are the focus of this book. These conversations reveal that joy in work means different things to different people. To some, joy is a spiritual experience. Joy can mean delivering a baby; forging a relationship with a patient; comforting patients and families; making patients well or better than they were; saving a life; teaching and mentoring students; simply having a patient say "thank you"; or living and working in alignment with their purpose, doing what they are meant to do. Some said joy is doing a job supported by colleagues, supervisors, and mentors—being part of a team. Others say that joy means being unaware of the passage of time; a sense of peace; of taking satisfaction in doing one's best; and, as one operating room nurse told me, being dog-tired with swollen feet at the end of the day. One surgeon says his definition of joy has changed over the arc of his career, from the time he was just starting out, to the time he was laser-focused on building a practice and a reputation, to today, when he is a grandfather and retirement is on the horizon.

It is clear from talking to these dedicated professionals that joy often emanates from within. Their abiding joy is sustained by their love of their chosen field and whatever drew them to healthcare in the first place. Those who treat the underserved domestically and globally exude a particular type of joy—their idealism, their deep commitment to connecting with and treating the most vulnerable among us, has particular resonance today. Some talk about their work with enthusiasm and effervescence; others with earnestness, focus, and commitment. Many say their tenacity and resilience are essential for overcoming inevitable obstacles, frustrations, setbacks, and failures. For these people, the glass is always half full, regardless of transitory circumstances.

Yet, the workplace can either promote, diminish, or destroy joy for even the most positive people. For those I interviewed, when joy is diminished or destroyed it is *always* diminished or destroyed from the outside. For the many nurses, social workers, physical therapists, technologists, and others low on the organizational totem pole, the proverbial "pebbles in your shoes"—a phrase that implies relatively circumscribed problems that can be easily fixed if only they can be identified, such as cumbersome electronic medical records, slow computers, or not having needed supplies within easy reach—are not what diminish or destroy joy in work for those I talked to. What diminishes or destroys joy in work for these healthcare professionals, as these interviews reveal, are entrenched organizational problems that go much, much deeper and are much harder to identify, admit, and resolve: problems like blame, pressure, denial, disrespect, understaffing, and—always—lack of time.

Even when one loves one's profession, joy can be eroded by the stressful nature of the work itself; pressure by leaders and managers who fail to listen and who put "relative value units" over clinicians' time with patients; by the lack of autonomy and control over one's schedule, one's time, and one's tasks; the expectations and demands of payers; lawsuits and the fear of lawsuits; fear of being fired for speaking one's mind; disillusionment when speaking one's mind leads nowhere; disrespect from administrators and co-workers; and the moral and emotional distress that results when one's values conflict with those of the organization. Nevertheless—and heroically—many of those who shared their stories explained how they manage, often struggle, to find joy when and where they can, and they keep going. Dissatisfaction is common. Burnout is rare among those I talked to, although the fear of burnout seems ever-present for many.

I was surprised to find few burned-out doctors and nurses. Why so few? Where were all the burned-out physicians that others have written about? One retired, burned-out physician, who contacted *me* to talk, described being burned out as walking dead--her own take on the Maslach Burnout Inventory. One nurse told me she became so burned out that she left a hospital job she'd always wanted for home healthcare after only four years. A volunteer EMT described the burnout of a colleague as being equivalent to post-traumatic stress disorder. This man's emotional state was so fragile that the EMT was unwilling to ask him to talk to me. Those who *were* willing to talk about joy in work or the lack thereof seemed, for the most part, not burned out—in essence, a self-selected group.

None of the interviews in this book was rehearsed, and only a few people asked to see the interview questions beforehand. I sent each person a copy of their interview for review and approval to be sure I'd represented their thoughts accurately. In some cases, interviewees edited their interviews to clarify points they'd made, to add context, to exclude statements they later thought better of—particularly those expressing anger, frustration, and other negative emotions about their workplaces—and to include ideas that didn't occur to them when we first talked. I have tried to capture their voices and personalities as much as possible, following the technique used by journalist Studs Terkel in *Working: What People Do All Day and How They Feel about What They Do*. And like journalists Pete Hammill and Jimmy Breslin, I have always thought the most compelling stories are those people tell themselves, in their own words.

I did not reach out to groups whose mission is to help physicians cope with burnout. Other books and many articles have focused on burnout admirably. I did talk to three experts on burnout whose interviews comprise the final section of this book. Their perspectives affirmed my decision to focus on joy and helped me to understand why I didn't find burnout where I'd expected to. These experts' experiences align with what healthcare professionals themselves told me about what promotes, diminishes, and destroys joy in work.

Maintaining anonymity was a primary concern for most of those I interviewed, and some edited their interviews so they would be even less identifiable. Three women, feeling unable to disguise themselves adequately, decided to withdraw. Even in a book focusing on joy in work, healthcare professionals' stated sense of vulnerability and fear of retaliation by their organizations when they admit problems runs like an invisible undercurrent just below the surface of many of these interviews. The liberal use of pseudonyms and some highly disguised identities shows how deeply this fear runs. In terms of their most negative workplace experiences, a handful of these interviews are a shadow of what these healthcare professionals told me over the phone. I interpret their fear to be a commentary on their organizations and the healthcare industry itself, which I find both sad and disturbing.

My goal in writing this book was to learn what a wide range of healthcare professionals, each of whom is vital to patient safety and the efficient running of any healthcare organization, have to say about joy in work. But while organizing and editing these interviews, I realized this book had taken on a life of its own to become something more: each of these stories represents a tiny mosaic; and when these mosaics are put together, a picture emerges of what healthcare delivery looks like in this country to many of the people who deliver it, from the top of the healthcare hierarchy to the bottom. The picture is not always pretty. The few people who decided to withdraw their stories, and the many who had second thoughts about publishing their most negative reactions, showed me that fear and intimidation are real, though silent, partners in the healthcare landscape. So, was everyone completely honest in answering my questions? In the immortal words of Oscar Wilde, "The truth is rarely pure and never simple."

Finally, I finished writing this book when the COVID-19 pandemic was just beginning to sink its teeth into the people of this country, as it continues to do here and in other parts of the world. How long this scourge will last and how many people will die no one knows, although as of this writing 70,000 people in the U.S. reportedly have died; the actual number of deaths is surely much higher. During the weeks my manuscript was being reviewed in March and April, my friend Gene Lindsey, MD, was consumed in writing about the pandemic from multiple angles in his *Strategy Healthcare* newsletters (strategyhealthcare.com). In his newsletter of April 3, 2020, I responded with a paragraph that seems like the most fitting way to introduce this book and the ethos behind it:

> "In all the sadness, grief, fear, and anxiety we are feeling in this moment, I hope we will always remember the heroism of the doctors, nurses, and others who risk their own health and lives every day to take care of us, especially in the face of their own exhaustion, anxiety, and fear. This is who they are and what they feel called to do. They are brave. When we think of this pandemic in years to come, may their caring and courage be what we remember most."

E.S.
Bethesda, Maryland
May 2020

Acknowledgments

This book was built on relationships and networking. It took a village. Thanks to all those who took the time to talk to me and who connected me to friends and associates, past and present, across the country. Your help and generosity made this book possible. You know who you are. I am grateful.

Thanks to John Ball, MD, Charles Kenney, and my husband, Howard Shapiro, for opening doors and introducing me to inspiring and thoughtful healthcare leaders. Thanks to Lauren Di Renzo, Elizabeth Bernstein, Douglas Shapiro, Louis Chrostowski, Zachary Kazzaz, and Raphael B. for putting me in touch with dedicated and thought-provoking social workers, psychologists, nurses, physicians, and emergency management personnel.

Thanks to Paul DeChant, MD, Beth Lown, MD, Allan Frankel, MD, and Bridget Duffy, MD, for helping me understand burnout and keep my focus on joy.

Thank you, Gene Lindsey, MD, and Don Berwick, MD, for validating the idea for this book and for encouraging me to write it when my hunch about its importance was punctuated by doubt. You are my heroes. Thank you, Gene, for reviewing the manuscript.

Finally, thank you to copyeditor Jane Moody, production editor Todd Perry, and to my editor at Taylor & Francis, Kristine Mednansky, for supporting the idea for this book, for encouraging me, and for giving me joy-promoting autonomy and control along this fascinating journey.

About the Author

A medical writer since 2007, **Eve Shapiro** has focused her writing on patient-centered care, patient safety, systems improvement, physician–patient communication, medical errors, medical ethics, and other subjects for audiences ranging from researchers to clinicians to patients and families. She has written for the Agency for Healthcare Research and Quality, the Institute for Healthcare Improvement, The Joint Commission, the Robert Wood Johnson Foundation, the University of Pittsburgh Medical Center, Consumers Advancing Patient Safety, and other organizations. In 2017, Eve co-authored, with Anthony M. DiGioia, MD, *The Patient Centered Value System: Transforming Healthcare through Co-Design* (Taylor & Francis, publisher). Eve is keenly interested in relationships within healthcare, and the stories people tell about themselves and their experiences, whether they are on the "sharp" or the "blunt" end of care. www.eveshapiromedicalwriter.com

Introduction

This book is about what promotes, diminishes, and destroys joy in work for 100 men and women who work in the healthcare industry in our country today. Most of the dedicated men and women who told me their stories did so on condition of anonymity either for fear of losing their jobs or otherwise being retaliated against, to protect their privacy, to protect their institutions, or to protect their colleagues. Those who wished to remain anonymous did not want their institutions to be identified or hinted at: most did not want to be identified by city or even by region of the country. I have respected their wishes to remain anonymous so I could learn about their experiences and perspectives and to share them with others. Most, although not all, of those who agreed to be identified were men—and these men tended to cluster at the top of the healthcare organizational ladder.

I make no claim about the generalizability of these interviews to anyone not represented here. In essence, this book is a snapshot: a picture of the way these people felt about their careers and their workplaces on a particular day in 2018 or 2019. Some were preparing to leave their jobs and move on to others, or to retire, at the time of our interview; one man, who loved his job, died during the writing of this book. My conversations with 100 people who work in different areas of healthcare in multiple settings in different parts of the country revealed common themes about what promotes, what diminishes, and what destroys joy in work. The first three sections of this book are organized around these themes. The final section, focusing on what experts have to say about what promotes and diminishes joy in work, aligns with the perspectives of the healthcare professionals I interviewed.

For the healthcare professionals who shared their experiences and perspectives, it seems that where one stands on the subject of joy in work depends, in part, on where one sits in an organization's hierarchy. For those working for the same institutions, physicians—who are accorded the greatest degree of respect in their organizations and who tend to have the greatest degree of autonomy and control over their days despite the demands for documentation—expressed more joy than nurses, technologists, social workers, or residents.

Those on the lower rungs of the organizational ladder describe three types of leaders—CEOs, medical directors, and nursing directors—who influence their joy in work, for better or worse: 1) those who communicate clearly, completely, and regularly with staff to listen to their concerns, understand their problems, and collaborate in trying to solve them; 2) those who attend grand rounds and hold annual meetings, appearing to listen to problems staff raises, yet, nothing changes; and 3) those who do not communicate with staff, blame them for the problems they raise, and in effect, silence them, sending the unmistakable—and sometimes explicit—message, "If you don't like it, you can leave."

The leaders who fall into the first category meet regularly with staff in monthly town-hall style meetings, often come to the floors and offices where care is delivered, are still involved in delivering care themselves, listen to what staff at all levels have to say, and work with them—as well as empower them—to make needed changes. Physicians and nurses at one such organization describe their CEO as "our lighthouse" and "our north star." A once burned-out physician in a different part of the country recalls a medical director coming to his office and asking the startling question, "Are you happy?" The changes that medical director set in motion after getting the honest answer quickly transformed that physician's burnout to sustained joy in practice. I interviewed ten leaders who fall into this category. They are deeply dedicated to creating and sustaining optimal conditions for clinicians to work and to learn, and for patients to receive care. They are as concerned with their organizations' culture of safety and safety practices as they are with financial solvency and the bottom line, and they have found a way to promote both.

Many professionals in different parts of the country working in different sized and types of organizations say their leaders fall into the second category. They describe a virtual chasm between leadership and staff. Such leaders rarely, if ever, come to the floors where clinical care is delivered. They don't deliver care themselves, and many—if not most—have business rather than clinical degrees. They don't ask those with "boots on the ground" to attend meetings or serve on committees where decisions are made that affect the care they deliver every day. Isolation—leading from on high—needs to give way to interaction and communication, they say, but are pessimistic that this will change. Why change, after all? Such leaders, I'm told, know that healthcare professionals' love of their work, concern for their colleagues and patients, good salaries and benefits, and vestment in retirement plans will keep them in their jobs regardless of their daily dissatisfaction, making the need for change a matter of little urgency. Too many healthcare professionals say they feel undervalued, disrespected, and overloaded, tied to their jobs by "golden handcuffs."

Those who told me their leaders fall into the third category have felt angry, powerless, exhausted, abused, and disrespected. Some left their organizations for positions elsewhere or planned to leave shortly after these interviews; others looked forward to retiring. At more than one large institution, veteran nurses say that newly hired, newly trained nurses tend to stay for a year or two, then move on. An operating room nurse in one hospital says new nurses on her unit are leaving at rates as high as 70% a year. Although some leave for personal reasons, nurses say many leave because their organizations are understaffed, the nurse : patient ratio is dangerously low, the culture is demoralizing, and patient safety and, sometimes, their licenses are at risk.

While professionals all over the country say the emotional costs to staff do not seem to prompt change in their organizations' cultures, neither does the cost of turnover. According to the 2020 *National Health Care Retention & RN Staffing Report* by Nursing Solutions, Inc., "The average cost of turnover for a bedside registered nurse is $44,000, resulting in the average hospital losing $3.6–6.1 million" when nurses walk out the door. Yet, nurses have said not even concerns about losing money have led to needed change.

As a dermatologist working in an integrated health system once told me, "I love my work, but I hate my job." This sentiment was echoed by many people intent on salvaging some joy and meaning from their day even when they have to fight multiple forces to do it. Some dig deep to find joy in caring for patients but clearly struggle to recognize it in the face of stress, fatigue, being treated with disrespect, or spending late nights with the electronic medical record (EMR). Too many say they love what they do in spite of—not because of—their workplace, their supervisors, or their leaders. They worry that dissatisfaction, if left unaddressed, will eventually lead to burnout.

What, then, promotes and sustains joy in work? Apart from enlightened and visionary leadership, the answer seems to stem from one's internal characteristics—enthusiasm, tenacity, resilience, passion for one's chosen profession, and the feeling that one is doing exactly what one is meant to do—combined with some fortuitous external characteristics, such as living and working in alignment with one's core values; having autonomy and control over one's day; working in multiple roles, especially when one of these is teaching or mentoring; having supportive bosses and colleagues; and insistence on finding work–life balance. Those who treat the underserved domestically and globally talk about the joy of helping the most vulnerable among us and, in so doing, reconnecting with their own higher purpose.

What diminishes joy in work, these professionals say, is pressure, stress, and fatigue brought on by the nature of the work itself combined with the ever-increasing volume of work; the complexity of illnesses, an increase in comorbidity, and the need to keep up with exploding information; the pressure to be both accurate and fast; an organizational culture in which there is little open, two-way communication between leaders and clinicians, and a culture that excludes rather than includes front-line staff in evaluating and solving problems; administrators whose primary concern for the organization's bottom line comes before their concern for patients; lawsuits; and the disrespectful treatment of doctors by administrators, of nurses by doctors, and sometimes of emergency medical technicians by nurses in an industry known for its hierarchical culture—one in which bad behavior by those who bring in the most money is tolerated while the collateral damage they inflict on other professionals is too often ignored.

What destroys joy in work? Older physicians say it is the EMR that eats their time and has erased the autonomy and control they once felt in practice. They have been expected to transition from concise hand-written notes in a paper chart to clicking box after irrelevant box on computers they were never trained to use. Many find the EMR so onerous that they either don't use it and pay a penalty, feel emotionally and physically depleted by the end of the day, or retire. Several older doctors whose organizations have invested in the latest-generation of EMR software—especially those with voice recognition—say this technology saves time and has reduced their burden.

Younger physicians and nurse practitioners who have good computer skills and have come of age using the EMR accept this tool as a given part of practice. One young physician chafed at his hospital's use of paper charts *and* the EMR, believing all records and communications should be electronic only; older physicians, in his opinion, are holding them back. Another told me she loves the EMR because it gives her confidence that the next physician who sees her patients will have complete and accurate information. A third praises the EMR because it helps her to stay organized. Yet, for many physicians regardless of age, the burden of the EMR increases as the number of patients they are required to see each day grows. "Pajama time" is common and can make work–life balance virtually impossible.

Moral distress, clinicians of all kinds say, never fails to destroy joy in work. Moral distress results from the collision of one's personal, deeply held, core values with the organization's demands and expectations. Alignment of professionals' values with those of the organization contributes to joy; non-alignment inevitably destroys it. When the tension between what one believes and what one is expected to do becomes untenable, clinicians leave. If they don't, they burn out.

People often report a mixture of emotions where their jobs are concerned. Many people, for example, work hard to find meaning, if not joy, in their day and try not to be ground down by their dysfunctional environments, although many are. This book is divided into three major sections, but most of these interviews could easily have fit into more than one category. There is certainly overlap, with multiple themes addressed by almost everyone. What I perceived to be the strongest themes guided me in placing the interviews where they are. (The fourth section, much briefer, focuses on the perspectives of three experts in the field of physician burnout.)

I hope these interviews will help healthcare professionals of all kinds to acknowledge and respect each other, and to see that they are more alike than different when it comes to what promotes, diminishes, and destroys joy in work—regardless of age, gender, ethnicity, degree, or their place in the organizations' hierarchy. I hope these interviews will prompt leaders to rethink their values, communications, expectations, and actions; increase appreciation for those in healthcare who tend to be undervalued and invisible; listen to and collaborate with staff to make changes that will help to increase their joy in work; and continue to inspire the search for improvement among healthcare leaders across the country.

Eve Shapiro
Bethesda, Maryland
May 2020

part 1

What Promotes Joy

Taking care of others, helping others, ultimately is the way to discover your own joy...

The Dalai Lama

Introduction to Part 1

In this section you will meet people who express joy, satisfaction, and a deep sense of purpose and meaning in their roles as healthcare professionals. Simply put, these people exude thoughtful enthusiasm for their work. They are nurses, doctors, social workers, educators, psychologists, organizational leaders, an office manager, and a music therapist. They like talking to people and developing relationships with them. They respect their patients, their colleagues, and they cherish their roles because they are able to do what they most love: to help others. They are grateful to have found professions and organizations that enable them to use their varied skills in ways that are aligned with their own values.

Some took direct routes into professions they knew would be theirs from childhood, others took long and winding roads, and still others found themselves plunged into circumstances that led them to "aha!" moments when, suddenly, they knew, beyond all doubt, that this was what they were meant to do. Many of these people seem hard-wired for joy. Their glass is always half full. And they are strong, tenacious, and resilient in the face of forces that, sometimes daily, challenge their emotional and psychological well-being. If they feel joy in work it is sometimes despite, not because of, their leaders, their organizational cultures, their colleagues, or their circumstances—a tribute to just how deep their love of and commitment to their ideals and their professions run.

Several themes about what promotes joy in work emerged during the course of my interviews for this book. The first of these is passion: passion for the work, passion for leadership, and passion for treating the underserved globally and domestically. The other themes about what promotes joy in work, regardless of one's professional status or affiliation, are autonomy and control; working in multiple roles; being part of a team; and finding work–life balance. When I realized I was hearing completely different yet remarkably similar stories and perspective over and over, regardless of who and how many people I talked to, I knew these categories would be the themes around which this section, What Promotes Joy, would be organized. I am privileged to present their stories to you now.

Passion for the Work

1.   Sebastian P., MD, Primary Care Physician and Instructor of Medicine

> Sebastian P. is a comprehensivist—a primary care physician and a hospitalist. He works in the same urban, academic hospital where he did his residency and was chief resident 22 years ago, and he works in the same primary care practice. Sebastian spends his time taking care of patients, teaching and mentoring residents, and, as he says, "thinking a lot about wellness."

I remember growing up as a young adult thinking, *I want to be a Marcus Welby.* Not necessarily a country doctor but just like one. *I want to go to people's houses and know how they live.* I like that role and it's lovely to be able to do that now. I don't exactly work in the country, but what I do isn't far off in terms of the kind of relationships I've established: I go to people's houses and hold their hands as they die. It's an amazing privilege.

I'm moved and fueled and energized by helping people feel better and lead fuller, richer, more thoughtful lives with the bodies they've got. I like the detective work involved in finding out why people aren't feeling well and figuring out how to make them feel better. If I couldn't have been a doctor, I might have been a travel agent (seriously).

I'm a salaried employee of the hospital. My clinic looks like a private practice but of the six doctors, five are salaried and one is private. This hybrid model allows us to hire and fire our own staff and gives us some autonomy. I spend 70% of my time treating adults 18–102 and 30% of my time training residents and teaching.

My spouse and I share responsibility for our kids about 50–50, but I'm the primary parent. I shifted my hours when the kids came to make sure my schedule would be more in sync with theirs. I round at the hospital at 6:30 a.m. and take care of my patients. Then I go back home, make three breakfasts and pack three lunches for my three kids, and get them ready for school. Then I'm in my office. I pick my kids up from school when they're done on Mondays, then I'm a dad. That's why Monday is always a half day.

I work three and a half days in the office: Mondays from 9:00 a.m. to 12:30 p.m. are patient-booked hours. On Tuesdays I have a full day of work, starting at 8:00 a.m. and going all the way through, with no lunch break, so I can leave at 2:00 p.m. to pick up my kids from school. Wednesdays and Fridays are my full, long days. I round early in the morning on patients in the hospital and I see patients in the office from 9:00 a.m. until 5:30 or 6:00 p.m. Thursday is the day I teach. I chair the advisory system for the residency program, teach in the primary care center of a hospital, precept the residents, and run a wellness program for the residents. I think a lot about wellness.

I'm in the middle of my career. I've paid my dues and now I have some control over my time. I pushed hard to create flexibility in my schedule, so my work hours are more in sync with my kids' school schedule. To figure out how to structure my time in the office I had to ask, first, whether such a schedule would be consistent with patients wanting to be seen very early in the morning or during their lunch hour and, second, what kinds of support systems I would need—and whether my medical assistant and secretary would be willing to work those hours, too. It turns out they were thrilled to work early and end earlier on Mondays and Tuesdays.

On Joy in Work

I definitely feel joy in work. I think you find joy in work when a moderate amount of work makes you feel good about yourself and about the difference you make—and that you want to do more of it. That doesn't mean you feel like you're on vacation the whole time or that every moment is happy. It just means that, overall, at the end of most days, you feel deeply positive about the work you've done and that you've made a difference.

I think people often feel, *that was such a cool diagnosis, I just nailed it.* Or, *this is such a complicated case and I did really well.* But for the most part, what's important to me is the sense that people appreciate the time I've put in, or that I've made a difference in their lives, or that I've made them feel understood.

I do a lot of end-of-life care. When somebody dies, one of the most moving experiences is to hear the family say, "thank you so much." At the beginning of my career I would respond, "Why are you thanking me? Your dad died." Or, "Your mom died." But obviously there are moving experiences all along that journey and I think those experiences fuel me. I feel engaged and energized when I know I'm making a difference.

When a young person dies, if it's a young parent, it is so tragic. I've had two patients within the last year and a half commit suicide, and it was devastating. But even in such hard times, knowing that I have the capacity to feel so deeply and be so engaged is a good thing. Some people spend their whole lives desperate for a relationship. I have a relationship with people every 15 minutes.

I'm married to a physician. We're a two-doctor household. My husband is a psychiatrist who is also deeply engaged in his work. I think he has a stronger drive to advance professionally than I do. In addition to patient hours he teaches and is a dean for educational programs, is involved in curriculum development, and so on. On top of everything else he has evening meetings and events. I don't have that in my makeup. I do a lot of primary care and teaching and curriculum development—and I've been eligible to be an assistant professor for the last ten years—but I just don't feel the need to climb through the ranks. It won't get me more money, it won't get me much more of anything, frankly. I'm doing exactly what I love to do, and I feel glad about it.

Promoting Joy: Wellness Programs for Residents

According to the literature on wellness in training programs published within the last three to four years, interns should have one day every two months or so to go to their dentist, see their doctor, get a physical, make sure they're honoring their bodies' need for sleep and restoration, that their nutrition is appropriate, and that their sleep patterns are compatible with humanity. There's a lot being written about the need to make these requirements acceptable so they become the norm: "Well, of course you need those! Why wouldn't you have that?" But that's not the way it is right now. If you have healthy 26-year-olds I guarantee they haven't seen a provider for a few years. They just don't. There's no space. There's no time.

I champion a wellness program to ensure that residents are not only learning medicine and how to take care of people but learning how to take care of themselves so they can do their best work. This wellness program includes organizing social activities for residents. For example, I founded a corporate rowing league; in the summer, the residents are out on the water and they train one evening a week for six or seven weeks. It's a wonderful time for residents to bond with each other and to be part of a team. There are lots of really good endorphins there! Our hospital competes with other companies and training programs. In the middle of winter, I organize a rock-climbing activity for residents. I also run a humanism program, taking the residents to the art museum every other month, which is fantastic.

I've also looked into how to offer confidential, non-insurance-based access to mental health treatment for residents. I've received funding for a program in which residents can access mental health services confidentially, without the knowledge of leadership. If residents feel overwhelmed, or if they're having personal or marital problems and really need to talk, they should be able to talk to someone who isn't responsible for grading or evaluating them. We fund three visits. After that, if they need more, whoever sees them helps them to use their insurance to find a provider for more extended treatment.

Maintaining Joy: Mindfulness

Mindfulness is helpful to me. For example, I have one work partner who whines a lot and he can easily get me into a whining mode. I'm particularly mindful of saying, "Don't go there." I have learned how to gently get him to stop whining—for himself, for me, and for the rest of the office. Deep breaths.

I ask him, "Why are you whining and complaining so much? Nothing is quite right so how can you make it right?" Or "Can you worry less about it?" Or "How can we change your *attitude* toward what's wrong, if we can't change what's wrong itself?"

I'm mindful of the fact that some problems can affect the other moving parts of my day so I want to nip those in the bud whenever I can. When I've had a really crazy, complicated day I'm less patient with my kids at home. I'm acutely aware of that.

What Diminishes Joy

Difficult patients, the electronic medical record (EMR), and exhaustion diminish my joy in work.

Difficult Patients

Patients who are very difficult make me feel imbalanced, depleted, and exhausted. There are some people who, no matter what you do, will not be pleased. Nothing is ever good enough. Often there's an underlying psychiatric problem with some of these patients. Sometimes patients like that diminish my joy.

The Electronic Medical Record

No question, the other huge factor in diminishing joy is the administrative burden of our work, by which I mean the EMR in general. Our world is codified. Everything has a code; we have to write our notes in way that is dictated by the billing system. Sometimes we spend a chunk of time in front of a computer that we could or should be spending with a patient. I'm 51 years old and I grew up in the era of paper charts but, even then, there was a sophisticated coding and billing system in place. I think this administrative burden has arisen from the need to do something with the incredibly expensive healthcare system we have.

Historically, we would bill for the amount of time spent with a patient—so for more complicated patients, we would bill more than we would for less complicated patients. During the last 30 years we began to bill for the complexity of thinking about the disease process. How do you document that complexity? Out came complicated billing systems to explain complexity, required by the Center for Medicare and Medicaid Services (CMS).

When I first started working, I would inherit charts from really good doctors who were on their way to retirement. There might be a little postcard stapled to the paper chart that said, "Made a house call. Pneumonia. Gave this antibiotic. Will follow-up in four days." That was the note. With undoubtedly excellent care. You can't do that now. You would be fired for fraudulence.

Fast forward to today. Let's say I see 20 patients on any given a day. If it's a particularly crazy, complicated day for whatever reasons my notes are not completed by the end of that day. We have a fairly new EMR system called Epic that enables administrators to see how many incomplete notes there are. They look at it every Monday. If I have a hard day on Friday, my notes will be done by Monday afternoon. But I occasionally have gotten an email from the administrators on Monday morning saying I have 20 incomplete notes. Sometimes I ignore that. Sometimes I say, "Do me a favor. Look at productivity. I don't want you sending these emails, they just piss me off." And sometimes I'll just answer tongue-in-cheek, "Thank you for letting me know. Appreciate it."

Exhaustion

I have felt exhausted. No question. But I've never felt exhausted to the point where I've thought *I'm just not cut out for this.* Or *I need to go and be a travel agent.* I love what I do. But at the end of the day, after seeing 20 patients in the office and I have 20 phone calls to make, I just don't have it in me to call some patients back. I need to go home and get a hug from my kids. When I'm not calling people back that tells me I need something, so I have to think about what I need. I need to remind myself I'm not a bad person and it's ok not to call certain people back. I let my secretary know, "just tell her I cannot call her back right now, but if she needs me, I'm happy to see her." This is how I cope.

I tell people that telephone medicine is not good medicine. "I can't see you, you can't see me; if I ask you whether anything is worrying you about your headache, I can't look in your eyes and see you look away. Is there a tear I'm missing, because this is how your mom presented with brain cancer? And is this why your migraine is worrying you? You don't have brain cancer. But I can't see that on the phone. Come in and see me so we can do this right."

Reflections

I started my professional life at a time when people knew who Marcus Welby was, and at a time when a lot of our learning was done through mentorships. I think mentorships have gone away and should come back. The 80-hour work week for residents and the shift work, the focus on teamwork rather than individuals, diffuses responsibility for the patient. When there's a whole group of people taking care of someone as opposed to when it's just you—you and your patient and you're on, and if you mess up it's up to you to worry about and fix the problem—the sense of personal responsibility for the patient is diluted.

On Control

The blue-suited people watch the white-coated people's bottom line, so you do have to work hard. But, in general, I think physicians believe we have less control than we actually do. I think that as a breed we may need a little help trying to understand what we need, what would be particularly helpful, and how we can get there.

For example, for three years I served on the executive board at our hospital. Those board meetings were held twice a month, on Wednesdays, from 8:00 a.m. to 10:00 a.m. And because office hours start at 9:00 a.m. I had to block two hours a month to attend those meetings. When I was no longer on that board, I decided not to open up those hours to patients, but to use that time to look things up, to call people back, to do all sorts of things that are patient related. Exerting that control gave me some extra time for myself, which gives me a little more peace and calm to do these other tasks.

On Burnout and Resilience

I think there's a lot of data, particularly around burnout, that says if you ask physicians straight on, "do you feel burnout?" they say no. This is what a study with residents found in 2014 based on their answers to questions in the Maslach Burnout Inventory, which defines burnout as positive answers to three questions: 1) Have you lost your sense of efficacy—that you're good at what you do and you're effective in making people feel better? 2) Do you feel a certain depersonalization, do you objectify people—e.g., "I saw pneumonia today;" 3) Are you getting cynical about suffering and about your work?

Some people find that when you no longer feel joy, it may be because you are burned out. Some people think of burnout as "anti"—you've lost the joy. But there is also the concept of resilience, which allows you to get back up in the face of adversity. When times are really hard, when you have a lot of difficult patients, or when your own kids are sick and people demand a lot of you and you're thinking, "I can't do it all," there's a way to cultivate resilience.

Cultivating resilience is a way to combat burnout. And they key to cultivating resilience is to find joy in the work you do. Some people just have it, other people need to go and find it by figuring out what gives them joy. Finding joy in the face of burnout takes a little work. We are trained to not complain and to keep our heads down, to keep doing the work. It is very tricky to convince administrators that *most* people start with a joyful attitude in their approach to their work. Some people are able to sustain that throughout their work life and some people aren't.

I think we have to figure out how to do our work in a mindful way that gives us a sense of purpose. Ask yourself, *what parts of the work do I enjoy most and why? And how do I carve out my day job to make sure those elements are prominent?* There will always be parts of your work you don't like. But it is extremely important to be able to mindfully and thoughtfully examine the pieces of your work that give you joy and to make these *really* prominent in your workday. Otherwise you're not going to make it. This job is tough if you don't like it. If you don't like it, you're going to be bad at it and you're going to end up in a bad place.

Support systems are necessary to prevent people from getting burned out in the first place. And that is really tricky because to put energy and dollars, presumably, into a system before the person is broken is complicated.

On Gender

I'm a primary parent and a male, and I've never once felt pressure to be both a super-dad and a super-doctor. I do think my female counterparts feel that pressure. I worked incredibly hard for ten years before my eldest daughter was born: I did everything, I was on every committee. So, by the time she was born I had a little clout. After that, when my bosses would tell me I needed to come to a meeting from 6:00 p.m. to 8:00 p.m., I had no problem saying, "I'm sorry, you cannot have me then. My pie, my work hours, is between this and this. I can cancel patients if you think the meeting is important enough and you want me there. I can do work later at night online. I can email with you. But I'm childcare. I feed my kids; we do family dinners every night. I don't violate that."

I haven't suffered for this as a male, but I think a woman would. If you're a woman and you have young kids, I'd bet you might think twice about doing what I do. You might tell yourself *they're going to think I'm weak if I don't go to the meeting and I'm going to be angry with myself more than anything. And if I do go to the meeting, I'll want to be home with my kids and they're going to be cranky for the next day or two because we missed part of our routine.* I do think people struggle with this differently, and I think gender has a lot to do with it.

Around two years ago I was the chairman of the nominating committee for officers for the executive board of the hospital. The president and vice president at that time were women. They asked the nominating committee to present a slate of people for us to vote on. As committee chairman, I said, "I can't. I have something at my kids' school." The next person, a male orthopedist, said, "I can't, either. It's band night at my kids' school." So, the men on the committee couldn't go and the women on the committee presented the slate. It may be that over time this will become less of an issue because there's much greater gender equality now, but I do think gender figures in this somewhere.

I feel badly for the women on my staff who don't have the autonomy or control I have. They might be told, "Sorry, you just can't go." Or "If you go, you'll be fired." Or something to that effect. Ultimately, if I have something to do that's really important—if my kids are in a play at school at 2:00 p.m. or they are at graduation at 10:00 a.m.—I would probably block the day and go. Or block the hour.

On the Power of Awareness

Howard Stevenson, a retired Harvard Business School professor, wrote a book on happiness about 15 years ago. He and his colleagues interviewed about 250 people from all walks of life and asked what makes them happy. It wasn't about joy in work, but about happiness in general. They found that four buckets, with the acronym HASL, determine happiness.

The first letter, H, is for *Happiness*. Some people are just wired happy. There's something about your own wiring that contributes to being happy, no question about it.

The second letter, A, is for *Achievement*. People feel a certain joy and pride that comes with achievement. Achievement is subjective and can be measured in any number of ways—you've raised your kids in a way you feel really proud of; you've accomplished something professionally; you've conducted yourself in such a way that makes you feel good; or you're a teacher in the school system and you've gotten really great feedback.

The third letter, S, is for *Significance*. To whom am I significant? Meaningful relationships are important to happiness and I think this is true for me, in my career, which is full of relationships.

The last letter, L, is for *Legacy*. What am I leaving behind, whether intended or unintended, as I plow along in this world? It could be anything: a reputation, something you invented, your wonderful family, friendships, your baking skills, anything at all.

You don't have to have all four buckets full at all times, but when you have these little pow-wows with yourself about the need to reinvent yourself or redefine yourself, or the need to find more joy or to combat burnout, it helps to remember which of these buckets is filled with what, and which are a little emptier. Think about how you're going to fill those.

2. *Miguel G., MD, Former Military Medicine Primary Care Physician; Surgical Resident in Obstetrics and Gynecology*

Miguel G., MD, is not your typical resident. At the age of 36—having served as a primary care doctor in the military, including a tour of duty in Afghanistan—he realized that his passion was for surgery and, specifically, for surgery in obstetrics and gynecology. Miguel's joy in work is palpable and abides despite long hours, and his frustration with insurance companies and administrators whose primary concern is the business of medicine.

I was born and raised in Puerto Rico. I live and work in Ponce, the largest city in Puerto Rico after San Juan. Nobody in my family worked in medicine or healthcare. My father was a businessman, my mother was a federal employee for 38 years. But as a child I was always inclined toward the sciences and from a very young age I said I wanted to be a dentist.

As I grew up and went to college I shifted toward medical school. Something about being able to help people appealed to me. I was always the kid who looked forward to the positive side of helping people, whether it was picking up something they'd dropped or helping them if they hurt themselves in a soccer game. Something just drew me toward helping them. And that, combined with sciences, is what drew me to healthcare.

Once I was in college it became very, very obvious to me that I wanted to be a physician and care for the sick and people who are in need. Even if they're not sick, but if they just have no idea what's going on with them—being able to explain it to them without their having to search through the literature and try to interpret it was something I wanted to do. I liked the idea of being able to help people who wouldn't have the capacity to understand this on their own.

When I started medical school in San Juan, I was offered a scholarship from the United States Navy. They would pay for my schooling and give me a stipend in return for service. I joined for the opportunities. This is probably the least expensive school of medicine in the U.S. and is accredited by the American Council for Graduate Medical Education. Seven thousand dollars a year for a medical degree is nothing. Not everyone can afford even $7,000 a year, but my parents were ready to help me out financially. I look back ten years later, and I don't regret it one bit.

I finished medical school and I wanted to pursue a career in general surgery. The Navy said I should finish my one-year internship, take my licensing exam, get my permanent license, and go to work as a general physician in the military. I finished that one year in general surgery training and loved it but had to move on to complete my military obligation.

My Career

In the Military

In the Navy I was first assigned to a Marine Corps unit in military medicine. That program takes care of Sailors and Marines assigned to units in the Marine Corps. The Marines don't have their own private medical program, so I was stationed with a Marine Corps unit in Camp Lejeune, North Carolina, where I was a primary care physician for the battalion. I did everything for them: morning sick call, everyday complaints, and so on. They're Marines but they get sick, too.

The other part of military medicine is deployment readiness. We did a lot of annual exams and keeping all the kids' (I say "kids" but the majority of them were 18- to 25-year-olds) vaccines up to date so that whenever their name came up for deployment, they were ready to go.

About seven months into that first tour of duty I got called up for the deployment to Afghanistan. I prepped for that and, sure enough, I was out there. I say this with all honesty—I don't want to take any credit for what I didn't do—I was in a very sheltered position while I was deployed in Afghanistan. I was a primary care physician for a unit of maybe 2,000 Marines. We (myself and some of my Corpsmen) were on a base, we were in logistics command. We didn't ride in convoys and we didn't take part in gunfights or anything like that. We were basically the ones who made sure the guys on the front lines got all their ammo, all their needs for shelter, uniforms, supplies, everything. And I was the one who provided primary medical care for all those guys who were providing logistical support. I was also supporting the logistics of medical supply and keeping the medical clinics in the smaller, forward bases up to date.

It was never my intent while in the military to be engaged in battle. I was able to experience, first-hand, what it is to be in combat by seeing the guys on the front lines without living the combat part of it myself. I felt the actual tension of *being* in a combat zone. We were in a sheltered base but every so often we'd feel an occasional blast from an improvised explosive device outside the base; receive threats that there may be something incoming and we had to take shelter; and the simple part of having to give bad news. Part of my job was getting that call from some physician in the States saying, "You know, so-and-so's mom is not doing well, and we need to send that Marine back home." I was the liaison for that.

The Red Cross in the U.S. has a liaison with all the armed forces. It's the one legitimate way of communicating between civilian and military medical services and deployments. For example, John's mother is sick in Arkansas and she doesn't have any Marine captain to call in Afghanistan. So, she calls the Red Cross, the Red Cross contacts the unit and sends a message to the liaisons, and that information gets relayed to us. While I was in Afghanistan, I would get those messages, and it was part of my job to call that doctor in the States and be the liaison between that doctor and the military personnel in my unit. Once I had to tell a kid his brother was in a car accident back home and wasn't going to make it. It's hard to tell a kid who's in a combat zone, who's doing what he thinks is right for his country, that his brother is dying from a car accident back home.

It was a very rewarding, very fulfilling experience and that's why I never regret having joined the Navy. I was in Afghanistan for 11 months. I was the general surgeon for an entire regiment, which is Marine lingo for the second-largest unit that's deployable. The larger the unit the longer the deployment. I was a third-grade officer in a job that was probably meant for a higher officer, but I was the one they got. I developed a great relationship with very senior folks. I had daily meetings with the colonels and the generals over there. I also sat down with the lance-corporals on a regular basis and saw every level of what it is to be in combat in medicine.

Coming Home

I finished my deployment after 11 months and came back home. While I was deployed, my fiancé at the time, who is now my wife, was finishing up her medical training. This is intertwined with where I am and why I'm here. She and I met while I was doing that one-year internship in general surgery. She was finishing up her general surgery residency. She became a general surgeon and went on to do a fellowship in breast cancer diseases and became a breast cancer surgeon.

We moved to the Washington, DC area and I worked at the Washington Navy Yard, providing care for Marines including those who guard the White House and who accompany the President, those who stand guard at Arlington Cemetery, those who play in Marine bands, and those who live and work in the Marine Barracks on Capitol Hill. The Navy also provides the White House with culinary services—so all the chefs who work in the White House were our patients, a lot of members stationed at the Pentagon, and those on several other military bases in the area. The smaller bases don't have their own clinics, so we were the primary care providers for them. Our patient volume was dispersed around DC, Maryland, and Virginia. They came to our office at the Washington Navy Yard.

Because of my experience with the Marines and my previous duty, I was called to the Officer Candidates School in Quantico to help them with some of their medical logistics. I was there for a couple of months, but I was back at the Navy Yard for the rest of that tour. I spent the last two years of my Navy obligation at the Navy Yard.

While I was deployed, I'd hoped to get back into a general surgery residency program within the Navy and the option came up to try once I was back home. When I came to the Navy Yard, I looked at applying but I would have had to start residency with the Navy after my active duty obligation was done. I still had some small amount of reserve duty left to do. My wife and I got to thinking about our future, and we really wanted to come back to Puerto Rico. It was a hard decision to leave the Navy after I'd discharged my obligation but, in the end, it was the best decision for us.

Puerto Rico

In Puerto Rico, I took a couple of years to work as a general practitioner and a hospitalist taking care of patients who had been admitted to the hospital for a variety of reasons. I applied for residency in obstetrics and gynecology after realizing there was the potential for a surgical field in gynecology. And the obstetrics part of it was very appealing to me; it seemed very interesting and rewarding.

Ironically, I started the program looking more toward the gynecology part and less toward the obstetrical part. But every day I'd be more and more interested in the obstetrics and I learned to like it a lot more. That occasion of putting the baby on its mother's belly, there's nothing like it. I've enjoyed a lot over the past year and a half, and every delivery is exciting. That sums up why I'm here.

I am currently a resident training in obstetrics/gynecology at an academic medical center. It's a four-year program and I'm now in my second year. So, I've worked as a general practitioner, I was in military medicine for four years, and now I'm back to being a resident. I think I've seen it all.

As I've grown—I've been a physician now for 11 years—I've been able to really appreciate the decisions I've made in life. And every patient—every patient!—teaches me something and gives something to be happy about. I really enjoy the interaction with patients and being able to do something for them.

Residency

Regulations say we can work 24-hour shifts. I do 24-hour shifts and within the next four hours I'm out of the hospital. I'm only doing what I couldn't get around to in those 24 hours. I delivered a baby, but I had to do the paperwork, the orders, and all that's required afterwards. When the baby's coming out, I can't be writing orders. I've got to take the baby out. So, our usual 24-hour shift becomes 26, 27. Sometimes it's 24½. Sometimes it's a very easy shift. But the usual routine is 13-, 14-hour regular workdays per month—you come home, study, sleep, and wake up the next day and do the same thing. We're on call every third or every fourth night. We spend the night at the hospital. We work about seven shifts of 24 hours per month; some months it may be six, some months eight, but we spend the majority of our nights in the hospital. That's why they call it residency.

It's going to give you grit. The faculty have said it, and they're right on about it. You spent 24 hours in the hospital Tuesday night because you had three patients in the delivery ward, and guess what? Wednesday morning you have an office full of patients waiting to see you. And they're waiting to see the best of you. Not the sleepy, groggy, I'm tired, I'm going to cancel, you. No. Residency is going to give you the endurance and the grit to overcome that. So, you get out of the hospital after delivering a baby at 6:00 a.m. and you shower, get to the office at 8:00 a.m., and work a regular day.

Our program is very good about making sure that once we get out of a long shift, we have enough time to recover. For example, I got out of work at 9:00 a.m. today. I have the rest of today and all of tonight off to recover. And I don't go back to work until 6:00 a.m. tomorrow. That's almost 24 hours off. I'll work again all of Friday to Saturday but I'm off all of Saturday and Sunday, then I'll go back to work Monday.

When Things Go Wrong

As a resident the first thing that happens when something goes wrong is that you get pulled aside and someone says, "Hey, this happened, you did this wrong" or "why did this happen?" The majority of our faculty members are open to listening to why it happened. In residency there's a hierarchy. When you're a first-year resident you've got a second, a third, a fourth year above you, and they're going to be your indirect supervisors. The blame is not always on you. But they're also on top of you making sure you do things right.

To take a simple example: if a patient is allergic to aspirin and I order a pain medication that has aspirin in it, if something happens to the patient there's going to be a medical incident report and administrative involvement. The nursing staff will talk with the physicians and make sure we all get with the program to fix the problem acutely and then make sure it doesn't happen again. There are protocols and ways to try to prevent those incidents from happening.

But from the residency perspective, you're going to have the hierarchy of residents who talk to you from a second, third, and fourth level up—then you'll talk to the faculty members and program directors. There's a process of learning because we're a teaching institution. So as far as events that result in an adverse event for the patient, these are usually seen as opportunities for teaching and learning and are not handled punitively.

But, as a resident, if something occurs because your oversight was lax or you weren't paying attention to the details you should have been, then it becomes an issue. The first time you'll get a warning saying you need to pay attention, you can't do this, and you can't do that. The second time they'll say, next month you're going to get an extra shift to encourage you to be more thoughtful. If there's not an extra shift available, they might tell the resident to give a presentation to all the residents so none of us makes that mistake. They turn it into a teaching opportunity. There is a committee in the residency program that provides overview and decides what action to take.

On Burnout

Let's talk about the words we've been hearing so much about: "physician burnout." This happens because our hours are very long. I can't say that I've felt burnout. I've had episodes where I'm more frustrated than usual because of the intricacies of residency or the interactions with peers and faculty. There's always that one faculty member who will get mad because I didn't call him at 3:00 a.m. to tell him his patient is fine. I'm competent so I didn't call you to tell you the patient is fine. That kind of stuff can get me angry.

There are occasions when I get out of a 24-hour shift and think, *oh my God, is this really worth it?* Putting in the hours, doing the hard work, and everything—and then just getting beaten over the head for something like that. I didn't make a mistake—I just didn't call. But have I ever been tired to the point where I can't deal with something myself? There've been times when I get out of a 24-hour shift and I'm literally debating whether I should drive home or sleep in the hospital. But I live three minutes from the hospital. I slowly make it home, shower, and crawl into bed.

The first year of residency is usually the hardest in terms of the numbers of hours a day and the volume of work, but I think the path I took earlier in my career is helping me now. When I was deployed, I spent many hours on edge. I spent many nights sitting there, staring at the tent above me. Because I wasn't tired, I wasn't sleeping, I was just antsy. During the first year of residency the hours are so crazy; I felt like I was working but I wasn't really getting anywhere. I didn't really know what was going on. It wasn't a matter of feeling burnout; it was more a matter of feeling frustrated with the long hours. At some point, I thought, *this isn't right. There can't be an expectation for us to do all this work.* But I think this is part of the weeding process in the medical training program.

It's the same in every specialty. Yes, I have long hours. But at the end of the day, when it's in my hands to take care of someone—and it's a life or death situation—I can't be tired. I can't be burned out. And if I am, I'd need to get help. And so, for the last four or five years, residency programs have been pushing resident wellness. And they should. Residents are giving their best. They are getting their time off and it's a lot better than it used to be. That's not to say we don't spend 26, 27 hours in the hospital. Sometimes I get out of that long shift and the next day I'm presenting some topic to the faculty. It's hard and it's long and it's tiring. But most of us do well and we're able to get through it.

As I've grown and have moved farther along in residency, I've learned to appreciate that I put in the hours and the extra time because there's an intrinsic reward. I may not have seen it at first, but now I see how much I've learned and how competent I feel when I go in to work the next day; I know what happened, and I know what I'm doing and I feel I've grown professionally. I may be tired, I may be sleepy, but when it comes to doing the hands-on job, I've always been able to get through it and do it well.

On Joy in Work

I define joy in work very simply: When that baby comes out and I grab it and give it to the parents. They were not expecting how joyful that would be. When my first baby was born it was a regular, vaginal delivery. The joy that my wife and I felt when they put that baby in our hands was unbelievable. Our second baby was a C-section and I was, literally, scrubbed in. Now, I've delivered very, very premature 28-week-old babies who will be spending a lot of time in the neonatal intensive care unit. The baby is born, I wrap it up and take it right to the pediatrician and do whatever needs to be done. But when it was my baby, in my hands, I totally froze. When I'm delivering a baby, I know that mom and dad are feeling the joy I felt when it was my own baby. And that just gives me a sense of, "job well done. Take care of this one and move on to the next." Joy in work is that for me. Delivering a baby.

There's joy in everything. I walk through the maternity ward and I see a mom breastfeeding her child and to me that's joyful. Because I know she spent nine months worrying about that little thing in her arms. Likewise, I walk into a woman's room who's 72, has had a biopsy for cancer, and is waiting for us to take the cancer out. We perform the surgery, take out the cancer, and she's "cured." She needs postop care and chemotherapy, but we've given her another five years of living. That's very rewarding.

On Money and Joy

I think there's a relationship between money and joy only when you don't have enough money to live reasonably comfortably. But do I think you need to have a huge luxury house, a condo on the beach, and a five-car garage? No. I don't expect to be a millionaire. As I say to my friends, "If you want to be a millionaire don't be a physician." To me what's important is to have a modest income and do right by your patients. The reason I didn't stay a general practitioner is that I wanted to be happy every day I woke up. I didn't want to take care of more mundane problems, which are important, but just not what makes me happy. Am I happy as a 36-year-old second-year resident? Yes, because I'm doing something I'll enjoy forever. The financial compensation, as it is, is fine for me.

What Diminishes Joy

I don't want this to sound like a rant, but a lot of physicians would say the insurance companies take the joy out of work. I'm a resident. I don't contract with insurance companies. I don't get paid by insurance companies. My salary is paid by the Department of Health, just like every other resident here. But at the end of the day, we are limited a lot by what we can do for a patient because the plan won't pay for this or the plan won't pay for that.

For a mom who recently delivered a baby who needed to stay in the hospital, the insurance company would have sent her home without her baby. They didn't want to pay for that extra day. So, we had to navigate around them, saying, "Well, she had a fever yesterday," or "she has too much pain." At the end of the day it should just be, "You know what? Just let her stay 12 hours." We have to fight against the resistance from health insurance companies. I understand the business. But you're doing it for the patient. Just do the right thing. It's what the patient needs. Often, the journals and the literature in medical sciences describe what you're supposed to do in this type of situation. But when you try to do it, the insurance companies will put up a fight.

The non-medical part of medicine is very frustrating in terms of the limitations it places on us. For example, there may be a shortage of supplies or some medications are unavailable because they're more expensive than others and the plans won't cover it. Some would argue that this helps us learn to juggle the difficult aspects of caring for a patient. I think it makes us learn to be creative, but not always with the best result for the patient. And that's frustrating.

The only other thing that obviously takes the joy out of medicine is having to tell a mom that her baby is going to be sick for a while. Or doing a second sonogram and having to tell her the baby has a heart defect. We do a few months of residency in the maternal–fetal center. The specialist in maternal–fetal medicine diagnoses bad things every day. It's high risk. And you have to give bad news. So that takes the joy out. You do three great things in the morning and then you have to talk to one patient about something not so good and it's hard. I've had times when I've gotten teary-eyed and I cry with the patients. At the end of the day it's heartbreaking but it's part of what we have to do.

Advice

My advice to my colleagues is, it's better to learn earlier that your colleagues aren't meant to be your friends. They also don't need to be your enemies. There's a lot of competitiveness— I've seen it in my training, and I've seen it in every specialty in medicine.

My advice to my hospital administrators is, every once in a while, get in the shoes of the patients. Or the physicians. Realize you may be running your business, which is keeping this hospital afloat, and you may have a budget. But we're trying to save lives. And you can't be that constricting. If there are two medications that will do the same thing for the patient, I agree that we'll choose the less expensive one. But if there's only one and it's expensive, then that's what has to be given. Administrators need to stop seeing only the financial mission of the hospital and realize it's about the patients. The hospital is not a hotel where you're wondering *how many beds can I fill up tonight, and how many will be empty in the morning so I can fill them up again?* You're talking about patients and you need to focus more on making sure they get healthy. And if they're not, then find out why and ask what else we can do.

3. *Theodore B., RN, BSN, Insurance Company Healthcare Consultant*

Theodore B., RN, BSN, was born in central Africa. His ready smile radiates light, warmth, and caring. A filmmaker and videographer in his native country, he entered a hospital for the first time the day his son was born. That moment changed his life, leading him first into nursing and then into roles as a leader and trainer of nurses. Today he educates patients in preventive care for a private insurer. Driven to help people, he divides his time between the U.S. and his farm in his native country where he uses "food as a catalyst to promote health." I met Theodore B. in 2010 when he was my husband's unforgettable bedside nurse.

I started out as a documentary filmmaker and videographer making educational videos about HIV/AIDS in Kigali, Rwanda. I witnessed such poverty and saw children who had no one to help them. I remember feeling helpless, asking myself what I could do for those kids. I could see myself in them. I had a feeling of responsibility toward them. And then my son was born. I think it was at the hospital with my son that I decided working in a hospital was really what I wanted to do.

I hadn't thought I wanted to be a nurse. But when my son was born, I couldn't bear the thought of not knowing what to do to take care of him. I didn't want him to be like one of those kids I saw in Rwanda. I thought, *just let me learn how to take care of you. Just let me learn how to do it.* At that point I didn't know there was such a thing as male nurses, whether nurses were paid, or even if you had to go to school to be one. I had no clue about that. I just felt taking care of people was what I was meant to do.

I returned to the United States in 2002 after my son was born. I started working at a community hospital. I learned that you had to take classes and get a degree to become a nurse, so I signed up for classes at a local community college. On weekdays I was a stay-at-home dad so I could take care of my son. During the evening I would take classes. On weekends I worked as a caddy at a country club because I was an avid golfer—I'd played golf competitively while working in Rwanda. I wanted to stay with the game, and I enjoyed the game, so on the weekend that is what I did. In talking to the guys at the country club I met the CEO of a local hospital who told me, "If you want to work in a hospital, you can come to mine and see if that is something you would really like to do."

So, I went to the hospital to check it out. And I never left the hospital until I was a registered nurse. I fell in love the moment I went to the hospital. I was there for eight years. I started as a unit secretary, then became a patient care technician, and then a registered nurse.

For me, "how long have you worked in a hospital?" is a better question than "how long have you been a nurse?" I do not separate my passion for helping people when I was a nurse compared to when I was a patient care technician or a unit secretary. I still had the same joy and the same excitement. I couldn't care less what role I played. I just wanted to be in a hospital. I just wanted to serve people. I just wanted to be in that environment. So that started in 2004. That's when I was hired to be unit secretary. That's where my journey started in the hospital.

Theodore's Ascent

The environment of my work didn't really affect me. I always look at the bigger picture. I was a little bit different. Maybe it was the friendship I had with the CEO of the hospital—but from the get-go I was the kind of person who was on all sorts of committees and volunteered on days I wasn't working. I was at work trying to do *something.*

The hospital administration was so understanding and accommodated my passion for doing more than simply being a bedside nurse. I set up an initiative to calculate how much waste we incurred every day from little things like lights that are left on when there's no one in the room or water that is left running. I asked how we could cut these kinds of costs so we could spend that money on our patients. That's how I always thought.

When I was still a nurse at the community hospital, I was interested in going back to school for further education. I went for my MBA and got a graduate certificate in the business of medicine. Then I did one more certificate in leadership development. Then that wasn't enough. I wanted to be more—I wanted to be a hospital administrator, so I did medical services management at a course that was being given at a prestigious university. I did all this while being a full-time nurse.

When I graduated a position became available at a nearby hospital. It was an out-patient clinic and they needed somebody to run it, making sure that patients who were having joint replacements were cleared prior to surgery and dealing with any medical issues, such as infection, that would come up. I stayed there for two years.

Then a third hospital was looking for a registered nurse who could help them understand the patient experience, which was a brand-new concept then. When I became their patient experience leader I thought, *how weird to be teaching the administration something I'd assumed everyone had been doing all along.* I trained nurses and helped them to see themselves as nurse leaders, not just to say, "I have an assignment." I trained charge nurses to think of themselves as extensions of the nurse manager—to know what's going on and actually make those tough decisions themselves. I also used role-playing to train nurses to take better care of patients.

Now, as a consultant to a private insurer, I create preventive care plans for individuals. For people with diabetes, I help them with education. I help people with chronic diseases that are prevalent in this state by creating programs that are going to slow down those diseases or help people manage them better.

On Joy in Work

As a bedside nurse, joy only comes the moment when I am with the patient—the interaction. When your husband was brought onto the unit, I couldn't wait to meet him. I was told I had a patient coming from the operating room. I read his paperwork, I read a little bit about him—what type of procedure he had, whether he was alert—the things I needed to know. The moment I knew he was on his way I was waiting for him. And I started a conversation—not in the room, but outside. That's how it is for me. The excitement is when I'm doing something for the care of the patient. That's not me working, it's me having fun.

I like to be in an environment where I am not constantly judged by what I do. I like what I'm doing to mean something. Not just to me, but to the person I am with. If I were a basketball player I wouldn't be happy to be on the bench, I would be happy when the game is on and I'm playing and everyone is cheering for me. And that's how I looked at it during the time I was a bedside nurse. That was the time I was performing and the patients were cheering for me, and the family members, and that just brought me joy. When I'm not around that when it comes to work, the joy disappears.

When patients aren't happy with me it doesn't stop me from feeling joy in what I do. I just ask myself how I can do my job better. Because my job is always about my customer. It's hit or miss. You're always evolving. If I make you unhappy on the first day, on the last day we are hugging and kissing on your way out of the hospital and you don't want to leave. That's just the kind of nurse I am. When I was at the bedside that's what I did. I do well because what I do has direct impact on people. I feel rewarded every day. My patients mean everything to me.

I feel joy in my current role. It's a little bit different. I do miss bedside nursing. There is no substitute for that—the bells and whistles and noise of the hospital environment. The emergency codes that go on. The alarms that go off and the helicopters landing and the commotion—there is just nothing that can substitute for that. You miss that. Your adrenaline is pumping all the time. You look at it as the beginning and the ending of life and everything in between. Somebody's life being saved. Somebody's life being mended.

The Opposite of Joy

The opposite of joy in work happens when care becomes a transactional interaction with a patient, when you are calculating the things you have to do. When you reach the ninth thing you are happy and when you reach the tenth thing you shut down. When asked to do the 11th thing you say, "That's not my job." There is nothing wrong with that per se because you cannot be fired for that. I've witnessed people who are like that.

When you see that and read patient comment letters it's easy to point out who is not finding joy in what they do. I don't think these nurses are consciously thinking what they're doing is wrong, it's just how they see their jobs: I'm getting paid to do ten things. And you don't pay me enough to get to the 11th thing. It's not a bad or a good thing, it's the expectation. Maybe it's a hiring issue. Sometimes you see people who get happy when they come to work; other times you see people who get happy when they leave.

Reflections

The patient experience means understanding that when someone is in the hospital, either a patient or a family member, you treat them as you'd want yourself to be treated. You're looking at safety first. You're looking at the quality of care, and you're looking at communication with the patient. If you do all these things the patient's perception of their experience is going to be positive. The patient experience and quality of care are intertwined.

If I want change, I'm not going to complain about a situation—instead, I'm going to suggest changes to my leader. When I was on the orthopedic unit at the community hospital, we were sometimes told we didn't have enough patients, so we were transferred to other units. We weren't always mentally prepared for that. Sometimes it was a good thing, sometimes it wasn't. Instead of just complaining we approached our leader asking to be our own independent unit that handled our own staffing. She championed that change for us and made it work. No one on that unit left because they were burned out. Everyone wanted to be on that unit.

In central Africa we don't have a healthcare system that looks like this. Not even close. We have very few hospitals and access to care is very difficult. In my country there are very few cases of obesity, very few cases of hypertension or stroke. But cases having to do with communicable diseases and conditions that can be prevented are rampant. The things that lead people to the hospital in my country are malnutrition and lack of access to clean water.

As a person who has worked in healthcare for this long and who now works for an insurance company, I didn't have an appreciation for preventive medicine until I started to develop the program I'm working on now. Now I get it. It's unfortunate that people have to come to the hospital. It's fortunate to have staff with the medical talent to take care of patients. But the greatest impact is outside of the hospital, in the community, where you can help patients stay out of the hospital.

I feel the need to practice preventive healthcare in my home country, so I bought a piece of land and started a farm there. I'm using food as a catalyst to promote health. The people who work on my farm are those who wouldn't otherwise have any hope in life; they are people society has forgotten. I've given them a second chance. Nine people are working for themselves on my farm. We're raising chickens, goats, pigs, and we just started selling chickens, which is my next phase. I travel back and forth between here and there. If it works there, I will use my farm as a model for helping inner-city kids here, those who society has forgotten and who risk being labeled as "bad" kids.

Advice

In terms of advice for my bosses, I think the employee knows best. The employee knows the environment they're working in and the employee knows exactly what needs to be done to improve patient safety and the culture of care. Those who are successful leaders take time to listen to their employees. Your job as a manager is to identify the potential in people—and if you listen to those who are doing the jobs, by listening you will help them.

Using role-playing as part of a training program can help nurses to empathize with patients. As a trainer I would ask nurses to be patients and give them call lights. As imaginary patients they would really have to go to the bathroom! They'd press their call light, and no one would come. After a prolonged amount of time I'd ask them how they felt when no one came. That was the "Aha!" moment for them: "Wow, I didn't realize…," they said. That's when I could see that my approach to care was influencing and changing them.

4. Emily P., MD, FACP, Retired Internist and Medical School Teacher and Mentor

Emily P., MD, FACP, retired from her small group internal medicine practice where the advent of the electronic medical record upended her autonomy and drained her joy in work. Emily now teaches at two medical schools, mentoring first-year students and teaching third-year students in the art, science, and joy of taking a good medical history and physical.

I had a book on the human body that I must have gotten when I was eight years old as well as my favorite toys, the "invisible man" and the "invisible woman.'" In camp we dissected frogs. I *loved* that stuff. There was something in all that that really caught my interest.

I started in nursing, having been given a choice between teaching and nursing. In the old days of nursing—the diploma programs—we spent enormous amounts of time on the floors. It was beaten into our heads that we were the only ones really taking care of this patient, that we were the ones who knew everything about this person. And I really developed the feeling that I *did* know everything about this person. I was that person's advocate. I was going to make sure that everything went right for that patient. This has always stayed with me.

Floor nursing was not challenging enough so I pursued a master's degree, became a nurse practitioner, then became aware that I just didn't know enough. I didn't like that I had to keep going to the attending for help. So, I picked up physics and organic chemistry, took the MCATs, applied to medical school, and went to medical school, which I found exciting and challenging. The clinical years were terrific!

My internal medicine residency was one of the last every-other-night programs in the country. That means on Monday I would go to work, work all day, take all the admissions and work all night, work all the next day, and I'd get home at about 6:00 in the evening on Tuesday. I would sleep Tuesday night, and start all over again on Wednesday. I actually loved my residency and I didn't mind the schedule at all.

And those patients—oh my God, I was so possessive of those patients—I wanted to make sure everything was right for them. I would always make rounds that second night. If I was on all night and the next day, I'd always check on my patients before I left at 6:00 p.m. I'd make rounds on all my patients, listen to their lungs, and say, "OK, I'm going off and I'll see you in the morning." They'd say, "You're leaving?! What do mean you're leaving?" And I'd say, "Well, I really have to sleep." They were so used to my being there *all the time*. We always had to make sure our patients were tucked in. It was a matter of pride that nobody got called on our patients when we were gone.

There was value in being there all the time. I could admit someone who was half dead with pneumococcal pneumonia. I'd stay up with him all night—meds, treatments, and I'd watch him, watch him. I'd see him every hour. And then by morning he'd start to get a little bit better. And then in the afternoon he would be a little bit better. And then I'd go home and sleep that night, come back the next morning, and he'd be up eating breakfast. I saw what happened to people in the course of a day and the course of a night. I really got to see the course of a disease. Students today never get to see that. And it's very important.

So that's how it was. On weekends I'd come in and it was Friday, Saturday, Sunday, and I'd go home Monday night. But because there were so many of us, each of us would have fewer admissions; we'd have more time to spend with those patients, we got to know them better. It was a plus that the main hospital was new and beautiful. There were all private rooms, so we could sit down in a quiet place and get our histories and physicals done. It was a very nice experience.

I had clinic duty every week in medical school. Every Tuesday morning was my clinic, so my patients all came on Tuesday mornings. And I always followed my patients. My patients came from part of the state that was dirt poor. They were illiterate and would take a bus that would wiggle-waggle to bring them to see me, a doctor who had been out of med school for one week. It was a big responsibility, I'll tell you.

When you finish medical school, you realize that residency is really your time to take all of what you learned and become the doctor you want to be. I finished my residency in 1985.

I worked for eight years at the student health clinic of a large academic medical center. With one veteran physician, who would become my long-time colleague, and a couple of other doctors and nurse practitioners, we took care of all the students. We then left the clinic when our medical director was replaced by an administrator and our work situation quickly deteriorated. We became faculty at the medical center with an office in the suburbs. When the medical center decided, for financial reasons, they did not want us to continue, we affiliated with a community hospital for a while and then started our own small internal medicine private practice.

On Joy in Work: The Art of Medicine

Now I teach the students how to take a good medical history and physical. Incorporated in this is my attempt to have these students gain an appreciation for the joy and importance of what they're doing—it's not just checking things off a list.

It's difficult to get a good history. It takes time. Patients don't always understand that some of the things they have experienced are actually important. And patients don't tell you, not because they're being obstructionist, but because they don't understand how important an event, or a symptom, might be. Maybe something happened to them just once, or maybe it happened a long time ago and they just don't think to tell you. Your questions and the history have to be probing enough to make them feel comfortable, to let them know you're interested, and to take away any embarrassment they may feel in bringing up something you really need to know. It's the art of medicine, not the science of medicine. It means looking the patient in the eye, probing, and looking interested. It means not looking at your watch.

The way I teach students to take a good history is by having a one-on-one experience and it's unique. I don't have five students in a room, I have one student at a time. I go to the hospital and I go up to the floor. I have cultivated a group of nurses who know what kind of patient I want: I want someone who's really going to give us a good history. I don't care what the diagnosis is, what's wrong with them medically. They could be in for a hip fracture. I want a patient who will play ball with us. I generally let the student take the whole history, tell them what I want them to include in the history—which is way more extensive than what they are used to—and then I take notes while we're in the room. When they are finished, I tell the patient, "I just have to ask a few more questions." And then I can get the real story.

One of the things I try to do with the students is to find something the patient needs that people have not focused on. For example, one patient was a double amputee, diabetic, homeless man. And he was pretty dirty. At the end of the interview, right before we left the room—I also like to give the patient something at the very end so that they feel this was a good experience—I said, "I want to ask you a question. When did you have a shower last?" And I could see him thinking, *I have no idea.* I told him, "You know, you're in a big medical center. They have shower rooms. So, when we leave here, I want you to put your light on and I want you to tell the nurse, more than anything, I want a shower. A good shower. And when you get into that shower, I want you to stay in there. I want you to enjoy it. I want you to soap up 100 times. Do whatever you want. But I want you to feel really good when you get out of the shower. Will you do that for me?"

And he said yes. When we left the room, the student had a quizzical look, as if to ask, *really?* And I said to him, "You know, there are a lot of things we can do for this patient but I'm willing to bet you getting him a shower is going to be the most important. And then he's clean, he feels good, he may actually listen to what someone has to say to him."
So, it's those little things that sometimes really make you a better doctor. It's the human side of medicine. I always, always try to do that.

Here's another story I had with a student. We saw a patient; I don't remember what his problem was. The student took a very thorough history and when he got to his educational history, he asked, "How far did you get in school?" The patient said, "11th grade." I waited until we were all done and were ready to walk out of the room and I told the patient, "Listen to me. You're obviously a smart guy. There's no question in my mind. Would you mind telling me why you left school in 11th grade? You had one more year till you graduated." He said, "Because I was a dumb kid." I said, "Well you're not a dumb kid now. What are you going to do about it?" He said, "I have a number. I know where to call." And I said, "Okay. I want you to shake my hand and promise me you're going to do it.'" In medicine the handshake is a very important thing. Sometimes people won't shake your hand; that tells you something. And he shook my hand and said, "I'm going to do it!"

And then, just by chance, I saw him again within a week. I asked him if he would let us take a history again with another student and he was all on board. The student took the history and then he started the physical. And the patient is correcting everything: "No, that node's right here." And "Oh, my arm's not relaxed. You're not going to get that reflex." It's obvious his patient's no dummy. If he listens to me explain a physical one time around and he remembered it enough to repeat my words back to the second student, I was standing there as if to say, "I have nothing to do." He was obviously relishing this. We were about to leave his room and this time he called me and said, "Wait a minute before you leave. I want to tell you something. I already signed up for the GED. I'm going to do it."

And then we went out into the hall and I said to the student, "I want you to just think about this for one second. We walk into this stranger's room. We're not his doctors. I come in and I say, I'm doctor so-and-so and I'm working with third-year students. My job is to teach them to do a good history and a physical. Would you like to work with us today? That's all I say. We've never even looked at his chart. We do not do anything to help his care. I have no relationship with him whatsoever. But we come in there as doctors and put this idea in his head last week that he needs to get his GED. And today he's proudly announcing that he's going to get his GED. Do you understand the power you have as a doctor? Do you have any idea what we just did for this kid?" And I really try to drive that home for them because, to me, that is the joy of medicine.

Sure, you take care of the medical stuff. Even when I was in private practice there were so many days when someone would come in with a sore throat or something. And I would look at them and we'd finish the sore throat workup and I'd say, "Okay, now do you want to talk about what is really going on?" And then the tears would come. Because I could *feel* it. And I think the patients knew I would figure it out.

On Money and Joy

There is some relationship between money and joy. I think you have to be paid enough money. I've taught these salary negotiation classes for the medical society. I say, "Look. We'd all love to be making $10 million a year but that's not going to happen. So, what you have to do is ask yourself, what amount of money—what number—will make me feel I'm being compensated fairly? You really have to think of that number. And then when you go into negotiations with a big employer, go above that number for your ask and realize that you can't come down any further. Because if you come down further, then you're going to feel like you're being taken advantage of." Women are the worst at negotiating salaries because they want to please people. And women always are offered lower salaries than men. Absolutely always. I tell women, "You decide on your number. And you hang in there with your number. Then you're not going to be paid less than someone else."

If you're a doctor in private practice you really have to depend on what insurance companies will pay. The smaller you are the less negotiating power you have.

You don't get rich being a primary care doctor. You don't get rich being a pediatrician. You don't get rich being a geriatrician, a family doc or internist. You may get rich being in orthopedics, or dermatology, or neurosurgery. But not this.

What Diminishes Joy

The Electronic Medical Record

In my practice, we debated and debated and debated about using the EMR. Theoretically you'd think this would be great. With the EMR we could share information. The problem is, when Congress pushed the EMR there was one concept they totally forgot about: that these systems needed to be able to talk to each other. Now, use of the EMR is a federal regulation. But they never put in standards for EMRs. At the medical center where I started working, the EMR in the emergency room (ER) wouldn't talk to the EMR on the floor, which didn't talk to the EMR in the clinic.

And then there's the expense. We went looking for an EMR and I found one that is actually free at first. It doesn't do a lot of what other EMRS do, but it's not bad. We started using that and by then our practice had grown to four doctors. We knew it was going to be rough going for a while. Little did we know that we would be there sometimes until 10:00 at night trying to get everything into the EMR. Everybody's nerves were completely frayed. Now, my partner and I had worked together at this point for 15 years and never had an argument, OK? Bring in the EMR.

The problem is, EMRs are written the way a computer programmer would write a program. There is no doctor's brain in this system, nothing that reflects the way we think. So, we ended up having to do a lot of free texting. With the EMR everything has to be in a different place. When we used paper charts, we would always keep a medication list. I'd go over their meds with the patient, asking them if they were still on each one. In that way I'd reconcile my meds. I could do that in five minutes. With the EMR it's one screen, another screen, another screen, another screen, all over the place.

When we used paper charts, we'd keep a piece of paper in the front of the chart with a huge list: a problem list, an immunization list, and a prevention list. I would write mammogram, with date; colonoscopy, with date. At a glance, when a patient came in, I could open this up—let's say it wasn't my patient—and I'd see the problem list, all the medications, all the allergies, all the preventive care. It was all right there. With the paper chart I would look at that front sheet before I walked into the room, so when the patients would tell me what was wrong with them that day, I would instantly know their health history. With the paper chart, I'd have an idea of how to put their story on that particular day into context. With the EMR, you have to look at screen after screen to find out all of this information. With the EMR, when I'd sit down with the patient, I'd have to go to the computer right away. With the EMR you can't look at the patient. The screen is a barrier.

There's a place on the registration screen where you have to fill in a blank about the patient's language preference. What difference does it make? If someone is a Peruvian diplomat who speaks perfect English, don't you think their preferred language would be Spanish? What is the good of that question? With the EMR we had to get all that data put in when we first started; we had to go back through hundreds of charts. Then we'd have to check this box about what is a patient's language preference every time. With paper charts, if I was taking a history on a Spanish speaker I would write in my history, "patient's language is Spanish. We made do as best we could." Or, "a friend came to translate for the patient." Or, "there is a number to call for translation help." I would always make a note in the chart, anyway. What happens with the EMR is as well as you think you're doing, there's always this crap.

What I would see happening at the medical center, which I found horrifying, was that people would cut and paste on the EMR. They would literally be cutting and pasting physicals. The attending would be doing physicals, and everyone would be cutting and pasting them into theirs. And everyone was rushed because, get 'em out, get 'em out, get 'em out to the insurance industry.

The EMRs are not in doctor-speak. Did you know there is a doctor-speak? This is a very clear way to present data. In the past, pre-EMR, if I got a note from the ER, it would say, "The patient presented with chest pain" and describe that. You'd have the physical, you'd have the electrocardiogram (EKG) results, you'd have other information, you'd have the impression, and you'd have the plan, probably on one piece of paper. Now, when I'd get a note from the ER it would be about nine pages long. It would have every minute they took a vital sign, the second listed when they started the intravenous line or changed it, it has all this garbage I didn't care about. They do that because it all has to be documented for billing. But at the end I'd wonder, *so what was wrong with this patient?* We have lost the forest for the trees.

I am very active in the medical society and I have not found one doctor who has said EMRs have made their lives better. And now there's a lot of data showing that EMRs have been written for insurance companies so they can get information on patients that you probably don't want them to have. A lot of these things have nothing to do with a patient's healthcare but with better pricing. The trouble is the insurance industry has so much power. We should have gone on strike a long time ago. We should have said "Either there's an EMR made by doctors for doctors, or we're done." And they cost the doctors a fortune. The insurance companies get all the data, but the doctors pay for the EMR.

With the advent of EMRs, if patients think they have privacy, they're just kidding themselves. None of us has privacy. Our information is out there, and the wrong person can access it. Back in the days of paper charts, we locked the charts; they were under our control.

In my current role as a teacher I don't have to deal with the EMR. But my students are under so much time pressure, which is why I try my best to help them see the joy in practice. To let them hear the patient say at the end of the visit, "Thank you so much. This was such an enjoyable experience." And I tell them, "You realize the patient has just *thanked you* for taking a history and physical." I really want them to feel that because there are so few times when they're going to feel that. And I get joy from showing this to them. I think that's what patients love. That's why patients love their doctors.

Lack of Control

I would say that back in the old days, doctors derived satisfaction that was based on their ability to control their environment and provide what they considered to be really great medical care to patients who were happy to get that medical care and who realized it was good. There was no adversarial relationship—there was a relationship. Now, care is very fragmented. Appointments are shorter. You may not see the same doctor twice. The doctors in a lot of these circumstances don't feel as though they're being dealt with as professionals because the administrators of the world do not deal with doctors as professionals, they deal with doctors as adversaries.

This is not Marcus Welby anymore; it's more of a Brave New World. Here's an example: Let's say a patient comes to see me for his high blood pressure. He's 90 and it's not easy to get him in the office. I check his blood pressure and then he says, "Oh, and by the way, my ear is really clogged," I can rinse out the wax. But if I do both of those on the same visit Medicare won't pay me. On the other hand, if I take care of his blood pressure and I tell him, "Come back tomorrow," and he comes back tomorrow so I can rinse out his ear, then I get paid for the visit today and I get the procedure code for the visit tomorrow. But if I do them both today, I don't get paid, even though doing both in one visit is better for the patient. Doctors opt for what's better for the patient all the time, but then it's not fair to them. Why can't I get paid for both of them, when I've done both of them? It's a Medicare rule. All these rules have been imposed on doctors and they make us crazy.

Another thing that has happened is the insurance companies and Medicare have forced patients into these *extremely* short hospital stays. And their interest is to get them out. Because if you don't get them out fast enough the hospitals face penalties, they lose money. If you can't say the patient needs an IV or needs more IV medications or we need to do this other test or he's going to have this procedure—if you can't prove that this patient must stay in the hospital, you've got to let him go. Discharge planning catches some of what patients need. But when you do things rapid-fire and you have a lot of patients coming and going on a daily basis, things fall through the cracks. This happens everywhere, all over the country.

What's Missing Today

I think that some of the younger physicians have a new normal. If I see somebody and feel I haven't taken care of that problem, I am very bothered by that. I'm very dissatisfied. I'm very upset. But younger physicians are not. They'll say, "It's all I could do. They may have to come back for another appointment." What if it's an 85-year-old woman who takes three buses? Oh, well.

If you know your patients, you are far more selective in the tests you order than if you don't know your patients well. When you don't know your patients you always order more tests because you're not sure what's going on. The less you know your patients, the more expensive healthcare is. Students in medical school today have no follow-up. Which means they have no relationship-building. As doctors we have let this happen, which makes me incredibly sad. Because I think sometime in the future when things turn around and the pendulum swings back, they're going to ask, "What the heck did you people do?"

Advice

At medical school back in the '80s—and I didn't fully realize it at the time—there clearly was a preference for the guys, the golf-playing doctors—" I've got a time slot on the golf course; who wants to come golfing with me?" I always declined. I now tell women to learn to play golf.

The main thing I would like administrators to know is if you let doctors be doctors, if you let them get to know patients and really take care of patients, the patients get much higher-quality care and it ends up costing a lot less—despite all their formulas and rules and regulations.

My main message is, take care of your patients. Care for them like they are your friends or parents. Cherish the doctor–patient relationship and do not let anyone (insurance companies, hospital administrators) or anything (EMRs) get in your way.

That is the joy of medicine.

5.   *Derek van Amerongen, MD, Vice President and Medical Director of Humana of Ohio*

Driven by a keen interest in health policy, Derek van Amerongen, MD, moved from practicing obstetrics to working in healthcare administration and the health insurance industry. In his role as Vice President and Medical Director of Humana of Ohio, Derek is helping to move the industry toward value-based care and strongly believes that "this is absolutely the best time to be in medicine."

I was always interested, even way back in high school, in the concept of medicine and the history of medicine, and I thought these subjects would always interest me. One of the best pieces of advice I ever got when I was going for my medical school interviews—and interviews for med school, at least then and probably still, are really, really important—was "When they ask why you're going into medicine, for God's sake, do not say to help people! Because if you want to help people, join the Peace Corps. Go work for the Salvation Army. You don't need to be a physician to do that." So, my answer during these interviews was, "I think it would really be fun. It would be fascinating. I think I could do this for the rest of my life and never get bored." And this has been true. The answer must have worked because I got into medical school and here I am.

I trained at the University of Chicago and was in practice in suburban Chicago for about seven years, then was recruited to Johns Hopkins and spent seven years there as chief of obstetrics and, ultimately, vice president of medical affairs for their ambulatory services group. While there I got my Master's in healthcare administration and then came to Cincinnati initially to work for Anthem Blue Cross. I was their national medical director and then in 2000 I was recruited to Humana to be the medical director for Ohio. Now I serve multiple states beyond Ohio and also oversee other commercial medical directors.

What brought me to this side of the industry, or profession, is I've always been interested in health policy. I've always been interested in history and the way things happen and evolve. Early on in my career I saw too many of my peers taking things at face value: that this hospital just magically appeared, and when I walk into the operating room, magically, there are nurses and instruments. I tell somebody I need XYZ and it just shows up. It's all magical thinking. It occurred to me that there is more to it than that. If you study the history of medicine, and I think my interest in history intersects with this, we had a totally different environment before World War II. Very few physicians had hospital privileges. Most hospitals were run by MDs as opposed to administrators. It was a very, very different environment. What is it that changed? How did we get to where we are now? Why is healthcare so complex? I became more and more fascinated with these questions.

At about the same time I started to think about these questions, I realized that although I did a pretty good job in the examining room, my patients would go out into the most dysfunctional world imaginable. The ambulatory services group at Hopkins was the largest Medicaid provider in the state of Maryland. I would say that 95% of my patients were on Medicaid. I'm talking to them about how they need to take their birth control pills and how they should stop smoking and then they go out the door and their issues are: "How do I get home because I have no money?" "My kids are getting a horrible education." "I'm pregnant with my third baby and I don't have a job." "Where am I going to sleep tonight?" "How am I going to eat tonight?" I'd say, "Here's a prescription. Go get an x-ray. Go get an ultrasound." For someone who has low levels of health literacy, how do they figure out how to do that? There are things that you or I have trouble figuring out and we have high degrees of health literacy.

For 50 years, we've had probably the world's most dysfunctional healthcare structure—I hate to use the word "system" because it's not a system—and, of course, up until the Affordable Care Act millions and millions of people were uninsured. Many still are, but fewer. And I thought, *here we are, spending billions of dollars on cancer, and people are dying because their most basic needs are not being met.* We see hospitals buying million-dollar robotic surgery devices and meanwhile, kids are in the emergency room having asthma attacks because their parents can't afford medication—generic medication that costs three dollars a month. Where is the disconnect and how can we address that?

For 15 years I lectured at the University of Cincinnati to third-year medical students as they were going through their obstetrics rotation. I would give a two-hour presentation on very, very basic health policy issues just to give them a little insight into some of the issues they would be facing. They've since created an entire course on this, but at one point, except for my very brief exposure, the vast majority of students would never hear about these issues.

What My Job Entails

I work with employer customers, meeting with them on a regular basis to help them analyze the performance of the insurance plan from a clinical perspective, help them strategize about benefit changes, and help them with utilization and medical issues their populations are having. I also spend a lot of time giving presentations with sales folks about the value we bring. I spend a significant amount of time on trend issues: analyzing utilization trends, cost trends, and coming up with strategies and tactics to address cost issues and improve our picture.

I spend time on purely clinical work—I'm an obstetrician by training so I do a lot of work with our maternity program and with many of our clinical management programs. We have a very active care management program across multiple conditions. In fact, I think we're one of the first plans to focus on analyzing the risk profile of members as opposed to saying, "Let's go for people with asthma" or "let's go for people with heart disease," to get away from putting people in buckets and to say, instead, "Let's look at the red flags, the indicators, that might suggest that a member is at risk for an adverse event, or a complication, or poor health that leads to utilization."

We employ close to 10,000 nurses nationally and their job is to reach out to members who pop up on our algorithm-based predictive model with a certain score and help them with their care coordination issues and questions. A lot of this revolves around member education to address issues of compliance and adherence. We want to make sure we're helping people with chronic diseases to access the right systems, to be paired with the right specialists and the right facilities, and to make sure they're getting their care as expeditiously as possible while avoiding unnecessary care.

I'm also involved, along with my colleagues, in helping to move the entire industry toward a value-based system, trying to align reimbursement with outcomes as opposed to the quantity of care. It's a huge initiative and nothing unique to Humana, but certainly we're very involved with this and, of course, the CMS is very involved with this as well. I think the entire industry is going to get away from paying x amount for a knee surgery, for example, because for every knee surgery performed, we have to ask, "How did the patient do? How quickly did he or she get back to work? Were there complications?" In other words, we've started to link reimbursement to how the patient performs and their outcomes, as opposed to the scenario immortalized in that famous saying, "the operation was a success, but the patient died." That, quite frankly, is how most medical care has always been reimbursed.

I have lots of interactions with customers—that is, employers—and I make many presentations for them. Recently there was what we call a "lunch and learn," where I went to our employers and gave a presentation on nutrition. There was a great response, I really enjoyed it, I got great feedback. Those are enjoyable activities for me; they're opportunities to get out and educate and meet one-on-one with members. I have a meeting today with an employer to go over data. We have good, enjoyable, productive meetings.

One metric of our success is, what is our success rate in keeping these customers? A lot of customers have been here for years and years, which must mean we're doing a good job and they like what we are doing for them. I'm a piece of that. I'm one component of that. And that's enjoyable, too, to be part of a larger team.

Healthcare Reimbursement: Moving Toward Value

Certainly, in the last 50 years, there has been no connection between quality—that is, outcomes or performance—and what healthcare professionals and hospitals have been paid. What you were paid as a provider was really based on completely non-medical considerations: how much market power did you have? What was your specialty? Were you able to drive a good enough deal with the payer? And so on. The real shift now is toward how we link payment to what people are receiving and experiencing. Ultimately, that's all-around value: it gives providers the accountability and responsibility for outcomes while giving them the latitude to do whatever they think is right.

I'm going to be very simplistic here: If I give you $10,000 to do a knee procedure, I really don't care what device you use. I really don't care how you do it. What I care about is, how did the patient perform? Did you come in under our mutually agreed financial target? Did the patient have a low complication rate? Did the patient get back to work quickly? Did you not have to use an excessive number of resources like physical therapy visits or medications?

The kinds of huge databases that payers have access to tell us the average cost of a knee procedure, the average resource utilization, and the average time it takes a patient to return to work. Of course, every physician will tell you that he or she is the best. If the average surgery costs $10,000, why don't we agree that if your cost comes in under $10,000, we'll split the difference? And that if your patients return to work in three weeks while most patients return to work in four weeks, you'll receive an incentive? I'm being very simplistic here. But the point is there are certainly ways to encourage or reward providers who have great outcomes.

In medicine I think we sometimes have very much of a Lake Woebegone attitude: that is, all doctors and all hospitals are above average. That's just not true. I think the public is coming to understand that more and more. Where the industry is going is to reward the providers who really are doing outstanding work. If your patients are going back to work in four weeks, great, here's $10,000. If you're best in class and your patients are going back to work sooner than that, maybe we'll give you $12,000.

The flip side, which I think is critically important—and we're not fully there yet but it's where the industry's going—is that if you fall below the average, maybe we'll give you only $8,000. And maybe, if you really are a poor performer, we'll remove you from the network and tell the members, "you can't go to ABCD orthopedics anymore because they just don't do a good enough job." And that's a sea change from where we've typically been, in which every doctor and every hospital is in the network, and patients have no idea whether one is better than the other.

On Joy in Work

I think joy in work means having some level of satisfaction that you're doing things that are meaningful, and some level of success in getting them done. I think it is also important that I have respect and positive consideration from my associates and people I work with.

One of the things I had to learn when I moved to this side from being a practitioner is that there's a lot of delayed gratification. Physicians, especially surgeons, work very much on instant gratification. Deliver the baby, everybody's happy, everybody's saying, "Oh, doctor, you're so wonderful. Can I take your picture? You're the best. I love you, I love you!" And then you come to this side and you may work on a project for six months or a year before it finally gets rolled out and then once it gets rolled out it takes another year for you to get the data so you can answer the questions, "Okay, did this work? Did we get the data for where we need to be?" It's a very different set of metrics. There are many days that aren't good days, but that's just like everybody else. You don't always have to be happy or ecstatic.

I do miss clinical care in a way. I mean, it was fun. I enjoyed it. But it was physically exhausting and there were many holidays, nights, and weekends I was at the hospital. And at least one Christmas I was on the phone listening to my kids open their presents while I was sitting in the labor and delivery suite. But, you know, that's part of clinical practice. I didn't leave clinical practice because I didn't like it or because I was bored or tired. I just got pulled into this side and I had an interest in it.

I really enjoy what I do now, I've always enjoyed it, and this is a much more tolerable lifestyle than being in clinical practice. Back in the '70s and '80s, people who were medical directors or vice presidents/medical administrators of hospitals were typically people who were semi-retired. I remember at the hospital where I worked in Chicago, the vice president, medical affairs was a surgeon who didn't want to operate anymore; he was more or less marking time until he moved to Florida, and the hospital needed a doctor to approve and sign things. This was a totally different role then; nowadays I don't think you can get the kind of position I have without an advanced degree. Twenty or twenty-five years ago administrators would say, "You've been a doctor for a while, great, you can do this." But now you really can't.

One of the things I think is important is work–life balance. I think as much criticism as millennials seem to get, especially from people in my generation of baby boomers, I think they have it totally right. You must have work–life balance. Of course, kids today want to work, but they want to work differently. One of the criticisms I've heard is that they jump around, they change jobs all the time. But if you look at the research on this, millennials are looking for a job that meets their ethical perceptions/objectives. Whereas we would look at it as a mark of honor to work for 20 years for a company we hated, today millennials are saying, "This company doesn't meet my needs and it isn't what I want. And I will switch jobs to find a company that does and is." They are far more altruistic than we ever were.

Attitude is so tremendously important. I've always tried to, as much as possible, instill that in my kids. That the glass is half full. Every day you have a chance to get up and make the day as positive as possible. Sometimes that's not possible. There are always going to be externalities. But a lot of these things can be fixed. I'm very grateful that I've had the opportunity to get the education, and to have had the experiences, I've had.

What Diminishes Joy

Boredom and frustration diminish joy in work for me—if I'm working on something and it's just not coming together or if I keep hitting roadblocks. In many big organizations there's a lot of passive-aggression. I can really be driven up a wall by the ways people can subvert what you're trying to do, like saying they're excited about your new project and once they're out the door they drop your proposal in the trash. But I'm not sure that's different anywhere else.

It's sometimes hard for physicians because many physicians, especially older physicians, are used to being the lone wolf, the captain of the ship. To be part of a larger team is a transition. I've worked with a lot of docs who have come into this industry and mentored them, and some of them really have trouble with that change.

Reflections

One of the things I would tell my students, and I still think this is quite true, is, "This is absolutely the best time, *ever*, to be in medicine. Now there's all this gloom and doom and people say it's terrible, I'd never tell my kids to go into medicine today." And then I'd tell them, "I first heard that statement in 1975 when I was a freshman medical student. An attending told me that. And, of course, he called me *son*. And it really upset me because I thought, *my God, I've made a horrible mistake. I should have gone to law school like my roommate*."

And then I realized that everybody thinks the golden era of medicine ended ten years ago. This guy in 1975 was all upset because of Medicare. He said, "Ever since Medicare, it's been just terrible. All the people I know are retiring." And so, I've heard that, essentially, for 40 years. One of the things I'd tell my students was, "In 2035 you're going to tell your students, '2018, now *that* was the golden era of medicine. And everything today is just awful and terrible. I'll never tell my kids to go into medicine.'" The golden era of medicine always ended three years before you started.

For people who say the golden era of medicine is in the past, I say "Stop a second. So you want to go back to—pick a number—1995 or 1985 or 1975—when millions of people didn't have coverage; and we had no idea why people were dropping dead from heart disease and diabetes; and we had no ability, and no interest or tools, to make sure that when someone was discharged from the hospital they wouldn't be back in three days with a complication? Do you really want to go back to that era?"

I think this is absolutely the best time to be in medicine because we know so much now about what drives quality. We understand the concept of outcomes. We are making progress in beginning to align reimbursement with outcomes and to really strive for value in healthcare, which we never, ever have. People throw around the word "value," but we've never had a value focus. We understand so much better what really leads to healthy people. You can build a billion-dollar building but if you're not addressing the social determinants of health then you're wasting your time. You're wasting your money.

We know so much more today than we did before, which is what makes this such an amazing time to be in medicine. We have so, so, so far to go but we can't begin to get to the better place unless we understand what the challenges are, and unless we develop some tools to address them. We have so many pieces of technology that are going to be helpful. You know, we don't have to reinvent the Internet. We don't have to reinvent Skype and the kinds of things that are really going to drive, for example, telehealth in the next decade. All that stuff is here. We just have to figure out how to best implement it. And for all the hubbub about the Affordable Care Act, we're never going back. Progress is always up and down and up and down but in general, hopefully, it still moves forward. The pride when you look in the rearview mirror—where we are today versus say, ten years ago, 20 years ago—it's pretty dramatic.

6. *Neal G., MD, Emergency Medicine Physician; Family Practice and*
    Urgent Care Physician and Entrepreneur; and Chief Medical Officer
    for His State's Federal Health Insurance Program, Retired

Neal G., MD, had a passion for emergency medicine and practiced at a community hospital for seven years until, exhausted by the erratic shift work, he needed a
change. His love of emergency medicine, commitment to patient care, and an insati-
able need to learn prompted him to start a family practice-urgent care center in 1980.
But the grind of seeing 30 patients a day for 15 years while running the business
wore on him—and by the time a hospital pressured him to sell his practice, which left
him devastated, he admitted he needed a break. Reinventing himself yet again, Neal
became the chief medical officer for the federal health insurance program in his state.
He is now retired to a consulting business.

I knew when I was 12 years old that I wanted to be a doctor. I thought I wanted to be a
psychiatrist. My first memory is wanting to know why babies cried, which may have been
a surrogate for wanting to understand human beings and the human condition. My mother
thought a lot about life and big pictures and people, and our next-door neighbor was a
cardiologist, who I knew when I was growing up. My dad was a cigar manufacturer's
district sales representative. My mother, a college graduate, sold carbon paper.

I knew I was going to go to medical school when I was in high school. When I entered
the university, I looked at the admission requirements for medical school and took the
courses I needed to get in. I studied the philosophy of religion and lots of other things,
including the arts and economics. Philosophy, not science, was my major. I applied to medical school and they gave me a scholarship. Not many medical students had a degree in
the arts. I went to a private high school for the performing arts and I was really good in
physics, but I knew I'd rather work with people than with machines. Medicine appealed to
me because it's a combination of science and the humanities.

When I went to medical school, I took a rotation in psychiatry at an adult mental hospital,
and for a couple of weeks during school break I worked for pay in an adolescent psychiatric
facility. I decided that I did not want to be a psychiatrist because the cure rate is too low, and
one ends up seeing patients forever. In terms of helping people get well, it wasn't dynamic
enough for me. I thought it was too wishy-washy. We didn't have a lot of drugs at the time.

I decided just after I did the psychiatric rotation in medical school that I'd switch to
emergency medicine. I took rotations in every single part of the body so I could learn
every specialty of medicine: orthopedics, ear-nose-and-throat, ophthalmology, surgery,
obstetrics/gynecology, everything. Then I took special classes. There were no residencies
in emergency medicine when I was in medical school and there were only two residencies in emergency medicine in 1972, when I graduated. There was no board certification
in emergency medicine until 1980. Emergency medicine was the last field in medicine to
become a specialty.

My Professional Journey

Emergency Medicine

I took a rotating emergency medicine internship at a county hospital in a medium-sized
town where there was a lot of action and I was allowed to do a lot of things. There was

no university affiliation at this county hospital. The interns were taking care of really sick people and we didn't have to go through a hierarchy to treat a sick person. I received a lot of responsibility right away, which is why I picked the county hospital. By contrast, patients at the university hospital were esoteric. I saw more patients with lupus than appendicitis. I needed to see front-line stuff, like the Mayo brothers saw when they were starting out in Rochester, Minnesota. My first day on the job in the ER was a .45-caliber slug to a man's right pulmonary artery. We gave him 45 units of blood and we saved him. That was pretty exciting. There were lots of cases like that: drug overdoses, cardiac arrests, gunshot wounds, stab wounds, crazy people, everything. I hired on to work extra shifts in the ER for extra pay so I could see more patients. I was working 100 hours a week and I loved it.

What it means to be an ER doctor is to see everybody's worst nightmare. Working in the ER was really exciting because one's expertise makes a difference right away. I could see everything. I wasn't limited to one part of the body. I saw psychiatric cases and ingrown toenails and everything in between. I only had to put on a white coat and a stethoscope to have an instant practice. I'd just show up. I didn't have to open an office, put out a shingle, or try to solicit patients. I'd just walk in and many patients were waiting for me. So, I decided to do that—and I thought it was great.

When I started most hospitals didn't have emergency medicine groups staffing their clinics. They just asked members of the medical staff to be available when anybody came in. There was no formal emergency medicine anything. The hospitals learned that having an emergency department was a good way to get patients. So, more and more hospitals improved their emergency departments. Then they needed doctors to staff them. This was in 1970. Then some entrepreneurial doctors decided to set up emergency medicine groups and bring in doctors to staff the hospitals with contracted doctors.

I was in the ER at the county hospital in one town, and a town north of us had a community hospital with an emergency department of three rooms and a couple of beds. The ophthalmologists were staffing it. When I finished my internship and was working as a staff doctor in the county hospital ER, the community hospital administrator contacted me and asked if I could staff their hospital emergency department too. Remember, there was no residency and I had just finished my internship. So, with one of my intern friends, and two of his medical school friends from across the country, we formed a group to staff the emergency department. Even without any residency training, we were better than the limited specialists we replaced.

Our model was becoming the force du jour in hospitals all over. It was all happening in 1973, 1974, 1975. Everybody wanted to have an emergency department and there were no doctors who specialized in that because there was no specialty certification until 1980. I became board certified in 1981. At that time, I was one of only 500 doctors in the whole country who was board certified in emergency medicine.

By 1981, I had left the emergency room. I'd worked the emergency room for seven years—from 1973, when I finished my internship, to 1980. I left the emergency room a year before I was certified because I couldn't stay up all night anymore. I was 34 years old and had to work 24-hour shifts. And as the emergency department grew busier and busier between 2:00 a.m. and 6:00 a.m., I couldn't sleep because there were too many patients coming in. I came to the point where I could not have two hours of sleep in a row, which disrupted my REM sleep and the next day I would be a zombie.

But I loved it! Here were patients coming in and they were sick: death was on one side, and I was on the other. I had all this knowledge and all these skills—I saw people who should have been dead—but my life was a mess. It would take me a day to recover from a shift. I talked to my partners and said I couldn't do this, rotating nights, days, back and forth. We needed to have a schedule like the police have, where they work three months of nights, three months of days, three months of afternoons—eight-hour shifts instead of 24. I said we couldn't continue to do it like this because was bad for our health. They wouldn't go for it. They said, "No, no, no, we want 24-hour shifts so we can have two or three days off and go skiing." So, I left.

The other reason I left, and this gets to the question of joy in work, is that I didn't have any continuity of care. Emergency medicine is everything you can do in 30 minutes. And then you never see the patient again. Maybe they'll come back for something else and they'll say, "Oh, yeah, I was here three years ago, doctor." Or maybe they need a follow-up and for some reason or other they come back to you. But, in general, you never see them again. You might wonder, when you're done with them, were my diagnosis and treatment correct? I've taken you this far, but we don't have a final diagnosis. We have to try this and see what happens and we'll figure it out over time, but we're going to keep you alive until then.

In those kinds of cases I didn't have any patient follow-up. So, I'd have to call up the patient's doctor and ask, "What happened to Mr. Jones?" Or I'd take their names and I'd call them up two weeks later to see how they did and what happened to them. And I was able to find out. Patients were flabbergasted. That was the only way to develop my skills as a doctor—I had to know the final outcome. I felt that the expansion of my skills as a doctor was being limited because I didn't receive any follow-up.

I decided I wanted to enhance my skills further and my knowledge of how to diagnose more complicated non-emergency cases and mitigate disease progression, so I thought I needed to go into more comprehensive primary care. But I liked taking care of really sick people. I thought primary care practices, like those of a family doctor, were boring because most of what they did was manage chronic disease. And even then, they only managed simple chronic disease, along with immunizations and vaccinations and well checks. It wasn't as exciting as I wanted, and I wouldn't see many urgent diagnostic problems. I wouldn't see people with appendicitis, acute gall bladder disease, kidney stones, things like that.

Family and Urgent Care: Building the Practice

I decided in 1979 that in order to have a joyful work experience I would start a family and urgent care practice. I wanted to staff an office where the doctors work both days and evenings seven days a week. I figured I'd have a daytime family practice and an evening urgent care practice. Soon I realized that if I really wanted to have patients use my urgent care practice, I'd need to keep it open for urgent cases all day long. I'd have to somehow market it to people so they'd know they could come in whenever they were sick. I decided I would be open from 8:00 a.m. until 10:00 p.m. and have urgent care availability—walk-ins—all day long, plus appointments. I started out with one doctor, myself, and I had an open schedule. People would walk in and I could see them, but not necessarily right away if I had a scheduled appointment. In 1980 I knew I'd need at least two doctors and eventually the practice would expand to five, and then to seven, doctors. My first time-sharing associate was a doctor who left the emergency department at the same time I did.

For marketing, I wrote letters to every doctor in my town who had been sending patients to the emergency department if they got sick at night. I had been taking care of their patients for years because I was working in the hospital emergency department. I knew all the primary care doctors and I'd visited them when I was in the ED, checking out their practices, so they all knew me.

I told them, "I'm moving across the street. You can send your patients to me instead of to the ED. They'll get the same good care they got from me in the ED and it will be a lot less expensive. And, on top of that, I'll take call for you during the evening until we close. You won't even have to answer the telephone. On top of that, when I see the patient, I will write up an encounter form to explain what was wrong with them and what you need to do for follow-up. I will send it to you that evening by fax. And you know it takes three days to get the record from the hospital. So, you'll know when you go to work the next day exactly what happened to your patient in my office. Whereas if you send that same patient to my colleague in the ED you won't know for three days. And on top of that, I'll make sure that nobody disparages your reputation in case one of us finds something about your care that needs to be changed."

As a result, when we opened, half the patients who had been going to the ED came to my office. Typically, one patient per practice per day was referred. Twenty to twenty-five doctors signed up with our service, so we were busy immediately. The ED volume dropped but the hospital still had plenty of business. My colleagues there were a little testy. They there were a little angry for a while because my new service took away a lot of their bread and butter business—sore throats, ankle sprains, asthma attacks, and minor lacerations. These were easy to treat, they'd get a lot of money for each case, and none required much time.

But I thought there was a lot of room for my business, which gave me the opportunity both to see sick patients and do follow-up. That enabled me to be a better doctor because I could learn what was causing someone's symptoms over time. The patients loved it because if they became sick, they could come in right away. We helped the practices of the family doctors in town who sent us their patients for urgent problems. The referring doctors were our customers. Unattached patients could request that a doctor in our group become their regular doctor, follow them and, if they had problems, manage their case.

I think this is what later came to be called a "medical home" model. If I had a patient who had a lung problem, or a gastrointestinal problem, or I couldn't figure it out—or if they needed a procedure like a bronchoscope or upper gastrointestinal endoscopy or colonoscopy—I would refer them to the specialist. I'd make a copy of the patient's record with all the tests I had ordered. Patients would go to the doctor with a copy of the record so the specialist wouldn't have to repeat any tests. Then I'd tell the specialist, "When you're done, I want a letter telling me what you found and what you did."

If the condition was managed by the specialist long term that would be fine. But when they didn't have to manage the patients, they'd tell me what to do, send the patients back to me, and I'd take care of them. If a doctor didn't send a letter back, I'd say, "I need a consultation letter, or I can't send you any more patients." And with each of these letters I'd see what the specialist did, and then I'd start doing it myself for the next patient. I would learn from the specialists what I didn't know so I could be a better doctor. That's how the Mayo Clinic did it. It got to the point where I didn't need internal medicine consults as often. More often I'd refer patients only when they needed a procedure that I couldn't do myself.

I'd see several esoteric diagnoses that I'd never seen before and sometimes I'd figure it out and sometimes the specialists would figure it out. I remember calling a doctor about a patient who had a disease called Cushing's syndrome. I looked at her and said, "You look like you're taking steroids." She didn't know what steroids were. I looked at her and said, "You must have Cushing's syndrome." I called the endocrinologist on the telephone and said, "I think I have a patient with Cushing's syndrome. What tests do I order?" He gave me the list of tests and I ordered them and then I sent the patient to him with the test results. She had Cushing's syndrome caused by a pituitary tumor. She had seen six doctors before she saw me. I didn't know how to work it up because I had never seen a case. But I studied it in medical school, so I knew what the signs were. I was impressed in medical school that diseases of the endocrine system were the hardest to diagnose. That's just a little example of what it was like in my practice. Talk about joy! It was thrilling to be able to figure out what was wrong and tell patients what they had. I found joy in helping people and joy in constant learning.

Expanding the Practice

We got so busy in those first four years that we moved to a bigger office in another location with nine exam rooms and three nurses' stations. By 1995 we had 10,000 patients. By then we had seven doctors: six full-time doctors and doctors in the community who wanted to come in and help out weekends and evenings. We didn't want nurse practitioners because we specialized in diagnosing and treating sick and injured people, and nurse practitioners don't have enough training for that. Instead, we hired all board-certified family doctors. I was a board-certified emergency medicine doctor. I trained my colleagues in emergency medicine and they taught me how to manage chronic disease. We helped each other. Some of my patients thought I was an internist. If patients had to see a specialist for a chronic condition we couldn't manage, they still saw a specialist and came to us for primary care. It was a team approach. I had this family practice-urgent care center for 15 years, from 1980–1995.

Closing the Practice

The hospital offered my partners $1.1 million to sell the business to them. Which they did, excluding me. I couldn't hire new, well trained family practice doctors because the hospital was offering them more money. So, we closed. What I would have done if this hadn't happened would have been to work with the hospital to help them transition from this greedy, self-centered, fee-for-service environment to an environment where the needs of the patient are the only things to be considered. The hospital wanted to run the business and I said, "I can't have you run this business. You're not doctors, you're administrators." But that didn't matter.

After my clinic was destroyed, and I couldn't get really good doctors to work with me and my patients weren't happy, I got sick from the stress. I solicited financial help from a hospital five miles away in exchange for joining its managed care network. The cross-town hospital competed with my hospital across the street. I asked for subsidies for my newly hired doctors so I could compete with my hospital that was subsidizing the income of doctors in its network. We worked out a deal so I could stay in business. With temporary competitive subsidies, I thought I could keep our service alive. But the next year, the two hospitals merged. They fired the CEO who was helping me. The subsidies for my employee doctors was cut off. For a while I subsidized their income from mine. But after a few months, I realized that I wasn't going to make it, that I couldn't compete without hospital subsidies.

How did I feel when this was going on? I had a gun in my car that belonged to my father-in-law and I had fantasies that I was going to shoot the CEO in the head. That's how I felt about it. So, I decided to get rid of the gun. I was on the edge. I had to back up. That's how angry I was. I was screaming in the shower every day. I was completely devastated. My wife left me. We got divorced. I was a total wreck. Emergency medicine with continuity of care is what I had always wanted to do. This was my calling. My business was my child—I didn't have any kids. The joy I had was destroyed because the hospital wanted to take over the practice. It was all about money.

To be honest, in 1995, after doing this for 15 years, I needed a break. I was getting tired of solving problems all day, seeing 30 patients a day; I was getting a little tired. I just needed a little break—I didn't need to quit. I miss clinical work a little.

From Practice to Policy

When I saw that I couldn't compete financially with the hospital I applied and was hired to work as the chief medical officer for the federal insurance program in my state. My job was to make coverage decisions for five million people. The man who hired me saw something in me I didn't see in myself. If you were a doctor and had any concerns about getting paid, or if you weren't sure what the government would pay for, you had to talk to my company or me. I was "the man" for 60,000 doctors. My job was to make sure the doctors were not impaired in their ability to properly diagnose and treat their patients. I thought this was absolutely fabulous. Writing coverage policies was as compelling to me as treating someone in the ED who came in with a heart attack. With my first policy paper, which took nine months to write, I affected psychotherapy coverage for the entire northern region of the state. My job lasted over six years.

The power I had to influence healthcare went up a thousand-fold in that job—from treating one patient at a time to treating a system with all the other doctors treating patients. I could make the system work better so the doctors were empowered, and the patients became empowered. The patients received what they needed, the doctors were paid on time and correctly, and almost everybody was happy—it worked. The medical care system was my patient.

On Joy in Work

For me, joy in medicine means constant improvement, constant learning, helping people in ways that really matter to them, and curing disease. The other thing that brought me joy was helping people die.

There is another part of the real joy I had in work I'd like to share. In my living room, over my fireplace, is a Japanese picture. On the side of the picture are three dolls: one with red hair, one with black hair, and one with white hair. Those are in my house because a patient, a Japanese woman, gave each one of them to me when I went to her house to see her husband, who was bedbound from multiple brainstem strokes. She used a Hoyer lift to get him out of bed, and he was in a vegetative state for five years. He was 6'2", she was 5' tall. I would walk by their Japanese garden and into the house to take care of him.

She first contacted me because he was going back and forth to the hospital for a urinary tract infection. She called to see if I would see her husband at home. I agreed to do it. When I saw him, I said, "We can fix this with a Foley catheter and daily irrigation with diluted white vinegar." I instructed her what to do. I told her he would never get another urinary tract infection and she wouldn't have to take him to the hospital. The treatment worked. He never developed another urinary tract infection and never went back to the hospital. She'd call me every quarter to visit him, which I did. Every time I saw him, she gave me a present. She was so grateful. And these gifts are sitting in my house today. I saw him for about two years until he became so sick that he died. But he died at home. I had ten patients like him who, because of their condition, couldn't leave their homes.

When you go to somebody's home you get to know them much better than you do when they come to your office. You see the way they live, their family. It's also joyful when the family's so grateful. The patients are overcome with joy. It's so completely weird for a doctor to go and see a patient in their home today.

One of the joys I had as a family doctor is that I assisted in the surgery of all my patients. I've done 1,000 surgical assists. What does that mean? Internists do not assist at surgery. When my patients needed surgery, I told the surgeon I'd like to assist. I've assisted on just about every surgery there is. I assisted on open heart surgery, brain surgery, foot surgery, vascular surgery, appendicitis, C-sections, penile implants, gallbladders, total hip surgery, you name it, I've assisted on it. Just about everything where a surgeon needs an assistant. That brought joy because I was able to work with my hands and I learned who the good surgeons were. I could watch them work. I learned who the best urologist was to take out the prostate. I learned who the best one was for any surgery because I had watched them all operate. When a patient needed surgery, I chose the best surgeon for the case. I could even match the personalities of the surgeon and the patient.

On Money and Joy

When I had the family practice-urgent care business, which was fee for service, I made toward the top end of what a family practice doctor makes. And about the same as, or maybe a little less than, what an emergency room doctor makes. Our rates were set so that the hairdresser without insurance could afford our care. Our regular office visit cost twice what it would cost to get your hair done. Because we wanted to take care of people, we accepted uninsured patients. We didn't want to have exorbitant rates or gouge people, so we had reasonable rates—our average visit cost $65 with everything included. It would be five times as much if you went to the emergency room for the same thing. I made enough. I funded my individual retirement plan. I didn't make enough money to have a Mercedes, but I didn't care about that. If I had had kids and wanted them to go to private school that would have been a problem. If I lived in a different part of the country, I could have made more money. But for me and my wife the income was enough.

For the most part, doctors make enough money to live a very comfortable life. That doesn't mean they're going to have a boat in the Caribbean or a string of polo ponies, but they make enough money to live well. You don't have to be greedy. But there's greed out there. Some doctors cross the line and abuse Medicare and a lot of them get away with it.

Advice

Eventually it became obvious to me that the only way healthcare can go forward is to practice the way the Mayo brothers did it. They were exactly right—they were just 100 years ahead of their time. There's too much information for one doctor to practice alone. The practice of medicine must be a group effort. The Mayo brothers were also exactly right that doctors compete with each other for money and to get rich. The only way to make the practice of medicine work is to put the doctors on a salary so they work together as a team, not as jealous competitors. Under fee for service, doctors are cutthroat with each other. I saw it all the time.

To have joy in medicine in an integrated health system, doctors have to be in charge of how long they can spend with each patient. They can't have a bean counter telling them they can only have 15 minutes with a patient if the patient needs half an hour. Collectively, doctors need to be in charge of the part of the business that allows them to take proper care of patients; they can't let the bean counters control them. Either raise the premium or figure out a way to reduce waste and abuse so there's enough money left on the table to do the right thing in managed care.

There has to be respect on both sides between doctors and administrators so they can solve their problems together instead of feeling that they have to fight with each other. You can't have a battle. You have to work together. You have to have a set of values that embraces putting the patient first and figure out how you're going to make that happen. You can't take care of patients if your business goes south and you don't have a place to work. You have to have a facility, and workers and doctors. The devil's in the details. There has to be shared decision-making. You want to work in a place that puts the patient first, where number crunchers don't interfere.

Medicine is partly logic and partly magic. You have to understand the human being.

Addendum from Neal G.

In March 2019, five months after we talked for this interview, an investigator from the state district attorney's office visited me at home. He asked me to verify a copy of a medical record I had created in 1978 when I was an ER doc. It was from an unsolved rape case. I had collected the evidence from a woman following a "rape kit protocol" and sent it to the sheriff, protecting its chain of evidence. Then the investigator told me what happened:

The sheriff's office kept the file, including the sperm sample, which I took from the victim's vagina. During the past several years, a police investigator who was still looking for the rapist compared the DNA in that sample to the DNA in various DNA and genealogy databases. Based on that DNA sample, 50 suspects were identified as potentially being the rapist. DNA from each suspect was obtained. Most were eliminated but three remained. One sample I had obtained from the victim was an exact match. DNA samples obtained by other ER docs from two other rape victims were perfect matches as well. Joseph James DeAngelo, Jr., called the "Golden State Killer" or "East Bay Rapist," was identified as the criminal. He raped and murdered scores of victims. DeAngelo is now in jail. www.cnn.com/2019/04/24/us/golden-state-killer-one-year-later/index.html; https://en.wikipedia.org/wiki/Golden_State_Killer.

Today, 42 years later, I feel proud I was well trained in emergency medicine and perfectly performed my job on behalf of the rape victim and all concerned. Professional training matters as well as precisely following protocols! Learning a skill that helps other people is a blessing.

7. Mary R., MSN, Perioperative Educator

Mary R. is a perioperative educator at a large academic medical center. She comes, she says jokingly, "from the era of things that aren't there anymore." A hands-on, roll-up-your-sleeves powerhouse and self-described "true workhorse," she's worked in the operating room (OR) of six different hospitals—as a staff nurse, a supervisor, an educator, and a mentor—for a total of 47 years.

Becoming a nurse was something I always wanted to do. When I was a little girl, I used to play doctor with my cousin. Back then, here were your options: you became a nurse, a teacher, or a secretary.

I think my attraction to the OR comes from my childhood. I have three sisters, and of the four of us I was the tomboy. When my dad needed help with things, I was the one who would help him. I painted. I hung up awnings. I was the carpenter. That kind of thing. I was very hands-on. That kind of goes with the OR because we're dealing with instruments; we're always fixing things. Dealing with the instruments, using my hands, and troubleshooting equipment appealed to me.

I like the procedural caring for a patient as opposed to the medical caring for a patient on the floor. When you come into the OR with a bad gall bladder, we take it out and hopefully you're better. In surgery something needs to be repaired or removed and hopefully the problem is resolved, although that's not always the case. Sometimes the best we can hope for is an improved quality of life. Patients on the floor usually have a medical diagnosis and all we can do is control the medical issue. It's as though you can never really fix it, it's always there. But there are nurses who like to do that.

A staff nurse in the OR circulates. In the OR the staff nurse is the unsterile person in the room, besides the anesthetist. The "circulator" does exactly that—circulates. He or she is the person who makes sure the patient is secure on the table, the one who gets the patient ready to be prepped and draped for the procedure and is free to get the sterile team what they need. The OR nurse is the patient advocate.

My Professional Journey

From Operating Room Staff Nurse to Operating Room Supervisor

I was a diploma grad and when I graduated, I started my career as a floor nurse at my hospital. I worked for six months on the floor until there was an opening in the OR. I worked there for five years and then moved to a hospital as a staff nurse in the OR for about six months before becoming the OR supervisor. I was in my early 20s when I became the OR supervisor, probably the youngest person in that position in this city.

It was a 200-bed hospital with a very progressive management style. They were forward-thinkers and had a proactive approach to everything. But it was a small independent hospital and we struggled a lot. In the late '90s, a large tertiary hospital that was also struggling bought us thinking we might be able to help them. In turn, they closed us. I transferred to the larger hospital and assumed the position of OR director for surgical services at the larger hospital. We worked hard to save the hospital but that didn't happen, and both hospitals closed within two years of each other. The smaller hospital eventually was demolished. By that time, I had moved on and took a position as director of outpatient services at a level I trauma center. That hospital was struggling a little bit. They did some restructuring, had some layoffs, and of course those of us who were new to the organization were laid off.

And at that point I said, "Okay, I've closed two hospitals and I've been laid off from a third in a matter of five years." So, I took my severance and stayed home for about four or five months. I received a call from a recruiter saying he had a hospital looking for an OR director at a small rural hospital. And I thought, *Oh, Lord have mercy, I'm a city person.*

I said, "I don't know."

He said, "Well, come and check it out."

In the meantime, I had also sent my resume to a large, 500-bed hospital in the city, had interviewed there, and I was waiting to hear.

I went to the rural hospital and checked it out. It seemed like a nice little place and I thought, *this is different.*

I received a call back from them saying, "We would like you to take this position, come up for an employee physical," etc.

So, I headed up the highway to that hospital. While I was on my way, I got a call from the big city hospital. I was in the car thinking, *What do you want to do? Do you want to work in the city? Do you want to work out here?* And I thought, *you know what? For some reason I'm being sent in this direction.* So, I went to the rural hospital.

This was a small rural hospital, about 200 beds. I took that position and stayed there for about two and a half years, then received a call from the vice president of a different hospital downtown. This vice president had been my little sister in nursing school, believe it or not.

She said, "Mary, we're building a new OR, would you come and build it?"

I said I didn't know. She told me to come and check it out, which I did.

I went down there, and it was just girders in the ground. And I thought, *the OR is my life. Working in rooms, you kind of know what works. If this were my OR I would build it this way for patient flow, and our flow,* and so on. So, I did. I went down and helped finish building the OR. It was a wonderful experience. It really was. They had plans in place before I got there but I had input. I could say, "This should be here because…" and "We should do this because…" So, we did make some adjustments to it. It turned out to be a beautiful OR.

I was there for about two and a half years and one day they said, "Thank you very much, but we don't need you anymore." I was let go. The vice president was let go. She took a job in another hospital and told me to contact the OR director because she'd heard they needed somebody with my experience. So I did, and that's how I ended up here in 2008.

When I got here, the OR director said, "We really need your years of experience and your background to try to develop a program and make sure everybody is on the right path."

Developing a Simulation Program for Operating Room Nurses

I wanted to develop the simulation program to train nurses for a couple of reasons. First, because there was no formal education for the OR and nurses just received their training on the job. This was very confusing for a new nurse because as they went from one preceptor to another, everyone did things differently and the new nurse didn't know if it was right or wrong. Second, it was very difficult for a nurse whose heart was in the OR to get hired because no one would ever take a nurse without experience.

When I was director, applicants would say, "You probably won't take me because I don't have experience."

And I'd say, "You're not going to get experience unless someone lets you in."

I was a new grad once and lucky enough to be taken in and mentored, so I've always felt a responsibility to return that opportunity.

Once on board, I developed a simulation program for OR nurses. I took them down to our sim lab—which had an OR—and put together scenarios, let them practice, and then we reviewed the scenarios on video to critique their practice and correct bad practice.

When I built the simulation program, I did some research with AORN—the Association of periOperative Registered Nurses—they are the guiding light for OR nursing. AORN developed a program called Periop 101, which is an online program of basic OR fundamentals. It's licensed, it's their program, you purchase it. So long story short I ended up getting corporate administration to sponsor the program knowing there was going to be this huge exodus of nurses coming down the pike. Our health system is a large corporation. We have several hospitals, lots of ORs, and I thought, *how are you going to keep things running if you don't have nurses to keep it running?*

Training Nurses in Operating Room Fundamentals

Eleven years ago, I got together with corporate nursing and I told them we needed to implement Periop 101. They were very supportive. The goal at that time was to get the new graduates as they came out of nursing school. I wanted to focus on presenting this program to the new grads because they don't get much, if any, operating room exposure in training. What these nurses get in the periop program is what I got when I was in nursing school. It's a lot different now, though.

Since this is a system-sponsored program it's gone out to all our sister hospitals. I train the trainers at our hospitals outside of the city. We have educators in all those hospitals. I train the educators and they train their nurses in the program. That way, we have standardization as far as orientation to the operating room. We also run a program for all new nurses in the seven hospitals in the city. If nurses transfer among hospitals, we know they've all had the same orientation. Different hospitals do different things, but we know they've all been taught the core basics.

Matching Nurses to Operating Room Cultures

Every operating room has a culture. It's a combination of the management team and the surgeons on the one hand, and how well you, as an individual, fit into that environment on the other. For instance, I'm at a level I trauma center. There's not as much warm and fuzzy as you would find in a community hospital because it's all about the critically ill. The culture here is very matter of fact, think on your feet, be quick, and think way beyond. There's a higher expectation. A nurse who's timid and shy wouldn't survive here because everything is critical and matter of fact.

I match nurses who want to come to the OR with a facility where I think they will bloom because it's important to fit into a culture. New nurses may say, "I want to be at this hospital because I want to see all that stuff that's cutting edge." And then they get in here and they're stunned by the size. We have 44 operating rooms and they're like deer in the headlights. They can't get into that gear.

And then I'll say, "Okay, let's move you to another place. Maybe you need a smaller place where you'll have time to grow, where you can work with patients who come in for elective surgery versus having emergencies all the time." Sometimes a nurse just needs to be in a different type of atmosphere to thrive.

I get a lot of nurses who transfer from the floor to the OR. I ask them, "Why did you decide to transfer to the OR?" Because I want to know, why are you here? Are you here because it's what you always wanted to do? 99% of the time the answer I get is, "Because I only have to take care of one patient at a time. When I'm on the floor I have six patients and I can't spend time with my patients, and I feel I don't give them the care they deserve." They're frustrated with that.

Sometimes they just want a mental break. And when they get down here and see that OR nursing is not floor nursing, that it's a whole new way of nursing, they'd have to get on a whole new career path to work here, they don't want to do it. They may sit in the classroom for two weeks and say, "I'm going back to the floor." Because they don't really know what it's like to run an operating room. They think, *oh, it's only one patient, I can sit in the corner and just chart.* No, you don't just chart. You chart at the end of the case.

I think because my whole life has been in the OR I can look at a nurse who comes to the OR on the first day and say, "Oh, she's not an OR nurse." When they have these pie-in-the-sky ideas I think, *they're not going to make it.* And I'm honest with them, I just tell them.

On Joy in Work

Working in the OR was my heart. I think you must have heart to be in the OR. It must call you. But I think that's true of any specialty area, including med-surg. I consider med-surg a specialty area. In today's world it takes special nurses to be on the floor. They work so hard. My joy now comes from looking at the new nurses who I've trained and seeing them develop into good, strong, professional operating room nurses, just taking care of the patients and providing quality care. I see them growing, I watch them. That's my joy.

A trauma hospital is a hard place to work. We've got critically ill patients. And, you know, you watch these nurses. You can see them making these little leaps and they kind of settle a bit. Then they make another big leap. You just see them getting stronger and becoming more critical thinkers and able to handle these stressful situations.

I feel that I've done my job. Lord forbid, if I ever need to be on the table, I'd feel safe knowing I taught these nurses, you know? I can say, "I know that you know what you're supposed to do because I taught you. I don't have to worry. And I know that you're giving patients what they deserve to have."

On Money and Joy

With today's nurses I think there is a relationship between money and joy, unfortunately. In my era we didn't care what we made. We got satisfaction out of watching our patients come into the hospital, get fixed, and go home. Today, and I just think it's the way the world is, it's "I'm working really hard, so I deserve to be paid X dollars." And they do work hard, they work very hard, and I do sometimes feel that they deserve more than they get. We're dealing with a different level of illness today. There's a lot more responsibility on them today than there was when I started. Even in the OR you see the difference. I just think that's the way things have evolved.

What Diminishes Joy

What diminishes joy in work is frustration. The frustration is sometimes caused by not having a smooth operation. Not always being included in what's going on by upper management. I think it just depends on your management team. Some might think if they tell you something you don't like, you'll pick up and leave. What also contributes to the opposite of joy is the distraction of cell phones, administrator–clinician disconnect, favoritism, and fear of speaking your mind.

Being Left Out of the Loop

If I know things are tough and I know you're trying to fix them, I'll hang with you. I'll give you an example: when I was at my first tiny little hospital, because money was tight back then, our purchasing director would say, "Oh, I can't get that from this company. Are you ok if I get it from this other company?"

And I'd say, "Yeah, okay, fine."

And when things were really tight, I'd tell the nurses, "Don't open anything unless you absolutely need it because things are tight and don't waste supplies if you don't need them."

I also involved the doctors in that. I'd tell them, "Don't ask these nurses to open things up if you don't really need them."

You know, it was like one big family. We all worked together to get the job done. But when you're left out of the loop, you think, *all I'm doing is coming in here, punching in and doing my work, punching out, and getting a paycheck.* And you don't feel like you're "part of." When staff are not included that's all they feel they're there to do—punch in and punch out, work on the assembly line.

The Distraction of Cell Phones

I'd like to take the cell phones and collect them at 6:00 in the morning and give them back at 3:00 in the afternoon when nurses go home. The cell phone is a huge distraction and we fight that every day. I fight it in the classroom. I'm teaching and these nurses are on their phones. The doctors have complained but they've contributed to the problem because they'll say, "Text me when you're ready for me, I'm going out on the floor." They don't carry pagers anymore; they use their cell phones as their pagers. You don't hear any pagers going on unless there's a code.

Everything is, "I want it right now." But when we walk in and you're on Amazon or on Facebook, or the doctor's asking for something and you're so absorbed in your phone that you don't hear what he's asking for, that's a problem.

And then nurses don't know how to have personal interaction, which is why you see less patient interaction. They don't know how to talk to people. They talk to that telephone. There's a time and a place for everything and I always say to them, "You think of that person on the bed as your family member. Do you want your nurse acting like this, taking care of your family member on the table? You know, that person deserves 100% of your attention as long as they're there. They can't speak for themselves."

Administrator–Clinician Disconnect

Administration is running the business. That's their job. They have budgets they have to stay within. They're looking for ways to increase business; how we're going to keep patient flow going; how we're going keep moving this bus along. They have their restraints and they have their strategies, and they look at what's coming down the pike or what they see in the next five years. As opposed to worker bees, who just want what they need when they need it. And it's not that administration doesn't see that. I know they see that. They know you need what you need to be able to do your job. But I think because they don't walk the path, they don't realize how difficult it can be sometimes.

Favoritism

Sometimes staff feel there's favoritism. I think it does exist. Sometimes administration migrates more to some staff members than others instead of being neutral across the board. There may be a nurse who, with the right mentorship, could turn out to be the best and strongest charge nurse; she has a real desire to excel, to grow, and to take on that role. But if she isn't particularly verbal—and some are not, they're just workers, nose to the grindstone, they want to be the best nurses and want to learn everything they can and they're not always chitchatting with administration—she won't get noticed.

So, when you say, "I think we should do this with so-and-so," administration will snap back and say, "No, I don't think so." Because she's not their favorite. I think what makes a favorite is being someone who has the gift of gab. You know, those who are politically correct, who say the right things. They're always talking to the administration and making the brownie points, as I call them. There are some magnificent people who administration doesn't see; and even if you bring those people to their attention, they don't want to see because those people don't fit into their personal plan for advancement. They have their eyes on their favorites.

Fear of Reprisal

Staff is asked what they think on surveys, but they are too intimidated to answer honestly. They feel that even though they're on the computer and the survey is anonymous, the administration will know who they are. So, I don't know that everybody is 100% honest. Staff always feel there will be a repercussion even though they're told there won't be.

I'm not saying that administration hasn't heard and made changes, they have. They most definitely have made changes based on what's come out of those surveys. For example, in general, people say that cafeteria food is boring. So, they'll change things in the cafeteria. Or that we need a little bit more variety here or there. Or that the shuttles don't run as often as we would like. In other words, the changes they've made are general as opposed to what's going to make someone feel better personally, like changing their schedule for a better work–life balance. People feel, *if I'm not going to get what I really need, why should I bother to ask for it?* And *if I'm not going to get what I need anyway, why would I stick my neck out and risk reprisal?*

Reflections

I have many thoughts about what is needed in healthcare today:

- If I could get administration to walk the walk with nurses and really listen to them, that is what I would do. Not "I hear you" but "I'm listening to you." There is a difference between hearing and listening. If they would just listen, they wouldn't have the turnover. Staff would stay.
- I truly, honestly worry about what's going to happen with healthcare down the road. I worry because maybe we're turning out nurses too quickly. When I talk to them in class and ask them, "Did you learn this?" they say no. I think there's a different curriculum in nursing today. When I was in training, I had a lot of hands-on. These nurses come to us and they've never put a Foley catheter in a patient. I'm not saying they don't get the clinical experience, they do. But it's minimal.
- I don't think nursing can be those three rigid shifts anymore. There is some movement to change that, but here's the thing: If you're going to tell me I can work three 12-hour days so that I can have four days off, well, you know what, at my age I'll be dead soon.

And studies say none of us is that good at the ninth hour, anyway. So, what else can you do? Maybe administration needs to be a little more creative.

- I had great mentors when I first started out and I've always felt I must give back. That was always my underlying motivation as an OR director. I must make sure that I mentor, that I have something to give these new nurses, because the OR is pretty much all baby boomers across the country. It is projected that in the next few years there will be a tremendous exodus of nurses because everybody's up in their 50s and 60s.

- You're always going to have ORs. You're always going to have illness. But I think medicine has gotten to the point where physicians are so busy doing their thing that they don't have the time to do some of the "personal" things involving care that used to be their role. Today healthcare is a business. It's big business, unfortunately, and I think that's one of the frustrations that nurses feel today.

- I've always been a supporter of our folks in central processing—you know, they're the folks who sterilize our instruments—but I don't think people in human resources (HR) understand how important they really are to patient care. I mean, these folks have hundreds of thousands of instruments that they must take apart and clean and put back together again properly or they're not going to work when the doctor needs them in surgery. HR people are HR people; they were never clinical.

  They'll say, "Well, these jobs are only worth X number of dollars."

  I always say, "You know, I can go back 47 years and say that when I started out, central processing cleaned bed pans and urinals. But today that isn't what their job is. Today their job is much more complex."

  And yet these healthcare workers are in the same classification as housekeepers, who are the other most important people in the hospital.

- My boss always tells me, "You don't toot your horn enough."

  And I say, "I don't need to toot my horn. I know what I do. And if I have to toot a horn to be noticed, I don't need to be noticed. I need to do what I need to do to take care of my patients and I need to make sure the nurses I educate are doing what they're supposed to do. I don't need to tell you every ten minutes that I did this, that, and the other thing. I just do it."

Advice

If you empower your nurses and you keep your staff in the loop and they know what's going on, they're more apt to be responsive to your needs.

To upper management I say, "Your nurses have more ideas than you'll ever have. You have a whole staff of people who are walking the walk every day. If you want to know what's going on, ask them."

At times the administrators don't have a sense of what the staff needs are. Administration doesn't really understand what nurses go through every day. Walk the walk with staff one day and watch what they have to do to get from point A to point B, or to get the patient from here to there to somewhere else. Administrators should do more shadowing. I think then they would understand how hard their staff works. Not only nursing, but ancillary support personnel as well, areas we rely on in order to deliver quality care.

Listening is a first step toward needed change. And sometimes it's just little things. You know, let staff have a little more flexibility in their schedules. Work–life balance is so important for folks now. *It's not all work, we want to have a life.* You have to be able to balance that. And if you can really balance that, they'll be happy here every day. Give them flexibility, you know?

I've always believed in three basic principles: simplify the paperwork; standardize the products; and streamline the processes. If these three principles are in place, people are happy, work gets done, and there is a smooth-running department.

8.   *Rachel M., MD, Pediatric Radiologist and Professor of Radiology*

Rachel M., MD, is a board-certified radiologist and certified in pediatric radiology. She is chief of pediatric radiology at a large academic medical center and a children's hospital and is a professor of radiology. Rachel started residency in radiology in the mid-1960s and has been devoted to this field ever since.

I went into medicine by following my own interests. I was interested in practically everything in school, but I was *most* interested in the sciences. I thought of medicine as a science-based field, which of course is only part of it, but I thought it was an important part of it. In high school and college, I knew I wanted to go to medical school and that I really wanted to be a doctor. But I didn't decide I wanted to go into pediatric radiology until I was a resident in radiology. As a resident you rotate through various subspecialties of your field—and as I rotated through pediatric radiology, I knew that was for me. After medical school, internship, and residency in radiology I did a two-year fellowship in pediatric radiology with the intention of being a pediatric radiologist. I felt from the very start that I was born to do radiology and I'm still born to do it. I love it every day.

What appealed to me about pediatric radiology was that I love children. I work indirectly with kids for the most part—because except for one or two subspecialties in radiology, you're a doctor's doctor, not a patient's doctor. You're helping the other clinicians caring for the patient, pointing them in the right direction as to what that patient needs. Diagnosis is the bedrock of medicine, without which you really can't begin to take care of the patient. You don't know what's wrong with them. Every medical subspecialty relies at least in part on radiology for diagnosis. My job is the ideal combination of an intellectual puzzle with a practical outcome. First you have to figure it out and then you can help somebody. Of course, that is largely true of medicine in general.

On Joy in Work

Joy in work means you get up in the morning and you're eager to go to work—you're not thinking, *oh darn, I have to go to work,* even though you have a long commute. And when you get there, you feel energized, you feel, *okay, let's see what we have today!*

There is the pressure of work but that doesn't bother me. Let me tell you why: I don't have any children in the house anymore, my husband is a big boy, and I simply stay until I finish what my tasks are for that day in whatever time it takes. I *love* what I do. My advice to others is, find something you love and do it.

It helps a lot that this is a residency program because, equally important as taking good care of the kids I call "my babies," is teaching the next generation. I love spending time with the residents, I love guiding them and giving them advice, and I love working with them. I'll tell you what I love the absolute most: it's when we come across a situation that's a little bit of a mystery, a little bit of a puzzle to us. The residents don't know what it is, and I don't know what it is. And we sit down together and research it and figure it out together. It doesn't get any better than that.

I don't interact too much with children. I don't have day-to-day contact with them, and I don't have any long-term contact with any one child. But when we do procedures on children as opposed to simply interpreting their imaging, I do spend some time with them and guide my resident as to what to do and how to do it. Then I usually speak to the family and give them the results verbally. People are *exceedingly* appreciative for the most part. So that's nice.

When you get to be my age, sometimes you think about your legacy to the world. What are you going to leave? I feel fortunate and happy that in doing my job, which is half patient care and half teaching medical students and residents, I get to multiply my legacy to the world by orders of magnitude. Because when I'm gone those guys will still remember what I taught them and will use it.

Lots of people teach but don't do; lots of people do but don't teach. The ideal combination is to do both. It keeps me fresh. Residents ask questions and I'd better know the answers, or I'd better find them out if I don't know. They want difficult things in medicine to be explained to them. It's a challenge and a joy. I still get emails from former residents who email me with puzzling images and ask me what I think. That's both a compliment and a job I enjoy.

I think of all the pediatric specialists in other fields, like pediatric gastroenterology and pediatric oncology and pediatric pulmonary disease, and so on—these guys *depend* on me. I meet with them at different intervals, depending on the field. I meet with pediatric oncologists every single week and we go over all their new imaging. I go to their tumor board once every two weeks. I meet with pediatric gastroenterologists once a month and we go over all the interesting and puzzling cases we've had over the month, and so on. It's so rewarding. It's an exchange. They give me clinical information, I give them radiological understanding, and they're *most* appreciative. One of the things that makes life feel good is being appreciated.

What Diminishes Joy

What diminishes joy in work is feeling *I have to do this job, I wish I didn't have to, and I will retire as soon as I can.* I've never felt that way, but there are negatives.

Most of the negatives involve the increasing administrative work over the years. For example, I participate in a number of committees that run the department and run the residency program. The federal government requires that every three months I log detailed information about how I spend every half hour of the day over a two-week period. Nobody ever tells me why. I don't exactly know what the government has in mind. But there are a lot of things like that, which take time and when I'm not productive. There's increasing regulation of medicine in general by various authorities, including state authorities, health departments, and others. I don't think they're ever going to back away from it. It's an annoyance but I just live with it.

Then there is stress, different kinds of stress. First, there's just the normal stress: you have three patients to do procedures on in an afternoon when you usually do no more than two—and all of a sudden there are two emergencies that *must* be done this afternoon. For the moment this feels stressful, but you just have to live with it. That's the way it is with work sometimes. Sometimes it's just uneven.

But then there is emotional stress, the stress that comes when there's a problem with a patient—say we're trying to do a procedure and things are not going the way they should. I worry about the patient; I worry about how to get out of whatever situation I'm in that's not good. Fortunately, that's very, very rare.

In many fields of medicine, you have to deal with difficult people. You have to deal with patients who don't follow your instructions. And patients whose families get angry when things are not going the way they think they should be going. Largely my work shields me from that kind of thing. I'm not the most patient person in the world, and I just don't think I would do well if I were dealing with a lot of that.

I find it a little odd that as they're building up this relatively new children's hospital and building up the pediatric department by hiring lots of extra staff and specialists so that we're geared up for almost anything, there's only one pediatric radiologist. They have made several periodic attempts to hire—but pediatric radiologists happen to be really hard to hire nowadays. So that's one thing. And another thing is, I stay late and finish the work, so what's the pressure to hire someone else? I have a wonderful chairman who I think understands, but you know, as long as there's no fire to put out...

If I could change anything about my job it would be to have a better backup system when I'm on vacation or on days when I'm not at work. Sometimes when people pick up the slack, I find all kinds of things that haven't been done that are waiting for me, or things that have been done poorly and that I have to re-do. Right now, I just have to fix things the best I can.

On Burnout

Any information I have on burnout is purely anecdotal, as I do not have a wide circle of medical friends beyond my colleagues at the hospital. A number of them, while not using the word "burnout," seem to fit the description. In addition to administrative time wasters, there is a great deal of pressure to be "productive," meaning that working fast is a bigger priority than being meticulously accurate. You can imagine how this feels to a person who takes the Hippocratic Oath, or that of Maimonides, seriously.

As for me, I work at a reasonable pace, give lots of time to those who are learning, and accept that I get home late every night. But that wouldn't work for those with children at home or those who have demanding spouses. Needless to say, people who work part-time or who work fixed hours are less likely to feel exhaustion.

9.   David L., MD, MPH, Ophthalmologist

> David L., MD, MPH is an ophthalmologist, medical director, president, and managing partner of a large suburban multi-specialty ophthalmology private group practice. He started at this practice after training in ophthalmology from 1986 to 1991 and has been an ophthalmologist for 30 years. David says his work gives him a profound sense of purpose, but passion is what comes through most clearly when he talks about his work.

My Career

Choosing Medicine

My father always encouraged me to go into medicine, however I was hesitant. People often rebel against what their parents suggest. There are many doctors in my family, but my dad was not a doctor. He recognized my capabilities and my need to be challenged during my career. There's something about my persona and who I am that my father, thank God, identified. And he pushed me a little bit. He passed away when I was 27, a little more than a year after I graduated from medical school. There are other rewarding paths I could have taken with my life but I'm not sure I would feel as fulfilled if I'd been a university professor or an ecologist or the head of the Sierra Club.

Toward the end of college I realized I had an opportunity to study medicine and it would be really interesting and rewarding and would keep me challenged my whole life—and that for me, my other interests would probably be better served as avocations. When I told my friend and great mentor I was going to apply to medical school, he was taken aback and said, "I had no idea you were interested in medicine."

Finding Ophthalmology

I didn't choose medicine with the passion that I imagine a lot of other people choose it. I chose it because I thought it would be a good field. For a couple of years in medical school I wasn't even sure what I was going to do with it. And then somewhere during the third year I found ophthalmology. It was both an emotional and intellectual choice for me. My mother has had eye problems since I was in high school, and she had a cousin who was an ophthalmologist who lived far enough away that I did not get to know him until I was in medical school, when I studied for a few months in his town. He became another mentor for me.

I also thought about how I wished to practice and realized ophthalmology is the best medical field there is. You take care of patients of all ages, although in my chosen subspecialties I take care of mostly older folks; you deal with quality of life rather than quantity of life; and most importantly, everybody understands what their eyes are for and holds them in such precious, high regard. Think of the alcoholic who drinks until his liver goes bad or the smoker who can't quit smoking even though her lungs are destroyed. Most folks don't know what a liver or spleen is for. But everybody values their eyes.

I have two very different degrees, an MD and an MPH, a Master's in Public Health. In medical school, where you get a Medical Doctor degree, they teach you how to cure a disease. A patient comes to the doctor, "Doc, you gotta help me. I'm dying." Doctor intervenes, does a heroic procedure that's costly, it's a big ordeal, takes a lot of patience and resources. Patient gets better. "Thanks, doc, you saved my life, thank you so much."

In MPH, the *P* should stand for *preventive*. The doctor goes to the "public," into the community, and observes, "Gee, a lot of people are dying from cigarettes and obesity and car crashes." And the doctor plans a program for the community to stop smoking, lose weight, and wear seatbelts. Even though these interventions are relatively simple and inexpensive, many patients say, "I'll do what I darn well please."

Cataract and Glaucoma

Ninety-nine percent of my patients have one or both of the conditions that are my subspecialties. One is cataract, which is cured by surgery; the other is glaucoma, which is managed but rarely cured. The procedures done by ophthalmologists are, by and large, scheduled at a convenient time, at the discretion of the patient, and usually are brief. Cataract surgery takes 10–15 minutes and glaucoma surgery can take 30–45 minutes, and they're scheduled at elective hours, e.g., 9:00 a.m. on Tuesday. Since they're of limited duration, the surgeon's leg does not go numb while sitting in the operating room chair. Cataract surgery accounts for most of the surgeries I do. Patients elect to have cataract surgery when their vision is inadequate for their needs due to clouding of the natural lens of the eye. Surgery involves exchanging the cloudy lens for a clear artificial lens. Nearly all cataract patients do well and are happy and grateful.

Glaucoma is a paradigm public health illness. The doctor usually detects it on examination before the patient does. The treatment is to use an eye drop, or to have a laser treatment, or to have an operation to reduce eye pressure. The goal is to reduce eye pressure in order to preserve existing vision so the patient can see well their whole life. A patient who has glaucoma treatment usually does not see better or feel better, but they maintain vision for a longer time, usually their entire life. Glaucoma treatments do not always succeed but even then, most patients gain peace of mind knowing they've done everything possible to maintain their vision for a longer time than if they hadn't had that surgery, that laser treatment, or used that eye drop. This is in sharp contrast to the cataract patient who can see better soon after surgery and who is usually delighted.

My Practice

Patient Care and Office Management

Three other doctors and I own this practice. For 12 years I have served as the president and managing physician partner. There is a full-time administrator and a staff of 50 people who support the dozen doctors who work here. Over the course of my career doctors have retired from ownership and other doctors have bought in. Doctors work here as employees before and after they are owners.

Part of the privilege of ownership is the burden of management. That's sort of a double-edged sword. I supervise the administrator and work with the accountant and the lawyer. I recruit new doctors and negotiate with them and with doctors who want to become owners. Many younger doctors don't want that commitment. They just want to see their patients and go home at 4:30 p.m. It's not even 5:00 p.m., it's 4:30. So it's hard for them to understand we have a meeting scheduled at night to talk about management. They don't understand that. Much of my managing partner work occurs at night and on weekends.

My hours are better than other doctors' but they're not as good as other eye doctors because I'm in management. My typical patient care hours are 8:00 a.m. to 6:00 p.m. in the office and 7:00 a.m. to 4:00 p.m. in surgery. There are ten doctors in my practice and seven of us take call. The older docs who have retired from ownership don't take call. But call is not painful. If I'm on call on the weekend, I carry my phone and do my usual activities including going for a run and going to synagogue. And if I have to answer a few phone calls or go in to see a patient for an hour or so, that doesn't destroy my weekend. If someone calls on a weeknight, and the problem is not urgent, I can tell them to come in the following morning. I don't have to travel to see clients or work late into the night like some other professionals.

I interact with patients and I interact with colleagues. I like working in a big group because I like the camaraderie and the peer review that goes on. We bounce cases off each other casually. My partners are all wonderful people, and each has some personality quirk that usually serves more as an asset than as an annoyance. To dissuade them from thinking I'm the head guy, I say "Look, we're all in this together; this is what I think we should do; now tell me what you want to do." There is open discussion about most issues. It's a good group and we usually come to consensus about management issues.

Research and Teaching

Between 1991 when I started in practice until about five or ten years ago, I was in two National Institutes of Health-sponsored multi-center clinical trials in glaucoma. Most of the other centers are universities, but because our practice is large, we were able to participate in these studies to recruit patients. That was fun and prestigious because I got to interact with academic ophthalmologists. My involvement in that is minimal now. I continue to teach residents at two medical schools about glaucoma and cataract, and the practice supports this volunteer teaching. Teaching is rewarding because you interact with young doctors and pass your knowledge and skills to a new generation.

On Joy in Work

Flow

How do I define joy in work? A whole day can go by and I don't look at the clock. I'm not aware of time. I arrive at my office around 8:00 am and sit down at my desk and one of my assistants tells me the first patient is ready. I go to the first patient, around 8:15 a.m., and then the next, and the next, and I scurry around, standing up and sitting down, hurrying from room to room all day; I don't get tired sitting at a desk, as I imagine some professionals do.

I get engaged in my work. I get in the flow. Before I know it, the hour is 12:30 or so and someone tells me I'm with the last patient of the morning. I grab a bite for ten minutes and then I'll do it all again in the afternoon. At the end of the day I'll look around and see no more patients, and I work at my desk for another hour or two. Flow happens in the operating room even more than in the office. I feel exhausted at the end of the day. I go home and exercise.

Seeking Truth

A nice thing about medicine is that medical decision-making is done by consensus. I have the joy of working in a field where, even in a formal conference where someone presents a patient and we're stumped about this person's disease, the path of the discussion is always toward resolving our differences by consensus. Medicine is much more consensual than, say, law. In medicine, everybody wants to get to the truth. There's not a winner and a loser; the goal is to help the patient. That's a wonderful part of medicine.

Purpose versus Passion

Going into medicine for me was an intellectual decision, not a passion. Instead of passion I feel a sense of purpose coming to work every day and I find that very valuable. Very cherished. And I'm very grateful for that. But there are other things I'm passionate about. I have a wonderful family, I'm healthy, my family's healthy, and I have a wonderful religious community. I have so many things to be grateful for. And I have a great career and a great place to practice my career. The frustrations are so small compared to all that. I feel very fortunate and very blessed.

We ophthalmologists are so privileged. We're so lucky to have such great jobs. We get to help people, solve problems, and study about an amazing part of the human body, and we get paid for it. That's pretty good.

Practicing in my location involves seeing patients who are nationally prominent and are in the newspaper and on nationwide television. This introduces some added stress, but the eyes of these patients are the same as those of my other patients. My wife keeps a photo album for me. She takes pictures of all the gifts and cards my patients bring me. There are hundreds of photos. One couple named their child after me. That is a great honor.

What Diminishes Joy

Patients Doing Poorly

The worst thing that can happen is having patients who are unhappy. They might have done well technically but if they're not happy, I'm not happy. Even worse is when they *don't* do well and they're unhappy; I do what I can to get them technically better and sometimes they improve and are satisfied and sometimes they're not. I don't have control over everything.

Which patients do I spend more time with, the ones who are doing well or the ones who are doing poorly? Definitely the ones doing poorly. I might see dozens of patients who are doing well and one patient who is doing poorly. And the one I spend a lot of time with, and then "take home" with me and think about at night, is the one who is not doing well. Most of these patients improve eventually. They need more time than the other patients. Nature takes care of most things most of the time.

There's a saying, "If you tell a patient about something before the surgery it's called an expectation; if you tell a patient about the same event after the surgery, it's called a complication." Before surgery I try to tell patients all the possible things that can happen to lower their expectations to a realistic level. If happiness is accomplishments divided by expectations, you can increase happiness either by increasing your achievements or by reducing patients' expectations. I try to do both, honestly and realistically.

The only surgeons who don't have problems are those who don't do much surgery. It's like riding a toboggan downhill: you have to enjoy the ride and know you're going to tip sometimes. You tell every patient that things don't always go as planned but you'll do everything you can to have things work out great. And usually they do. But not everybody does well; that's how the world works. The one out of a hundred who fails despite your best effort, you did the same as you did for the 99 who succeeded. Since you gave your same best effort to both the many successes and the rare failure, to be consistent you really can't take credit for the many successes. You've got to pass the credit to Mother Nature or God or whatever you believe regarding risks of surgery and healing after surgery.

Keeping Patients Waiting

Some of my patients end up waiting for me. It must seem very inconsiderate, but I surely do not intend it. You'd think I could have a schedule where I don't keep people waiting. It's downright annoying to both me and my patients.

I've gotten my biggest slams on doctor websites, where patients rate doctors, about keeping people waiting. I feel terrible about that, but the length of time I need to spend with patients varies tremendously and is not predictable. Some patients I spend five minutes with, and others require half an hour or more.

Severing Relationships

In my role I occasionally have to dismiss people from their job. Usually it is personality or a poor fit with our office culture rather than a competence issue. We have an administrator who hires and fires people but I'm often in the room when it's a high-level employee. Usually I explain, "The job is not a good fit for you. You will be happier elsewhere."

And almost always these people *are* happier elsewhere. We hire competent people, so after working for us, they do get a job elsewhere. Mostly they are then more valued and more fulfilled, and their skill set is better utilized and so they're a better fit. But at the time you terminate them they can't see that. It's awful. I hate that. Fortunately, I don't do that often.

The Electronic Medical Record

Seven years ago, after much deliberation, my colleagues and I decided to change from paper charts to a government-mandated electronic medical record (EMR). One of the other doctors and I took the lead in our office, shopped around, and identified what was the best available system. The other doctor who helped pick the system is one of four doctors *not* using it, five years after we bought it. I feel a little betrayed by this. He tried to use it a couple of times, and said, "I can't do this," and walked away from it. I thought, *what do you mean you can't do this? You helped choose it.*

All the doctors under the age of 50 and I use the system. And four senior doctors, including one who's 52, don't use it. They say, "It's too time-consuming, it's faster just to jot down a quick note and get on with it." They say, "Whatever the government penalty is, I can make up by seeing another patient or two each day—because I'm not going to be taking my time to fill out the computer form."

One problem with the computer form is that it asks unnecessary questions that doctors don't consider on a paper chart. So, every time a patient comes in, the EMR wants to know if you've checked the patient's blood pressure, their obesity index, and have you counseled them to stop smoking and lose weight? These issues are not perceived as the role of an ophthalmologist.

It's really not a question of fulfilling the government mandate to use the computer, but of the government mandate to use the computer for what the government calls "meaningful" use, which doctors refer to as "meaningless" use. In our practice I use the EMR, so I get a modest bonus—and the doctor who doesn't use it gets a modest penalty. At this point I've been doing it for five years. Instead of opening a paper chart and flipping the pages, which is tedious in its own right, on the computer I click-click-click-click.

If the government were to say, "Use the computer however you think is best," that would make life a lot easier. And that will be the case eventually, I think. The doctors who don't use the computer go home earlier and see me using my computer and going home later. The EMR sucks up time and does not help me or my patients.

Reflections

There are three types of doctors. The first uses all the latest technology available. Anything new becomes available, she wants to buy it—the new device, the new lens— and if there's a fee to use the new technology, she wants to pass the fee on to the patients; she thinks if the technology can be a profit center, all the better. Doctor number two is the opposite. He just wants to do what he learned in residency 25 years ago because it works. And he thinks, *why do we need these new techniques and why are we asking patients to pay for new medicines when they're no better than the old ones?* The third type, which probably describes most doctors, falls between these two extremes and describes me. I'm not the first to accept a new technology; I want to be sure it benefits my patients. I'm not going to ask patients to pay for something I'm not confident will help them. And I'm going to ask my patients what they want to achieve before I ask them to pay an out-of-pocket cost to achieve it. A doctor who does more procedures paid by patients out of pocket rather than paid by insurance companies makes more money than a doctor who does fewer.

There are a fair number of procedures in ophthalmology in which patients don't really know what we're doing or what we're using, and we can choose to be ethical or not. I always try to be transparent in discussions with my patients and utilize techniques that will be best for them. A surgery rarely proceeds without my using a technology that was paid for; but when that happens, I always refund the insurance company's or patients' out-of-pocket money promptly. I sleep well at night.

Advice

I have advice for people considering going into medicine: if you enjoy helping people, and solving and preventing problems, and studying the science of the human body, then it's great. If you're going into it to make a buck, then don't go into medicine. If you're doing it to feel important about yourself, don't go into medicine. Whatever you do, go into a field where achieving your goal is the point of the job. Medicine has money and power, but if that's your reason for doing it, those are bad reasons, and you'll probably be unhappy. Go into medicine if you like helping people, and solving and treating problems, and studying about the wonders of the human body.

10.   Owen R., BS, MS, City Director of Emergency and Safety Services

Owen R. was a born caregiver. Always wanting to help people, he worked in the fields of occupational safety and health, emergency medical services, and volunteer firefighting. Owen served as fire marshal for a university, for the last seven years had been director of emergency and safety services for a municipality, and for the last five years added teaching to his resume.

One night in late January 2020, I learned that Owen died unexpectedly. In my last correspondence with him, he approved this interview for publication and said he was looking forward to reading this book on the beach. While this introduction is written in the past tense, his interview follows in the present tense; these are his words, recorded here as he spoke them in the summer of 2018. Thank you, Owen, for all your good work, and may you rest in peace.

On all the personality tests I've ever taken I always come out on the caregiver side. What feels fulfilling to me is knowing I'm making a difference for the individual and the community as a whole. I've always felt that way. When I worked in industry, I helped people do their jobs safely—I made sure they had the right equipment so they would be protected. That carried over into doing fire prevention work, making sure buildings were safe for firefighters and the public.

After college I started out in industry, focusing on occupational safety and health for two chemical manufacturers. Then I worked in the environmental field doing Superfund site cleanups as a safety industrial hygienist. We were trained in first aid, cardiopulmonary resuscitation (CPR), and firefighting because when you're on a site or in a plant you're the first line of defense.

At some point I got tired of traveling and I got interested in firefighting. A lot of my family members were in the fire department. In the mid-1980s I became a volunteer firefighter and also spent a number of years in a rescue squad doing EMS work. I always liked sports and being part of EMS is like being part of a team.

I then became the fire marshal for a university. Part of my job was code enforcement—doing inspections and making sure buildings and fire suppression and detection equipment were up to code. The other part of my job was emergency management—making sure we were prepared for a variety of disasters, that we had the right responses and recovery planning in place.

The four broad categories of emergency management are *mitigation*—preventing something or lessening the blow. A good example is a hurricane coming. You can't stop that, but you can do things to lessen the impact and help people. Then there is *preparedness*—being prepared for whatever emergencies arise. An emergency manager has to make sure people are prepared with plans, equipment, and other things to handle whatever their town or city faces, whether it's flooding or a hurricane or other weather events. And, of course, now in the world we live in, everybody has to be ready to deal with a *terrorist attack* or *an active shooter*. Emergency managers have to make sure they have a response for all these situations—that they have fire, EMS, a hazardous materials (HAZMAT) team, things like that. Another big category is *recovery*. How do you recover from whatever happened? The fire, police, and EMS are all part of an emergency management plan. That work for the university has carried over into my current job.

For the last seven years I've been the director of emergency and safety services for a municipality. I have the fire department and the fire marshal's office under me, so I have my hand in all of it.

Joy in Work

Joy is being a servant-leader. Taking care of my people—taking care of the community—is what gives me joy. That gives me a sense of purpose. People's lives matter. Making sure they're safe, making sure they can do things like have picnics or see fireworks safely, that they can enjoy themselves without having an incident take place. The joy comes from being able to work with people, resolve issues for them. Helping people get back on their feet and rebuild their lives when something does go wrong. There's something different every day. Variety is what I've always liked about this work in general.

I loved doing EMS work. To me, there's nothing more fulfilling than being able to help a person: you're on-on-one, you and your crew members, and someone has an issue; you're able to give them some resolution in the field and get them to a medical facility quickly so they can get the help they need. Someone may be in cardiac arrest and it's a chaotic scene; someone else may be a bit of a hypochondriac and just need somebody to talk to who can take them to the hospital to see a doctor. Then you have everything in between. I still jump in when I can. I really like to do that work.

The thing I liked best about working for the university was working with some of the student groups. In theater groups, some of them would want to have open flames or pyrotechnics and I would have to work with them to set these up according to code and make sure the local fire officials were satisfied. I really enjoyed the diverse interaction working with the university because there were always lots of different things going on. I'd go from being with students working with chemicals in a laboratory to working with a theater group doing fire extinguisher training.

I've always liked teaching. Now, in addition to the other things I do, I'm an instructor at the fire academy. For the last four or five years I've been teaching classes on fire department health and safety at the local community college. I like being able to teach young people who want to get into the field of fire and emergency management. I also like teaching on the job. How to do the job. Teachable moments when things don't go right. I never thought way back when that this is where I'd end up, but it's been an interesting journey and I'm actually very happy with where I am and what I do.

On Money and Joy

There is some connection between money and joy. People need to make money to live. If you make a fair wage for what you do—if people are compensated properly—they are generally happy. But I also think that just making money can make a person miserable because they can become a slave to whatever it is that's making them a lot of money.

I don't think money affects your joy. You either love what you're doing and you'll do it regardless, or you won't.

What Diminishes Joy

I once worked for a manufacturing company where the work became mundane, repetitive. Although there's paperwork in every job I like to move around. Doing the same thing every day gets boring and takes the joy out of it.

One of my least favorite things about work is dealing with personnel issues because they suck the life out of you. I've been through litigation because people have been separated from their positions and, of course, thought they were wronged. Those things tend to wear on you.

I loved my work at the university but the circumstances around my job made me feel I had to move on. A new director who was trying to clean house made my job miserable. Everything I did was suddenly called into question. He nitpicked, looking for problems. He was passive-aggressive. There were days when, as much as I liked what I did, it was hard to come to work because I'd wonder, *what kind of game was this guy going to play today?* My ability to function well in my job was definitely affected by this. Things I'd normally do—and was contractually obligated to do—he would question. I'd either have to tell him what I was going to do, or just do it and end up having to explain it. This level of disrespect was difficult to tolerate. Finally, I thought, *I'm done with this and it's time to move on.* So, I found another job.

I've learned a lot from tough situations like that. I should have spoken up sooner, requested a meeting with my supervisor, and decided what I needed to do. Looking back, I see I spun my wheels a lot. I wouldn't do that today.

Advice

Leaders need to be good listeners. You need to be able to really hear what people are saying. And be up front and direct with your staff: let your "no" be no and your "yes" be a yes.

Anyone in emergency response or medicine needs to have compassion toward people. Whether you're a doctor, a nurse, or first responder you need to have compassion because 99% of the time you're going to meet people on their worst day.

11. Rebecca L., MS, Clinical School Psychology, Retired Psychologist in Private Practice

Rebecca L., MS, was a practicing psychotherapist for 30 years. Her rewarding career was not planned but, rather, unfolded as a result of her talent, bravery, determination, wisdom, optimism, and passion.

When I was in college I started out as a chemistry major and then switched to psychology. I thought psychology was interesting. I ran youth groups, I always worked with kids, but I didn't know what I wanted to do professionally. I thought school psychology sounded interesting, so I went back to my hometown to get a school psychology degree, which was essentially a master's in clinical psychology. The people who taught the courses were lay analysts who had private practices. I learned all the testing. I loved it. It was a great program. I got a research assistantship and was periodically asked to teach. I was very interested in developmental psychology and worked with some of the developmental psychologists on their research projects.

My Professional Journey

I was going to get a PhD in developmental psychology, but my husband was drafted, and I joined him on a military base in a foreign country where I became an army psychologist. I volunteered for a month and they loved the work I was doing with teenagers, so they hired me. I treated adolescents and families in a clinic and had great supervision. That was the beginning of my career.

My goal was to get back to the States and get back to school. But it didn't happen exactly the way I thought it would because I followed my husband around the country when he did his professional training. I worked at a hospital for a year in the child outpatient clinic and had two fabulous supervisors.

The following year we moved, and I worked with children in a family therapy clinic with an outstanding staff. I was the only master's-level person there, other than the social workers. I continued to grow despite the lack of the PhD degree that I wanted and should have had for the positions they kept giving me. I did testing, I did a lot of community work. Because I worked with children and families, I went into the community to work with pediatricians and schools on behalf of children I was treating at the time. It really suited me.

We traveled for a year and then I was home with two babies, trying to figure out what I was going to do. I wasn't quite ready yet to go back to school and I was pounding the pavement without a PhD. I realized I was in a city where one building on a major avenue has more therapists than some towns, and they had MDs and PhDs. I thought, *where the hell was I going?*

A psychologist friend of mine who had supervised me for a year came to visit with his wife who had just gotten her PhD. I told him about my feeling that I couldn't do anything without a PhD, and I wasn't at a point in my life when going back to school was an option. I had three kids—five, four, and a newborn. As we sat and talked, he said, "You're starting a practice." I said, "You're crazy. I don't have that doctor title yet." He said, "The hell with the doctor title—when you get out there, they're going to see how talented you are and you're going to do it." I thought he was dreaming.

He spent three hours trying to convince me and I thought, *I'm going to be brave.* I started telling people that I was starting a practice and one day somebody called and said, "I'm looking for a therapist." I almost dropped my baby and I said, "Let me get back to you." I scurried around trying to find an office where I was going to see this person, and I did. I ended up there for ten years, until I built an office attached to my home where I saw clients for the next 15 years.

I decided that if I was going into practice alone, I did not feel comfortable treating children without the support system I had had in the community mental health clinic. Instead, I decided to see people ages ten and older. That worked out beautifully for me, because I always had a family model in my mind. When I treated people their families always came into the office with them—not literally, but they were there. People are always talking about their kids, their husband, their parents. Along the way I did training in family therapy, gestalt therapy, hypnotherapy. You name it, I did it. I had a whole bag of tricks in my pocket and I had a whole framework around which I worked. I saw people individually from ages 10 to 80, couples, and families.

My practice largely revolved around client referrals. Whoever I saw would send me referrals of colleagues and friends. My first client was a journalist and I ended up seeing many journalists. Then I saw a physical therapist and I ended up with many physical therapist referrals. And this is how it went. If I saw a physician, I saw several physicians. If I saw a lawyer, I saw lots of lawyers. You get the picture.

I really thrived on the client referrals. It's not that I didn't appreciate referrals from some physicians I knew and from close colleagues, but the client referrals were very special. They came in trusting me on a level that anybody coming to someone for the first time wouldn't or shouldn't trust. Some of the comments were, "So-and-so said you're great," or "I noticed a real change in so-and-so and I asked who's your therapist?" that kind of thing. That's how the referrals came.

Going for My PhD

I was about six years into my practice and still felt a terrible loss over that PhD I never got—so I decided to go back to school and get it because I'd always felt "less than." Not because the practice wasn't going well, the practice was going fine. I just felt I hadn't done what I needed to do. I applied and I worked like crazy for the GREs. I did stunningly. I did much better than I did when I was younger. I did so well that someone called me up and said, "We're offering you a spot in this PhD program because we don't believe a 42-year-old person could do that well." They didn't understand—those tests don't say how smart you are. They say how determined you are, and I was on fire.

I was determined that I was going to get into a program. But I hadn't thought well enough about what it was going to be like to be in the program. My friend/mentor Richard laughed when I told him what I was doing and he said, "You're crazy. You don't have the personality for this. You can't tolerate bullshit. You are going to be crazed by the bullshit in the PhD program. I don't think you're going to like this." Another mentor said, "You need to do this because you do PhD kind of work and you need to have the definitive degree." That was the controversy. But they both supported me and they both wrote beautiful letters.

I got into the PhD program in counseling psychology at the state university and to a clinical program at a private university. They were excellent programs but the only one that would let me go part-time was the state university and I needed to maintain a part-time practice for financial reasons. I was in for a couple of months when I realized this was not working for me.

They put me in a class teaching me how to interview, and I thought, *this is the craziest thing I've ever seen.* I went to the head of the program and said, "Listen. I don't have time for this. I am one of your few people who don't need this program to do clinical work and it's not mandatory for certification. Get me involved in some research. Give me something I can sink my teeth into."

I realized if I were younger and less experienced, it wouldn't have been an issue. But since I was 42 and trying to juggle a lot of balls in the air, I didn't want to waste my time. From the get-go I was dealing with this nonsense, and they put me off every week. Long story short, I walked into the administration office one day and said, "I'm out of the program." I had all my classes deleted, walked out, and never thought about the PhD again. There are some programs around the country that would have been good for a seasoned therapist, but this wasn't it. I never looked back. My professional life continued, and I kept adding patients.

Looking back on the whole PhD saga, I know what I missed. I missed out on a richer professional experience—balancing teaching, research, and clinical work; however, realistically speaking, I am somebody who likes to be with her kids. I always worked three and a half days a week and Friday I always cooked and had a lot of company over the weekend. It was very important to me to spend a lot of time with the kids, particularly because my husband's job was so demanding. Weighing everything, I am most grateful for the balancing act I did create. It suited me.

On Joy in Work

I don't think of the word joy. It feels an inappropriate word when you're dealing with people who are in pain. I think more of tremendous satisfaction. I think of a therapy space as a sacred space. It's a place where people talk about things they don't talk about to anybody else. I feel their gratitude and I am enormously grateful for their trust. It's work, but it's very creative work. You're listening hard and trying to sort through what's going on.

You expand your own horizons when you sit with people. You understand so much more about the human condition, how alone we all are and the challenges we face. I was most fascinated by the issue of resilience—is this hard-wired? Is this environmental? People can go through the same things, and some seem to cope incredibly well, and others can't figure their way out of a box. I think given today's data, people would say a lot of it is genetic, but resilience is definitely informed by one's environment. That's where therapy comes in.

I learned that educating clients was extremely important. Sometimes people just didn't have the tools or were too anxious to think creatively about their problems and were amazed when they found out there could be paths to take they simply hadn't thought of. It was such productive work. It was like an aura in the room surrounded me and my client as we worked together. Nothing compares to it. I often told my husband, "I don't even know why I get paid to do what I do, it's so amazing."

I had the most wonderful working relationship with three female psychiatrists, with whom I consulted for the one-third of my clients who needed antidepressants and antianxiety drugs. If I had a client who was clinically depressed and called any of them to say, "I think this client needs her meds tweaked," they saw those clients immediately. I was truly blessed, because I don't know how I would have had my practice without them. It was critical to me that my clients were well taken care of and that wonderful working relationship with the psychiatrists benefited me and my clients greatly.

What Diminishes Joy

There were times when I had clients who were very angry, and it was difficult to get through that. There were clients who were ill, who were deeply depressed. You don't feel joy when you're worried that somebody could possibly commit suicide or otherwise harm themselves. I always made sure that in those instances that I got support and, if needed, mentoring.

I vetted my non-client, non-colleague referrals carefully. I spent a long time on the phone making sure that the fit was right. I also was particularly careful because for 15 years I had a home-based practice. One day I received a call from a woman who said she saw I was a family therapist on some website. We talked for a long time on the phone and she asked if she could come to see me. I agreed. By the third session, I learned she was highly suicidal. I didn't follow my own best practice and I was really worried. She ended up being the most extraordinary client I ever had. Where she went, and what we did together, was remarkable. So, you never know, but I had many weeks of worry.

Reflections

I'm a very optimistic person. I can't help but think that little ingredient helped my clients. My message was that most problems could be solved one way or another. There had to be some way to get beyond "whatever" was always my feeling. Maybe it was growing up in a post-Holocaust community and watching people who had gone through the worst of the worst and managing somehow to not only survive but to embrace life. My mother taught me "this too is for the good." You can always learn.

I think some people have a lot more resilience than others. They bounce back. They don't get into their brains and relive all the ugly details about their experiences but manage to move forward. Manage to compartmentalize. And they do it naturally. But I think you can teach people to do that. To what extent, to what degree, I don't know. I'm not a scientist. But I believe that people have a lot of room for growth, that we are restricted by our environments or our place in this world, and that if you broaden that the lightbulbs go on. You'd never believe that people could come into therapy and make the changes they make. It's remarkable. I am humbled by my clients' willingness to put themselves on the line.

I have many interests. I don't believe that I'm suited to do just one thing, but I did land a "winner." I think I could have been happy doing a whole slew of things, but clinical work was very well suited to me.

Advice

Trust your clients. They know more about themselves than you do. Listen carefully. They have a lot to teach you before you teach them. Embrace people. It feels good.

12.   Grace Y., RN, Operating Room Nurse at a Large Academic Medical Center

Grace Y., RN, has been a nurse for 25 years, and an OR nurse at a large academic medical center for 15 years. Strong, confident, and resilient with a wicked sense of humor, she has a low tolerance for what she calls the "predatory culture" of the operating room; the OR administration's inequity; substandard staffing; and tolerance of bad behavior by administrators, surgeons, and nurses alike. Grace's love of her work emanates from within. She finds joy in work despite, not because of, her work environment.

I am an operating room nurse at a research facility and a teaching hospital. We have residency programs for physicians, occupational therapy, physical therapy, a nursing school, a physician assistant school, and a radiology program. There are a lot of new faces, a lot of young blood, a lot of learning, a lot of teaching.

I think medicine is something you must have a love for. There's the scientific end of it, where you're trying to cure diseases like cancer or Parkinson's or Alzheimer's. And then there's the clinical end of it, where you really have to want to help people get better. This is especially true in surgery, where so much of it is life and death. You have to care about what's going on with these people, not just about their kidney stones. You can't teach someone to care. That has to come from within. Joy in medicine has to come from wanting to be there in the first place.

When I work with surgeons, I can absolutely tell whether they love what they do. I can tell because even the ones who are inexperienced have a thirst for knowledge. They want to improve. They're not interested in the status quo. And you can tell that from a first-year intern, whose daddy got him in. He *will* graduate, even though his skill set is half of what it would be if he didn't have a hook. To be a surgeon you need a certain amount of confidence. But there's a very fine line between cocky and confident. Some of them cross that line daily.

I've been in the OR now for 15 years. I've been a nurse for 25 years. I worked in a sub-acute rehab nursing home with dementia patients for five years. When the hospital across the street needed staff, I was ready to leave. I was hired quickly and went right to the floors. That I really hated because people don't get better on the floors. Most of that is from self-inflicted behaviors. I spent a year on the floors, then I went down to the OR. I like the OR; the patients are asleep. That was almost 15 years ago.

I was a veterinary technologist for 11 years. I love animals. I'm not a big fan of people. It was the best job I ever had, and I was there for 11 years. We did surgery every day. We did 15 surgeries a day, we did all aspects: the hospitalization of animals, well visits for animals, anesthesia, pretty much what I'm doing now minus the brain surgery and heart surgery. The vet I worked for was wonderful, fabulous. I'm still friends with him 35 years later. I was going to get my license to be a vet tech and he told me not to do it. He said he couldn't afford to pay me enough and told me I should be nurse. He said nursing would give me the chance to pick and choose what I wanted to do with my life because I'd be getting a real paycheck. So, I looked into it and went to nursing school.

My very first job was in a nursing home. The place was horrible. Management was so corrupt, I felt I was taking my license into my hands. I have stories that would curl your teeth. I was in the office every day because I would stick up for my staff and the patients, naively thinking that was the right thing to do. The soulless woman who was the nurse manager explained to me, "I understand you just bought a house and you'd like to continue paying the mortgage." I lasted there for three years and then just couldn't do it anymore. Eventually I got to the point where I was getting knots in my stomach. There was absolutely no humanity in that place whatsoever. It was *all about the money.*

Now I work in the main OR at this academic medical center. I'll end up staying later for a surgeon I like. I've worked off-shift my whole career—I'm not a morning person.

Cases come from everywhere. I work on whatever surgery needs to be done. I circulate or I scrub. When I circulate, I gather all the surgeon's equipment, I do all the documentation, I make sure that the case stays fluid—that the surgeon has all the instruments needed to perform whatever surgery it is. And each surgeon, besides their own proclivities, needs certain instruments. I do whatever the surgeon needs in the OR.

I have a nice life at home. My job is ten hours out of my day, and I try to do, absolutely, the very best I can. But I have a life outside of work. There are many people here whose job is their life. Those are the most miserable ones.

Operating Room Culture

The culture of the OR here is predatory, and it takes a certain personality to survive in the OR in this hospital. There's almost a hazing that goes on. People are absolutely brutal. I would say 30% of the people who work in surgery have no other life. The operating room is their whole world. There is a lot of need to be superman, to be "the only person who knows *exactly* what a particular surgeon's likes and dislikes are," as some nurses actually say. Bullies in the OR are rampant: doctors, nurses, anesthesiologists, everybody. It's sad because we're all supposed to be on the same *team*! The patient is supposed to be the star of the show! If you stand up to the predatory ones, they back off.

My boss, the vet, was completely insane. He would throw scalpels and surgery packs on the floor and smash things. He had a psychotic temper, he still does. But I worked with him for 11 years, so I learned to work around the crazy—best training I ever had in my life. I worked in cardiac surgery for five years, but I never go there anymore because I hate the surgeon who's down there. Cardiac is its own little dysfunctional entity, although the nurses there are very devoted. I play well with everybody and I'm very capable, so I get put into the lion's den to defuse many situations.

Everyone was terrified of one cardiac surgeon, because he would scream and yell and curse and tell you that you were a fucking idiot and didn't deserve to crawl across the face of the planet and be in his air space. They made him retire eventually because his hands were so bad, he couldn't tie knots anymore. Plus, a number of his patients were brought back in, and that cost the hospital money. They brought in foreign-born nurses to work with this guy because nobody could take him. Three of them survived, the others left because they couldn't stand it anymore. He could turn his anger on and off like a spigot and used these nurses as whipping boys. He turned his anger off when I would confront him but then turned it right back on when he saw one of these other nurses. We have a few surgeons who are like that. They are not the majority. This kind of thing doesn't affect me. I know how to handle this stuff. But we lose a lot of nurses.

Our salaries are substantially lower than salaries at other hospitals around us, so that has something to do with why nurses leave, too. The turnover rate in the OR is at least 70% a year for the new people. It's a constant revolving door. We're constantly training. And it's sad because some of them are really good nurses and decent human beings, and either they're bullied out, or they take the training because we turn out really good nurses, and they run somewhere else where it's not as vicious and it's $25K more to start. Somebody is supposedly looking at the turnover rate but it's probably cheaper to pay overtime than to hire new people with benefits. Why do I put up with it? I have 19½ years in so at 20 I can get a pension.

People report abusive behavior, including me. When I was working in cardiac surgery a few years back there was a female anesthesia attending who was teaching the residents. When a resident went to pull the bed close to the surgery table to prepare for the patient's transfer, the anesthesiologist ordered residents not to do that "scut work—that is for nurses." I wrote an email to report what happened, and it rocketed up to the chair of anesthesia. He went after her with a vengeance. I got an apology from him. I got an apology from the cardiac surgeons. Because I handle my own problems 99% of the time and don't complain, when I do write an email like that, I have credibility with the physicians, the anesthesiologists, the nurses, and the nursing management. I was told that despite that email, this anesthesiologist would do it again. She really does think she's better than anybody else. She didn't talk to me for about a year and a half. She would tell someone else, "Tell the nurse that we need this." She is the exception, not the rule.

To a degree, the OR administration is separate from the hospital administration but, ultimately, nursing has to answer to the higher-ups in nursing, the doctors have to answer to the higher-ups of the hospital. I have no idea what those at the very top of the hospital hierarchy are like or what's important to them, I've never met them. I've seen them in the hallways, always with a flock of people around them. I'm positive they know what's going on, but they just choose not to do anything.

When something goes wrong in our organization there is often a lot of blame. Ultimately it is the attending surgeon's responsibility. Foreign bodies are still retained in patients after surgery. People have had the wrong grafts sewn in. Often, we can fix it before the patient leaves the OR, and then it's not an incident. But if the patient rolls out these doors we're screwed, and they do a deep dive. Nobody's ever been fired that I know of. Ever. People will be remediated. Systems are reevaluated regularly. Bottom line is, *nobody* gets fired, no matter how egregious the error. We have to keep the operating rooms running.

On Joy in Work

I feel joy in work. I love what I do, despite all these problems. If I didn't, I wouldn't be there. I love what I do because, for the most part, we fix people. There is immediate gratification in that. For example, a 26-year-old kid who was studying to be a fireman had a minor fender-bender very late one Friday night—a big, strapping, beautiful specimen of a 26-year-old. He went over to see if the lady in the other car was okay and he got creamed by a car. His feet looked like they were where they were supposed to be but, unbeknownst to anybody, they had both been twisted around 360 degrees. The bones and the muscles were crushed and shattered. The surgeon who was in the OR when this young man was brought in that night was either ill equipped or unwilling to try to save his legs. When he told me what he thought he was going to do, it was as though somebody had sucked the air out of the room. Mercifully, the St. Jude of broken bones was on the next day. The more hopeless the case, the more interested he is. He is fantastic when things are beyond all hope and somebody else might say, "I can't fix this." And he does it. This kid was in the hospital for six months. He walked out. Those are the days I like. The job itself brings joy. Fixing people is the biggest part of it.

Another big factor in finding joy or finding solace, which may be a better word, is my work husband. That's a really, really big deal. We've been following each other around professionally for 20 years. He works in the OR with me. We worked together in the nursing home and then we went to the hospital together, worked on the floors together, and then went to the OR together. If something bad is going on and we see each other in the hallway or have lunch together, having him as a companion who has my back no matter what makes things easier—and I have his. He almost quit. He almost didn't stay in the OR because of the predation that goes on there.

The OR surgeons and those in anesthesia are very good to me. They recognize, appreciate, and are grateful for what I do and that absolutely adds to my joy. I feel that gratitude. And it's a two-way street. The surgeons I adore are decent human beings and dynamite surgeons. They're good, good people. Their humanity is off the charts. It's like a bell curve. You have the ones who are fantastic, you have the ones who really suck, and everyone else falls somewhere in the middle. My mom had a stroke. She ended up needing eight hours of vascular surgery, eight hours of general surgery, and 16 hours of anesthesia. She spent the week upstairs on the surgical intensive care unit. These surgeons donated their time to us, saying, "You've been through enough." I never got her back. Those are the ones I'll stay late for. And they appreciate it. They are incredibly kind and go out of their way to help me. One hand washes the other. That brings joy.

Another part of my joy is learning and being good and capable. That, and good music in the OR, enhances my joy in work.

What Diminishes Joy in Work

One day a week I truly feel I have had my insides sucked out and resistance is futile. I have a rapport with some of the surgeons and anesthesiologists so that when I walk by, and they ask me what's the matter, I can talk to them. It's a friendship. With these people I can bang m head against the wall, and they'll put their hand up to make sure I don't bloody myself.

There is a serious lack of communication here. But as long as they are making money, as long as all the ORs are going, as long as nobody dies, as long as we don't hit the newspaper, it's status quo.

Inequity

What diminishes joy in work for me is the unfair distribution of assignments, people who don't pull their own weight, and people who are allowed to stay when they're not good at what they do. I'm kind of "plug and play," you can put me in anywhere. I've been here a long time and I take a lot on, learn how to work things, and make things run more smoothly in the OR. But there are people who have been here for years who say, "Oh, I can't do that," and administration doesn't get rid of people who don't function. It's not an environment where you can have "dead wood." We have a lot of dead wood, and age has nothing to do with it. These people get the easy cases. Our acuity level is, if not the highest, then one of the highest in the entire hospital. The ER is on parallel, but they don't really fix; they stabilize. We fix. Along with the acuity level is the added stress of dealing with some of the people here, the dead wood they don't do anything with.

Administration tolerates the dead wood because of the large number of operating rooms we run. What administration does is work around their weaknesses. They are put on the simple cases. Which leaves the people who function at a high level to go to cardiac surgery, neurosurgery, orthopedic surgery, or one of the other services that requires a high level of skill and attention. I occasionally feel overloaded by work. The overload comes from picking up the slack for people who are not dedicated, smart, or good at what they do. Some nights I come home and ask, "Why am I doing this?" but I don't leave because I'm vested, and I *love* what I do.

There are no consequences for negative actions. No one gets fired, no one gets written up. The bad apples are treated the same as those of us who try to make things work, try to make it a pleasant environment, and try to make it more bearable. The bad apples are predatory to new people: they try to make them cry, try to make them look stupid, try to make them look incompetent. A nurse educator was teaching me to scrub cardiac surgery. She opened up the chest retractor tray that has about 100 instruments in it, left it open for about 30 seconds, pulled one instrument out, closed it up, looked at me, and asked, "What is this?" I looked at her and said, "I have no clue." She responded, "What are you, stupid?" I have heard her do this to others. And she is as vindictive as they come.

A lot of intimidation goes on here. Administration knows and does nothing about it. Favoritism, nepotism, and cronyism are rampant. I would be passed over for a job in favor of someone less qualified, even though I have a resume that would choke a horse. A shocking example of racist behavior by a nurse was tolerated because he is a friend of the nurse manager. Up went the carpet and everything was swept under it. All he had to do was apologize to the victim. But when she first thought someone she did not like was responsible, she was ready to fire him.

There are surgeons who are chauvinistic and one who is misogynistic. They are part of the culture here. It happens, although it's rare, that they don't renew someone's contract. There is a complete lack of respect for humanity—patients, co-workers—among the people who work down here. And most of them are very, very nice to administration, so administration has no clue as to how vicious and evil they really are. These people are made of Teflon. They look out for each other. If anybody blows the whistle on some of what goes on here, they will end up with every lousy assignment, in every rotten barrel. There is retribution, retribution, retribution.

Dysfunction

If I could change anything about my job it would be my immediate administration. They need to be flushed out. We need someone from the outside because a lot of the answers to the problems raised are, "Oh, it's this place. That's our way." Homegrown physicians do very well here because they know what the politics are—who not to piss off, and who to suck up to. And you don't go from A to B. You go from A to B via the Channel Tunnel in England and then you come back and take a loop around the Pacific Coast Highway and then you can go to B. That's the way things are. When we get physicians who are highly trained and highly skilled, or anesthesiologists who are highly trained and highly skilled, they say, "this is insanity." Someone from another academic medical center once told me, "Your institution is the most constipated thing I've ever seen in my life." That was a perfect description.

You cannot train someone to care. You cannot train someone to be kind. Either you are or you aren't. When they hire people who aren't, those are the ones who stay because they can't get a job anywhere else.

There was a surg tech here, let's call her Morticia, who made one of my colleagues cry. I walked into my boss's office and said I'd had it, that a nurse was crying because of her. My boss said she can get carried away, but she is very good at what she does. I pointed out the economic arguments against keeping her, given the fact that Morticia had intimidated and chased off at least one nurse and one technologist a year during the 11 years she'd been here. Knowing that it costs between $50,000 and $90,000 to train an OR nurse to fruition, I told my boss that I estimated Morticia had cost the hospital anywhere from $550,000 and $990,000. All my supervisor said in response was, "I have another meeting now."

Advice

The sight in everybody's binoculars should be the patient. That gets fogged over, lost, in the pettiness and the arrogance.

My advice to my colleagues is, don't judge people. We do a lot of abortions. Don't judge them. That's their decision, they have to make peace with themselves. But some do judge. Funny how everybody finds God when there's an abortion to do. Don't judge. It's not your job. Your job is to achieve the best outcome for the patient for whatever reason they're there.

If I had any advice for my bosses it would be, "Resign."

Passion for Leadership

13.   Gary Kaplan, MD, Chairman and CEO of Virginia Mason Health System and Practicing Internal Medicine Physician

Gary S. Kaplan, MD, is chairman and CEO of Virginia Mason Health System in Seattle and a practicing internal medicine physician. His organization is nationally recognized for innovation in advancing quality and patient safety. The Virginia Mason Production System, his organization's unique management method for continuously improving the delivery of care, is based on principles of the Toyota Production System. Dr. Kaplan is past chair of the Institute for Healthcare Improvement (IHI) Board of Directors and is chair of the IHI Lucian Leape Institute. In 2019, *Modern Healthcare* magazine included Dr. Kaplan on its annual list of the 100 Most Influential People in Healthcare for the 11th time. "Healthcare leaders must look ahead with courage, embrace change and commit to identifying new ways of doing things rather than relying on yesterday's solutions," he says.

I knew I wanted to be a physician when I was about 14 or 15 years old. I worked in my father's hardware store from the age of five until I was 26, when I was in my senior year in medical school. I was fortunate to be able to continue working there and I learned many, many things. When I was about 14, a family physician who'd been a long-time friend and customer asked me if I would like to spend a day with him. It was a day in the office but also rounding in the hospital. He was an old-school general practitioner—he did surgery and participated in a tonsillectomy that day. It was very formative for me. Following that day, I was convinced that was the kind of work I wanted to do. I thought I wanted to go into medicine just because I found it interesting, I liked science, but more importantly, I liked people and wanted to have an impact in their lives. That day just cemented it.

I knew what I wanted to do when I was a college undergraduate, so I needed to take the prerequisites. But I also wanted to maximize the time doing other things—reading great books, philosophy, political science, things that interested me that weren't going to be part of my career path.

I've been Chairman and Chief Executive Officer of Virginia Mason Health System in Seattle since February 2000. I held progressive leadership roles in the organization up to that time and was vice-chairman of the medical center for five years before becoming CEO. In addition to being CEO, I'm still a practicing internal medicine physician. In fact, today was one of my clinical days. I spend about 10% of my time each week delivering patient care.

There are many reasons why I still practice medicine. I'm the seventh CEO in the 100-year history of Virginia Mason, and every one of us has been a practicing physician. Even though my board says I don't have to practice, I say "Yes, I do. I'm not going to be the one who's going to break that tradition." Even more important is that practicing medicine is part of who I am. In some ways, seeing patients is the best part of my week. My practice has evolved so that I see people I've known for decades and that's very, very special for me. And it's important to my patients. The gratification of taking care of patients is more immediate than that of leadership. I believe being a practicing physician makes me a better leader: When things are clunky for our physicians, they're clunky for me. Being a practicing physician is important to who I am as a person and who I am as a leader—and, I think, it is important to our organization's culture of quality and safety, which is a major area of focus in my role as CEO.

In the early 2000s, I led a transformation of the organization from one that was physician-centered to one that has become patient centered *and* a great place to work for doctors, nurses, pharmacists, social workers, and every member of the healthcare team. This transformation included adapting Toyota Production System principles for healthcare to create our unique management method called the Virginia Mason Production System. We embarked on a journey to truly put the patient first in everything we do, and this has served as our true north ever since. Our strategic plan is illustrated as a pyramid, with the patient at the very top. Every member of the team is valued, respected, and empowered to "stop the line" if something doesn't seem right.

On Joy in Work

Joy in work is a psychic reward, an emotional reward, not a monetary one. Joy in work doesn't come from the reward of praise or even gratitude, although I think those things are part of generating joy in work. Joy is the emotions that are generated, or can or should be generated, by one's work experience.

As a physician, it's the gratitude I get from sharing with patients and the interactions I have on a regular basis with people I've come to know. What a privilege. And what joy one can get from patients who allow you into their lives at their most personal, intimate, vulnerable moments. For me, that's very, very meaningful.

As a leader, joy comes from the ability to have impact and the ability to broaden, or scale, the impact I can have. It's the opportunity to see individual growth and the joy in others. I've been a CEO for 20 years and the average tenure is about four and a half, so I've had a long history of experiencing these kinds of meaningful interactions, of seeing the impact. I know the challenges and the hits we take in our work. I help people develop resilience, help them be the best they can be and develop their full potential. I think the most important thing I do is to help those I lead be successful.

Waste Diminishes Joy

Waste diminishes joy in work for me, both as a physician and as a leader. That's the big one, and that's something that my whole career has been about. By waste I mean things that have no value. Things we do either because we think we have to, or because it's habit, or because it's the way we've always done things. Like making patients wait. Waiting rooms—waiting rooms are a waste—where patients can hurry up, be on time, and wait for us. It's embarrassing. It's the antithesis of being patient centered. We spend millions of dollars building waiting rooms. That's just an example of something I think we can control. We're working hard at my organization to eliminate waits, delays, non-value-added tests, and unnecessary treatment. So many wasteful things exist in healthcare. There are thousands of examples. Waste is everywhere.

In our health system we use our innovative management system to reduce waste. We're the furthest along of anyone in applying Toyota Production System principles in healthcare and we've been doing this for almost 20 years. It's a journey. Our management system focuses on continually reducing and eliminating waste, improving quality and safety, and improving satisfaction for patients and our team members. This is both top down and bottom up. The top down part is identifying and prioritizing the things we'll work on, and the bottom up is where all the answers are—people on the front lines are the ones who drive the improvement work.

Leadership at Virginia Mason

One of the things that gets in the way of joy is a feeling of loss of control. I think that's true for everybody. The biggest fear that the elderly have is losing control. In healthcare there's a lot of feeling around loss of control, whether it's because of the regulatory environment, the productivity pressures, the electronic medical record mandates, or any one of a number of things.

It is possible to give control back to the people who are on the front lines of care by engaging them in the improvement of their work. That's what we do at Virginia Mason. Nobody knows their work better than team members on the front lines. So, to the extent that we can, leaders need to engage them in improvement, particularly to help them regain control and make a meaningful difference. I remember when we first did this, some team members were telling us, "I've known what we needed to have happen for 20 years but either nobody ever asked me, or there was no way for my ideas to come to the fore and be acted upon."

Our management system is all about the people on the front lines improving their own work. This is done through organized events and multidisciplinary teams. It's also done through what we call daily management and everyday *Kaizen*, and using methods and tools of our management system to enable and empower team members and leaders.

We also innovate from the ground up. Every team member is encouraged to share their suggestions and look for ways we can improve. By submitting ideas and participating in *Kaizen*—continuous improvement—activities, everyone is empowered to think creatively in making things better for our patients and our teams.

Being a leader at Virginia Mason is not about being a boss; it's about being a coach, a facilitator, and a trainer for those who have the content expertise to redesign and improve their work. We're not anywhere close to perfect but that's what we're working toward, and that's what the management method we've created allows us to do. At Virginia Mason, leaders get out of their offices and go to the *Gemba*—the shop floor. We are visible, we are vulnerable, we engage in humble inquiry because we are genuinely curious about what's happening on the front lines. On the shop floor, leaders can inspire and catalyze innovation. It takes perseverance, it takes strong senior leaders who make it their work, not just things they delegate.

Every member of our executive and leadership teams must become certified in the Virginia Mason Production System, which means we don't just have to know it, we have to teach it. We have to lead workshops every year or we're not "fit for duty." That's true for me, too. I lead workshops every year. Every year I also lead a two-week study mission to Japan where we—physicians, leaders and others on the trip—work in factories to further our understanding of Toyota Production System principles.

We have a very thorough recruiting process when hiring to fill positions. We need the right people in the right places to grow and help lead us into the uncertain future of healthcare. Diversity is important. So is the willingness to be part of a collaborative team because our work is about today and the future. Job candidates, particularly physicians, spend two-plus days in interviews, back to back, meeting lots of people. Behavioral interviewing. It's as much for them as it is for us.

When physicians apply for an opening, they get a letter that, among other things, introduces them to our Physician Compact. Ninety-five percent of the time people say, "This is really good, this is really cool." A small number will say, "I'm not sure I want to work in a place that's that clear." So, we hope to identify people early on who truly want to come and work with us.

The Physician Compact explains the gives and the gets. It was put together about 20 years ago, before we ever discovered the Toyota Production System, by front-line clinicians when we realized that doing things the way they'd always been done wasn't going to allow us to move forward. The compact explains what every physician has every right to expect from the organization, and what the organization has every right to expect from its doctors. We also have a leadership compact and a compact for our board members. These are similar to our Physician Compact. Together the compacts provide the foundation for necessary change.

When we began the cultural revolution at Virginia Mason, people would say, "Are you kidding me?" or "Over my dead body," or "This, too, shall pass." Today, it's, "Wow, I want to work in a place that's working on their work and where there's an opportunity to keep getting better. I want to have an opportunity to engage in improvement."

Respect for People

Respect for others is woven into the fabric of our values of Teamwork, Integrity, Excellence, and Service. I don't believe we can have effective teamwork or consistently achieve excellence if we aren't treating each other appropriately, with kindness, courtesy, and respect. We recently finished our second cycle of Respect for People training that is required for every physician and every staff member. We hired an improv acting troupe and staged sessions in the morning and evenings, weekdays and weekends, and everybody had to attend. This troupe acted out vignettes about disrespect that were all written by our team members. The response from our team members was very positive.

As leaders, we have tremendous opportunity to make a difference. One of the most important things we do is help people who report to us be successful. That's the default mode: How can we help you to succeed? Our management system helps each team member do his or her very best work for our patients. And our organizational culture is predicated on deep respect for each other, our patients, and the community.

We also do a lot of recognition for staff for their good work. Our "Applause" program provides recognition in the moment and is very effective. Our "Good Catch" award celebrates team members who identify near-misses and patient safety issues. We have awards for outstanding leaders, outstanding front-line leaders, and executive leaders, as well. We also honor physicians in many ways. Feeling valued is important for job satisfaction and to finding joy in work.

Advice to Leaders, Staff

My advice to leaders is: Get involved. Understand the current state of your organization. Be a good listener and be curious. I think these traits, in and of themselves, will lead to huge learning and improvement opportunities.

My advice to staff: Find the best pathway to speak up, knowing your organization and its culture. Be a hammer, not a nail. Make your thoughts, your ideas known. This can be done well and constructively. Don't just complain—come forward with concrete, creative ideas. If leaders aren't listening to you, help them listen. We're all in this together.

Leaders and staff members never need to be satisfied with the status quo. Complacency is the enemy of improvement and success. Be innovative. Lean into change together rather than back away from it.

I can't think of a better way to explain the importance of being a learning organization. How better to evolve a culture than by being curious about what is possible and capitalizing on the full potential of your people? This is the journey we are on at Virginia Mason. It's a work in progress and, in many ways, never ending.

14.   Gene Lindsey, MD, Retired Physician and CEO Emeritus of Atrius Healthcare

Gene Lindsey, MD, is a retired physician, CEO Emeritus of Atrius Healthcare, and is active on the boards of several medical organizations. He is a thoughtful, passionate leader and advocate for social justice and improving the experience of care, improving the health of populations, and reducing the per capita costs of healthcare—that is, the Triple Aim. I was introduced to Gene, although we have never met, when he wrote the Foreword to my last book, co-authored with Anthony M. DiGioia, MD, entitled *The Patient-Centered Value System: Transforming Healthcare through Co-Design* (CRC Press, 2017). When I asked Gene to talk to me about the subject of joy in work, we did so twice for a total of more than three hours.

Part of the rhythm of my week is receiving Gene's electronic newsletter, *Healthcare Musings* (www.strategyhealthcare.com), which punctuates my inbox every Tuesday and Friday afternoon. He has addressed the subject of joy in work and his reactions to our interviews in several of these newsletters.

Gene and I are intellectual cousins of a sort, having discovered that we both studied—25 years apart—with a brilliant, beloved English professor named Jack Russell, gone but not forgotten. May the circle be unbroken.

I do not practice anymore, but I have not forgotten the full range of experience from unsurpassed joy to utter frustration and a sense of victimization by a system gone off the tracks. I am no longer heading out early each morning to discover what joys or frustrations await me in the office or at the hospital, but I do spend a lot of time thinking about all the ups and downs of almost 50 years of training and practice. I also know both the joy and frustration of having the responsibility to make the experience of practice better for those working in the delivery system, as well as the experience of trying to work through others to improve the experience of care for those seeking service.

I didn't have an "aha" experience but gradually came to realize that if I was ever going to have any fun practicing, or if I was ever going to be secure in the joy, I needed to find joy in the problem. The real joy is in the problem solving. Most people want to tell you what they personally experienced. I try to get under the covers of *why* I was feeling the way I was—understanding the forces that were creating suboptimal conditions for me and then working to change them.

My Professional Journey

I can break my career up into little pieces. Between 1967 and 1971 I was in medical school. I was an intern and resident in cardiology at the Brigham and Women's Hospital from 1971 through 1976. I started in practice at Harvard Community Health Plan in July 1975. From that time until the end of June 1976, the Brigham allowed me to be both a fellow in cardiology and a cardiologist at Harvard Community Health Plan. It was a nice arrangement.

From 1972–1980 I did a lot of ER work. I worked at the Lowell Hospital in Lowell, Massachusetts, which had a very mixed patient population—inner-city people, suburban people. At this hospital there were no interns or residents so at night on call in the ER, I was the only physician in the hospital. Anything that happened in the hospital that required the immediate attention of a physician, I was the person who had to do it. What I learned doing that was how to rely on my own judgment. What you don't realize, when you're in a group environment or in a huge hospital environment, is that if you don't know what to do you can just turn around and find someone you can discuss the case with. It's different when there's no one to look to but yourself. That's more or less the way it was in the office. You didn't want to interrupt other people's office flow to ask questions, although you sometimes did that. I think that had a lot to do with my development as a physician.

I was delighted just to be a primary care physician/cardiologist for the first ten years of my career and really didn't have any leadership responsibility. I was just going to work, doing my job, being a physician. Harvard Community Health Plan at that time was rapidly expanding. When I joined the organization in 1975 it had 80,000 members and ten years later it had 500,000. We went from having two sites to having about 14 sites—multispecialty buildings with pediatrics and internal medicine and surgery and radiology and a lab and pharmacy and dental—they had everything a hospital had minus an overnight stay.

By the mid-1980s, when I had ten years of practice under my belt and developed a reputation for being a good patient-sensitive physician who carried his fair share of the load, I made a couple of attempts to become a medical manager because I thought I'd like to make a change in the system. Initially I wasn't identified as someone who had any managerial ability, but I wanted to move in that direction.

The organization had a strong-willed CEO who was not a physician; I thought he didn't understand the original principles the organization was founded on, and he was focused on business rather than on clinical innovation and things of that sort.

The medical director was the interface between the front-line staff and the administration. We would have regular meetings of groups of several hundred physicians who would meet to discuss challenges to the organization three or four times a year. He would manage these meetings. There were lots and lots of meetings in addition to these. Each site would have its own meetings and each department would have its own meetings. There was a hands-on sense of interaction with management, which was good, but people often came away from those meetings feeling they weren't being heard.

There was, in our organization, because of the way it had evolved, something called a Physicians' Council. The Physicians' Council was essentially a board that interacted with management—it was almost like a union—over issues of compensation, work requirements, where we practiced, etc. I ran for the Physician's Council three times and finally won on the third try. Once I got on the Physicians' Council, in very short order I became its chairman and was the person who interacted with management over these issues. Being chairman of the Physician's Council made me a member of the board of the entire organization, both the insurance function and the care delivery function. When physicians met, they met with me on the podium. In the first five years I learned a lot.

The medical director had a five-year term and could not be hired for the next five-year term without the approval of the Physician's Council. The CEO was fired; the physicians refused to work with him any longer. We eventually changed the management of the organization. There was tension all through the '90s that played out in terms of organizational change.

Losing patients because their employers had changed insurance companies began to bother me so much that I became part of a movement to take the medical practice out of the insurance company (which is what created Harvard Vanguard) so we could actually be open to all insurers. That was a piece of work that involved a lot of politics, working with lawyers, haggling with boards. I did that through the mid-1990s and began to understand the nuts and bolts of how healthcare works based on many frustrating attempts to ensure that anybody who wanted to get care from this organization should be able to come and see me.

I began to understand the business from both sides and how the tensions developed between practitioners—who always felt rushed—and management, whose primary concern was keeping the organization in the black. As pioneering healthcare leader Sister Irene Krause said, "No margin, no mission." She was absolutely right. You can't fund healthcare these days on philanthropy. You actually need to have a business that meets all of the requirements from human resources to investment strategy that an ordinary business would have. I didn't go to business school, so I was learning all these things around the edges of being a practicing physician.

I was working in tandem with the administration. But by being chairman of the Physicians' Council and chairman of the board, I was not only in conflict with the administration but I was part of the senior management team; I was essentially there representing the interests of the physicians in all the business issues that came up. For instance, if the administration wanted to change a vendor, we'd discuss whether this represented an improvement in quality or whether it was all about cost, and what additional burdens it would put on the shoulders of clinicians. Our doctors were coddled to the point where their experience was quite different from that of the rest of the world. Once you had a job there, nobody left. It was a competitive advantage.

On Joy in Work

Joy in work, for me, was the direct realization that I had a meaningful relationship with another individual who had expressed confidence in me, and I in them, and together we created what we called a therapeutic relationship. It's like being in an effective marriage, in a way. It's the understanding that existed about what my role was, and what their role was, and together we jointly pursued their health. I got great satisfaction out of seeing them succeed in being healthier, recovering from whatever it was they'd been challenged by. That was worth a lot to me. There was nothing more emotionally satisfying than a good clinical outcome for a patient who came to me with a life-disturbing problem.

I also got joy from removing some of the barriers that hampered the relationship between the patient and me. For example, if I had a 15-minute appointment with you and you'd been frustrated by my office staff and felt you'd been treated disrespectfully, then in the first ten minutes of the encounter I was trying to do what's called in business "service recovery." I was trying to make it better and that's a steep hill to climb. Truth be told, the patient was *right*. You had a bad experience and you had every reason to hold me accountable for it—because from the looks of things I should have been in charge, right? And you didn't want to hear me tell you the problem was with the office manager, or to say, "Yeah, it's a terrible system." To which you may have responded, "Why should an intelligent guy like you work in a terrible system? Why don't you do something about it?' The "doing something about it" is what got me into management.

Harvard Community Health Plan was small and a tight-knit sort of family in the beginning, a supportive environment where we looked at issues of dysfunction as opportunities for improvement. Early on, we had a grant from the Robert Wood Johnson Foundation to have a Balint group, a "touchy-feely" group, as we called it, which met once a week for lunch. The goal of Balint groups, according to the website of the American Balint Society (www.americanbalintsociety.org), is to present clinical cases to improve and better understand the clinician–patient relationship. In our best moments we talked about the emotional challenges and stresses of practice in ways that allowed us to be more empathetic and patient centered. We learned that our relationship with the patient was potentially a powerful therapeutic tool. We physicians and nurses would sit around the conference room table and talk about our feelings associated with practice, which was sort of forward-thinking for 1975. That was a very good experience for me. I think in retrospect it helped diffuse some of my frustrations. We would also just sit there and bitch to each other about how bad, how difficult it was. We would complain about administration, we would complain about all the things that people tend to go inward with now, I think, when they feel so isolated and alone and burned out. That was beneficial for me. After about a year or so I became one of the associate leaders of the group. That conversation continued maybe until 1978 or 1979 when some key people left.

What Diminishes Joy

Anything that challenged my relationship with patients—for example, a dysfunctional system that made it difficult for patients to access me—diminished my joy.

When I was practicing in an unsupportive environment I didn't understand where the pressures were coming from and I felt inadequate. I felt like I was climbing a hill that was impossibly high. Like I was an agent in the injury of other human beings who were labeled "patients," because they weren't getting the care, they weren't even getting the attention, I felt they deserved from me. I felt like Old Mother Hubbard who had so many kids she didn't know what to do.

In the beginning I thought of Harvard Community Health Plan as a little island; we had our own sort of internal economy, we controlled everything in the way we thought was optimal. But the external environment became harsher and harsher as we got bigger, maybe going from 100,000 to 300,000 patients, and we had to build a sort of "causeway to the mainland" in terms of healthcare. Once that happened, we were subject to infection by any bad virus that was affecting healthcare in general, essentially in the context of financial issues and business functions.

We had an EMR going back to 1969! At that time doctors dictated or made short, hand-written notes that were input into the system by someone else and then transcribed. By the early '80s we were trying to develop an in-house EMR that was connected to billing and that allowed (or forced) clinicians to input the information themselves. I don't think people realize how much work inputting our own notes added to the life of the average physician. So many people my age have very little or nonexistent keyboard skills. Many still can't type. They're having to spend too much time documenting lots and lots of activities.

We were a prepaid medical group, so our patients' employers paid a fixed number of dollars per year for all of their healthcare. At the end of the year the organizations' financial status was a function of the number of people served minus the cost of serving them, and there was constant pressure from the finance department to bring new patients into the organization.

There was a lot of pushback and resistance to that pressure. What some physicians ended up doing—which created a lot of tension between the workforce and management—was creating ways of blocking new patients from their schedules because they didn't actually get any personal increase in remuneration from seeing more people. We were all salaried, but a minority of physicians don't perform as well if they are salaried. (I preferred being salaried to running on the fee-for-service treadmill.) We could go into our schedule and say, "I need an extra 30 minutes with this patient because she's complicated." The other thing some physicians did was to bring back patients they already knew more frequently than they really needed to be seen—because if you already knew the patient and there was no problem, and you were just checking their blood pressure since you added their last medication, the patient would be delighted. The administration was not happy with that because they'd think, "We don't want you seeing the people you've already seen and who are well. We want you to see the people you haven't seen before so we can grow the organization. Because our total revenue is a function not of how well you take care of the patient but of how many patients you take care of."

At the same time, we were encouraged to do what was needed for patients, to practice thoughtfully and be good stewards of resources. I was never told not to provide a procedure or a test I thought was clinically indicated, even if it was ordered only for psychological reassurance. In the 1980s, Harvard Community Health Plan paid for one of my patients to go to Stanford and wait for a year for a heart-lung transplant simply because I said it was the right thing to do; at that time, no hospital in Boston performed this surgery. That patient is still alive!

I don't think people think about the ethics as they're doing things. They think about survival. We rationalize what we're doing in the context of what's best for patient care, whether it's adding an extra test or adding an extra appointment. It's what's in my best interest translated into what's in the best interest of the patient. I get to see no new patients on my schedule, I get to see people I know and already have a relationship with, and they get to see me. We have a little chat, and we check their blood pressure, and I get to know their family better. There are a lot of positive things about that.

If there were a need for me to see another two or three patients at the end of a day—or if someone walked in unexpectedly who needed service, say at 3:00 p.m.—then the rest of the afternoon would be a disaster because I would be behind. I would be spending more and more time doing service recovery and less time in practice. Then it occurred to me one day that the last patient I saw long after 5:30 p.m. had every right to expect the same level of attention from me as the first patient I had seen at 8:30 a.m.

Fixing the Problems

Fixing broken systems will enable joy in practice. Bonuses don't work. Money doesn't create joy. I dealt with the frustration of burnout by realizing where it came from and trying to do something about its origins. In our "touch-feely" group it was helpful to get in touch with our feelings, but we needed to go from knowing where our feelings were coming from to doing something about their root causes. There were a lot of remarkable people around, like Don Berwick and Atul Gawande, to learn from and be involved with. We did a lot of innovative things that helped physicians: we maximized the use of what we used to call "mid-level clinicians" or "advanced practiced clinicians" but we literally invented the concept of the nurse practitioner back in the 1970s. Instead of telehealth we had telephone help. We had 24-hour call services in the '70s. We brought all of the laboratory tests in-house to minimize costs.

We established guidelines for an optimal number of patients to be seen and we established concepts of what a reasonable work week was. It was never perfect. We established something in the '80s called the "model practice unit." The model practice unit was essentially an innovation center, where we developed a call center and a variety of other things to try to optimize the relationship between the practice and our patients, with the idea that if it was better for them it was better for us. We tried lots of things.

When I became CEO in 2008, we really upped it by introducing Lean. At that time, we were all into quality improvement but had no system to improve performance. For example, we discovered that a mother who had a pediatric appointment with a child would spend over an hour in our facility waiting for a 15-minute visit. Forms to be completed for school, and for camp, would either pile up on the pediatrician's desk or be filled out by hand at home. All of those systems were examined using Lean engineering technology. We put in systems to automate the filling out of forms so they didn't have to be done by hand, and we implemented improvements so the time patients spent waiting for an appointment dropped by more than half.

Reflections

I've felt frustration as a physician and I've felt frustration on the other side, as a leader, being unable to fully explain why things are the way they are to people suffering either as patients or as clinicians.

The most important thing about practicing medicine, for me, was interpersonal interactions. I never thought of myself as an engineer but I became cognizant of the interdependency of everything in medicine: between the physician and the medical assistant; among the physician, office staff, and patients seeking to come in; between the nurses and physicians; and the interdependence among physicians. Medicine is so complex now that no one of us has universal knowledge of all things. And so instead of learning simply how to practice, it's more important to learn how to practice as part of a complex process.

What you begin to discover is these complex processes are not well engineered at all. Inherent in them are inefficient handoffs. Patients don't know what frustrates them about healthcare, but I think a lot of it is that they sense it's poorly coordinated. You hear it in the context of a patient saying, "Well, you're asking me the same question the last person asked." And their expectation is there's been a transfer of information that really hasn't occurred. As a physician, I feel a responsibility. I also understand that a lot of what doctors consider burnout—and the origins of their burnout—is doing the same things again and again and again. It doesn't have to be this way.

A good question to ask is, what part of the problem am I? I tend to be a self-examining person. It's best not to look at problems and blame somebody else because the truth is, we don't have any control over what somebody else does. The only place where we have any agency is over the part of the problem that we are. The problems have to be fixed by the people who are living with the problems themselves. You can't bring in someone from the outside to fix them for you, and only fixing broken systems will enable joy in practice.

For example: One day in the mid-1990s I asked myself why so many people were on my schedule. I went down the list and saw that everyone was there because I told them to come. So, then the question was, was I right to tell them that they needed to come at this time? The truth is there were a variety of reasons why I told them to come. I realized I told some patients to come back in three or four months who could have come back in six or eight months. Some of it was my insecurity, some was their insecurity, but that was a productive thought process.

When you do this you realize that the frustration you are experiencing in this moment is probably the outcome of what was happening three or four months ago that you didn't manage well at the time; what comes back as a dividend today is payback for that day's dysfunction. Thinking about what diminishes joy in practice from the point of view of practical, bad mechanics is an opportunity. What happens in the real world is that people don't often think that way and feel victimized by circumstances they feel are beyond their control. Or their managers don't think that way and continue to make unnecessary and burdensome requests of them. To have heuristic joy, as author Daniel Pink acknowledges, there has to be a little bit of control in your environment.

To get clinicians—doctors and nurses—to understand the external realities that are creating the pressures they feel internally is a big concept. When there are fewer people on the job, the people who are on the job are working harder and harder in the bad system. I personally believe this is at the heart of burnout. There's a limit to the clinical load any of us can carry. That clinical load varies from individual to individual. Most of the time, the people who are carrying the heaviest loads are either working way too hard or they're not doing what they should be doing for each of the patients they're caring for.

Each of us has emotional, intellectual, and physical limits that can be overwhelmed. I can't run my car for hours and hours at 5,000 rpm and expect that it will last long. I believe that part of responsible professional behavior is to recognize one's limitations and ask for help when the limits of responsible performance are approaching. It is not productive to complain about the incessant demands coupled with the non-compliance of our patients. It is also not healthy to sense that everything "depends" on me.

Collectively, as physicians, we are our own worst enemies. We need to heed the maxim, "Physician, heal thyself." This has more to do with the profession and its dysfunction than with the individual physician and the individual physician's health. Yet, as the system becomes more dysfunctional, the dysfunction has measurable impacts on physicians' health and well-being; you can't work in chaos even if you're the cause of the chaos for very long without being affected by it one way or another. If you're so depressed that you're hardly getting to work and you're a problem for yourself and others when you're at work, you're unlikely to be willing to stay after work to make the system better.

The biggest issue in quality improvement is getting exhausted, burned out physicians to see that Lean is the way out of the woods for them. We have horrendous institutional ineptness that has created the burnout that a lot of physicians feel. Dissatisfied physicians are not growing professionally, their autonomy is being violated, and they forget why they're there. Their sense of purpose is lost.

The medical literature provides a sort of treadmill concept about what diminishes joy in practice: physicians don't spend enough time with patients, they're running faster and faster, they're being asked to do more and more tasks in a shorter and shorter period of time, and all of a sudden they have this automated medical record that's turned them into a secretary. And now they're up at 11:00 at night documenting what they did the previous morning at 8:00. And they can't remember what it was. They feel like they need to fill out the form completely because if they don't fill it out correctly then it'll be rejected, or they'll get less credit and not maximize the yield on the income they honestly earned. These become self-reinforcing problems.

The conversation about joy in practice is one of the most critical conversations in healthcare today. The work–life and staffing issues ahead of us will soon move ahead of access and finance as the most significant and rate-limiting issues in determining our pace toward the Triple Aim. We are behind in understanding our frustrations and disappointments, and our lack of understanding and lack of clarity about potential solutions threatens the health and safety of patients and providers alike.

15. Mark Huth, MD, President, CEO, and Family Physician at Group Health Cooperative of South Central Wisconsin

Mark Huth, MD, started his career in the music industry, playing and manufacturing organs for churches and concert halls. "Mine was a circuitous path to medicine. I didn't go to medical school until my late 30s and finished residency in my early 40s," he says. A compassionate physician with a love of patient care and leading teams, this president and CEO believes that following one's heart and listening to others is a pathway to finding joy in work.

I'd always wanted to go into medicine. I grew up in a small town. My mother worked as a registered nurse for small-town doctors who were wonderful men and women. I remember looking at them and thinking, *I would love to do that. I would love to have people look at me the way we look at these physicians—as people who are truly helpful and compassionate.* I thought that was a pretty neat role to play within a community. It was the quintessential small town. It was doctors stopping by people's houses on the way home because that was easier for them than coming into the office. Or people coming to see the doctors on evening and weekends. Physicians always finding a way to accommodate patients. So, I thought that was really what I wanted to do.

But, truthfully, I nearly failed every high school math class I ever took. I could not solve for x, I didn't understand how you found the area of a triangle, I mean it just did not compute. I was also really involved in music and a very smart guidance counselor said, "If you're struggling with math it's going to be tough to do the college math you need to get into medical school. You should do music." That led me to study music at the college level. I loved it and got involved in church music.

A few years later, I got noticed by a local organ manufacturer; they hired me to help design and build the instruments and play them when they were finished. (When you bought an instrument, you'd often get a free concert.) I worked at the factory and played concerts and was promoted within the organization over time. Now, I was managing people and projects. I went back to school in the evenings to get a business degree.

But I still had the desire to be a doctor, and I didn't want to retire from the music industry and think, *I wish I'd pursued a medical career.* So, I went back to night school and, wouldn't you know, for reasons I still don't understand, math made sense. I got all my prerequisites done and applied to medical school in Portland, Oregon. I was accepted, and, frankly, to this day I'm still surprised! I guess I didn't really think I'd get in. I was 35 when I started medical school, and 39 when I started a family medicine residency. And, at that time, my goal was just to see patients. I wasn't thinking about leadership at all.

My Professional Journey

I chose family medicine because it's what really felt right in my heart. I had thought about orthopedics because I love sports and thought musculoskeletal surgical care would be fun. I also thought about dermatology, as well as a number of other subspecialties. Then, I worked with a family physician during a clerkship in my third year; I was with him for an entire year. I would see patients with him on Monday afternoons.

I remember the first week I was in his clinic, a woman came in with a positive pregnancy test. It was the first time she met this doctor, it was the first time she met me. And it happened to be that Monday was her day off. So, throughout her pregnancy she came in on Mondays and I always saw her.

During spring break that year I had no classes for a week, and I got a call from the doctor, who said, "She's in labor. If you can be here, it would be really cool." So, I went in and helped with the delivery. For the last three months of the year we saw her and the baby. That experience—the continuity of care and the chance to develop relationship with patients—was the thing that really hooked me. It took me back to my small-town roots, reminding me of the doctors I had known as a child. I knew it was the right fit.

My residency was at the University of Wisconsin Department of Family Medicine, where I was chief resident in my third year. I had a chance to stay on as part of the faculty after graduation, which was a great way to start my medical career, seeing patients and teaching residents. A year later, I was recruited by Group Health Cooperative of South Central Wisconsin. I've been here since 2007.

At that time, I just planned to see patients for the rest of my career. And I would have been very happy with that. However, a few years after joining Group Health, our Executive Director approached me and said, "Hey, you're a physician who also has a business degree, you should be my chief of staff." I'd never thought about leadership in medicine before that point but agreed to try it.

Looking back, the decision to enter leadership within my medical group was kind of an experiment for me. I wasn't sure how long I wanted to do it. It also felt a bit like blind luck, just being in the right place at the right time. A few years later, I moved from chief of staff to chief medical officer and then president and CEO after that. Although my role is mostly administrative, I still see patients when I can get to clinic.

My work hours are pretty regular. Typically, I'm in my office by 8:00 a.m., work till 5:30 p.m., and almost always eat at my desk. My wife and I have an 11- and a 14-year-old at home, and it's really important to me that I spend time with them, taking them to soccer practices and games, helping with homework. I'll often look at email after that, sometimes until 10:00 or 11:00 p.m. That's pretty much five days a week. And then I come in either Saturday or Sunday morning for four hours. So that's probably pushing 60 hours most weeks.

Clinical practice is typically about three hours a week but it's not every week. My job is almost 90–95% administrative with very little patient time. But I love seeing patients so much that I just couldn't give it up; even an hour or two is restorative for me. It fills me back up.

On Joy in Work

I definitely feel joy in work. This is something I think about a lot and something I've been working on quite a bit. I have a peer group of CEOs, not in healthcare, and we often talk about finding joy in work.

In my mind, joy in work and joy in life in general are related to two things. One is, I want to make a positive difference in the world. I don't have the idea that it has to be some big, sweeping thing. If I can make even a small positive difference in one person's life today, that's special to me. I want to feel that I'm leaving the world a better place than when I came into it. Second is, I want to fill my life with meaningful relationships with people I love—at home, at work, and in other places in my life. Feeling that I'm making a difference and having meaningful relationships really fills me up.

That's why I still see patients. I actually went through a period when I stopped. I read journals that said physician leaders at the C-suite level should stop seeing patients because our time is best spent elsewhere. So, I gave that up for nine months and found that my joy in work went down dramatically. And I thought, *I know I can't carry a panel of patients; it's not fair to patients to be assigned to me as their physician because they'd never be able to see me—just two hours here and there—but I can do urgent care, seeing people who need to be seen but can't get in with their regular provider.* The second I started doing that I felt centered again. It reminds me of why I do all the administrative work, why I love medicine, and why I feel fulfilled by it. It was tough when I lost that connection to patients.

With administrative work I feel that I'm making a positive difference but in a different way. As a leader, I enjoy working with individuals and teams, helping them contribute their best work while pursuing a common purpose and a common vision. I think the people on my senior leadership team are all smarter than me! They each do their jobs better than I could. And I love that because they each have a tremendous impact on our organization. My role is to help them work together for a common purpose. That's very satisfying to me, and that's why the administrative job is appealing to me. I feel I'm making a difference and I have strong relationships with people I care about, so it's a great fit.

What Diminishes Joy

Feeling I don't have any power to help improve a situation diminishes joy in work for me. If we're saddled with a challenge, if something is happening that is a threat to our business or the way we want to practice medicine or provide health insurance and there's nothing I can do personally, that's very stressful for me. An example is what's happening with the cost of care right now. This unsustainable cost trend makes it more difficult to provide the care that people deserve, and it's a significant source of stress for me.

Lack of Control

The best healthcare is worthless if nobody can afford it. We already spend more on healthcare than any other country in the world, while the rate of medical inflation continues at an unsustainable pace. As both a health insurer and a delivery system, we have to find that very delicate balance of providing insurance and care which is both appropriate and affordable. A few years ago, we had to figure out how to cover the cost of a few medications that cost more than $50,000; now we have one that costs over $2 million for a single dose. There's just not enough money available to support that pricing scheme. So, we have to decide which care is in the best interest of the patient and we have to find a way to keep it affordable.

The lack of control over pricing creates a lot of stress, not just for me but for many of our providers and leaders. It often feels like we have to come up with a solution for a problem we didn't create. The flip side is that there are victories, times when things work well. And, when you find a solution in a very complicated situation, that win feels bigger.

The cost problem also affects what is now expected of providers and nurses who see patients. There is a tension between the amount of work the providers have to do and the need to keep our clinics financially healthy. The request to add resources (more providers, for example) has to be balanced against the financial impact. Staffing and running clinics is expensive; the more we staff up, the more expensive our products become and the more difficult it will be for people to pay their premiums.

We are constantly trying to balance two challenges: 1) how do we run efficiently enough that people can afford to buy our insurance and come to our clinics, and 2) how can we have enough staff so that when patients come to our clinics, there are enough people to perform all of the necessary tasks in a way that's not only sustainable but that helps staff to find joy in work? It is a challenge that we deal with every day. Luckily, our providers understand the tension and are motivated to work with us to find the best balance.

Fixing the Problems

It's really impossible to find solutions in a vacuum. Maybe there are brilliant minds somewhere who can fix problems perfectly without consulting others, but that certainly isn't me. Although there are times when a single person has to make the call, generally I feel that tackling problems as a team is a vastly superior process.

Embracing Conflict

First, we have to embrace conflict. Too often, people avoid conflict or try to push it to the side. When we do this, we rob ourselves of the chance to gain valuable perspectives. Conflict is a wonderful opportunity to learn from others. It is also a chance to pull a team together. Rather than push conflict away, we have to embrace it. But when we embrace conflict, the embrace has to be genuine.

We have to replace, "I don't agree," with "Tell me more about that." Acknowledge that other peoples' views and feelings are valid. Embrace the moments of discomfort because that is where the solution is. Conflict is a great opportunity and it is easier to handle when we see it as a positive thing. What's more, when we embrace and welcome conflict, we start to move people from being adversaries to becoming teammates.

Listening

People are more resilient and better able to handle the stress of this job—and this job is incredibly stressful—if they have a sense of empowerment and trust that leaders listen.

The most salient example is a conversation we're having right now with providers about the length of appointments on the schedule. Some of our providers are advocating for longer appointments, moving from 15-minute appointments to 20-minute appointments for problem-focused visits. Their feeling is that even five minutes more per patient throughout the day would allow them to provide better care, leading to better health and less demand, as patients will be healthier and won't have to come in as often.

On the other hand, if you have longer appointments, you are seeing fewer patients per day. If you're seeing three patients an hour rather than four—and you multiply that by eight hours a day, five days a week, across 75 providers in primary care—you end up with a big decrease in clinic capacity. That could mean there are patients who really need to be seen who can't get in.

There's the rub, right? How do we balance length of appointments with demand, all while keeping the care affordable and not burning out our providers? The key is, it is critical to listen to our provider experiences and perspectives and avoid the temptation to move to a solution too quickly. When we listen, empathize, and embrace someone's point of view, they are more able to become a partner in the solution

Communicating

In the past, the response of the leadership, at least in our group, may have been "We're sorry, we can't do that, everybody needs to see patients every 15 minutes." One of the ways we've been able to improve is to say, "We want to hear your point of view and understand where you're coming from; we want to hear more about what your experience is." After that, there will be plenty of time to share what we are dealing with—how much it costs to staff a clinic, how much we can invest in providers and nursing staff, the number of appointments that are really required each week, and how we will balance the tension among all of those factors.

We can't add significant costs to the system by adding lots of providers. But at the same time, it doesn't help us if we're burning people out or if our staff feel they can't do their best work because they're always running in the red and they're at their breaking point. It's a complex issue, one that many organizations struggle with. But we are more likely to get to a workable solution if we attack the problem as teammates.

Advice

I think people know that I love what I do. Frankly, I have loved all of the jobs I've had. I loved being in the music business, I loved being a performer, I loved building instruments and dealing with customers and leading teams. I've loved being a physician. I actually loved residency. Most people say residency was terrible. It's true I wouldn't want to work the 80-hour work weeks again, but it was a wonderful time of learning and experiences with great residents, faculty, and patients. I loved being a physician full time and I love the leadership I'm doing. It's not because I'm happy-go-lucky. I actually work every day to try and manage the stress that comes with this job and with the work of raising a family. But I am able to find joy in my life.

Part of it is feeling that I'm making a difference and that I'm in relationship with people I care about. However, that sense of joy also comes from a life lesson I picked up many years ago: I don't have to be perfect. I can struggle and fail, and things will be okay. I think that's particularly hard for doctors, because we have the perception that everyone expects us to be perfect in all that we do. And, somehow, we accept this mantle of responsibility even though it is impossible. I have to allow myself to be imperfect and know that I am still good enough. Keeping this in mind allows me to step back and say, even in my imperfection, "Look at the richness of all the experiences I've had in my life. Aren't I lucky to be in this place doing this stuff right now?"

Identify Your Core Purpose

I believe that people need to identify what is most important, their core purpose—what is truly meaningful? For some people, their core purpose may be prestige. Or financial gains. Or it may be achieving excellence in a particular discipline, whether that's sports or business or banking or being a physician. Maybe they want to be recognized as being at the top of their field. I interact with some people who feel the salary they make is more important than anything else. Others are focused on prestige, being recognized as an expert in their field and earning the respect of peers and community. And then I find people who feel much the way that I do, that it's really about patient care. That's where they feel the most filled up. For most of us, it's not just one thing, it's a blend of many things. What you need to think about is, what are the most important things on my list? What will fill me up? Then, make career decisions that are most in keeping with what you really want to achieve. I certainly enjoy the success I've had as a physician and a leader, but I would be very unhappy if I were not able to balance my work with the experiences I have as a husband and a father. Figure out what's on your list, what fills you up. Then, position yourself to find the job, the life, the personal relationships, family structure, whatever it is, that best fits your core purpose. If there's a mismatch between your core purpose and what you're doing, I think it's incredibly difficult to be happy.

For example, there was this top student in my medical school class, a very bright and driven learner, someone who could have gone into just about any specialty. She chose her specialty based on how short the residency was and what the earning potential was in practice. Essentially, "How quickly can I get working and how much can I make?" The last time we talked, this student shared that she was miserable because she is in a specialty she doesn't enjoy.

Medical School Debt

It's hard to ignore the amount of debt most people acquire in undergraduate school and medical school. For many of us, it's a pretty big number. However, I think it's risky to go into a specialty for the sole purpose of paying off medical school debts quickly. The reality is, as a resident I made more money than I ever did in the music industry. And I made so much more than that in my first year as a salaried physician. It's true that when I got out of medical school I had two big loans: one was a mortgage and the other was my school debt (and, for the record, my school debt was bigger than my mortgage.)

But I have said this to roomfuls of doctors: I don't agree with the image of the poor doctor who has school debt, because we have the earning potential to be able to pay that all off. Even if your medical school was expensive, you gained significant earning potential and even the lowest-paid physician will be able to pay it off and have a good lifestyle. So, pick a residency that is the best fit for you and don't worry about your ability to pay off your debt. You'll have the earning power in your career. It is so much more important to pick a specialty you love.

Finding Balance

The most successful and fulfilled people I know are masters at finding balance. Even though they face challenges and stress, they also have enough experiences that fill them up, moments that serve as stepping-stones, allowing them to cross a creek without getting their feet wet. In my practice, it's the patients that fill me up. As a leader, it is the people on my teams and those I work with all the time. At home, it's the experiences with my wife and family.

We need to make sure we get enough experiences that really fill us up because there are many, many things—both in the administrative world and the care provider world—that empty us out.

16. Thomas Foels, MD, MMM, Chief Medical Officer of a Not-for-Profit Health Plan

Thomas Foels, MD, started his career in 1984 as a pediatrician, first with one and then with two practices. He gradually became interested in the links between patient outcomes and the quality of patient care, first as delivered in his own practices and then in the practices of other physicians. Over time his focus shifted to population health, he earned a master's degree in medical management, and, in 1997, joined a not-for-profit health plan to facilitate the transformation of clinical care delivery and patient outcomes in hundreds of practices in his community. Tom retired in 2019, less than a year after this interview, but by then the changes he helped to usher helped many doctors to recapture their joy in work.

I went into healthcare because I was driven by the science and I was influenced by the strong and enduring ethic of doing good with a degree of personal sacrifice. What I mean by this is a commitment and accountability to the patient for good care. It sounds kind of "old-school." It wasn't about lifestyle, it wasn't about income, it wasn't about title. It was really devotion to doing the right thing, and to not letting people fall through the cracks. That was important. Unlike many others, I didn't have a personal health event, I didn't have experience or exposure to hospitals and was enamored by what I saw, and nobody in my family was in healthcare.

I still see glimmers of that old-school medicine here and there, especially among providers who work with recent immigrants. Immigrants have come here from Southeast Asia and the Middle East but that's slowing down quite a bit. It's a real struggle to work with these people—there are many language barriers, multiple cultural barriers to think about and address—and these doctors just roll up their sleeves and do it. Doctors overcome these barriers by engaging immigrants who arrived here a few years ago to help more recent immigrants acclimate. They provide breastfeeding education, mentoring, and care coordination. They operate on the thinnest margin known to man, and their services gain traction because the immigrant community is very tightly interwoven and, slowly, doctors win these patients over. These professionals are paid, and they're employed within a federally qualified health center. They are very committed to what they do. That's real, mission-driven stuff. I love it.

I went into pediatric practice in 1984 and started as a two-person group. My partner unexpectedly died in his 30s. I hired another doc to take his place. We had an approach to care that attracted many patients: we had quality-driven open-access scheduling. We provided many services for obstetricians, including deliveries in small local hospitals, and the practice built up quickly. Before long we had six or seven docs.

By the time I opened a second group practice things were getting bigger and busier and I was doing a lot of administrative work. Long story short, I was doing a lot of work with the early EMR, which was very rudimentary at the time. I said, "We need to have a quality assurance program in the office around things that result in children being hospitalized, asthma being one of the more common. Let's start looking at every asthma admission in the hospital as a failure on our part until proven otherwise—let's assume we screwed up somehow. Either we didn't triage these patients into the office in a timely fashion, we undertreated them when they had an exacerbation, we weren't available on a weekend and they got worse until they finally came in on Monday, or anything else. Of course, some of these will not be our fault, but let's go in with that frame of mind." When we did that we found, *Gee, this patient should have been on a controller medicine for asthma,* and *this could have been prevented if they'd had the right therapy weeks earlier.*

I began to dig a little deeper, thinking, *we all trained together, we all are the same age, there's probably not going to be a lot of variation in the way we treat asthma.* I started to pull records and saw we all more different than we were similar in the way we treated asthma. We couldn't all be right. We were still having what I thought were avoidable admissions to the hospital, but we couldn't tag them to any particular provider. So, I said, "Let's develop a common guideline for the practice. It's the least we can do for our patients since we all swap our patients when we're on vacation. Let's develop a uniform guideline and work to adhere to it. Let's do some quality assurance checks." That's what got me interested in stepping back and thinking about a population of healthy individuals.

That was the "Aha!" moment. I began to take some courses, became more population health focused, and one thing led to another. With this blend of some insight into practice innovation and thinking about population health, I got to know people at the health plan. They asked if I'd work part-time, I said I'd be glad to, and things went on from there. Then I got my master's degree in medical management and I was really smitten. When I couldn't spread myself so thin between the practice and the health plan, I knew I'd have to fish or cut bait. I went with the health plan and I've been here since 1997.

What My Job Entails

I am the liaison between our health plan and provider network to facilitate the transformation of clinical care. I examine providers' systems of care delivery and decode what might be necessary to improve them. By system of care, an example is the way a practice is set up to remind patients whenever they come into the office about the preventive care they need, such as mammograms or colorectal cancer screening. Our health plan is sophisticated at profiling physicians' panels of patients on a variety of preventive healthcare measures. Of course, there are always weird variations in providing preventive care that supposedly can't be explained: one doc is a superstar and one is not doing well at all.

When I ask the higher-performing docs, "What is it that allows you to be the best in class with mammography screening?" often they won't have a clue. They say, "I don't know, I talk about it a lot." I say, "You may have some systems in place in your office that aren't even visible to you that allows this to happen. Maybe you have someone at the front desk who is always looking at the medical records and is the first to remind the patient that it's been a year since she had her last mammogram, ask if that's something she'd like to schedule now, and offer to help make the appointment then and there." There's always down time in an office, and care gaps such as these have time to be addressed. Physicians may think they're the strongest contributors to providing preventive care but so much more can be achieved through accountable individuals up front in the office.

When I ask low-performing docs why their rate of breast cancer screening is so low, they say, "I come in every day trying to do my best. It's not like I set about to deny services to people. I don't understand why my rate is 20% and the doctor's down the street is 80%." It is usually because these doctors have a system of care that is not optimal. If they go in every day just attempting to *try harder*, their results are not going to change; they'll stay at 20%. So, docs have to think systematically about how to approach improving rates of screening in their offices. It may involve delegation of responsibility.

In any physician's practice they need to look at cost, they need look at quality, and they need look at access—these things often have to do with how their system of care delivery was developed, how they delegate to others, and how they retrieve information from the EMR. Obviously, on a given patient visit, the doc who has an EMR pop-up reminder box showing five quality measures and the gaps in preventive care that need to be filled will be able to do a better job of filling those gaps than those who have a less sophisticated EMR. Docs may try hard but trying is not enough; I help them to find tools and enhance systems of care that will enable them to improve.

On Joy in Work

When I was in clinical practice the thing that brought me the most joy was seeing the patient heal—and healing could be physical, behavioral, or emotional. In pediatrics the turnaround time is pretty quick—I usually saw the results of my work, although not in every case. There was joy in that. If I hadn't been there, hadn't brought the knowledge that I had, and not delivered the care in as patient-centric a way as I had, the outcomes would have been different. Some of that was about saving lives—that's incredibly powerful—but just altering the course of a child's illness for the better brought me joy.

It's very different in my current role. The challenge, which I always think of and encourage my staff to think of, is this: *Many of the people we will impact and whose lives will change for the better, we will never meet. Ever.* We're going to put a policy in place and we're going to do something at a population level. I'm going to work with primary care practices to redesign their work so physicians can spend more time with their really sick patients. All those things are going to open new doors for patients and result in better things happening. For example, our health plan has tremendously high scores when it comes to managing diabetes, and that's due to how we interact with our providers in the community. This means, as a patient, you lower your A1C levels, you get your blood sugars under control, you get your blood pressure under control—that's like saying there's one less amputation, one less renal failure. I'll never see those people. I just have to believe they're there. That was hard for me because I don't get the feedback. Through mindfulness training I've become much more conscious of the important indirect effects of what I do.

Sometimes physicians tell me I've changed their lives. That came to light for me was when I spent three hours in one physician's practice after I'd worked with him to implement needed change. I told him I would spend the morning in his office, that I wanted to see everything that was new, and that I wanted to talk with his staff. When I got to this physician's office, I thought, *Oh my God. This is the happiest group of people I've ever seen.* Everybody had defined roles; there was no role confusion. Physicians had more free time than I would have imagined. I was always used to a fast pace—run, run, run. This physician said, "I've delegated work to staff, it is all going to be done. I'm going to answer a couple of emails of patients I'm checking up on for their diabetes and hypertension. I used to bring them all in but now they simply report out to me and the information is more accurate than what I'd get as their blood pressure in the office, anyway. I tell these patients, just communicate and we'll schedule a time in two more months when we can touch base." The waiting room was empty. It wasn't because they weren't seeing people, it was that nobody had any wait time. You could see the joy in the faces of staff. They had optimized their EMR so they could do things that had been busy work before. They were paring down their notes, so they were more readable. The EMR is probably the single biggest and most commonly listed contribution to burnout. In this practice, they were finding ways to engineer around that. That made my day, it made my year.

The Road to Improvement

I was able to facilitate improvements in that doctor's practice because my colleagues and I had begun to work with Don Berwick at the Institute for Healthcare Improvement on office redesign. Primary care is in the most desperate state of any component of our healthcare system right now. People don't want to go into the field, it's drudgery, there aren't young primary care docs anywhere, and those who are in primary care are being burdened by patients who have more complex diseases than ever before. Their tools are antiquated, they're trying to manage all on their own, they're under-resourced, and they can't afford to bring in registered nurses who could be very helpful. I felt that primary care was dying on the vine and it would be catastrophic if it were to disappear. I was one of multiple voices here who said, "We need to do something differently. Maybe we can take some of Berwick's teaching and think about redesigning." So, we began to develop some courses.

I brought a group of primary care docs together; this was the first time I went to see and talked to the doctor I just mentioned. I said that if we could get a group of doctors together, a group of patients together, and start to talk about what improvement would look like, I wonder where that would lead. So, we started to do that. And we started to pull in some of the old Berwick fundamentals. At about the same time, although we weren't conscious of it until a little further down the road, there was this bubbling up of the patient-centered medical home concept nationally. We looked at what those design elements were, we looked at what we had already put on paper, and we realized these were the same. On a national level and on our local level, we were looking at the same root causes of problems our doctors were experiencing. We needed to figure out how to do things differently.

One of the fundamentals was we'd need to start paying doctors differently. First of all, we'd have to put more money in their pockets because they had to invest. And we had to get them out of fee for service, which was killing them. At that point, the only way doctors would be paid was by bringing patients in to see them, whether those patients needed to be seen or not. I used to give telephonic advice to keep patients out of the office—I wasn't terribly successful as a pediatrician—but I was keeping the cost of care down. I'd say, "You don't need to come to see me, that's crazy." But fee for service doesn't align with a sustainable business model if you give services away like that. So, we started to redesign the payment model. We dabbled in an early form of alternative payment, referred to as "pay-for-performance" back then.

Then we realized we'd have to provide doctors with good data, give them meaningful incentives, and teach them "best practice" to drive improvement. We became laser-focused on diabetes control measures and, sure enough, diabetes control numbers started to improve overnight. It was dramatic. We realized that if we could get docs to focus on a narrow set of problems that are a high priority, such as diabetes—since they can't focus on everything—and give them really good data on what they're doing, the data would surprise them; it would show them their patients weren't as healthy and well-managed as they thought they were. So, good data was number one. Number two, we put meaningful incentives in place to reward doctors for better health outcomes, sizable enough that they could begin to invest in additional staff and better systems of care. And number three, we'd teach doctors best practice. We used to call it "improvement science" or "improvement literacy." We said that putting together all three of these things—good data, a meaningful incentive, and improvement literacy—would lead to magic. At the time, everybody in the country was futzing with the first two and they'd say, "We'll give the docs the data, we'll put incentives out there, and magic will happen." But change never occurred because they forgot the third element: teaching doctors how to improve.

There's a footnote to this story: We didn't provide the doctors health plan data; we asked them to extract data from the medical records with a very simple sampling methodology, and to just feed the data back to us. We put together profiles and sent them back to the docs so they could see where their peers were performing. I got two kinds of phone calls afterward. One was from doctors who said, "I can't believe my numbers are this bad. Your data systems are terrible." I'd remind them that, "This was the data *you* gave *us*." And they said, "Oh, okay. I guess these outcome numbers are accurate then. I'm really not achieving the outcomes I'd like to see." And the second kind of call was, interestingly, "Look, you wanted five pieces of information on the diabetic patient: their last visit, their A1C, their renal function, blah blah blah. Do you know how long it takes me to get that information? To get it out of the chart, to fill out one of these forms? It takes me five or ten minutes." So, I said, "Wait a minute. When a patient walks in and you're seeing them face to face, does it take you the same five or ten minutes to pull that data so you can have a conversation about their diabetes? That's not going to work for you. How are your charts, how are your medical records arranged?" I'd hear silence on the other end of the phone. Then they'd say, "Oh yeah, I think I have a problem there." I'd tell them this was the root cause of the problems we were talking about and say, "Let's start reorganizing your medical records so this information comes up easily at the time of the patient visit." We now use a population health software system that pulls data out of the EMR, combines it with health plan data, and then puts it back into the EMR as alerts and reminders, so doctors don't have to wade through pages and pages of screens to find it. There's a little alert box on the screen and they can customize it any way they want. This is very recent.

What we haven't fed into the system yet, but which will come very soon, is a tool to help doctors see the gaps in preventive care for each patient at a glance. We're reformatting and restructuring data in the doctors' medical record and making it easy to format as a pop-up. A pop-up might tell them a patient is a year overdue for breast cancer screening, or overdue for three immunizations. Boom, there it is. Docs won't have to do mental calculations about them. Pretty soon the health plan data will tell the doc that the patient still has high blood pressure, and the doc will be able to see whether the prescriptions they wrote were filled. If they weren't, then the doc will be able to say, "Oh, you're struggling to be compliant with your medicines. Let's talk about what would help you take your medicine every day." Then they can ask why their patients aren't taking their medicines. Is it cost? Side effects? Something else? This systematizes information that would otherwise be unavailable. Better outcomes bring joy and professional reward into their everyday work. Administrative burdens are reduced and pathways to better care are made easier. I've heard physicians say more than once, "This helped me to be a real doctor again!"

The real challenge of all this is, how can we scale these improvements rapidly? We have almost 900 primary care physicians in the community. We're an open network, so they're all independently practicing doctors. The health plan does not employ physicians. We're using intensive training and dedicated resources to just under 200 of these practices to help them adopt and spread improvements that are already working in others. We're working with some practices to test how quickly and how extensively we can make changes if we throw the kitchen sink at the problems. In other words, how rapidly can we deploy what works?

What Diminishes Joy

I've become jaded after being in healthcare for so many years, seeing everything from blatant criminal behavior to lack of accountability in patient care.

In my perfect world there would be fewer distractions, because distractions slow me down. A lot of what I need to do is thought- and time-intensive. I can't do something in five minutes, then drop it and come back and drop it and come back. I have to stay with it, finish it over the course of a couple of hours, and be done. We're in a crazy world. The doctors will say this, too. Information is coming in every door and window and we're not the multitaskers we think we are.

People on the front lines of working with office practices in our health plan say what really drives better care is office practice culture. This gets to the practice's burnout factor. One of the first things they do when they go into an office is an assessment of all the staff and physicians. They ask many general questions, among which are: "Do you feel valued? Are duties well defined? Is there camaraderie in the workplace?" And they can almost predict, based on the results of that assessment, whether they're going to make any rapid progress in that practice.

Burnout is a contagious disease. We might think it resides solely with stressed, overworked doctors and often it does. But it's contagious in practices. People lose vitality in work. Physicians and staff lose intrinsic motivation and, basically, lose interest in thinking about how to do things differently. They don't have any energy to change. Change is hard, we all know that. It's emotionally hard, it's physically hard, and in certain practices it's just not going to happen. We're teaching and professing improvement science. The culture of every office is different. The culture of an office can either facilitate or hamper our progress for many reasons. If there's no doctor leading the initiative, and if there's resistance from the staff because they think changes may jeopardize their job in some way, it won't work. There are landmines all around.

Part of my angst involves how best to engage these practices. All of this is time-consuming, all of this is resource-intensive, so how do we scale it in a timely enough way? Sometimes, when we take a practice's data, bring it back to the docs, get everybody around a table and say, "This is where we are—is this where we want to stay?", all these good conversations begin to percolate. People will say, "What really diminishes me is X, Y, and Z." and our response is, "You know, we can probably fix some of it. We can't fix it all, but let's start working on that. Because we really can't institute change or have dialog until we begin to address some of these more foundational problems."

17.   *Donald L. Lappé, MD, FACC, FAHA, Executive Director of the*
      Cardiovascular Clinical Program; Chairman, Cardiovascular Department;
      and Chief of Cardiology at Intermountain Healthcare, Salt Lake City, Utah

Donald L. Lappé, MD, is Executive Director of the Cardiovascular Clinical Program; Chairman of the Cardiovascular Department; and Chief of Cardiology at Intermountain Healthcare, an integrated health system that includes 25 hospitals in two states, 120 clinics, 1,400 employed physicians, and another 300–400 advanced practice clinicians. It also includes a health plan that insures 900,000 people in the Intermountain West. A practicing cardiologist who has worked here since 1979 and who has held leadership positions for 25 years, Donald speaks reverently about his profession and eloquently about the importance of continuous improvement, organizational values, and a culture of safety.

Probably like most people in healthcare, I was driven by wanting to help others and save lives, applying science to the enhancement of care. I'd graduated from college with a degree in electrical engineering. I think I chose cardiology because of my engineering background. Cardiology made sense. Electrical signals are part of EKGs and can be measured.

My Roles

When we were in the process of forming this integrated health system, my colleagues and I asked ourselves how we wanted to ensure the highest clinical quality, service quality, and value. We understood that 80% of healthcare can be described by about 100 common clinical processes of care, and these aggregate into areas. For example, there's cardiovascular, which is probably the easiest one; women and newborns are another area. Under cardiovascular we manage heart failure, arrhythmias, open heart surgery, and so on. And what we said is, let's bring together physicians, nurses, administration, and finance to optimize these processes of care in a collaborative way to get optimal clinical outcomes, service outcomes, and value.

In my three jobs I'm responsible for people who need cardiology services, both as inpatients and outpatients. I try to bring to the forefront best practices and evidence-based medicine, and then provide goals—and measures around those goals—to continue to improve the care we deliver. I spend 20% of my time as a cardiologist seeing patients so I'm grounded in reality.

For my clinical program I bring together teams of people with fundamental knowledge of appropriate use criteria from the American Heart Association and the American College of Cardiology for managing conditions such as heart failure, management of defibrillation, and optimal care in the cardiac catheterization lab. We then develop best practice models, condensing this information into a few digestible pages, tools that help us to reduce variation in the way these tasks are performed.

We don't standardize—we reduce variation. I don't think telling people what to do works well because I don't like being told what to do. But I like to be educated as to how to do things better and work as part of a heart team. We meet with physicians and at other times we meet with nurses because nurses are key to the consistent delivery of care, and nurses are the ones who do it in the hospital. Physicians can do procedures, but nurses are the ones seeing the patients and taking what doctors are asking to be done and then doing it.

I meet with operational people to talk about how we can continue to improve the efficiency, effectiveness, safety, and quality of care. Operational people are, for example, nursing directors, echocardiogram directors, and directors in all the modalities we work with. I share with them best practices from all the regions of our system. Sometimes one hospital may be doing something better than another; by sharing these experiences and successes we can continue to improve the workflow, consistency, and quality of care we deliver based on our evaluation of best practices.

Championing Measurement and Dissemination

Fundamental to determining outcomes is measurement: you manage what you measure. Our health system has a robust measurement system, which we use to produce reports of both final outcomes such as readmission mortality, and intermediate outcomes, such as whether patients were sent home on the right medicines (for example, for heart failure and coronary artery disease).

Then it's important to disseminate widely the resulting information. Our website makes these measures available to anyone in our system, and I meet with people in all our regions to share that information. At least once a year I go to each of our 25 hospitals and give them cardiovascular updates about, for example, what's new in managing people with chest pain in the emergency department, and enhancements in heart failure management.

I'm also a leader in our flagship hospital, where our heart team can take these best practices, deliver them, take what we've learned as a result, and then disseminate them further to other care givers throughout the system. This gives us a good grounding not just in the theory of how care should be delivered, but in the results of that care delivery. Our weekly cardiovascular grand rounds, which are broadcast throughout our system, cover all areas of cardiovascular knowledge and is presented both by internal and external speakers. Also, I organized regular meetings of our multidisciplinary care teams to focus on specific cardiovascular processes of care including heart failure, coronary heart disease, prevention, rehabilitation, imaging, cath lab, open heart surgery, and electrophysiology. As a result, most team members develop subspecialty expertise in these disciplines.

We have a robust cardiovascular research team, which I also help with. We use rigorous data definitions so that when we do something, we can review what we did, what changed, and what the outcomes were. It's informative, and we publish information about what we've learned and how we can prove that it works. We typically publish 50–60 manuscripts and about 70 abstracts each year.

Encouraging Continuous Improvement

There are opportunities to improve, in which we've asked, "How do we take care of people with heart attacks in our emergency departments?" We thought we could do better. We distilled existing guidelines, developed new guidelines, shared them across our system, and brought teams together to communicate what would be needed—such as in the handoffs from the emergency department to cardiology—and within a year we had a superb program that has provided exceptional and timely care to all heart attack patients presenting to our heart hospitals or who are transferred in.

And it turns out, our facility has some of the lowest readmission rates for heart attacks in the country. The same is true for heart failure. It's really complicated but we keep building more and more to help those people. Then we work with our primary care providers because we need to do a better job in preventing people from going into heart failure. We've improved our treatment and management of people with high blood pressure, diabetes, and cholesterol. All these opportunities to incrementally improve result in making our population as healthy as possible.

We weren't always this good. In the 1990s people with coronary artery disease were being sent home with the right medicines less than 50% of the time. We worked out a system with both paper protocols and a decision support approach and within a year, more than 90% of patients were being sent home on the right medicine. About 400 lives a year were saved and 400–500 readmissions each year were reduced just by sending patients home on the right pills.

On Joy in Work

Joy in work means feeling you're doing something positive—whether you're helping the patients you serve or the colleagues you're enabling to be as productive as possible in a rewarding environment. If I can set up an organizational structure or workflow that makes things better for people who are part of our heart team, that's great; and if I can see patients getting better care because our system works, how much better does life get? We save lives every day. There is no more joy in terms of job and life satisfaction that lets me know my life has been worthwhile. There's no profession that's more noble and rewarding than healthcare. It's demanding and challenging—but the rewards and fulfillment that come from being such a constructive member of society are unsurpassed.

The most exciting advances in healthcare have taken place over the last 30–40 years in treating cardiovascular disease more than any other area. It's very hard and stressful, what we do. If you don't find it stressful, you're not showing the right level of concern for patients. Every time you take on the care of a patient and do procedures, you must be 100% focused and committed. It should take 100% of your concentration. That's taxing. But the reward is, each time you have a success, it doesn't get any better.

This is the most fulfilling life endeavor that you can take on. It takes effort and time and you must work with the intention of perfection. And when you do, it's amazingly rewarding in terms of the joy that you get. I mean, when you're not in this profession, how many lives in a lifetime can one person save? We do this frequently.

What I don't like is imperfect care. The care we deliver needs to be perfect. Every life is precious.

I give everybody my personal phone number so if they need me, I am there; I think as physicians that is what we are obligated to do. But the joy of what we can do as a healthcare professional exceeds any personal, additional demands on our time or other commitments.

The values of our system are paramount, and I adhere strongly to them. I also believe people in our system do, too, and we make sure everybody understands them. I can recite them by heart because they are so important. Our mission, vision, and values, which are the foundation of everything we do, are respect, accountability, trust, excellence, and integrity.

I do feel sufficiently rewarded by my administrators for my work. On the other hand, the more you have confidence in your value, and values, standards. and results, the better off you are. You shouldn't have to exist based on the adulation of others. Having grateful patients is probably the best reward that I can see.

On Money and Joy

It's better to have money. When working this hard and taking on these responsibilities I think having a good salary adds to your ability to enjoy life. Remember, the other problem we have is that this takes a lot, both in terms of time and emotion. When you're not working you want to have enough money to be able to do things that bring you additional joy outside of work.

On the Essential Culture of Safety

In terms of culture, our system has always been committed to patient safety, quality, access, and stewardship of the patient experience. We do everything we can to minimize care defects including overutilization, inappropriate procedures, or medical errors, and we put in place processes, checks, and balances to that end.

Important to success is having a highly communicative, collegial heart team. This isn't a sole proprietorship, where if you're seeing that doctor, you're seeing no one else. We always discuss cases. All the doctors talk to each other during the day; we sit in one room and say, "What do you think of this echo?" "What do you think I should do on this patient?" No one is perfect. But when you start getting two or three opinions you reduce the chance of misdiagnosis or misdirection. We establish many layers of safety by empowering the other three people in the cath lab, for example, to be part of the knowledgeable, procedural oversight team. So, if somebody sees something on an EKG that looks abnormal now, it isn't just the cardiologist or the surgeon doing the procedure who sees that and says something. We make sure that the entire team in the room is both knowledgeable and empowered to speak up. We've been doing this for 25 or 30 years.

We make sure that physicians are respectful because our values are critical in our system, and we make sure they apply to everybody. And by doing this, we reduce errors. We make sure people who have found anything that has the potential for improvement to come forward quickly to share what they found with all the members who participate in an area so we can all improve.

Not being bad does not mean you're good. Having leadership who like to gravitate toward adversity doesn't get you very far. What you really want is to set standards that raise the bar for excellence. In cardiology, we have rigorous guidelines for maintaining privileges to do procedures. Let's say you want to do a percutaneous coronary intervention, which is stenting, or balloon angioplasty. First, you have to be highly trained so you won't have privileges unless you've had experience and training as required by fellowship training standards and board certification in that procedure. But as important is maintenance of privileges. We say someone must have a minimum of somewhere between 50 and 75 procedures a year to maintain privileges. You don't want somebody taking out your gall bladder who does only one a year. So, we set a minimum number. We monitor and measure adverse outcomes and if you don't meet the standard, then you are asked to stop doing those procedures. When you set the bar high, and you set it in an environment of excellence in patient safety, you don't spend a lot of time dealing with negatives.

On the Electronic Medical Record

In terms of the EMR, you've got to put these things into perspective. There are a lot of rules, a lot of regulations out there that can swamp you. But this is the structure within which we work, and you just do it. There's nothing out there that is encumbrance-free. You have to have a driver's license to drive. You've got to fill the car with gas. If you have an electric car you have to plug it in all the time. It's part of life. If you let that get the better of you, then get out of the game. If part of my day consists of doing piddly things like paperwork, then that's what my day consists of. My time may be underutilized when I'm not focused directly on patient care but that's how our healthcare system is. It's sad that no

EMR works very well and that it does distract, but we're a long way from modernizing our healthcare system to facilitate efficiency and effectiveness.

Advice

What's important in healthcare is assuming good intent. People in healthcare—whether doctors, nurses, or administrators—are there to help others and save lives. If you come in with an expression of trust and take seriously people's dedication to this very noble profession, they will help you do it and contribute to the enhancement of care delivery. Take people with this intent, break down any barriers, and communicate what you have learned and what has been shown to have good outcomes.

What do I mean by barriers? Healthcare delivery is complicated and there are a lot of people involved. To continue to improve things there needs to be infrastructure support for delivering the care—meaning enough staff, nurses who are well trained and fully empowered to be part of a heart team, and people who get together to discuss cases from a multidisciplinary perspective. It's also important to spend time in bridging specialties. We spend a lot of time with our primary care doctors, emergency department docs, and their leadership teams to say, "How do we do these handoffs better?"

You can only do well as a healthcare professional if your values, priorities, and ethics match those of the organization in which you work. If there isn't a match, then you should move somewhere else.

My colleagues and I always talk a lot. I ask them for advice, they give me advice, I learn from them. These people are impactful leaders who are very skilled. Cultures take on the personality of their leaders. Watching how they behave, even more than how they talk and the words they say, will serve as a guide to emulating behavior. You learn not just from what they say, but what their priorities are, which may be unexpressed. A lot of management has to do with helping the culture to evolve. You can't really create a system of excellence through strategies. You need to do it by enhancing the culture. This health system has a great culture.

18.   Chris DeRienzo, MD, MPP, Neonatologist and Chief Quality Officer for a Large Integrated Health System

Chris DeRienzo, MD, MPP, a neonatologist and healthcare leader, was chief quality officer for a large integrated health system at the time of this interview in 2018. Today, he is chief medical officer and system vice president of quality for a different health system in the same state. His first book, *Tiny Medicine*, was published in 2019 and is filled with real-world stories of hope, humility, and humanity in medicine from his life as a doctor. In this interview, Chris reflects on leadership and what's needed to "scale joy" throughout an organization.

When I was in high school, I joined one of our neighbors in her lab one summer. I've always enjoyed science, and she was an oncologist. The science in her lab was fascinating—she was doing some interesting prostate cancer research. But then I went to her tumor board and just loved the connection to people. These folks were having really hard conversations and doing their level best to find the best way to treat people. I knew then I had to be a doctor. I couldn't imagine anything more challenging or more important to get right than this hard work for patients.

In college I went into the sciences. I got my emergency medical technician license and really enjoyed being able to treat people. I worked as an emergency room tech at a local hospital right out of college and a spent little time on an ambulance. That was great.

I've been at this health system for four and a half years. I was hired right out of fellowship to work in patient safety. When I started here my role was chief patient safety officer, and I became chief quality officer in the spring of 2016. When I came on, I was hired 50% as a neonatologist and 50% as a patient safety officer, so I worked half-time as an inpatient clinician. Now, I spend about 95% of my time in my leadership role. I serve as a part of the executive leadership team with accountability for quality, patient safety, patient experience, analytics, and population health across our network.

The patient safety team within our department focuses on preventable harms—on how we analyze serious events to learn from them, including root cause analyses. On the performance improvement team are people with both clinical and engineering backgrounds who help to strengthen Lean processes and align best practices in workflow.

On Joy in Work

I don't think there's necessarily one definition of joy in work. To me, it means having a clear purpose—knowing why I get up every day to go to work and connecting with that purpose. The best driver of joy in work is the alignment between what I find rewarding and what the organization wants me to do, the match between "this is what I'm built to do" and "this is what I get to do."

Resiliency, in my mind, is resistance to things that can cause burnout. Scaling joy, I think, is equally important. At this health system, the two most common answers to the question, what brings me joy, are "spending time with my patients" and "spending time with my team." People connecting to people.

What Diminishes Joy

Clinicians face incredibly challenging patient cases that can really deplete our emotional well. But a classic paper on the neonatal intensive care unit showed that symptoms of burnout don't necessarily correlate with negative clinical outcomes because emergency room teams or intensive care unit teams band together and say, "We're going get through this." There is a level of camaraderie that, even under exceptionally challenging circumstances, can yield some positive return. So, under such circumstances, people are simultaneously challenging their emotional wells and refilling them.

I think each of our internal thermometers has a different upper limit. Some people may like to live a little bit hot but at a certain point our thermometer is going to break. As physicians, classically, we've not been as well attuned to knowing when that threshold is challenged. I think we're getting better as a profession at identifying that. Calling that out and acknowledging that as part of life and part of practice—and knowing when we're reaching the bottom of our well and ideally finding ways to fill it back up before we get there—is essential.

Some people are built to work under incredibly intense circumstances. They thrive on that intensity. Part of their resiliency comes from knowing they were built to do this. Put other people in those circumstances and they might be able to handle that once or twice, but then they're done.

Leaders' Roles in Changing Organizational Culture

When we're talking about a leader's role in culture, I think we have to communicate the vision, we have to live the vision, and then we have to repeatedly reinforce it. For example, in healthcare, in the days before the patient safety movement, there was a more punitive response when an error happened—you know, fire the person who made the error. In order to overcome the perception of that kind of culture, we couldn't just say, "Now we're different." We couldn't just say we use root cause analysis or that it's rare when an individual is to blame, and that the vast majority of the time there's a process problem. We could have said that until we were blue in the face. But until our team members experienced that change for themselves—which took *years* of root cause analyses after which the results weren't punitive, when folks were not fired for making a mistake (unless it was willful or unwarranted)—they wouldn't believe the punitive culture had really changed. Repeating an action that is contrary to an old belief is the only way to get to a new belief.

About two years ago we started a program to identify barriers to joy or things that really bother us, and to teach continuous improvement methods so teams could call those out, fix what they had control over fixing (and make that permissible and okay), equip them with the tools, and teach them to use those tools to make change happen. That's empowered teams to eliminate barriers and scale joy.

Within my team, one of the barriers to joy has been not having control over our days. About four years ago we knew we had folks who had the skills, knowledge, and expertise to begin taking control over the way they interacted with their clinical program teams, but no one had given them the authority to do that. We went to our patient safety officers and said, "Instead of waiting for an assignment, you now have the authority to work within your program and go where you need to go." We explicitly changed expectations and, in the process, empowered those patient safety leaders. Within just a couple of months, they went from reactive mode—just waiting for assignments—to taking the steps they needed to take on their own. They said they enjoyed not only the flexibility but the trust we placed in them to move the program to its next step.

Any time we as leaders have an opportunity to empower our people to practice at the top of their license that generally brings people joy. Specifically, in this case, with our patient safety officer team, it not only brought them joy, but the number of challenges they were solving within their programs not only changed, but significantly increased.

Advice for Leaders

Good leaders listen and communicate—and if something can't change, they need to be open and honest about why that's the case.

I also think there are circumstances in which what's needed is a small handful of bright minds. And if there are folks stuck in an old model who aren't willing to come around to patient- and family-centered care, or who aren't willing to come around to the organization's shared values, leaders have to be willing to say, "This is the time to find your success elsewhere."

Part of leadership, in my mind, is being clear about our purpose and our values, hiring those who share those values, and doing our very best to align what people want to do with what they get to do. That's not going to be 100% of the time, but the more we can do that the better.

Leaders need to have an open mind and communicate so they know when things are going sideways because, inevitably, we are going to face challenges. Build the right teams so when things are challenging, people can draw on those teams and the strength that comes from the camaraderie. And be aware that everybody, at some point, is going to reach the depths of their well and will need support to rise back up.

19. *Virginia J., MSN, RN, Chief Population Health Officer for an Integrated Health Plan*

Virginia J., MSN, RN is a nurse by training and a leader by nature. Working 12-hour days and more leading her organization's strategy for population health, she finds joy in teamwork, in mentorship, and in working to improve health outcomes for patients and populations. Virginia has worked at this health organization for 35+ years and has no plans to retire.

Some of the early influences on my career were my mom and dad. They were not in healthcare. My mom wanted to be a nurse but never went to school. A friend of my mom's was a nurse—and what she did intrigued me. I ended up in nursing school and was president of the state nurses' group at my school. I've always gravitated to stepping up and taking a leadership role.

Fresh out of nursing school I worked at a small community hospital for about two years. I then had the opportunity to move from hospital-based nursing to chronic disease management in the ambulatory setting. This new role gave me the opportunity to help create a new diabetes management program, which I did for almost 20 years. The program started with a focus on the design of an educational program, but the role ended up allowing for a collaborative model with providers to help build clinical programs targeted at special needs within diabetes management.

I had a strong mentor early on when I worked in diabetes. The physician who hired me really took me under his wing. He literally invested in training me. And when I say training, I'm talking about the deep clinical training perspective I needed to gain confidence in my ability to develop new programs. I suspect my leadership skill set was always there. Maybe that's because I'm one of seven kids—next to last—and I had to figure out how to fend for myself.

The doctor who was my first true mentor had a wealth of clinical experience and knowledge. He was also very collaborative, so even from a leadership perspective he taught me how to be part of a team. He was a soft-spoken and kind physician, so I learned how to be that, too, as well as to hone some of my more independent, stronger skills. It was a nice mix.

When I transitioned to the financing side of healthcare in the health plan, I was fortunate again to work with two physician mentors. One was the chief medical officer and the other was the new CEO. They both saw something in me and really coached me in the leadership role. One was quite transparent. He'd say, "You're coming on a little strong here," or "Think about this approach." He was very direct, but in a non-punitive, noncritical way. I knew he just wanted to see me succeed.

Now, I lead strategy for the organization around population health. This means answering questions like, what gaps can we identify in our communities and the people we serve, both on the clinical delivery side and on the health plan side? What is our vision and strategy for developing interventions to tackle population health issues? I'm responsible for care managers, community health workers, social workers, and peer support individuals who help build programs and deliver services, coordinate care, and work to close the gaps in the social determinants of health.

I generally come in to work by 7:00 or 7:30 a.m. and leave between 7:00 and 7:30 at night. And then I probably spend an hour in the evening, if not two, catching up on email and other things. I also put in an hour or two on Sunday. I work a lot of hours. I don't know if it's just how I am. There are days when I wish I had the weekends. It would be nice if I didn't always have to think about work on Sunday. But there are weekends when I really do blow Sunday off and just have fun. But I never feel like I've got a hammer over my head making me work. There are just things to do. I've been afforded a great opportunity to make changes, so that's how I look at it. I've been at this integrated health system for 35+ years. My longevity in this organization speaks to the joy I have in my work.

On Joy in Work

Joy means going home at the end of the day feeling I've contributed to improving a health outcome for a patient or a population—and that I've been able to help other colleagues, peers, and nurses who report to me, to watch their growth, and to help develop staff by passing on the mentoring I had.

I derive a lot from working with a team. There are days when sometimes I get in the slog and think, *what in the world?* And then I sit back and watch one of the folks on my team just knock it out of the park in a presentation. Or watch when our staff bring forward a new strategy and their reasoning behind it. I just think, *yes, they get it!*

Mentoring younger nurses, and not just nurses now, but administrators and administrative fellows, gives me joy. I've been very fortunate that people want to come and mentor with me, whether formally or informally. It's just a good way to spend my day. I hope some of my folks someday, when they're listing their mentors, mention my name.

On Money and Joy

I think at a leadership level there's probably not a relationship between money and joy. Of course, let's face it, there are people who are less fortunate than I am and who struggle to make ends meet. I have to think that what they get paid contributes to their ability to support their family and also to their sense of self-worth. I think that's less true the more you make. There are certain people who feel they need more money every time they take on more work. I look at it from the perspective of, do I like what I do? Do I feel what I do is contributing to a health outcome or to the value of the organization? I don't get all of my reward from the paycheck.

What Diminishes Joy

Sometimes the politics diminishes joy in work for me—the layers of leadership that can get in the way. For example, we have a real gap in palliative care for the end of life and advancing illness. I've been tasked with trying to develop a strategy, particularly on the ambulatory side, to start to address community-based management of advanced illness. And it's well-known within the organization that I'm doing this. But a couple of days ago I heard that a lead physician somewhere else in the organization gathered a group of stakeholders to identify opportunities for management of advanced illness in healthcare. I have to admit I was extremely disappointed—I wasn't even invited to attend.

Organizational Politics

For me, it's not about who owns leading the strategy. I like to be part of that sort of effort, but I don't have to lead it, I don't have to own it. I like to be a contributor. But now we've got this duplicative effort and it raises questions and concerns among, probably, both teams: *Is the organization really gathered around this in a formal, organized way, or have I just gone off on my own trying to develop something else?* I think this duplication can lessen the credibility of the strategy we want to put forward.

Sometimes certain leaders plant a stake in the ground, whether it's in the right place or not. And because of who they are in the organization, it's considered okay. Or, it may not be okay, but it's not addressed or managed. That's probably the most frustrating thing for me—when we have known leaders, or people in positions of influence, who make everybody roll their eyes and say, *this person has been a problem for years and it's just never been addressed.*

Over my 30+ years here, my approach has always been the direct approach. Which is, I will talk directly to a provider. I don't have any difficulty talking with providers. I think I'm well respected in the organization by physician leaders and I've learned how to work with them. And in a healthcare organization, physicians are essential to an organization's outcomes. They don't always have all of the leadership skills others may have, either because they haven't been trained or they just don't have the skill set—some of these skills are innate and some of them are learned. So, I've learned how to engage physicians as partners rather than as adversaries. I will pick up the phone and we'll talk, and we'll work out some resolution to a problem. It may not be totally the way I'd like it to work out, but if it's good enough and it's going to point us in the right direction, I try not to lose sleep over it.

When something goes wrong in our organization, what happens depends, to some extent, on who you are. If I were to make a mistake, I think because of my role and my track record I'd be given more latitude than someone else might. I'm a bit of a risk-taker and that's what they like about me. I've been able to help build programs that were not well established. I build new things. And sometimes when you build new things you make the wrong choice or veer off course or it doesn't come out perfectly the first time. And that's how you learn. But then there are others who, one mistake, they're met with a little harsher attitude.

We recently had somebody who made a pretty giant mistake that threatened a strategic partner, but we were able to bring it back. Some people felt that something should have happened to this person, who is well respected in the organization. Then there were those who said, "Listen. We all make mistakes, we've all made a bad choice, let's learn from it and move on." I've never felt afraid that if I were to do something wrong the organization wouldn't keep me on.

Difficult Personalities

When a physician or other leader has been behaving in the same abusive way for 12 years with no consequences, and that behavior is tolerated just because he's a physician or leader, that not only feels undermining but it can be dangerous. The fact that there are no consequences may be irritating to other leaders in the organization—but where I think it's most dangerous is for front-line staff who, potentially, have to be partnered with this person and may need to push back.

I think that certain types of behavior—bullying, arrogance—means people may *not* be willing to come forward when they see an issue. What if a surgeon were doing something wrong? Or had an oversight, like leaving a sponge inside a patient? I'm worried that because of the way some people behave, those working with them might never highlight that kind of a lapse in patient safety. Would staff ever stop it, do a time out, and say, "Doctor, you left a sponge in the incision" or, "the sponge count is wrong"? If we tolerate this behavior, then we're allowing this behavior to go unchecked and, in the end, this could cause greater harm.

Lack of Time for Self-Care

I don't take as good care of myself as I should. I work 12–13 hours a day, I'm tired by the end of the week, and sometimes I go home and I'm a little grouchier with the people I love. I save my best behavior for work. I don't necessarily practice what I preach but I often tell my team, "We all need to be good colleagues and partners here at work, but you really need to take your happiness home. You need to not leave it at this door." And sometimes I find I'm guilty of that, particularly if I've got some timelines and commitments that need to be met. I think I'm much more cognizant of this now than I was maybe five years ago or ten years ago. Some of that has come along with some maturity on my part.

Reflections

There are things that leadership could do to enhance my joy in work. I think that just continuing to be more transparent would help. Just being a little more up front, sooner rather than later from an organizational perspective about things like strategy; being as truthful as we can about how well we're doing versus "drinking one's own Koolaid." I think recognizing where we're not doing well and being honest and up front about it is okay if we're ever going to make it better. Sometimes I think we are not as honest in our performance and we forget that we still have a lot of work to do. And that's okay. We're going to continue to get better at what we do and take better care of patients. I think most people realize that no healthcare organization is perfect, and it's okay to be transparent about that.

I think the further away you get from the work the more disconnected you are from the problems of those on the front lines. I'm one of the senior leaders—and although I don't still practice, I do home visits and get on phone calls with patients so I'm a little more involved than a lot of leaders at my level. I think if you don't stay on the pulse of the organization—and the pulse for me is, what are we doing every day to take care of patients in our community?—you tend to lose sight of your goals and get too far away from what your front-line staff is experiencing.

I do think that what front-line people put forward as issues are not always what the top-level staff see as issues. Here's an example: we just looked at a survey of our front-line staff in the hospital—mostly nurses and technologists. I heard somebody who reviewed the data comment, "Well, we scored really low here, but everybody does, so we're not so bad." So, I said, "If 35% of those surveyed think we're knocking it out of the park, is that what we want to subscribe to?" versus, "Maybe the benchmark isn't what we really should strive for we and should be ashamed of ourselves in this particular area." One of these areas was, "Do I have enough staff on my unit to provide safe care?" Another was, "There won't be any retribution if I bring a problem forward." I think the survey responses were 35% for one of these questions and 37% for the other. That's what I call a write-off, particularly when we start to compare ourselves to benchmarks instead of looking at what we could be doing. We met the other day to review these data as a senior leadership group so we could develop an improvement strategy based on what we found. But many of us walked out of that meeting thinking it was mostly spent in tolerating the findings rather than strategizing how to address them. We will go back and try again.

I've been doing my job a long time. I still like to get out of bed and come to work. I'm not in any hurry to think about retirement. I don't know that I'd be happy retiring. But when I don't feel like I'm contributing to an outcome—whether that's quality or cost improvements to patients, the community, or my staff—then that will be the time for me to go and find something else to do.

There's so much left to do in healthcare, especially now that we're starting to focus on the community's health needs and not just patients who show up in our organization. That just opens another whole host of opportunities for us, and a host of other colleagues and partners to work with in solving the problems. It's not just about the hospital figuring it out, or the clinic or the physician. It's about people in the community who have great ideas and actually great resources. This is an exciting time to be in healthcare.

Advice

I think that to some extent front-line staff, depending on the environment, tell top leadership what they want to hear. I know what they tell others and what they tell me. There are several executive leaders with whom I have a matrixed relationship on the clinical side, in operations, and in finance. I might share with them that people aren't necessarily being open and honest with them, and that they need to ask questions in a different way to get at the crux of the problem or the crux of the potential issue. You can get the kind of answer you want depending on how you ask a question, or you can get to the real answer if you ask the right question.

My final advice for my colleagues is, do yourself what you expect from your team. If you expect your team to do X, Y, and Z, then you'd better do it, too—and do it faster and better or do it alongside them and help them. Sometimes at a leadership level we forget that we need to do some of that work, as well. I'm all about the front-line team seeing me be part of the solution, and not just talking the solution. For me, this might mean starting a workflow, doing home visits, or taking the lead with a workplan to get things started. And I don't just go and observe. I actually go and do some work. I'm not afraid to pitch in. If a nurse needs help with some outbound recruitment I get on the phone and I'll call patients. Or if we've got a problem with workflow, I'm not afraid to roll up my sleeves at the white board and help them map it out and listen and offer suggestions or whatever they want me to do. I like to keep my hands a little dirty and I think sometimes when we get too far from understanding the business, then we lose credibility with the front-line staff.

20.   *Charleen Tachibana, DNP, RN, FAAN, Health System Senior Vice President for Quality and Safety and Chief Nursing Officer*

Charleen Tachibana, DNP, RN, oversees nursing practice, works with schools of nursing on curricula development, recruits nurses, and helps to develop the careers of those she hires at an innovative health system. She also oversees "the work, culture, policies, protocols, and practice of nurses within our system." This health system, a source of joy for Charleen, is characterized by a culture of respect; teamwork; rapid and continuous process improvement; ongoing staff training and support; and the seamless delivery of high-quality patient care.

I went into healthcare because I had a personal desire to serve. I knew I would be in some type of service career. That's part of my childhood, my background, my faith belief. My parents instilled a deep value for service to others, for helping others, for using the talents that are given to an individual to do the most one can with them. For me that was important. I loved the academics of the science and social components of nursing, so the academics were enjoyable and challenging to me. But mine was really a mission-driven decision to go into nursing.

My hours are mushy, let's put it that way. I'm usually heading to work around 6:30 in the morning on weekdays, and I leave somewhere around six at night. So, I work about ten- to twelve-hour days. That said, this is not a task-driven job. It's always on my mind. I never turn off my brain. I'm the kind of thinker who needs to massage thoughts around a bit and look at them in different ways, so I do that when I'm out working in my garden or doing other things. Even though I spend ten to twelve hours a day at work, nursing and leadership aren't my job, they are part of who I am.

I oversee nursing practice across this two-hospital health system. I oversee the work with schools of nursing on curricula development, and recruit and place nursing students in our organization. In addition to working with nursing schools and nursing students, I work with the 1,500 nurses in our two hospitals. I don't directly supervise them, but I oversee the work, the culture, the policies, the protocols, and the practice of nurses within our system. I also work with our nurses to help develop their careers while working to create programs that meet the needs of the patients we serve and the organization itself. That might mean examining models of care, how we look at nursing roles, and how we develop new roles for nurses. Essentially, this means matching what our nurses do with the needs of our patients.

For example, some of our needs have shifted over the last number of years from being illness-focused—that is, taking care of patients who are sick and need procedures—to focusing to a greater extent on health promotion. Many more people in our community are living decades of life with multiple chronic diseases than they were in the past. They are trying to manage those diseases to optimize their health and live their lives to the fullest. We want to help people stay healthy or to manage their diseases. People used to die of heart attacks; now, they live with and have to manage their heart disease for decades.

The question is, how does one work with individuals to help them optimize their health? We've seen a pretty significant shift from hospital-focused care to care that's focused in our clinics, and to care managers who work with patients over extended periods of time to manage their diseases. We've developed different types of roles because our patients' needs are different than they were in the past.

Our turnover rate is different in different areas of the health system and it varies among different age cohorts. We are able to attract people. Our first-year turnover is significantly lower than in the rest of healthcare. And we're slightly lower when benchmarked against other health systems. There are probably different types of roles that turn more quickly than other types of roles, or locations or departments. Some of this is good turnover because people are going back to school or doing more. I would say our voluntary turnover—where people are irritated and leave saying, "I don't like this place"—is quite low. But we usually measure all-cause turnover.

Organizational Culture

I'm blessed to work in an organization with such a healthy, vibrant culture. We have a culture here—and this is atypical in healthcare, I would say—of high respect, value for teamwork, and for the contributions that everybody brings to the table.

Intentional Improvement

We work hard on our culture here. I don't do that alone. I do that as part of an executive team of many different types of professionals. Leaders are important to culture; culture is set by the actions or inactions of leaders. We pay attention to what is going on out there. Of course, people tell us there is a need to further improve the culture of our organization. We consider that kind of dialog really healthy and we encourage it. We have town hall meetings to talk about it, we ask people about it, and we want people to know how to raise issues.

We use the Lean approach in our organization. Every day, people in the organization are encouraged to speak up, regardless of their position in the hierarchy. A housekeeper can "stop the line" as much as a surgeon can if something doesn't seem right.

We hold rapid process improvement workshops in which we work to quickly improve particular patient experiences. We bring in people who are involved in a certain process, for example—physicians, nurses, nursing assistants, secretaries, and patients themselves—to work through problematic issues and create a new and improved process. For example, a leading cause of death in hospitals is sepsis. So, in about 20 of our rapid process improvement workshops we focused on our sepsis management process. Part of the challenge is that patients with sepsis need rapid treatment. The longer it takes to treat, the worse the condition gets. We're talking hours.

One of these workshops focused on a process for reducing the time it takes to manage sepsis. The result was that a nurse would be given a protocol and could initiate it as soon as she or he saw the conditions for sepsis line up—as opposed to the older process, in which a nurse would need to call a doctor; explain what she or he was finding; the doctor would have to find time to stop what they were doing, come to the bedside, do their own evaluation, and maybe start thinking about doing some lab tests and other things—which usually spans about a three-hour period, just to get the treatment started. Now you might think that's pretty fast. But that process was reduced to less than 45 minutes when we put that nurse-initiated protocol into place.

There are protocols for other conditions that we continuously re-evaluate through rapid process improvement workshops. We have them for patients who are having strokes, and for patients in other situations that require a rapid response. These workshops are effective because there's value, there's trust, there's respect for colleagues.

Respect

These workshops and resulting protocols depend on respect. It's not, "I'm the doctor, I need to do this, I'm the boss, the nurse isn't good enough, they're not going to be smart enough, they're going to screw it up," which were all the old kind of tapes one would hear. Now, it's "That's a good idea. Let's try that and see if it works. Let's monitor it to see if there are any issues with it, and the let's get it implemented." That's been our protocol for three or four years now.

The other thing that I think drives respect is our focus on the patient. In those workshops and in a lot of our other improvement efforts, patient and family partners work alongside us. In the rapid process improvement workshop I just described, three people who either had sepsis, or had a family member or a loved one who had sepsis, worked with us. It's really hard to look at a family who has suffered and say, "I'm the doctor, I'm the smart one, we're not going to go there." Working together with patients and families is a great leveling experience, and a way to build an engaged community that asks, how are we all going to contribute to make this better for our patients?

A number of years ago, as part of our quality work and our lean work, we decided to take a deliberative approach to respect and consider what respect looks like in an organization. With our employees we worked through an iterative process, asking, "What does respect look like? When you receive it, what does it feel like?" We came up with ten respectful behaviors. These behaviors are:

1. Be a team player.
2. Listen to understand.
3. Share information.
4. Keep your promises.
5. Speak up.
6. Connect with others.
7. Walk in their shoes.
8. Be encouraging.
9. Express gratitude.
10. Grow and develop.

These ten behaviors have become part of our culture, each of which is framed as a positive statement. We use these words when we talk to each other. We have trained all 5,500 members of our workforce in these respectful behaviors. We make personal commitments to respect each other, and our respect for each other is visible to our teams in whatever areas we're working to improve. This gives us a common, positive language to give each other feedback.

We recently examined these respectful behaviors more deeply. We wanted to understand not just the behaviors, but *how we feel* about them. We also explored the concept we call "second-hand respect," or "second-hand disrespect." Like second-hand smoke, you might not smoke but if you're around smoke it still affects you. If you are watching an interaction that is either respectful or disrespectful, that affects you as well, even though you might not be part of that interaction directly.

All our 5,500 our employees also participated in a two-hour session in which we used actors who role-played different scenarios that arose from employees' not-so-positive experiences in our organization. We then reflected on these scenarios to understand how they could have been handled differently. These scenarios focused on diversity, sexual respect or disrespect, and other issues related to race, ethnicity, and gender. We wanted to bring greater awareness to how these issues might play out and be handled with greater sensitivity in a healthcare organization.

We spend a lot of time on culture, and our culture is constantly being reinforced. At our meetings and presentations, we ask, in terms of respectful elements, "what did we just hear?" We spend time talking about this. This is how respect becomes embedded into everything this organization does.

But people slip all the time. We're human. We don't always treat each other with respect. One of the respectful behaviors is to speak up. Part of what we do in these scenarios and role-plays is to bring up disrespectful behavior to someone in a way that calls it out but also helps them grow, and helps them to understand what the impact of their behavior was on the person who was on the receiving end.

Crucial Conversations

We have a series of training modules, and one teaches people how to have crucial conversations to provide feedback; how to give feedback to another person, how to structure that conversation, and how to get help if someone is not comfortable doing it directly.

A variety of tools are provided to staff and have been over time. Over time, staff and leaders have helped to build and continue to improve this culture. For example, how does someone receive feedback? How does one express gratitude for the feedback given? It's about modeling that, too. As a leader, it means being vulnerable enough to say, "I apologize. That was totally inappropriate of me, insensitive. You must feel terrible being the recipient of what I just did," or something similar. We model this behavior and make it safe to be this way in the organization.

And it isn't just the culture here. It's how are we with people in general? What do our personal relationships look like? It's amazing when we get feedback from staff and from others saying, "Wow, that improved my marriage." Or "That helped me with my kids when I was struggling." These are life lessons; they're not just work lessons.

On Joy in Work

The culture I've just described is part of what brings me joy in work. I define joy in work as making a difference in people's lives. For me, this means a life of service. I want to do things that are going to help advance the human journey or to raise our humanity in whatever our circle of influence might be. When I was in clinical care, when I started in nursing, I did this typically with one patient at a time or one family at a time. But as I've learned through leadership, leaders have bigger circles of influence and can build programs that help others. We can model that, we can change culture, we can reinforce behaviors or make certain that negative behaviors are nipped in the bud immediately and not tolerated in an organization. Those kinds of things bring me joy—and seeing other people being able to optimize their contributions.

Promoting Joy in the Workplace

I think the work itself is rewarding if you have the right culture and if you are focused on the right things. We focus heavily on experience and quality, and for most people there is great reward and joy in that. There is an intrinsic reward we try to optimize here, including our teamwork. Most people who go into healthcare or who go into service want to feel there is a personal connection to their work—that there is a deeper connection, a vocation, or a calling they are fulfilling. I believe we reward people by creating an environment that allows their intrinsic reward system to be activated. But we have financial rewards. We have different tangible rewards, like applause programs, where we thank people. Ways of expressing gratitude and celebrating the successes of our teams. Some of the deepest, most meaningful rewards are the recognition given for exceeding expectations relating to the patient experience and for our quality and/or safety work. We acknowledge service excellence of our provider group. We read letters that patients or family members have written to recognize individuals. We put some of those letters out on our Intranet so everybody can see them. We do a lot of leader rounding in which we express gratitude and highlight the successes of teams.

To our staff we say, "We want you to give good care, and we want to help you do that while getting more patients in." In using lean, we ask, are you doing work you should be doing? Are we supporting you with other people who could be doing some of that work? Are your processes efficient so you don't ever have to leave the exam room because you don't have what you need? Is everything set up for you, reliably set up? We look at problems in different ways and try to find a third option to resolve them. We believe you can have quality time with patients if we eliminate all the waste that is associated with processes outside of that sacred time you and your patients have together.

What we have tried not to do is interfere with the time the provider has with the patient or do things to minimize that time. But what we have worked on is reducing the time around the visit, asking how we can make those visits more efficient. During surgery, all a surgeon has to do is hold out a hand to get what he or she needs. How does that look in an ambulatory setting, in a clinic visit? That may sound extreme, but that is how we look at it. We want to set up that physician to optimize exactly what needs to happen when the patient walks into the room and the door closes—what we call that "magic moment." That's the value that this patient has come for. Nothing else should distract from that. And that has to be streamlined. I think we've done this to a huge extent in many of our clinics, and we continue to work at it. We don't say, "did it," check the box, and then move onto what's next.

One of the things we did when we started on this journey in our clinics was to implement what we call "flow stations." We pair a medical assistant with a physician and put the medical assistant right outside the exam room with a computer. The physician is set up by the medical assistant and directed on what will happen next. The medical assistant sets the patient up and has all of the reports available for the physician; the physician is free to just flow into the room. If the physician has to return a phone call, the medical assistant sets that up, too, so the doctor knows exactly what to focus on. If the physician has to endorse labs, the medical assistant sets that up. As long as physicians follow the medical assistant's direction, they remain in flow so they can move through the visit; document, code, and bill it; and move directly to the next patient.

We used to see doctors waste time running around: they didn't have the supplies they needed in the exam room, they were searching for things, they would be interrupted by a phone call or by something else. Then they'd come to the end of the day and they'd have to document everything that had happened. At that point they'd have to think about billing. They were getting home late in the evening with all this work to do because they weren't helped to be efficient and effective. Now, the flow of the clinic day is much different. The critical resource of physicians is optimized. They make their greatest contribution when they're with a patient. We want to minimize all this other type of work.

What Diminishes Joy

Uncertainty

What diminishes joy in work for me is feeling there's more I want to do, and I can't move fast enough. Or when I can't cut through the noise—when there's too much swirl around an issue and there's a lack of clarity about where we're going. Fortunately, here, we have a lot of clarity about where we're going. But there are still moments when there's confusion— "where is this going?" Or "why is this taking place?" Or "this seems like a distraction"— because some of the issues in healthcare are outside of our control; for example, rapidly shifting economics or the consolidations we have to respond to in the marketplace. We live in a dynamic world, and politics have contributed to uncertainty in healthcare. We have to pay attention to that, too.

In a "noisy" environment it sometimes feels unclear and uncertain, for example, who is going to pay us? How much are we going to be paid? Will we be able to afford to deliver tomorrow the services we're providing today? What do we have to consider for tomorrow? Sometimes that's clear; but at other times there is just so much uncertainty out there that we feel as if we're in a holding phase.

Staffing

We have challenges in this market around staffing, being able to recruit talent, partly because it is such a competitive market. We compete not only with healthcare, but we compete with everybody who's trying to hire a front-line workforce. This market is expensive to live in—the cost of living here has skyrocketed and, frankly, has become unaffordable for many people—and wages have not risen to the same level. Housing costs are through the roof. So, we are working with some challenges to our staffing, and that has been of some concern.

Technology

When you bring in a workforce of millennials who compare your technology to what they're living with in the rest of the world, healthcare is behind. We're hearing more and more from our workforce that our technology is like a dinosaur, when compared with whipping out your iPhone and doing anything and everything you want. I don't think our health system is further behind, but I think that healthcare in general is behind other industries. We're considered one of the most wired hospitals, but it does not compare to the rest of the world we live in. We do a lot of enhancement work on the technology we're using here. We work on communicating more broadly on what's being done now and what we're planning to do. These are ongoing challenges in all of healthcare.

Some people can use the electronic medical record much more effectively and efficiently than others do. One of the challenges is, how do we help people understand the most effective ways to use the EMR? If you give me an iPhone and you give my kid an iPhone, my kid is going to be way more effective in using it. That doesn't mean I can't learn. It just means I *haven't* learned. You look at the two different levels of participation in that piece of technology and they're quite extreme. We have that divide in our workforce. We're working on ways to bridge those gaps and engage the rest of our workforce in finding solutions.

21. *Carol M., MD, Hospital Internist Specializing in Allergy/Asthma,*
     Hospital Executive Director, Director of Graduate Medical Education,
     and Medical Director for Provider Services

As hospital executive director, Carol M., MD, along with the hospital vice president, is responsible for hospital operations. As director of graduate medical education, she oversees the training of residents in surgery, internal medicine, anesthesiology, radiology, and urology, and directs several graduate medical education fellowships. Carol is also medical director of provider services and an internist who specializes in allergy/asthma and practices one day a week.

I was on a science track in college. I realized that in science, many groups in this country are doing the same thing, which made me wonder, *how am I really going to make a difference?* That's why I decided to go to medical school: I wanted to make a difference. For me, it was the perfect choice. I love the work and I've had no regrets, ever.

I'm an internist first and I subspecialize in allergy/asthma. I think people go into areas that fit their personality, and internal medicine really fits me. I'm obsessive–compulsive about details. I love nothing better than sitting in a cardiac care unit and tracking blood pressures and heart lines. And as an internist I get to spend a lot of time with patients. I've been in practice now for 30 years and I've taken care of some patients since they were practically kids. There's nothing better than that.

I was an inadvertent leader. In the past, which is no longer the case, leadership positions were elected. There had never been a woman on the physician compensation committee, so all of the women pooled their votes and asked me whether I'd be willing to have my name put in, and I said yes. I got elected to the compensation committee, which the CEO and the president were also on. That's how I ended up becoming known and visible. The rest of my career just progressed one little job at a time. Our CEO would call me into his office and say he wanted to give me a project. He was an incredible mentor and gradually this became my path.

Unless we walk in people's shoes, we don't know what they're going through. And that's why, although I only see patients one day a week, I try to make sure that I see patients for that whole day, with no holes in my schedule, just like everybody else. That helps me to see how frustrating it is when the EMR isn't working, or when the computer doesn't have enough memory so there are pauses in how long it takes for the machine to come up. Or to experience how many times people get interrupted. I shadowed a hospitalist one day and her pager went off five or six times in ten minutes. Well, until I stood in her shoes, I didn't realize what she was really dealing with. I think we probably don't do enough of that. If we don't stand in someone else's shoes, we won't understand their challenges and we'll just wonder why people aren't more engaged.

On Joy in Work

For me, joy in work means waking up in the morning and looking forward to the day and to what I'll be doing. Seeing patients, for me, is always the very best thing because I get immediate feedback and I can make a difference on a day-to-day basis. Leadership is much more long-range. Very few people say thank you when you're leader. That's why seeing patients even one day a week is so important for me.

On Money and Joy

I agree with Daniel Pink that there really isn't a connection between money and joy. I believe in the intrinsic reward of the work. But I do think you have to have enough money so you match what society says is reasonable for, let's say, a pediatrician in 2018, and anything beyond that probably doesn't bring joy. But taking money away is very demotivating. Our docs are paid mostly on productivity. When salaries go up, they're happy. But if they ever go down—let's say they took a long sabbatical or for some reason their productivity went down and their salary went down—the impact is negative.

Our doctors have templates for patient visits. In primary care, everybody has the same length visit and the same visit template. We don't have patient quotas, but we look at how many RVUs doctors generate, which are based on the amount of time they spend with patients.

What Diminishes Joy

A couple of things diminish joy in work for me: a day when there are just a ton of "rocks in my shoes"—the little things, things that don't work right, can get to me; it could be anything, like a glitch in the EMR. When I'm in that kind of mood, then it's everything, right? I've watched the doctors, and if there's one thing that doesn't work in the EMR then they say nothing's working in this organization. We all feel like that some days. Sometimes docs feel they have no control over these things and it's the organization's fault. I would argue that we have control over probably 80% of things. My job as a leader is to get people engaged in thinking about the control they do have and in working together to find solutions.

Recently, one group of doctors had gotten to the point where they felt powerless, that they couldn't make any changes, and that their problems were somebody else's fault. I talked to every member of the department in 34 one-on-one conversations and learned that everybody in this group wanted the same thing. The problem was, they not only didn't talk to each other, but they demonized each other. No one was happy and they blamed everybody but themselves. The whole department was like that and gossip was rampant.

We had a powerful half-day-long retreat, where all we talked about was respect; and with this group of doctors, to say we were going to spend four hours talking about respect was a little risky. But it was amazing, because these doctors started talking to each other. We did a gratitude exercise in which they realized how much they cared about each other, that they really had the power to make change, and, in fact, they had the responsibility to take ownership and make the changes that needed to be made. What happens is we get really busy—for instance in the OR it's case after case after case. And in the clinic, on a day when I see patients, it's every 20 minutes. We never have time to talk to each other or to take a break. So, taking some time out to think about these issues is a luxury. And because we had a good facilitator to help us to talk with each other, it was extraordinary.

Organizational Culture

The culture of our organization is patient centered. The vision of our organization is to be the quality leader and to transform healthcare. That really resonates with our people. Our organization is relatively small so we're probably more aligned than most in terms of our vision and our values. Our visual strategic plan, which has the patient at the top, is on everybody's screensaver and everybody's bulletin board, and we start every meeting with it.

As a physician leader I spend more time with the physicians, although I work very closely with my administrative leader and partners and we all share the work. I find that if I really want to get people engaged in the work, I remind them why they came here to begin with. And that brings it back to the patient. Almost without exception, when people go into medicine, it's a hard road. There may be a rare person who does it just for financial security, but there are jobs that are a lot easier if money is what they want. People come there because they really want to make a difference for patients. So, if I just push that button and remind them why they're here, it's magical.

For example, we have exercises in which we examine processes that could compromise patient safety and hurt patients to varying degrees. We bring together everyone involved in a process, from the physical therapist to the physician, nurses, environmental people, and others. Sometimes they'll say, "Well, he didn't give me a good handoff," or "They never do X, Y, or Z." Then we ask, "How are we going to make this process better for the patients, make it safer, and make it work better for everybody?" Boom, everybody just gets engaged. Reframing things so that people remember why they're here always makes a big difference.

We have a physician compact that we created early in our history because this had been a physician-owned organization. It's on my bulletin board. On one side it has the physicians' responsibilities and on the other side it has the organization's responsibilities. I use that compact all the time with docs; I bring it to annual reviews. The physicians' responsibilities are to focus on patients, collaborate on care delivery, listen and communicate, take ownership, and change. The organization's responsibilities are to foster excellence, listen and communicate, educate, reward, and lead. There are sub-points under each of these headings.

A physician once yelled on the phone at someone in admissions. He was really frustrated. He had a patient who was in the emergency room in a different state with an unnamed arrhythmia. He had seen the patient in our hospital not long before, but he couldn't remember what the EKG showed. And he didn't have the EMR at home. He wasn't particularly computer savvy. As his backup, he would call the ED. There was a nurse there whom he knew well, and she would look up information for him. But she wasn't there that night and the ED was really busy, so he called the referral center and they were really busy. And he just lost it. He really wanted to take care of his patient, but he just lost it with this person. I was able to take that compact to him and say, "Look, it says here that you have to collaborate on care delivery, and you have to respect everybody on the team. You can't practice here if you don't do that." But we hadn't lived up to our side of the compact, either: it is our responsibility to make sure our docs have the tools they need to do their work. We sent a computer expert to his home to upgrade his computer and load the program he needed so he could look at EKGs. We took that "rock" out of his shoe so he wouldn't be frustrated. Both sides are accountable when things go wrong.

We talk about saying thank you and expressing gratitude to each other, but we don't do it nearly enough. We do give out awards for people who catch problems that could have compromised patient safety. We also give teaching awards, research awards, best patient satisfaction awards, and other awards that recognize people for good work.

Healthcare is a different world today than it was 15 years ago in terms of being constantly in touch, with our phones going off and our continual need to multitask. The world is really complex. Even that four-hour retreat. where we gathered people to talk to each other, had to be on a Saturday, which took people away from their families. Our very full schedules and other obligations make it hard to stay even an hour after work. In this day and age, that's asking a lot of people who have other responsibilities. The question is, how else can we help people connect?

22.   *Peter R., MD, Former President and CEO of an Integrated Healthcare System and Strategic Advisor/Consultant*

Peter R., MD, president and CEO of an integrated healthcare delivery system at the time of our interview, has since left that post to become a strategic advisor and consultant. He talked to me in 2018 about joy as a "three-legged stool" that depends on regular, honest communication between leaders and teams; helping people to remove the hassles and barriers in their daily work; and identifying contributors to joy and working to spread those throughout the organization.

As a kid I'd always wanted to be a physician. I loved science, and even when I was a patient going to the family physician's office for a vaccine, I thought everything they did was cool. I loved being around the process of what physicians did and the way they did it, and that was an essential part of who I wanted to be. That was powerful. I didn't have any physicians in my family. The first house I grew up in didn't have complete indoor plumbing. My dad was a barber, my mother was a school secretary. We were poor but happy.

In college, I was exposed to a lot of new people and ideas. One of these was the Robert Wood Johnson Clinical Scholars program, in which physicians and others would go to designated universities to earn a degree in a different discipline. The Robert Wood Johnson Foundation wanted to create a group of interdisciplinary healthcare professional scholars who would bring different perspectives to their work, recognizing that healthcare is a complex interplay of science, business, social morés, policy, and more. This program continues today. Most of the participating physicians I interacted with were earning their MBA as their second degree. I have an undergraduate degree in economics, a master's in business administration, and a medical doctorate.

I became fascinated with the intersection of healthcare delivery, health policy, and evidence-based care. What drove me to the business side was that, from my perspective, the one-on-one patient interaction, while meaningful and rewarding, was too slow. Serving one person at a time is never going to create system-wide change. You're going to impact those *individuals* and that's emotionally rewarding, but you're not changing the course of care for the country. I wanted to have a bigger platform and scale to make a larger impact. That's what led me, first, to found a healthcare information technology company and later to become president and CEO of a large integrated health system. I've been in this position for a little over eight years. I was a practicing physician only during my clinical training and, for a short time, I saw patients in a homeless clinic.

This is my first job as the CEO of a health system. My primary responsibility is to apply overall leadership, vision, and strategic direction for the health system under the guidance of our board of directors. This means trying to navigate the waters of an incredibly complex healthcare environment with many barriers to care delivery, among which demographics is the most significant for our system. While a typical health system might have 50% governmental payers, we have 70%. Our patients are older, poorer, sicker, and less likely to be insured than state and national averages. That's caused us to be both innovative and cost focused. We've always been focused on high quality. I define quality as depending on three attributes: first, patient experience; second, evidence-based care; and, third, clinical outcomes. As one example, since I arrived here in 2010, we've reduced our risk-adjusted mortality rate by more than 40%.

On Joy in Work

I think the definition of joy in work is different for different people, although there are some commonalities. These include believing in the purpose of what we're doing, and believing our work has an impact beyond ourselves, regardless of the field we're in. For me, being good at what I do and being able to play to my strengths gives me joy, as does feeling that I have a degree of autonomy and control over my work. Finally, joy in work comes from being part of a team and a social infrastructure that's bigger than myself alone.

I want to change the way healthcare is delivered in America. I want healthcare to be higher quality, more patient centered, more evidence based, and I want it to be developed in a way that's scalable within and across organizations. Whenever I'm doing work to that end, and when I can see the outcomes of that work, I feel incredibly joyful.

Because I want to work around people I respect and enjoy being with, I carefully select those I work most closely with. I select people who embody the attributes of the organizational culture we want to promote. These cultural attributes, meaning our approach to care and the way we are committed to treating each other, are listed in our ten guiding principles: patients first; safety focused; evidence based; team approach; interdependence; value focused; great place to work and practice; benefit of the doubt; mutually accountable; and select for shared values. Posters listing and explaining these guiding principles are on our walls and elsewhere. When people are hired to work here, they must agree to follow them.

I strongly believe that joy can be understood as a three-legged stool. The first, "leg 1A," is the way people interface with their leaders and their teams, which are dynamic rather than static. Each week every team leader, who is not necessarily one's "boss," asks team members three questions: "What do you need from me?" "What did you love about your week?" and "What did you loathe about your week?" The answers to these questions give team leaders insights into people's highs and lows in the moment, enabling them to help their team members rise out of the lows quickly.

The second, "leg 1B," is identifying and eliminating hassles and barriers in the workplace, such as barriers in one's daily workflow. No matter how great the mission or how great your team, if every single time you try to do something—your computer doesn't work, the printer won't print, you don't have the supplies you need, you can't spend time with a patient—you can't be joyful. As part of our effort to remove hassles and barriers, we've created teams of people—clinicians and information technology professionals and performance improvement specialists, people trained in six sigma and lean processes—who do nothing but go around the organization and watch what happens, look for hassles, and then talk to people to figure out ways to remove them.

The third, "leg 1C," is identifying and spreading joyful moments in daily work, both for those working on the front lines as well as for executives. Here's some background to a perfect example: Puerto Rico, which was devastated by Hurricane Maria, is where a lot of pharmaceutical manufacturing occurs. One of the products manufactured only in Puerto Rico are "small IV piggyback" bags, low-volume fluid bags used to mix medicines that nurses can hang with IV pumps to infuse the medicine into the patient. Well, the hurricane destroyed those facilities and, overnight, those bags became unavailable. The entire globe's production was affected. So, we had to adapt. The alternative to a small IV piggyback is to have the nurse stand at the bedside, put a needle into the IV, and slowly push the syringe over the course of five or ten minutes to infuse the medicine. They can't just squirt it all in at once, since that would cause trouble.

The same teams that look for hassles throughout the organization also look for joy. So, here's what happened: these teams were roaming around and saw that when the nurses were at the bedside and pushing the syringe in slowly over five or ten minutes, those were typically moments of intense emotion and joy between the nurse and the patient or family. Normally nurses come in and out of patient rooms and move quickly because of their workload. But, suddenly, they had to stand there for five or ten minutes and they were observed laughing at times, tearful at others, but regardless they were incredibly connected to the patient, and vice versa. The observers would talk to the nurses afterward and say, "Wow, you were so engaged—you were laughing," or "You were crying. Tell me about that." And, to a person, they said, "That's why I became a nurse." Now manufacturing has started again but we're not going back to buying the small IV piggybacks. We're hard-wiring that IV push so that every nurse can have those experiences during the day at some point.

What Diminishes Joy

The most common complaint that physicians and nurses have relates to information technology—they say all they do is spend time at the computer, they don't spend time with patients, it's annoying, it's a hassle—but not to have information technology here wouldn't make any sense. So, we created processes improvement teams that go to one floor or unit to watch, see what's going on, and create lists of problems that are systematically getting in people's way. Then they fix those things, whether it's a broken piece of equipment, a needed tweak in the electronic medical record, or something else. If we don't observe the daily workflow, we can't appreciate what the reality is for people on the front lines.

In short, we have an absolute, abject healthcare crisis in America. And it's not just the stuff we see on TV that politicians focus on. Healthcare professionals carry so many burdens—regulatory burdens, financial burdens, emotional burdens. Over half of doctors are burned out and 50% of nurses have compassion fatigue. I think many professionals who are burned out are also clinically depressed. This is a problem that is going to grow and escalate at the exact same time that baby boomers are aging and need more care. It's time for people to *wake up*. Anything that can be done to support those who care for others is a good thing. That's exactly what I'm trying to do.

Passion for Treating the Underserved Globally and Domestically

23.   Laura Spero, MSW

"What is my degree and job title? That isn't even an easy question to answer." So began my wide-ranging, three-hour long, riveting conversation with Laura Spero at the kitchen table of her parents' home in November 2018. Laura, a passionate advocate for social justice, is impossible to categorize. She has a master's degree in social work; founded Jevaia Foundation (www.jevaia.org), a primary care rural dentistry program in Nepal; is a certified integrative manual therapy provider; and is an independent radio producer and maintains a multimedia blog, www.allthepiecesof.com. I have known and admired her since she and my daughter, Lauren, met in kindergarten at the age of five. Laura has a lot to say about the joys, frustrations, fears, failures, successes, and rewards of creating, sustaining, and trying to systematize basic oral health services in the government healthcare system of Nepal.

My Journey to Nepal

I received my bachelors' degree from Williams College in anthropology with a minor in neuroscience—basically, I studied people and brains. I never decided to go into healthcare. But I'd been attracted to Nepal for a long time. I didn't even know anything about Nepal, I just had kind of a fixation on going there. I loved the mountains, and I read *Into Thin Air* and different books on exploration. I was drawn to all things Asian without really knowing a lot about what that meant; I had an interest in alternative healing and the spirituality of Asian cultures. My dad worked in Japan when I was growing up and I remember him coming back from a trip to China when I was in high school and telling us about conversations he had had there dealing with business and economics in China. I was so fascinated with the perspective he described. And also, I was lucky to grow up with a lot of security and opportunity, and I was restless to deconstruct that experience by spending time in the developing world. In some vague way, by the time I was in college these forces combined into a growing desire to travel to Nepal and be in the mountains and immerse myself in Nepali culture.

I took my first trip to Nepal between my junior and senior year of college. I joined a Canadian program that was taking a group of people to study medicinal plants. That excited me because of my interest in natural and alternative medicine. So, I went on this trip and met some really interesting people. I was part of a group of Canadians, Americans, and one man from Japan, and I really had an amazing time with them. It was my first time visiting a completely different part of the world and traveling with strangers, so there was a lot of discovery in that. But I was also very aware that I was part of this unit of foreigners.

I had dreamed about going to Nepal forever. In that context, there was a specific moment on this trip that changed everything for me. We were walking through a village and we passed a woman who was leaning in the doorway of her house, maybe 20 yards from the road. She was leaning in the doorway and there was a child standing next to her, and I thought, *Oh my God, that would be such a beautiful picture.* And I started to take out my camera and I just had this moment where I thought, *I've imagined this for so long, and now*

I've come all the way here, and all I can do is take a picture of this woman. And I realized, *I'm not really in Nepal.* I knew then that I wanted to come back in a different way, where I could be part of a community. The way I experienced that realization was with the exact thought, *I want to stand in a doorway and watch people walk by on the road.*

So, when I graduated from college a year later, I returned to Nepal with a volunteering agency. I was placed as a teacher in a village called Kaskikot and stayed for two months the first time. Then I went back later that year and stayed nine months. I've been going to Nepal once or twice a year since that first trip for the past 16 years, and I still call Kaskikot my home.

So here I was, 22 years old, I didn't speak the language—this was not the Peace Corps where they gave you six months of training, but a short-term program with one week of orientation. It was before cell phones, before social media. I had to take a two-and-a-half-hour bus ride—no, it was longer—on a bumpy road to a city to send my parents an email. And I had this idea in my head that made absolutely no sense—I was going be in Nepal, to live in a village, be absorbed into some family, and experience life in Nepal. *And* I had a picture of what it was supposed to look like. Looking back, it was pretty self-centered and crazy. But as it turned out, that is what happened.

When I first arrived in Kaskikot, I was placed in a very welcoming home with the headmaster of a local school named Bhim Subedi. He was a kind, well-educated man and his family spoke pretty good English. They had hosted volunteers before me. It was a logical setup. But after three days I told them that I wanted to move, because I wanted to live with a family who got up every day and went to work in their fields. I would never do that now! These people were showing me hospitality. But I was young, and primarily concerned about my vision for myself, of how I wanted to be in Nepal.

Bhim Subedi is someone who changed my life, too. Because after first being understandably perplexed by my request, he somehow just understood something about me. I didn't want to experience a household more similar to what I knew, I wanted to be lost, to connect with people whose lives were completely different from mine. I think Bhim showed a great deal of intuition. He actually took me around to meet several different families and guided me to move into the place that became my home with a lifelong second family.

I moved into a small house with a widow, who I call Aamaa, and her two daughters Malika and Bishnu. Bishnu, Malika and I were 20, 25, and 22 at the time. Very quickly— this is one of the unanswerable mysteries of my life—I was welcomed in and I became the middle girl in this household. And then I just wanted to do everything. Every time someone was going somewhere with a sickle and a rope I'd say, "I'm coming, too, to chop things and plant things and carry things!" And they looked as if to say, "Please don't do that." And I'd say, "Why? I can do it!" I very quickly established myself as this crazy American twice the size of anybody else who was very excited about doing difficult field labor. Which was amazing, because it gave me a chance to do what I had hoped to do, which was just to connect with people. And Kaskikot has a road that runs right through it, so I ended up doing exactly what I had imagined: standing in the doorway and watching people pass by.

So, in that scenario, I often got into conversations about what people were thinking and what was going on with them as part of everyday life in a community. Because I was a foreigner living in that area at the time, people would come over to see if I could assist with all kinds of random things, simply because I was a foreigner. Even all these years later, if somebody cuts their finger they'll often come over and see if I have bandages because that's the kind of stuff foreigners bring with them. I mean, what would you pack if you were going to go live to in a village in Nepal back in 2002 and you really had no idea what that was like? I had antibiotic cream and Bandaids® and ibuprofen and my whole little packet of useful little items. I mostly used them with the neighbors.

People had a lot of questions I was unprepared for. One woman asked if I would get her daughter adopted to the U.S., where she would have a chance of a better life. People had questions about their family members who had traveled abroad, or how to further their education. Keep in mind that at this time, there were no cell phones or internet. There was one satellite telephone at a house up the road, and if someone called you on it, that family would have to walk over and find you and tell you to go wait for a call back. So, a basic phone call was an irregular occurrence for the majority of people. This has obviously changed in the intervening 15 years. But what it came down to then is that I came from a world most people in Kaskikot didn't have access to.

Starting an Oral Healthcare Project

When I was living with Aamaa and Malika and Bishnu during those first two months in 2002, people used to come by our house with all kinds of issues and questions. And among the most common problems was toothache. It would usually be someone asking for medicine during an acute pain episode. If you've ever had a serious toothache, you know I'm talking about discomfort that can be severe to overwhelming pain that interferes with sleeping, eating, working, everything. Our next-door neighbor had recurring dental issues, so I would see him regularly while he was suffering. But all I could really do was offer some ibuprofen and suggest going to a dentist. And I could tell from people's reactions that nobody was following up with visits to a dentist. I started to feel like I should have better advice, so I decided to find out specifically where I should advise neighbors to go for dental treatment. That's when I started to understand the problem better.

It was true then and remains true now that dentists were in the city, which, at that time, was a three-hour, expensive, bumpy bus ride away from Kaskikot. Then you'd get there, and there would be all sorts of logistics: you'd have to arrive early in the morning to get a ticket, and there's no guarantee that you'll be seen or be able to afford the treatment, among other things. It's cumbersome, time-consuming, and expensive, and on top of that treatments like root canals actually require multiple visits. Then, as I learned over time, there were many common misperceptions about dental treatment, such as fear that dental extractions can cause blindness, deafness, or cognitive disorders. So, there were a lot of obstructions to people taking any next step after swallowing some painkillers I might offer in our yard in 2003. The only other option was really to get antibiotics at the nearby government Health Post. But there was no viable, specific dental care for the Kaskikot community.

That's what gave me the idea to start working on dental care in rural Nepal. I had no training in this area whatsoever. I literally started by Googling something like, "dentistry in Nepal," and went from there. There was no point at which I said, "I'm going to start an organization and it's going to look like this, and we're going to do these things, and then we're going to try to grow it in this way, and then we're going to work to model something for the National Healthcare System of Nepal." At each point I did the thing that seemed like it was the next step based on where we were.

At that time in 2003 I was a volunteer teacher at a primary school, so I started by working with my dear friend and co-teacher, and eventually co-founder, Govinda Paudel. Our initial thought was to get dentists to come to Kaskikot and do a dental camp, because that's the prevailing model for bringing dental care to remote areas. But from our perspective within the community, it pretty quickly became obvious that didn't make sense. For one thing, the camp model is not a human rights approach. It's limited, transient, sporadic, and non-responsive to local needs. Communities have no authority or power or say and the timing is dictated by what works for the dentists. There's often no follow-up and therefore very little accountability. Our problem was simple, which was the neighbors coming over to my house needed to be able to access dental care whenever they needed it. Camps obviously wouldn't achieve this.

And secondly, 2003–2004 was the height of a civil war in Nepal. So, dentists and dental students didn't want to travel to remote areas anyway. That meant we had to think from the vantage point of our own community and work outward. It was ultimately a huge advantage that I was positioned alongside a community trying to get a basic need met on its own terms. It's different from conventional "expertise" as a dentist or a public health professional, but it's a perspective centered on real humans and their experience. These conditions set us on a unique path and made us more willing to try things outside standard approaches.

Nepal has a centralized, socialized healthcare system with government-sponsored facilities at the central, regional, and local levels. Every village has what's called a Health Post, and that's the first formal facility that people living in a village like Kaskikot would rely on for primary healthcare. Our project went through many false starts and modifications, but the strategy that emerged was to establish primary care dental clinics in Health Posts, where a midlevel provider who is local to the community delivers something called the basic package of oral care, or BPOC.[1] The BPOC was developed by the World Health Organization in the late 1990s. It's a set of dental procedures designed for use in limited-resource primary care settings.

Let me describe our program model. First, a local healthcare provider gets trained in the BPOC. Interestingly the BPOC has been taught to midlevel providers in Nepal since the early 2000s, but when we started, nobody was supporting those providers *after* the training. They didn't have an appropriate clinic setup that included cross-infection control, full sets of instruments, or basic materials needed for the procedures they had learned, not to mention any sort of monitoring or professional support. So, we started by supporting a midlevel provider who had taken BPOC training to actually deliver the BPOC with an appropriate clinic setup in Kaskikot. (Actually, we started outside the Health Post, and eventually figured out that there were a lot of reasons we needed to work inside the government facility.) The first few years were devoted to watching the provider operate and learning how to make an improved care delivery environment within the constraints of a limited-resource Health Post without electricity or indoor water. I'm talking about basic stuff nobody had thought about, like a portable dental chair and an autoclave. Things that speak to people's dignity, like formal dress.

We named the provider a "dental technician." And guess who our first dental technician was? It was my adopted younger sister Bishnu, who by then had obtained an 18-month community medical assistant degree. We connected her with BPOC training, and she became the Kaskikot dental technician.

With the clinic going, we quickly learned that we needed to couple this with specific types of oral health promotion and screening out in the community. So, we developed a school outreach program and then, based on the learning from that, a community outreach program. We realized we had to work specifically with shopkeepers, for example, to make sure the toothpaste being sold locally was fluoridated. It was a few years before we began establishing daily toothbrushing programs in schools. In the last few years, we've tackled sugary packaged junk food that has become popular among schoolchildren, and we do this by working year-round with schools, shopkeepers, and parents in a variety of different community settings. And for each of these developments, we've had to figure out who can successfully implement the concept in a way that is genuinely locally based and sustainable. Suffice to say that the dental technician spends a lot less time sitting in the clinic waiting for patients than getting out into the community.

In 2008, we started a second clinic in the neighboring village of Sarangkot. And it was soon after that that Govinda and I realized that we had to get the government to take over our clinics in Health Posts or we'd be trying to fundraise for them forever. By the time we launched in our third village, we said from the start that it would be a two-year seed program that we would hand over in two years. That was in 2011. But our early seed programs failed at handover. We didn't have our first successful handover until 2015. My point is that each of these steps involved a major learning curve that was achieved through trial and huge amounts of error.

In the last few years, we've gotten more traction and our model is running in eight villages with varying levels of government funding. And our natural trajectory has led us to the policy level. So, at this stage, the majority of our effort is focused on advocating to establish primary oral healthcare services in the national healthcare system. Oral diseases comprise the most prevalent noncommunicable diseases *in the world.* There is research showing these diseases affect the ability to eat, sleep, and even perform in school. There can be major social consequences to poor oral health. At this stage, we want to point to what we've done and say, "The government should be doing this in every Health Post in the country. Here are the inputs. Here are the protocols."

I want to emphasize that it's not about growing our organization. I think that's something more unusual for a healthcare enterprise in this arena. It's about seeing the public system in Nepal establish dental technicians that offer the BPOC and have the training, supports, and supervision our project has modeled. It's about advocating for technicians to be local professionals who are based in Health Posts and have an intimate familiarity with the community. And making sure institutions support these providers to spend time mostly in schools and community spaces doing free screening and health promotion—because that is what's best for people like my neighbors in Kaskikot.

Regardless of the future, I think it is an achievement that we've earned the opportunity to be able to say, "Don't take our word for it. Go to Kaskikot or Sarangkot or Rupakot or Hansapur. Do your own evaluation. Talk to the community about whether or not this works for them. It was created by the community."

Advocating for Dental Care

In my role as the executive director, I'd say I'm the big-picture thinker and the person who's mainly responsible for hiring and making organization policies. I have to think expansively what it's like for a dental technician to come in and do their job, and I have to both imagine and observe what it's like as a patient to walk through the door and encounter the treatment environment. What do those two people need around them to make sure that interaction goes well?

At this stage, my role is not front and center with respect to the public-facing side. In the field, I show up and take notes and photos. I'm the person on the back end saying, "We should do this! Here's an idea! We should fix that! Here's another idea!" Usually the process is, I have an idea and I get really excited about it. A bunch of people tell me that's not going to work and it's not a good idea. I say, "No, it's definitely going to work. And it's definitely not only a good but a necessary idea." And then we go back and forth for a while and then finally somebody else says, "Okay, fine, but let's do it this way." And I say (laughing), "That is a much better idea."

There's an important role that I play, I think, in bringing another perspective. And also just the commitment, the conviction that this should be solvable and this is something we *can* do. If nobody else is going to do it in an excellent way, then we're going to do it a subpar way, but something is going to happen. That's not to say you settle for a subpar version. It just means you have to be ready to take a first step and see where you are. But then of course you have to be accountable to all the ways your first or thirty-first idea fell short. Excellent solutions happen version by version, not all at once, so you can't get there if you can't weather the uncertainty and frustration of all the middle steps. I suppose that's the slightly deluded yet useful enthusiasm I bring.

I've had to develop a sense of humor about myself and an appreciation for that sort of back and forth. That's critical for my happiness and my ability to be a little bit of a bulldozer and be really committed to breaking through challenges in any way possible. But I also have to do all that and still be able to recognize when we have to do something different than what I originally thought, which is most of the time, and know that's not a failure. That's actually a success. I've played an important role in helping a team to develop something new. Being ready to laugh at myself goes a long way in that process. I think that without that sense of humor, I would long ago have abandoned this line of work as being very frustrating and unrewarding. I think that's true for any person who's creating something: you have to go through that process of constantly renewing and destroying things and then putting them back together.

Facing Failure

I can't say it's not scary. I do get invested. There are moments that can be very demoralizing, when things just don't hold together, or alternatively, when things fail dramatically. The clinic we started in Kaskikot closed when we handed it over to the government in 2012. And I had to let it fail because I knew that ultimately, it was unrealistic and unhelpful for us to run it forever. And then, after lobbying from people in the community, the government restarted it in 2018 and now it's completely integrated into the Kaskikot Health Post. It's a model clinic with a beautiful mural painted outside. But I didn't know that was ever going to turn around. This was the same community where people had sought me out for help with their pain and suffering. I had to sit on my hands for six years while neighbors asked me, "Why did you close the clinic?"

In that situation, the other option would have been to stick with something that on some level I knew hadn't achieved the vision or wasn't really working. But to be afraid to let go of something that isn't working is actually worse than the disappointment of trying something new and having that fail. Otherwise you stay stuck hanging on to something that's not fully realized. I think you have to have that experience for a while before getting a visceral understanding that the cost is too high, and the risk of reinventing your idea is worth it. Not all of the clinics and ideas we've let go of have been revived in better form; some stayed gone. But all of the letting go has freed us for the next round of creativity and discovery.

In our case, we're working against the inertia of an entire system. Inevitably, if we aren't actively shedding layers, we get weighed down trying to singularly manage all the pieces that the environment hasn't put momentum behind. Sometimes I feel that and it's absolutely exhausting. The failures have often been the spaces where that vacuum got filled, where others picked up the mantle and systems around us started to change. Or where we learned critical new tactics for achieving what we wanted. But only after we risked or experienced failure.

On a personal level, I didn't want to spend the rest of my life raising money and feeling the responsibility of keeping clinics in existence. That didn't feel like a fulfilling future for me, it felt overwhelming. I came to see that it actually felt better to me to advocate with the Ministry of Health and risk failure. Some of that is my personality; I think I get more joy out of the advocacy process than the administrative process. I am happier pushing the envelope than maintaining things as they are. It gives me more freedom to keep creating and being challenged in fresh ways.

We've founded 13 clinics and eight of them are being run by local level government in Nepal. A couple of them have—full stop—failed. But in the places where it's worked, the government has budgeted its own funds and is actually looking to upscale. We've worked our way to the table in new policy drafting processes at higher levels of government, where we're actively involved in making recommendations for turning our model into national health policy. So, at each frontier we've moved on to the next challenge, up to the highest systems level. I think that's a great example of realizing a human rights approach to healthcare, where a marginalized community organizes to solve its own problems and then pushes the institutions around it to change the rules to serve their needs better.

On Joy in Work

My joy comes from making people feel better. I think that's what anybody working in healthcare will say. Even the creative aspect of running something and starting an organization—well, I don't love fundraising or writing business proposals—some people love that stuff, but for me that's more like eating my vegetables. What makes me happy is being able to go to a clinic and see somebody walk in and see them walk out feeling better. That's the payoff that makes the rest of it worth muscling through.

Working at the macro level, running something, is frustrating but it's also fun. I've really found joy in getting policymakers involved in the conversation—looking at what's driving how resources are being used, asking why this hasn't been made a priority, pushing to make it happen. Like anywhere, there's a small group of people making decisions that influence the majority. And the majority of people in the community don't have a voice in that conversation. The advocate is the fighter in me, who gets to say: "These politics are in the way" and "This policy is in the way" and "These competing interests are preventing something that needs to be done, that could be done, from getting done, and now we're going to fight for it."

I'm happy working when I'm part of a team. There's just no question that collaborating with other people, having a shared language and a common mission is rewarding. I've been an athlete my whole life and the feeling of being on the field with your team, being prepared and part of one coordinated mind, is exhilarating. It's wonderful when you can find that in your work.

Something unique to me is that I love being part of a rich world that's so different from the one I was raised in. That's more fun for me than doing something that's safe and familiar and stable—although it's important to me, too, to have a piece of that. But I have a persistent restlessness that can be either a barrier or a source of energy depending on what I do with it. I want to have something to digest, to write about and talk through at the end of the day, to have a story to share, to stretch my experience of the world. I want to have absurd things happen and to laugh hysterically about them. I want to be surprised and humbled and out of my element. If I can have that in my life, it makes me happy. That means I'm going to put myself in situations like these. I am happy when I'm challenged.

What Diminishes Joy

What diminishes joy for me is feeling alone. Starting and running something is in certain ways an inherently lonely process. You're out there doing something different, without a roadmap, and sometimes it's just not fun. Then of course you have some of those predictable joy-draining things like bureaucracy, challenges that feel superfluous and turn what should be meaningful work into periods of obstruction and drudgery. That probably happens in most types of work from time to time. Then again, in my setting we've chosen to work at that frontier, challenging a healthcare system to evolve, taking on the bureaucracy of government. So, we signed up for that.

Ultimately, I think that to experience joy, you have to know what you enjoy most about your work, and seek out work where you get to do a reasonable proportion of those things that fill your bucket. I've actively spent time thinking about this. I know that when I sit down at the end of the day, I am happy if my day has included people but also provided adequate time for reflection and focus. In my line of work, that means a high proportion of on-the-ground interaction in the community, teamwork with my co-workers, and a balance of quiet time to pull it together. If I spend too many days looking at spreadsheets in front of a computer, inundated with administrative responsibilities, I'm miserable. So, I've tried to organize my life so that it doesn't get out of balance in that direction.

Reflections

Well, we should acknowledge that in my case, there are major things to confront about the power, which I did not earn, that comes with being a white American from an affluent suburb who has chosen to work in vulnerable communities in Asia. The first time somebody asked me to get their child adopted to the U.S., obviously that wasn't a thing that I felt I could act on. But I remember standing on a stone path in the woods and asking myself, *is that actually a thing I'm capable of doing? Because if it is, I'd better understand why I'm not going to do it. I need to understand why someone would ask me that.* It was a life-changing moment in which I first confronted what that ongoing responsibility would mean, and when I realized I would have to deconstruct the power differential of my situation and take responsibility for how I would handle it.

In terms of working with communities that have less power, that have less say, that have less voice, I think I have struggled to reconcile that I was born into my world, and Bishnu and Malika were born into theirs, and that mother who couldn't afford a safe upbringing for her child was born into hers, and none of us had any hand in these original placements. Randomly the world gave me a bigger microphone and access to more resources than many of the people I work with. So, what am I going to do from that platform? One option is to make myself heard, to seek accomplishments where I am in the center. Another is to try to make more space for others on the platform. I've tried to move in the direction of the second.

I have a deep love for Nepal and for the people who have become such mainstays of my life there. I still live with Aamaa, and Malika is married with two sons who have always known me as their aunt, and I adore them. Now I am an old hand at a lot of the chopping and carrying, and I speak Nepali pretty well. Actually, there are teenagers in Kaskikot who have called me "auntie" their whole lives, which is an incredible gift. Bishnu now lives in the U.S. with her family. I kept a daily journal for many years in Nepal, and a few years ago I started moving my writing to a blog called "All the Pieces of Heaven" (that's a line from Bishnu). I post a lot of reflections there, as well as stories about our dental project and other stuff I've worked on in Nepal. The blog is my outlet for sharing this beautiful place that welcomed me as a daughter.

Advice

First, I think it's important to be honest with yourself about what you're here for. There's nothing wrong with being in a job because it pays well, the hours are good, and the people are nice. But I do think when you're working in healthcare, if you're not there mainly because you're invested in patients, that's going to have an impact on the work you do and on the people around you. It's inevitably going to create conflict and it's definitely going to reduce joy. And the reverse is true too: there is always joy in helping someone feel better. Regardless of your specific role in healthcare, patients offer an eternally renewable source of fulfillment. When I feel unanchored or tired, it's always grounding to re-center myself on the people at the other end of all the effort.

The second is, as I said before, it's healthy to have to have a sense of humor about yourself and events around you. That's probably truer the further away you get from a conventional role with predetermined rules. Maintaining the ability to laugh at yourself or ridiculous events actually requires an intentional attitude in the face of frustration, embarrassment, fatigue. It's about how you see things when they don't work out or when circumstances beyond your control make your work difficult. If you can maintain a sense of humor, it keeps you light on your feet. It leads to openness, flexibility, adaptability. Those traits really go a long way in finding courage to take worthwhile risks.

Note

1   Frencken JE, Holmgren CJ, van Palenstein Helderman, WH. *Basic Package of Oral Care: WHO Collaborating Centre for Oral Health Care Planning and Future Scenarios.* College of Dental Science University of Nijmegen, The Netherlands, 2002.

24. Myron Glick, MD, Family Physician and Founder and CEO of Jericho Road Community Health Center

Myron Glick, MD, is a family physician and CEO of the federally qualified community health center, Jericho Road. Driven by his sense of social justice and his Christian faith, Myron explains the importance of being a family doctor and of treating the underserved and marginalized in his community, in this country, and around the world. About his work in Africa, Myron expresses pain and frustration at the deaths of people from diseases that were long ago eradicated here, of the lack of access to clean water and sanitation to prevent illness, and of the absence of basic medical equipment, technology, and tools. "When we complain about our lives," he says, "these things give us perspective."

I grew up as a Mennonite missionaries' son in Central America in a country called Belize. My dad was a school builder/church planter in a very rural, remote area, and we owned the only vehicle in that village. He would often be called to transport people who were sick to the hospital a couple of hours away. I would often ride with them and saw things that made me realize there was a real need for medical care. I remember being in the car when a baby was born. Maybe I was ten or eleven. I decided I wanted to be a doctor. We eventually moved back to the States.

I went to medical school in Buffalo. I didn't really understand poverty in this country until I went to medical school. I didn't realize the way the poor were treated here, especially in the hospital system where I worked. As I went through that experience as a medical student, I realized that what I was really called to do, or wanted to do, was to stay in Buffalo and design a practice that would treat people differently. So that is what I did.

I am a family physician by training. I always knew I wanted be a family doctor because I love the idea of taking care of the whole person, of building relationships. I love talking to people and I love delivering babies, so for me it was not a hard choice. Family practice is what I wanted to do from the beginning. I've always liked working with my hands, but I knew I didn't want to do surgery eight hours a day.

Jericho Road

I graduated from medical school with an MD in 1993. When I finished training in 1997, my wife and I started a family practice, which would later become Jericho Road. We got a bank loan and started as a private practice on the west side of Buffalo. The mission was to provide family medical care to whoever needed it, regardless of their ability to pay. When we started, this was primarily a working class, poor neighborhood; over time, the neighborhood became very diverse. Large groups of refugees have moved to Buffalo over the last 25 years; through a series of events, Jericho Road has become the place where most of these refugees have come to receive medical care. Many of these refugees never received medical care before coming to America.

For 16 years my wife and I owned this as a private practice. Starting as solo docs, we grew into a $4 million organization. In 2013, we became a federally qualified community health center, so we no longer own the practice. We are employed by Jericho Road. I transitioned from being the owner to the chief medical officer. We have a board of directors. This year our CEO resigned, so I took over as CEO and hired a couple of younger folks to be the chief quality officer and chief medical officer. This organization now has 30 doctors and nurse practitioners and employs about 300 people here in Buffalo. We also have four medical centers in other countries, which we established when we followed refugees back to their home countries. Jericho Road has a global reach.

Jericho Road is a very cool place. We are a family practice in the old-school sense: we deliver babies and take care of the whole person from birth to death, regardless of people's ability to pay. There's huge diversity—I believe we're one of the most diverse health centers in the United States. We also have a very diverse team.

I decided early in my career that every one of us is different, and for me to build Jericho Road and to get good people to serve as clinicians I'd have to be willing to hire people who would be really productive from a patient-numbers perspective, and be willing to hire some who might not be as productive but who are really good doctors and put them on my team. If some people need more time, they need more time. We try to be flexible so each of the 30 physicians has a slightly different contract, slightly different schedule, slightly different interests. We say, for their own good, "Listen, you've got to learn to see a patient, write the notes, see a patient, write the notes, so you're not going home at night with this work." And if they are going home at night with this work, we ask, "What we can do to make sure that doesn't happen? Because you are going to burn out if that happens."

We've really had to be flexible and make sure that our definition of productivity isn't just about numbers. It's also about time, and quality. One of the things I've noticed is that patients in some ways self-select. Some of them prefer providers like me: I will see them on time and give them ten minutes; they tell me what they need, I tell them what I need, and they're done. Other people need more time and don't mind waiting an extra hour or two. So, we have a real mixture of providers. I don't want everyone to be like me and I don't want to be like everyone else. That has been a really important lesson from a management standpoint.

Jericho Road has a faith component. I'm a Christian so I think of what Jesus would do as a doctor. We serve the most vulnerable people in Buffalo and follow some of these folks back to their countries, working with them in Sierra Leone; Goma, in the Democratic Republic of Congo; and in the villages of Hagam and Hapra in the Himalayan mountains of Nepal.

I am CEO of Jericho Road, I see patients four days a week in the office, and I still deliver babies. I have a job that allows me to still practice medicine but also to lead the organization. I spend about 70% of my time being a physician and about 30% of my time being a CEO. I love being a doctor and if I had to choose between the two I'd choose to be a doctor. I think the organization benefits from my being the CEO because I can focus on our mission and vision and allow others to do the day-to-day administrative work, which I think is healthy.

How do my roles as a practicing physician and CEO inform each other? I think there are pluses and minuses to being both a practicing physician and the CEO. My identity is that of a family physician. Being a practicing doctor on the ground does inform certain decisions I make. Many decisions are practical, not theoretical. If we have to decide about something like investing in a nursing team or cutting a nursing team, such decisions affect me because I'm physically on the ground. My role as a practicing doctor enables me to understand the operations and to feel the impact of my decisions on those operations. And I do feel the impact. On the downside, I probably can't always be as objective as I should be—I mean, I'd find it hard if I ever had to make major cuts because I'd know how those would impact the front-line providers.

I think the reason I'm able to do both jobs effectively is that I've been here for 22 years so I know this organization really well, and I know the people and our mission and can speak to that very clearly. Also, a good set of people report to me—the chief financial officer, the chief operating officer, the program officer—there are a lot of people who work full time in administration. I enable them to do their work, I hold them accountable and don't micromanage them, and I can focus on being a doctor, which what I most enjoy about my job.

Jericho Road Globally

We work with the refugee resettlement agency in Buffalo. When refugees arrive, they need to see us for health screening within 30 days and then they become our patients. A woman who fled with her family from Sierra Leone during their civil war in 2001 came to see us. Soon, her family became our patients and she became a friend. She was a nurse in Sierra Leone, and we needed a medical assistant. She started working for us, went back to school, and got her RN degree here in the States.

In 2009, she said, "Dr. Glick, I really want to go back to my country and start a clinic—would you help?" I said we would. She wanted to lead it, so we visited Sierra Leone a couple of times. In 2013 she moved back, we raised the funds, and she built a clinic that is now a hospital. We raised a lot of the funding to support it, but she runs it with a full Sierra Leonean team. They do all the basic surgeries and take care of people as inpatients and outpatients. It's very cool. We send our Buffalo teams there a couple of times a year to support their work. That's how our outreach in other countries came about.

Our work in Congo started a little differently. One of the main groups of refugees who have come to Buffalo in the last ten years, and especially in the last two to three years, are from Congo, and we've come to know many of them. We brought some folks back to work in a clinic there through some of these connections. A similar scenario is taking place in Nepal as we've followed some Nepalese refugees back to their country.

That's how we choose the countries we do. We follow folks back to their countries and then support local teams to do the work there. We provide financial and educational capacity-building, but we don't do the actual work. It's been a huge win for our organization because it's created a holistic cycle in which we take care of local health in Buffalo and local health in other countries. A lot of folks working for us now really are committed to this, and we give them opportunities to take short-term trips.

I typically visit these countries twice a year. I'm there for two weeks at a time, which is the longest I can be away. When I go to Sierra Leone or to Congo, I see things I normally don't see in this country and that no one should really see. For instance, we see malaria all the time in those countries, but we never see it here. I was in Sierra Leone the first two weeks of December and admitted a baby with malaria. This baby got really sick overnight and ended up having a seizure. I was called in, was working to resuscitate him, and while I was holding him, the baby died right in my arms. This was a perfectly healthy nine-month-old who, two days ago, was fine.

In America people die, obviously. But I tell people that in Sierra Leone, death is more real, and life is more real. Everything, life and death, are right there in front of you. You don't take anything for granted. When I was there, I saw a little child with swollen glands and because I was worried about HIV, tested for that. It was. I tested the mom and she tested positive, too. Suddenly that family's life has changed. We see kids with malnutrition. One day we were in a village clinic doing hernia repairs. The word got out that we were there, and 24 men were soon in front of me with huge hernias that had affected their lives but that they'd never been able to fix, because they couldn't afford the $25 or $50 or $75—which is an exorbitant fee for them but nothing for us.

We take a team of five or six people from Jericho Road on these trips. Some are going for the first time and others are going back on repeat trips. While we see hardships like those I've just described, we also see that so many of these people live their lives and have joy and play soccer. When we see people living in those circumstances and then come back to the States, we find it a lot harder to complain about the things we complain about. These experiences change our perspective.

To prevent illnesses in Sierra Leone and the Democratic Republic of Congo, like yellow fever and malaria, people need access to clean water and sanitation and basic public health measures. It has to start there. But when it comes to actual medical care, we could use things like x-ray machines and computed tomography (CT) scanners and Pap smears and treatments for cancer. There are so many things that people face in sub-Saharan Africa and other parts of the world, treatments for conditions that are available here and that we take for granted but are not available there.

In all of Sierra Leone there are five or six dentists, five or six ophthalmologists. Most elderly people can't afford glasses, let alone cataract surgery. For most people who get diagnosed with a cancer, the only treatment is surgery. There's no chemotherapy in the whole country. There are no mammograms in the whole country. There are no working CT scanners, much less magnetic resonance imaging machines in the whole country. They live with a whole different set of problems. But, there's no obesity in those countries. There are fewer motor vehicle accidents, there's no opioid addiction. Hospitals in Sierra Leone and Congo have no narcotics at all. They treat pain totally differently. So, we see things that give us perspective.

On Joy in Work

I think there's something bitter-sweet about joy, a sense of peace in the midst of a storm. I think you can work with someone who's dying of cancer and feel joy, but that doesn't mean you're feeling happy. Joy is a sense of perspective and meaning and peace, even though you're dealing with something that's really hard.

In medicine we see tough things in our work, but joy is the sense that there's nothing else I'd rather do than this meaningful work and having meaningful relationships. And feeling that this is where I should be. I'd say that's what joy is.

I haven't made the most money in the world, but what's most important to me, and what has brought the most satisfaction, is the relationships I've had with patients for more than 20 years now, and of having built a lasting organization that is doing good work.

One of the things that brings me joy is taking several trips a year to Sierra Leone and Congo to visit our clinics and work with the teams there. The work we do with people from all over the world, who really need our services, has brought a lot of meaning to my life.

Vulnerable people are open and honest with us most of the time. I find this work meaningful because I see that my work can make a difference. For me, at the end of the day, that's enough.

What Diminishes Joy

Inequity

In 2012 I started to journal my time in Sierra Leone, Congo, and Nepal. I would send an email back to our Jericho Road team about my experiences. At first, I thought it was for other people—to give them an idea about the work we were doing and to raise funding. But, ultimately, I realized my journaling was for me—it helps me to think through what I'm experiencing in the moment. I do some of this in Buffalo, too. When I'm in Sierra Leone or Congo or Nepal, there are some resources I can work with. When I'm in Buffalo there are a whole different set of resources. I don't really try to bridge the gap, but journaling helps me to see the world the way it is. I don't like it. If someone were to give me a fraction of the money that we spend on healthcare in this country and say, "Go do something good in a place like Sierra Leone," I could change the whole healthcare system in Sierra Leone with a fraction of what we spend here.

Preauthorizations, Precertifications, and the Electronic Medical Record

I don't like to do paperwork. I'm an advocate, but I get frustrated when I have to talk to insurance companies and argue that we should be able to get this procedure done or that medication prescribed. What gets me discouraged sometimes is the way money has taken over healthcare. We have to worry about costs—and I'm not saying we shouldn't worry about them—but I get frustrated when I have to convince someone to let me do something I know is necessary for a patient's health. And the way we have to document so many things and check so many boxes in the electronic medical record—I live with it but I don't like it.

Burnout

I don't ever feel burned out. I sometimes feel overwhelmed, which is different from burnout. Burnout is evident, for example, when a colleague says she doesn't know if she can do this anymore, she doesn't know if she made the right choice by going into medicine, and she's losing the sense of compassion that drove her into this profession in the first place. She goes into survival mode and her only motivation is to get through the day. To me, that is burnout. Seeing things we shouldn't see in this world but being able to do something about them is the antidote to burnout, I think.

I do feel overloaded by work sometimes but I don't necessarily feel a loss of control. That's an important distinction. I'm scheduled to see patients every 15 minutes and I typically see 25–30 patients a day on a full day. But I've known many of these patients a long time, so it's not as though we have to get reacquainted. For me, overload is not necessarily based on the number of patients I see in a day, but on how challenging their conditions are and on what else is going on. Am I trying to fix some administrative crisis at the same time I'm trying to see patients? Is someone in labor, do I have to run to the hospital, and is something up with my kids? There are days when everything comes together and that can feel overwhelming.

Being overwhelmed is possible to ignore in some ways. There are days when I have a lot to do, and even though I'm feeling overwhelmed, I'm not feeling as though my life or my work have no meaning and I don't question why I'm doing this work. I don't feel disenfranchised. I know exactly why I'm overwhelmed, I know I'm doing good work, and I know I've just got to get through the day.

Advice

I tend to look at things from a justice standpoint. Healthcare is a basic human right for everyone in the world. People across the world should have access to good, basic healthcare regardless of where they're from or how much money they make. Somehow, we've got to shift resources so that poor countries aren't exploited.

In this country, we need a single-payer national healthcare plan. Change the system and take the money out of it as much as possible. Healthcare is so expensive in this country and it's such a business. We don't care for the poorest the way we should.

Clinicians should be able to work in settings where they are supported to do the best they can for patients. I think 80% of our docs should be family docs.

25. Mark K., MD, Primary Care Internist for a Rural Integrated Health System

Mark K., MD, a primary care internist who spends a portion of his time working with patients with diabetes, has worked with the underserved in public hospitals for his entire 36-year career, in both urban and remote rural areas. Mark has a lot to say about inequity, the essential role of public hospitals, the personal struggles of patients, and the need to really listen to their stories to be able to understand the social determinants of health.

My father was a doctor. My parents are Holocaust survivors. My dad went to medical school in Germany *after* the war. He went from a displaced persons camp to a university. He left Germany after medical school and came to the United States in 1951. It was his dream that his son would be a doctor and work with him. So, it was in the cards that I would become a doctor. As an undergraduate I got a degree in physics, but I didn't think I had what it would take to get a PhD in physics.

Having the parents I did and coming of age in the late '60s–early '70s, I saw my childhood through the lens of social justice informed by my parents' experience. I heard what was happening in terms of the Civil Rights Movement and other events that were in the news, like the war in Vietnam. I had a sense that there were real people who were harmed and benefited and that there were principles of justice that were at play. It wasn't particularly well-formed, but I remember being drawn to Michael Harrington's book, *The Other America*. This is jumping way ahead, but I thought, *okay, I'm meant to be some kind of worker for social justice.*

I read the book by Isabella Wilkerson called *The Warmth of Other Suns*, about the migration of blacks from the South to the North. When I read that book, I thought, *these people are just like my parents.* They left hardship suddenly, under difficult circumstances, they broke family ties at times in order to do it, and I can imagine some of the kitchen table discussions that they would have had in terms of trying to make it in a hostile environment, of raising families, of having some sustenance. And these were the same memories of my childhood.

I crossed this boundary of going from the suburbs to the inner city and of working in an environment of relative wealth and stability to working in an environment of poverty and instability. You can see that you are reaching out, thinking that you're doing things with people who are different from you. But when I read that book, I realized they were just like my parents. That's why it felt comfortable. I only realized this ten years ago. You tell yourself a story that you're going someplace else to work with people who are different, but it's cross-cultural more often than not. Rather than making a sacrifice, I was in my comfort zone because of what felt normal to me growing up.

My Professional Journey

I started in residency at a large public hospital and practiced there for almost 30 years before I came here. Even before I got there, there was a very idealistic—and I would even say politically motivated—group of physicians who had been around the country as an outgrowth of the Civil Rights Movement and the politics related to the anti-war movement. The city had a great medical community, and that way of thinking was not unique. We all supported each other. We all challenged each other. We all added to it. People didn't always get along and people were rough with each other, but at the end of the day I think the health community there had a very, very, very strong development of a social justice consciousness. I started there in 1983.

People who preceded me did very formative work in the institution. I started in this large urban public hospital in the division of general medicine. Over time I did a handful of different things. There was a very big general medicine clinic; the residents were all trained there as well as all of the clinical staff—the preceptors, supervisors, all of us in general medicine saw patients there. When the job of director opened up, I took that job and did it for five years. It was a gigantic operation with over 55,000 patient visits a year. I saw patients and had administrative responsibilities, including listening to and addressing complaints from patients and providers. There was a gigantic staff of doctors in that clinic. A lot of them were residents or were just there one day or half a day a week. But the point is, it was either them or nobody to take care of these patients. I tried to set a tone of respect and caring within the clinic as much as possible.

It was a tough job and part of what was also happening at that moment was that the administration was ratcheting up their demands for the number of visits. They wanted more appointments, more visits, and increased productivity. I was getting tired. In a public setting there's always a kind of difficult relationship between volume and quality. At some point, when you turn up the volume, you risk sacrificing the quality. It was clear that this was not going to be something that would be a discussion; greater productivity was going to be a demand.

They weren't really interested in my productivity, but they wanted me to be the enforcer of somebody else's productivity quota when they didn't explain it and there was no way to know whether productivity helped or didn't help care. They were not measuring patient satisfaction—and if they said we'll stop driving productivity when we're hurting patients, I could have lived with that. I could have stayed. But they had an idea of what the industry standards were, and I just felt that this wasn't an industry standard sort of place. I didn't want to be their enforcer. I felt they really wanted to take away my autonomy as a clinical director.

There were bigger changes going on at the institution, too. They were building an ambulatory network. Different power centers existed, and we didn't all get along. I felt that this would either have to be a very messy fight—which is not my temperament most of the time and didn't seem like something I was going to win—so it just felt that after five years of doing that job, I didn't feel I had the oomph to keep going. And given my family obligations, I thought my continuing as clinical director would be too much. I didn't leave the hospital then, but I left that position. I stayed and got more involved in internal medicine, I got more involved with preventive medicine, and then I became the director of preventive medicine.

That was a perfect job for me. I loved that. My boss was great. She had done some really wonderful work around alcohol in the institution. I learned from both the person who had been the director before, and from her, how to bring population health into these clinical environments. We're used to thinking one person at a time but really thinking about the population's needs is important. Think about it: on any given day, x number of people are admitted with substance use, x number of people are admitted with alcohol problems, and x number of people are admitted with tobacco issues, or coming to the clinic with those issues. We know that these are major barriers to health and well-being and, in the case of alcohol and substance use, are also barriers to the delivery of other parts of healthcare. If you don't address those problems, you're not going to be very successful. So, you can actually build programs that are more systematic and reach a good proportion of the population—you never reach everybody just because of how healthcare flows—with simple, broad-based interventions that would really affect people.

After working at that public hospital for 30 years, I came to work with underserved populations in a remote, rural integrated health system. Half of my time is spent delivering primary care, which is intended to be face time with patients. This involves a fair amount of administrative work. I spend a portion of my time working with a program to prevent and treat diabetes. I work, on paper, four ten-hour days, from 8:00 a.m. to 6:00 p.m. On average I probably work about three to five hours more than that.

One of the things that's really nice about this place is they've been able to recruit bright, very capable providers. By and large people want to be here. Those who are starting their careers come from very good residency programs. There's a movement here of being attuned to global health needs. Many people here have worked or trained in global health and see working here as being connected to that work. So, the provider group is really solid. When someone leaves after three to five years someone else wonderful comes to take their place.

That said, in my job at the public hospital we developed clinical buddies over time. These clinical buddies were as honest as people could be with each other; where no question was a stupid question; and where we could really let our hair down, express our doubts, ask someone in an honest way what they thought. And there was even a range of people—if something was more of a medical issue, I might have gone to one person; if it was more interpersonal, emotional, or psychological I might have gone to others. These relationships developed over years and years and years. I miss that. I don't have the same kind of clinical buddies here that I had there.

On the other hand, I feel like the luckiest person because I walked into a great model of care, the kind of team-based approach that people talk and write so much about. In this setting, community members—some, but not all, without bachelor's degrees—are trained as health coaches and work in the primary care setting. They are bicultural and bilingual and are available to help answer patients' questions and to clarify plans of care.

There are many times these health coaches have saved me from myself when I see things going poorly. For example, let's say somebody with diabetes is on a group of medications and has poor glycemic control. I will talk to the patient and we agree on a plan of care. Then the health coach will spend more time with the patient than I do, and in the process learns that the patient really doesn't want to do what I suggested—the patient may think the plan of care is too hard to follow, or is just not ready to do it. People may perceive an illness or a set of treatments in vastly different ways. Having these health coaches, who have a little more time to spend with patients and who can read cultural cues in a way that I never could—and who establish relationships with them—can make patients go from resisting treatment to accepting and following it.

People have very different health beliefs and not all want to take medicine. They aren't always forthcoming about their reasons for not wanting to take the medicine I prescribe. Over time I've gotten a tiny bit better at being able to anticipate problems, at being able to see if there is something they're willing to do, to seeing if they need more explanation, more time to think about things. While there are people who are resistant and locked into their positions against taking medicine, there are many, many people who, if you explain things well, will jump on board and are amazingly good at following the plan of care.

On Joy in Work

I see joy as moments of connection with patients, times when people reveal what they've held onto as private and that are important to them. I spent over 20 years running a tobacco cessation clinic. It's the same discussion over and over again on some level, but every six or nine months I learned something new, I heard what people were saying with more depth. Sometimes if you're an attentive listener it's almost as if people speak to you in poetry. And when you can hear that—the depth of what people are expressing in simple ways, the challenges and the conflicts—those are the joyful moments. A lot of it comes with relationships where you feel frustrated and maybe think things are going nowhere, and then there's a breakthrough.

For example, years ago a patient kept coming to the clinic smelling of alcohol. I'd give him the speech about why he shouldn't do this and sometimes he would still come in smelling of alcohol. Finally, I just got annoyed with him, seeming to ask, "Why are you coming here? What's the point?" And then at some point he showed up and told me he had stopped drinking. He was dressed nicely, much nicer than he had ever dressed before, and much better put together. His face, clothes, and hair all looked better. It was clear that he did it without me, but he did it with my annoyance. After he stopped drinking, I realized he was really this nice guy, a likable sort. He taught me that, in his case, underneath the alcoholism was a vulnerable human being. He didn't change with my dismissal of him, with my annoyance. I realized that treating him that way was a mistake. As a physician I wanted there to be space for his vulnerability even when he was drinking, by being there and present. And of course, realizing that informed the way I treated others. I became even more curious about patients.

I did a lot of learning about how people change behavior, which was really helpful and useful. A colleague and I went to a Jon Kabat-Zinn mindfulness retreat at the University of Massachusetts Medical School and in Rhinebeck, New York, which was a source of enormous joy. And then I did a teacher training in Worcester, Massachusetts. Learning the principles of mindfulness made me a much better listener, made me much more aware of my own stress and reactivity and irritation and how to deal with that better. But this also led to an ability to hear that in other people and, I hope in some small ways, helped some people to be less hard on themselves, more loving toward themselves, more willing to trust themselves to make some changes. I think it made for better relationships.

I feel really lucky learning about mindfulness. At some point I had this realization that joy is despair's next-door neighbor. It's never far away. It's always right there. And sometimes you just have to open your window, or go out the door, or just look at things a little differently, or open your heart a little more to think about things in a different way. There's always room at the table for one more. And particularly when that one more is joy, then you've got to make space for it.

I do feel joy in my work. For better or worse my parents taught me resilience. I grew up with their hardships. There's a kind of early education in experience—I don't wish it on other people, I don't know whether it was healthy, and other people I knew suffered and struggled with it—but for me, hardship isn't exactly new.

I feel I've also been really lucky to have had jobs that are not full-time clinical. It would have beaten me down to do that all the time. I also feel so lucky because my work has given me such a clear sense of purpose. And when you go to work with a sense of purpose, even if it's hard, you feel connected.

On Money and Joy

I feel terrible that so many people have enormous debt. To be in a position where you're paying down debt for years and years is very hard. I think if I were doing a hard job and a gigantic portion of my salary was going to pay off my debt, that would make me unhappy. I didn't go into medicine for the money, but I was never uncomfortable. I had minimal debt. I almost never worried about money. How do you do something when you need to be emotionally available to other people and have part of your thoughts consumed with things like, how do I pay my rent?

I've been very lucky to be working for public institutions for my whole career. But even in institutions like federally qualified health centers, the business model is a pretty tight and narrow one, where you're serving strata of the working poor. Both the issues of physician compensation and productivity are right at the fulcrum of the question, will the business model work, or not? I think it's right that people have some expectation of being, on a certain level, comfortable, though we might disagree about what being comfortable means.

What Diminishes Joy

Documentation

Typing notes is the biggest thing that diminishes my joy in work. It's a lot of work. It's hard. I probably use a different part of my brain to be with patients. It's trying to make relationships with people from many, many different walks of life. People who are super quiet, people who are very chatty, people who are angry, people who are sad, people who are happy. So, working with this very big range of clinical issues, emotional issues, health beliefs, styles of interacting, levels of trust. You're working with all of that in a limited timeframe of 15–30 minutes per person. The more I'm engaged the better that goes. On top of it there are questions like, is this the right dose or the wrong dose? Is this a drug interaction, not a drug interaction? Do we have a correct diagnosis or an incorrect diagnosis and what does that mean in this individual? There's all of that going on. It's intellectually very stimulating and personally it's very engaging. And at the end of a session, I'm done. But I'm not done.

I'm of the school where I don't feel it's right to type and see people. I think in general it's disrespectful. I also risk missing things when my eyes aren't on the patient. To work in a place where the question, "Do you respect me?" given the historical context of where I've worked, gives this issue added weight. I write my notes at the end of the day or the next day, depending on what's going on at home, too. I try to get them done within 48 hours.

I don't think the administrators care when or how we write our notes. This is not the kind of environment where there's productivity reporting. They don't care whether we're typing in the room with people or not typing in the room. There's nothing prescriptive about any of that. There is an awareness that it's important to treat patients with respect. Because I have a dual position, I'm in clinic a little less often than some of my colleagues; if someone else has six outpatient sessions a week, I have four. I think this suits me. I don't know if I could have six. My dual roles give me a little bit of flexibility during the week so if I haven't finished all of my documentation, I know there are places in my schedule where I can do it.

The experience of primary care is often that year to year the demands are greater, medical care gets more complicated, we need to be on top of more things and different things, and organizational initiatives look to primary care doctors to do them. Suddenly we're responsible for meeting more institutional requirements. This raises the issue of the need to do things uniformly to do them well—particularly anything that involves communication—and that is really hard to do.

Emotional Hardships of Patients

Medical care tends to be a little streaky, where you'll get busy streaks and less busy streaks. Emotionally it can be overloading sometimes. Many of the people I take care of are lovely, wonderful people, but there are hardships in their lives. One of my patients attempted suicide. I asked myself what was the sadness that led to this suicide attempt? He's a pretty reticent guy, not a big talker, not emotive. Is there something I should have known that we could have talked about before it came to this? When I ask myself such questions, I feel really, really sad. There's also a quality of feeling overwhelmed. Their heart disease or diabetes pales in comparison to their sadness and being alone in the world.

Fatigue

I realize this will be my last full-time job and when I can't do it anymore, when I've emotionally had enough, I'll quit. I'm 62 and I don't have the oomph that I had 20 years ago. I get tired and I need to rest, and if I don't, I know I make mistakes. Just having that experience of myself is important. There are times when I'm fatigued, or a patient's demands seem unreasonable and unmeetable. Some of this is related to people's existential suffering. They don't have anyone who is helping them with that. More and more I answer some of those calls slowly, put a little delay between the time they call and the time I get to them, because it's too much.

Inequity

During those medical staff years in the inner-city public hospital I learned about how systematic racism worked and was structured. This created an apparent difference in health and well-being in which black people were blamed for their conditions. Systematic racism underscored how important public institutions were for people who were poor, who were African American, and who were immigrants. Members of those communities knew the importance of these public institutions, but the white community didn't see or care because the need didn't touch them. And so, you had this political process where the health and well-being of an institution like ours was dependent upon white politicians, most of whom didn't give a damn about the place. How things were structured to create all that was the education of a lifetime.

You can read about social determinants of health and then if you really listen to people, you can hear these through what people tell you about themselves. Whether it's the violence in people's neighborhoods and what they do or don't do, or the losses people experience of going to the funeral of a cousin who was murdered, or the ways they are treated at their jobs, the mercurial nature of being employed or not being employed, or the experience of losing their home—you can just hear how that happens. And so, you have to be interested, and maybe a little trustworthy, to show that you care about that; or leave things quiet at the moment; or spend an extra five or ten minutes with people. But sometimes not. You can't experience it, but it becomes more real. And then in a smaller way history becomes more real. And then, over time, for me at least, a sense of purpose deepens. Instead of things becoming routine they become filled with depth.

During the time I worked at the public hospital, within the medical staff but also outside it, we talked about what makes a public hospital different. Urban areas should be supporting a public hospital. What does it mean to be a safety net? I think having a place that doesn't means-test people provides an element of access. It's important to have an institution among institutions that stands for those things, that challenge other places to not turn people away but rather to serve the community.

Places that have strong public hospitals also have better community hospitals. Maybe that's because people who work in the public hospital go to the community hospitals. Public hospitals talk about what they're doing, whether it's education, or education and research, or serving particular communities. These are places that are innovating and delivering a very high level of technical care—but within that mix people talk about the gigantic unmet needs and having to marshal our resources to deal with it. That just has an influence on the community at large.

I think that when you're bigger you touch more people. When you touch more people, you have more community acceptability. When you have more community acceptability, it's not such an outrageous thing to have a political discussion about your funding because everybody's either part of it or knows somebody who at one point in their life went there. And the reaction becomes, "Well, of course you need it." In a city like ours the public hospital was chronically underfunded, caught in efforts to reduce the local tax allocation to the hospital, so that fewer and fewer and fewer people felt they were part of it. When the Affordable Care Act was signed, 900,000 uninsured people were living in the county I worked in. There were more uninsured people living in this county than there are people in the city of Baltimore.

When I was a kid, I had an aunt who lived in New York and I once went to visit her. She was elderly and asked, "Would you come to the doctor with me?" She went to an eye doctor at one of the public hospitals of New York City. Here I was, walking with my aunt to a public hospital so she could get services. My mother would no sooner go close to the public hospital than she would stop eating brisket. She just wasn't going to do that.

26. Andrew M., MD, Professor of Family Medicine and Family Physician

Andrew M., MD, graduated from medical school in 1985, worked in a family-urgent care practice, volunteered for two years in the Sudan and Kenya, worked in a federally qualified health center, and for the last 30 years has divided his time between teaching and practicing family medicine. Recently appointed to the board of directors for the American Academy of HIV Medicine, Andrew is devoted to his patients, committed to his students, and passionate in advocating for healthcare as a human right.

As a kid I was a little nerd-cake and decided that whatever I was going to do for a living, it had to matter. It had to matter to people. Early on I decided I might become a farmer, because that's pretty concrete: farmers grow food. I briefly toyed with the idea of becoming a priest. My parents were devout Catholic—my mother was, anyway—and when I presented that notion to her, she was appalled. Another option, interestingly, was to be a funeral director because there's emotional content in doing that. One can be present with people, doing something that matters a great deal. And healthcare/medicine was the other one. I took the MCATs on a lark. I had been out drinking the night before and I was horribly hung over the day of the test. I did really, really well, which was unexpected. I applied for and interviewed at a number of schools and got accepted to the one I decided to attend.

Everyone probably knows, though few people may speak of it directly, that one's choice of career is often an attempt to get affirmation from one's parents. That was certainly true in my case. My folks are rather reserved. I still have and treasure a letter I got from my dad after I was accepted to medical school; this was unexpected, because my dad was never a letter writer and didn't tend to reveal his emotions.

I grew up in a small town. In that part of the country, Marcus Welby was the definition of what a doc was: a generalist, a really caring person. So that was my model. But it also suited me. I loved my rotations in medical school—I loved obstetrics, I loved psychiatry, and I really loved surgery, which surprised me. I considered applying to psychiatry programs and ER programs and surgery programs and anesthesia—I'd done a two-month anesthesia rotation in 1983 and had a blast with that—but when it finally came down to it, I wanted to do everything. So, family medicine was a slam dunk. And I'm a people guy. I like looking after people. I'm not a super-brainiac by any stretch, and there are certainly professionals with specialty designations whose brain power exceeds mine. But I've got a good heart and I decided this would be a good match.

After my residency I worked for two years in an urgent care-family practice, then volunteered for two years oversees, first in the Sudan and then in Kenya with a refugee relief organization. I came back to the U.S. to work off my medical student loans for two years, then went to work for a federally qualified health center. I was then offered an academic position at the university here, so I stayed.

I am a professor of family medicine at a university that is the parent organization of the clinic where I practice. I am employed 70% by this group and 30% by the university. I have a busy practice and I teach. I spend 60% of my time seeing patients and 40% teaching, or 70% seeing patients and 30% teaching, depending on the week. My university has about 8,000 students. It's growing and vibrant and highly thought of.

I see patients four days a week for at least a half day, sometimes more. At intervals, my partners and I rotate teaching rounds at the hospital. I spend other parts of the day precepting family medicine residents, lecturing medical students, or leading small group or practicum exercises for learners.

The day starts with what we call "huddle," when the whole team meets together at 7:45 a.m. We talk about the day, any safety issues, affirmations from people, and any announcements. The huddle builds collegiality, and starting these huddles put us on the path to seeing each other as peers. Everyone has a role to play, a reason to be here, and we look after one another. As a result of the huddle, this office is much better today around warm handoffs and the respectful interface among us. It's actually pretty cool. This distinguishes us from many other places that are very hierarchical. The hierarchy levels out quite a bit here.

The first patient is in the exam room at 8:00 a.m. I usually finish seeing patients at 2:00 or 3:00 in the afternoon, often working through lunch, then chart or tend to phone calls and messages, typically heading home between 5:00 and 6:00 p.m. My schedule is about the same on the days I teach. Sometimes I get home a little earlier, sometimes a little later. During my teaching weeks I generally teach Monday to Friday, all day long.

Today a woman I've taken care of for years, who doesn't live here anymore, drove in from a neighboring state. She was ready to get back on the road, but she needed a procedure. And it's lunchtime. I think many people would have said, "We can't do this right now. Next time you're in town we'll get it attended to." I was working with my medical student and said, "Go set up the procedure room and let's get her added to the schedule. Let's get this taken care of while she's here; we're going to work through lunch, and we'll take a little break afterward." You know, it worked out fine. My student loved it because she loves procedures, so we were able to attend to this woman's needs then and there. Working through lunch was no problem. That was actually fun.

On Joy in Work

I would say joy in work revolves a lot around one's sense of competence and mastery, as well as pacing. I think mastery is a key part of joy. I can go to my office manager and say, "I really love caring for people with HIV. It's what I'm called to do and it's my favorite thing to do, so if folks are looking for that please send them to me." And when they do, I absolutely love that. In terms of pacing, a day can be too slow if the weather is bad and patients don't show. I get anxious when I don't have enough to do. But often it's the other way around, when there's so much going on it's just chaos. Those are hard days. But every once in a while there's a particularly great day when there's a really nice flow that's neither too light nor too heavy, and the pacing is good. Days like that are great.

My biggest satisfaction comes from having happy patients who give me affirmations that they like the way I care for them, that they trust me, and that they're delighted that I look after them, their kids, their spouses, and their families. I'm a hugger. I like hugging and I like those affirmations from people. I love my little practice, which is very inclusive. We take care of the third richest guy in town and the folks who live under the bridge and everybody in between.

About four years ago, on my 30th anniversary of graduating from medical school, I turned to my department chair and said, "I'm going to pay somebody to take my night call now. I don't want to do this anymore." After 30 years of night call I said, "This is killing me—the next day is almost impossible. I'm willing to pay out of my own pocket to have someone cover that." She agreed. I now have call coverage at night; I almost never have to take call anymore. Life is good.

My bosses are very good listeners. If I go to them with a problem or say I need something, and if I outline why or what it is, they work really hard to accommodate me. I don't think this is just for me. I think they're trying to make sure everyone is healthy and happy at work. Certainly, within the day-to-day context of the folks we interact with and who look after us, this group is pretty supportive. I do not deliver babies or practice obstetrics and it would be awful if my boss came to me and said, "We're going to make you do obstetrics now." It's not my area of expertise, I don't have mastery there, and I don't want to do that anymore. It would be very difficult if those changes were unilateral. I'm fortunate because generally I can call the shots.

One of the easiest ways to tap into joy in the practice of medicine is to have some learners around, because you can watch them get fired up over learning something new or gaining mastery over a procedure. It can be something as simple as doing a respectful, graceful Pap smear for the first time. Or sewing up a laceration. Or peeking into a child's ear. Watching a learner get comfortable with something and having them express awe and joy around that, too, is infectious. And it makes practicing medicine much more fun. When I teach I feel I'm serving something bigger. People talk about this all the time, but there really is a nobility to teaching. We're doing something that matters and it's a little bit bigger than just meeting budget next month. Teaching is a great way to renew joy.

On Money and Joy

I'm very well paid. But I'm also family doctor-paid, which is not like what an orthopedic surgeon is paid. But for a family doctor I do really well. What happens week to week and month to month in the office is not reflected in any discernible way in my paycheck. I live rather frugally. Except for plane tickets to crazy places, we live carefully, and I don't need anything. I have the luxury of saying money doesn't matter but that's because it's gone so well for a long time.

What Diminishes Joy

What diminishes joy in work for me is people who do things without letting me know, people who make unilateral decisions: when I look at the schedule and there are two more people who walked in that I hadn't heard about. I try to be inclusive and accommodating but I don't like to be stepped on.

Unrealistic expectations, in which I sense injustice for the people I serve, diminishes my joy. Say one of my patients tells me, "I got a bill that I don't understand, and I can't get anybody to talk to me about it and they won't fix this. They tell me they're sending me to collections." I understand we've got to have margin for mission, but this needs to be done in a respectful, humane way. That gets my dander up and I usually intervene around things like that. I take it to my office manager and say, "We're not going to treat people this way and I'm relying on you to have a phone conversation with this person to get this fixed." That almost always works. There are countless little examples of times I get to be the defender of the downtrodden because that kind of stuff, when I see it, really pisses me off.

I have partners who get upset about people running late but I'm pretty good about seeing the flip side. You know, sometimes people are running late because traffic's bad or they have a flat tire, they don't have transportation, or they're rounding up their quarters from the sofa cushions to get on the bus.

I do feel overloaded by work. I've attempted to be rather forthright about that. I went to my department chair and said, "This job is too big. I've been at it long enough that I want to do less, not more. I want to start off-loading some things." I made a list of all my tasks, from the courses I teach to the clinic work to the committee work to the state board involvement. I asked myself, *what no longer brings me joy? What costs too much emotionally?* and decided to start off-loading those things. I'm fortunate to be in a place where I can do that. Most people don't have the luxury of being able to tell their boss, "I don't want to do X,Y, or Z anymore. I just want to do A." I feel that's remarkably rare. My boss is very cool, and I'm good enough at the work I do that she wants to work with me to find someone to take over the things I no longer enjoy. It's very much a work in progress. I wish there were a couple of younger, more energetic folks with values similar to mine who would take over my patients, whom I care greatly about, as I toy with the notion of winding down.

Financing Healthcare

Value-Based Care

This organization is moving more and more into value-based care; that is, for x amount of money, we're going to take really good care of people. We have care coordinators in the office, a social worker, behavioral health professionals, physical therapists, occupational therapists, a diabetes educator, and radiologists on salary. There's still a bottom line, there are still budgets, but we're moving more toward value. We've reduced the number of people using the emergency room. We look for novel ways to reach out to the community for A1C reduction, for example, trying to meet those quality indicators.

Paying for Healthcare

One of the biggest challenges to having a healthy community is the whole issue of insurance and medical payment reform. I wish we would have a national referendum, a day off from work when the whole country would have to vote, with only one question on the ballot: Is healthcare a right, or is it a commodity? Are we going to work on making healthcare accessible to everyone or are we going to continue to let the marketplace control who receives care? We need to decide, today, what it's going to be. And once we've decided that, then we as a nation, as a community of people, can decide how we're going to structure healthcare delivery and how it's going to be paid for. The work we are doing here, in this neighborhood and in this community, is constantly being thwarted because we don't have ways to pay for it. Or people don't have a way to pay for it. How is a patient going to pay for that magnetic resonance scan? How will he be able to see the surgeon? How can we get that pregnant woman into the prenatal clinic?

Work–Life Balance

My husband retired this year, which has prompted the conversation about how much longer I'm going to be doing this job full time. What is our life going to look like? That's weighing on us right now and is driving some of our decisions about what's going to happen next. We acknowledge that we are *incredibly* fortunate because there's this rare nexus when people have the need, the money, and the time to go hiking for two weeks in Peru, or to go run a marathon in Mongolia, or to go and see your host parents in Australia whom you haven't seen for 40 years. We've done all these things in the last year and we've got all kinds of adventures planned. There is a sort of rebalancing of the life outside of work and the life within work and trying to get that right, where it's mostly energizing and joyful and not too spirit-sapping. By and large, I think I get it right. I'm lucky to have bosses who support me in this.

27.   *Ruth F., BSN, Public Health Nurse/Community Health Nurse at a Rural Integrated Health System*

Ruth F., BSN, became a nurse when she was 59 years old. An international board-certified lactation consultant who spent almost 20 years as a midwife before going to nursing school, Ruth has been a public health/community health nurse in a remote part of the country for the last six years.

My going into healthcare started when I became a midwife in Canada, which really happened because I was having babies myself. I had been a leader at the La Leche League, which is a peer support group for breastfeeding. I heard a lot of women's birth stories and their dissatisfaction with their births, and I literally just got drawn into midwifery.

The primary problem women talked about was lack of choice: lack of respect for the mother, doctors wanting to deliver babies in a routine, assembly-line kind of way, and mothers wanting to do something different during labor like not being in bed and standing up. Really, fairly simple things that at that time the medical establishment was just not willing to entertain. Doctors had their routine and they wanted to stick with it. I primarily got into midwifery to empower women and to champion the idea that they had the right to make their own choices. I did that for almost 20 years.

I had been on call for years and I was tired to being on call, I was tired of staying up all night. I was just tired. Midwifery is really beautiful and wonderful, and the births are fabulous—until they're not. I think I was also worn down by being constantly on guard, constantly watching and then reacting to emergencies, which I think just contributed to my being tired.

You don't just walk away from midwifery. You have to quit nine months before you want to stop, because you have clients. When I left, I had no idea what I was going to do. I just knew that at 4:00 a.m. I wanted to be in my own bed. And I wanted to have control of my own time. So, for about five years I did some odd jobs. I was able to work as a medical assistant in a dermatology office for a while because I had some medical background.

And then I decided I wanted to live here, in this beautiful part of the country. I loved it. The natural beauty of this place was the main draw. I had been coming here often because my daughter had moved to this area. I started to meet people and I had a few friends, so I didn't feel like I was walking in cold. I realized if I were a nurse I could live and work here because there were so many opportunities.

In Canada, midwives are not nurses, and nurses are not midwives. There is no overlap. If you're a nurse and you want to become a midwife, you have to go to midwifery school. And if you're a midwife and you want to be a nurse you have to go to nursing school. So, I came here and went to nursing school. I felt I had a good base for working here when I finally graduated.

Now, I work 7:00 a.m. to 5:30 p.m. four days a week. Every other weekend is a four-day weekend, so I have Friday and Monday off every other week. It's wonderful. I'm not on call—no nights, no weekends.

This is an extremely isolated area with long distances between places where people live. To get from one of these remote areas to the hospital would take about an hour and a half for those who live farthest away, assuming they're not dealing with mud. Mud is a huge issue in terms of travel. The main highways are paved but off the highway are dirt roads. These roads are sticky clay, almost impassable when wet.

When I first came here, I worked in a clinic where the only people we saw were 75 and older. Primarily I assisted the doctor, inserting IVs for hydration because that's an issue for the elderly. We also did assessments and met with families to try to make living at home safer for their elders.

Public Health Nursing

Public health nursing is extremely varied. Although we see individual patients, our focus is on population health. Right now, we're finishing up our flu shot clinic, where we go out into the community and the schools to give as many flu immunizations as we can. We respond to referrals from physicians to visit individual patients in their homes: we provide safety evaluations, deliver prenatal and postpartum care, assess newborns, and provide their parents with needed education. We help people manage their chronic diseases, especially diabetes assessment and education, in the home.

We also have individual projects. Mine is breastfeeding. I'm an international board-certified lactation consultant. I take referrals for breastfeeding. I also take on breastfeeding projects like community awareness and a lot of staff education.

Public health nurses investigate to try to stop the spread of contagious infections, like whooping cough. If we are aware of someone with whooping cough, we try to find as many people as we can who may have come into close contact with that person to treat, immunize, and prevent its spread. We do the same thing with diseases like salmonella. If we see someone with salmonella, we'll try to determine how that person got it and who else in the family may have been exposed.

On Joy in Work

I define joy in work as wanting to be where I am, being happy to come here in the morning, and feeling periods of satisfaction and accomplishment at least once a day—for example, when I feel I've connected with a patient and the patient has heard what I have to teach them. This is difficult to achieve in the community where I work.

There is resentment and suspicion of healthcare professionals here for many reasons. I have to break through that to get people to trust me. And I don't have long. I have less than five minutes to make that happen, to give people the information I need to give them, to assess what I need to assess and get out of there. We don't often—occasionally, but not often—have ongoing relationships with patients. We get a referral, we respond to the referral, next patient. I don't know exactly how to describe how I get people to trust me, but I do something with my eyes and my voice that says, "I'm a mama and a grandma and no threat to you. But I care about you." I don't touch them, hardly ever, because that's really invading their space; I'm still a stranger. If they're upset, if they're crying, and if I feel that they are open to it I will hug, I will put an arm across the shoulders, I will put my hand on a shoulder or hold a hand. But not as a general rule. And I have to really judge their openness to that. I think I learned to judge that as a midwife.

Connecting with individual patients and getting them to trust me doesn't happen every day. But there are other things that bring me joy. We had a flu clinic at the local high school, and we gave 572 shots in two and a half hours. I organized all of that. I felt a lot of joy in that. That was a major accomplishment. If I've done breastfeeding counseling with a mother and I find out months later that she is still breastfeeding, I feel a lot of satisfaction. If I have inspired another staff member to be more supportive of breastfeeding, there's a lot of joy in that. Sometimes there are just small things that I can't even describe but I feel, *Yeah, that was good.*

I had one instance yesterday, when I had gone to see a patient who wasn't expecting a visit. She felt I was checking up on her. I wrote, in my brief note, that she'd had that attitude. And I got a note of apology from the doctor, saying "I'm sorry, I thought I had communicated it better with the patient, and I realize I put you in an unfair position." I thought, *Oh, my God, that's never happened before.* It really made me feel good. And then, when a doctor sent an email about how I inspire him, I thought again, *Oh, my God.* It was wonderful!

When people feel better after I see them, that does change their attitude for the next time. Definitely. Sometimes even just seeing me again does that, even if they weren't responsive the first time. Nurses and doctors here come and go; they may be here for two or three months and then they disappear. People feel there's no point in creating a relationship because their nurses and doctors are just going to leave. When they say, "It's you again, you're still here," and I tell them, "I'm not going anywhere," that really helps the connection.

On Money and Joy

I think there is a relationship between money and joy because money gives you options. I know that a lot of money can create stress, but enough money can relieve stress. I'm paid well enough that I can go to visit my grandchildren three or four times a year.

What Diminishes Joy

Office politics diminishes joy in work for me: territorialism, control, other people's laziness. Sometimes territorialism will show up as, "This is my idea, my job, my plan and I don't want you to step into my space." But territorialism also applies to, literally, land. Here's an example: public health nurses here are assigned areas, or territories. In my opinion, the borders are gray. If I get a referral and it's a mile outside my border but I'm already out there, I just go and take care of it. But some say, "This is my area, I'm not stepping over the line." The people who don't want to go outside of their territory are implying, "Oh, well, I can pass this off to somebody else."

People bring their own baggage to each job. I work with people who are passive-aggressive—they don't seem to know how to say, "I have a problem; I need you to do this." Instead, they'll go and tell everyone else they have a problem with you. Gossip is a huge problem. Psychologists call this triangulation. It makes me crazy. And I hate my boss; that doesn't help.

My boss makes unreasonable demands; he's a bully and enjoys putting people on the spot and shaming them. He is this way to everyone, not just to me. I hate it. The way this organization deals with problems is to have a training. So, if we complain that our boss is a bully, we'll have to go through a training on how to deal with bullies. Our boss won't have to attend. The way I deal with this is to ignore him. I try to stay off his radar and I try not to care. The good part of it is I have a lot of autonomy, I'm not in the office every minute. And the money is good.

I hate my boss, but I don't let him get under my skin. I did. I went to a therapist who said, "You're taking him home with you." I said, "You're right." I don't take him home with me anymore. I not only don't take him home with me, but he doesn't come into my office. He doesn't come inside my head. Because, really, people only exist the way they live in our heads. I let him pass through, but nobody gets to camp out here.

This is an extremely dysfunctional organization, which is a big reason people leave. Turnover is frequent. Every year a handful of people leave. They hire new people. It takes a long time. While waiting for new hires the people who are left carry the load. We're taken so much for granted. The attitude of leadership is, "That's life. Get on with it. If you don't like it, leave."

I occasionally feel overloaded by work, but I have learned that if I don't get it done, nobody really cares. I have a good work ethic, but I have learned not to make myself crazy. If I don't get something done it will still be here tomorrow. My patients don't pressure me; most of them don't know I'm coming. It's not as if I have a clinic full of patients waiting to see me. They're just doing their thing at home and suddenly I appear, out of nowhere.

Apart from money, I do not feel sufficiently rewarded by my bosses, administrators, or colleagues for my work. When I do hear something good it doesn't sound sincere; it sounds canned. Because of my work ethic, and partly because I'm older and know how to manage my time and prioritize, I get a lot done. Way more than anybody else. And nothing. Just nothing.

Becoming an international board-certified lactation consultant is a big freaking deal. It involves a year of study, at least, 500 hours of breastfeeding counseling, and the hardest exam I ever took in my life. As I said, it's a big freaking deal. Nobody here even blinked when they found out I had this certification.

If the administration sees a problem in delivering care, it's because they think the nurses aren't doing enough. I may see a more systemic problem but, somehow, they just don't see systemic problems.

Advice

My advice for anyone in a work environment is, find your own path. Find your own satisfaction. Find your own way of dealing. Your own strengths. As opposed to constantly looking to your co-workers and looking to your boss to make you happy. Most nurses are codependent. We're serving, serving, serving, serving in order to feel complete. In order to feel we're good enough. I think it's possible to serve without being codependent, and that's what I'm working on, to see serving the patient as an act in itself, by itself; that I'm only an instrument, and that my self-esteem is not on the line. I don't want to let myself be defined by what people think of me. I'm good enough on days when I'm not good enough because, overall, I am good.

28. Eliot D., MD, Internal Medicine Officer for a Rural Integrated Health System

Eliot D., MD, has worked for an integrated health system in a remote part of the United States for almost two years. He was drawn to global health work first in South Africa and then in this country, feeling most fulfilled when working with the underserved.

I took a bit of a circuitous route into medicine. I grew up in a suburban, relatively affluent environment and was exposed to many people in medicine. I didn't think much about it at the time, but I was aware that looking up to my mom, who was a physician, and to my grandfather, who was also a physician, played a huge role in my wanting to go into medicine. In college I was interested in engineering and became a history major. I floated around for a while and ultimately finished pre-medicine courses after a summer working in an HIV research lab. I thought that was fascinating. But what I thought was missing in research was the patient. I really wanted to see the impact of that research on people. That's when I decided to go to medical school.

I took a year off after college and worked at odd jobs. I realized that my strength was talking to people. And there's no better way to help people and get to know them on an intimate and deep level than to be a physician.

I loved medical school. They were the four best years of education I've ever had—my teachers, my peers, my patients, everything about the training was great. My trajectory from there was residency. I chose internal medicine for a couple of reasons. For one, I wanted to work with underserved populations. I think that probably was true before I went to medical school. Doing global health work and working in HIV research landed me a rotation in South Africa. Seeing the extremes of poverty and lack of health access resonated with me from an early stage in my medical training. That stayed with me as I saw inner-city patients at the public hospital during medical school. I had very meaningful relationships with some patients. I learned so much about their hardships and their lack of access to care.

As a medical student I'd gone to a noontime grand rounds lecture and, at the time, I was considering doing global health work in Ethiopia. At the lecture, a former chief resident talked about his wonderful experiences working with the underserved in a rural area in the United States after his training and residency, and highlighted many parallels between global health and working with the underserved in such areas, whether this had to do with life expectancy, later presentation of pathology, or a stark lack of access to resources. I was impacted by that ground rounds and thought about it when I was applying for jobs at the end of my own residency. I wanted to go into rural primary care here, but I was also thinking about doing global health work. I finally decided that working with the underserved in this country would be the perfect situation. I was drawn to working with this population and to learning about a new culture.

The population with which I work lives very remotely and faces large health disparities. I'm not sure of the exact numbers, but a considerable percentage of our patients don't have running water or electricity. There are six to eight clinical sites scattered around this part of the country. Our town has very small population, yet I'm told we serve a clinical population of about 30,000 people who live around the area. People have to travel far for their care.

My job title is internal medicine medical officer and I work in a clinic. Before this I worked as a hospitalist. This is a small community hospital with fewer than 25 medical/surgical beds and only a handful of intensive care beds. We have capacity to treat certain things, but the challenge is in the triage and management of more medically complex patients. In my role as a hospitalist there was variety in the types of patients I treated. Patients would either come in sick to the emergency room or they would have gone to their clinic appointment, wouldn't feel well, and because they couldn't be managed in the clinic, they would be admitted.

As a hospitalist, I would be on cumulatively for 80–90 hours each week and off for about 10–12 hours each day. More recently, I'm working at our facility's clinic, where the hours are quite good. There, I work four to five days a week, from 8:00 a.m. until 6:00 or 7:00 p.m., which amounts to about 50 hours a week, with most weekends off, and occasional overnight call. I like working with sicker patients and taking care of them in the hospital, but after my first year in that role, I started to realize how tired I could get and know I have to pace myself.

Almost all of our patients are medically complex. If a young, healthy person were to come in with pneumonia, the hospital would be a perfectly fine place to treat her. But if somebody were to come in with diabetes, and he's already had bilateral below-the-knee amputations, is wheelchair-bound, has had three heart attacks, is morbidly obese, had complicated bloodstream infections last year, and comes in with a fever and pneumonia and requires intubation, that is not the kind of person we can sufficiently care for here with limited resources. We have to triage those patients, fly them to a hospital where they can be treated. We do have many patients who are that complicated because of lack of early diagnosis and a high prevalence of diabetes and obesity.

Another of my roles is medical educator. We have partnerships with medical schools across the country, and students and residents rotate through for a month as part of their clinical training. There is a strong public health nursing team based in our hospital and clinic. They drive to remote places to be sure the patients' medications are working, for example. The students and residents go out with public health nurses once or twice a week and they love it. They get to see how people live.

We can get to know how people live when we take care of them in the hospital, too. My wife and I both took care of a patient who was in her mid-40s and has five kids. She suffered from severe alcohol use disorder. She often had to be in the hospital for weeks. After being discharged from the hospital, she stayed sober for nine months; but her liver failure progressed, and she had to be readmitted. She was highly motivated to try to get a liver transplant but died before she could be treated by a transplant team. She was trying so hard. We are confronted with that a lot here.

On the hospital side of things, I would sometimes keep readmitting the same patients for complications of diabetes. Some patients' complications from diabetes would be preventable, but the underlying psychiatric component of severe depression plus generational post-traumatic stress disorder often causes people to struggle with their self-worth. They don't feel able to take care of themselves, and some are constantly readmitted to the hospital.

On Joy in Work

I think joy in work means making a connection with the patient. It is very rewarding when patients feel I listen to them. And I can pick up on that in subtle ways, whether it's that they are eager to show up or that they smile or joke at the end of the encounter. Joy for me is establishing a connection with a patient, making a patient feel empowered, letting patients know they can come to me and that together we can try to better their health. Joy is a partnership between the patient and the physician.

I love it here. I find it really rewarding. There are a lot of hard days and tough patients, both clinically and emotionally; but when we talk to our peers who work in the inner cities, we feel sheltered from some of the demands they face. It's an adventure.

Working with my peer group is highly rewarding. My group here is very close. We all live in the same section of housing near the hospital and we all work together; we socialize together; we work long hours at the hospital and then we come home and make dinners or have potlucks. We do home improvement projects together. I'm off today and we're about to drive off to go camping for the weekend. There are probably 30 or 40 doctors here. They come from all walks of life. Some of them have been here for decades and they are great role models.

On Money and Joy

I think there can be a relationship between too much money and not enough joy. Too much money and you won't be happy, too little money you definitely won't be happy. Moderation is key. I took a slight pay cut to work here but I also have minimal cost of living. I didn't go into medicine to make money. If I had wanted to make more money, I would have chosen a different career path.

What Diminishes Joy

Administrative responsibilities can diminish joy in work for me. Our training isn't designed for us to be administrators, it's designed for us to be physicians. Sometimes, the number of administrative tasks that have to get done drives me nuts. For example, if someone is supposed to be in the hospital for less than 48 hours but ends up staying longer, I'll have to justify why they stayed, in writing, even though I've been taking care of the patient and documenting the patient's condition daily in all my notes. It may not sound like a lot from the outside, but when you break it down to having to review their case, take the time to fill out their paperwork again, find the person to give the paperwork to, have the paperwork be refused and then send it back, that's time-consuming, distracting, and frustrating.

Cutting down on some of the administrative demands of work would enhance my joy. We're responsible for documentation, billing, and medical records. All that takes so much time. Just coming out of residency, with the electronic medical record being the reality in which I trained, it's not too bad. But for other physicians the EMR is a huge time drain. We don't have specialists here, so we refer patients elsewhere to see a specialist. Our healthcare system has grown so much that we have almost too much information on everybody and it is challenging to utilize the most important information.

The average age of our patient population is 37—very young. But we have quite a large aging population in their 80s and 90s. Probably one-third of the patients I manage in the hospital are elderly with dementia needing end-of-life care. There are three rooms in the hospital that we use as an inpatient hospice. We can accommodate them for about a week. But if they live longer than that, an awkward scenario ensues, and I am caught in the middle between the hospital and the family. I want to do the respectful thing for the patient and family. That's a challenge because I'm not a very confrontational person.

Often, in a physician role, we sometimes have to step up and take responsibility when something goes wrong with a patient's care. It may not be something I necessarily did or caused, but I think it's my role to convey why an error was made, how it happened, and what we are trying to do to make it better. If you have trust in the patient and the patient's family, they often trust you and you don't feel blamed. That's the fundamental truth. I think my shift to clinic work will be good for my continuity of care and relationships with patients. But there are definitely times I do feel blamed when something goes wrong.

Overall, I love my job and wouldn't change anything on a big scale. Even in the busiest times, it's important to remember the patient comes first. We were taught in medical school to remember this: As bad as your day is, the patient who is sick in front of you is probably having a worse day.

29.   *Paula C., MD, Orthopedic Hand Surgeon*

Paula C., MD, has been an orthopedic surgeon—still an uncommon specialty for a woman—for 20 years. Having worked in private practice and hospital settings, she talks about the pitfalls of private practice, her perspective on hospitals, and her feelings about the health insurance industry, the electronic medical record (EMR), and sexism in the workplace.

My dad is a doctor, so I grew up around medicine. I thought everyone's father worked 15 hours a day. He was very old-school; he saw his patients in one little office, had a nurse and a secretary, and that was him for over 40 years. He made house calls. I would go with him on Sundays after church and I'd get to carry his little black bag. I thought going around to see patients was just the best; they were so happy to see us. I knew how to take people's blood pressure when I was nine years old and by that time, I'd decided I wanted to be a doctor. It seemed like a very rewarding field.

As I went through the clinical subjects in medical school, I really liked the hands-on kinds of work, so the surgical specialties appealed to me. I especially liked fixing things and I was athletic, so I gravitated to orthopedics. There was a female physician in our town who was an orthopedic surgeon. I'd known her all my life and thought she was so awesome and inspiring, and I thought, *I can do that.* Female mentors in orthopedics remain somewhat rare. We still make up less than 10% of orthopedic surgeons.

I trained in an urban center in the 1990s. Cases included multi-traumas, total joint replacements, spine surgery, pediatrics, sports, oncology, and hand surgery. I was fascinated by the intricacies of hand surgery. Trying to piece someone's hand back together or correct deformities was such powerful, transformative work. Preserving hand function can make a huge impact on people's lives.

I decided to do a hand fellowship to hone these skills and to learn more specialty-specific skills like wrist arthroscopy, ligament reconstructions, and tendon reconstructions.

What My Job Entails

I'm currently on staff at a 200-bed community hospital outside a city with a population of about 155,000. I work for the hospital. I've been in this area of the country for 19 years. I have had other hospital affiliations and practice settings but have geographically stayed put. I like working here because it's an underserved area and that appeals to me.

My hours vary. Meetings or OR start times bring me in at 7:00 a.m. Clinic days usually run until 4:00 p.m. After seeing patients there is usually paperwork to finish and phone calls to make. Days rarely finish before 6:00 p.m.

My job entails seeing patients who might be referred to me from either their physician or from emergency rooms. There are post-operative patients who come for re-checks and cast changes. I have some patients whom I've taken care of for years who have various conditions, like rheumatoid arthritis. I'm fortunate that my patient base has been fairly stable. Some patients have been with me for all my 20 years in practice.

My Professional Journey

The Realities of Private Practice

For nearly a decade I was an independent physician in a small group practice. The office was small, and we ran a pretty lean ship. The guys I worked with were great. Two of them have since retired, and the other is employed by a local hospital. Our practice was there for a long time but with ever-declining reimbursements and a high percentage of patients who were either uninsured or on subsidized care, it became increasingly difficult to keep the doors open. The costs kept going up and our reimbursements kept going down.

Even though a hospital's money is tight, they do get federal funding and they do get at least some pennies on the dollar for service to underserved areas. They may be able to write that off more readily than I ever could in private practice. In private practice if I'd do surgery on someone, and provide all the aftercare a patient would need and that person had no insurance, our practice would eat that. And we would have all the liability. The hospital has at least some mechanisms to recoup some of that. The business of medicine has changed dramatically in the 20 years I've been in practice and this will likely continue.

Hospitals

Although similar, not all hospitals are the same; each has its own culture. That's often dictated by whomever is the leader of a particular hospital. Some hospitals do a better job than others to provide the framework and infrastructure so that doctors can function effectively, others not so much. The widespread consolidation of medical entities and the effect of turnover can disrupt the hospital environment. You can't keep track sometimes of how much things change—people who made really bad decisions, or really good decisions, might be gone in another year. It's very hard to develop relationships with anyone on the administrative end if they're going to be gone in less than a year. But that seems to be the way of the world these days.

On Joy in Work

What does joy in work mean to me? Being able to help others is a central tenet for me. You can make such a positive impact on people; that's a huge driver and brings a great deal of satisfaction. Treating the underserved appeals to me. Our profession has a responsibility to do that, and that aligns with many of my values personally.

On Money and Joy

I am the sole breadwinner in my family. Knowing that I'm providing for my family makes me feel good. I want to help them do the things they want to do, aside from the obvious things like providing a house, food, and other necessities. I want them to experience unique opportunities and get a good education. To make these things possible for my children is really important to me, and it does bring me joy.

What Diminishes Joy

The Health Insurance Industry

Patients often are overwhelmed by the whole complexity of the insurance industry—and this is true whether they have subsidized insurance or insurance of another kind. They don't realize that certain physicians or healthcare entities don't subscribe to whatever insurance plan they have, and this narrows their access to care a great deal. I think the inequities in our current insurance system create an urgency for patients that doesn't need to exist.

Access to care can shut down in short order if insurance companies and hospitals can't come to agreement on rates. Also, businesses are changing their insurance companies frequently in an effort to stem rising costs. And, all of a sudden, their employees find they can't go back to see Dr. so-and-so. There are all sorts of complexities like these that add to the burden of access for patients, and that is frustrating. That's what I take umbrage at—that this has been allowed to propagate.

The Electronic Medical Record

The EMR definitely diminishes joy in work for me. The EMR is the source of a lot of frustration for many physicians. It was not borne out of clinical need but rather a financial one. Despite what the various companies will tell you—I mean, we're not going to get rid of it now, it's in the water supply, we have to deal with it—EMR documentation is hard. It's good to have standardization; I get it, we want to cover certain bases clinically. But when I do my documentation it's the story of that patient that is meaningful to me. So, the next time that patient comes in, I can see what our conversation was about, what I found, and what the differential diagnosis was and what plan we came up with. I don't need my staff to be taking their blood pressure every time they come in; I just don't. But a lot of tasks are done to click off boxes so we'll get paid and not be accused of fraud, which, with all the complexities of documentation, is an ever-present risk—not because of malfeasance but just because the process is so complex. My office is burdened with a very un-user-friendly EMR. We will be switching to a larger one, supposedly sometime this year. There are a lot of manual workarounds the staff has to do, tasks that can chip away at both their time and emotional energy.

Responding to the Opioid Problem

We're under a lot of pressure in regard to the use of opioids and there have been a slew of regulatory changes. I think these changes are good, but the double-edged sword is that responding to these changes is burdensome. We have to take a certain number of continuing medical education credits. We have to look up the medications on the website each time we prescribe something. Now insurance companies have jumped on the bandwagon, and they're making it more difficult because now we have to get preauthorization for narcotics in some instances.

Work Overload

I often feel overloaded by work; I just never quite feel done. Trying to keep the life-work balance is a constant challenge. When I finish seeing patients at 4:00 or 5:00 p.m., I have to make phone calls until 6:00 p.m., and start dictating or doing whatever paperwork or documentation I need to do for however many patients I saw that day. Let's say I see 30–32 patients a day—I've still got to document all that. Some of it is quick, but some of it's not. The OR can run late, and cases can be delayed. All of that can drag the days out and be exhausting.

Lack of Work–Life Balance

I often joke that I am not the poster child for life-work balance. Work can easily upend plans and can chip away at family time. Mindfulness and learning to say "no" to some demands can protect family time, but it is hard. Then there is self-care: trying to get in enough exercise and recreation. Having entered my 50s, I'm keenly aware that I need to spend more time cultivating my own friends, my own contacts. I think a lot of parents feel that way, that as their kids get older, they have a lot of kid-related activities but not as many of their own.

Sexism

In training there was the garden-variety kind of sexism such as other residents thinking female residents were not "tough" enough; getting mistaken for nurses; being talked over; being talked down to; all the usual. Thankfully little of that has carried over into practice. The people I've worked with in my private practice settings I got along with very well. In my first practice coming out of fellowship the guys were great. I did not feel that I was treated as a second-class citizen. My senior partner's daughter was a general surgeon in town, so they were very comfortable with the idea of a female surgeon. In practice I've tried to be mindful to be inclusive and to amplify the voices of the other female physicians. There are still not enough women in positions of authority. This is changing but just so damn slowly.

Advice

There are many challenges and burnout is real. I know doctors who have checked out a little early because they could. They retired, they got out. We're going to be facing a critical shortage, I think, in the next five years. But despite these challenges, I think medicine is still a very rewarding field. Medical students need to know that. I'm very lucky. I don't meet many people who get to do what they dreamed about doing when they were nine.

30.   Angela DeVanney, BA, Executive Director of the AMD3 Foundation

Angela DeVanney is Executive Director of the AMD3 Foundation, an organization focused on research and education in joint replacement and arthritis. The primary program of the AMD3 Foundation is Operation Walk Pittsburgh, which provides joint replacements free of charge to those in need in the Pittsburgh community and throughout Central America. Angela manages the operations of the Foundation and acts as translator on Operation Walk missions in Central America.

Operation Walk Pittsburgh, sponsored by the AMD3 Foundation, is a volunteer humanitarian medical organization that aims to provide life-changing education, service, and surgery free of charge to patients in need in Pittsburgh and throughout Central America.

My job is primarily focused on the operations of the AMD3 Foundation. I make sure that both from a fundraising perspective and an operational perspective, we are prepared for our missions and provide promised services to the patients we've identified to receive them. This means everything from fundraising locally and nationwide—because our teams come from all over the country and not just from Pittsburgh—to working with the ministries of health and administration teams in the countries and hospitals we partner with. We identify patients who will receive joint replacements ahead of time and teach our partners abroad how patients should be prescreened. We do this by phone and by email.

Our volunteers take time off from their jobs to work with us and pay for own their trips. It is a huge commitment. For our trips to Central America, we take every type of role and process that exists in the United States and replicate them there: surgeons, surgery teams, nursing staff, physical therapists, medical assistants, central sterile processing techs and surgical techs, and x-ray techs who are cross-trained to do other things. Many of these volunteers make minimum wage at home—so their commitment is awe-inspiring and speaks volumes as to how much they get out of these trips.

I started with Operation Walk when I worked at the IHI. It was our very first trip, in 2009. The IHI had given me 50% of the time to go on the trip. One of the requirements was to give a presentation at a staff meeting when I came back, which I did. I remember meeting with my boss, a nurse, who asked, "You're going to leave us, aren't you?"

One of the things I enjoyed at IHI was having a connection with clinicians. I supported them in data-crunching, report writing, and process improvement efforts. I spent probably eight hours a day on conference calls with them and heard what their daily lives were like. That gave me a glimpse into the chaos that exists in healthcare, but also into their dedication to delivering outstanding and high-quality patient care. My experience at IHI led me to take that leap into the unknown. I wanted to share, somehow, in the joy that clinicians expressed in their daily work.

I worked as a Spanish translator starting on that first Operation Walk trip to Guatemala in 2009, and I have done this for the last ten years. That first year, I was the only translator and it was a "trial by fire" in the truest sense. I translate from clinician to clinician and from patient to clinician. The first time I did this it was overwhelming. I was worried I was going to say something incorrectly or make a mistake because I'm not a native speaker. It was exhausting because I was constantly having to do the mental flip of switching back and forth. But it's gotten much easier over time.

On Joy in Work

Being a translator has brought me tremendous joy because the patients look to me and to the other translators for everything—everything from pain relief all the way to asking, "Can you call my family and tell them I'm okay?" Patients have always thought we translators play a critical role. We tell them we're not clinicians when they ask us questions about their care, but they would look to us as their lifeline because most of them have never been in a hospital, never had surgery, and many of them are afraid. This is the only chance for most of these people to have this surgery; it makes all the difference between their being active, productive members of society and being stuck.

When we start to see patients go home and see how excited they are because they can walk—and many are crying because some of them have never walked in their entire lives—that is really when I feel the most joy. Patients are happy, our staff is on Cloud Nine because the patients are happy, and they quickly see the fruits of their labor. In most large hospitals here you don't see a patient through the entire care process; you just see whatever your piece of the silo is. But there you get to see everything.

For me, now, the only thing that diminishes that experience is knowing I will never have those new eyes again. That's why it is really fun for me to work with people who have never had an experience like it, to try to put myself in their shoes, and see that experience through their new eyes.

In the U.S., with the hustle and bustle and the many distractions, the human side of healthcare can be lost. On our missions we truly get back to basics. What provides me with daily joy is seeing the excitement on people's faces who are often burned out in the U.S. by their work—to see the joy on their faces remembering why they went into healthcare to begin with. One of the surgeons who goes on these missions always says, "Everyone is very well trained to do exactly the job we do. But when we do it in a different place, we feel like rock stars." He is absolutely right.

Autonomy and Control

31.   *Amir F., MD, FACP, Internist and Vice President of a Small Internal*
        Medicine Group Practice and Chair of a Group of 25 Practices
        Based on the Patient-Centered Medical Home

> Amir F., MD, FACP, has practiced internal medicine for 38 years. As partner and vice president of a small group primary care practice, his lack of autonomy and control over his work—including the daily need for preauthorizations and precertifications, pressure to see more patients in less time, and payers' unreasonable demands for quality metrics—led to burnout. When a payer's enlightened chief medical officer came along and asked, "Are you happy?" his blunt answer released a cascade of resources that coincided with the start of value-based, rather than fee-for-service, care. All this, plus his involvement in a CMS pilot project, has led Amir to recapture his joy in work.

I knew I wanted to be a doctor when I was a young boy. I was interested in medicine and biology and the health sciences. Being a doctor was the only thing I had in mind. I didn't think of any other line of work at all. My father was a businessman and always supported us in whatever we wanted to do. I had a passion for medicine, and I wanted to serve other human beings by treating and maintaining their health.

Our small primary care practice has seven providers: two family physicians, one nurse practitioner, and the rest are internists like me. In terms of administration, we are three partners. One of the partners is president. I am vice president. We also have an office manager, a non-clinical supervisor, a clinical supervisor, and 35 staff. We have about 10,000 patients. I also have another job: I am chair of a group of 25 practices with 180 doctors based on the principles of the patient-centered medical home that continues to grow. That is my administrative work. Twice a week I do that.

Let me define my workday to help explain how I juggle between my clinical role and my nonclinical role. I leave home at 6:45 in the morning. By 7:00 a.m. I am in the office. I turn on my computer and there are a few things waiting for me, which include refilling medications, looking at lab results, and finishing triages that I couldn't finish the previous day. At 7:20 a.m. we have what we call "huddle." Huddle is a brief meeting of people from the administrative office, the manager, the receptionist, the clinical supervisor, and the nurses. In the huddle, staff go through the slots open for that day for all seven providers to see which are available for same-day appointments. We promise our patients we will see them within 24 hours to prevent them from going to the ER or to an urgent care facility.

In the huddle, the nurse goes through all the patients we are scheduled to see that day so we can try to close those patients' clinical gaps as soon as they come in. For example, if they've not had a colonoscopy in ten years, right away the patient will be informed that they need a colonoscopy. Or immunizations. Things for which I want to improve our quality metrics. Huddle takes about two to three minutes and we know our "battle plan" for the day.

On average I see about 16 patients a day. I used to see between 24 and 30 patients a day. I started reducing the number because of the burnout and exhaustion I was starting to feel. We have developed a new strategy for taking care of our patients. We've started acting more smartly. We can do a lot of things online—in the past ten minutes I've had two e-visits for simple things like nasal congestion and a rash. There was no need for these patients to come in. They sent pictures, they asked questions, and I responded.

We are part of a CMS pilot project, which I'll talk more about soon. We are very lucky to have been chosen for that; as a result, we have gone the virtual way of taking care of our patients and, as a result, we take care of patients in a more proactive way than we used to. For example, a patient with diabetes whose diabetes is well controlled does not really have to come and see me. She can send me her numbers online through our secure automated system. About 41% of our patients interact with us through computer. A portal system allows us to take care of our patients without having to see them face to face.

When our reimbursement model changed from fee-for-service to value-based care, there was really no need to see as many patients in the office. Value-based care is almost capitated. The insurance companies give us a global payment, in which there's a base payment, which means there is a regular cash flow to run the practice and we don't have to deliver care in the old fee-for-service model. That global payment emphasizes alternative ways of managing patients. One of the things we wanted to achieve was to control the cost of care. For example, we make sure the patient gets the right kind of medication but there's no need for a brand name; we can use generic medications that do the same thing at lower cost. With the global payment I don't have to document unnecessary information. It's a win-win for everybody—for the payer, for us, and for the patients.

On Joy in Work

Going into work with all my heart with a passion to see my patients, being able to meet their needs, and having a positive outcome is how I define joy in work.

Today I saw a patient who has Alzheimer's and she came in with her husband. Of course, the person who has Alzheimer's doesn't feel it, but the spouse feels it. For a couple of years, we've been talking together, and today her husband gave me a card. He couldn't say it, but on the card, he wrote, "Thank you, doctor. A special thanks to you from me." Those are the things that bring me real joy.

My administrative work absolutely gives me joy—it's just taking care of our patients from a different angle. For example, payers place a burden on providers to define quality metrics and outcomes. What I struggle with is to make sure the payers don't put so many demands on the physicians in the 25-practice group I chair that their joy is depleted. For example, the payers would like physicians to take care of 125 quality metrics; I tell them we will focus on five.

On Money and Joy

Is there a relation between money and joy? This is a very good question. A few years ago, we were incentivized by a payer who gave us a bonus to start something. The joy lasted, maybe, for half an hour. So, forget about it. I think money doesn't bring joy. The joy, really, when you go into medicine, is to see your patients getting well. Or improving. Or taking care of them during their terminal stage of life.

Yesterday, my first patient was a patient I've known for the last 24 years. Her husband had died. When she came to the office, of course she broke down. We hugged each other and I sat down next to her and talked to her and helped her. At the end of the session she said, "Doc, that was really helpful. I feel so much better." When a patient tells you that, that brings me more joy than any amount of money can bring. Of course, money is important. We need money. But it doesn't bring joy to your heart.

What Diminishes Joy

Prior Authorization

Unnecessary bureaucracy, such as the need for prior authorization, takes away from my joy in work. Why do I as a doctor have to ask the payer to authorize treatment? Ninety-five percent of the time they do authorize it. It's unnecessary work for me and for my staff. For example, I prescribe a medication that requires prior authorization. I ask my staff to call the insurance company so we can get approval for that medication. So now I have to deal with my staff; they get on the phone and sometimes I have to talk to the medical director of the insurance company. Or, I'll write a prescription and it goes to the pharmacy. The pharmacy sends a note back saying this medication needs a prior authorization. I have to talk to the pharmacist. I have to justify this medication, which sometimes is a common one. But because it is not on the formulary of that insurance company, I have to go through another layer of bureaucracy to get that approved. This takes away the joy of patient care.

Getting prior authorization from payers has always been a big burden. We struggle with them all the time—it is just ridiculous. If you want to put your patients first, why do you need prior authorization? Fortunately, we have a good payer that works in partnership with us, listens to us, and helps us with the process. With our payer on board there's more joy in practicing medicine. Payers typically put demands on doctors that overburden the whole system, not just clinicians, but nonclinical staff as well. Not a day goes by without needing prior authorization for something. I have a good staff who spends two hours every day working on this, which they could utilize in a more productive manner.

Quality Metrics

Our autonomy is gone in relation to quality metrics, too. Because we did not take charge of our destiny, payers have taken over. And we depend on their money. We have to show the payers that we are improving the quality of care. And how do we do that? We can't interview thousands of patients; we need some numbers. So how do we quantify the quality of work we are doing? We did not quantify it ourselves, so now payers are putting the onus on us to do it.

Burnout

I felt 100% burned out when I was seeing 24–30 patients a day. There was always two to three hours' extra work waiting for me after I finished seeing patients, no doubt about it. Burnout is emotional fatigue and physical fatigue. When I was burned out, I felt exhausted. When I got out of bed I felt as if going to work was another chore and there was no joy in it. Burnout manifests itself in being grumpy, skeptical. Small things could make me flare up. Taking blood pressure felt like a burden. That is burnout.

From Burnout to Joy

I don't feel burned out now. Number one, I reduced my workload. Instead of seeing 24–30 patients a day I see close to only 16 patients a day. I can sit and listen to my patients, discuss with them and sort out their problems. I have modified my schedule. My schedule is 20/40: I see one patient for 20 minutes, the next one for 40 minutes. So even if a patient comes in with a small problem like a sore throat, I take advantage of the time. Sore throat treatment may take three to five minutes. But I take the next 15 minutes to talk to the patient and identify those clinical gaps that need to be filled: we talk about their need for a colonoscopy or a mammogram, for example. I have more time now. I don't have to rush through and write notes and all those other things.

Moving from Fee-for-Service to Value-Based Care

Our switch from fee-for-service to value-based care came about because we had one insurance company that was proactive. The chief medical officer came to my office eight years ago and asked me whether I was happy at work. I looked at him and thought, *what is this guy dreaming of?* I asked, "Can you repeat the question?" and he asked me again. It was the first question he asked. I told him of course I was not happy, I was just feeling like a person on the assembly line, doing the work and getting out of here at the end of the day. I was not feeling satisfied. I was not doing the work I was cut out to do. Before he asked me that question I felt like a hamster on a wheel. There was no happiness, no joy. I was burned out.

That chief medical officer asked me to join the patient-centered medical home advisory committee, where I had a chance to interact with patients. That started the ball rolling. There were five patients on that committee. I realized that when the patients come into the office we talk about their clinical problems. But I didn't know they were also suffering the pangs of system dysfunction. They talked about segmentation of care and duplication of tests and multiple other things. They were getting burned out going from one specialist to another specialist. They didn't know how to navigate the system. They wanted somebody to coordinate care.

We formed a team of what is now 25 physician groups with 180 physicians and multiple sub-teams. One of the sub-teams, the integrated care team, has worked hard to develop strategic partnerships with specialists. We've looked into how to evaluate quality metrics by asking, what quality metrics are important for all patients, not just for the purposes of data collection? And then, of course, value-based reimbursement was coming along to control costs, which was a win-win for us, because we'd always struggled to maintain a cash flow to pay the staff and ourselves and to run the practice. We have made tremendous progress, and, in the process, have de-burdened ourselves. Our value-based care really started last year. But even before that the payer was putting into place quality incentives and resources to help us reduce burnout. They weren't tackling burnout directly, but they did reduce burnout by helping us to improve the system and our processes.

The payer helped us with care management, care coordination, and placed someone in our office, whom they paid for, who was dedicated to taking care of our high-risk patients: patients who had multiple admissions to the hospital, patients with multiple diagnoses, and those who ended up in the ER or urgent care. Of course, the ulterior motive was to reduce costs, but it helped us, too. We did that for three to four years and we no longer have that person here. Instead, we became participants in a five-year CMS pilot project and employ our own staff person to fill that role.

Practice Transformation: The CMS Pilot Project

As participants in a five-year CMS pilot project, we employ a registered nurse who serves as care manager and care coordinator. We are just finishing our first year. We already feel the difference, absolutely. Reimbursement has improved. As I mentioned, we have more e-visits; and because patients don't have to come into the office, we have more time. We hired two more staff members for our performance improvement team. These two people make sure we aren't burdened with paperwork. They fill out the necessary forms. Primary care is inundated with so many forms from so many angles. They take care of that, they take care of getting prior authorizations, and they help fill the clinical gaps in our quality metrics. They don't scribe for us—we write the notes—but they have access to the EMR and can pull out all the pertinent information from the EMR, which they can use when they ask for prior authorizations.

The process of transforming our practice has saved so much time, both clinical time and non-clinical time. Here's an example from the receptionist's point of view: Our receptionist calls patients every day to remind them of their upcoming appointments. That used to take about two hours. Now, we have in place an automated reminder system. There are three ways of reminding patients: we use a phone system, we use email, and we use our portal system. Patients love it, and our staff loves it because the reminder process now takes them less than 20 minutes. The other process we improved was the patient's insurance verification. That used to take the receptionist another two to three hours. Now, a patient's insurance can be verified in five minutes with a process known as "batch" verification. An automated check-in kiosk in our office enables patients to check in themselves rather than having to see the receptionist to check in. We think these changes alone will save eight hours a day of nonclinical time for our staff.

I love the computer. But I don't want to be a slave to my computer, I want the computer to be my slave. My documentation is more refined now and geared to what the patient really needs. As a result, the documents have become smaller and everyone loves it. And as I said, I don't see more than 16 patients a day, so I have more time to document. And I have people to help me. We are one of the first sites to have a new tool called Arcadia population health software and we're really excited about it. It is amazing.

Advice

First, be aware that the system is changing very fast—and accept that. Once you are aware of it, I think it's easier to accept.

Second, if you are at my stage in your career and you feel burned out, recognize it. Accept it. You are a human being. Don't hide it, don't sweep it under the carpet. Seek help. Talk to people. There are a lot of people who are exhausted, burned out, and some of them are outright depressed and addicted to alcohol.

Third, communicate with payers about your differences in how you define quality metrics. My definition of quality is that I take care of a patient, prevent disaster, resolve his acute problem, and the outcome is good. The patient is ambulatory and has not lost his capacity to function. But payers, who are subject to CMS rules and regulations and to insurance regulatory bodies, define quality metrics in their efforts to control how we deliver that care, prevent disaster, or take care of that acute problem. Go out and talk to the payers. Don't be stuck in your lab doing colonoscopies day and night. Talk to them with your colleagues and say this is not the way to define quality metrics. That could lead to reduced stress and to your regaining joy in practicing medicine.

Finally, the medical school curriculum needs to change. New students who are coming out of medical school are being pressurized. The curriculum is still the old-fashioned curriculum that focuses on the science of medicine and research papers but not on the delivery of care. The delivery of care in the marketplace is quite different from what it was. The moment residents become employed, they think, *wow, this is quite different from the way I was trained.* I was never trained in the business of medicine. I had to learn as I went along, which caused frustration. I want the new kids who come out of medical school to be happier when they come out, with full knowledge of how they are going to deliver care, because down the road these doctors will have to fulfill the mandate to improve the quality of care, decrease costs, and improve both provider satisfaction and patient satisfaction. The only way this will happen is if payers demand that the business of medicine becomes part of the curriculum. Payers have a lot of influence on medical education because medical education is university-based, and their hospitals are university-based hospitals. The community needs to demand it, and the payers need to demand it.

32. Cathy U., MSN, Administrative Director of Perioperative Services for a Large Academic Medical Center

Cathy U. has a master's degree in nursing with a concentration in education and leadership. She has worked in surgical services at three hospitals in a large academic medical center for 28 years, with responsibility for everything that happens before and after surgery: pre-operative services for same-day surgery, the preadmissions testing area, and the recovery room. Cathy oversees the OR educators, the OR schedulers, family lounge staffing, and more.

I wanted to go into healthcare because I've always loved taking care of people. There was no particular event that made me want to become a nurse, although I did have a cousin who was about four years older than me who was going to nursing school. Everyone always said how similar we were in personality. She would come back and tell me how much she loved nursing school and all the stories and things she got to do. If there's a story it's that I followed in her footsteps. I even went to the same university as she did and she actually capped me.

On Joy in Work

I love my job. I always have. My biggest joy, when I first started working here, was seeing the many types of patients we would take care of come full circle. I'd see patients and their families who were very anxious about having surgery and I would help bring their anxiety down, keep them calm, educate them, get them ready for surgery, and then get them off to the OR. And then, on the other end, I would see them come back and help take care of their pain or nausea or whatever their issue was, and then educate them and actually see them go home that day and know that they were going to get better. Seeing the process through full circle with those patients was very satisfying compared to what happens on the floor, where patients could be there for days or weeks at a time and you never really heard or saw anything after that. They moved to different floors or you weren't always assigned to them. There wasn't that closure.

My role now as a director is to care for employees, and that is where I find my joy in work. I oversee what happens with patients, but it's seeing staff advance in their careers, educating them, working through processes with them, and seeing the great outcomes we have that gives me joy.

I'm autonomous in my work. My superiors, my managers, have always given me the flexibility to make my own schedule as long as the work gets done. I've always been given the message, "You make the decisions, we will support you." Every manager I've ever had has let me make decisions and run it by them if I had any questions, but they would always support me in those decisions. This has always been a great benefit and has given me joy in working here. That's been true no matter who's been in charge.

I have control over my schedule and have had this control ever since I've been a director. I don't really work fixed hours. I generally try to be here between 7:30 a.m. and 4:00 p.m. on really quiet days, but most of the time I start at 6:30 or 7:00 a.m. and I could be here until 5:00 or 6:00 at night. I base my hours on what's going on that day and what meetings I have.

I report to the hospital vice president of operations and he reports to the president of the hospital; the communication up and down is very solid. They listen to me. If I have an issue,

I take it to them. An issue is taken up, or over, or to anyone it needs to be communicated to. These people are not clinical so there may be clinical things they don't understand. But if I explain it in lay terms—and I think they've been here long enough—they understand what I'm telling them. They try everything to give me the resources I need to help fix the problem.

I've worked myself up from a staff nurse and up through management to where I am, and I don't believe I'd want to go any higher than where I am right now. I'm very satisfied with my work and challenged at the same time. I don't miss patient care because if I want to go out there and go into the rooms and start working with patients, I can do that at any time.

I haven't really felt the effects of the nursing shortage until the past year. But the tension is real and I'm feeling it. The fact that I've had a pretty steady staff helps in my joy. Once you have staffing issues—and I hear horror stories from a lot of other departments and directors—you just don't have the staff, and the directors are working the night shifts and filling in the holes and coming in on weekends. I've never, ever had to do that. And if I had to start doing that, I don't think I'd like my job too much anymore. I'm lucky.

What Diminishes Joy

What diminishes joy in work for me is a patient and family who are dissatisfied with the care they receive. That's always something that brings me down; it disappoints me that they are disappointed or frustrated. It makes me even sadder if there was something we did or didn't do to make a patient feel that way.

Recently a patient who was scheduled for surgery, and her mother, were very upset. A couple of patients were scheduled for surgery before her, and there were complications in both of those cases. The surgeries ran way over the blocked time and ran well past the 3:00 p.m. mark, which is when the anesthesiologist on our first shift usually leaves. By the time this patient could have gone into the OR for surgery it was 4:00 or 4:30 p.m. and the anesthesiologist was not available to take her case. They ended up cancelling her surgery and asking her to come back. They had driven from home, which was four hours away, and were really upset. I work very closely with our chief of anesthesia and administration and others and I think maybe, if we'd all been aware of it at the time, the staff might have been able to escalate it up to us and we might have been able to do something different.

After this happened, we talked to all the staff involved, and I met with the patient and her mother and sat with them for a long time. I cried with them, actually, because these are people who come in and out a lot, every few months, and they were disappointed. The patient talked about her relationship with her mother and said her mother was so put out by it all, that she drives all this way and takes the time to bring her in for this procedure and she's been doing it all her life. Then she and her mother started crying, so of course I have that heavy heart, too, and when someone starts crying, I tend to get tears. So, we cried together, and we really connected because I showed that side of myself. The whole thing made me sad, but I was glad I was able to help with that service recovery; that's part of my role. I promised them it wouldn't happen again. The patient has actually emailed me a couple of times in the last two weeks to let me know when she's coming in next, so hopefully she won't have that experience again.

My meeting schedule is very demanding. I am the voice of my areas to administration and to other departments. At the same time, I need to be here for my staff and the department and not always in meetings. While I'm in meetings being the facilitator or the communicator, the staff often needs me or one of my peers needs me or another department is calling and asking something. People will call me and I want to help everybody, which is my problem. I just have to determine what the priority is at the time. Of course, if I have a staff member who's having an issue and I'm supposed to be at a meeting, I just call and say I can't be at that meeting because I'm dealing with an issue with a staff member. If the meeting is really high priority, I apologize to the staff member and say I'll get back to them. It's very important that you always follow through—so if you tell somebody you're going to get back to them, you need to do that.

I have system responsibilities for all the hospitals I work with. I run the peri-anesthesia leadership group, so I frequently get emails and other things from people in the system—directors in post-anesthesia care units and same-day surgery, for instance—who say, "Can you give me any advice on this?" and "Can you give me any advice on that?" I juggle a lot. I just have to prioritize what's going on right now or that day.

The administration has given me all the tools I need to feel joy in work. In general, they allow me to have the staffing I need. The problem I'm seeing now is related to the nursing shortage, so we might have a position open a lot longer than we used to—and that causes my staff to work harder, me to work harder, and gives me more issues to deal with. I believe the people in human resources try their best to help us keep our positions filled but the staffing holes really make things difficult.

On Leadership

When problems come up I never blame a staff member for anything. I always say, "Tell me what happened with this patient" or "Tell me what happened with this issue." I think the biggest thing when dealing with staff is, never be accusatory or defensive but let them tell their story. There are always three sides to any story—I'm a big advocate of that. So, I want to hear it from the patient and the family, I want to hear it from the staff member. Whatever the story is, I want to hear their side of it.

Experts say you should always give three positives to every negative. So, I'm one to talk a staff member up and say, "You do this really great and you do that really great, but maybe next time in that situation can I suggest you try this?" And then just talk through it. Always end on a positive so you retain your employees and keep them satisfied. Satisfied employees make satisfied patients.

We have had longstanding nurses here. Lots of them have been in the ambulatory surgery area for 25–30 years because they feel supported and cared about. Although I have to maintain consistency in making decisions among staff, there are always special circumstances and I try to help everybody as best I can.

Reflections

I guess because of my age, I'm about 55 years old now, I would like to work from home one day a week. I travel an hour and a half to get to work and to get home from work because I love my job so much. People think I'm absolutely crazy to have a commute like that. The general expectation is that I'm here five days a week to make sure things run smoothly, which I understand, but as I get older it's getting a little harder to make that commute every day and then work nine or ten hours a day. If I could do some of this computer work at home that would be on my wish list.

In my 33 years as a nurse I've never experienced any of the sexism between doctors and nurses that people often speak of, but I have experienced the hierarchy. I certainly have the utmost respect for all doctors but there are some who are very demanding ("You will do this") and they don't want to listen to any suggestions the nurses have—and the nurses are the ones who are dealing with all of the patients. There are more male nurses nowadays. It used to be rare to have a male nurse but in my areas, which have well over 100 people, there are at least ten male nurses.

Advice

My advice to my bosses is, be visible. Be visible to the staff on the floors so they know upper management cares. My bosses are visible right now, but I would say they're more visible in the last six months than they ever have been. They are making changes in what they call the patient and employee experience. They send out surveys that are designed to measure and improve employee engagement. The staff has filled out these surveys for several years now, which ask what staff wants to see happen, what they want changed, and so on. The administration has worked very hard to take all their opinions and themes and to make these changes. I have seen a huge change in employee satisfaction because our administrators are rounding on all the floors and talking to the staff and having town hall meetings and such. In general, I would say to administrators throughout the country, go out and see your employees. I'd say rounding on employees is probably the number one thing administrators can do to make a difference in employee satisfaction.

My advice for staff and colleagues is, don't assume you know what your patients want. Back in my early days, we would get together and have all these meetings and talk about what's going to improve patient satisfaction, that we should do this and we should do that. Some of us have been patients before, and that therefore we think we know what our patients need and want. But until you go out there and directly ask patients and round on them, you should not assume you know what your patients want.

The other thing I'd say to healthcare professionals is, take care of your own time. I think time management is so important. Cut out the things you've always done or attended to because they've always been on your schedule. If a meeting doesn't have a purpose—or if you can meet every other month as opposed to monthly—don't meet more often just because it's always been done that way. Think outside the box and really take control of your schedule. Cancel meetings, even at the last minute, because there's really not a lot for you to discuss that can't wait till the next time.

I find that a lot of nurses on the unit don't want to raise their hands and say, "I need help" or "Can you give me an extra hand here?" because they think of it as a sign of weakness or that they're not doing a good job. I will frequently have just rounded on the unit and everything seems fine; everyone's busy and everyone's smiling. Then I'll come back to my office and within ten minutes someone might come to see me in tears, saying, "It's just so crazy out there." I ask them why they didn't let me know. I think nurses, in general, tend not to raise the flag and say they need a little help because they think it reflects badly on them, that it means they can't handle the job. And so they just don't ask. I think they would find more joy in their work if they did ask because there are lots of people around who *can* help them. But we can't read their minds.

My advice to doctors is to treat nurses as team members, not just as people who are going to do all the work with your patients. I think sometimes doctors look at nurses and think, *these are all things you need to do for my patient* as opposed saying, "Let's talk about this patient." It's more of a one-way street: the doctors are always telling the nurses what to do—but sometimes, when we try to give advice back, there's that doctor-nurse divide, and doctors are always on the higher level.

33. Elana G., MD, Pulmonary and Critical Care Physician and Medical Director of an Adult Medical Specialties Group in an Integrated Health System

Elana G., MD, delivers pulmonary and critical care medicine, and is medical director of an adult medical specialties group, in a 109-year-old integrated health system. As a physician, autonomy in practice—and as a leader, removing barriers to progress—contribute to Elana's joy in work.

I grew up in a small, remote, agricultural town. I wanted to go to college and become somebody. I had many different interests. In college I studied neuromuscular disease; I worked in hearing. I was guided toward engineering because it was a profession my parents thought I could make a decent living at. I chose biomedical engineering because I was interested in medicine.

I went to graduate school, but I always thought I would go to medical school. I knew I wanted to impact people and their health directly, and that as an engineer I would only be able to impact people indirectly. So, I went to graduate school, defended my thesis, and four days later started medical school.

In medical school the field I chose to specialize in, primary critical care, aligned with the training I had in engineering. Primary critical care involves a lot of physiology, and a lot of the instrumentation and design work I did as an engineer is used in pulmonary and critical care: extracorporeal membrane oxygenation pumps, ventilators, magnetic resonance scanners, that sort of thing. When I chose pulmonary and critical care, I still had an interest in research, so I chose to do a research fellowship.

My Professional Journey

Through serendipity—the research funding for my fellowship had shifted—I returned to my hometown to work on what we would fondly refer to as "the dark side:" private practice in a hospital with no involvement in basic science research.

I became medical director of a hospital, took on various other leadership roles, and volunteered on a number of committees. After a year I was asked to open a new hospital in the area. I was medical director there for six years when I was asked to lead the adult specialties service line. The adult specialties service line is a group of internal medicine-trained specialists who subspecialize in pulmonary, rheumatology, endocrinology, neurology, sleep medicine, gastroenterology, pain and spine, and wound care. I supervise and advise on the clinical processes in this service line and lead the implementation of telemedicine and telehealth for this hospital.

I also deliver patient care. When I was hired at my first hospital, I was offered an 80% administrative and 20% clinical role. At that point I had just turned 40 and my answer was, "I am too young to give up that much clinical time." I was still learning my craft. I insisted on it being 60% clinical and 40% administrative. Which really meant that I was 60% clinical and 80% administrative. I learned my lesson over time and over the last seven years I've flipped it the other way: 40% clinical and 60% administrative.

What My Job Entails

I deliver patient care only in my specialty, which is pulmonary and critical care medicine, and I practice only on the inpatient side. There's a different balance of burden versus joy in an all-inpatient versus an all-outpatient practice. When I work a shift on the inpatient side in the intensive care unit, I come in at 7:30 a.m. I take care of 12–14 patients on any given day, perform procedures, meet with families, talk about serious subjects like death and dying—but when I'm done at the end of the day, I go home and I don't have any further responsibilities because my partner, who's covering at night, is taking care of everything. The work ends. I just need to show up the next day and continue to take care of my patients.

For physicians who work in clinics exclusively, their work never ends. They show up in the morning and patients come in every 15–20 minutes; I can spread my work with 14 patients throughout the day in a way that suits me. I have a lot of autonomy and choice in the way I deliver care to my patients. Clinic physicians have to show up at a certain time, see patients within a certain period of time, and must be open to questions from medical assistants, nurses, other physicians, patients via pagers, cell phones, texts, and patient portal emails. I don't need to do any of that because I take care of inpatients exclusively.

When I'm on clinical duty my hours are 7:30 a.m. to 5:30 p.m. Administrative questions come up all the time. When there's an administrative emergency I try to shuffle my clinical responsibilities while still putting patients first and maintaining high-quality care. If I have downtime because I've taken care of everybody—say I don't have very complicated patients on a particular day, or I don't have a very high census—I can work on my administrative duties. One has to be organized and know how to balance those work cues. If I have to attend a meeting, I can defer my clinical work and stay late.

Organizational Culture

This organization is 109 years old. We're one of the first healthcare facilities in this part of the state and we've continuously remained an independent healthcare organization. We haven't been purchased by national organizations and chains the way so many other healthcare organizations have. We've been able to remain a private, not-for-profit, fully integrated organization with a healthcare facility, a medical group, and a health plan.

Thirty years ago, there was a missed opportunity for this to be a truly physician-led organization. I think we've changed dramatically in the last five years when we reorganized. Now we have a chief medical officer over the entire integrated enterprise, the health plan, the individual facilities, and the medical group. I think that has brought much greater engagement from physicians and advanced practice clinicians in this organization, which is demonstrated in our engagement scores year over year. You can just feel that engagement in terms of conversations and the way decisions are made. Our decision to change our electronic health records system was physician led. That was a huge investment, so to have physicians make that final decision was important.

Trust is an important part of the culture on the intensive care unit. I rely on the bedside nurses to give me all the information I need about each patient. I need to have a great deal of trust in them in order to write the orders I do. These are life and death therapies, they're minute-by-minute titrations, so I need to have that trust. And the trust has to go both ways. The bedside nurses need to feel that if something doesn't work out, or if they have a question, then I will be responsive to them, that I will treat them with respect, and that I'll support them.

This year we're deploying a five-year strategic plan, called Elevate, geared toward improving the satisfaction of all those who work in our health system. Elevate focuses on enabling all our employees to work at the top of their license, and to have the autonomy to stand their ground and to grow their business. We're working with all our teams, not just clinical teams but with administrative teams. People who may not participate directly in patient care are, nevertheless, very much a part of the care we deliver to our patients. We want to focus on what the employee experience is like so they can fee that they're thriving. We conduct physician and employee engagement surveys and organizational health surveys every year. We've seen scores improve each year since we started this program.

We involve nurses, respiratory therapists, physicians, and clerical staff in talking about the programmatic growth they want to engage in, the type of work they want to engage in to feel joy in practice, and the barriers they would like to remove to help increase their joy. A lot of this relates to autonomy: for example, being able to solve problems without having to go up "the food chain" to get approvals and then have those approvals come back down. To a great extent, this is about flattening the hierarchy, about identifying things that staff can do autonomously versus things for which they need approval.

In an initiative to increase physicians' joy in work, one of our practices converted from a fee-for-service to a salary model using what we call a "citizenship guarantee." In this model, the physicians commit to seeing no fewer than 16 patients a day between 8:00 a.m. and 5:00 p.m. The physicians understood that to receive the benefit of a salary guarantee, they would lose some autonomy. The tradeoff was worth it to them. Not one physician has left in the two years since we went from fee-for-service to a salary model. They're the ones who asked for a salary guarantee; we said, "give us a citizenship guarantee" and we all signed on the dotted line. The transition took about nine months overall. Physicians were involved in creating the citizenship document and in deciding on the total number of hours they would work per day or per year.

We have many programs here to reward our staff. For example, we have a Catch Me program. Catch Me are little post-it notes that we give to people if they do something above and beyond. It's an on-the-spot thank-you note we write to them, saying, for example, "Thanks so much for helping me out with producing that A-4 document," or "Thank you for walking that patient out to her car because she needed assistance." If somebody receives five of these notes, they get a coffee shop gift card. We have lots of programs like that. We also have an employee engagement fund; if, for example, our patient satisfaction scores are in the 94th percentile in one clinic, then we use that fund to cater a lunch to celebrate. We use funds like that in order to reward our staff. People say they appreciate all those things, but there may be things we haven't been paying enough attention to.

I reached out today to my lab staff because they had a flood in the lab and resolved the situation so patient appointments weren't cancelled. I sent them an email saying, "Thanks so much for doing all that and making sure that our patients had great care. You guys are extraordinary. Please let me know what I can do today to help you." Earlier in my career, I didn't realize how impactful that type of recognition could be. I've learned that personal acknowledgment of someone, in public, for even small things they do, is extremely valuable.

We've grown in the last five years from 9,000 employees to close to 13,000 employees. Turnover has been about 12% for physicians per year. We'd prefer turnover to be closer to 8%, which is the national benchmark. I think every region of the country has some unique challenges. This is a beautiful area and the cost of living is low. However, the lack of big shopping, restaurants, and top-rated schools makes this a bit of a recruiting challenge. I can't say how much of that contributes to turnover.

On Joy in Work

Autonomy, I think, plays a major role in joy in practice, whether someone has administrative responsibilities or does purely clinical work. When that autonomy is taken away, joy in practice is much more difficult to achieve.

I do feel a lot of joy in my work. First, what fuels me is taking care of patients; that sustains me through the administrative side of work, where I don't get that immediate gratification of helping people. I need to be able to touch people, and to help them heal. What gives me joy as a leader is being able to reflect back on the past six months, year, or other period of time and to see where we've been and how we've grown, and to see how, through my influence, things have been accomplished.

At this hospital we each have what we call our personal "eggs" and our organizational "eggs." These eggs are our unifying purpose. We exist to improve the health of the people of our state. My personal egg is to deliver healthcare to patients when and where they want it. What's behind that statement is that my mom still lives in a rural part of this state. If I can help deliver population health, to practice total medicine, to provide preventive healthcare, to deliver specialty care outside of our brick and mortar clinics and take it to patients where they need it, then that's what I always go back to. When I feel frustrated in my administrative role, I remind myself that I do this work for my mother. And for people like my mother.

On Money and Joy

I think that, across the board for physicians and clinical staff, people often go to money as the solution to finding their joy. But there's no amount of money that can truly give one joy. They reach for money because that's the easiest thing to say. It's so much harder to say, "I don't have autonomy," "You don't trust me," "I don't trust you," or "my colleagues are not helpful." Typically, the way the problem is presented is, "I need to get paid more. I look at our competitors and they pay more." What I think is important is to delve deeper and to ask the question, "Why would you think about leaving your organization and going to the competitor? What is it about this job that makes you think that you should be paid more for it? Is there something else that I can resolve for you that would make you feel more joy in work?"

When you take the time to talk to people, that's when they're able to tell you all the problems that are causing them to reach for the money lever. Often, when clinic managers ask for money we ask, "What is it that's making you feel overworked, overburdened, and unhappy?" The answer is that we often assign task-like work or we don't trust people enough to allow them to just take care of their own business. They lack autonomy. When we're able to take away the task-like work and allow these managers to connect with the doctors to whom they report and the patients they take care of, they're much happier. If you give people meaningful work and take away the meaningless work, there's so much more joy because that's a value proposition. They feel more valued when they're not having to do tasks and can focus on doing important work.

What Diminishes Joy

Negativity

When I'm surrounded by people who are more focused on barriers than on reaching the goal, that diminishes my joy in work. Let's say I'm at a meeting with our administrative folks and we have a goal in mind—for example, refining our telehealth program. When people in the meeting are more focused on all the reasons why we *can't* do this rather than on how to get it done, that diminishes joy.

I've grown over the last seven years in this regard. In the past, I would have been outspoken about my frustration and would probably have expressed myself very negatively: "I am upset that you aren't willing to engage to get this project going." But I think I'm much more positive now; I explain what my personal egg is and what I'm trying to accomplish. I share my connection to my own goals to help others make similar connections to theirs and, in so doing, to overcome barriers to reaching our shared, organizational goals.

I think that's certainly much more effective than ranting and raving and being upset. I think it helps when I ask the question, "What is your connection to purpose? What brings you to work each day?" If I can connect their reason for being here to what we're trying to accomplish at that moment, then it's much more effective. I try not to put anyone on the spot when I ask them what their central "why" is, but I try to use my own connection to purpose to show why I'm so passionate about a particular project. I have found this new approach reduces barriers.

Here's an example: we were working on a project to enable patients to schedule their own appointments. There were many perceived barriers as to why this wouldn't work: people said we didn't have enough standardization to do it, we didn't have enough access to do it, we couldn't trust patients to schedule their appointments at the right time, etc. When I pointed out that we were much further along than we have ever been, and that the whole reason for doing this is to improve patient engagement and patient access in our very rural state, I found that resonated with people. People started to come up with ways to overcome these perceived barriers. This project is now in process.

Lack of Autonomy

A good third of our turnover occurred as we began to implement EMRs. That put a big strain on physicians who had not trained in an electronic world and then were being held responsible for documenting on a computer. Before, they could just focus on patients and scribble a few things on a piece of paper and keep their paper charts. Everything was great. Now with the EMR there is so much more of a burden of clicking and typing than there ever was before. During the transition to the EMR many people left trying to find a place that wasn't using them. That was five to seven years ago, and that phase has come and gone. Most of those physicians have reached retirement age or have gone into private solo practices, boutique work, or have left healthcare altogether. The EMR really sucked a lot of joy out of people because it took away their autonomy. There are standards or templates you have to follow.

More recently, turnover has been related to the lack of a different type of autonomy. Clinic physicians have patients scheduled every 15–20 minutes. Physicians who are 100% clinic-based have very little control over how many patients they see in a given day because the schedule is made up for them. They can't control whether patients are going to have more problems than they expected, whether patients are going to show up late, or whether they're going to get angry. To be able to feel their own joy, physicians have to focus on the relationship they've developed with patients over the years, on that personal connection. Because if they are unable to make that personal connection, I don't see how they can keep working in that environment. There's always pressure on physicians to increase the number of patients they see in a day. We have conversations that sound something like this: "Your compensation model is based on productivity. And if you're not seeing enough patients and billing and coding the right way, then you can't make the type of money you think you should be making because you're not productive enough."

34. Harlan Z., MD, Total Joint Replacement Surgeon

Harlan Z., MD, is a total joint replacement (also known as arthroplasty) surgeon and entrepreneur who has been in practice for over three decades. He speaks passionately about his love for his work, his freedom to practice reasonably autonomously in a collegial environment within an increasingly tightly controlled milieu, and his joy in helping patients to achieve a newfound quality of life. Harlan also speaks with some degree of frustration about the loss of professional autonomy related to corporate oversight of medicine, bureaucratic obstacles, and policies such as relative value unit-based compensation models that tend to reduce physicians to "employees" and contribute to the growing and serious phenomenon known as physician burnout.

When I was a kid growing up in the Bronx you either became a doctor, a lawyer, a teacher, or an engineer. My family was dominated by attorneys. My grandmother may have been the first woman to graduate Brooklyn Law School. When I was 15 years old, I clerked for my Dad and I remember saying to him, "You don't seem to do anything all day but talk, Dad." Of course, he was not happy with that comment! But I recognized then that I didn't have the personality for a career in law, so becoming an attorney was ruled out. I exceled in the sciences in high school. During my junior year we were exposed to physicians in a mentoring program. Bingo, right then, the decision was easy. I knew at that moment I wanted to become a physician and would focus the next four years in college on meeting the rigorous requirements for admission to medical school. I was lucky, and got accepted.

Once in medical school I soon began to think about what I wanted to do for the rest of my professional life—a series of simple algorithms came into play: First, do I want a cognitive medical practice versus a technical specialty? For me, that too was an easy choice. I had a natural inclination for tinkering and fixing things, so the hands-on technical skills of surgery excited me. Becoming a surgeon was unquestionably the best fit for me. Then there was the decision about *which* surgical subspecialty—yet another decision with a number of different practice options. I initially considered becoming a cardiothoracic or vascular surgeon, but I didn't enjoy making life or death decisions or amputating poorly perfused extremities. As a rotating surgical intern, I was offered a position as an orthopedic resident (twice) because the chairman thought I'd make a good orthopedic surgeon but (foolishly) I turned it down (twice). Orthopedic surgeons, at the time, had a reputation for "not being doctors, just carpenters and technicians." But then one day I had an epiphany: *I think I actually do enjoy fixing bones and I want to be an orthopedic surgeon.* Life just unfolded from there. "Yuan fen," it was just meant to be, I never looked back or second guessed my decision.

That's how I decided to be an orthopedic surgeon. But then there's more. The next decision was, what did I want to be, a general orthopedic surgeon or a subspecialist? And, if a subspecialist, what type of subspecialist? Being a frustrated carpenter, I migrated to joint replacement surgery (arthroplasty) for two reasons: first, we use really cool instruments and tools! And second, for the sheer joy of helping patients regain their mobility and function and eliminate their pain. That was my journey to becoming an arthroplasty surgeon and I have been truly blessed to have had this opportunity.

I'm 66 years old now and after 33 years in practice I still work 12–14 hours a day. Folks have asked if I ever think about retirement or slowing down. "Why? That is the furthest thing from my mind," is my usual reply. My professional satisfaction has never changed, and I remain bullish on the future of healthcare.

But that is not what I often hear from my colleagues. These physicians seem disgruntled, frustrated, freely use the term "burnout," and speak of early retirement. This has puzzled me and prompted me to ask, "Why?" An understanding of human behavior is helpful to begin to pry open the answer.

The Importance of Autonomy

I lead a specialty center of excellence that has had, over the years, a great deal of success in creating an exceptional experience for our patients, with a uniquely positive energy and culture. I've often asked myself, *why has this been so successful? Why are my physician partners professionally satisfied?* We don't make more money than other joint replacement surgeons.

I am an admirer of the author and behavioral scientist Daniel Pink and have read his books and watched his TED talks. When I viewed his TED talk, "The Puzzle of Motivation," I found the answer. Pink talks about three intrinsic motivators that can modify human behavior and cultivate creativity and personal satisfaction (one of them is *not* money, which is an extrinsic motivator). These are autonomy (control over one's time/team/techniques), mastery (the desire to continue to improve at a particular skill), and purpose (the urge to contribute to something larger than oneself). And when I listened to his concepts, I realized that is exactly why our program is so successful. Our surgeons have been given the autonomy and the opportunity to develop mastery and purpose. I can assure you, in terms of importance, for a surgeon, retaining *control* will trump income any day. But do all physicians enjoy access to these intrinsic motivators? If not, could this contribute to the growing problem of physician burnout?

Our company comprises a group of surgeons who belong to different, and competing, private practices. We came together many years ago, all equally dissatisfied with the hospital environment where we were practicing at the time: it was inefficient, not value driven, had no plans for the future, had no physician control, and was largely ill equipped to manage the impending onslaught of arthroplasty business related to the aging of the baby boomer generation. We put aside internecine differences and established a shared vision: to create a world-class destination site for total joint arthroplasty.

We also agreed on two fundamental principles: to adopt a standardized, protocol-based approach to care delivery, and to make data-driven decisions. With that, we launched our patient-centered value agenda. There is a delicate art to leading and practicing in organized medicine: you simply can't tell a physician what to do for their patients. It just doesn't work. But you can work with them to co-create consensus-based protocols and policies in which everybody can weigh in and have input. If 80% comply, the 20% of naysayers will quietly come on board when you can show them which patients actually did better.

Standardized healthcare means care that is protocol-driven and therefore that outcomes can be measured. This takes time and patience. In our program, it can take months to develop a single protocol. But because all stakeholders have input—including our surgeons, anesthesiologists, medical consultants, nurses, physical therapists, and our physician assistants—we get broad acceptance and buy-in for the protocols we produce. The process develops collegiality, teamwork, and levels the playing field; all caregivers' perspectives are respected and it's an approach that works. In the end, we not only arrive at the best protocols but there is also a sense of shared ownership. Once a year, we review these protocols, measure the outcomes, and we continually improve based on real, actionable data—our data. *This* is exemplary of Pink's first intrinsic motivator, autonomy.

Our management company entered into an agreement with a local hospital to manage and oversee the day-to-day operations of the Institute, a service line within the hospital.

It is a facility wholly owned by the hospital—we don't own one-square foot of it. The agreement stipulates that we provide the hospital with consulting, administrative, and managerial services for which we receive a fair market value stipend. The hospital then provides us with the support services we need to manage the service line and it is incumbent upon us to create exceptional quality outcomes and patient experience while reducing costs. This has worked out extraordinarily well for our patients, the hospital, and the surgeon members.

Over the past decade, many hospitals across the United States have had significant challenges to maintaining their financial independence. Three years ago, our local hospital was acquired by a national healthcare system. Like most large healthcare corporations, this one had certain standard enterprise policies, model structures, and rubrics, some of which often differed substantially from our pre-existing model and culture. The added layers of regional and national administrative oversight initially created the potential risk for a "collision of models" and a sense that this could stifle entrepreneurialism and innovation of our high-performing organizations. Although there have been occasional differences in approach to care delivery, over time, and with the development of trust and effective relationships, experience, and demonstrably favorable outcomes, these issues have become far less frequent and easier to resolve. New, highly effective partnerships have emerged.

On Joy in Work

I remain a full-time practicing high volume arthroplasty surgeon while president of our management company, medical director of the Institute, and leader of the orthopedic service line at our local hospital.

How many hours a week do I work? Maybe an easier question is how many hours a week *don't* I work? I wake up every day inspired to deliver excellence in patient care and quality outcomes with an unsurpassed patient *and* employee experience with a unique team of energized, dedicated teammates and professionals.

Substantial progress has been made in the urgent need to transform our healthcare system in the United States. Our organization has been contributing in many ways to these efforts in our region. Playing a role in this grassroots endeavor has also been a source of immeasurable fulfillment.

A typical day for me? Before seeing patients in the office at 8:00 a.m. today, I attended a meeting with a large primary care provider (PCP) group with whom we want to work to develop a population health management model for all musculoskeletal conditions and all patients who present to their PCP for evaluation. PCPs are most often the front line for musculoskeletal problems, but they are not formally trained to manage these conditions. Our hope is that we can bridge trust and demonstrate to our colleagues that if we work together to co-manage these patients, higher value (better quality, lower cost) care will result. At noon, I had a meeting with an implant vendor to discuss better pricing options before seeing patients again until 4:00 p.m., when I had a conference call followed by a dinner meeting with regional hospital administration to discuss marketing strategies. This is a typical *non-surgical* day. Two days a week, I am in the operating room performing joint replacement surgery. Before and after surgery I often have organizational meetings.

Our team's administrative achievements and our outstanding patient outcomes are why I am grateful for each day. And, I must admit, I have never experienced anything coming close to what has been described as physician burnout.

Helping Patients Walk

For me, administrative and clinical responsibilities generate absolute joy and professional satisfaction. But the supreme joy, and why I love arthroplasty surgery, is watching folks who have been immobile, in chronic pain, and with no quality of life get up and walk without pain on the day of their surgery. The ability to help these patients is a privilege not to be minimized.

Arthroplasty is an elective practice and the patient is always the decision-maker. I have never had to say, "You must have your joint replaced" because, in point of fact, they don't. Some patients are so terrified of surgery that they may suffer needlessly. Since we are compensated for performing these procedures, arthroplasty surgeons often walk a fine line and cannot be construed as "selling" the surgery. How do I reconcile this dilemma? Given a patient with radiographically severe end stage bone-on-bone arthritis of their hip or knee, I ask probing questions to determine their current functional status as well as how their arthritis has impacted their ability to function at peak desirable performance. If a patient feels their functional losses are minimal and tolerable, they are not in my view a candidate for a joint replacement procedure. The bonus question is this: "Is your quality of life acceptable to you now?" And if they say yes, then they don't need a joint replacement. My job is to try to guide them through this shared decision-making process. Finally, all of this has to be balanced against a given patient's surgical risk profile and modifiable risk factors.

Administrative Empowerment and our Employees

When we launched our Institute, we recognized that we had two fundamental customers: the surgeon and the patient. Simply stated, no surgeon, no patient. The third essential group is our staff, who are employees of the hospital. They are the folks who are in contact with our patients every day. Seeing our employees happy, inspired, and actively engaged in decision-making is another source of personal satisfaction. It starts with creating and then sustaining a unique identity and organizational culture. Empowering all employees is vital. Even the people who sweep the floors know how to do that job better and more efficiently than anyone else and their voice should be heard. To foster this culture, we have quarterly luncheons with all of our caregivers to listen to their concerns and their suggestions on how to improve our program. I also take great pride in seeing our staff advance their careers and rise through the ranks.

As yet another show of support, in addition to holiday bonuses, the surgeons give back approximately 15% of our administrative stipend to our employees in the form of an annual holiday party, cookouts, team-building events, and educational support, which surely supports our esprit de corps.

We are a certified ISO 9001 healthcare facility. ISO 9001 is our quality management system where policy or protocol "non-conformities" (medical errors) are never addressed as *individual* failures ("it's your fault") but rather as *process* failures. Within a complex ecosystem such as healthcare, problems are never related to one person's error but, rather, to a systemic or *process* failure. This mindset of no blame-no shame fosters a culture where silos are effectively disrupted and the playing field is leveled.

As a mission-driven individual, I thrive on data measurement and using clean data to realize excellent outcomes. We are proud that 99% of our patients would refer a family member, that we've been recognized by numerous ranking agencies as the number one program in our state for ten years in a row, and that we were recently listed among the top ten programs in the United States by the CMS. We remain focused and humble, understanding there is substantial work yet to be done while always working toward *the most* patient-centric and sustainable model for joint replacement surgery.

On Money and Joy

An association between income and joy remains shaky at best. As singer Sheryl Crow sang in *Soak Up The Sun*, "It's not having what you want; it's wanting what you've got." Dan Pink postulated that financial dependence and extrinsic contingent motivators narrow one's entrepreneurialism and creativity by focusing primarily on numbers—"If I do this, I will receive that." Money brings a certain level of security and perhaps a sense of accomplishment. But, unchecked, there is often a tendency to want more and then the relationship between earning more money and achieving greater joy falls off quickly. Will having a second or third car buy incremental joy? I doubt it.

What Diminishes Joy

Wasting time diminishes joy in work for me. Certain administrative tasks seem duplicative and don't add measurable value. Meetings to solve problems that don't exist or that can be solved without formal committee approval, and complex bureaucratic policies that stymie innovation, are examples of what can detract from joy in work. In healthcare we must become leaner, more flexible, nimble, and responsive to patient needs. We simply cannot take months to get something done that could be accomplished in a few days. For me, those delays are a major source of frustration.

Relative Value Units

How did we ever become obsessed with RVUs? We don't live in a relative value unit world. By definition, an RVU is an assignment of work effort for a healthcare activity a provider is performing. It has become accepted as a measure of productivity for physicians and mid-level providers—and the foundation for provider performance compensation models for employed providers. But there are unintended consequences that may *not* be aligned with the patient's best interests. Who defines "relative value"? RVUs are part of the resource-based relative value scale. Historically, the American Medical Association's Specialty Society Relative Value Scale Update Committee, with input from a number of specialty societies, has largely determined Medicare's RVU physician work values. In practice, real value may be unmeasurable and unaccountable. For example, if a provider spends an hour communicating with a non-English-speaking individual who needs a minor surgical procedure but doesn't understand the language and therefore requires substantial additional time (time largely uncompensated by RVUs), the procedure will not be as financially rewarding as the same procedure performed on an English-speaking patient. Yet, for the non-English-speaking patient, unquestionable value has been delivered.

When I hear that a provider generated x number of RVUs and is (or is not) eligible for a monetary bonus, I turn and run! In my view, RVUs are one of the fundamental and primary reasons why physicians are experiencing burnout today. Imagine being a diligent, caring physician providing optimal patient care (time) and being advised, "We know your benchmark was the 50th percentile for the RVU-based bonus but you're in the 42nd percentile. Sorry." Or, "You only see three patients per hour, and your contract stipulates that you see four." What impact would this have on *your* perspective? Healthcare systems are now beginning to look beyond this outdated metric and create outcomes-based, risk-adjusted compensation models. In private practice we typically don't use RVUs to determine compensation. In fact, I didn't know what an RVU was until I got into healthcare administration.

Now, factor in the burden of administrative paperwork and the hours per day of endless forms to complete while also keeping up with the EMR. This has become an enormous, valueless burden to all clinicians, and a major contributor to burnout.

I am fortunate. My colleagues and I have not experienced burnout, largely because of the degree of autonomy and control we've been able to maintain. And because we don't receive RVU spreadsheets with productivity targets.

Advice

Physicians are naturally independent-minded individuals, focused on and driven toward excellence. A prominent healthcare consultant once said, "Physicians may be employed but will never be employees." In either environment, their mindsets are the same.

To healthcare organizational administrators I would recommend this: set reasonable, measurable enterprise goals and objectives, provide the necessary support to achieve these outcomes, and then allow physicians to create the pathways for success.

Finally, I would advise that you understand what really motivates and inspires physicians. Unburden them. Help them achieve their goals. In some sense, this is actually remarkably simple: give physicians some level of autonomy and burnout goes away.

35.   Edward B., MD, Medical Director of an Alcohol and Drug Detoxification Program

Edward B., MD, is the medical director of a suburban alcohol and drug detoxification program in a 180-bed men's rehabilitation center. An internist in private practice who loved treating patients for 36 years, Edward has found a new level of freedom in his current role: the freedom to focus solely on being a doctor; to learn as much as he can about patients and their conditions; and to establish relationships of trust and respect that underpin successful treatment.

My father was an old-time, small-town general practitioner and I think I went into medicine because of him. I admired the one-on-one care he gave to his patients; he was beloved and respected by his patients and the community, and their devotion to him made a deep impression on me. I took over his solo practice in 1979 when he became ill and couldn't go on. I maintained that solo practice in internal medicine until 2015. I didn't have time to specialize at that point, but I didn't want to. There is nothing I love more than general medicine. I treated everyone, with every condition, who came through the door.

I left my practice in 2015 and became the medical director of a suburban alcohol and drug detoxification rehabilitation program. Men come in addicted to alcohol and/or drugs; the ones who are still actively using upon admission require detoxification, which is usually a five-day process. My role is to detoxify the patients and treat them for medical illnesses while they're here. After detoxification, patients attend counseling and lectures, Alcoholics Anonymous and Narcotics Anonymous meetings, and group therapy.

Most of these men haven't taken care of themselves in the past 20 or 30 years and never see a doctor, so I have to triage what needs to be taken care of immediately and refer them for medical care after they've completed the program. My primary focus is their alcohol and drug rehabilitation. My job is to keep them stable, which draws on my years of treating patients from head to toe.

I work 9:00 a.m. to 5:00 p.m., Monday to Friday. Now that I work for an organization the only thing I have to do is my medical work, which is a pleasure. I'm in a perfect position now where I can just go to work, be a doctor, and focus on doing what I love.

There are no programs in place to support me here, none whatsoever. I'm the only medical person, with 180 patients plus three medication nurses who hand out medicines and one triage nurse who sets up my appointments and screens the patients. The only person writing orders is me. Before I started here they'd never had a full-time medical doctor.

I'm quite independent here. I come in, I have a schedule of five or six people in the morning and six or eight people in the afternoon. I take my time, I get a history and physical on every single person I see. Administrators don't pressure me to see more patients or to do anything differently. It's a very good situation.

On Joy in Work

I feel joy in work every day. I try to have a positive influence on every single person I see. I find I've been fairly successful at that. I get people to trust me. That is difficult to do with this population—these are drug addicts, alcoholics; they don't have respect for anyone, they don't trust anybody. They come in for the first time with a little sideways look at me. But after 20 minutes or so I've established a relationship with them and they believe in me, they trust me, and that's the first step in my being able to help them. I feel joy with just about every person I see.

I get people to trust me by listening and talking. Probably more listening than anything. I've always been a good listener. I was always called a good diagnostician, not because I'm a genius but because—in addition to understanding the body and its physiology and pathology—I listen. I still drive to work every morning and look forward to it, then come home in the evening and feel I've had a really good day.

In this job, I have a lot more time to study and read up on the conditions I'm treating than I did when I was in private practice. I'm up until 11:00 or 12:00 at night reading about the types of patients I've seen or their illnesses. There's a wonderful app called UpToDate®, which is a fabulous medical tool with the best descriptions of diseases and patient information. It's a luxury to have the desire to learn and the time to do it. I never had time before. I spend a lot of my time educating my patients, too. That's rewarding, as well, and I think it's important.

There are doctors who spend two hours a day or more charting and doing paperwork. In my program I see a patient, I dictate a note, and that's it. I bring nothing home with me other than once a week, when I bring home about 20 lab results to review in the evening. I look back at the day and think *what interesting patients I've seen* and look forward to studying more about them.

I've never felt burnout. Never. Maybe at the end of a long day I feel tired but that's not burnout. I love my work too much to get disgusted with it or tired of it. It's too enjoyable. I set out to help people. That was my only motivation. I've succeeded in doing that, and along the way made enough money to live a comfortable life. But it was never about money. It was only about having a positive effect on people.

One of the things that keeps me going is the tremendous respect I feel from patients, the staff, and the administration. Especially from the patients. These are addicts, alcoholics, but everyone acknowledges me with respect. It's lovely. It feels good.

What Diminishes Joy

The Business of Medicine

In my office practice I had to be involved in the business of medicine, which I never liked. I was a bad businessman. I don't enjoy billing, I don't enjoy advertising, and I don't enjoy the insurance business. But over the years the patients certainly made everything worthwhile. Now, because I don't have to be overwhelmed by the business of medicine, I am free to focus on what I love.

Lawsuits

I'd say the opposite of joy in work is malpractice. Being sued is my one overwhelming and pervasive fear. I was sued once for malpractice and it was a terrible, destructive, devastating experience. I misdiagnosed a patient. It was a mistake. It was a rare neurological disease and I just missed it. I thought it was something else entirely, so I had very little defense. The lawsuit went on for probably three years until it was over. In the end, we settled the case and the patient was compensated. Did I let that affect the way I practiced medicine? I don't think I did.

I keep using the word devastating. But maybe the better word to describe how it feels to be sued for malpractice is *degrading*. I made it personal and I shouldn't have done that.

I know it's nothing personal. But because of the relationships I developed with patients and families in my practice, I felt sabotaged and betrayed when they sued me.

Being sued is still a fear I have but I try not to focus on it. I don't practice defensive medicine, although when people come into this rehab center and they're sick, I don't hesitate to send them to the nearby emergency room to get that second opinion. When I was in private practice I could send patients to specialists, I could admit them to the hospital, but here at the rehab center, I'm it. I can't call people to ask questions or refer patients out. It's all on me and it's a *lot*. It's a challenge. But it's okay.

Advice

It's important to balance things out. Life can't be all doctoring, can't be all medicine, can't be all patients. If that's all that I did or if I were killing myself at work I would not be happy. I have a nice balance in my life now. I'm motivated to get up and go to work, I'm motivated to leave work, to play golf or see a movie, and to spend more time with my family. There should be more to life than work.

36.   Meghan Pillow, MSN, Critical Care Nurse

Meghan Pillow, MSN, began her career as a writer focusing on the subject of patient safety. During her three years in that role she became passionate about improving patient care and wanted to actually do it, not just write about it. She went to nursing school, was a critical care nurse in a community hospital for ten years, and the day after this interview would start a new job as a university nurse. I met Meghan when she was my editor in 2006.

In nursing you can make good money and there are endless opportunities that support family life. I was able to work evenings and nights while my kids were growing up so I could be home during the day. Now that they're in school full time I'm making another shift to work in the university setting so my work schedule will align more closely with their school schedules. It's hard to find part-time work that pays well and provides a flexible schedule. Nursing checks all the boxes for that.

My Healthcare Journey

I started my nursing career at a suburban community hospital. I've been there for most of my ten years. But six years ago, after my son was born, there were problems with the economy and I wasn't getting as many hours as I needed so I took a job as a house supervisor managing a different hospital during "off" hours. That job involved staffing, patient care issues, family complaints, and even safety. I was a critical care nurse and there were only two nurses in the critical care unit; and because it was a small hospital, I would also run code blues. I did that for only six months because I didn't feel that the organization was safe. I felt that my license was being put at risk. That hospital closed in 2018.

When a position opened up at my old hospital, I went back as a clinical nurse consultant. In this role I've been a clinical supervisor. I'm not in charge of staffing, I'm not really dealing with patient or family complaints—I'm there to help the nurses when they have questions. If they don't know the answer to a question, they go to a charge nurse and if the charge nurse doesn't know they come to me. As a critical nurse consultant, I respond to all emergencies in the hospital, which include being part of rapid response and code blue teams. I get paged and go to the emergency room to navigate care for patients with acute stroke symptoms so they can get the medications or procedures they need right away. I take these patients to the interventional suite, get anesthesiologists involved, and do whatever else is needed. It's an extremely fast-paced and exciting role when there are emergencies.

When there aren't emergencies, I do a lot of IV work, putting IVs in for patients. This became a passion for me. I really hate it when patients get poked too often and we aren't successful inserting IVs. We weren't having a 100% success rate with anybody and I thought there has to be a better way. So, I spearheaded a project to use ultrasound to insert IVs. Our boss was really supportive and bought us a $20,000 refurbished ultrasound machine. We're still learning—ultrasound-guided IVs take a lot of practice so people get discouraged and often give up. But it's an amazing technology and it was awesome to bring it to our hospital. I've done this for about five years; it was one of my biggest accomplishments during my time here.

When I go to rapid response or code blue calls, I have to work with nurses I may not be familiar with and who may not be familiar with me. In the beginning it was difficult because they didn't know who I was. They wondered, *how was I going to treat them? What was I going to say to them? Was I going to order them around?* I told them, "We're a team. We work together. I'm not better than you, you're not better than me. We come to this team with different expertise. Please don't feel intimidated by me." I tell them to speak up, to tell me what they're thinking, to let me know what I missed, and to tell me what I need to know.

I just had my last shift because I'm going to transition fully to the university health setting on Monday. I've worked there part-time for the last year. It will be quite a transition to go from critical care to community health, but I'll be working with young people, which is something I've always wanted to do. They come in when they're sick, they come in when they have sexually transmitted infections, urinary tract infections, and other problems. You're there to help them navigate the healthcare system and to treat their symptoms. Every university health clinic is different—some have doctors on staff, some have advanced practice nurses or physician assistants on staff, and some have only nurses on staff. A physician oversees me but she doesn't usually come to my clinic. If a patient comes in with pain, I can give them ibuprofen or acetaminophen based on a pre-established, physician-approved nursing protocol. I've decided to go back to school and get my family nurse practitioner certificate.

On Joy in Work

I think joy in work means you're fulfilled by your job, you have purpose, and you're helping people. I think people go into healthcare because they want to help others. As a clinical nurse consultant, I'm here at an emergent time in people's lives—if they're having a stroke or chest pain or difficulty breathing, I'm there to support them. Their family members are often extremely grateful; they might not voice it at the time because they're so nervous and scared, but later they'll say, "Thank you so much for being there. Thank you for explaining those things to me." That's so fulfilling. That's why I got into nursing. I've always felt fulfilled working in critical care because patients always say, "Thank you, thank you, thank you." I don't often get awards from my bosses or managers and that's fine—I feel rewarded by my patients every day.

At my hospital, I've felt a lot of joy in work. We have great teams with people trying to be positive and help each other. I try to model that with the rapid response teams because the leader sets the tone. Put on a smile, try to remember people's names, try to be kind, try to be patient. When you're working in emergencies people start to get a little tense. I try to be that calming and compassionate presence.

We have great educators at my hospital; they are super-supportive. You can come to them with issues and they'll start working on them, educating, and improving. Everyone puts patients first, wants the best for them, and is trying to do their best.

At this hospital, I've had multiple opportunities to serve on committees to improve care. I worked on a central line committee, worked on improving IV access for patients, and trained nurses on improving IV access. I've had protocols changed so we could include pain spray for patients when we do IVs. When it's put into the protocol it's easy for the nurse to do it—the nurse doesn't have to call the doctor and ask for an order and then order it from the pharmacy. It's there and the nurse can just grab it.

What Diminishes Joy

We get bogged down by systems that impede our ability to care for patients well and safely. We're all here to help patients but when the system prevents us from providing safe care—or when we're on teams that are not practicing as safely as possible—that really can take away joy. Patient safety can't be the responsibility of only one group or one person. It takes the whole organization to support the front-line staff—to let them know that in this hospital, we follow evidence-based care and we follow these processes to keep our patients safe and to keep *you* safe.

Teams change all the time and that's part of the problem. Certain teams just work better together than others and some nurses have an expertise that other nurses can't match. When you work with those nurses you think, *we've got a great team tonight and we can handle anything.* But if there are teams with weaker nurses—people who are not as experienced or people who just don't work as well together—then you're up against barriers to provide care. When the healthcare team doesn't work together well that takes away the joy.

When I was working at that small hospital as a supervisor there were not many education programs for the nurses and, as a result, there was very little evidence-based care. The nurses were doing their best, but they were working in the dark, without knowledge. It was extremely scary. You don't know what you don't know and because of that you're putting patients at risk every day. I didn't feel comfortable working there. Patients and families were often not satisfied and that's not a good environment to work in. I left because leadership wasn't going to make changes, they weren't invested in patient safety, and they weren't interested in educating nurses.

When I'm not feeling joy in work, I do have some control. There's always a chain of command. I can go to a director or I can bring more help into the room. In our hospital we have intensive care/critical care doctors we can go to, lean on, and get help from with our rapid response or code blue teams. We have great working relationships with them, and they support and help us. My colleagues and I always feel we have backup layers of support.

Advice

Leaders have to be keyed in and listen to the front-line staff. Acknowledge their insights as to what will work and what won't. Always make time for rounds on the floor and know what's going on with your employees so you know how to support them, how to get them resources, how to have enough staff, how to give them enough time to do the work you're asking them to do. We're always asking them to do more but how can we make sure that what we're asking them to do is possible?

Include joy in work as a goal for people working in your organization. If you can't focus on the joy of the caregivers by making sure they feel supported by the system, then you're not going to be able to make changes for the patients. The staff won't be motivated to make things better if they feel pushed down by the system.

It takes leadership to change culture—whether the challenge is decreasing central line infections or implementing checklists routinely, these will become part of the culture only at the insistence of leaders.

We always need to improve our communication in healthcare. Doctors need to make nurses feel heard and *really listen* to them. Don't intimidate them. In healthcare we have that problem—nurses do it to each other, physicians do it to nurses, and physicians do it to each other. This also applies to respiratory therapists, physical therapists, radiation technicians, and so on. Treat people as you want to be treated.

Nurses are asked to do so much with so little. Resources and time are always getting pulled back. When there are emergencies those resources really get tight, so people get stressed and communication degrades, and people can be rude and impatient with each other. Nobody's perfect, but we can always say, "I'm sorry I responded to you that way. I'm sorry I was impatient." There is a time when you can debrief and clarify that situation so next time you will all have a better understanding and work better as a team.

For nurses starting out in this field today, don't expect to know everything. Learn to be comfortable with not knowing. Humble yourself and be ready to learn. Ask a lot of questions. As I always say, "Ask a dumb question before you do something dumb." You can always ask a dumb question, but you can't take back a dumb action. The nurses who make me the most nervous are the ones who think they know everything. They're going to run into problems because they think they know it all.

37. Sarah D., MD, Physician and Practice Manager of a Small Group Gynecologic Private Practice

Sarah D., MD, former co-owner and current practice manager of a small group gynecologic private practice, has been a gynecologist for 28 years. She gave up the obstetrics part of her practice after the terrorist attacks of 9/11; eventually gave up surgery; and, most recently, sold her practice to a larger organization. Sarah's experiences in letting go and her willingness to embrace change have led to increased control over her work life, greater peace of mind, and enhanced joy.

Since I was in middle school there was something about hospitals I liked. I was a candy striper as soon as I was old enough to be one. My mother frequently told me how obnoxious I was about my uniform and my little nurses' shoes. I was very compulsive about my shifts and being there on time. Literally, my job was to fill up ice buckets and water buckets. But I remember when we worked a certain number of hours, we got our caps; and then with each additional little milestone we got stripes on our caps.

Originally, I thought I'd be interested in going into hospital administration, in running hospitals. My two aunts were nurses and they were the first ones who told me, "You know, you should be a doctor." This was back when that wasn't really something women did. I also have four brothers, and my father, at that time, thought girls were there to cook and clean and were not good for much else. When I told him I wanted to go to medical school, he asked, "What's your backup plan?"

I was one of these kids in high school who worked hard and got okay grades. In my freshman year of college, there was a meeting for premed students. There are a few things I remember in my life: they put up a slide that said, "Based on your SAT scores what is the likelihood that you could go to medical school?" Next to my score was the little comment, "You may want to consider a different profession." I was a bad test-taker. That comment pissed me off.

From there I went to a school career counseling center and took all these personality tests that tell people what they would be good at. I sat with the counselor who told me that, based on my scores, I should be a stewardess. You can't make this stuff up! I thought, *you've got to be kidding me!* I decided I would do what I wanted and go for it. When I was a junior taking the MCATs, which I didn't do very well on, I had a premed advisor who told me he didn't think I would get into medical school. There was a program in my state geared toward getting students from small, rural places into medical school. I got into that program, did get into medical school, and got into a top-ranked residency program. I became chief resident in my senior year.

In medical school, while doing the rotations trying to figure out what I wanted to do, I really didn't have a good sense of what I wanted to focus on. My first rotation was psychiatry at a facility for veterans, which I thought was scary; then I did general surgery, which I didn't like; then internal medicine, where people were very sick and weren't getting better; and then pediatrics, which I really liked, but kids at that teaching hospital were so sick and sometimes they died. That didn't give me a good sense of general pediatrics, which would have meant taking care of much happier, healthier babies.

Then I did a rotation in obstetrics/gynecology (OB/GYN). The patients were relatively healthy, we made them better, most of the time it was happy, and we could empower them so much with their choices and their health. Then the pediatric part of OB/GYN, which I didn't realize one could do, felt good. OB/GYN as a specialty involved some surgery, some emergency care, and preventive care. Once I made my choice, I was very sure that's what I wanted to do. I had some great mentors and professors in medical school and residency. From there I decided I really didn't want to go into academics, I just wanted to go into practice.

I finished my residency in 1990 and worked in two different private practices before this one. My first year was in a private practice affiliated with a hospital in the city where I'd done my residency. I was there for only a year because I got married, moved, and joined another private practice. Eventually my husband and I moved here, I went into my third private practice with my father-in-law, and eventually became an owner. In those first two practices I was the most junior with the least experience, but I learned a lot from the people who ran those practices about staffing models and what makes for a well-run practice.

My "Aha" Moment

I stopped the obstetrical part of my practice after the terrorist attacks in 2001, which had a huge impact on my life, professionally. At the time my children were quite young: three, six, and nine years old. Those attacks took place just before the High Holidays that year. Our rabbi gave a sermon about the fact that no one calling from those planes was calling work to let people know they were about to die—they were all calling their loved ones.

At that point we were four female obstetricians and a nurse-midwife. We had two very busy offices, but we hadn't structured our practice very well. It would have been better if we had insights into how to share call, and how to take off after being on call instead of going right back to the office. But since we didn't, I'd go for days without seeing my kids. And then when I did see them, I was so exhausted I was not being a good parent and relying on childcare too often. My husband was a very busy surgeon, so we were often out in the middle of the night. I was sitting there, exhausted, during the rabbi's sermon thinking about life, and I just decided to reprioritize. Before that day I had never even considered it because I loved my work—there's nothing like delivering a baby—but I decided to stop the obstetrics part of the practice.

At the time, two people in our practice were moving out of the area and I was interviewing candidates to come into the practice. We were good and empathetic obstetricians and all women, and we were always busy. But the week after hearing that sermon I put a stop to the interviews and decided not to hire anyone. That week, any new obstetrical patients who called were told we were not accepting new patients. We delivered all our current patients' babies, which took us to that summer, and saw fewer and fewer patients. We consolidated our two offices into one, cut down on our staff, cut down on our malpractice insurance, and I had a very different lifestyle—one in which I could sleep and be the parent I wanted to be.

Early on, we brought in a business consultant who said we needed to identify who was running the practice, which is how I got into the role of managing this practice as well as seeing patients. Today, I am a full-time physician and practice manager of a small group private practice in gynecology and gynecologic oncology. Including me, we have five physicians, two physician assistants, and one nurse practitioner.

I work Monday, Tuesday, Wednesday, and Friday. I see patients starting at 8:00 a.m. and see patients probably until 4:30 p.m. Tuesday afternoons from 2:00 p.m. to 5:00 p.m. is my designated administrative time for the office, when I meet with the practice administrator and the billing manager. Once a month we have a manager's meeting, which includes our front desk manager and our nurse manager, to go over everything from our profits and losses to approving purchases, hiring, staff reviews, new technology, and new equipment to bring into the office. We now do ultrasound in the office, and three months ago we brought pelvic floor muscle training nurses in for the first time, so we monitor all of that. Physically, I spend 10–12 hours a day in the office. I also log in and answer patient portal messages over the weekend. We share call one week at a time but it's all just by phone.

I no longer practice surgery—hysterectomies, pelvic surgery, ovarian surgery, and vaginal surgery—which I used to do, so I'm completely office based. I stopped surgery because surgery was not my strength. As I get older, I appreciate my strengths and weaknesses. As a surgeon I was too anxious and too tentative, and I didn't enjoy it. The practice has three gynecologic surgeons, who perform surgery more often so I could focus on seeing patients in the office—which is what I like to do—without having to send patients out of the practice for surgery.

On Joy in Work

Relationships

I love my patients. I can have true impact, even on people coming in for well visits who aren't sick, if they are open to what I have to teach them. The beautiful thing about my job is that I've been taking care of some of these women since I delivered their kids. And now I'm taking care of their daughters, which is *wonderful*. I love seeing the women and their children grow and developing these relationships. It's not just about their gynecologic care but about asking how they are doing in life? Since I have been seeing some patients for many, many years, I enjoy hearing about the wonderful things going on with their families and their work and can share with them during sad times as well.

I have a subspecialty interest and certification in pediatric and adolescent gynecology, which has been an interest of mine since residency. I think I'm the only community-based gynecologist in my county who will see children. Establishing relationships with pediatricians has been rewarding. Seeing young adolescents with menstrual problems and working in the whole contraceptive arena is great for me as a specialist in women's health.

The Role of Personality

What I have found is that joy in work comes from the type of person you are when you're not at work—from your personality. If I find people who are not so happy at work, they're also not so happy when they're not at work. If you're generally a happy person in your life, you're happy at work. I see it in the people who work with us.

The Electronic Medical Record

I took typing in high school—we called it "keyboarding" then—so I can talk and type at the same time. I love the EMR. I used to drag bags of charts home with test results every night. Then I couldn't find the charts I needed, and within the charts I couldn't find the information I wanted. With the EMR, I can log in and look at lab results while I'm talking to someone, which increases my efficiency tremendously. Like most physicians, I'm a little type A, so I like my inbox to be empty. The EMR just helps me organize.

We went through different changes with the EMR and until we could get all the data in one place, it was painful. But now we have everything, and we have the notes from the previous year, so it's much easier for me to see patients and get to the information I need. I do a lot of preventive and well visits, so with our EMR I can bring over a patient's history and exam from the prior year. That makes it so much easier because I can just note any changes, and I don't have to ask everyone every year, "How much calcium are you taking?" I can just ask, "Are you still taking X amount of calcium that you were taking last year?" Or I can say, "Last year you mentioned Y," and follow-up on that.

Other Technological Innovations

We've tried a number of different approaches to charting—we had virtual scribes for a while to help with that. Now we're conducting a trial with a company that uses artificial intelligence to document the notes using a watch. I dictate notes about my assessment and treatment plan into my watch, either while I'm in the exam room or as soon as I leave it, and the program in the watch puts it into a computer. It's learning my voice, my cadence, my rhythms, and puts the notes into the chart. At the end of the day, I just have to make some corrections and sign off. Some of this technology is great.

Managing the practice, I get to make decisions about some of the products we're using and set up the templates and so on. There is some benefit to being able to make the decisions. I have a lot of control—over my time, my environment, the technology we use, my workload. For me, that's been very helpful.

On Money and Joy

I'm sure there is a relationship between money and joy, but I hope money doesn't motivate me. We try very hard not to put the incentive of direct financial gain into what people do at the office. For example, when someone wanted us to bring in a vaginal rejuvenation laser because it's a great money-maker for other practices, I said, "Absolutely not" because I don't believe in the technology or what it represents. That was my decision. Ultrasound, yes. Pelvic floor strengthening, yes. These are things that have science behind them. I'm not in a position to sell things to my patients. I don't like to go into other offices where people start selling me products or services. The good news is I'm in a position to say no.

I think people need to be compensated fairly for what they do and the expertise they bring to their jobs. I think there's comfort in knowing I don't have to live paycheck to paycheck like so many people do, and that if there's something I see and would like to buy, I can.

What Diminishes Joy

What diminishes joy in work for me is the frustration that comes from knowing I'm not having an impact on a patient's health or their lives. I know some patients do not hear me and I'm not going to have an impact on their lives. They're just not open to it. I find joy in giving people accurate medical information so they can feel better and live better; but if a patient is not open to it, it can be frustrating.

Some of my most challenging patients are those who are overweight. I see women as they age. I see the women who age well because they keep their weight under control, exercise, and manage their stress. And I see other women who have horrible diseases and horrible things happen to them. What tends to motivate some women to lose weight is that they have a reunion or a wedding to go to, rather than hearing, "You're going to have a heart attack." I'll ask, "What would you have to hear to change what you're doing now? Because until you're open to doing something differently, nothing will change." Sometimes I think, *why am I wasting my time and your time?*

Necessary Change

About 15 months ago, after much soul-searching, we sold the practice. I still run the practice, so for all intents and purposes my day-in and day-out decisions are the same. We decided to become part of a large umbrella medical group, so some of the processes are different—but for our patients and our staff, things have been pretty much the same. We could see that hospitals were buying practices and doctors were moving into larger groups. We needed to be in a better bargaining position with insurance companies, with purchasing, and even with group health insurance—for our employees, the larger our group, the easier it is. Now that we're part of a much larger group, the premiums are less. This organization has bought quite a few OB/GYN practices in the area. They have much greater bargaining power to go to insurance companies for better reimbursement rates and bundles, which is great. As a solo practitioner, insurance companies wouldn't even call me back.

We became employees and had to sign employment contracts. We have a business meeting once a month. They've helped us bring in the pelvic floor nurses and do some of the things I'd wanted to do but just didn't have the resources for. They're helping with alternate income streams for the practice. They're the ones who brought in the new watch technology and, like millennials, they want us to make appointments and do everything else online.

Being a physician is a marvelous calling. I don't consider it a job—it's part of my personality, it's part of who I am. When you find something you're passionate about and something you're good at, it becomes part of who you are.

38.   Kevin S., MD, Senior Vice President and Chief Medical Officer for an Integrated Health Plan

An internist by training, Kevin S., MD, has always liked combining clinical with administrative work. His joy comes from helping patients access the care they need and nurturing talent in his organization. Bureaucratic drudgery, the culture of blame in medicine, and the failure of leaders to listen is what diminishes his joy in work. Kevin's antidote? To listen to, observe, and try to understand the people he works with. He also suggests taking some risks to try to move things forward.

My father was a primary care doctor, which probably had something to do with my wanting to go into healthcare. My mother was a nutritionist. When I was 15 my grandfather, who lived with us, had a cardiac arrest and collapsed in our house. My father and I tried to resuscitate him and bring him back. It didn't work. That indelible memory, plus the fact that I've always liked helping people, made me want to make a difference and set me on this path. My major in college was not related to medicine yet I completed all my premedical training. I always liked that bigger picture perspective—being challenged by multiple things and having a broad point of view rather than working in a specific area. After some debate I decided to go to medical school and then completed my residency.

My Professional Journey

After my internship and residency, I was asked to stay on as chief resident. The chief resident's role had an administrative focus: making schedules, managing residents, troubleshooting between departments, teaching, leading morning rounds, and managing conferences. I started doing clinical work half-time and spent the other half of my time working with the chairman of medicine. I took on more training and educational roles for the program and residents and got involved with the business side of the department, with oversight of about 80 internists in training.

When I started in practice, I continued to do administrative work half-time. I've always had an eye toward doing both. I've always felt that either you're managed or you manage, and I like to be in a position where I have input and say, and to work in areas that are creative or developmental. I've been doing this for more than two decades. Over this tenure my clinical role has stayed about the same, but the administrative piece has evolved.

Almost 20 years ago, when health maintenance organizations were starting to come into their own, I became president of an independent practice association, which had a group of about 400 physicians. This group of physicians came together to work with the major health plans in our market to take on and learn how to manage risk.

I was on the board of my health plan for ten years before transitioning into my current role. Prior to that I was vice president for community practice, chief of internal medicine, and maintained a part-time practice. I still practice two afternoons a week for about three hours each day. I see about ten people a week on an ongoing basis. So, I'm still kind of "real" from the perspective of knowing what clinicians are dealing with on the one hand and knowing the needs of the management side, on the other.

My hours are not fixed. I'm a salaried employee. I work at least 40–50 hours a week. It varies. Some days can be lighter, and other days I will have meetings in the evenings, dinners, or conferences to attend. I don't put in any less than 40 hours a week, but it would be unusual for me to work as many as 55 hours a week. With the exception of about six hours a week it's all administrative now.

On Joy in Work

Joy in work means feeling I've accomplished something at the end of a day or the end of a period. That I feel I've made a difference by what I'm doing. It's feeling that what I'm saying and what I bring to the table matters. And that my work makes a difference to the product we provide for people. We're dealing with people as patients, not just members. What we do for them makes a difference to their health and well-being.

I get satisfaction from helping high-performing individuals to move up the corporate ladder. One of the women I worked with, a director who is African American, was working on issues related to cost management. She and I worked for a period of time on diversity strategies. We wanted to convince people this was something we needed to do and get traction around, and she sponsored a number of programs. Long and short of it, she became our vice president of diversity. It's nice to see someone move in that direction. Those are the kinds of things that make life fun.

The positives in work are being able to help people get the care they need. When we were able to support the state with additional money to buy and distribute a medication to people with substance use disorder—and when we were able to educate women who needed in vitro fertilization that implanting a single embryo was safer than implanting multiple embryos—that felt good.

I'm very happy in what I do. My job has allowed me to do the things I'm interested in. At my level I have a lot of latitude to participate in things I may not have gotten to do otherwise. It has allowed me to get off the treadmill of what healthcare is these days.

Organizational Culture

We tend to be an extremely collaborative, consensus-driven organization. Tensions are generally resolved well but they are also rare. Most of the time there is ample time for input and conversation and processing of what we're trying to achieve. We tend to work in groups and toward consensus. So, the number of times we're going to clash or butt heads with somebody directly is fairly infrequent, which makes it a very positive place to work.

It's a transparent organization and a judgment-free environment. In many of our meetings titles don't mean so much—in a meeting with senior vice presidents, managers or coordinators will feel comfortable raising things they are concerned about. On the other hand, people have different agendas, different priorities. Frequently this requires reconciling points of view and trying to prioritize needs. That's where the friction occurs, where there are limited resources and limited time, which determines who gets bigger band width today versus tomorrow.

At my level the overarching feeling is that the organization is overwhelmingly supportive. We each do an annual performance evaluation, a 360-degree approach. We get input from peers, from our superiors and reports, and people we work with on a regular basis to get a composite point of view.

What Diminishes Joy

Joy in work is up and down. There are days when I feel I've hit one out of the park, and there are days when I just feel like I'm slinging mud. It's the nature of work. The mud slinging is dealing with the bureaucracy, some of the rules and regulatory issues that simply challenge, on a day-to-day basis, our ability to get work done. These are things over which I have limited control, usually related to fulfilling regulatory requirements.

What else diminishes joy in work for me? It can get frustrating when I don't feel I'm getting ahead: projects are getting bogged down or I'm not being as successful as I'd like to be in moving things forward. Sometimes it's the nature of a project—a lot of the things we do are very complex. We're dependent upon vendors, IT support, and others. It's not a lack of communication but sometimes a lack of understanding of what each person is trying to accomplish that can be frustrating at times. It can be frustrating when you have different people with very strong points of view. I think I'm a rational and reasonable person; when I see other people for whom a decision is an emotional call it can be frustrating.

There sometimes are personality differences that can diminish joy in work. The challenge is trying to work on relationships to understand where someone is coming from and what their point of view is. Like many other organizations we've taken personality tests that can help you and your peers to understand each other better. There are people we align with and people we are completely, 180 degrees opposite from in terms of how we see the world. There are the alpha folks and the analytic people, the social people and the collaborators. It's helpful to understand who I'm dealing with and where they're coming from. It doesn't mean they are right or wrong, but I have a better sense of what their point of view is, and how best to interact with them, if I can understand their personality traits.

The Opposite of Joy in Work

The opposite of joy in work is being caught in bureaucratic drudgery; feeling that what you do doesn't have relevance to anything; that you're just doing it, going through the motions; that there's no appreciation of what you're doing by anybody. It is rare in healthcare on the provider side that people acknowledge the positives. It's almost expected. But they do tend to recognize the negatives or the failures—and that goes right back to residency. It's sort of, if you're doing your job and you're doing it well nobody says anything. But if something goes wrong then they're all over you.

The opposite of joy in work is recognizing there are things that should be done differently and that you could contribute to improving, but you're being completely shut out of that process—only to see the thing fall flat on its face a year or two later because the intrinsic flaws in what people were doing were evident, they knew it, but the senior person wasn't going to listen to anybody. It's like that old joke, "I've made up my mind so don't confuse me with the facts." It's very frustrating to get into that kind of negative feedback loop.

Advice

My advice to bosses and colleagues is to understand the points of view of your people. Listening and observation are huge. If you don't understand where people are coming from it's really hard to have a conversation that will move them anywhere. Whether it's someone above me, or someone working with me, the better I know them the better I can understand their priorities and the better I can anticipate their concerns over time. Often that understanding eliminates or minimizes any kind of friction.

On some level, part of having joy in work is being willing to take risks and being in an environment that allows you to do that. Whether those are risks in career moves, or risks in business activities, having something that's challenging, that pushes you a little bit, creates a level of excitement in what you're doing. Of course, there's a balance between excitement and panic—but the ability to move things forward even a little is a good thing for people to do. If you're getting too comfortable in what you're doing, sometimes that's not as interesting.

39.   Haley N., MA, Music Therapist

Haley N., a board-certified music therapist for the past 12 years, has a BA in psychology with a minor in music studies and a master's degree in creative arts therapy. Haley has worked as a music therapist at a day program for adults with severe mental illness, in a rehabilitation hospital, and now works in a facility providing long-term care, rehabilitation, and hospice services.

When I was an undergraduate, I thought I wanted to study child psychology because I always loved working with kids. I worked at camps and I worked with children with special needs. When I worked with children with special needs, I played a lot of music for them and I saw a lot of engagement and response. I realized how powerful music was before I knew music therapy was a profession.

I found music therapy in a career book, which suddenly made so much sense because I had been practicing it for so many years without knowing it was a real profession. When I found that I decided to add music studies as my minor because I was already halfway through college. Then I took the GREs because I realized I wouldn't be able to do anything in psychology with just a bachelors' degree. I applied to graduate school and wanted to learn about not just music therapy but about art therapy and dance therapy. I found one of the only programs that was clinically focused: it was focused on psychology, on the healthcare professional side, rather than on the music side, as many programs were.

I work at a facility that provides long-term care, rehabilitation, and hospice services. I work eight hours a day, five days a week. I work later shifts when I take the residents on outings, which I do about once a week. I like to take them to a free jazz concert once a month. And then a lot of really wonderful nonprofit organizations give away tickets to basketball games, baseball games, plays, musicals, and more. The residents meet to discuss which outings they'd like to take.

The residents are here for a range of problems. If they are here for rehab, then they're expected to be discharged to home after a certain amount of time and discharged by either the occupational therapist or the physical therapist. They may need hip or knee replacements, and some have had many falls.

In the morning I check in with my boss, let him know I'm here, greet the residents, and pass out the newspaper. Not everyone's eyesight is good enough to read the newspaper, although those who can read it like to know what's going on. We discuss the news and what they think about it. The size of the groups can range anywhere from five to 15 people. The youngest resident in my group is in his mid-30s, the oldest is 99. Some are here for brief periods and some of them are here for good.

Every day we stretch doing seated aerobics—the rehab folks, the long-term care folks, and those who are there for hospice care. Depending on their ability to get up and about in their wheelchairs or with walkers or canes, they'll come to my group. Sometimes I'll have residents who aren't participating at all, but who are there for auditory stimulation with the music.

We move to the music. Usually I put on music that they know, like Motown, funk, soul, disco, even going back to big bands and doo-wop. It's a lot of fun. I'll even get some staff and volunteers or family members involved, which is good because a good percentage of the staff is overweight. I work with a dietitian on fitness. If we don't have healthy staff, then we can't take care of the residents. I'm trying to encourage the staff to do some seated aerobics. They don't even have to stand up. You'd be amazed at how much you can sweat just doing seated aerobics.

Some of the residents, who don't participate in the current events session because understanding and cognition are difficult, will be able do seated aerobics. They'll see me doing movements, they'll recognize the songs, and they'll do the movements, too. Or they'll just clap. Or their moods will just brighten—you'll see it. Some residents are hard of hearing, so I keep the music pretty loud. Sometimes someone will ask, "Can you turn that down?" And I'll say, "No, actually!"

My title is music therapist, but I do way more than that. I wear many different hats. I'm involved in many committees. I do stretching sessions three to four times a week. I play music trivia and Name that Tune with the residents as a memory exercise. It gives them time to reminisce, to socialize, to remember the songs, and to talk about where they were when the songs were popular. And we make it a game, so I might say, "We're going to do teams." And I know which people know a lot about the music, so I won't put them all on the same team. Other times it's every man for himself.

On Joy in Work

Joy in work means bringing joy to the residents' day, seeing them laugh and smile, or giving them a new experience, whether through an outing or providing entertainment that's not a regular occurrence. For example, I have brought in some of my magician friends. I have a lot of creative friends so it's easy for me to find people who are willing to volunteer for a few hours to do what they usually do for the residents.

My boss likes to know what we're doing and, for the most part, I let him know what's going on. He is a big music fan, so he enjoys talking music. He lets me do the work I need to do, and he trusts me to do it. He gives me a lot of creativity and free rein. I try to make sure I'm asking him things just to make sure. I have a lot of autonomy. He's a good boss.

In addition to my salary and benefits, which are good, I do get recognized by my bosses and colleagues. We recently had a staff meeting about what supervisors can do to reward employees for a good job. I definitely feel recognized. I've been given different awards throughout the years for things I've done. I've been featured on the website and on the radio. Community groups take note and we get donations because of it.

What Diminishes Joy

I have a very low tolerance for sounds, and there is a lot of environmental noise here. They're doing construction. They have a wandering management system for residents who are at risk for elopement. These residents wear bracelets with sensors, and they go off all day long. It can drive me crazy. There's also a lot of beeping on the unit. Many people can tune that out and ignore it but I'm not one of those people. I hear it so clearly and I have a hard time tuning it out. I close the door or put on headphones when I need to focus on my documentation.

I sometimes feel overloaded by work. I'm the only creative arts therapist, so I have a lot of demands on my time. It would be better if I had at least one other. When I had an intern it was amazing, because for the first time I could be off work and my groups were covered. Now when I'm away nobody really covers my groups.

I'm never really on top of my documentation, like writing in the charts all the things I do with each of the residents. Part of me thinks, if I were always on top of my notes, then the groups would never have any activities. People see that. If I'm not writing a note every day, at least for the quarterly team meeting I'm writing a note of all the things the residents did in the last quarter.

The purpose of this documentation is accountability: that when our long-term care surveyors come in, they see that all aspects of person-centered care are being addressed. So, not only are the residents being treated for the condition they're here for, but are they engaging psychologically? Are they getting cognitive stimulation for mental health? What are they getting for range of motion? Are there pleasure foods—even though they may have a special diet, are they still able to enjoy a piece of cake now and then, like at the birthday parties we have every month? Especially in the long-term care setting, we have visiting animals, including birds and therapy dogs.

The physical space in our office is really small. I don't have a designated space to hold one-on-one sessions or groups. I have to make do with what's here. I've gotten used to it, but the physical space has always been an issue. I would like to have a designated space for my groups and to have additional staff for music, art, and dance.

I feel so fortunate that I found a career that is creative and keeps me thinking. I never know what I'm going to run into. It's a healthcare facility and hospice and there are a lot of deaths on the unit, so I have to deal with those. But I've learned that with the sadness comes joy: I was fortunate to know these people in the last season of their lives, they had full lives, and they're no longer suffering and no longer in pain. After the first few deaths I really didn't cry. I felt sadness, but I felt privileged to have known them and to have cared for them even for that short period of time.

40. *Marianne S., PhD, Counseling Psychologist in Private Practice and Adjunct Professor*

> For Marianne S., PhD, a counseling psychologist in private practice, joy comes from being able to relate to and help people; feeling valued and appreciated for her work and getting paid for it; and having the autonomy, control, and flexibility that comes from being her own boss. Marianne's last job, in which she felt overworked, disrespected, and controlled, has heightened her appreciation for and pride in the practice she has built.

From a young age I always liked helping people. I found it very fulfilling. I was always fascinated that talk therapy could be helpful for people—how exploring the past could provide insight, almost like a puzzle—and I wanted to learn more about it. I learned more about it when I majored in psychology in college and talked to my professors. I wasn't sure whether I wanted to go into academia or not, but that was one of the options. I graduated with my degree in 2011. I worked as a therapist and taught while I was still in graduate school. I've worked at different university counseling centers and worked at my last one for four years.

A couple of things led me to go into private practice. I never really thought I'd want to work in private practice full time. I thought it would be too lonely or too stressful. But my job at the university became very stressful. There were leadership issues and the administration made too many demands on staff. College counseling centers have historically been great places to work because the work is interesting and you're helping people through a very difficult time in their lives. But counseling centers have moved toward short-term work, with less therapy and more crisis intervention, and often decisions are made by people without degrees in psychotherapy.

My last counseling center job had a high risk for burnout because I was working and working and working; I wasn't paid much; and I was being told what to do, which had more to do with organizational politics than with ethically sound care. For instance, if a student went to the hospital intoxicated and made a flippant remark about wanting to hurt himself, the university wanted us to persuade the student to waive his right to confidentiality while he was still intoxicated. That is unethical. I just didn't feel comfortable working there anymore.

And then things changed in my life. I had a child and realized I wanted more flexibility. I started a part-time private practice while I was still employed by the university, then decided to stay in private practice full time because I realized I loved the work.

I work about 25 hours a week and see from four to seven patients a day. The bulk of my clinical load is Monday-Thursday, when I work five to eight hours a day. In addition to psychotherapy, I also provide supervision sessions for doctoral students in psychology as part of their training.

The bulk of what I practice is individual therapy. I typically meet with people for 45 minutes or one hour for weekly sessions. Some people meet with me for short-term work, say 10–20 sessions, but most people meet with me for longer-term work. I've been seeing some people for years.

People come to see me for so many different reasons. Often, they come in because they're struggling with something. It may be a transition issue. Much of it is family related.

Or they may have some trauma in their background. Often these things contribute to their being anxious or depressed. It really does vary from person to person.

I try to tailor my work to the person. We often will explore their history, their patterns, and try to gain a deep understanding of why they're experiencing the things they're experiencing. Why they're having the conflicts they're having. Why they're having the anxiety they're having. Why they're having the interpersonal issues they're having.

On Joy in Work

I think about joy a lot in my work with people. When it comes to joy, I think it comes down to being able to make your own definition of success.

I love my job. It's the best job I've ever had. I think it's because I feel valued, I feel I have connection and, especially on days when I feel I'm doing good work, I feel very excited to be doing what I'm doing.

I also feel a great sense of accomplishment in having my own business—it's exciting and something I feel passionate about. It's a combination of feeling that I'm doing something useful and being compensated for it or appreciated and valued for it.

On Money and Joy

I do think there's a relationship between money and joy. I'm still relatively new at this. I've been in full-time private practice for about two and a half years, definitely long enough to feel I'm getting compensated for what I do. It feels really good that people value my services enough to pay for them. So, I feel valued, I feel that people take my work seriously. As a business owner it's really good to see that I'm contributing to my family and that my income is going up on a regular basis—that gives me a sense of accomplishment.

What Diminishes Joy

What can diminish joy in work for me now is working with someone and not feeling I'm being helpful enough. Many people come in feeling hopeless and it's a wonderful thing when I can give somebody hope. But that doesn't always happen. It can be very difficult, very challenging, to not know what to do to help someone. To be really worried about someone's life. What do I do if I feel that way? If I'm really worried about peoples' safety, I can hospitalize them. I've had to hospitalize people before.

One thing that really helps me when I'm feeling this way is participating in a consultation group, where different therapists get together. Someone who is very knowledgeable and established in the field leads the group. We talk about our patients and challenges, de-identified, of course. In private practice we don't have colleagues, people we can help and learn from. So, this group provides that, and I find it really helpful. I go to this group when I feel de-skilled or have doubts about my ability to be an effective therapist. It's a place to be centered and grounded. Something I knew I would miss about not working in a counseling center anymore was not having colleagues.

What diminished joy in the counseling center was feeling underappreciated—not by my clients but by the larger system; feeling overworked; feeling that parts of the job just didn't make sense; and being around people I didn't trust or who didn't seem very competent. There were lots and lots of crises and lots of hours without breaks. I was there eight hours a day and then had to be on call on a regular basis. I'd be responsible for being by the phone and could get a call at any point.

The crises were difficult, but it wasn't just the crises—it was the walk-ins when I had no way of knowing why someone was there. I would have no idea what to expect when someone walked into my office; I was never told who was coming to see me, or why. During walk-in hours students could come in any time and be seen. I would just see people lined up on my schedule. Was somebody in crisis who would need to go to the hospital? The situation felt totally uncontained.

It was a very reactive system where I couldn't say no. There were no boundaries, like telling someone they could wait for an appointment while someone else couldn't. This person is in crisis, this person can't wait. When the person walked in, I may have thought, *this person could have waited until next week.* The hours weren't advertised as crisis hours. They were just advertised as walk-in hours. Even if someone could have waited, we still had to see them.

It was all very short-term work where I wasn't really forming relationships with people; I was putting on a bandage and saying, "Here's an option you have, but I'm not going to be the one to help you with it," or "Here, try this," or "Here's a workshop you can try." It was frustrating, stressful, and it made me think, *what am I doing here? This isn't why I got into this.*

Staff retention was a huge problem there. Staff were dropping like flies. Nobody wanted to stay there. From what I saw it didn't seem they were doing much at all to retain staff. It was more like, "let's just try to get what we can out of them. If people leave, they leave, that's okay." People kept leaving and nothing changed. When I started there, a lot of people had already left so there were very few staff. While I was there, rounds of people would leave suddenly. On a regular basis people would announce they were leaving. In the four years I was there, they were never fully staffed. That turnover definitely led to burnout. It's demoralizing when people you really care about leave and nothing is done to get them to stay. They would hire new staff, but people wouldn't stay long. And the staff that remained would be even more overburdened because there were so few of us, which leads to burnout.

I only feel overloaded by work now if I want to be. I can tell myself I'm only going to do administrative work on Fridays, or I'll do makeup sessions on Fridays. But then I'll get calls and I'll think maybe I should schedule people on Fridays. Or some Fridays. But if that proves to be too much, I'll want to have more flexibility because I have kids. So, I have to decide what I want. It's all up to me now.

I have limited experience with all of this but being my own boss was very, very hard to picture, looking back. Being my own boss is a different kind of stress, a different type of pressure. I felt grateful that I had an experience that made me feel I had to leave, because I think I could have gotten complacent. Being my own boss is the best thing ever.

41. *Irene J., MD, OB/GYN Hospitalist for a Small Community Hospital*

Irene J., MD, has been an OB/GYN since 1990. She reduced her level of stress and found the flexibility she needed in her life by transitioning from owning and running a private practice to becoming a hospitalist.

I've always wanted to be a doctor. I thought it was a way I could help people and I always thought that was exciting. I always knew I wanted to work *with* people. My grandfather was a physician—he died when I was about ten years old—and he was the only physician in my family.

I decided to be an OB/GYN when I was in medical school. Going into medical school, I thought I wanted to be a pediatrician. I always loved kids and loved babysitting growing up, but when I did my pediatrics rotation, I wasn't super-excited. Then I did my OB/GYN rotation and thought it was the be-all and end-all. I loved the fact that it combined continuity of care with the element of surprise—I loved the high adrenaline, fast decision-making, think-on-your-feet, never-know-what's-going-to-happen-next nature of labor and delivery. I loved the idea that OB/GYN combines the best of both medical and surgical care. I really liked the idea of taking care of women, especially over the course their lifetimes. It became obvious what I wanted to do, so in my third year of medical school I decided to become an OB/GYN.

I worked in private practice for 25 years, two-thirds of those years in a group practice and the last third as a solo practitioner. The number one benefit of being a hospitalist is the flexibility it offers. When I worked in private practice, I had very little flexibility to take care of acutely ill and terminally ill family members and friends in need. Flexibility is the most positive thing about being a hospitalist. That was the number one reason I made that change in my professional life, but it was a really hard decision to make. Many of my colleagues look at me as a glorified resident and say I'm not in charge. Yes, I am on a payroll; yes, I'm paid by someone else; and yes, I'm someone else's employee now. But when I walk through those doors I am in charge and make my own decisions.

I work in a small community hospital with about 300 patient beds. My title is OB Hospitalist, although I am also responsible for gynecological patients in the emergency department, and OB/GYN consults throughout the hospital. I spend the majority of my day in labor and delivery and rounding on the mother-and-baby unit. I round on our high-risk antepartum, or undelivered, patients and on all of our postpartum patients. I don't work in the ED, but I go down to the ED when they call me. Almost daily, I connect with our social workers and with my colleagues who work in the neonatal intensive care unit (NICU).

A handful of us here do what I do. Each of us works different days each month and a different number of shifts varying from five to nine shifts a month, but we all work 24-hour shifts. I really like this schedule. It provides me with a lot more time off. This allows me to more regularly volunteer my time at a free clinic. I also need more flexibility because I have elderly parents who do not live here and who need me.

I spend my day taking care of and admitting active labor patients, doing scheduled inductions and scheduled cesarean sections. I usually make rounds, then sit down and do all my documenting at once. Documentation can take a long time, and, of course, how much time depends on how many patients I have. It's the part of my work I enjoy the least, but it's critically important to make sure I'm communicating everything I do for each patient to the next person who will provide care to that patient, or to someone who will act on the care I provided. Documenting is laborious and time-consuming, but it is the only way to convey information other than when I'm talking directly to the nurse or the patient or another doctor. It makes it possible for people to know what's going on with our patients.

On Joy in Work

Helping Patients

Joy is the satisfaction I get from doing my job well for the patients I serve. The vast majority of the time, I walk out of work feeling really satisfied that I made a difference. It's a good feeling when I prevent a patient from hemorrhaging, or shorten their hemorrhage, or deliver a baby who might not have made it if I hadn't been there. That's rewarding and exciting, but at the same time emotionally draining. I can't think of many jobs where we can use the skills we were taught to bring happiness or a better outcome to someone else. That, to me, is complete satisfaction.

High-risk patients have to come in for antenatal testing, like monitoring and sonograms, weekly toward the end of their pregnancy. I see a lot of those patients every week for the last three or four weeks, and then take care of them in labor or do their C-section. Even in my role as an OB hospitalist, these high-risk patients are super-excited to see me because they know the doctor who is going to be delivering their baby.

I get instant feedback from being an OB hospitalist. I'm often called emergently to the bedside or to the C-section operating room because the obstetrician needs additional help to get a wedged-in baby out of the abdomen or to relieve a baby's shoulder dystocia, or a nurse calls for help with a postpartum hemorrhage. It's high adrenaline, but it's so satisfying and rewarding when the mom and baby come out okay.

I can see the burnout in a lot of my colleagues. I feel I had a new beginning when I changed to this job, but I know a lot of people who wouldn't want the inherent stress level that goes with my job. Some people find it stressful, other people find it fun. Some people balance it better than others, and people want different things out of medicine. I think I'm very fortunate.

More Time with Family

My kids love my schedule now because I have more time with them. When they were young, I always had to be very selective about what I could and could not volunteer to do for them or their schools. For example, I could co-chair field day—because I could do some fundraising earlier in the year, attend a few organizational meetings, then show up for the event, but it wasn't an ongoing commitment. I also volunteered for every book fair and went to every school program and concert I could possibly attend. Some parents were in the classroom every week, but I couldn't be like those parents. I had to walk a fine line between wanting my kids to know I was involved and not wanting to upset my OB/GYN partners.

Relationships with Nurses

I tend to get along extremely well with my charge nurse and the coordinator of labor and delivery. Technically I feel I work under them because they're the ones who call me when they need something. We each have different skill sets, but they're in charge. They'll make sure I am where I'm needed, and I think we work great together.

I get almost daily feedback from the nurses. I love the nurses I work with. They are amazing, sweet, caring, they give of their hearts, and they're so smart and so talented.

They're such good people and they are incredibly dedicated in their roles. I come into labor and delivery and I am met with huge smiles and five hugs before I even get to my desk. They ask, "Oh, are you on?" There is happiness. That makes my day right there. I come in and get all these warm greetings.

The hospital where I work gives an award every six months to acknowledge respect, integrity, stewardship, empathy, and other qualities of their "top physician." I received that award and I think the nurses I work with were a huge part of my getting it. I was only the second person in my department to ever receive that award, so I have felt very acknowledged. I've only been here a few short years, so to get that award was very, very touching and it meant a lot to me. It's the nicest compliment I could get, especially from the people I work with day in and day out.

On Money and Joy

I'm not sure I'm your "typical" physician, whatever that means, but I have a roof over my head and I can pay my mortgage. I have two children, one who will be out of medical school soon and one who is in the middle of working on her doctorate. My kids are going to come out of school debt-free, which I know a lot of people don't think is their responsibility. But I don't want my kids to have debts that will bias the field they go into because they have to pay loans back. My daughter who's in medical school wants to work with underserved populations. My kids are very service-oriented. I've been very lucky. I have a husband who contributes, too.

I can't complain. We can take at least one trip a year and I can fly out to visit my parents when I need to. Do I know people who have a lot more money than I do? Absolutely. They have a lot more things and nicer things, but I feel very fortunate. There's a difference between needs and wants; I have no needs and I'm very content.

About once a year we network, and we know what other hospitals pay people to do what we do. We probably are underpaid compared to a lot of neighboring hospitals. We haven't pushed too hard on that because we push on other things that are more important. We choose our battles carefully.

What Diminishes Joy

Stress

There was a lot of joy but also a lot of stress that went with running my own business. Every two weeks there was a payroll and a mortgage—I owned the space in which I practiced. I always had multiple employees, some of whom worked part-time and some full time. My productivity and hard work guaranteed that those people and their families would be secure and happy. Becoming a hospitalist has taken a lot of that stress off my shoulders.

Time Away from Family

What diminishes joy in work for me, maybe, is sheer fatigue and time away from loved ones and my family. This is the cost of being a physician. The sacrifices I make are part of the job, but I don't dwell on them because there's not a lot of choice there. There are times when I don't go to certain events or even think about attending them because I'm on call.

No Long-Term Continuity of Care

The negative of being a hospitalist is that I don't have the same long-term continuity of care that I had in private practice. On the other hand, of the patients who are transported to us, some are here for just a day, but some are there for weeks. In a matter of a couple of days, these patients come to know us very well and to trust us. A woman was transported to us recently who lived in another state was pregnant with a high-risk condition and was here visiting family. She became ill on Wednesday, went into labor, and we had to deliver the baby on Friday. The baby will be in the NICU for a month, but if she hadn't come to us, she would have lost her life and her baby. I guarantee that today, that patient would say she knows me better than any of her private practice doctors and appreciates the care we have given her and her baby. Even though we delivered her baby prematurely, she would say we took care of her when she needed the most care and we had a good outcome in the bigger picture. So, although we don't have the same long-term continuity of care, we do have short-term continuity of care and tremendous patient and personal satisfaction.

42.   *Francine J., MD, Internist in a Solo Concierge Practice*

> Francine J., MD, a doctor of internal medicine, has had a solo, private concierge prac-
> tice in a relatively affluent area of the country for the last 12 years. Describing the
> upsides and the downsides of being in solo practice, she says the positives of conci-
> erge medicine far outweigh any negatives. Francine relishes the freedom, autonomy,
> control, and emotional reward of being the boss while working for a company that
> pays her salary and lets her practice as she sees fit.

I've been in practice for almost 30 years. For the first 18 years of my career I was in a group
practice with two other physicians. For the past 12 years, I've practiced concierge medicine and have been an affiliate of a national network of primary care doctors. To become
a patient in my practice, the patient must first join my network. Joining my practice as a
patient is somewhat like joining a gym: patients pay a membership fee every year to the
network; I am not involved in that transaction. I do accept payments from patients' insurance companies when they come into the office to see me.

Doctors are not as well paid as people think. Because of our high overhead costs,
doctors can't afford to practice with only the co-pays and payments from insurance companies, which are minimal. I'm salaried by the network and paid every two weeks. I probably wouldn't still be in practice if I didn't have this additional source of income. My
network allows me to have complete autonomy in running my business and my practice.
They don't dictate how many patients I should see per day or how much time I can spend
with them. They want me to be happy. They want my patients to know they're getting the
best medical care possible.

There are 550 patients in my practice. I am limited by my network to a practice size of
no more than 600 patients so I can spend enough time and give enough attention to each of
them. I may see some of them ten times a year and others 25 times a year. Sometimes I have
to beg patients to come in and see me.

I have a staff of four plus an office manager and billing company, all full time. I'm
off Wednesdays and I work half a day Fridays. The rest of the week I work 9:00 a.m. to
4:00 p.m. I have complete control over my schedule, but it does seem that I work all the
time. That's my choice. Being a doctor is a full-time, out-of-the office job, in addition to
time in the office. Administrative paperwork takes me about ten minutes a day. Paperwork
related to patients takes me about an hour a day. And then there is computer work and
reports to go through, which takes me about three hours a day. Staff concerns take probably ten minutes of my time a day. On my day off my staff calls me all day because they're
still running the office even if I'm not there. For example, a patient can leave a urine sample
or have blood work done even when I'm not in the office. I never mind being contacted
about any questions pertaining to my patients or my practice.

On Joy in Work

Here's the perspective of somebody in a solo practice: it's amazing. It's all mine, I'm so
proud of it. I take care of everybody, so if a good job is done, honestly, it's a reward for me.
Not a financial reward but an emotional one. I have nobody else to ask for help besides
specialists, and they're a very important part of my team. It's really nice being the boss.
I hope I've mastered it by now because I've been doing this by myself for almost 12 years.

Unless you're the boss, and you're by yourself, it's hard to imagine how nice it is to be in that position. It's a great feeling to not have to ask permission to do things.

On the other hand, practicing alone can be a stressor. I generate all the income myself, and all the overhead is my responsibility. I am also responsible for all bad decisions. If something goes wrong, I have to fix it. And I have to pay for it.

I am happy to say that practicing medicine has been very enjoyable, and my patients seem to be very happy with the care I give them. I work hard and I have a very active non-professional life. So, basically, I'm exhausted. But I like to be busy. It's a lot to juggle. But life is great when things are working well and when people are happy. On balance it's totally worth it.

On Money and Joy

I am well aware that a lack of money depletes joy. It's not what you make, it's what your expenses are. I'm a solo practitioner. So, every time my IT person comes in to update and upload my computer, it's $3,000 in two hours.

One of my staff just asked me for a raise. My biggest question is always, do they deserve it? And usually the answer is, I'm not sure. But then I try to put myself in their situation and if they don't have a lot of money, and they're single parents and they need money to pay their expenses, I usually give them a raise. It's really important for me to have staff I can trust and who are hard-working and honest people. I try hard to be a generous employer and I know how difficult it is to survive in these times.

What Diminishes Joy

Lack of communication from other doctors and my fear of missing an abnormal finding for a patient who has seen a specialist or visited the ER diminishes my joy in work. When specialists don't send me information after I refer patients to them, it's difficult for me to understand what they did for those patients. Communication between providers is critical to ensure proper medical care. A lack of communication really slows me down. There are always things to follow up on.

For example, let's say a patient of mine goes to the ER because he has chest pain, and the ER rules out anything cardiac and sends him home. But during that evaluation they do a chest x-ray. And the chest x-ray shows something abnormal and they tell the patient, but the hospital doctor and staff forget to tell me. The patient doesn't remember because he's only human. I always request records from the hospital, which all doctors should do, and I see an abnormality on the chest x-ray that needs to be followed up on. Had I not requested and received this report, and if the patient hadn't remembered to tell me he went to the ER, this abnormality never would have been addressed. Similarly, it is very stressful when I'm reviewing 20 pages of an ER evaluation and I happen to miss one paragraph explaining an abnormal result. I just have to be very meticulous and make sure I don't miss anything.

Yesterday two patients came in and told me they'd been to the ER. One went to the ER because he hurt his thumb and didn't think it was anything worth bothering me about. The other one went to the ER because she cut herself. All minor issues, but I should know about them because I'm their primary care doctor. I never mind patients calling me or seeing me. That is my job.

There are positive and negative sides to computers. Computers enable us send information to other people more quickly—but we are given and have to send way too much information. With all the incredible changes in the medical record world, I now spend three hours a day on the computer. There really should be another system.

I sometimes find it hard to gauge patients' understanding of my instructions for follow-up care. I often wonder whether they understand the need to have particular tests within a certain period of time. I wish there were a computer program that would enable patients to take my typed-up note and explain it to them clearly at home to reinforce what I told them in the office.

I find It stressful when my office atmosphere is not pleasant. I'm the only boss and it's a small office. I have four staff, and sometimes they have to deal with their own individual problems and with problems among themselves. I have to be compassionate not only to my patients, but to my staff. I have to diffuse any type of stress that may be caused by friction among them. I am happy to say that I have wonderful staff and they have kind and friendly dispositions. But when they have personal problems or problems with each other and stress results, I deal with it.

All that said, I love what I do. I love to talk to people. And, of course, I love to help people. I love to make myself available to my patients and family members at all times. For me, joy is based on having successful interactions with others and keeping patients healthy, happy, and safe.

Working in Multiple Roles

43.   Anthony M. DiGioia, MD, Practicing Orthopaedic Surgeon
      and Medical Director of the UPMC Magee-Womens
      Hospital and the UPMC Innovation Center

Anthony M. DiGioia, MD, has always been interested in bridging the gap between engineers and physicians in the clinical practice of medicine and in having an impact. He has been a practicing orthopaedic surgeon for 25 years. During this time, he established the Bone and Joint Center (BJC) at UPMC Magee-Womens Hospital; the UPMC Innovation Center; the not-for-profit AMD3 Foundation, which runs a mission program in Central America called Operation Walk; and the start-up company, GoShadow. He also serves as faculty for the Institute for Healthcare Improvement and adjunct faculty for Carnegie Mellon University. One of the most rewarding experiences of my professional life was to co-author, with Tony, *The Patient Centered Value System: Transforming Healthcare through Co-Design*, published by Taylor & Francis in 2017.

My pathway to medicine was a bit circuitous. I started out training to be an engineer. In all ways, I'm still an engineer in my orthopaedic practice, even today. However, early on, I had not envisioned going into healthcare to provide direct patient care. My interest in mechanics of the body and sports led me to get a master's degree in biomechanics. Then, a physician mentor at the University of Pittsburgh hired me as an engineer to work in their orthopaedic research lab. He felt strongly that there was a need for engineers in medicine. I then had the opportunity to attend their Grand Rounds and was able to observe surgery. Because of this experience and with the encouragement of my mentor, I decided to apply to medical school.

As background, I have a BS degree in Civil Engineering, an MS in Civil and Biomedical Engineering, and then received my MD degree from Harvard Medical School. I then completed my residency in the Department of Orthopaedic Surgery at UPMC and my Fellowship in Adult Reconstructive Surgery at Massachusetts General Hospital.

A personal priority has always been to try to have a high impact in the efforts I undertake. And, certainly, in performing joint replacement surgery (my specialty), I have a very positive, high impact on patients by improving the quality of their lives, "curing" their hip or knee arthritis.

As Founder and Medical Director of the BJC, one of the leading centers in our region for the evaluation and treatment of knee and hip arthritis and joint reconstructive surgery, I'm responsible for developing and maintaining a unique program for patients. The BJC was developed as a "focused care center" or, put another way, a "hospital within a hospital." You can think of the BJC as a free-standing subspecialty hospital that just happens to be inside the walls of an existing hospital. Over the years, we have grown; there are three other full-time orthopaedic surgeons and one part-time orthopaedic surgeon, and we are one of the busiest programs in our region.

The BJC positively impacts patients as well as staff by focusing on meeting the needs of patients and their families through their whole care experience, from the time they first come into the office for a consultation to the time they return from surgery—and then annually thereafter—and everything that happens in between. It's an improved, updated system of healthcare delivery based on the patient-centered value system (PCVS) (the subject of the book *The Patient Centered Value System: Transforming Healthcare through Co-Design*, published in 2017 by Taylor & Francis).

The PCVS is an approach to co-designing improvements in healthcare delivery based on the experience-based design and team-building sciences. For example, our unique care teams include any provider who "touches" the patient's experience, from the surgeon and anesthesiologists to physician assistants, nurse practitioners, nurses, OR staff, rehab, office, and even the parking staff. We cover the entire patient experience and view all care through their eyes.

In other high-impact efforts, I am the founder and medical director of the UPMC Innovation Center, where the PCVS was developed (www.DiscoverDrD.com); founder of the start-up company, GoShadow (www.goshadow.org), a digital shadowing tool for clinicians; and founder of the AMD3 Foundation, which coordinates Operation Walk medical missions in Central America (www.operationwalkpgh.org/). Great teams have been critical to the success of all these efforts.

I call my non-practice activities my "hobbies" because I enjoy them so much. Having these outlets is important to help me maintain joy in work. Taken together, these activities have fulfilled my dreams of going into medicine. Being a surgeon is just one part of what fulfills me. If I were "just" an orthopaedic surgeon I could have continued to help many patients by performing hundreds of surgeries a year, but that was not my goal. My "hobbies" have permitted me to continue to function at a high level and have extended my career as a surgeon while helping me to maintain the balance I need to feel joy in work.

On Joy in Work

Joy in work means having the option (and time) to develop programs, and to work on tasks, that I would work on whether I were getting paid for them or not. It's a high standard. Part of my joy, particularly at this point in my career, does not necessarily come from my doing "things" myself, but more from building programs and teams that allow other people to participate and achieve their goals. Yes, it's always fulfilling to have a positive impact on an individual patient. But one of the joys for me now is being able to build programs that can impact many, many more patients, families, and care providers than I could ever impact alone.

Another effort that gives me joy is our effort to scale and export the PCVS so that *many* leaders and organizations can learn about this updated "operating system" of care delivery, and so their patients and staff can also benefit. So, at this point, my joy comes from the scalability and the broader impact that my work potentially has, not necessarily just from what I do as an individual.

As one example, we have been leading an effort to develop centers of excellence in joint replacement surgery by implementing PCVS at several hospitals. Recently, as a result of our efforts, these hospitals have been recognized as centers of excellence, resulting in better outcomes and efficiencies, and best patient experiences, for an increasing number of patients. These impactful, ongoing wins bring me joy in work.

Everyone Needs a "Safe Haven"

You'd be amazed at how serene, calm, and efficient our operating room is. We have a great team. Everyone knows exactly what their role is, and we all work very hard. For any surgeon, I've always thought the OR should be a protected "safe haven" away from everything else, and that this safe haven is necessary to help maintain joy in work. As a surgeon you should be able to focus solely on the surgery you are performing. Don't worry about what's going on in the office, don't worry about what's going on in the C-suite, just focus on what you need to do to help this patient. It creates a great work environment for the OR staff, too, not just for the doctor, and promotes joy in work for everyone involved.

Being Part of a High-Performance Team

The staff and doctors who work in the BJC really feel they're part of the team. Because the BJC is "hospital within a hospital," everyone has the same focus, which creates a much better sense of teamwork than you'd have in the usual hospital department structure. In addition, we're always re-evaluating and updating processes and protocols to try to provide the best outcomes and experiences for our patients. Everyone is part of the team. Always.

On Money and Joy

There is some relationship between money and joy, but I think it may be overly emphasized. When you look at the factors that make you happy, there's probably a minimum financial requirement because having that gives you options and freedom you may not otherwise have. But other factors are equally important, such as picking a career in which you can feel satisfied and fulfilled. You must feel fulfilled by the job itself. You can't just do it for the money. It's really about engagement—the feeling that you *are* part of a team, that you have some control in your work environment and you can have a positive impact—that's all-important. The financial part gives you sort of a minimal "threshold," but engagement, teamwork, and impact are very important—plus the feeling that you're a valued participant and that your voice is heard.

The Joy of Medical Missions

The AMD3 Foundation sponsors our medical missions, Operation Walk, to Central America in which we perform free hip and knee replacement surgery for those in need. The patients in Central America are different from patients here because their society is so different from ours. Our patients here are very thankful, but you can magnify that by 1,000 for patients in Latin America. Every culture in Latin America is a walking society. If you can't walk, you can't participate in society. People feel they've won the lottery when they are selected to have surgery.

We've now gone on ten missions since we started the program a decade ago. I always tell travel team members before we go that the trip provides a two-way benefit. On the obvious side, we're helping patients who could never afford to have a joint replacement and, in a walking society, all the benefits that go along with that. But there are unexpected benefits for the team members as well. Operation Walk takes us back to the basics of why we went into healthcare—to take care of patients and to have that special relationship with them and with our colleagues. These missions remove all the layers of regulatory and administrative tasks that sometimes get in the way and take us back to basics. I think a lot of people in the United States, just because we've grown up in the system, don't realize how many layers there are that affect the way we care for patients or relate to our colleagues. It's a real eye-opener for travel team members. I warn them, "You'll come back changed," because it happens on every single trip.

One of the nice facets of our trips is that each year, of the 60–70 travel team members we take, approximately one-third are on their first trip. And for the folks who are team leaders and for people who have been on three, four, or five trips, it's really neat to watch the experience through the eyes of the first-time participants. Because that restores the same kind of feeling in all of us—it reminds us of the impact we have on patients and care providers alike. I think that's a very important part of why the trip impacts everyone in such a positive way—it gives us another boost, another way to get through the next year when we return home.

Operation Walk has evolved over the years and one of the most satisfying aspects for me, personally, has been to be able to build the team and organize the logistics for each trip. Our team is big. We bring everyone and everything we need. This past year we brought a record 70 people. More than a third of the team members were on their first trip. Many don't realize how important the logistics are and how much work we do ahead of time to pick the team, put the supplies together, raise the money, and make sure the supplies get there in time.

There's also an educational component to all our trips. We're always partnering with the "home team," which includes the local doctors, nurses, therapists, and care providers. They become part of our team and learn about taking care of patients. We're helping them, they're helping us. Our travel team members often maintain connections with both the patients and the local staff through social media long after the trip is over.

Every team is unique and special. It's amazing that even though many of us have never worked together before, everyone comes together and quickly becomes a team, which is a great experience in itself. Over the course of seven days it's amazing how people come together, become colleagues and friends, and these relationships last for a long time. Operation Walk has ripple effects. Each trip is like one raindrop falling, and the ripples extend far in space and time. This is a very satisfying facet of the program for those of us who plan and organize the trips so that many, many team members can have these unique experiences. More than 300 people have participated over the last decade.

A unique component of our Operation Walk program is that our families also join us on our trips. My wife, Cathy, and all three of our daughters have traveled with us on past trips. In fact, my granddaughter, Eleanor, at four years old, has already been on <u>three</u> trips and has been our youngest volunteer.

What Diminishes Joy

On the flip side, if I perceive that people aren't adopting commonsense and impactful approaches to patient care, that can be frustrating. It can be frustrating at times if I feel that the PCVS or the centers of excellence model isn't being adopted or spread as quickly as I think it should be.

Another downer are negative attitudes, and people's unwillingness to re-evaluate and change, which can be really discouraging at times. However, I try to view each of these hurdles as just another challenge to turn a negative into a positive. I enjoy overcoming challenges coupled with the interim "wins."

In my role as medical director, I often have to mediate situations between providers, hospital leadership and staff, and sometimes even with patients. This is a part of my job I don't really enjoy. However, I view this mediation role as one in which I'm supporting both staff and patients by bringing people together and building a consensus; things are never as black and white as they may first appear. Many times, conflicts result from simple disconnections or miscommunications. My approach to these challenges is to look at problems through the eyes of the person coming to me. If an operating room tech who works with us in the OR comes to me with one problem, and then the CEO of the hospital comes to me with another problem, these problems and solutions are going to be very different. But to understand both, I find it's always best to put myself in their shoes. This gives me a place to start and a perspective that is helpful in coming up with solutions that will help everyone.

Advice

My guiding principle is, it's always important to view everything through the eyes of your end users. It's a simple theme that can be universally applied with patients, families, leadership, and staff. Our tendency is to provide detailed guiding principles that no one remembers and that no one can operationalize. You may have a limited opportunity to provide a guiding principle to your colleagues, so keep it simple. Following this principle is a great way to build high-performing teams and, after all, it's all about team building; the results are very fulfilling.

The Evolution of Joy in Work

Joy in work is an evolution. If you would have asked me what joy in work was in 1992, when I started practice, you would have gotten a completely different answer than you would have ten years later and a completely different answer than I'm giving you now. I think people need to be aware that their definition of joy in work is very likely going to change over time. It's dynamic, not static. I think that's something people sometimes forget. Re-evaluating joy in work, for me, also happens around life-changing, family-oriented situations; most recently, this happened when my first granddaughter was born. Joy in work is a moving target (in a good way).

I have two pieces of advice about how to improve joy in work based on my years of experience. One is to create and maintain your own "safe haven" at work. The second is to include your family members in some aspect of your work and hobbies.

44. *Connie E., DNP, Level 2 Staff Nurse at a Quaternary Care Pediatric Hospital and Assistant Professor of Nursing*

Connie E., DNP, has been a nurse in the medical-surgical intensive care unit of a quaternary care pediatric hospital for the last 30 years. She also teaches two courses: one in end-of-life care for the hospital's critical care program, and another for students about to take their nursing boards. For Connie, having dual roles is essential for maintaining joy in work.

As corny as it sounds, I think I've always wanted to be a nurse. If you go back to my kindergarten scrap book, where it asks, "What do you want to be when you grow up?" it says, "I want to be a nurse." And that's never changed. I've never oscillated on that one. I've always had a desire to help others. I think I've always had an affinity for children. I've only primarily worked in pediatrics. Kids are interactive, they're fun, they're resilient. They get better much faster than adults. They can be barfing from chemotherapy one minute and the next minute they're off to the playroom.

I'm a level 2 staff nurse providing part-time, hands-on bedside care at a quaternary care pediatric hospital. My other role is teaching undergraduate nursing students. I spend 75% of my time teaching and 25% providing clinical care. In the summer I do more clinical work. My title is assistant professor and I teach a course in transition to practice. It's the last class students take before they graduate and take their nursing boards.

I have a clinical doctorate in nursing practice. My doctoral work examined how to use simulation to teach newly licensed nurses to provide end-of-life care in the intensive care units. Now I offer this end-of-life simulation program to the whole critical care program within the hospital, which is especially important for new nurses who have had very little personal or professional experience dealing with end-of-life care.

In the clinical setting I work 12-hour shifts: 7:00 a.m. to 7:00 p.m. I give two to three hours of lectures a week and also spend time creating lectures—interactive lectures and facilitating simulation.

When it comes to taking care of patients, I do the same work as other RNs. I provide direct patient care in a highly specialized environment to children from birth to adulthood in a 30-bed intensive care medical-surgical unit. We treat kids who are the sickest of the sick, whose conditions are hard to manage and come from throughout the world.

I worked in general pediatrics at another hospital for about a year and a half and for the last 30 years I've been here. For the first five years I worked in the bone marrow transplant unit and for the last 25 I've been in the medical-surgical intensive care unit.

On Joy in Work

Joy is the level of fulfillment, the feeling that you've made a difference in somebody's life, helped them through the most difficult time in their life. Having some small role in helping a child recover.

Physicians here are not put on a pedestal. They're part of the team—the pediatrician, the nurse, the child, and the family. Physicians tend to respect nurses more than might be the case in other hospitals.

Balance helps me maintain professional joy. I think I'm one of the few who is this posi-tive 30 years in—and that's due, in large part, to the fact that I've always had balance. I've never worked full time in critical care. I've always worked 20–24 hours a week. I started to balance my work life when my children were younger. Now that they are older I can do other things. Most people with 30 years of pediatric intensive care unit experience are hon-estly, quite burned out. For my work colleagues, this means they are counting their years to retirement if this is the only thing they've done.

On Money and Joy

I don't think there's a relationship between money and joy. I don't think I'd be happier if I made more money because nurses in this area are used to a certain caliber of pay. But I do think the annual $1,000 bonus we used to get five to ten years ago was a really nice gesture. People felt appreciated. We don't get that anymore.

What Diminishes Joy

What diminishes joy in work for me is just not getting a break sometimes. As the acuity level of patients continues to rise, I can't catch a bathroom break or eat lunch until 3:00 p.m., and that's three-quarters of the way through a 12-hour shift. Sadly, it's become part of what we do. If it's not my patient(s) who are super sick, it is my lunch relief's patients who are. Sometimes it is hard to manage four very sick patients for an hour so that your colleague can go to lunch. We just have to figure it out. Bringing snacks to hold you over is a must! We put our patients' needs before our own and typically don't complain to leadership because this is the new norm. There are some good and some bad days. On some days you might have a single-patient assignment and a nice family and a child who's transitioning well and is going to transfer to the ward. There are definitely good days. However, it has become more commonplace that so many of our patients are more acutely ill and we can't get to lunch until 3:00 p.m., and we've come to accept that as the norm.

Understaffing

It's all about numbers now—staffing. We have a census of 30 patients with only 23 or 25 nurses and the acuity continues to rise. We're being told to manage, to do more with less. In a perfect world there would be one nurse for every patient in the intensive care unit (ICU), but that doesn't happen. If there were a ratio of one patient to one nurse we'd feel better able to support all of our patients' and families' needs.

In our hospital we're so good at what we do that we sometimes forget how acutely ill these patients are. Sometimes it's not safe to double-assign them. We just can't be in two places at once. And we definitely can't support two families in crisis at the same time. The staffing issues, including the lack of bathroom breaks, diminish my joy.

Because we are so understaffed, we are never able to have patient coverage to attend any hospital-wide programs or meetings. Our unit is grossly under-represented throughout the hospital. I miss being able to be part of the bigger hospital system. I'm not so sure I feel like I'm part of the team anymore compared to when I started here.

Leadership Response

The administration knows about the issues that are difficult for us. I personally haven't said too much. It's just unspoken. There's a kind of quick rebuttal and people get shut down. I'm part of the leadership group as a level 2 nurse, so if people say "The staffing, the staffing," I know administrators don't want to hear it. They're just not open to listening.

It's "the elephant in the room." Nobody really talks about it too much. Either that, or nurses just complain among themselves rather than to leadership—I think that's how most people tend to cope. If we were to tell leadership they would say, "Well, you know, we hired three full-time people who will be off orientation in three months." Sometimes this can help a little but it's not enough in real time.

Reporting Errors

After a mistake happens there's supposed to be a debriefing immediately afterwards. But I've noticed that doesn't happen as often as it used to. We are deemed a high reliability organization and people are supposed to speak up and say they made an error and rectify it and be transparent with the family.

Here's some background: a few years ago, two nurses were covering a very sick patient who came back from the operating room. One of them, a friend of mine and a phenomenal nurse, noticed that the infusion pump was running at the wrong rate, double or triple what the amount should have been. The patient's blood pressure naturally started to drop and at first the nurses couldn't quite figure out why. The pump had been running at the wrong rate for about an hour, which isn't horrible as these things go. But they figured it out, corrected it, and then changed the pump to run at the right rate.

My friend wrote an incident report and did the right thing by reporting the event so it could be investigated. She was doing what she was supposed to do, disclosed her error, was transparent, and was then unfortunately made an example of. Even though her name wasn't mentioned in the mass email that went out reminding all staff for two nurses to double-check an IV pump, people were asking, "Who screwed up and who forgot to check the sedation infusion?"

Mistakes and oversights in critical care, when you're dealing with high-risk patients, do happen more than they do on the ward with less acutely ill patients. The nurses corrected the mistake in time. This might even have been an incident where the family might not have had to be notified because it was during the one-hour post-recovery period where the parents aren't even at the bedside. But my friend was troubled by this event and wanted to have the process looked at: why did we miss it? Were two nurses there? Was it because we were busy? She wanted to elevate the error to the systems level, trying to understand so this kind of thing wouldn't happen again. But the focus of the hospital staff became the scuttlebutt on who screwed up.

The colleague went on to require employee counseling after this medication error. Administration does take the supportive approach when mistakes happen. About a year after this incident, my friend decided to leave our unit.

Reflections

In the "trenches" there is a saying that it's not patient-centered care, it's family-*driven* care. Parents are part of the patient care dyad or triad. They're part of the team that includes the physician and the nurse and are equally as important, if not more important, than the child because we have to explain to an adult, on their level, what's going on with their child and what we're doing to support them. We really have to get their buy-in and work with them to support their needs. This can be challenging, especially when the parents don't really want to pursue what we think is best for the child.

Parents worry and their anger can get displaced onto the staff at the patient's bedside. We try not to personalize it too much, but rather walk in their shoes and be empathetic. If it were my kid, I'd probably be pretty angry, too. My joy comes from helping a child and parents understand and reminding them that, hopefully, this illness is only a temporary setback. Trying to be optimistic and offer hope to support parents.

My decisions are sometimes countermanded by parents. For example, when a patient was struggling with narcotic withdrawal and really needed a low stimulation environment, I kept reminding the parents to please let her sleep because, at this point in her recovery, she really needed to sleep. We tried to do several things at once to give her long periods of rest in between. And even though I told them and asked the physicians to talk to them—which they did (the beauty of being there 30 years is that they have my back and I have theirs)—the parents were constantly irritating her. I think they meant well. They kept whispering in her ear and talking to her, trying to cheer her up. But then she was awake again. And she really needed rest. I'd feel a little insulted, like "Did you just not hear what I said?"

I once took care of a child who was diagnosed with a large tumor and was in the hospital for about a month because he was so acutely ill. The parents did not want the child to hear the word "cancer." The mother was really upset when someone sent the child a get well card and it used the word "cancer." The mother was upset and the child had a really difficult time with it. Despite our advice and that of the physicians and support staff to be transparent with this bright, alert child, they insisted on not telling him his diagnosis.

Advice

Parents have rights—they make decisions, sit in on rounds, and sometimes dictate what they want if they've been here long enough. Parents are here from the minute we come in to the end of the day. They're there at night and don't sleep well, so they're a bit angrier and edgier because they've been sleep deprived for so long. Parent rights trump nursing rights. Don't personalize it too much, or just find other things to do. My advice to colleagues is to strike a work–life balance. Find other ways to feel fulfilled.

For me, it's important to strike a professional balance—not just doing bedside nursing, but doing different kinds of nursing at the same time. Teaching, which I've done for more than ten years, just mixing it up, has helped me maintain my professional joy.

45.   Tyler M., MD, Chief Medical Officer for an Integrated Health System

Tyler M., MD., chief medical officer for an integrated health system, is both a manager and primary care physician. He has worked for this health system since finishing his residency ten years ago. Tyler is philosophical about finding joy in a tough profession; he finds joy, in part, in the variety that his dual roles provide.

I chose to go into healthcare when I was a teenager. I had an older stepbrother who was in medical school. He would study at home and I would peek over his shoulder to see what subjects he was working on. I was curious about it. I'd always liked science and math, but the health sciences were particularly interesting—seeing how everything in the body works together and how you can make changes, fix things, and keep people healthy. Since I really enjoyed the health sciences, I thought it was something I could do. I also thought I'd enjoy working with people and helping people. So, before I graduated from high school I knew that was the direction I wanted to go in; I continued in that direction and here I am today.

I knew in medical school I was probably directed toward primary care, but I didn't close myself off to anything else. The continuity and the variety were what really appealed to me. I could have been a cardiologist or a rheumatologist or a surgeon, but I didn't want to deal with the same thing or do the same thing—work with the same organ system or the same set of problems, if you will—every day. That really works well for a lot of people. But I really liked the idea that when I put my hand on the doorknob it could be any number of things. I could see kids, adults, or older adults with any number of medical issues. In fact, I delivered babies for the first seven years of my career. I like the variety and absolutely the building of relationships, which I still get to do because I carry my panel, and my panel is primarily made up of people who have continued to stick with me despite my decreased availability in clinic.

I had no idea when I was in high school, college, medical school, or residency that I was going to take a leadership track. Being a clinical guy fulfilled my dream of going into medicine. I still have great relationships with some families I've known for a decade or more now. That's what I was looking for when I went into practice and I got that. I still get that a bit, but currently I'm on a tangent in my career. A welcome one, but not what I thought it would be.

When I first started at this integrated health system, which has both a clinical side and a health plan side, I was a full-time, 100% provider. I see patients about 20% of my time now: eight hours a week on Monday and Wednesday afternoons. The other 80% of my time involves managing the health system's medical division: providers and internal specialists (mental health, physical therapy, occupational therapy, clinical health education, complementary medicine, eye care, and so on). Our care management department reports to me, along with our population health department and our quality department; each of these departments has directors or managers who report to me. I also act as liaison with external provider groups, typically from our health plan but also with our medical group. My goal is to maintain good partnerships so our patients get good care as they transition across the system.

On Joy in Work

Joy in work means having an overall sense of enjoying what I do and looking forward to the next day. It means having some sort of excitement as opposed to dread about the days to come. That's what keeps me going. That being said, everyone can and does have difficult days or periods where things are tougher, when we're facing professional and personal challenges that sap our ability to really enjoy the day. If that happens here and there, it's okay.

I like both roles, as manager and physician. There's a part of me that likes the variety. I can see the landscape, look around and identify patterns; I can think of fixes, I can think how to cut through red tape—it's a skill I have. Not a lot of people want to do that, want to manage people, manage conflict. Having to say no to people is difficult.

I go home feeling fulfilled even if my day was really hard. You know, it's taking care of people or working to improve a system that I believe is mission-oriented and is passionate about prevention, and taking really good care of people while keeping costs down—not so that our shareholders profit, but so that we can reinvest in ourselves and expand this system of care that I think does a really good job. So even if I have a hard day, or a couple of hard days, I always know I'm working for a place that makes a difference, and that balances things out. That mission is there for me.

I wouldn't change anything about my job. There's a certain level of stress inherent in having to make decisions and then living with them and owning my mistakes, but I'm always learning.

What Diminishes Joy

What diminishes joy in work for me are difficult patient outcomes. I've never been sued for malpractice but bad things do happen, and I sometimes look back and wish I had done something different. For example, if someone has a cancer diagnosis or they get really sick or some other bad thing happens, I look back sometimes and wish that I had done something different or seen it earlier. There may not have been an error or a misstep but dealing with those cases is hard on me personally, regardless. I sometimes feel that I should be omniscient and at the same time I understand that's impossible, and that hindsight is 20/20. I know I can only do the best I can with the information I have in the moment, but that's hard for me.

Difficult social interactions with patients—especially with people I don't know, or with patients who are very needy, who have personality disorders, or who I know I'm going to have an unpleasant conversation with—can be draining. They're going to get mad at me specifically. Interactions like that don't lead to a good day. I dread the day when I know those are coming, and when I look back, they're either the lowlight or the headline of the day. Luckily this doesn't happen too often, but these increase with the current opioid epidemic. I don't have anybody who's been in a really bad way, but I have a couple of patients who need to do a bit of tapering for safety reasons. And 99% of patients get all that. But sometimes I have to tell people things they don't want to hear and that they're not going to take well. There's a sense of dread there, knowing I'm going to have a really hard conversation with somebody and tell them they have to do something they're not going to appreciate.

I have colleagues who drive me nuts or who are selfish or they're not team players—you name it—personality issues one finds in any workplace. So sure, they're impactful, but not in a systemic way.

The Electronic Medical Record

I don't enjoy the paperwork but I don't think of it as the thing that would make my life super unhappy. I don't like it, but I get through it. It's the cost of doing business.

I don't think the EMR is a bad thing. Frankly, I think the blame on the EMR is a little overblown nationally. I trained and started my career when EMR and Epic prevalence was just coming up. I was in a couple of hospitals and systems when they were instituting these things and I remember the "before" state.

I think there's a romantic notion of how great paper charts and all that were, because the grass is greener in retrospect. But there were a lot of problems with paper charts, too. It's not that the job was easy before there was an EMR—I think the EMR is a scapegoat sometimes. No question, a poorly designed EMR will create terrific frustration. There may be places where the EMR is really bad. We have our own dedicated EMR, Epic, that we can control and focus on outpatient primary care, and so it's a wieldy tool. Other people may find their system less responsive or that there's less caring for how their tool works. If it doesn't work well that could absolutely make every day one of those "I'm going to dread this day" scenarios.

Burnout

I have not experienced burnout. The inverse of burnout is resiliency and I think I tend to have that as part of who I am. Obviously there are periods of ups and downs in life, but I would not put myself in the same boat as others who I know are feeling the down sides more.

When I was a 100% provider I had even less burnout than I do now, even though now I have more control over my time. Now I have more varied kinds of responsibility. There are different types of pressures on me now and my failures and successes are very public. If I didn't have a great day when I was a provider nobody would really know.

Burnout is multifactorial, it's personal. We have people who are burning out. We don't have an answer. Being a provider is a tough job. Every month, our senior leaders have lunch with all our new hires. I often acknowledge, especially to new clinical staff, that primary care is really hard. Nobody said it was easy and there will be hard days.

Managing Conflict

There's clearly a tension between me as a leader and people who have problems, people who want things that seem right and obvious to them but may not, objectively, be right. Their arguments may sound convincing; but if you look more broadly and get the perspective of other people on the same problem, their perspectives and suggested solutions might be different.

For example, within our care teams there are areas where people have challenges, such as burnout or performance issues. Our nurses may feel they're not being heard; they're the cornerstones of our team, they're answering the phones and nobody is helping them, and they're going to quit. They don't like where things are and that's affecting the entire team. But if I look more broadly and get the perspective of other people on that site who interact with that team, they'll say, "Those nurses are great but they refuse to let anybody else help because they have sort of a professional martyrdom or they don't trust their partners to do it, so when people offer to help they say no, you're never going to do it right, so why should I bother asking you?"

People can be shortsighted. I try to run people through a series of explanations for a problem and come up with an idea and vet it, so people can consider the idea and what its impacts and ripple effects might be. It's important to not decide what the problem is or what the solution needs to be until you've vetted it. Trust but verify. If you go with a first explanation for a problem, you're getting one side of the story; you need to flesh out the different perspectives so you're not being reactive to one side and causing problems for another side.

Managing conflict is similar whether the people are front-line clinical staff, claims and billing staff, or sales staff. We identify problems and opportunities from where we sit, and so people's perspectives are different. Talking and listening to both sides is important. You need to flesh out the problem so you have an accurate understanding of what the problem is and the circumstances behind it, because if you go off half-cocked you're just going to make mistakes.

It's hard to be in the position, as I frequently am, of being in conflict. It's something I have to deal with and I feel well equipped to do that; but I don't like being a punching bag when I have to turn down a prior authorization. People don't understand the circumstances and think health plans are evil.

Advice

I think you have to institute a lot of transparency as a leader. You have to listen to people; if you say no, people have to feel heard and know why you don't grant them what they want. As long as you're fair and transparent, people don't *have* to feel great about it. From a system's perspective and from a management perspective, I can't say yes to everything. That would be irresponsible. But if people have felt heard, and if they see that sometimes the system does process changes and that change is possible, then they won't lose faith in their system. On the other hand, if they feel there's just a black box, or always a "no" stamp, then people will lose faith with their organization and feel that improvement is impossible.

46.   *Joseph B., MD, Retired Professor, Researcher, and Practicing*
      Gastroenterologist; President of a Board Review Company in
      Gastroenterology; and Head of a Monthly Gastroenterology Journal Club

> Joseph B., MD, has felt deep satisfaction, if not joy, in his career as a professor of gastroenterology, a researcher, and a practicing gastroenterologist. Now retired from private practice, Joseph remains involved in academia as president of the gastroenterology board review company he started 35 years ago and in his role as head of a monthly journal club in gastroenterology.

My father ran a restaurant that was very well-known in its day in the neighborhood where I grew up. I thought I should be a restaurateur like him. He made people happy. But he forbade me to consider that because he thought it was a very tough field to go into for so many reasons. I was always interested in biology and science. There were no doctors in the family. But it just seemed like a natural flow for me—biology, science, medicine—and when I went to college, I was premed from the beginning and then went to medical school at the biggest teaching hospital in the city.

I was drafted into the military during the Vietnam War and I spent 18–19 months in the Air Force. I was a doctor. In those days you were considered a doctor if you'd finished your internship. I got drafted in the middle of my internship, but they let me finish. I went into the Air Force as a general medical officer and went to Okinawa. When you're taken out of your own sheltered community and go elsewhere, it's a tremendous experience.

My Professional Journey

In the Air Force I worked in a clinic and made myself into the clinic's venereal disease doctor. Someone needed to do that. I did that in the mornings and that was eye-opening for me, a kid who had lived a sheltered life. I did my first study comparing one antibiotic to another antibiotic for the treatment of gonorrhea. That was how my academic leanings started. I couldn't get that study published because I could not prove that people who still had symptoms of the disease after treatment had not been re-infected.

After the military I went to a university for my first year of medical residency. In those years there was a different system and you didn't need a third year of medical residency. Now you do. In those days you could go into subspecialties after two years. But I wasn't sure what I wanted to do so I went for a third year and finished my internal medicine training. After taking a year off to travel around the world with my wife, I went back to complete my GI training.

I decided on gastroenterology because I wanted a specialty that required a mix of cognitive skills and procedures, which boiled down to cardiology or gastroenterology. This was early in the days of scoping. It was the mid-70s and modern scopes were just coming of age. It wasn't super-procedural when I started; now it's *super*-procedural. But I liked the mix—doing things with your hands, doing things in the office. I did my fellowship in another state.

The great majority of fellowships are almost entirely clinical. But I went someplace where I was exposed to research. I did clinical lab research for a third year to see if I wanted to stay in academia, which I decided I wanted to do. But I never was trained properly. In order to be a research doctor, you need to train in the basic sciences, which I never really did. But I enjoyed the academic activities and I enjoyed doing clinical research, and so that third year sent me in that direction.

I pursued what's called the "academic trifecta:" I had an animal lab and did research, I taught, and I saw patients. I had the lab for seven or eight years. Getting funding was hard. By then I was conducting clinical research with colleagues at my academic medical center and published articles in the best journals from 1979–1999.

I branched out into medical education and made that my big focus. I was still writing clinical papers, which I always enjoyed, but no longer involving animals. I thought I was advancing the field. I have always found research and writing as a way of contributing to medical knowledge very satisfying. In mid-career I went into private practice and remained involved in medical education.

I worked in two practices during the course of my private practice career. The first was a small all-gastroenterology practice where I stayed for six years. I didn't like the practice for various reasons and switched to a large multispecialty internal medicine practice with about 25 doctors. I was the only GI doc there when I started. There were primary care physicians, pulmonologists, an endocrinologist, rheumatologists, and I loved the mix. I loved not being with just GI docs. I started a monthly academic program for the docs to include a case conference, monthly guest speaker, and a journal club.

Being with docs of other specialties, I thought, enhanced medicine and I loved it. That practice gave me tremendous flexibility in the number of hours a week I worked. I was very fortunate to have other sources of income from my medical education company so I could see fewer patients and spend more time with each, and this practice afforded me that opportunity.

I continue to have an abiding interest in medical education. I've directed a board review course in my field for the past 35 years, which I began in academia and continue to pursue. It is the largest course of its kind in the U.S. The clinicians who take this course have to take a periodic exam to remain board certified and my course provides the information they need to help them with their studies. I hire the best faculty from all over the U.S. to lecture.

I've also been the editor of a monthly journal club in gastroenterology for the last 35 years. This is another academic activity I still enjoy. There are ten reviewers, each of whom have certain journals to review.

On Joy in Work

I like to do a lot of different things. I enjoyed the mix of academic activities. I did research, wrote papers, taught, and saw patients. I ran my course and the journal club while I was in academia and then continued these activities in private practice. That's how I've kept my—I don't know if I'd use the word "joy"—I would call it job satisfaction. Joy sounds religious. I can't speak for others, but I would not use the word joy.

In practice my area of focus in gastroenterology was the pancreas. Very few people subspecialize in that, so clinicians would ask me all the time for consultations on pancreas cases. But most of what I practiced was general gastroenterology. Doing research and writing papers were also very high up on my list of what gave me satisfaction. I enjoyed taking care of patients and helping them. That's a huge part of what I found satisfying. I enjoyed the challenging cases.

Medicine is wonderful. There are constantly new cures being discovered. It's a fantastic field to be in. Suddenly there's a new medicine that helps people, that's revolutionary, that changes everything. You'd like to be the genius who invented it but you're not. But you can use that medicine to help your patients. As an example, in the last few years Hepatitis C has been wiped out by incredible medicines that hardly have any side effects and that are 98% effective in eradicating the virus. I mean, to be part of that, okay, you use the word joy, but there's excitement. Enthusiasm. Being part of that has been a very wonderful thing. It's been a great career for me. I've had a wonderful experience because I was able to develop a varied career of clinical practice and academic activities.

What Diminishes Job Satisfaction

Lawsuits

Medicine also became defensive over time, where docs felt they had to do every test in the book to protect themselves from malpractice. That wasn't great. That was the downside over the years, but that wasn't a huge problem for me.

I was sued early on, which was very traumatic. In this case I didn't do anything wrong, but the patient sued everyone: me, the surgeon, the pathology department, the hospital. When you bring in a lawyer everyone is sued because everyone has malpractice insurance. So, the lawyers sue broadly to get as much money as they can.

That lawsuit went on for months. It was a terrible experience. Dealing with the legal profession and seeing how juries are selected in malpractice cases is awful. The attorney for the other side wants to get the least educated people on the jury because the less they understand the medical issues, the more they rely on emotion.

Over the years I became an expert witness in malpractice cases because I found them interesting and, in the vast majority, I wanted to defend the docs. Every now and then I saw things that were *horrendous*, and I didn't defend the doc. This was another aspect of medicine that I found educational.

Computers

Medicine started to become computerized about 15–20 years ago. The trend continues to increase. Although there are some clear advantages to computerization, to an old-timer like me the disadvantages outweighed many of the advantages. It takes time to learn a computer program and each unit or hospital has its own program requiring its own training. And then there are the periodic updates that require retraining. I dropped out of hospitals the minute their computer systems changed. I didn't want to go through this time after time. Many clinicians whose typing skills were not very good or non-existent would have to type computerized notes while talking to patients. This became and remains a most troubling development. However, the new generation of docs will not find this a problem because their computer skills are much better.

Evolution of the Field

One of the things I was dissatisfied with was the way the field of gastroenterology evolved. When I started, as I've said, the field wasn't super-procedurally oriented. We'd do diagnostic scoping if patients had symptoms. But when insurance started paying for screening procedures things changed.

The practice of gastroenterology became highly influenced by screening colonoscopies. More than 50% of a gastroenterologist's practice was devoted to this. About 5% of the time we'd find something significant. And 20% of the time we'd find little polyps, and who knows if those were significant? And then patients would get into every five-year or every ten-year cycles, and that's what most of GI has become. To me that was not particularly satisfying.

What I got my greatest pleasure from was seeing patients who had difficult problems and trying to help them. And holding their hands. The more senior a clinician becomes, the more that clinician's experience can help many kinds of patients.

47. Adam B., MD, Pediatric Pulmonologist and Sleep Specialist at a Quaternary Care Children's Hospital

> Adam B., MD, has been a pediatric pulmonologist and sleep specialist at a quaternary care children's hospital for the last 17 years. In addition to direct patient care, interpreting sleep and pulmonary studies, and teaching medical students and residents here and abroad, Adam volunteers in Latin America as a pediatrician and, one-on-one, as a teacher and mentor to pediatricians there.

I'm not certain what pulled me into healthcare. I have no family members who are physicians. When I was 18, I was quite sick with mononucleosis and wound up being hospitalized with its complications.

I also spent some time on a kibbutz after high school and really enjoyed the time spent in the sheep pen. One day it was time for the ewes to give birth, so I attended multiple deliveries. I really connected with that experience. I guess I had the same sentiment watching the deliveries of human babies, and in medical school I was seeing hundreds of those. If you were to cut off somebody's finger, the finger is just dead. There's nothing you can do with it, really. But when you cut the umbilical cord you have a living being, completely independent. There is something absolutely magnificent about witnessing that.

After medical school there is a year's rotating internship and I started in pediatrics, really because I knew I didn't want to be a pediatrician and I wanted to get it out of the way. And I actually enjoyed it. The doctors I was with were really nice; they were constantly giggling and were kind of silly. It was a happy rotation. Of course, there were tragedies that came through every so often, but for the most part kids are designed to get bigger, better, stronger, and healthier. That's one of the little secrets of pediatrics.

Then I finished my two-month rotation and went into general surgery. I felt as if I couldn't take my hands out of my pockets for two weeks. It was as if, after all these beautiful babies and children, I suddenly had to start touching hairy bellies. That wasn't for me. So, I started thinking maybe pediatrics would be a good fit.

I started my residency abroad in 1996. I came to the U.S. for my fellowship in 2001 and had to re-do a couple of years of residency training to become certified here. I came on staff at this hospital in 2006.

My job entails caring for patients with respiratory disease and sleep disorders, primarily sleep-disordered breathing. I see patients, on average, four half-days a week. I interpret sleep studies, I interpret pulmonary function testing, I attend on the floor in the hospital. I teach medical students, resident fellows. I teach elsewhere in the United States and abroad.

I've been quite active in global health over the last several years and I try to volunteer a couple of weeks a year in Latin America with their affiliate of Partners in Health. I have also been engaged in working closely with various physician groups there.

Broadly speaking, the clinical care, the direct patient care that I provide, takes up between 40% and 50% of my time. Then I spend another 20% of my time interpreting sleep studies. The rest of the time is focused on other things I have to do, including teaching and the global health work, writing, and doing research if I'm working on a project.

When I'm in clinic the hours are 8:00 a.m. to 12:00 noon and then 1:00 p.m. to 5:00 p.m. Depending on what I'm doing I might be there a full day, or I might be there a half day. If I'm not in clinic I have more flexibility but, generally speaking, my hours are 8:00 a.m.

to 5:00 or 5:30 p.m. I'm on call about six weeks of the year when I'm on service, and I also cover night call for the sleep lab one in every six weeks.

I have half an hour for return patients and an hour for new patients. That's supposed to include note dictation/writing, and many times that's enough. This may sound luxurious compared to what doctors in other systems have but remember, the complexity of our cases is greater. Patients are referred to us by specialists who don't know what to do. For the most part, probably 70% to 85% of the time, I have completed my work—my notes included—by the time I leave the hospital. I may stick around for an extra hour of work outside of my clinic session, but I generally complete my work before leaving the hospital. But others don't. And it really depends. If I have a patient booked into an hour slot who doesn't need a full hour, and patients who are booked for a half hour slot who really need 45 minutes, then that gives me a kind of freedom.

Global Health Work

What I do for global health can probably be divided into two parts. Over the last three to four years I've been working with a Latin American affiliate of Partners in Health. About seven or eight years ago this group identified an underserved region in the southern part of one country. When I go there, probably two-thirds of my time is spent sitting by the side of a doctor in the clinic, just listening to the interaction. Sure, maybe asking a question or two but making it really clear to everybody that the Latin American doctor is the doctor. And then we'll step outside and that doctor will tell me what he heard and what he saw and what he thinks. I may ask him some questions and then we review the plan together. And then we'll go back in and the doctor will proceed. If I notice things, I'll point them out. And if I have observations, I'll describe them. So that's how it works. It's one-to-one precepting and mentoring.

And then the second thing I do with them, which I've been doing for a couple of years now, is teaching a course called Helping Babies Breathe, which is a newborn resuscitation course that is meant for underserved areas. This course teaches one how to resuscitate a baby who is born and not doing what a baby should be doing—not breathing well, has bad color, is not moving. And, basically, clearing secretions, drying the baby off, maybe using a bag mask to help give him a few breaths but no meds, no compression. But it's enough to save, on average, 98% of all babies who otherwise might be deemed stillborn. I've been teaching that to doctors and their nurses who rotate into the local hospital as well.

The third thing that I do with them is provide long-distance consultation if they have questions about patients, if they're not sure whether something is a pulmonary disease or a pediatric disease. They just reach out to me and we talk.

This is all volunteer. I use my vacation time. Although I did get a travel grant from the hospital that covered a couple of trips, I do this all on my vacation time. I buy all my own supplies.

On Joy in Work

I derive most of my satisfaction from my interactions with my patients. And it really is an immediate, unfiltered, undistilled interaction that I have with them. It's not mediated through other people. That's what I really like.

I find that my interactions with my patients and their families are immensely satisfying. I rarely come away feeling something went badly or that I shouldn't be doing this. I can't remember, since my residency, questioning why I am doing this.

Volunteering in Latin America

I derive a lot of satisfaction from my work in Latin America for several reasons. For one thing, when I go down there it's planned. They will very often arrange for pediatric patients to come to the village where I'll be so I can see them. I tell them I don't do general pediatrics much and that my experience is kind of stale. And they say, "Well, there's no pediatrician within a three-hour drive so thank you very much. It's awesome that you're here." So, there's that piece. And really identifying that I'm making a difference, both in terms of teaching and medical care, is satisfying. And again, I make sure it's the local doctor who's given all the credit for it.

I also like giving moral support to this organization. The people leading this organization are mostly in their 20s and are living in this village where you can't even buy a newspaper. Half the houses have dirt floors. We take our meals with one of the families. I pay the family but not very much. The meals are generally beans and tortillas, with maybe a little bit of cheese, and once or twice maybe a little bit of chicken. It reminds me why I went into medicine: to help people who really don't have access to resources. I think this is valuable and worth investing in. And it grounds me. It's a reminder to be grateful.

On Money and Joy

Do I think there's a relationship between money and joy? I once had that argument with my father, who's an economist. He said, "There is a well-defined relationship and it's been studied." So up to a point, yes. After a certain point there's not a relationship, and joy may even go down. If you're living in a one-room shack with a dirt floor and your kids are malnourished, that weighs on you. If you are comfortable money's not an issue. That's pretty obvious and it's been studied a lot.

Beyond a certain point, though, how much does a person need? Growing up, this question and answer was always really important in my school and in my family: "Who is happiest? The person who is content with his lot." If you always aspire for more, you'll always feel you're not there. But if you're happy with what you have, there's less pressure.

What Diminishes Joy

One of the things that diminishes joy in work for me is the regulatory nonsense we have to deal with. We should not have to get approval from insurance companies for services that should not be called into question.

The Regulatory Environment

One of the areas I practice in is the identification and treatment of sleep-disordered breathing in children who choke on their throats while they're sleeping. A few months ago, I put in an order for a sleep study for a ten-month-old who had symptoms of this. We had to make a decision about whether or not she should undergo surgery. Permission for the surgery was denied. I had to call the insurance company and set up a time to talk with the doctor. Ultimately, the reason it was denied was because in my clinic note I hadn't emphasized that this patient's likely sleep apnea was impairing her ability to drive. That was one of their criteria, except this was for a ten-month-old girl!

That wound up wasting my time. I wish I could say that was an isolated occurrence but it's not. That, unfortunately, is the kind of crap we have to deal with and, thankfully, it doesn't happen to me too much—but it happens. That's the face of modern medicine right now in this country. That does take away from joy.

We do a lot of things as part of our work that are not direct patient care, but we have to do them because of the regulatory environment in which we practice. That's getting worse and worse. And that sometimes gets me down. On the whole, it's not enough for me to want to stop doing what I do.

Lack of Recognition from Leadership

While I receive great satisfaction from my own interactions with patients, I feel there's perhaps not enough recognition from the people who are responsible for us, meaning people higher up in the system. My colleagues and I often feel we're treated more as cogs in the machine—and it's not pleasant to know we're not recognized as we should be for what we're doing. The other side of the coin is the tremendous amount of recognition we get from patients. And that's what it's about. But I still think the hospital could do a better job of providing that kind of recognition.

I think the administration's recognizing people's achievements would enhance my joy in work. Our promotion system is based on the university's medical system, which is much stricter than most other places in terms of what they demand. I've heard that here you're generally one rank lower than you'd be almost anywhere else. So, if you're a professor somewhere else you might be an associate professor here. If you're an associate professor at another university, you might be an assistant professor here. One of the problems with that is promotion really is very difficult.

And then that becomes an issue because your value in an institution or workplace is recognized by one of two things: either an increase in salary (you work really well, and you should get more money for that) or a promotion. And if promotion really isn't available, except for a select few, then that's a problem. And if your raise is tied to your academic promotion, that's a problem. I think they're starting to recognize that here. But there's still a lag. And I think that causes frustration. It doesn't need to be that way and probably should not be that way.

Reflections

The administration has a much more macroscopic view of healthcare than I do. They're looking at levels of care that are far different from the ones that I'm looking at. I'm focused on my patients; I'm focused on doing things better. I personally look around and think about ways of improving systems and processes. The hospital administration is looking at things that are far beyond what I'm looking at. For example, they're looking at the effects of changes to Obamacare on our care mix: looking at how to integrate telemedicine, which is certainly up-and-coming, despite the fact that our state did not pass a bill that would have allowed that to happen. What reimbursements from Medicaid are going to look like. These are the things they're focused on, as they should be.

I'm quite fortunate having been here for 17 years in what is a culture of safety. We have morbidity and mortality meetings. If I had to put my finger on what is most punitive, it's when emails come out saying if you don't sign all your notes within ten days of seeing a patient, we're going to dock your bonus by whatever. I'm not aware of people being punished when something goes wrong.

If I could change anything about my job, it's that I would like to have a greater leadership role. I'm not quite sure in which capacity. I do find systems interesting; I do find healthcare disparities interesting. But I'm not that interested in leading committees or working on small projects and I don't have the training for the bigger things. I really enjoy what I do in the global health realm and I'm hoping to expand that because it's important to me and I get a lot of satisfaction from that. I've been able to carve out a nice work–life balance. Overall, I'm in a pretty good place right now.

I've changed quite a bit over the years. I've been able to redefine my focus and do things that are interesting to me on different projects. I became involved in pulmonary medicine, I became involved in sleep and breathing. For a while I was doing some writing for nationally recognized newspapers. I wrote a book. And then I became involved in global health and wanted to learn how to speak Spanish, so I studied Spanish. I've been doing lots of things. I feel I'm at a point where I'd like to define my next thing, my next multi-year project, which I will, and I'll start running with that.

Advice

Over the years I've come to realize that what works for me doesn't necessarily work for other people. But my advice for colleagues, especially younger colleagues, is don't waste time on things you don't really enjoy. If you don't have the fire within, then don't waste your time.

A piece of advice I got in medical school that I often share with trainees is, pay attention to the people you work with on the different rotations, because that's what you're going to look like for the next 50 years of your life. Where I studied abroad, obstetricians were nice but they were on edge, a lot of them smoked, and I think it was because in deliveries things go well until they don't. Until there's a crisis. I just didn't find that appealing.

48.   Caitlin G., MSN, Assistant Clinical Professor and Hospital and Home Care Nurse, and PhD Student

> Caitlin G., MSN, a pediatric nurse for 33 years, finds her joy in caring for children with special needs, helping their families, and teaching the next generation of nurses. As a PhD student, Caitlin's goal is to focus on research and continue to work in the home care setting.

I always knew I wanted to do something in healthcare, and it was really a matter of exploring what I wanted to do. I knew I wanted to be with patients for extended periods of time, as opposed to the in-and-out of short-term visits. That's what pointed me toward nursing. I didn't have any family members who had chosen that career path, so I didn't have a role model. As a teenager I volunteered as a certified nursing assistant to see whether I liked it. Back then it was called a candy striper.

I've always known I wanted to work with kids. I'd never had an interest in working with adults. I just love, I exude, children. I love being with them. I started babysitting when I was pretty young, and I worked in the recreation department in the summer when I was a teenager. I was always drawn to kids. If there was a family party and little kids were there, my mom would say they were just drawn to me. I was always the entertainer for the kids.

I have been a pediatric nurse for 33 years. I've always worked with children, providing direct care in the hospital and in the home care setting. I've worked for a number of home care agencies. Home care is so flexible; it's based on what the family needs and what suits their schedules. But there are not enough nurses who do home care. There's such a need. The agencies try to fill hours for families who have nursing-hour coverage within their insurance plans, but there just aren't enough people who do it. A lot of people who work in home care come out of working in hospital care because of the flexibility of the schedule. Our hours are based on the number of hours people's insurance companies cover. Some families will say they want a nurse for three hours a day in the middle of the afternoon, in the evening, or during the bedtime hours. Many people work part-time within the home care system because they're able to work four hours here, three hours there.

In the home care setting, I provide direct care for children from infancy through age 18 who have special needs and provide emotional support for children and families in their journey of caring for children with special needs. Children with special needs can mean many things, from mild autism to children who were born prematurely, to children who have tracheotomies and are on ventilators, to those who have gastrostomy tubes, to those who have other conditions.

Now I do more teaching than clinical care. I fluctuate between days and evenings. My schedule is now about 50% teaching, 25% home care, and 25% hospital care. I work 10–12 hours a day. Some days I work eight-hour shifts; others I work 12 or even 16 hours. On Thursdays I work six hours in the early morning, I have a little break, and then I work in the evening for a total of anywhere from 8–12 hours. I don't feel overloaded by work, either in the home care setting or in the hospital. I feel I have control over my time. I totally choose whether I want to do more. If I want to overload my schedule that's my choice.

I'm getting my PhD because I'm teaching in a faculty position. My PhD trajectory will enable me to work and do research in the home care setting. That's where my focus is.

On Joy in Work

My greatest joy is feeling the impact of doing something for somebody else. Not only for the children that I care for, but also for their families. I see their parents' appreciation. That brings me a lot of joy. As far as working with students, I love their enthusiasm as they prepare to embark on their careers. I love being able to light the fire of enthusiasm with them. I find joy in being a role model for approaching one's career with such positivity. Students often come across nurses who are mopey in their clinical work or who don't want to spend time with students. But these students are getting ready to embark on their careers; I want them to have positive examples.

My job has absolutely been the fulfillment of my dreams of going into healthcare. I've gotten even more joy since going into teaching because I have the opportunity to impact the next generation. Multiple roles are important to me. I've been teaching for six years. I truly love working with college students. They're a blast.

On Money and Joy

I don't think there is a relationship between money and joy. As I moved from nursing into teaching, my husband said, "Most people climb up the ladder as far as income and position. Honey: every time you make a job change you make less money!" But I told him that because we have three teenagers, with one already in college, the tuition assistance I get from teaching at the university is going to make up for it. I feel sufficiently rewarded by my bosses and colleagues for my work apart from money. The nurse managers have always been very supportive.

What Diminishes Joy

What takes away joy is people high up in the hospital bureaucracy making decisions that don't affect them but that do affect other people, such as decisions about what happens when we're short-staffed and don't have enough resources. That creates workload issues and requires having to do workarounds. I think administration takes advantage of the fact that nurses are caring and compassionate people who are never going to leave their colleagues in a situation of potential danger or one that compromises safety; administrators know nurses will stay and work overtime to cover the short staff. I feel they purposely schedule fewer staff knowing that nurses will pick up more shifts so as not to leave their colleagues "in the weeds," so to speak. Folks who go into healthcare, nursing, specifically, really look out for each other because, ultimately, if we're not looking out for each other there are poor outcomes for the patient. We really have each other's backs. Sometimes it looks like chaos, but it's really organized chaos. If one person has a complex issue going on everyone chips in. Teamwork is crucial.

Sometimes nurse managers don't always know all the intricacies of what goes on, especially on the "off" shifts. They might be there during the day, but they might not be there into the evening or on the night shift. Even if I don't get to see the night shift, when I come into the hospital for teaching purposes, I usually arrive at 6:00 a.m. to catch the night-shift folks so I can make my student's patient assignments for the day shift. I talk to the night-shift nurses, who were scheduled for eight hours but are working 12 or 16 hours because that particular shift was short-staffed. I think this increases burnout and increases the likelihood that burnout will happen more quickly in nurses' careers, and they will choose to move on.

I've heard nurse managers in different settings say new graduates stay for just a couple of years. Nurse managers invest in their training and get them used to the culture and then these new nurses quickly move on. They don't stay for five or ten years because they think the grass has to be greener somewhere else. I don't think the turnover is particularly high in my organization; it's probably average. I think dissatisfaction with working in hospitals is a precipitating factor for burnout. I don't find that as much in home care.

I think there's a bit of a disconnection between what I think of as problems and what the administration thinks of as problems. As nurses, we look closely at patient outcomes and patient safety—and I know they do, too—but, ultimately, it's a business for them and it comes down to the bottom dollar. Some decisions are made based on revenue and the nurses caring for the patients don't have a say in that revenue chain.

Advice

Administrators: come down to the floor to see what is going on. Give nurses a seat at the table and greater involvement in decision-making—not only nurse managers, but floor nurses delivering direct patient care. Include these nurses in managerial meetings. They are the ones with "boots on the ground."

Maintain a culture that invites learning, especially if you're working in a teaching institution. Everyone needs to be on board with teaching. Everyone involved with students, even if they're not instructors, should always be positive about student engagement.

Don't be a naysayer. Sometimes I walk onto the floor and I'll see nurses rolling their eyes about students. Seriously? Do you not remember being a student? That's something I think the administration should have a role in stopping. At the point of hire, nurses should understand they're being hired into a teaching institution; they should expect that they'll not only be working with nursing students but with medical students, nutrition students, physical therapy students, respiratory therapy students, etc. There are students everywhere. Nurses who are having a bad day should not take it out on the students. And if they do, the behavior should be called out and addressed from the top down.

49.   *Monica T., MD, Assistant Professor of Pediatrics and Attending Neonatologist at a Quaternary Care Pediatric Hospital*

Monica T., MD, is a neonatologist who divides her time among caring for critically ill infants and their families, teaching/mentoring, conducting research, and writing at a quaternary care pediatric hospital. She finds joy in this hybrid, which also gives her the flexibility she needs to be present in her own children's lives. Monica's joy in work is further enhanced by an organizational culture that supports the individual clinician when things go wrong, and that promotes physician wellness throughout the year.

I've always loved the combination of the arts and sciences. I double-majored in biology and premed as well as French literature. Melding the arts and sciences has worked well for me. I just loved children, pediatrics, and babies. I was born prematurely and received wonderful care, so I've always wanted to give back. I was fascinated by the work done in the NICU and find it really rewarding. That's why I went into neonatology.

What I love about being a neonatologist, which is a subspecialty of pediatrics, is that you care for the whole newborn who is critically ill. It's not just focusing, for example, on the pediatric heart, or the pediatric brain. It's caring for the entire infant as well as the family. I really like that aspect of it.

I also like working with my hands and there are some surgical procedures that I love in neonatology, but I knew I wasn't cut out to be a surgeon for so many reasons. I knew I could do the work, but I couldn't be in a cold operating room for hours on end. And, at the time, the atmosphere of that specialty wasn't for me. It's historically portrayed as not very welcoming to women. I knew I wanted a family, and the hours weren't likely to be workable for me, so I gravitated toward pediatrics.

I am an assistant professor of pediatrics and an attending neonatologist at a quaternary care pediatric hospital. I came here in 2012 after completing my fellowship training. I spent six years in pediatric residency and doing a neonatology fellowship. I've been on the clinical/academic track. I wanted a hybrid position combining clinical care with academics so I could also conduct research, teach, publish and write. In the NICU, there is high acuity and thus a high potential for burnout if you do that 100% of the time, so for me academic neonatology is a nice balance and a chance to contribute new knowledge to the field as well as mentor the next generation of neonatologists.

I spend roughly 60% of my time on the academic side teaching and mentoring, along with my scholarly work in ethics and professionalism, whether that's teaching, research, grant writing, or publishing. I spend about 25% of my time on clinical responsibilities—actual time taking care of patients and families in the NICU and other areas of the hospital. That can fluctuate depending on the time of year. I spend about 10% of my time on administration. I'm on several committees at the hospital that connect with my academic interests.

I'm on the Institutional Review Board, which takes probably about 10% of my time. It meets twice a month and we review all the hospital's research protocols to make sure they're scientifically rigorous and meet human protections and required regulations related to conducting research in the pediatric population. I enjoy it because I see what other research is going on around the hospital and what other divisions and colleagues are doing. And this aligns with my niche in the ethics of protecting vulnerable populations and with research ethics. It also helps me in my own research because I'm really "in the know" when it comes to making sure my projects meet all those regulatory standards.

I'm an ethics associate, which is a permanent member of the longstanding ethics committee across the whole hospital. In addition to providing ethical consultations as needed, there are monthly meetings with education, and discussion and review of cases. I've also worked in other hospital NICUs and I still work part of the time in another hospital NICU, as well as mentoring fellows and teaching.

My hours vary widely. When I'm on service—the clinical piece—I'm on during the day in two-week chunks. This is pure clinical care in the NICU. I could work for months at a time, but I prefer not to do that because of my lifestyle. On the clinical side, I work roughly 12-hour days: Monday to Friday, from about 6:00 a.m. to 6:00 p.m., but it can vary.

The other part of the clinical piece is nights and weekends. I work usually two to three nights a month and one 24-hour weekend shift per month in addition to all that, and that can be while I'm on service, too. But it's pretty flexible in total and it is balanced. Sure, a 24-hour shift on a Saturday means being apart from my kids and family, which isn't great, but I love my job. And my husband is amazing; he's so supportive. And we definitely give and take there. That helps. I don't know what I'd do without him. And I know that when I do have a night/weekend shift my kids are in fantastic hands. That helps a tremendous amount.

When I'm not on service I'm in my office in a different part of the hospital and it's roughly nine to five. But there's flexibility, so I can take my kids to the doctor if needed. I can leave early and go to the school play. As long as I get my work done and as long as I'm meeting my commitments, I'm usually in charge of my schedule and can schedule certain meetings during times when I'm not on service doing the clinical piece.

My philosophy is to try hard not to take work home with me. I have the capability with encrypted computers to work securely from home, and sometimes I do to meet deadlines after my kids are in bed, but typically with my kids now that's not the best way. I try really hard to finish everything during my time at work. That's what I love about my job, too: the clinical piece is shift work and so when I'm done, I'm done. I rarely take clinical work home. Notes have to be signed and billed for in a timely manner, so my philosophy is, get it done while I'm at work.

I have four children and I feel that, overall, I have a great work–life balance. That's partly due to how I approach it. I think being a mom has made me a better physician, particularly a neonatologist. I generally don't bring work home like I used to, pre-kids. I don't take naps anymore post-call; instead I play with my kids. It's given me a much better perspective about priorities and what's most important in life, and it's made me much more efficient and appreciative of my time. It also has enabled me to prioritize and say no when I can't take on additional tasks or something that interferes with my kids' schedules. When possible, I just say no, I can't do that, and I feel very supported here in saying that.

When I first came here there was no structured wellness program for our division, so my boss and I decided to start one. This has been going on for a couple of years now. Quick surveys of our faculty about what you love about your job, what you'd change, were all related to not having a wellness program. Over the past couple of years, we've peppered our conferences at least quarterly with topics like wellness, burnout, and other things people have identified as being of interest. Attendance at these sessions is mandatory. One was on financial fitness and how to pay for kids' colleges, aging parents' healthcare needs, energy banks, and narrative ethics—that is, exploring difficult conversations and situations, then writing to process and work through those. Other people have talked about call-room workouts and how to get a good workout in for 30 minutes when you're in your call room on the night shift. The feedback we get is great. One of my colleagues leads a weekly guided meditation, same time, same place each week, and anyone can just go meditate for 20 minutes.

I report to multiple bosses and they are all women with families and children. They are exceptional mentors and role models and they are very supportive. I am truly grateful for that. I know that isn't the case everywhere.

On Joy in Work

Caring for infants and families is where I get the most joy. The second part of what gives me joy is teaching and mentoring: teaching the trainees who are rotating through the NICU—our fellows, medical students, observers, and nurse practitioners—and having family conversations, counseling, and reviewing parts of the clinical exam with the trainees. Those are the parts of the job that are so rewarding. Doing a procedure. Teaching a trainee how to do the procedure. Mentoring a trainee. That's the most fun. But it has to be balanced with getting those notes done, which is not as much fun. I'm someone who really likes to be complete and I want as much time as possible to spend on the parts of my job that are more rewarding.

I haven't been on a clinical shift in a week and half and I'm getting itchy to see some babies and talk to some families. I do love my job. I just wouldn't want to have five shifts a week. There is a balance there. I love doing procedures. And this is a nice reminder that I could never do either a purely academic or a purely clinical job. I like this hybrid. In addition to working in the NICU, I need to research, write and reflect, and have some office time with a little more flexibility.

I love the fact that the hospital is supportive of some of the nontraditional research I'm doing in ethics and communication. When I first started out in this niche it wasn't as widely accepted as true clinical research compared to basic lab or bench research. I've been here for a few years and I'm respected, and that plays a lot into my joy, too. The fact that my family is happy is also a big piece of it. I wouldn't change anything about my job right now. Administration continues to provide opportunities for mentorship and modeling and leadership. They paid for me to attend a conference on women in medical leadership last year, which was excellent. They continue to offer these types of opportunities—not only mentorship, but sponsorship, for women in medicine.

On Money and Joy

As far as a relationship between money and joy, I think there's a certain level of income that you need to be comfortable and not worried about the basic necessities. But once those are met, I feel that excess is not exponentially related to joy. When I first graduated from training, all the debt I'd accumulated from medical school—which was enormous, I had roughly $250,000 in debt—was a burden. After deferring repayment throughout my years of training I had to start paying it off, and I paid off a lot of it, but it was difficult in those early years, when I was just starting my career, to pay off that kind of debt. I was trying to buy a house, raise a family, do research. I was fortunate enough to get an award to assist with loan repayment that has helped significantly, and I am truly grateful for that.

What Diminishes Joy

The electronic medical record definitely diminishes some of the joy. A lot has been written about this. When I'm spending four hours trying to finish all the notes and billing on a weekend shift, and I'm sitting in a corner of the NICU rather than talking to a family, that's not great. But it has to get done by the time I leave. Those notes have to be signed, they have to be correct, they have to be complete and updated. The billing has to be done. I try to find some joy in the art of making the notes easily readable and look good. At the end of the day it's work. It's not my favorite part but it has to get done.

I spend a lot of time writing notes, documenting procedures, and billing but I try to do that as fast as possible and as completely and accurately as possible; I want to make sure there's effective communication for the rest of the team as well as with consulting specialists and for the medical record as a legal document.

There are times when my schedule is clinic heavy and I'm missing time with my family, and that hurts a little. But that's not the majority of the time. Overall, it's very well balanced and my husband and I are fully present and active in our kids' lives. We take our kids to or pick them up from school, take them to sports practices, or attend a school play. For me that's a huge joy. When I miss too much of that in a row it starts to add up. But that's few and far between now. If I'd had kids during my training that balance would likely have been much more difficult. I started having children when I was a second-year fellow, so I was at the end of my training and early in my career.

When Things Go Wrong

We have, as do all areas in medicine, lots of quality assurance programs, clinical event reporting, and systems in place to find out what happened, from a systems-wide perspective, when something goes wrong. This is not in a blaming or shameful atmosphere, but to understand from a systems perspective what happened and what can be fixed in the future. The focus is not on blaming individuals, but on improving systems. We have monthly morbidity and mortality conferences, which are confidential and good for discussing events, what went well, and opportunities for improvement.

50. *Walter G., MD, General Surgeon*

Walter G., MD, has been a military general surgeon, professor of surgery, and medical illustrator. Calm, quiet, and centered, he explains why "the dreams of that little boy who wanted to be a surgeon have been fulfilled."

There were two choices for me professionally. I've done art ever since I was a child. While I theoretically had a choice between being an artist and being a surgeon, I always knew I would be a surgeon. When I was six or seven years old, I saw a *Life* magazine cover with Dr. Michael DeBakey on it and his heart surgery innovations at that time and it was fascinating. In medical school I started doing medical illustration to combine the two, so it's been doubly satisfying.

I entered the military right out of medical school. I served on active duty for four years and then continued working in the military health system as a civilian. I've never worked in a non-military setting but I can compare it to my civilian residency in surgery. The big difference, which was very striking, was that the military has a very different approach to interpersonal interactions from the civilian world. In the big city where I did my residency, when you walked down the street it was very impersonal—you never made eye contact. As soon as I went through basic training in the military it was evident that with anyone I met, especially a superior officer, I had to make eye contact. If they were a superior rank, I had to acknowledge them by saluting. So it was a very different and positive connection between people and an atmosphere of mutual respect. It was really collegial. I'm always interacting with people at the various levels of the hierarchy and there's always a constructive consultation environment.

Officially, I work 40 hours a week but often more, and my hours are quite variable. In the past my commitment was more intense. Continuously over a 30-year period there were times when I took emergency night call every fourth or fifth night and one or two weekends a month. I now have more flexibility and, overall, my schedule works well for me.

On Job Satisfaction

I get satisfaction from being a surgeon because I'm a type A and I like instant gratification. I get satisfaction from teaching students, from having patients who appreciate what I do for them and who let me know that they do. I have patients whom I've seen for 30 years. And these days, although I don't like it as a sign of growing older, a lot of patients say to me, "You're not going to retire, are you?" There are a lot of patients I've operated on who give me a big hug when I see them, and several patients will tell me, "You've changed my life" or "You're my favorite doctor." There's great satisfaction in that. I feel the satisfaction of helping patients—those I may have cured of cancer and those whose lives I've improved—and the response and appreciation I get from patients as a result of that is invaluable.

The second satisfying component for me is training generations of surgical residents who then go on to do great things; at the student level, as well, being able to train them regardless of whether or not they go into surgery. Anecdotally, I was coming back from California on a flight last weekend and one of the passengers—a young man who was coming down the aisle where I was seated—said to me, "Hi, Dr. G., I thought I recognized you. You were my teacher in medical school." He's a urologist now.

In terms of increasing my job satisfaction, efficiency in my work environment is key. The optimal situation for me is to have an efficient support system both in the clinic and in the operating room. And that entails things like turnover time and personnel who are familiar with the different procedures that I'm doing and can efficiently provide me with the support I need in terms of equipment and the function of the operating room. When it works well, that's good. Efficient turnover of the OR is an objective of any hospital. This is the nature of the beast. It happens in all hospitals and doesn't diminish my joy in work.

On Joy in Work

The human factor has given me a lot of joy in work. The collegial interaction I have experienced makes work intellectually stimulating, rewarding, and challenging. I don't think there is anything I would change about my job. I value the ability to do my job, to see my patients efficiently. I pretty much have control over the circumstances in which I work.

What Diminishes Joy

Administrative duties are a fact of life for all medical professionals and are negative intrusions on the pleasure of practice. When patients have difficulty with access to my care it is a stressor both for them and for me. I always see all the patients I'm scheduled to see even if they're late.

What is the opposite of joy in work would be hard to say. If the annoyances were to outweigh the pleasures, that would be a turning point for me. But the pleasures far outweigh the annoyances. This has been true throughout my career; I have been very fortunate to work among first-rate colleagues. The camaraderie in the military system is a daily pleasure, vs. the pressure of competition and the increasing bureaucratic burden in the civilian world.

Reflections

Going into surgery today is dramatically different from what it was when I became a surgeon. I don't know what course I would take now if I were to start out in surgery because technology has advanced so rapidly and the changes are so dramatic. I've always enjoyed working with my hands. Doing surgery the old-fashioned way was very satisfying for me. Now it's increasingly "Nintendo" surgery: laparoscopic surgery, arthroscopic surgery, interventional techniques have changed the face of surgery dramatically. So you have to find a niche that you really like in this new world, as opposed to the old approach to surgery, where you had a master technician who would accomplish things by manipulating the body with his or her hands.

The word for surgery actually comes from the Greek *chirurgi*, which means working with the hands. Now, although you're working with your hands, it's remote from touching the patient, using long instruments grasped outside the body. I of course adapted to the new technology. Before, if a patient got an abscess you would have to drain it with an incision. Now interventional radiology can put a catheter into the abscess to drain it.

I've changed my practice at this stage of my career in that I'm not doing as much laparoscopic surgery as I was, but I focus on doing breast cancer surgery, which is still manual. There's no robotic way to do breast surgery at this point, although that may change dramatically as the treatment of breast cancer changes. Even open breast cancer surgery has changed from more radical surgery to much more limited surgery over the course of my career.

When you're a physician, especially a surgeon, you always have to be at 100% when you're seeing patients and when you're operating on patients. Even during residency, it's amazing how resilient people are who make it through the program. Even with long hours, one can still operate efficiently and safely. Awareness of possible deleterious effects of sleep deprivation has led to a healthy ongoing debate about reasonable work schedules. There is also important attention being directed to resiliency and strategies to avert burnout for both trainees and practicing physicians.

51. Nancy W., RN, PhD, Nurse, Clinical Psychologist, Faculty Member, and Clinical Consultant

Nancy W. is a psychologist and faculty member. She teaches, conducts research, writes, and provides clinical consultation to children and their families, specifically to help them to cope with the emotional impact of childhood illness.

I started out wanting to be a veterinarian because I loved animals. But after working with animals in college I realized I didn't want them to be my work—I just wanted them to be my pets. One day my mother suggested I work with people, and that immediately sounded right to me. I knew I wanted to be in a helping profession. I switched into the nursing school at my university and it was the perfect fit. I absolutely loved every minute of it. I got my degree and became a nurse. I became a psychologist and got my license when I graduated with my PhD, and I carry both licenses in two states.

When you're a nursing student you have to try out everything. I gravitated toward psychiatric nursing. What I especially loved was working with children who have medical illnesses and, in particular, working with children and families to help them cope with the psychological effects of their illnesses. I felt there were so many people who could take care of the physical body, but there was a huge gap when it came to answering the questions, "What does this illness mean for my child?" and "What does my child's illness mean for me?" I felt my niche was to help the child and the family through that. For the first part of my career I worked with children who had traumatic injury or chronic illnesses in the ICU. It was helping them around the psychological aspects of coping with their illness that I really loved. I don't work in the ICU every day now, but it's easy for me to tap into that because I did it for so long.

I knew my first job was a disaster in less than a minute. I got my master's in psychiatric nursing, I thought I had a dream job, I was going to work on an inpatient child psychiatry unit at a nearby hospital. I'll never forget it. It was a locked child psychiatric unit. That locked door closed behind me and the senior nurse who was orienting me said, "Here comes one of your first patients."

This little boy was walking up the hall. And when I introduced myself to him, the first thing that nurse pointed out, with him there, were the deep cuts on both his arms. And I told myself, *I'm never going to last in this job.* I knew that. That was about a minute into that job. That's when I went back to my original idea of wanting to work with kids who have medical illness but to work with the psychological effects of their illness, the impact of that illness, rather than with kids' primary psychiatric illness.

I've learned that finding the job that brings you the fulfillment you originally sought in healthcare is a process of discovery. At that point I didn't know. I thought that was going to be my dream job and it turned out that it wasn't right for me at all.

Today I spend most of my time teaching nursing students. I have control over my schedule. I teach the things I want to teach. Some of it comes from nursing, some of it comes from psychology, but it's combined. The blended approach is what I find most meaningful.

On Joy in Work

Joy is feeling that I'm fulfilling my purpose, which is very much about service. There's something called the "concept of original vocation"—what you hoped to be, what you started out to be. It's the interface between where the world's needs meet what gives you deepest satisfaction. That is what joy is for me. I don't feel it all the time, but when I feel it and know I'm in the zone, and I know I'm doing something worthwhile and meaningful, it not only lifts somebody else up, it lifts me up.

To feel joy in work, it's important to be in a place where I feel I'm part of a shared mission. That there is a sense of esprit de corp. The feeling that we're all in this together. My personal joy comes from connection to shared humanity and relationships. I like to have opportunity and I love to be part of a team. I never just wanted to be off somewhere by myself. I could never have a private practice. It's too lonely for me. You have to know something about yourself. If you don't know something about yourself how are you supposed to find the right kind of position that will bring you joy, where you can really do your best and best serve your patients?

I'm a person who loves deadlines. I like to have goals. But what has never worked for me is feeling I have to push people. I want to work with other self-starters. And then it isn't work anymore.

I remember hearing somebody say once, "You know you've reached that joy when work isn't work anymore. It's your passion. You want to do it." And then you're in that zone. Once you've had it you just want to stay in that lane. And you owe it to yourself and to your patients to try to keep that going. It's not easy today, with all these cost-cutting measures, understaffing, and just trying to squeeze every ounce out of everybody.

Everyday Ethics

I have come to believe in what I call "everyday ethics." It's how do we treat a person? Do we pick up the phone and call someone? If we're late, do we apologize? If someone says they think they're having a side effect from their medication, we say, "Tell me why you think it's a side effect," or "Tell me more;" we don't just jolly them along, saying "There, there, there." This is what I've been thinking about and what I like to teach.

Mentorship

A piece of advice I once got at a professional workshop was that it doesn't matter who you are, what level you are, whether you've been working in the field for 40 or 50 years, if you're top dog or the new kid on the block, *everybody needs ongoing mentorship and somebody who is invested in our professional development.* I realized that when I was an intern and a fellow, I had fabulous supervision. It was exciting to wake up every day and feel that people were interested in my professional development. And then that just stopped, the plug had been pulled. All of a sudden, I was supposed to be this complete professional and there was no ongoing supervision. It wasn't until I went to that workshop that I realized I was missing that.

I came back, talked with a colleague, and we agreed to do peer supervision. She would supervise me and I would supervise her, mostly about our professional development and our goals and aspirations. That helped me to dream bigger and work to achieve my goals.

On Money and Joy

We have to have enough money to meet our basic needs. It's like Maslow's Hierarchy of Needs: if we don't have the basics, the foundations of what we need, it's very hard to go up that ladder. No one wants to live too close to the bone. Obviously, we don't do our jobs for the money and I think we probably can overcome being underpaid to some extent. But if I felt grossly underpaid or not compensated fairly that could be a stumbling block to joy.

If somebody doing similar work to mine was making more money that could really be a sticking point.

What Diminishes Joy

Going home and then having three or four hours of unpaid charting to do diminishes joy. But burnout—if you're still engaged with patients but you're not getting the joyful part, the energizing part, you're just getting completely drained—is the opposite of joy.

Burnout

Understaffing in nursing creates unsafe situations that are *extremely* stressful. Sometimes we have to talk about organizations. There's a fine line between how much stress we can absorb and practice safely, and the point at which the environment becomes unsafe. Nurses need a leader who says, "We will have adequate staffing here" or "We will not let it be unsafe."

A nurse is always available here if someone needs a mentor on the spot. But the nurses say, "I can't go to those support rounds. I don't have anybody to cover my patients." There just aren't enough people. Nurses don't have time to use the restroom.

Nurses may be feeling, *if I could just get more efficient* or *if I could just write these notes faster* or *if I could just make these conversations shorter* or *if I could get on top of superior time management, things would get better.* Sometimes people feel, *of course I should be able to do more, to take on more.* But that's going to take us only so far. We know when we're trying to make it work, and we're working harder and things are just not turning around. We might be up to date but we're not in a state of joy. When we're in it and struggling it's so hard to see what we're doing. That kind of situation leads to burnout.

I have a friend who went back to school, got her nurse practitioner degree, and is now a nurse practitioner. This was going to be her dream job but what's happening to her is devastating to see. She has young kids and is now working in a clinic where she sees between 20 and 24 patients *a day.* Someone else tells her how long she can spend with patients, like a bean counter. You feel you need half an hour with a patient, but guess what? They only booked you for ten or fifteen minutes. If she spends any more time she's going to get behind. And then she comes home, and this is not unusual, and spends two to three hours a night charting on her own time just to keep up. She's burning the candle at both ends. We are *completely* sapping people. And we're not giving them the supportive environments they need.

I'm so worried about new people. Like new medical students, whose empathy by the third year of medical school has tanked. They've taken these bright, energetic, motivated people and basically bled it out of them.

I once heard someone say, "In life, you can be a spring—always generative—or you can be a well, which just fills up and gets drained." Somehow that metaphor was very helpful for me. I knew I needed to cultivate that in myself and in my environment. I wanted to feel that internal rejuvenation: I go to work every day and I owe it to my patients and the people I work with to be at my best. Because they need help. If I'm fried or burned out or just barely hanging in there it's not only unfair to me, it's unfair to everyone else.

Feeling Out of My Depth

I remember once, in a hospital where I worked, I had been hired as a psychologist and was technically a psychiatric nurse. The staff went out on strike and the administration told me that I had to work as a nurse. I told them I wasn't qualified. It was horrible. I thought, *do I want to lose my job over this?* I ended up saying as long as there was somebody there that I could ask questions of—and that I was going to have a very low bar for questions—I would do it.

I worked in the NICU mostly with the babies who were ready to go home, so I felt comfortable with that. I worked with their parents. But I didn't like being pushed around. It was my license on the line, my judgment about what I felt qualified for and capable of doing. And when somebody says, "You're going to do something else," that is not joy. That is joy eroding.

I coped with that situation by making it my own. I got in there and I remember there was this premature baby in an isolette, doing fine. I was feeding him and he was doing well. And I noticed all these hand-done illustrations in his baby isolette. I asked people, "Where did these come from?" They told me they came from the father, who was in jail. I asked for his address so I could write to him, to send him a few photographs of his baby looking at these pictures. He wrote back to tell me the photographs were beautiful and to please keep sending them. And I did. That is how I coped. My strength was working with families. That is what I was qualified to do. My joy has always been to create circumstances where people feel they're the very best parents they can be under the circumstances.

I'm a nurse first and I'm also a psychologist. I can walk into a place and I can think like a nurse and I can think like a psychologist. I ask myself, *what legacy can I help build? How can I help this father feel there's a connection? That it is not irreparable that he's not here?* I don't think I could have done that with just my nursing background or just with my psychologist background. But with both together, I could.

Advice

My advice to colleagues is to take care of yourself well so that you can be at your very best to serve. Everybody has to figure out for themselves what that means. For some people it might be exercise. For other people it might be their animals, their relationships, their vacations. The obvious things, like making sure you're sleeping and eating well. Because people so often don't even do *that*. It gets so bad, nurses don't even use the restroom. They're not eating all day. I know anesthesiologists who basically say things like, "Never an epidural on a full bladder." You know that applies to a patient, but what about *yourself*? My advice is, you owe it to yourself and to your patients to take good care of yourself.

On Mentorship

We need to have mentorship and opportunities to get the bigger perspective. Sometimes we get so myopic because we're always on that hamster wheel, trying to make this one day okay. And we have no perspective. So those opportunities—through mentorship, through education, through taking retreats or vacations, and through our relationships—will give us perspective on our lives and our careers.

It's important to try to find someone in the organization who will take you under their wing, people in leadership who will take an interest in you. I like it when organizations have innovation grants. I'm talking small. You have a good idea, you bring it up, you write it up in one page, and somebody supports your good idea. It can get you into a totally different lane. It makes you feel, *wow, I did have a good idea!*

On Flexibility and Time Off

We all need to have our lunch breaks. When our child is graduating, we need to be able to take that time off, and to take vacations when it's convenient for us. Bring in some rent-a-nurses and other temporary staff so that people who need vacations can take them. There are all kinds of creative things you can do to give people needed time off. It costs money, but it's money well spent. When a nurse walks out the door, $100,000 walks out the door.

On Honesty

Ask yourself, *is this what I intended*? If not, be honest about whether there's a better place and a better fit for you. Don't be afraid of making change if necessary. Because as hard as it is, sometimes change can be extremely good. Even though I've sometimes made hard decisions, they've always ended up being the right thing.

What has been really important for me has been to recognize when something isn't working and to get out so I can change. In our society there's so much emphasis on, "hang in there"—but nobody talks about how hard it is to let go. I feel if I can't do something well, I have a responsibility to get into a better situation where I can fulfill my purpose. I think some people feel stuck where they are, and they just stay there.

It's important to be honest with our organizations, too. We need regular opportunities in our organizations to give candid feedback and not be afraid. It's important to create an environment where people can give an honest appraisal about what's working and share their ideas for improvement.

On Variety

It's important to have variety. If you're doing straight clinical work, although some people love it, I think it can be very draining. I've found that if I have a more varied portfolio—some clinical work, some teaching, clinical research, and writing—it is energizing. I love to go to conferences to present and learn because it gives me some respite from the clinical.

Employers should think about how to create more variety within different positions. Obviously, things like job sharing. Or sabbaticals. A friend of mine was in a sabbatical program where people could take a few months to study something, or recharge, or travel. She came back energized, with so much to give.

On Organizational Support for Self-Care

Why aren't we doing in healthcare something like what Google does? Why isn't there free food? Daycare? There are so many things we could be doing to improve the quality of life. Nurses worry because their daycare providers charge five dollars a minute if they're one minute late. And so here they are, trying to finish up their notes or do discharge planning or something else, and their child is waiting, the meter is ticking.

Before they renovated our hospital there was a cafeteria that served home-cooked food. The cafeteria now serves high-fat fast food, and staff are trapped inside with not-so-good food choices. The work culture and environment needs to be healthy. Instead, give people something nutritious that's going to sustain them.

On Relational Skills

In our training we used to talk about relational skills with patients and families. What this did—and compared to a lot of things it was really cheap—was to help people feel more capable of and comfortable with talking to their patients and having relationships with them. And that's where the good stuff is. Relational skills—what people tend to denigrate as "soft skills"—is what we should be emphasizing *more*. The point is to enable everyone to feel more capable and more confident at work. Because then at 3:00 a.m. we won't feel afraid when there's not a chaplain or a psychiatrist around; we will have developed these skills and we'll realize, *at least I can get through this and I know whom to refer to. We're going to be okay.*

Hospitals have morbidity and mortality rounds that focus on patient deaths and other things that go wrong. But why don't we have the opposite of that when things go well, and call them "joy rounds?" These would be places to examine what went well, and why. We need to carve out time to celebrate those things.

52. Nicole A., MD, MPH, Medical Director of a Neonatal Intensive Care Unit at a Quaternary Care Pediatric Hospital

Nicole A., MD, MPH, is the medical director of the NICU at a quaternary care pediatric hospital. First named the associate medical director of the NICU shortly after finishing her fellowship in 1996, she then became the medical director. Nicole is involved in every component of what goes into providing optimal patient care in the NICU: providing direct patient care and working with families; keeping all of the practice guidelines and policies up to date; making sure the hospital's practice of family-centered care, and the role of the family on the unit, is optimized; encouraging research of all stripes to take place safely; and managing logistical tasks related to schedules, teaching sessions, and the like.

I came to healthcare from a different direction than probably most people. I studied anthropology in college, and I always had the idea that I would do something global, something related to understanding people, and something that would be helpful. But I wasn't sure how I was going to pull that all off within anthropology.

In my junior year I was in an amazing program, where we lived in host countries all around the globe. We left the West Coast for Japan and lived with host families in different countries for about six weeks, circling the entire globe, ending in London. We each had a topic that we studied for that whole year. Mine was medical anthropology. I saw for the first time in my life the real medical problems, the number of terrible diseases people had all over the world. And I, too, had a couple of experiences with gastrointestinal illnesses. In the United States it's easy to not see any medical problems if you don't have any of your own, and your family doesn't, and you're young. You just don't see diseases. It became increasingly clear to me that medical anthropology was interesting, but it didn't really seem all that effective. That's when I realized I did not want to continue to study medical anthropology.

Then I got really interested in the possibility of going to medical school, which was something I never would have considered before. I was not particularly interested in the sciences and I had never given medicine serious thought. But then I met my father-in-law-to-be, who was a pediatrician who had done a lot of global health work. He came to medicine from a humanistic perspective rather than a hard-core biological one. The college I went to was a wonderful little school where there were a few mentors in the premed program who really worked to convince me that it was possible to go to medical school without feeling my primary driver had to be science. I decided to go for it. I applied. It turns out I had actually taken all the premed requirements except for one; I had to take organic chemistry, but the rest were done.

I went to medical school and of course loved pediatrics. During my pediatrics residency, I thought I'd be a general pediatrician and that would be a great fit with global health. I rotated through the NICU where I learned about neonatology for the first time. I didn't know what it was, I didn't know it was a field. And I just completely fell in love with it. But then I felt a huge conflict because neonatology is a very high-tech, expensive, first-world field that I thought wouldn't lend itself well to global health. But I decided to stay true to a basic decision-making tenet that had always served me well: Choose to do what you love, and things tend to sort themselves out.

I loved two things about neonatology right away: one was the efficacy of it. Some of my patients had conditions in which, without an intervention, it was clear they would die. Then we would offer a specific treatment, and the babies would improve and recover. These were sick newborns. Some of them were premature, some of them were full-term babies who had infections or congenital anomalies or inborn errors in metabolism, a whole range of problems. It was different from every other specialty that I had witnessed in medicine because the effect of the treatment was appreciable, and it was incredibly satisfying to see these babies do so great. Neonatology is often criticized for seeming futile or having patients with terrible outcomes. In fact, a big piece of what drew me to the field was the opportunity to play a role in these ethical dilemmas.

The other aspect of neonatology that I loved was thinking I would never suffer from burnout. I had heard of doctors getting burned out by taking care of patients with the same condition over and over again. I thought it was amazing to work with newborns because, regardless of what care providers might be thinking or feeling, the parents and extended family are the absolute opposite of burned out. So every time I was called to a delivery, even at 3:00 a.m., even when there was really no medical emergency that required that I be there, the mother, father, and extended family would be so thrilled that I would get caught up in their enthusiasm. To be part of that and know that I could ride this external excitement that would always be there, I thought I could never get burned out.

The delivery of a baby is never a blasé moment. I think all human societies find the moment of birth to be captivating. I really wanted to be part of that. General pediatrics, as much as I admire people who practice it, just wasn't the right choice for me. Parents sometimes seemed less focused on their children's well-being once they were into the day-in day-out challenges of parenthood.

I was also drawn to neonatology because I knew I wanted to subspecialize in a field. I wanted to understand one topic in depth. At the same time, I didn't want to specialize by organ system. I still wanted to take care of an entire person. To be a nephrologist or a cardiologist or a neurologist, I realized I would never again be able to think about the way everything fits together. If I wanted to specialize but still take care of a whole person, then I'd have to do it by age. That meant neonatology, adolescent medicine, or geriatrics. As a pediatrician, geriatrics was off the table. Adolescent medicine did not appeal to me. I thought neonatology was this amazing little narrow window, but a window that is so important and would allow me to learn in depth about a particular field, still take care of an entire person (and family), and think about how all the different body systems work together.

On Joy in Work

My definition of joy in work is tied into knowing that I am devoting my professional life to something I know is an important service to others. This gets immediately back to how much childbirth and newborns mean to parents. If something is all-important to your patient, or to your patient's family, then it's joyful to tap into that focus.

Variety

My hours are incredibly variable. I like that, but some people would hate it. In any intensive care unit specialty, because of the intensity of the work, generally people don't do it all the time. At the hospital where I work, we do a certain number of months of service per year—I do two and a half or three months—and that is broken up into blocks. When

I am on service, I'm fully in charge of many acutely ill newborns. My hours vary a bit but generally I'm in the hospital by 6:45 in the morning and then don't leave until 5:00 or 6:00 at night. I do this Monday to Friday with some weekend and night call responsibilities. It's incredibly intense. But then after half a month or a month, I'm done and sign the whole service off to somebody else and rejuvenate.

This gives me time to do research and global health work along with my administrative responsibilities. During this off-service time I get to do things that are totally different from clinical medicine, and that are exciting and fun. They have nothing to do with direct patient care with all of the emotional highs and lows that entails, working with families through dramatic recoveries, explaining tragic diagnoses, and thinking through difficult decisions. You give it your all until you feel completely emotionally drained. Then the service time is over and there's time to replenish and start again later.

I think it's fun to have these widely variable days. Today I'm thinking about designing a new medical device, developing a teaching curriculum, and making next year's service schedule. Then I'm on call tonight, so I'll do some patient care. This constant change makes my job feel rich and sustainable.

Recognition

I'm in a special position because I've had this leadership role for a long time, so I get a lot of recognition. Probably more than some people who work just as hard and have been here just as long but who have less leadership responsibility. I feel very lucky. Many times, when everybody is helping, I'm told, "Wow, you guys really did great at that." And I respond that I did nothing; I just happen to be the director of the unit. By virtue of having been in this role for a long time, I have become the most recognizable face of neonatology at this hospital.

There was a long tradition at our hospital that is finally giving way, in which people who did basic science research got more recognition than people who did research in other aspects of medicine. For a long time, I felt I was not recognized from an academic standpoint and that used to bother me. But in the last ten years or so, people have come to recognize that a lot of important research is being done that has nothing to do with cells and atoms and molecules. People in the hospital and the medical school have really come to appreciate a wider definition of research and are promoting doctors through new academic tracks focusing on all kinds of other topics, like bioethics, epidemiology, medical education and global health. For the longest time I felt as though I was working on topics that nobody was ever going to value academically. But now, these have become areas people are excited about; I'm getting a lot of recognition for my academic work and I feel proud that people value my contribution.

On Money and Joy

I think that in general, at least in pediatrics, no one goes into it for the money. It's one of the specialties that's relatively poorly compensated. Most of the people I know from college and medical school went on to make way more money probably doing way less work than those of us in pediatrics. I'm making enough money that I don't have to be constantly worried about it. There are people who work all around me who aren't making enough money to avoid worrying; that is a huge stressor for them and is detrimental to their joy. I don't know what it would be like to be making a massive amount of money because in my world nobody is doing that.

I do think some doctors are underpaid despite their incredible investment in time, money, and education. It always feels heartbreaking to see somebody who decides to go to medical school, make it through residency and a fellowship, become an attending, and then not have enough money and have to constantly worry. I have a colleague who has four young children; yesterday she told me she was feeling guilty because more than ten years after graduating from medical school, she finally decided to splurge and hire a house cleaner once a week.

We're not all starving; I can't say that anybody is in any kind of real financial peril. But I do think between the cost of living here, and the cost of education, many of the pediatricians I work with do struggle to make enough money to live somewhat comfortably.

I am not personally in a position to change anyone's salary, but along with one of my colleagues, we have organized a series of programs focused on wellness that all of our faculty can attend. One topic we picked was financial fitness; we learned about retirement planning and other kinds of financial planning. I think people felt better after making clear financial plans and goals.

What Diminishes Joy

Sleep deprivation gets harder to deal with the older we get. And neonatal intensive care, especially, has a lot of overnight shifts. Babies don't stop being born or getting sick just because it is the middle of the night. I try to lead by example, taking night call and working weekends, and that's getting harder and harder.

When I'm pulled away from my own family at a time when they need me, it always feels very controversial to me. Because I'm working with other people's families—especially when I had my own babies and I'd leave my babies to go take care of other people's babies—the conflict couldn't have been clearer. I have three children and have worked full time through all of that. There have been many important events I've missed or times I felt I wasn't being the mother I wanted to be. That's difficult.

Coping with Tragedy

When something happens to a patient that is tragic, I think we have two choices in how we respond: We can either be in such as state of depression and lacking in empathy that we don't care, or we can keep a human connection and really care about the baby and family, which can be morally and spiritually draining. There are several things I do in tragic situations to be sure I keep my human response. One is to be sure I recognize the tragedy for what it is. It might be a death or some other kind of medical event that's well beyond what we see every day. I set aside time for myself, by myself, to make sure I have a chance to emotionally process that. I don't want to burden my patients and their families by expressing a huge amount of emotion in front of them. But I also want to be absolutely sure that I'm honest with myself and can give myself permission to express my own emotions at a time and a place that's appropriate. I take some time, whether it's in the next hour or, at most, half a day, to privately recognize and experience what happened. That's very helpful for me.

There are lots of support services at my hospital. We try to support each other as professional colleagues. Sometimes, if a death is particularly upsetting, we'll hold a formal debriefing session separately with clinicians who were present at the time. Sometimes we get together with the family and take a moment to recognize the passing of this person who was important to all of us. One of the hospital religious leaders might offer a prayer or blessing. Those feelings are important to share.

We also have a specific series of conferences dedicated to discussing every death to make sure that we allow for the opportunity to learn any conceivable way we can improve our care. The way the hospital handles safety, I have to say, is excellent. We've all had an enormous amount of training in ways to make safety a top priority and to eliminate any barriers to safe care.

I ask all of our attendings to write a personal letter to families whenever there's been a death; I hope that's meaningful to both the parents and the attending.

Promoting Patient Safety

We've all taken many courses in how to communicate in a way that makes safety as likely as possible. For example, there are ways to ask clarifying questions if someone says something confusing and you are unclear about a plan; to make sure that if someone is acting in a way that's inappropriate, the behavior doesn't continue; and to be transparent with families, assuring them that if something does go wrong, we will disclose the situation promptly, honestly, make sure we accept responsibility, and learn how to change the system to ensure it won't happen again. From that standpoint I think this hospital really is a great place to work.

A selection of people in leadership roles in the hospital gather for a few minutes every morning to go through any safety concerns that have come up in the last 24 hours or that could come up in the next 24 hours. We go up to the NICU and report on any relevant hospital-level safety issues, discussing any concerns that pertain directly to the NICU. We then report any NICU safety concerns back to hospital leadership the next morning, so that there is a closed loop of accountability.

What counts as a safety concern is widely defined. Yesterday at our hospital-level safety briefing, I reported that nurses in the NICU had noticed the elevator doors were closing too quickly. The person who's the head of operations was there and said, "I can look into that." The next day he got back to us to say, "Yes, the doors were closing too quickly and now that's fixed." Through this system, it is easy for anybody working at any level to say, "I have a concern"; it may be minor or major, and it is listened to and addressed. This culture makes us all participate in the process of safety and look at our day through a lens of responsibility and potential improvement.

I think a lot of this focus on patient safety comes from leadership. Our chief medical officer has required everybody—literally, from the person who stocks the milk in the fridge all the way to the chief of surgery—to take safety courses in multidisciplinary groups. And then the leadership of the hospital comes around and talks to us about safety, how we're doing, how we are putting into practice the content of the courses, what barriers there are to patient safety, and how they can help.

Advice

When people explain what, to them, is an important problem or idea, try to be undistracted and listen intently, open-mindedly and non-defensively. And then, if you think it's an important problem, decide to put in the time and persevere until you get to the bottom of it.

When someone complains about something that at first blush sounds outrageous, hold your fire and learn about what happened from the other perspective. In general, people are reasonable, smart, thoughtful, and trying hard to do their job well. Jumping to a conclusion that presumes otherwise is likely to be incorrect.

In medicine there are a lot of difficult people with tricky personalities. I've found it incredibly helpful to recognize that these people are difficult in a way that has absolutely nothing to do with me. It's so much easier to handle all the potentially conflicted, hostile interactions by recognizing that I can take myself out of the picture and focus on what we can do together for the patient we are caring for. I don't try to take on the rest of what's going on with them. That's been hugely helpful for me. The organization has recognized these problems, has been responsive, and many of those difficult people have left.

This last piece of advice is, be proud of yourself and your choice to go into medicine. Whether patient care, basic science, or other research, you are doing something that's important to somebody regardless of how much you get paid. If you ask yourself the question, "If I didn't do this job, would the world be the worse?" the answer is yes. In medicine, people should be pleased that they've chosen a profession that is important, helping the sick get well, and the well stay well. Whatever your niche, it's important.

53.   Amy I., MD, Pediatrician and Chief of Staff at an Integrated Health System

Amy I., MD, has been a pediatrician for 18 years and chief of staff at an integrated health system for the past four years. Driven and passionate about healthcare delivery and administration, Amy talks about the pressures of time, as well as what it's like to be a physician and a leader—who also happens to be a woman of color—in her organization.

I'm a pediatrician and medical administrator with a half-time clinical practice at a not-for-profit, primary care-focused, integrated health cooperative that has both a clinical delivery side and an insurance side. My job is interesting and challenging in many good ways, and I work with many wonderful teams that "share the care" with me, so to speak. The work is also challenging in other ways because I tend to be a "driver"—mostly a driver of myself, but also a driver of the system. I want good things to happen for patients and the people who deliver the care. I really do believe good things can happen when well-intentioned people work to solve problems together. I put a lot on my own shoulders, though. My elevator speech about my role as chief of staff is that "I work to support a healthcare system that allows our providers and teams to do their best work on behalf of patients."

My Professional Journey

After high school, I was accepted into a combined baccalaureate-medical program, which essentially meant that I was already accepted into medical school as a teenager. By age 17, I already knew my plan—I was going to be an undergraduate for four years, then be in medical school for four years, and then I would do my residency for three years. My plan at that time was to work one year in practice, have a baby, and then work another year and have another baby. And that's pretty much what I did.

I had trained mostly at the same public university, in the same college town, for 11 years. Initially after residency I moved to a larger metropolitan area to work in private practice before returning home in 2002, when a job opportunity arose unexpectedly. My short time in private practice was an eye-opener. I witnessed some of the business realities of medicine and got my first job jitters out of my system.

Back home for about ten years, my focus was on becoming the best pediatrician I could be and also growing my family. Thankfully, my full-time practice blossomed, as did my two kids, and I was voted a "top-doc" among my peers in a local magazine. All of that felt meaningful and rewarding. I was also working on a handful of quality improvement projects because I felt compelled to contribute to the group. Like many young professionals, I was just trying to figure myself out. And then in my late thirties, during what I suppose is the usual time for a mid-life crisis, I thought, *I've reached the end of my plan. Now what?*

I started running for fitness and learned some Spanish but still wondered, *What am I going to be when I grow up?* Then a little more than six years ago a leadership opportunity popped up. While I had participated on a variety of committees in various positions throughout my career, I had not held any official leadership roles. My professional curiosity piqued with this new opportunity and I figured now might be a good time to try something new.

In 2013, I was chosen to be the site chief of my clinic, which included 20 primary care providers. In those first years of leadership I learned a lot about people, communication, and my own capacity to learn new skills. It was not all fun, particularly when I failed, which I did, though thankfully more often things went well.

After three years as site chief I found myself a better human being and a better leader. And I felt I was helping wonderful people do awesome work. I was figuring out that there was space in our organization for my type of leadership, in my shape and size, so to speak. I really enjoyed growing and collaborating with teams and "being in the room where it happens," as the quote goes from Hamilton, the musical. My desire to contribute to and support an organization that really had its heart in the right place continued to grow. Then, three years ago, I became the chief of staff, which means I have management responsibility for our entire medical group. Leadership has always been a leap that has made me feel vulnerable. But, despite the job being bigger and harder than I imagined initially, I have very few regrets. Leadership was not part of my original plan back in high school, but things have turned out okay.

Balancing Clinical and Administrative Roles

In my role as chief of staff, I hold management responsibility for our medical provider group, which includes 70 physicians who are MDs and doctors of osteopathy, as well as nurse practitioners and physician assistants. These are healthcare "providers," a term we use in our system to encompass multidisciplinary professional groups who work in primary care, urgent care, sports medicine, and dermatology.

People who held this job before me spent less time than I do, or no time, in clinical practice. I remember hearing my staff or my colleagues complain about how the administrators didn't know the realities of medical practice. That's why, when I became chief of staff, it was really important to me to maintain at least a half-time practice to maintain legitimacy, relevancy, and understanding of how care is delivered in our system. Between being chief of staff and managing a very busy practice, it often feels like I'm doing nearly two full-time jobs. And day to day, week to week, and month to month, the lines blur and my balance teeter-totters. Burnout is something I navigate personally as a clinician and as an administrator.

There are two different camps as to whether it is wise to combine clinical and administrative responsibilities, but I think the combination of the two helps me in my work on both sides. I am a better administrator because I also see patients regularly. I am a better clinician because I understand the administrative systems at play. There are very few people in my organization who navigate this blend of work, and it poses some serious risk for burnout. I have to protect my own restorative personal forces that keep me upright. I do a lot of talking about how to stay upright in the work we do, which ultimately boils down to intentional system structures and personal choices.

In our integrated healthcare organization, there's a set salary with very few areas for incentives in terms of pay. For the most part, our provider income is predictable from paycheck to paycheck. Because our providers are salaried, which is not the case in most healthcare organizations, our work is not based on RVUs, or fee-for-service production. We don't order tests or medications because it's in the doctor's best financial interests. We are more focused on what is best for the patient. There are limits to this type of system, though. Sometimes a salary model can be a barrier to change when we ask people to do things differently. Change always feels like more work initially. That said, I do think this is a better way to provide care compared to a productivity model. Our motives feel better.

On Joy in Work

Joy in work means being energized and figuratively "lost" in work that is meaningful and productive. By lost, I mean being immersed in the flow of the work. Joy in work is apparent when you're so into what you're doing that you're using all of your brain juices, when you almost forget about the rest of the world, when you feel energized by participating in whatever the work is. To me, joy in work is having the luxury, honestly, of not having to think about the outside world; when I can be in the moment, solving a problem, following my curiosity and being energized by it, and feeling that I'm connected to something meaningful.

I definitely experience those moments in the clinic and on the medical leadership side. When I'm doing project work, I enjoy the process of figuring out what to do next, talking to people and hearing their perspectives, making compromises, collecting data, and looking for the story in the numbers. And when I'm in clinic rooms, connecting with patients, hearing what they have to say, trying to help them solve a problem, offering suggestions that are helpful, and building positive engagement—there is so much fun and joy in that clinical practice.

What Diminishes Joy

What takes away from joy in work is not having enough time: not having enough time with patients; not having enough time to do all of the work that's important, including the tedious work; not having the time for communication and the meaningful interactions and moments between people. Foundational to having enough time is having the structure that allows for the work to fit the time available.

Tedium

Tedious parts of the job, by which I mean non-value added work, diminish joy in work for me. Things like coding. Things like charting to the extent that you're serving a different person's priority. Some of this has to do with reimbursement: there are rules about how to get reimbursed and how much charting is necessary to do. Although I do think regulation gets a bad rap and there are many things about regulation that are reasonable and helpful overall—and I understand some of why these rules exist (to prevent fraud, waste, abuse, inequity, etc.)—there are other aspects of regulation that simply seem disconnected from what is important. There's just never enough time to do the important stuff, let alone all the nonsensical baloney.

Time Pressure

Being a primary care provide feels like an endless stream of pop quizzes. At our organization we see patients who are scheduled every 15–30 minutes: 30 minutes for preventive health visits, 15 minutes for follow-ups and acute visits. We don't get off the treadmill until the end of the day, and even then there is charting to do. We're constantly on the treadmill of seeing this patient and the next patient and the next patient. We don't get to toggle up or down, because the next patient is waiting.

We're accountable to our patients. We want our patients to have access to us. There is a constant stream of patients waiting for us and we want to spend enough time with each of them. And because we're all human beings, and everyone's problems are somewhat different, and everyone's communication skills and literacy are slightly different, it is difficult for a system to accommodate the variability without layering pressure on the provider.

I don't think we'll ever be able to take away the feeling of pressure to stay on time when we have a series of appointments stacked up.

Furthermore, in healthcare, because it's science and technology, things are always changing and there are always new ideas to add on. If there's a new version of the flu shot and patients all need to have an informed conversation about it, that's three to ten minutes to add onto every single person's appointment. As a provider, if I want to do a decent job, I will want to invest that time in my patients. But that choice takes time away from something or someone else, such as another important health issue that may be more important to the patient, the next patient waiting for you, your own family time, or your own sleep and self-care. Technology or any good idea is a stressor unless there is a plan to integrate it into the work we are already doing. This gets back to being intentional about how we structure the work so it fits the time and resources available.

Time is finite. There are only 24 hours in a day, and we all have to make choices. As a provider I want to help people and I'm driven in that direction; the system wants me to do the most and be the best and to never make mistakes. Healthcare is a high-stakes game. We're dealing with people's lives. As I've said, to protect my own time, I sometimes need to stand up for what is realistic. We all do.

If I were being perfectly honest, I am an imperfect role model in this way. I have too much magical thinking about my own double work life. Sometimes I can create time through intentional choices and working more efficiently. Other times, I just try to squeeze more from the stone that is my day. This is metaphorical for health systems, I suppose.

In our system, we need to intentionally engineer the work to fit the time, space, and resources available. This is true for the work in the clinics and for the work in medical administration. On the clinical side, our work systems are not flexible enough to toggle up and down efficiently based on patient complexity. Healthcare providers can't answer ten health questions in a 15-minute appointment. It is not safe and it's honestly not possible. However, if we allot more time for each appointment then fewer patients can be seen each day, which pushes patients to wait longer for their appointments; and that is unsafe in its own way. Both scenarios are costly in one way or another, either through error and turnover, or through unused resources and the barriers of expensive care. The goal has to be to find a way to create a system that is affordable and sustainable. As we engineer the work system—the staffing, schedules, space, workflows, training, and tools—we affect quality, safety, access, service, equity, and cost of care. As complex as it sounds, we have no choice but to try to improve.

As a manager, I witness times when the providers are burning too hot, trying to accomplish too much, and when the system is asking too much of them. We need to innovate and engineer a healthcare system in which the work fits the time and the resources available. In my mind, it all comes down to the choices we make as patients, as providers, as organizations, and as a society. We will have to do things differently in the future. We need to be honest with ourselves about our resources and what we can afford.

The Primary Care Backpack

There is lots of other work that happens outside of direct patient time. I call it the "backpack of primary care." This backpack goes with the day's work. And the backpack definitely adds to our time pressures. Let's say I have a face-to-face appointment with a patient. I am the primary care provider. If someone comes in with fatigue, I collect a history, do a physical exam, decide whether I need to prescribe medications or order tests, and co-create the plan with the patient. And then I leave the room.

Although I am leaving the room I still have the work left of charting, coding, receiving and reviewing the lab results, communicating the lab results to the patient, sending a new prescription, maybe creating a follow-up plan, having that patient respond to me with their follow-up questions through the electronic health record, and then maybe conferring with my partner about the case, particularly if it is a complex one. I may read an article about the condition or do a little bit of research. I may look back at the patient's medical history to make sure I didn't miss anything and incorporate that into my follow-up care. I may need to reach out to our team nurse or social worker to help the patient arrange transportation for future visits. I might have to advocate for the patient if the care they need is not covered by their insurance plan. All of this work happens outside of the actual patient visit. If I have patients scheduled every 15 minutes from 8:00 a.m. until 5:00 p.m., and I have even five minutes of that backpack work for each patient, where does that time fit into my day? It goes into my lunch hour; it goes into my waking up early to do work at 5:00 a.m. before clinic, which we call pre-visit prep; it goes into my evenings, my weekends, and into my "pajama time."

When I had young children, I had to leave work at 5:00 p.m. on the dot so I could pick my kids up at 5:30 p.m. And that meant I would chart between 9:00 p.m. and 11:00 p.m. every night. Now that my kids are a little older, I might stay until 7:00 p.m. and finish that work before I leave the office, then have less work to do during pajama time. But the bottom line is that the backpack work has to go somewhere in my day and the time adds up.

Gender and Racial Biases

I consider myself a person of color, I am biracial, and so my life has always intersected with the issue of identity. There are pressures that people of color and women in leadership face. There are different standards. There is the extra pressure to have no dents in the armor. People of color and women in the workplace need to go above and beyond so that imperfections or infractions are not over-applied or over-emphasized. I think the pressure stems directly from our social structures and the history of the United States.

In reality, more positives attributes are presumed of my white, male counterparts than of my female colleagues. People assume that men know what they're talking about more than women do. At work, it's complex. I don't hear my boss saying, "You're a woman, you need to work harder." It's never that explicit. I don't think anyone here would overtly make that case. However, there are cultural norms in our society that are challenging to disrupt. It takes time.

I think for women it's about being heard in the workplace. Men have told me, "Amy, you need to take the emotion out of the situation." These men wouldn't say this to another man. If I start a sentence with, "I feel we should go in this direction," then it's, "Amy *feels* this. She doesn't *know* this."

This issue came up for me in one of the first forays I had in leadership, in which I was a physician representative at our board of directors' meetings. I am a sincere, intense person by nature. At these meetings I would contribute. I would say something about my pediatric practice, about my relationship with patients, about the services we provide to our members. At the time, maybe ten years ago, before we had a female board president—and before the board completely turned over—every time I spoke, one of the male board members would crack a joke. He wanted to "lighten the air" every single time I spoke—but not when others spoke, and especially not when my male colleagues spoke.

It was as though my sincerity, or my contribution, needed to be diffused. For the first few meetings I didn't really notice it. I had grown up professionally in my medical education environment where I felt there was a lot of gender equality and equity in our treatment as medical students. We were all lowly as medical students and residents, and I was blind to any bias among us. My board experience was my first exposure to a corporate setting. At one point, I leaned over to a male colleague and asked, "Have you noticed this?" And he said, "Yup, I've noticed it."

I didn't ask for any action at the time, but at the next board meeting this same board member said something typical to defuse my contribution. My male colleague interjected, "I agree with Amy. I share her view." Now, while I was grateful for my colleague's backup and he's one of the main reasons I'm still working here now, I really wished I hadn't needed him to raise my legitimacy at the board level. Unfortunately, despite my colleague's redirection, the jokes at these meetings did not stop and I ultimately removed myself from the board committee.

Now, years later, we have a new board and new leadership who are substantially more committed to diversity, equity, and inclusion, which makes a big difference to me. To reduce burnout for professionals from historically marginalized identity groups, you need leadership commitment from the very top combined with strategic deployment at all levels. I am grateful that we are headed the right direction.

Bias and burnout are bedfellows. Bias makes it all the more difficult for professionals from historically marginalized identity groups to find a sustainable work–life balance and take leadership roles. Addressing burnout needs to include efforts to address systemic and interpersonal bias in healthcare.

Burnout

Burnout has many faces. Burnout happens when you find yourself thinking you can't continue to do this anymore, when you know you need to make some change. Burnout is worse when you feel trapped, when you don't have resources. Pre-burnout is thinking, "I'm not sure I can continue to do this." Dangerous burnout is feeling stuck and not knowing where to go.

It's all about feeling upright. I ask myself, *am I upright? Am I doing the right work? Is this meaningful? Is it worth it? Do I feel I have the resources internally to be able to do this?* Then there are challenges that can push me over; it's a constant battle. There are constantly things that can topple me—mostly when I face failure and imperfection or unpleasant people. That's when I need to make different choices, create better boundaries between myself and my work, and set my own limits. If providers burn out it's a bad situation for everyone. So, we need to design the system to support a workload that fits the time and resources available for each position. Unfortunately, the current system can't always accommodate everything we ask of it, and improving the system takes time.

The manager side of my brain hopes people can understand these realities: some people need a reduced workload and a slower pace within the current health system in order to stay upright. The system cannot afford to give everyone full-time pay for much less work and doing so might not be fair to others who are able to balance the responsibilities. So how can we individualize support strategies in a way that is fair to others? I think it starts with asking good questions like, what will keep you upright? What work is joyful enough, fills you up enough, and protects your restorative and personal time enough at a paygrade you can afford? The provider and manager should walk that path together to ask, "What is possible?" I am always hoping for creative solutions in these discussions.

Sometimes, in the end, there is a still gap, or even a chasm, that a manager cannot fill and that the employee cannot span. This may not be the right situation for either of them. How do people handle this? Not everyone can afford to work part-time. Not every system can accommodate an individual's needs. It is a pickle.

I have never felt completely without resources, I'm grateful to say. There have definitely been times, and I wish I could say they were rare, when I have felt I needed to make a change. Or when I've needed to make different choices. There is personal ownership I feel to some of this. There has been a lot of talk about healthcare professionals experiencing "moral injury," rather than burnout. I am not a big fan of that narrative because it feels disempowering to me. Yes, life happens to us. Yes, the system of healthcare is happening to us to some extent. It is not all in our sphere of control to change. However, I still feel accountable to make it better. Only about 2% of the workforce is simultaneously burned out and checked out. Another 40–50% of us are navigating the pressures of burning out and are still showing up engaged. There is a lot of talent and goodwill available to improve our system. If we feel like victims, it is going to be more challenging to participate in the change that is needed.

Advice

It's essential to listen and aim to understand multidimensional perspectives within the healthcare system. It's more than a two-way street. The various parts of the system need to recognize and understand the various front-line staff experiences, the "pebbles in their shoes," and the boulders that they feel are insurmountable. I also think it's important for the front-line staff to understand the complexity of the system. No change is without ripples that affect real lives, real communities. We need to embrace a culture of standard improvement processes. *How* we do improvement is as important as doing it, because how we improve affects what we can create together.

Understand All Sides

This stuff is *complex*. As a manager, I make one tweak in one area and its ripples can be felt across the whole group. You can really see the shift in understanding when you go from being solely a provider to taking on even a little bit of a leadership role. In truth, to be successful, we will need everyone, and I mean everyone, to see themselves as leaders, to be systems-thinkers. Being accountable for a group and not just out for yourself really broadens your perspective. Sometimes individual providers can be a little blind as to how their choices or their behavior affects their team, the clinic, and the whole system; it can be hard for them to comprehend when they don't have a full spectrum view. Some are not even open to hearing a broader view, which is frustrating.

It may seem so simple for a provider to say, "I want to leave at 4:00 p.m. on Thursdays" so he can get to something in his personal life—it seems so easy, it's just one hour, it's two or three patients. But how does that schedule change affect the team coverage? How does that affect the nursing staffing? How does that affect patients who want to come in after their kids get home from school? How does that affect the organization's strategic plan, our backpack work, our bottom line, and the benefits we can afford for staff? There are so many things people want and need to be able to request for themselves. I need to be the type of manager who hears them and says, "Let me see how feasible that is, what the impacts are, and let me bring that information back to you. Let's see what is possible." But I can't just say, "Sure, whatever you want."

It would be nice to have more shared decision-making and shared accountability in the outcomes. But sometimes people don't want to do the work of understanding the system and some providers don't always want to hear that the system is complex. They just want the problem to be fixed by somebody else. They don't always want to hold themselves accountable to the system or to the organization, and the truth is, this impulse is a consequence of burnout itself.

When you feel that you have already given up so much to the organization, you may not feel up to being part of a systems-level discussion. So, there is the challenge. Healthcare is burning folks out, and then they don't feel engaged in the solutions, which makes improvement all the more difficult. We will need to inch forward together in order to improve—nurture group engagement, work on improvement processes, and build trust. There are no magic wands that will fix everything at once. Some of us healthcare providers are hurting. The pace of improvement will depend on how well we can recover, build relationships, and trust each other enough to create the innovation and change that is needed.

At the end of the day, even when folks feel burned out, disengaged, cynical, and disempowered, my job in being on both the clinical and administrative sides is to increase everyone's capacity to have the necessary, multidimensional discussions that will lead to effective ideas and choices and, hopefully, better outcomes.

Improve Medical Education

Upstream improvements in medical education would be very helpful. Medical education does not include enough systems training or process improvement science. Medical student training does not include enough in the curriculum about what it is like to be a nurse, or an audiologist, or how multidisciplinary teams work. Upstream educational changes could mean people would go into practice knowing more about what to expect, understanding a bit more about what's realistic, and having some familiarity with the systems approach to managing a healthcare organization. Furthermore, we need more "emotional intelligence" training in medical schools. We need to be better prepared to work with other human beings, individually and in groups, people with different life experiences and viewpoints. And we need more healthcare professionals, specifically diverse healthcare professionals. We need a better pipeline of talent in order to meet the needs of our communities. I could go on!

Have a Life Plan

I think there are a lot of people in healthcare—physicians, specifically—who start with life plans that began in their teens. To go to medical school, you really do have to plan ahead. (Not everybody, of course. Some people have had other interesting careers before going to medical school.) And I think it's particularly important for women to have a life plan, to help us figure out how to get through our training and still have the family planning options we may want to have some day. All that said, life is bound to throw us curves and our careers rarely turn out as expected. And that is okay. My journey led me here. What I am doing now in practice and in leadership feels challenging, albeit on some days too challenging, and it is mostly meaningful, which keeps me upright. In this moment I continue to learn and to strive to contribute toward a better way for everyone in healthcare. I hope that is enough, because it is all I've got.

Being Part of a Team

54. Justine M., BSN, Retired Hospital Nurse Manager

Justine M., BSN, looked back on her 45-year career in nursing just before retiring in 2019. A self-described "jack of all trades," she worked in intensive care settings with newborns, children, and adults before taking on the administrative role of nurse manager in 2005. As nurse manager, Justine co-managed the float pool and managed staffing, scheduling, budgeting, and the myriad details needed to ensure adequate daily resources for nurses and patients. Dedicated to her work and committed to her colleagues and her staff, my college roommate and friend of 49 years explained that her love of teamwork, and particularly her valued relationship with her boss, enhanced her joy in work and kept her going even during the most trying times.

I went into healthcare because I wanted to help people. My mother was a nurse. I was the oldest of ten children and I was used to helping with them. People are in need. Doctors are important but they're not there all the time. They come, they go.

I came here in the late 1970s as the assistant nurse manager in the NICU, after having worked for four years in the NICU of another hospital in this city, and for nine months in a cancer research hospital. I worked in the NICU here for two and a half years, then moved to the adult cardiac care unit (CCU). I'd really wanted to work in critical care. What drew me to critical care was the acuity of patients' conditions, the ability to make a difference, and the opportunity to collaborate with multiple team members.

In the '70s and early '80s, working in critical care was exciting no matter where you worked. It was very different from being on a med-surg floor, which never appealed to me at all. When I transferred to the CCU it was brand new. They had just renovated it, it had 12 beds, it was state-of-the-art. It was an exciting place to work. And, of course, adult patients could talk to me, whereas babies weren't able to say a word. A fair number of patients were at the end of their lives instead of at the beginning, but many did really well.

Then in the late 1990s a position opened up in the NICU for a nurse manager, so I left the CCU after two years and went back there. I still had hands-on responsibility for patient care then, although the role of nurse managers has changed substantially over the years and nurse managers are not typically involved in patient care today.

Moving into Administration

I worked in clinical care for 30 years before moving into administration in 2005. I work with unit directors and assistant directors. I work with teams of nurse managers, including the mother-baby team, the emergency team, the psychiatric team, the medical-surgical team, and the critical care team. I also work individually with nurse managers on all the units because I have to make sure we have the appropriate resources to take care of patients in each bed. I work with my boss, the director of operations and finance, to put together budgets; monitor budgets; hold people accountable for budgets; and determine whether they can explain variances, because they may not be appropriately budgeted for their average daily census. In the critical care unit, for example, sometimes the census may be four, sometimes it may be eleven on a twelve-bed unit. I work with everyone to be sure they have enough of the resources they need.

When I started as nurse manager, I spent a lot of time developing schedules, balancing schedules, and trying to keep everybody happy with the schedules. You can't make most of the people happy even some of the time! I tried to put together schedules that accommodated nurses' weekend patterns, their vacations, and their requests ("I don't like to work three days in a row" or "I'd rather do this than do that"). When I started doing this, many nurses were working 11½ hour shifts. Then the organization bought an application that could help to create schedules—but first, in order to make the application work, someone would have to enter the kind of detailed information I was used to entering on my own schedules. They asked for volunteers to create the schedules and I raised my hand.

Since I'd already created my own schedules taking into account nurses' weekend patterns, vacations, and requests, and because I wanted to prove to myself that this application worked, I put all that information into the application and clicked "create." And in less than a minute it created a schedule that was so much like my own I thought, *this is a good thing.* I'd spend hours juggling things and this was amazing. I became one of the people who trained the trainers in how to use the computer and this application.

But people are creatures of habit and change is hard, so most people weren't using it. Total waste of a lot of money. The director of nursing said, "No, this won't do. We need a champion (called a 'liaison' in those days), somebody who actually knows the application, who believes in it, and who's going to bring people into the fold." That was me. This put me in a different role in the hospital. I was no longer delivering bedside care.

My title was systems coordinator, and it took a lot of work to bring people on board. Many were my contemporaries but a lot of them were older than I was. Many people would say, "I can do this with paper and a pencil…" I'd say, "Sure you can. But you can just put all the requests in, push 'create,' and have a schedule. You can tweak it, but you don't have to spend all that time and energy doing it." People slowly came around to using it; slowly technology was working its way in. It was an interesting and a bit of a challenging time. Some people never really got on board, but many of those people were at the end of their careers.

I have no work–life balance. I work five days a week, sometimes six, at least ten hours a day, sometimes twelve. I work to ensure that nurses have what they need. I deal with budgets, and then there are contractual issues. There are reports to run for finance. We need to justify why we need to bring in agencies, for example. I can't just go to the CEO of the hospital and say, "I need ten traveling nurses to come in from an agency" that we have to pay top dollar for. People are leaving the profession for all sorts of reasons. But being at the bedside is *hard work* and patients are way sicker than they were when I got out of school.

On Joy in Work

Working with team members to achieve a common goal, working in teams to improve the way we deliver care, brings me joy. That was true at the hospital where I started as a NICU nurse. As a new graduate, starting in a new place, and seeing the impact I had—absolutely, my years there were very rewarding. I had good mentors there. It was a good environment: the orientation was structured, we had didactic time, we had clinical time, we had preceptors. I felt joy when I came here to work as assistant nurse manager in the NICU because I was working with others to change the culture and improve care for high-risk newborns.

Going into administration was exciting because I was helping to change practice. Years ago, nurse managers' responsibility for managing those who reported to them was minimal. Nurse managers evaluated staff and did the scheduling, but they also helped take care of patients on the floor. Times changed, demands changed, and nurses needed to spend more time managing their budgets and the like. Now, nurse managers are managers of what amount to little organizations on their own units. They have to collaborate with the teams they have. If they're in a teaching facility, they have to participate in rounds, educate staff, be responsible for consistent messaging, attend staff meetings, justify what they spend and how they spend it every two weeks, and more. They have dashboards and patient satisfaction scores to be concerned with. Patients determine their scores and that's what drives reimbursement. This doesn't affect my joy in work because, thank God, I'm not managing a unit.

My bosses and my peers appreciate what I do. My boss, who's head of operations, has a lot of respect for me. She believes in teaching people. We go to a monitor meeting every two weeks to go over the financials. Every unit. In the big room. Some people are good at managing their budgets and some aren't. For those who aren't, she'll make it a teaching moment and ask, "Okay, what stands out on this monitor?" She works to educate people so they have the knowledge to do their jobs well. She started as a nurse. She learned all this the same way I did, on her own. Her heart and soul are in it and she is trying to do the right thing. She tries to push people in that direction.

It's more important to me to have a boss I respect and who respects me than to have a good relationship with the chief nursing officer—because while I work with the chief nursing officer and will do whatever I can for her, I don't work with her every day. I work with my boss every day, all the time. We'll bounce things off one another and we have an understanding that we can tell each other anything. It's good to have that kind of relationship with somebody.

My staff are wonderful to me. They know me so well that for Christmas they went out and got a basket. And in that basket, they put Chardonnay, butter, bread, cheese, chocolate Twizzlers, and a bag of Smarties. All things I like. They went around and bought all that stuff. And they bought a gift card. That just showed how well they know me, and it felt great to know they went out of their way to do that for me. These relationships are so important. That's joy, right there.

Enhancing Employees' Joy

My staff know what I expect of them in terms of their job responsibilities. At a minimum, they know I expect them to come to work on time, do their jobs well, be professional, and listen to people. Most of them are very good at what they do. We all have days when we're not at the top of our game. But everyone knows they can come and talk to me. They know my expectations, and they also know I work just as hard as they do. I am fair. I ask people, "What do you think? How can we do this better?" I work collaboratively with them to fix a problem. My boss does that with me.

The organization does this, too. Members of senior leadership, the leadership of a unit, and staff round once a month and leaders ask, "How are we doing? What are your issues? What are your heartburn issues? What are the problems? How do you think we can fix them?" They're trying to listen to people to make their jobs easier and to make their experiences easier.

We have "town hall" meetings four or five times a year. The senior leadership of the organization for all shifts attend, and staff can come and tell them where we are and what are we doing. Then they open the floor to questions and concerns. The people who speak are heard. This organization's culture is positive and supportive.

On Money and Joy

For me, there isn't a relationship between money and joy. Obviously, salary is important because, besides the need to pay our bills, people associate money with respect. Money has never been a big issue for me. I do my job because I do my job. Do I feel I should be appropriately compensated? Absolutely. But is that what drives me? No. There were periods of time when the hospital didn't have the money for many raises. Some people left, and that was fine, but I had been here for a long time and I wasn't in it for the money.

What Diminishes Joy

I've always tried to make sure that everything gets done, gets done right, and is rectified quickly if it isn't. What aggravates the life out of me are things like class action lawsuits that are filed because things that didn't need to happen, did happen when oversights weren't acted on in a timely way. These things are absolutely beyond my control. I'll watch something happen, I'll warn against it, and I know it's going to implode. When it does, why is anybody surprised?

The CEO might be terrific and hold town hall meetings and do other things that enhance my joy in work, but those lower in the hierarchy do things that make it hard to do my job day to day. And there's nothing I can do about it. It's a fact of life, as in any job. And some things, like mismanagement of resources, just go against my grain.

Advice

My advice to my bosses and colleagues is, be clear with your messages about whatever your goals are, whatever your expectations are. People shouldn't need a secret decoder ring or a translator to figure out what you're really trying to say. People are unclear when they're not necessarily willing to lay all their cards out on the table. And there may be times when senior leadership can't lay all their cards out on the table. But be clear about your expectations and be clear about the message itself, because we need to take the message back to the people who work with us and for us. If the message isn't clear, then how can we present it?

Be respectful of one another. Everyone has their differences, none of us is perfect. People have different strengths. Work with people. Be flexible and adaptable. Listen.

When the CEO and other higher-ups don't go above the first floor because they're afraid they'll have a nosebleed in the elevator, they're not engaged with anybody. The staff need to know you care about them, even if you only round a couple of times a year. That's important to staff on the front line because they need to know that the people on the first floor, who are making decisions, really know what the front-line staff are doing.

Listen to what people say. One of the goals in this organization is to help people develop trust so they can say what they think without repercussions. We need to feel that people above us are going to listen to and value our opinions and if they can do something to change practice or provide us with resources, they're going to do it.

Managers need to collaborate with their teams. That's what the whole idea of a team is about. If you don't ask people what they think, or if they're afraid to tell you what they think, things are never going to get better. People need to feel heard—and when they offer an opinion, they need to believe that somebody's listening and that valid concerns will be taken to heart and acted on.

There's a positive association between employee engagement, employee satisfaction, and patient satisfaction. Happy staff, happy patients. Happy patients, better scores. What makes happy staff? That's the million-dollar question.

55. *Gail M., BSN, BS, Hospital Labor and Delivery Nurse*

> Gail M. has been a registered and certified nurse in labor and delivery in a community-based, not-for-profit hospital for the last 13 years. She started out wanting to be a doctor. Then with her marriage, wanting to support her husband through law school, and having children she decided that nursing would be a better fit. Gail has the calm demeanor of a woman who knows in her bones that she made the right choice.

I was 39 when I graduated from nursing school. I've been a nurse for 15 years and an obstetrics nurse for 13. I did my senior practicum in labor and delivery and was very lucky that the hospital hired me to go into obstetrics. I worked the night shift and got a little burned out because my kids—who were in elementary school, middle school, and high school at the time—had so many activities it was getting a little crazy. I really needed to be on their schedule for a while, so I took two years off and worked as a school nurse. It was great for my kids but I was so bored. As a school nurse my role was really that of a case manager. I couldn't wait to go back to obstetrics. I went back to the hospital where I started and have been there ever since.

I love working three days a week but sometimes the shifts are long—12–13 hours a day. But that's the tradeoff. We get there around 6:30 in the morning because we have to be changed and clocked in by 6:45 p.m. We usually don't get off the unit until close to 7:30 in the evening, so it's about 13 hours. But you get used to the fact that you work those long hours. I see the reasoning behind it—it's about continuity of care. We can literally see a person from start to finish. We can get an induction in the morning and take her to mother-baby in the evening. That's kind of nice because we've seen the whole story.

On Joy in Work

I find joy in my work every day. I really do. I can have some very frustrating patients, I can have some bad outcomes, but there's always, always some bit of joy somewhere in my day. Watching the birth of a baby is still, to me, an incredible thing. Every time. I'm so up close and personal to it and I get to do it every day that I'm at work. Seeing the looks on these families' faces and the tears and getting to be a part of that—most of the time it's such a joyous thing. Every day at work I always see something good. I just do. It's really just an amazing job to have.

My co-workers and I are a team. It's total team nursing. It has to be. That's the only way it works. And we're very much a team with our physicians, too. Some physicians, of course, not so much but most of the physicians very much rely on us. They respect us and we work as a team. They all cannot be there 24/7 so we're their eyes and ears. That's why when nurses come from other units to work on our unit they say, "This is like no place I've ever worked." I train new nurses. Younger nurses need to learn how to become team players. I try to gently guide nurses in the right direction. It's a group effort, it's not just me.

Every day is different. No two days are the same. Every day has a different feel because I'm working with different people. I like going to work never knowing what that day is going to bring: what I'll be doing that day, what my assignment will be, who I'll meet—I get to meet new people every day and I love that.

What Diminishes Joy

What diminishes joy in work are the very sad situations we have to deal with. That's the hardest part of the job. Seeing moms come in with babies who die after birth. Moms who have been going through in vitro fertilization over and over again and who just cannot sustain a pregnancy. To see that and to see their grief—that's the *very* hard part of our job.

To know just how to deal with it is very difficult. We have bereavement seminars. We have a loss committee and a nurse who's our birth advisor and is also a hospice nurse. She's very good at both. She's a very good resource, especially when we have a very bad outcome. We'll sit with her and have a little debrief. Or we just all sit and talk about it together. We seem to have more high-risk situations now than ever before. Women are waiting until they're older to get pregnant. And because they're waiting until they're older they have to use a lot of fertility treatments. And some fertility treatments come with risks.

Talking with co-workers is what really gets us all through. We have an employee assistance program, too, so if we need help that is available to us. Our nurse manager and charge nurse are also very supportive.

Probably what has the greatest effect on my work and everybody else's work is when we're so busy and so stretched so incredibly thin. We try really hard not to let the patients see that that's happening, that we're so busy—we're supposed to be very good about hiding that—but sometimes we can't hide it. They see us running all over the place. We're getting called from room to room to room, so they know it's busy. I always say, "Yes, we're very busy but we're not forgetting about you. If you call us, we will come, or some-body will come." I'm always trying to reassure them. But there are days when I leave and think, *did I give my very best care today?* Probably not, just because I was spread so thin. But I always try.

As far as pay goes, the hospital is notorious for not keeping up with the pay scale. Nurses sometimes quit their jobs after training so they can be hired somewhere else for higher pay.

Staff-Leadership Disconnection

There is a disconnection between what the administration says is happening and what's really happening on the units. The administration is out of touch with what's happening. The CEO holds periodic "town hall" meetings that focus on the goals for the hospital. But they're more "dog and pony" shows than attempts to find out what isn't working well and what administration can do to fix problems. At these meetings the CEO shows lots of graphs. Staff members are afraid to be honest about the problems for fear of reprisal. I fill out employee engagement surveys but never hear back about how the problems I wrote about have been addressed.

For example, medications aren't kept in the same places on each unit, so I just have to know where everything is. We've had to search for baby blankets and supplies that aren't always there. People ask us why we're wrapping a newborn baby in an adult blanket. Nurses don't always have enough scrubs. I've had to wear the wrong size scrubs because there isn't always a supply of scrubs in my size. Wearing extra-large scrubs doesn't work for me and looks ridiculous.

Advice

The president of the hospital should go to each unit to see what's going on and what the staff needs. They need to take seriously what's broken and fix these problems. When the hospital president did come to our unit, she didn't take any notes. She said the things we pointed out would be fixed but they never were.

My advice to bosses is to be fair. Don't play favorites. This can spill over into how assignments and schedules are made on a daily basis.

One of the biggest lessons I've learned is never judge a book by its cover. Never. You could have your very best day with a patient you thought was going to be difficult. You don't have to speak the same language. You can say so much with a look, a touch. It's important to give them a calm, positive feeling. We get to hear back sometimes what patients say about us because we have nurses who make follow-up phone calls and ask a series of questions about what they liked and didn't like. It's so nice to hear somebody say, "Gail was very calming and helped me get through it," because that's my goal. That gives me joy.

56.   Eric Cannon, PharmD, FAMCPP, Assistant Vice President of Pharmacy Benefits for an Integrated Health System

> Eric Cannon, Pharm D, FAMCPP, is Assistant Vice President of Pharmacy Benefits for the insurance arm of an integrated health system. A hard-working, small-town family man, Eric is guided in his work by certain core values and principles: love of helping others; readiness to seize opportunities for growth; building trust in relationships; and helping others to succeed.

When I was in high school, I had a neighbor who was a pharmacist and owned a pharmacy. I started working in his pharmacy as a delivery boy. When I finished college in 1987 and was trying to figure out what I wanted to do, I was feeling kind of lost. My mother wanted me to go to dental school; I didn't want to. Then the neighbor who owned the pharmacy said, "Why don't you go to pharmacy school and come to work for me?" So that is what I did. Still, on the long drive moving back to my hometown after graduation, I remember thinking, *I don't know if I want to do this.* But I reasoned that I'd always enjoyed interacting with people and this job would give me a chance to continue to do that. Besides, I had agreed to work there when I started pharmacy school. As simple as my responsibilities were as a delivery boy, I felt I'd helped people. I often found myself sitting in an assisted living facility just talking to them.

So, I started working at the pharmacy and for a while I really enjoyed working in the same place I had worked in high school. It was the neighborhood where I grew up so I knew everybody. I truly enjoyed interacting with people I had known my whole life and being able to help them with both simple and complex medication issues. I felt the same reward regardless of how simple or difficult the issue was.

When I started my new job, I was excited to go to work. I worked there for five years but after about three and a half or four years I found myself thinking, *I hate this.* As much as I enjoyed interacting with people, the things I liked doing as a pharmacist I wasn't getting a chance to do. I felt like just another cog in the wheel, I guess. There were only two of us running the pharmacy and as time went on, working 60 hours a week and not spending enough time with my family, the job really started to wear on me. I had three sons and worked until 9:00 at night. I'd get home and they'd be in bed. Some of the interaction I wanted to have as a father I was missing out on.

In July 1997 one of my dad's best friends from college came into the pharmacy. He lived a block or two away from us when I was growing up. He was a senior vice president for an integrated health system at the time. He came in at about 8:30 p.m., I filled his prescription and talked to him for a minute, and he started walking out. I followed him out to the parking lot because I didn't want to have this conversation in the pharmacy. I told him, "I don't like coming to work anymore." And what he said kind of surprised me: "You should love going to work. And if you don't, then you need to explore options." He was really gracious and said, "Let me make some phone calls in the morning." He called me the next morning and gave me the names of two or three people. I spent the next three months trying to find the job that was going to make me happy. Then I got really lucky.

I started working in utilization management as part of a health plan with patients and physicians. That was 22 years ago. When I started here, I would spend my day talking with patients and doctors, mainly on the phone, but every time I talked to somebody, we were talking about things that would improve a patient's outcome. Today, even though it doesn't happen as frequently, anytime I can communicate information or make a suggestion or recommendation or improve something for somebody, I am reminded that's the reason I went to pharmacy school.

Over time, as the health plan has grown and developed, my role has changed: I went from doing utilization management to being the director of pharmacy. When I became director of pharmacy, I had seven or eight employees in my department; now, there are 130. So, while I've been essentially in the same *type* of role, the scope and the challenges have changed and continue to change. What I do today is very different from what I did five years ago. This is what keeps it fresh and interesting.

I look at where I was 22 years ago—when I had one-on-one patient interaction to now, when I'm interacting with decision-makers rather than patients—I realize that what made me happy then is what makes me happy now: seeing a positive outcome as a result of either the work I do or the work my team does for a group of people.

Today in my role as a pharmacist I may not interact directly with patients, but I get that same sense of accomplishment when I sit down with clients and show them how to provide adequate coverage for their employees at an affordable price. Or show them how we've improved the outcomes for their employees.

On Joy in Work

Opportunities to Grow

I feel I'm most rewarded at work as I learn and grow and develop. I think providing opportunities for development is critical. By this I mean opportunities to do new things, opportunities to learn how to do things better. That involves training, creating new positions, and even within existing positions, having someone push me out of my comfort zone so I develop a new skill or become better at what I do. My current boss is doing a good job of this for me, providing additional opportunities and maybe some opportunities in areas where I wouldn't necessarily have said, "Oh, that's something I want to do."

Today I feel just as rewarded when my employees are successful and achieve their goals as when I achieve my own goals. This has been true especially over the last two to three years. Sometimes we are so busy—entrenched in our thinking, focused on our individual goals, or preoccupied with our performance—that we don't take the time to ask whether the people working for us are able to succeed: Have we created the right situation or the right environment for them to succeed? Ultimately, if I'm going to succeed then they need to succeed.

Communication, Partnership, and Trust

I try to ask my employees once a month when we meet, "Are you happy?" And they do say no to me. I have one employee who oversees all of our Medicare products in pharmacy. A problem arose and he'd made a mistake that affected the way we were displayed on the CMS Plan Finder. I walked down to his office to ask what happened and I could tell immediately, by looking at his face, that he wasn't happy. We talked about what was going on, how he was feeling, and what we needed to do. It was a situation where everybody, me included, was so busy we failed to see we were placing this huge burden on him—giving him additional work and additional responsibilities with no additional help. I think it's a credit to our organization's leadership that I was able to leave this person's office, walk upstairs, and tell the CEO, "I've got to get this guy some help." Her response was, "I trust you, that's great, go ahead and hire." And that young man could see the light at the end of the tunnel when he knew that help was coming.

On the other hand, if I were always in the CEO's office saying, "I need more help, I need more people," her reaction would have been different. Yes, I've got a really kind and empathetic and trusting boss, but at the same time I play a part in establishing that relationship so that when I *do* need something that trust is there. I think people forget trust requires a partnership. It's a two-way relationship.

On Money and Joy

People who are happiest taking care of patients are the ones who have been able to get beyond their personal agendas, the personal incentives. If your focus is continually on how you can make more money, you don't spend your time focused on the things that made you want to go into medicine in the first place. As much as I enjoyed the money I made while I was working in retail pharmacy, for instance, I didn't go to school solely because of the money. I went to school because I wanted to be able to help people. In today's world that may be an antiquated thought.

Other career opportunities have come up for me. I've flown to another part of the country to interview for a job where the culture is palpably and vastly different. What I've found to be rewarding and comfortable here makes me say no to other opportunities. There are certain environments where I don't want to work.

What Diminishes Joy

If there is anything that detracts from my joy in work, it's the hours and the struggle to find work–life balance. I'm supposed to work fixed hours. But in my role now, as much as I want to work fixed hours, I don't know whether that's realistic. I'll typically get up really early and go to work early, or maybe do a little bit of work from my desk at home and then drive to the office. Then I come home and have dinner with my wife and children. Sometimes, depending on the pressures of work that day, I'll wander off and do some more work.

I have a leadership coach and he and I were talking about how to balance work and family life. He asked how my working after dinner makes my wife feel. I said, "Well, she's got plenty of stuff to do, that's no problem." But of course, I'd never asked *her*. My assignment for that day was to go home and ask my wife. She was very open and direct with me. She said, "Sometimes it makes me feel bad or unappreciated."

I think having those kinds of conversations now does help me find my balance, I guess. I understand I'll probably never get caught up, but that doesn't mean you work until there's nothing left but work. Part of my finding joy in work is that I'm figuring out how to balance work, family and play.

Bureaucracy

If joy in work means helping people—whether patients, employer groups, benefits directors, or others—the opposite is the inability to help someone because of infrastructure barriers. For example, with Medicare or Medicaid products, regardless of how hard I try, there are some things I can't help people with because I have to comply with and follow a particular set of rules. Or, as much as I want to streamline something and make it better for a patient, I find myself caught in the bureaucracy of the organization.

Organizational Culture

One of the things you run into, especially in big companies, is this: as much as you want to believe everybody's working together, there are situations where everybody is literally working against each other. What you see quite frequently is someone who does a really good job managing up—their whole goal is to climb the career ladder. But in the process of doing that they don't mind working against, to some degree, the people below them because their primary focus is, *how do I make myself look better?*

For a time, our organization was divided into regions. Each of those regions was given goals and incentives to generate revenue. To generate more revenue, regions did things like put in more services. But instead of adding more services, patients might have been better served if we'd sent them 10–15 miles down the road to another facility that was better suited to their needs. The way the goals and incentives were structured, you kept them in your facility, you kept them in your region, because you were measured according to the revenue you generated.

Fear of Speaking Up

I have a different boss now from the one I had for years. My new boss trusts me and gives me room to work and make decisions. My previous boss, who is now in a different position within the organization, is someone I still work with. We talk through issues and he's a sounding board. It's nice to bounce what I'm feeling off of someone. We ask each other, "Well, should we say something, or do we just let it go?" And more often than not, we let it go because sometimes, when we really think things through, we find the issues are not as big as we'd originally thought.

In the past, I think people wanted to hear the truth. Our new leadership is great, they want to hear the good and the bad. We are expected to speak up but speaking up means I need to manage my fears. Since I don't know what their reaction will be, my mind immediately goes to the worst place. You know, *if I really tell them what I think I'll have to put my stuff in a box and security is going to walk me out.* Not that I have any reason to think that would actually happen, but it still crosses my mind from time to time.

The gentleman who was our CEO until 2009 lived near me and we were good friends. We had a relationship in which I could have told him anything, at least in a respectful way. He may not always have agreed with me, and he may have wanted to argue, but I always felt safe in that communication. When I look at the communication with the current CEO objectively, I think the same is true. I can't think of anything I couldn't tell her, as long as it was done in a respectful way, that would have any negative consequences. But within our organization, which has changed significantly in the past few years in terms of leadership and structure, some of those things are unknowns. Part of the uncertainty, I guess, is having new people and new roles. I don't have the same level of comfort I had at one point in time. So, I find myself re-establishing relationships, re-establishing levels of trust that I hope will provide the degree of comfort I'm looking for.

What I Have Learned

Finding joy is dependent on me. It requires me to be open and honest with myself and to be willing to prioritize what is most important to me. I have learned to control the things I can and not let my happiness be dictated by the things I can't control. For example, in my first job as a pharmacist I couldn't control the environment, but I could control whether I stayed or left. I mentioned early in this discussion taking three months to find the right job—that was stressful in that we had no money coming in, but it also allowed me to see what I was missing with my family. When I reflect on that time I don't think of the stress, I think of three months in the fall of 1997 spent with my wife and three young boys.

Fear is healthy in that it provides an opportunity to evaluate risk, but fear must be managed. As I have grown older, I have learned not to fear failure. Failures will happen but they should not stop you from trying something new.

57. *Jennifer F., MSN, Nurse Practitioner for an Integrated Health System*

Jennifer F., MSN, is a nurse practitioner for an integrated health system who is deeply committed to social justice. First as a teacher and then as an advanced practice provider working with the poorest and most underserved children in her state, she delivered care in public schools until the health maintenance organization (HMO) where she worked shut down the program for being unprofitable. Vowing never again to work for an organization that puts profits before people, she has, for the last six years, worked for an organization whose values and actions closely align with her own. After having experienced the polar opposite, Jennifer explains how enlightened leadership, along with supportive teamwork, sustains her joy in practice.

My undergraduate degree is in biology. I'm from a very left-leaning town, also a very white town. My parents were both professors and I grew up white, upper middle class. I was planning to get my master's in higher education. About two weeks before I was due to start there, I got a letter from that graduate school saying I had no student aid. It's embarrassing, but I literally did not read the fine print. I realized, *it's $12,000 a semester, not $12,000 a year—I can't do that!*

My Professional Journey

I started looking into the public-school system in my city, which served about 90,000 children at that time. About 80% of them received free or reduced lunch. It is one of the most racially segregated cities in the entire United States. At the time it had the highest rate of sexually transmitted diseases and teen pregnancy in the nation. I wasn't certified to teach in that school system, but I was able to get a job teaching in a parochial school system within the city. I taught third graders. It was trial by fire. I knew nothing. It was a fourth- to eighth-grade parochial school with 90% African American students. In the first week there was a drive-by shooting in front of the school. In the first two weeks I lost 15 pounds and my hair fell out in chunks. I've never been in the service, but it was the closest I think I'll ever come to boot camp.

Lightning Strikes

One day, one of my third-grade students pointed to his mouth and said, "Miss, this hurts." When he opened his mouth, I saw he had no teeth in the back of his mouth. It was this gaping, open wound. It was as if the floor dropped out from under me. I'd been suffering with these kids every day, it was total chaos in the classroom, I was shaking in my boots coming home every night. The Iraq war had just started, and it was a crazy time in our country. I thought, *I'm up here trying to teach seven times five, and of course they don't care. They don't have teeth in the back of their mouth.* That was my "aha" moment, the moment when lightning struck. It was Maslow's hierarchy of needs. These kids don't feel safe and secure. Their basic needs aren't being met, and I thought, *we've got to get down to business here.*

I made it through the year. In the beginning I thought, *I'm not going to let these children get me*, and by the end of the year it was hard to leave them. I loved them. I was totally on track by April. I stayed for only one year, then took a job developing a community outreach education program for the local zoo. I was there for eight years.

When I was teaching, I saw that my kids all got the same question wrong on a standardized test, part of the No Child Left Behind initiative. This was a great equity learning moment. It was a picture of a horse and the test asked, "Where does this animal live?" the options—A,B,C, and D—were "in a school;" "in a stable;" "at the zoo;" or "at the bank." What do you think all of my kids circled? "At the zoo." What the hell is a stable? Do you think these kids have any idea what a stable is? The only place they've ever seen an animal like a horse is at a zoo. They're not going to farms. They're not rural, they're urban kids. They certainly have never had riding lessons or privileges like that. They all got it wrong. I was so pissed off. Even well before I ever heard the word "equity," I knew inherently what it meant. I'd never been faced with this.

Years later, always in the back of my mind were my third-grader's teeth. I still wanted to serve those kids, I never forgot about them. So, I applied to a direct-entry masters program in my city, which would give me an RN and a master's in nursing and put me on an advanced practice track for a community health nursing program. I wanted to work in community health nursing because in impoverished communities people look to the schools for everything, so it just made sense. When I was placed in the school-based health division of a huge HMO, I thought, *this is the greatest thing in the world. This is my dream come true.* I was getting to do exactly what I was trained for. It was really exciting.

Reality Bites

I worked in that small school-based community health program, which was run entirely by a small group of nine women, all nurse practitioners, who were very close-knit and very functional. We treated sexually transmitted diseases in high schools and provided immunizations, physicals, and wrote prescriptions for a population in which 95% of the children and their families received Medicaid. All this predated any EMR, which sounds quaint to me now. We did a lot with a little. Our "clinic" was in the school basement and was like the inside of a janitor's closet, but we did a lot for those kids. We were not school system employees even though we practiced in the schools. We acted as satellite clinics. We had excellent outcomes.

Then new management came in and saw we were not a profitable segment of the organization and closely monitored costs. Conditions had been spartan before but now, we had to use only one glove to give a vaccine, not two. They nickeled and dimed everything. Our manager resigned and then the HMO shuttered the beautiful, robust, 12-year-old program that provided care for 27,000 children in one of the most impoverished areas in the state.

We billed the state Medicaid for all our services, but for whatever reason they decided to shutter the program. This had been a partnership between the HMO and the public schools. We had no say in this decision. They abruptly closed the program and their communication to the schools was minimal. I'm haunted by that experience. I remember someone knocking on the door for his HIV injection, and the door was locked. They brought in dumpsters and pitched medical waste.

I vowed I would never again work for an organization that leaves patients out in the cold. I so believed in that program, heart and soul, that I would still be there in the basement of that school treating those kids. It was my placement when I was in nurse practitioner graduate school. I was placed there for a full years' preceptorship, which I loved so much that I wrangled my way into a permanent position as an RN and then as a nurse practitioner. I did that for a year until they closed the program.

Onward and Upward

I now work as a pediatric primary care provider in an integrated health system where I've been a patient since childhood. It was my dream to work here. This unusual organization has been around for more than 40 years. There are many, many people who have been there 25 years or more. I am one of four members of the primary care pediatrics team. I have my own panel of about 820 patients—I am not a "physician extender"—which contributes greatly to my joy in practice. In my opinion, this is the best way for nurse practitioners to be used in primary care. I work four days a week. My three partners, who are all physicians and women, work 50% clinical time. I see patients until they're about age 23.

One thing I think is very ethical about this integrated health system is that we're not paid on productivity. That is very intentional. You could see three patients in a day or 30 and that does not change your salary. I have a full schedule. In pediatrics we do a lot more physicals than they do in adult medicine. That's the nature of children—there are seven well visits in the first year of life. We have a 15- and 30-minute model. We have 15-minute visits for sick visits and 30 minutes for physicals. If we were wide open, we could potentially see four patients in an hour.

I see the CEO at all-staff meetings once a month. He is our lighthouse. He is the center and compass and soul of our organization. He is known to me and I am known to him. I'll never forget, when I came in for my interview, I was super-nervous because I really wanted this job. As I said, it was my dream to work here. I was wearing a suit, and he said "Hello" and handed me a bottle of water. He shook my hand and asked, "Can I get you anything?" My heart just melted because I was coming from a completely different type of organization—one that was corporate, large, with tens of thousands of employees who were nameless and faceless to the CEO. That organization's ethics went against my own in terms of how people should be taken care of. To go from that to having the CEO shake my hand was wonderful. He is a really kind person and a very busy gentleman, but if I have a question or concern, I wouldn't think twice about picking up the phone. I could shoot him an email if I wanted to know what he thinks about something—I could even send him a Facebook message if I wanted to. I don't do that most of the time, but I know I could.

I have a full and busy practice so on any given day, looking five days ahead, I'm 80% full most days when I come to work. If kids get sick, if I need to do an ear check, or if a newborn is discharged from the hospital and my schedule is full, I double-book them. That's how I get by. If patients are late, I still see them, even if it's for an abbreviated physical, because these are children. They still need their shots; they need to be seen.

I pressure myself to see more patients, but I don't get pressured by the organization. I work hard on an extremely highly functioning team. We have very high expectations of ourselves and we pride ourselves on setting the standards for pediatrics within this organization.

On Joy in Work

I love primary care because of the ongoing, continuous, and evolving relationships I have with families. We develop intense relationships. What is more intense than guiding people through the experience of becoming parents, watching them grow and add to their families, and grow in their confidence? It's wonderful. So, the continuity piece is key for me. I work hard to have a connection with my patients even if they're coming to me for the first time. Yesterday three people came to me for the first time. I have the confidence to make that connection: "What were you for Halloween?" or "I like your shoes!"

I'm a bit fanatical about patient experience. Someone can have the greatest medical care in the world, but if they're not treated kindly, or if they're disrespected, they may never come back. They will remember what that felt like. I do a lot of pelvic exams for young women. If I mess that up for someone, they might not do it again for ten years. They might literally die if they didn't feel respected, if I didn't make them feel seen. I'm sure there are more brilliant clinicians, people who got better grades than me, but my job is not done, I did not do my job well, if patients are not just satisfied—I want them to be *delighted* when they walk out.

I truly feel that healthcare is such a privilege. I feel so lucky to see my patients every day. People are so vulnerable. It's an honor that in this job, which I get paid to do, I get to be a human interacting with other humans. We have opportunities to really see each other, face to face.

I have the luxury of working on a highly functional, very happy team. We have parties together. After my family, the physicians I work with occupy the most space in my mind, and certainly my work does. We spend an enormous part of our lives at work and are really invested. I feel incredibly satisfied, and this has to do with my team. Everyone I know says they value and appreciate me. I feel that on many levels. I feel respected. Nobody makes me feel like a second-class citizen even though I'm the only non-physician on my team. My patients don't make me feel that way, my colleagues don't make me feel that way. They treat me as an equal member of the team and that makes all the difference. There is no drama or backbiting on our team, which is rare in healthcare. I cannot imagine doing this job—this job is hard enough—if I didn't feel supported, if I felt I was walking on eggshells with my colleagues, if they didn't recognize my efforts and hard work, and if they didn't appreciate me or communicate with me. I would never have lasted.

Sometimes I ask myself, *what keeps me here? What keeps me coming back every day when it's really kind of crazy?* It's the love and respect I have for the people I work with. And my love for my patients. I feel loved and respected reciprocally by both groups of people. I love my organization. I trust my leadership. I feel listened to.

Mitigating and Preventing Burnout Organization-Wide

I co-lead a provider engagement panel at this integrated health system. It was formed about four years ago to develop a provider compact, which is something that a lot of high-performing organizations have done. These guiding principles are our promises to one another, a set of values and expectations, on topics such as communication. These are set out in two columns: listed in one column is what our providers will do, and in the other is what our leaders will do.

This group of about 20 providers found we work well together, and we meet once a month. This group is intentionally multidisciplinary, multispecialty, and comprises staff from all our clinics. We get a sneak preview of initiatives on the horizon, like one that would enable patients to access their EMRs. There are many medical–legal issues attached to this, things that made providers very, very nervous. So, the group discusses issues like this and hashes them out to help influence decisions. This panel is not bottom-up. It's not us vs. them. Its purpose is to be a voice together.

About three years ago, three of our group's members went to a conference in which burnout was the topic. We decided to look at our own level of burnout and took a deep dive into it. We developed our own survey based on Maslach's work, used validated questions, and administered it to our providers. The information we got back was really interesting. We look at trends and try to learn from them. A huge amount of what we've done for the last three years on this panel has focused on burnout mitigation. Who are the most burned out people in our organization? Full-time physicians. We're below the national trend of 50% but we are higher than we want to be.

We've sent out this every year for three years now. Information gathered is information that needs to be acted on. We found that advanced practice providers—nurse practitioners and physician assistants—want equal pay for equal work. Unequal pay is a big dissatisfier. Advanced practice providers are primary care providers in this organization. We see more patients per day than most physicians. We have more clinical contact hours than physicians, we get less time for continuing medical education, we accrue benefits at a lower rate, and we get paid a lot less than physicians. On our surveys, these show up as trends. Leadership has responded by reducing the number of clinical contact hours for advanced practice providers by two hours each week. This will give me more time in my week and will make my life easier.

Leadership

People matter. Our CEO matters. This organization is the exact opposite of the huge HMO where I worked before. Here, leadership gives ample opportunities for people to speak up in a non-punitive way. Then there is this incredible boots-on-the ground, get-it-done person who leads my team. She does the work of keeping providers happy, saying, "You asked, I listened, let's get the data on this and let's make a meaningful change and follow through." Who could ask for anything more? We're small and nimble enough that if somebody has a good idea, we try to act on it. This organization is much more horizontal than hierarchical. What makes people stay? It's the values of the organization.

On Money and Joy

There are a lot easier ways to make money than working in healthcare or teaching. When I was a teacher, I made about $19,000 a year. I don't look at my paychecks now. I'm not sure exactly how much money I make, but I make enough. Money is not my motivation for doing this. For me, doing what I do is a privilege. I think money matters only if you feel underappreciated or devalued in some way.

What Diminishes Joy

What's a bad day? What takes away from joy? Bearing witness to suffering is very difficult and takes a toll. If I have the time in my day to be human and step outside the room for a moment when someone has just collapsed in sorrow, I can reset. I can keep going. It's taken me a long time, and I've had to do a lot of very direct work on this to not feel I was "failing" when I didn't instantly fix something for patients with a combination of complex health conditions, inequity, and financial strife. There are things we cannot write a prescription for. When the "system" conspires to make it hard to give our patients what they need when they clearly need it, when our hands are tied because of insurance constraints—especially for the least among us—that is crushing to me as a provider. I have to make decisions about how I'm going to treat someone, what I'm going to do, when their insurance doesn't cover that. These are the broader issues that really bother me and have nothing to do with where I work.

58. Angela R., Retired Medical Assistant/Office Manager

Angela R. is a retired medical assistant and office manager who worked in a family and urgent care setting, as well as in pediatric urgent care, over the course of her 39-year career. "I've never worked in a private practice. It was always an urgent care or a walk-in setting. It was organized chaos," she remembers fondly. Angela retired five years ago when her health declined and her joy in work diminished. She misses work every day.

I wanted to go into healthcare because it's a rewarding job. I wasn't looking for a pat on the back. I always had compassion for people and wanted to help them. My dad was a police officer, a detective all his life, and he served the community. But I didn't want to help that way. I wanted to help people by working in the health department since high school. I hated school. I'm not a book learner, I'm a hands-on person. Ninety percent of what people know is learned from experience, and I learned more from being supervised by physicians than I learned in school.

I raised two kids as a single parent, so getting my medical assistant degree about 40 years ago was everything for me. My formal training lasted for about a year. I studied phlebotomy and I earned certificates in drawing blood, in terminology, in vital signs, and in CPR. I learned a little bit about casting and orthopedic procedures. I did so much more at work than I was trained to do because the doctors trusted me and trained me. All three of the physician partners at the family and urgent care center where I worked were such good working doctors, supervisors, and teachers that I learned so much. I learned every day what I needed to do. I was with them for 17 years, working seven days a week.

Learning medicine hands-on was always very easy for me. I saw every person, every patient, as a learning opportunity. I would read patients' charts and then read about their conditions. I would follow-up on people because that's what I liked to do.

When I moved to another city to be close to my children and grandchildren, I commuted 85 miles each way for five years so I could stay at that family and urgent care office. Then I took a job as a supervisor and manager at a nearby pediatric urgent care practice and worked at both jobs until I couldn't do that anymore. Splitting my time had been difficult, but I was a single parent with two kids, and I had colleges to pay for.

What My Jobs Entailed

I was a working boss. I was never one to sit behind a desk and tell everybody what to do. When someone couldn't come in, I would take their place. I was always hands-on. At my last job I was a supervisor or manager so I did not work as staff, per se, but if someone called in sick and I couldn't get someone else to work, I'd work the shift myself. At my other jobs I was part of an active staff where I would work from 8:00 a.m. to 5:00 p.m. taking care of patients.

Medical assistants are doctors' partners. When patients were called back, we'd take vital signs, hear their chief complaint, double-check their medications, prepare the chart for the doctor, and place the chart on the exam room door so patients' names couldn't be seen. If the doctor needed anything while they examined patients, we'd assist with anything from gynecological procedures, like Pap smears, to physicals and EKGs. We also acted as phlebotomists.

If patients would come in for vitamin B12 injections or allergies, we'd test for allergies and do urinalyses. We gave immunizations and assisted with sigmoidoscopies and vasectomies. We did suture removal and wound care. We were allowed to do all that. Now, insurance companies want either a physician assistant or a doctor to do those things because of concerns about liability and malpractice.

I hired the staff and they stayed for a long time. They stayed because of the teamwork, my appreciation, and the fact that I was flexible with their schedules, which I prepared 30 days in advance. Staff always knew what they were doing. I didn't mind their taking a day off as long as they had their shifts covered. And, if not, they would talk to me. I took care of things: if they weren't happy with the way things were done or if they had concerns about one of the doctors they worked with, I was always open to talking. For example, doctors would be chronically late and that would put their patients behind. It's not a good thing to be behind the minute you walk into the office. I was able to sit down and talk to the doctors. I also was involved in hiring doctors.

I would hire staff who felt the same way about taking care of patients as I did. I wanted them to treat the patients, the doctors, and the staff the way we wanted to be treated ourselves. When I'd hire the receptionist for the front office, I'd say, "You are the first person anyone coming into this office sees. Patients are going to get a sense of this office by how you treated them when they first walked in. Of course, the doctor is important, but if you're going to be a poor receptionist and give people an attitude, that reflects badly on the whole office."

When I hired medical assistants, I'd hire people with more than five years' experience. They had to be knowledgeable about medication administration and phlebotomy; they had to be friendly, tactful, and understand HIPPA (the Health Insurance Portability and Accountability Act) and other rules and regulations; and when they escorted patients back to the doctor's office, they had to treat people the way they would wanted to be treated. I was very open with the doctors when I'd first meet them. I would tell them we were here to try to be a good team, that sort of thing. They were fine with it. Our practice had a good reputation, which was the most important thing.

Everyone loved coming to their jobs. At the family and urgent care center, we probably had 25–30 staff, plus the doctors. We had medical assistants and x-ray technicians so we could accommodate patients who had minor injuries. We had this size staff because we had to pull two shifts, we were open seven days a week, and we didn't pay overtime. I had a lot of fancy scheduling to do.

When I moved to pediatrics, I supervised the scheduling of more than 100 doctors for about ten years. If I thought they weren't taking enough time with a patient, or if I thought they were taking too much time—or if they were conducting a sports physical when they really should just be treating a cold—I would say something. They were receptive. Most of my doctors were just out of residency. I would collect charts at the end of the day and one of the partners who owned that business would review them. I had three clinics under my wing in different cities.

I triaged very heavily in my pediatric group using protocols of questions we needed to ask. After giving the parent advice about how often to take their child's temperature, any over-the-counter medication to give the child and at what dose, we'd note this in the patient's chart and put it on the doctor's desk. The doctors would double-check and sign off on that, or would tell us to call the mother back if he wanted the child to come in. We did that every hour on the hour. When working with adults, we did the exact same thing.

I used to take a lot of the phone calls and check with patients on the weekends to see how they were doing. And if I didn't think they were doing so well, I'd connect with the doctor on call at home to let him know. The fact that I did a lot of triaging took weight off the doctors. I'd triage on Thanksgiving and Christmas because I couldn't get people to come in. I brought my kids to work with me when they were in the playpen. That's how it was. I just didn't want to miss work.

If patients weren't happy, they'd come to me. I'd give it a day. I'd always say, "I'm always open to constructive criticism." I always let the patients know they came first. If they weren't happy and they paid cash for the visit I might slide the urgent care charge for the office visit. And then I would document that to let the doctors know: "Mrs. Smith was unhappy because she thought her visit was too short," for example. If the patient was a chronic complainer, I would still give them a call, of course, but I would say, "You're just never happy! I'm sorry. There are other urgent care centers and we would hate to lose you, but the patient's always right." Just like the customer. We would just go with the flow. But I would let the doctor know that Mrs. Jones said you didn't even look at her ears; maybe you forgot. The doctors were fine with all that.

I was completely blessed with my bosses. The family and urgent care practice opened at 8:00 a.m. and closed at 10:00 p.m. When I started my second job at the pediatric urgent care center, I would work at my first job from 8:00 a.m. to 4:00 p.m., then I would go right next door to the pediatric group from 6:00 p.m. to 10:00 p.m. to make extra money. After I moved, I commuted for five years, working from about 9:00 a.m. to 9:00 p.m.

On Joy in Work

Joy in work, for me, meant talking to people and knowing they were better. I would have such a satisfied feeling when little ones were sick or hurt and then they'd be better. Joy in work meant calling people when they were sick and having them thank me for checking on them. This should be part of being human but there's just not enough of that. Joy in work meant connectedness, relationship, and just being there for people. I was there 24/7 for them.

I had only three jobs in my whole career. I left one because I moved, and when I retired it was because of my health. I just couldn't do it anymore. But it killed me because my brain and my heart and my soul is still there. I miss working tremendously. I connected with all the patients. I would take their phone calls at home, especially in pediatrics. I've known all these kids from the time they were five or six, and now they're in their 20s. That is so satisfying.

I worked all the time, but I never really felt overloaded by work. I loved what I did. That's why, today, I miss it so much—working was so much a part of my life. It was never a burden. Yes, I missed a lot of time with my family. But if I was ever able to make a ballgame, or something for my daughter—even for an hour—I was there. My life was chaotic, no question. But I always managed to step back and get it organized. My staff was always great. I could never have done it without good staff.

On Money and Joy

I don't think there's a relationship between money and joy. Money didn't mean joy to me. Joy came from being able to do what I loved.

What Diminishes Joy

Lack of time diminished my joy in work. I would get overly involved in what I was doing, and I'd want to give it 100%. When you're in an urgent care setting there's no time for holidays and weekends, so I spent a lot of my weekends at work. That took away a lot of family time. I think it's the same with doctors.

Being in medicine gives you heartache. Patients would bounce in one day—you knew they had leukemia—but they would have a heart attack the next week and they'd be gone. It takes a lot out of you when you can't fix something. We had a lot of HIV patients back when most doctors didn't understand how to treat them. We would bring those patients in later in the day, during the 2:00 p.m. to 10:00 p.m. shift, so they wouldn't be exposed sick people.

All of my bosses, with the exception of one, expressed appreciation for my work. That one was a micromanager. Secrecy among partners in that practice dominated, and I didn't work that way. I worked there for five years until my health declined and I just couldn't deal with it anymore.

Advice

- Know that if you're going to have a lot of patients, you're going to have book work to do. If I didn't understand something I'd go to the computer and books and would read for hours.
- You have to be ready to be on top of every rule and regulation. That is mandatory.
- Managers need to be open, they need to listen, they need to communicate—communication is very important—and don't let problems fester. Waiting another day is not going to help anything.
- You have to be open to any kind of help as a manager. You have to learn how to scramble when unexpected situations come up, and you have to learn how to calm things down.

59.   *Dana D., LICSW, Clinical Social Worker at a Pediatric Hospital*

Dana D. has been a dedicated social worker for over 25 years and has worked in multiple hospitals in a variety of settings. Her greatest fulfillment comes from working with children and their families, which she has done in emergency departments, intensive care units, and outpatient clinics. Dana, when asked about professional joy, discusses her sense of accomplishment and satisfaction in the workplace and what influences these feelings.

I chose to become a social worker because of several personal experiences as well as guidance from mentors who knew me well. When I was in my early 20s, I enrolled in a nursing program after completing my bachelor's degree in human services. I was unfortunately forced to leave the program in the first several weeks due to a traumatic car accident. I required several years of intensive medical care and rehabilitation. Following this life experience, I was guided to social work by a colleague who felt it would suit my personality and skills well. I enrolled in a social work graduate program and began working in hospitals in my second year, which led me to a lifelong career in medical social work.

I currently work in a consulting role at a pediatric hospital where I have worked in several positions over the past ten years. I provide guidance to nurses, doctors, and social workers, both in the hospital and in the community, about complex decision-making and protective issues. I have been in this role for several years. Prior to this, I worked in the ICU inpatient setting.

Over the course of my career I have worked with families in a variety of settings. As a social worker, I have supported families through some of life's greatest challenges, including receiving a devastating diagnosis, surviving a tragic accident or other trauma, and facing the end of life. It has been an honor and a privilege to be with families in moments of crisis, to help guide and support them, and to be present for their pain and sometimes their joy when a child recovers or makes progress.

On Joy in Work

I feel uncomfortable using the word "joy" to describe my own emotional experience in my role. I experience deep satisfaction, gratitude, a sense of accomplishment, worry, weariness, stress, empathy, and especially a deep personal and meaningful connection with children and their families and with co-workers. But joy itself feels too delightful an emotion to associate with the type of work I do, particularly when families are facing such significant distress.

There are factors that contribute to job satisfaction, including feeling valued and recognized, in this work. More than experiencing joy, feeling appreciated and respected is what is meaningful for me in the work I do. I believe there is a role for the administration in finding meaningful ways to acknowledge and appreciate staff. I also believe that co-workers contribute immensely to job satisfaction.

I do feel appreciated for my work, most often by colleagues who work in similar roles and therefore have first-hand knowledge of my work. Our ability to come together after a difficult case, share our experiences, and support one another contributes to my job satisfaction and my ability to continue doing this work. We talk and process, share our sadness and our success, and come together around very difficult circumstances to connect on a more meaningful level. I think these times are the closest I come to experiencing joy in my work, which I would really identify as satisfaction, a feeling of community and connection, understanding the support I can access from my team when needed, and the support I can provide to others.

The administration can also be supportive but often in a much different capacity. Broader decisions regarding finances, schedules, flexibility, and time off all contribute significantly to my job satisfaction. Pay is certainly important, as I imagine it would be for most of us, but sometimes it's appreciating staff in small ways that goes a long way. There have been times in my career when upper administration has recognized a challenging week for staff by delivering lunch to an inpatient unit or sending an email of gratitude acknowledging our hard work and dedication to the families we serve. These small gestures really do go far.

One of the things I have found most helpful and think is beneficial from an administrative perspective is that we have the flexibility and support from administration to change roles. I reached a point after six years in the ICU where I was feeling emotionally depleted and lacked the energy necessary to support my own children and family. As I considered all the possible options for changing positions as well as advancing in my career, I approached my administration, who were supportive and provided guidance as I made decisions about my career path. This was extraordinarily helpful for me personally and allowed me the flexibility to stay with my employer but in a different role, which provided both an opportunity for professional growth and a better work/life balance.

On Money and Joy

Overall, I really love what I do, I feel good about what I do, and I feel I'm contributing in a positive way to individuals and to society as a whole. I think this is something that other people, who have jobs that are high paying but less meaningful, can really struggle with. I feel grateful that I feel this sense of accomplishment in my work. This is a lower paying but high-stress and high-intensity job. Do I wish I made more money? Yes, of course. That would help me navigate my own family's financial needs, put my kids through college, save for retirement, and feel generally stable financially. But would I trade the job for something less meaningful and higher paying? No.

Advice

There are ways in which recognition from administration could improve, particularly from upper administration. I believe social workers, nurses, physicians, and other employees are recognized in different ways that aren't always equal or fair. I think these differences should be addressed from above, particularly in relation to pay, access to flexible schedules and vacation time, and other types of compensation and benefits.

If I could make a recommendation for administrators, I would highlight the importance of creating meaningful opportunities for growth and development within the institution, with a focus on staff retention. People work really hard and want to feel valued and recognized for the contributions they make. Part of this relates to pay, but part is creating an environment that recognizes staff in meaningful ways. I think it's important to acknowledge the extensive knowledge, wisdom, and dedication that staff with years of experience bring to their work. These staff members are so dedicated and so thoughtful in their respective roles. They don't work in a pediatric hospital just for the paycheck. They are here because they are dedicated and motivated to make a difference. It's important to retain staff with years of experience who bring not only clinical knowledge, but knowledge of processes and hospital culture in their roles.

My advice for social workers who are new to the field of medical social work: you could stay at work forever, 24/7. Make sure you take time for yourself and your family, whatever that looks like for you. Burnout is real. Boundaries are important to sustain you in your career emotionally and physically. Don't overlook small interventions or accomplishments. These are sometimes the most significant. We don't always see our impact in our first conversation. But we can plant seeds. These small interventions can have a long-term impact. Use your resources. There are always co-workers available to provide guidance and support. Don't be afraid to ask for help.

60.   Karen L., MSN, Board-Certified Family Nurse Practitioner at an Academic Medical Center

Karen L., MSN, has changed jobs several times over the course of her ten-year career as a family nurse practitioner. At the time of our interview, Karen had found the greatest joy of her career in a position where she was treated with respect, as a valued part of a team. She has since changed jobs once more, but her feelings about what promotes her joy in work remain.

I'd thought about nursing when I was younger and brushed it aside but decided when my children were young that I really wanted to be a nurse. I took courses in microbiology, chemistry and anatomy (along with other pre-requisites) and then enrolled in an accelerated second-degree nursing program. I got my BSN degree in 16 months; later, I earned my master of science in nursing.

Over the course of my career as a family nurse practitioner I've worked in college health, emergency medicine, and primary care. Then I finally found this job, which has brought me joy. It's the work, the place, and the people. I love being in academic medicine. Working in an academic institution is a whole different world from working anywhere else. It's a world where the expectation is that we're all here to learn. And we're all a team. There's so much opportunity for learning and for growth, which is encouraged and fostered because we're a teaching hospital. There are medical students, nurse practitioner students, residents, fellows, and attendings who all work here because they like to teach.

These patients are sick with a certain type of cancer. If they are ill enough to be hospitalized, they are typically in the hospital for about a month and then come to see me in the clinic for their first outpatient follow-up. Patients who have disorders that are not life-threatening come to see me in the clinic for initial consultations, as well as for regular follow-up.

The attending physician, a fellow, sometimes a resident, and I all see adult patients 18 and up. In primary care, there's nothing a physician can do that I can't do, although what nurse practitioners can do depends on the state. I take histories, examine patients, prescribe medications, and order tests. Nurse practitioners here have the authority to manage, diagnose, and treat patients independently. I often see patients for routine follow-ups on my own if the physician is away or on service taking care of hospitalized patients.

The doctors I work with and I are a team, which is a unique situation for me. We're all working together to make sure the patients are seen and taken care of. I'm so much happier now that I'm able to work as part of a team and to work collaboratively. I love being part of a team. I love that the buck doesn't just stop with me. It's a huge responsibility. It's nice to always have somebody here to ask, "What do *you* think?" I feel respected and valued as part of that team.

On the weekends, for the most part, I'm able to unplug. One of the nice things about being a nurse practitioner and not an attending physician is I don't have to be available 24/7. I'm not on call. When I'm home I can just be home. There are other things in my life that are important.

On Joy in Work

Joy is feeling I'm having an impact on a patient's life. Joy is having time to spend with a patient. Even if four other patients are waiting for me, I like making patients feel I have all the time in the world for them. Even if I'm only with that patient for five minutes and can sit and listen to them and not check my computer, and not look at my watch or my phone, the visit can seem longer than five minutes. I love that.

I love being able to educate patients. In some ways I am lucky because many physicians have so many more demands on their time and their schedules than I do. I have the luxury of being able to spend the extra time to answer a patient's question.

The other thing I love about where I work now is that this organization is very pro-nurse practitioner. The director of nurse practitioners has been here for many years. She sees our value and what we contribute to the organization, so I feel I have a lot of support. I feel empowered. If there were something I wasn't comfortable with, if I felt something wasn't right, or if I felt overloaded or pressured, there are many different avenues I'd be able to go down to address those issues. I feel very comfortable talking to the attendings with whom I work. I feel valued as part of the team and I would feel comfortable talking to any of them about anything. To be working among so many other nurse practitioners is great—there is power in numbers. And to feel valued and supported in an institution and in such a big group has really changed the dynamic for me.

On Money and Joy

There is a relationship between money and joy to a certain extent. I want to be compensated in a way that reflects my education, my training, and my hard work. Being compensated beyond that wouldn't give me more joy.

What Diminishes Joy

Many of my patients die, which is really, really hard. That is probably the hardest thing for me about this position. This is the first job I've had where I've had to deal with a lot of loss. Ultimately, I know we do everything we can for each patient and, I hope, make the time they have left good quality time, but it doesn't make the losses any easier.

Pressure to see too many patients diminishes joy. In other places where I've worked that came from the top down. In one place I worked I was expected to see x number of patients an hour. I'd receive reports every month about my productivity, which made me feel like a cog in a wheel. That's not why I went into medicine, that's not why I went into healthcare. I felt I didn't have enough time to interact with patients. I never pushed back. I never felt in a position to do that. In every job I've had before my current one, especially in the ER, everybody was drowning. It was all about seeing as many patients as possible; it was all about billing and productivity.

Advice

My advice for my bosses and colleagues is, take time to take care of yourself and make that a priority. This is not selfish. It's probably a cliché, but if you're not taking care of yourself—if you're not finding joy outside of work by doing what's important to you or just finding time to exercise and get enough sleep—you won't be able to take good care of anyone else. You can't show up for work burned out, sleep deprived, or hungry. You have to put the oxygen mask on yourself before you put it on your patients. I think this makes you a better provider.

61.   Gloria K., MSW, Hospital Neonatal Intensive Care Unit Social Worker

Gloria K., MSW, is a clinical social worker who supports families and nurses in a hospital NICU. Over the course of her nine-year career, she has worked in pediatric oncology and worked with children in community mental health, emergency departments, and inpatient settings. While Gloria found working in pediatric oncology stressful and painful—and while there is plenty of stress in her current job—she feels joy in being valued and supported by her colleagues, respected by leadership, and doing work she finds meaningful.

I went into this area of healthcare by chance. When I went for my master's degree in social work, I'd wanted to focus on advocacy and health systems. When I was in my second year, my field advisor told me I'd need to do a straight clinical rotation. I said, "No, thank you." I didn't think I wanted to do clinical work. But then I found myself on a year-long rotation on a pediatric floor and fell in love with it. I found it so meaningful and I thought the work I was doing made an impact. Even though I wasn't affecting large systems change, my one-on-one interactions with patients and families made a difference. Before this, I thought I was going to help populations; but then I found I loved taking care of individual patients and families and making things better for them, one at a time. Suddenly, I felt this was the right thing for me. I did a year of post-graduate fellowship in infant-parental mental health.

I had been diagnosed with chronic illnesses as a teenager and as a young adult. Social workers are always very careful not to bring their own issues into their work, which is probably why I initially shied away from direct clinical work. But I think my own experience with illness, so different from that of most other young people, helped to increase my empathy and inform my practice.

I'm a clinical social worker in the neonatal intensive care unit (NICU) of a large hospital. My job is multifaceted. I do a lot of direct clinical work with families, end-of-life and bereavement work, and both informal and formal work to support staff and families during times of high stress. I work four ten-hour days a week, 8:30 a.m. to 7:00 p.m. each day. There is a core group of ICU social workers who cover for one another, so my days off are always protected. I am very lucky.

On Joy in Work

Creating Moments of Joy

Part of my intention, in addition to providing clinical therapeutic support, is to create moments of joy for families in the midst of treatment and relapse and life-changing illness. I used to work in pediatric oncology. I once worked with a family whose adolescent had been diagnosed before I started and relapsed twice while I was working with them. I used to wear boots in the winter because it was cold and snowy. One of my patients called me "Boots," so I would start wearing different types of boots. If a patient liked a certain type of sneaker, I would start wearing them to clinic visits. I did these small, small things to create a little bit of joy and connection to my patients.

Teamwork

My joy in work is informed not only by the work I do but also by my gratitude to the team I work with. Because the members of my team understand the level of stress we all work under, we are extremely supportive of one another. I think that makes it possible for me to do my job and to find the joy in it. Of course, there's a shared joy, inherently, in the work we do because it's meaningful in and of itself, but also because we're doing it together. Our staff is large, diverse, multidisciplinary, and not hierarchical. There are nurses, attendings, and mid-level nurse practitioners. I work alongside the nurses. Everyone appreciates everyone else's expertise.

Regular Communication and Support

If a patient dies or has a serious injury, we do a debrief. Not only are we organically supporting each other in the moment, but we understand that everyone has his or her own process of coping when someone dies. If we work as a team long enough, we come to understand, to a certain extent, each other's experiences and ways of coping. During the official debrief, we talk through the entire experience of caring for the patient as a team and talk through what was helpful and what wasn't. We always talk about our emotions first. How far that goes depends on the team makeup. It changes depending on which team members are there, their level of comfort with expressing emotion, how connected team members are to each other, and other factors.

I think about narratives a lot when I work with families. I talk a lot about narrative processing, by which I mean telling a story as a way to explain their journey. Often parents will share their journey this way themselves. If a family has been outside the hospital for several months, one of the things that not only increases their sense of ownership but also decreases their feelings of helplessness is to share their story and the story of their child—of what their child is like and what their family is like, and how they've made their way through until now.

I feel supported by the hospital, too. I am part of the social work department and part of our NICU team, so I have a foot in both worlds. Being part of the social work department means I have a group of 200 people who understand the work and have a framework for it. We have peer supervision once a month, where we have a group of six to eight social workers who come together and talk about their work. We talk about things that were hard about the month or things we want to share that were joyful. Everything is on the table. People feel safe to be open and honest in these groups. I tend to forget that other healthcare providers don't have groups like this.

I also have individual supervision in the form of debriefings every other week. I talk about the families I work with, the emotions that come up when I work them, the hard cases, the joyful cases. How they impact my life, how they don't impact my life, or how I think my own past experiences may be coloring my work with families. I share frustrations I may feel about a family, or my own concerns about the ethics of a patient's medical care. I look forward to these debriefs. Our social work department considers these important, although they are not required. And I think certainly having a space that's protected and confidential allows us to process our frustrations and our sadness. Social workers always have to be very even keeled, and these debriefings gives us a space to express our internal emotional experiences.

As far as the top-down dynamic in our organization, we have a medical director and a nursing director who we see all the time. Every day at 10:00 a.m. we meet as a team. We all come together for five minutes and everyone checks in to review basic concerns, anything that anyone is concerned about. It may be, "Today we only have this many nurse practitioners;" or "We have this many nurses;" or "We have 15 intubated babies;" or "We want to be mindful that we have seven patients going to surgery." Any of these things may change the work we do and make things a little more acute.

We also have a hospital operations briefing, and the person who goes to that earlier in the day, who may be the medical director, the nursing director, or the clinical coordinator—someone higher up—also comes to our 10:00 a.m. meeting. If there is anything of concern about the hospital, then they report back to us. The communication is very good.

Feeling Valued

I feel extremely valued by my NICU team. I never question my value on the team. On other units in our hospital, social work tends to be dismissed or minimized, or unacknowledged or misunderstood, in terms of the breadth and depth of what we offer. I've never felt that way with this team. We are considered leaders and people to go to for expertise in certain areas. We express gratitude to one another. A social worker who left and I were honored with an award from our unit, which gives out awards every year. Our colleagues nominate us. It was surprising but incredibly moving that my colleagues appreciate me and expressed it in such a meaningful way.

Many hospitals are cutting social work roles. There's enough research showing that patient and family satisfaction scores go up when social workers are on staff but looking at financial balance sheets in hospitals across the country, we look like low-hanging fruit. Which is interesting because we make so little money. But at this hospital, there are over 200 social workers. And social workers in these odd, niche clinics that you'd wonder what we do. But social work is so valued here that social workers are considered part of the team. I definitely feel that value.

On Money and Joy

Social workers don't make as much money as nurses or doctors. People don't go into social work because they're super-interested in making money. However, in the past, I had to work two jobs to feel I had enough money. I don't have to do that now. I got a promotion and it's only recently that I have felt, *okay, I'm good.* More money wouldn't increase my joy, but less money would increase my stress level and would negatively impact my joy and my ability to do my work. In that case I'd be working more, and I'd feel stressed and resentful that I didn't have enough money to feel comfortable.

What Diminishes Joy

Being Overworked

One of the things that reduces my joy in work is feeling I'm not doing enough. I'm one of two NICU social workers who cares for really acute patients. Usually, we split the workload, but my colleague left at one point and I was covering all the patients and their families, without a partner, for almost six months. What I noticed during that time was I felt I wasn't working up to my standards. I didn't feel that I was supporting families in the way I normally do—I was just putting out fires. I worked more hours. I focused on families with the greatest needs, the ones who were in complex social situations, those with limited resources, those whose children were facing the end of life, and those who really needed to have conversations about diagnoses. For the families who were doing "okay"—okay for being in a terrifying life situation—I wasn't able to offer the same amount of support I usually do. And that was hard.

Yes, the administration could have brought in someone from the outside to help during this time, but our team is very particular and insulated, and they trust the people on the team. It takes two to three months for them to get comfortable with a new person. So, the task of training a new temporary person in our environment, versus just waiting to hire someone permanent and then training her, would have been a lot. I both sucked it up and was very intentional with my time. I'm lucky my husband is very understanding, which is immeasurably helpful. I was definitely emotionally depleted in a way that is not normal for me when I'm carrying just half the unit. Fortunately, I was able to plan a vacation in the middle of this time when I knew I would be alone. One of the ICU social workers covered for me and I was able to go and breathe and relax and disconnect.

Even with the second person sharing my workload on the unit, it's impossible—as grateful as I am for everything that goes on in our environment—not to get overloaded in our world. I would mistrust anyone who said they never felt overloaded, just because of the level of stress, of being exposed to trauma every day. The moments that get hard for me are sometimes personal. They're sometimes related to the families I'm supporting. They're sometimes related to the acuity of patients on our unit. Sometimes they're related to the cumulative death I experience. The hard part is, it's impossible to predict. And sometimes there can be a confluence of all of these things. I don't feel I have control over my work environment or my workload, not at all, but I think one has to have an orientation to the workplace. Knowing I have no control, that's helpful.

Conflicting Priorities

There can be a tension between what a family needs and what the team wants, or what I understand about the family and their thought process about their child's illness or end of life and what the team understands. Social workers are taught to be culturally competent and sometimes social workers do a lot of interpretation on behalf of families from different cultures, who speak different languages. Sometimes there's tension because I feel I'm doing an extra layer of work to try to get the same level of support for these families. I think it's hard. We do a lot of negotiation and compromise.

I have my ideal social worker response and doctors have their ideal medical response about what can happen in a clinical moment. Our unit is so acute that when a family doesn't speak English, it would be helpful to have an interpreter there to explain the child's medical state. That's not always possible, and because of my role I am mindful and a little anxious for families who come from different cultures and need that extra layer of support. In these cases, I try to educate the staff about how a family's experience or history of experiences with the medical field informs their reactions to things. I teach how a family's cultural differences or religious differences may cause them to view circumstances differently.

Being Made to Feel "Less Than"

I came into my job here with five or six years of experience. There is a clinical ladder here for most nurses and social workers and there are associated salaries at each level. I came in as a "level 1" social worker even though the standard for that level is two to five years of experience. I came in with experience in supervision, I'd had advanced training, and I was certified in some specific methods of trauma therapy. I felt a little resentful. I applied to be bumped up to the next level two and a half years after I'd started here. At another hospital I would have been hired at a level 2. This is something those of us who were "raised" outside this institution have immeasurable frustration with. I think this has to do with institutional culture. I have a really hard time understanding this; it's one of the things I probably struggle with the most. I get a bit resentful or irritated at the arrogance reflected in the attitude that training elsewhere is, by definition, not as good as training here.

Resource Management

If I could change anything about my job, I would love to hand off the resource management to someone else. Master's level social workers are very clinically focused. And sometimes people hear social work and think, they'll help me get funding; they'll help me get food; they'll help me with financial support. Which is true—we do all those things. But in the NICU it's so hard to hold both. And sometimes people think our role is a little more expansive. Managing resources also sometimes detracts from the clinical work I could be doing. It really varies, but sometimes resource management takes up to 30% of my time.

Advice

I think we often don't take enough time to acknowledge our internal experience and response. Take small moments or have small rituals throughout the day to just breathe or be mindful. I have rituals that are very helpful in grounding me at work. I have lunch, even if it's only sitting down for 20 minutes. I have a cup of tea in the afternoon. This is after nine years of practice. I didn't do these things for the first four years.

The work is easier to do if it gives you a sense of meaning. If you can make meaning of the work, then there's more joy in it. The joy comes from how you make sense of the work, why you came to the work, and what you see in your colleagues and your team. The gratitude and the meaning-making for me is why I continue to do the work and why I feel joyful doing it.

Finding Work–Life Balance

62.   Sharon D., BSN, Perioperative Nurse and Operating Room Educator

Sharon D. has worked at a large academic medical center for the last 28 years, commuting an hour each way to work. She started as an OR staff nurse and, eight years ago, took a position as an operating room educator. Sharon credits her ability to avoid burnout and maintain an essential work–life balance with being able to switch roles within the OR and to working off-shifts for the first 19 years of her career.

Growing up, I always used to play doctor or nurse. I just felt that nursing was the right career choice for me. It was between nursing and teaching. I didn't really aspire to be a doctor or choose another healthcare profession. There are many different career paths you can take in nursing. You don't necessarily have to work in a hospital, you don't necessarily have to work in the operating room. Depending on your level of education there are a lot of different career options in nursing.

I wanted to go into healthcare to help people. The healthcare industry serves a broad spectrum of people and as a nurse I encounter many types of individuals from all walks of life. Providing comfort and security and care at a time when patients and their families are most vulnerable is very rewarding; it's a way I've always felt I could make a difference.

I did leave once to take a job in a community hospital closer to home, but I didn't like it so I came back here. I prefer the academic medical center to the community setting for a couple of reasons. First, in the academic setting there's a lot more flexibility with your work schedule than there is in a community hospital. As an OR staff nurse, I worked in a department where there are more than 100 people, so there were always people I could change my schedule with. In the community hospital, staff didn't work as many hours or days; and because the staffing levels were much smaller there, I'd have to take call. If I got called in, I could be working for 24 hours with just one other nurse, the surgeon, and the anesthesiologist. That meant I could be working through a very long period of time without any break, including a lunch break. I just didn't like it. Second, in the community setting I wasn't challenged enough because patients there tend to be a lot healthier than they are in the academic setting. In the academic setting patients are a lot sicker and surgeons perform many more complex operations.

I work in a level I trauma center and I've done a lot of work in trauma surgery over the course of my career. You never know what you're going to get in terms of injuries, the type of care the patient is going to need, or the type of surgery you're going to be involved with. It really challenges your critical thinking skills. There are 45 operating rooms in this hospital. We do very complex and, at times, pioneering procedures. We have patients who come from all over the world for certain types of services and operations they can't get elsewhere.

When I was a staff nurse in the operating room my schedule was not fixed—I worked different hours, weekends, holidays, and I had to take call. Today I'm one of the operating room educators; I've been in this role for about eight years. I now work a fixed schedule, Monday to Friday, eight hours a day. No weekends, no holidays, no call. My primary job is to get new hires on board, orient them to the department, teach them about policies and procedures specific to the operating room, and so forth. I am involved in patient care now occasionally. If we're short-staffed I may staff a room. Sometimes I provide staff with lunch relief. As a staff person I know you have to feed your people. But on a day-to-day basis I am not directly involved in patient care.

On Joy in Work

One aspect of joy in work is being able to take care of patients. When I worked in the operating room, although patients were intubated and under anesthesia and didn't remember the care I gave most of the time, I was able to use critical thinking skills and get instant gratification when their operations were done. For example, if someone had a gallbladder that was making them sick, we would take it out. Providing there were no complications from surgery, they would immediately get better and be cured. That was very gratifying. Being part of a team in the operating room and collaborating with the surgeon, the anesthesiologist, and other healthcare professionals involved in patient care brought me joy.

Knowing what I did was going to make a difference for patients most of the time brought me joy. Sometimes there wasn't always a positive outcome, particularly when we were taking care of very sick patients. Sometimes we provided palliative care. During traumas, if patients would come in very, very unstable, sometimes they wouldn't make it. But even when they didn't make it, which was not a happy time, everyone was focused on saving that person's life. Saving lives is joyful.

Because I have a steady schedule with fixed hours now, I have a better work–life balance than I had before and that brings me joy. Because I know what my hours are, I know what I can do outside of work. Not having fixed hours can interfere with work–life balance because when you're on call you don't know whether you're going to get called in or if you can go ahead and spend time at home with your family. Working in a hospital and being a nurse, the expectation is that you should be able to work 24 hours a day, including holidays, because of the acuity of the patients in this type of setting. This takes time away from your family. Since you don't know what your schedule is going to be until you receive it, you really can't make any plans in advance.

On Money and Joy

I think there is some relationship between money and joy. I do think people like to be compensated for a job well done. I think that money is a factor but it's not the biggest factor.

What Diminishes Joy

Difficult Surgeons

What diminishes joy in work is the unhappiness that comes from working with difficult surgeons. A few surgeons, though not all, have challenging personalities and some have reputations for being difficult to work with. If I were assigned to work with a doctor like that—for instance, someone who liked to yell about everything, whether at me or anyone else in the room, including the anesthesiologist, the first assistant, the residents, or the medical students who were helping—I didn't want to come to work. I didn't like being yelled at all day; nobody does. Such behavior caused unnecessary stress in an environment that was fast paced, demanding, and high-pressure enough, an environment where I'd have to think critically and make quick and impactful decisions.

I understand the stress the surgeons are under sometimes, particularly if they are trying to save a life. Because of my years of experience, I knew when I was doing a good job in that type of situation and when I could have done a better job. In the OR, there really is no room for mistakes because a mistake could compromise patient care, it could be fatal. When assessing an unpleasant situation while working with a difficult surgeon, I would ask myself whether I was doing something to contribute to it or whether the unpleasantness was due to the stress the surgeon was under. If the situation was due to stress it was not ideal and not something I wanted to experience, but in those cases I didn't really internalize it. But when a surgeon yelled all the time just because he could get away with that type of behavior, it was extremely unpleasant; it made me not want to come to work and do that job with that particular surgeon.

Working Overtime

As an OR nurse, although I worked 12-hour days I couldn't necessarily leave after my 12-hour shift. There were times when I worked 20 hours in a row. This didn't make me happy but I was obligated to take care of the patient. Many times I would work my 12-hour shift up until 11:00 p.m. At 11:00 p.m. we're only staffed to run so many operating rooms. And we're a transplant facility, we're a trauma center, so if we have emergencies, transplants, and traumas that come in and there aren't enough staff, then people are mandated to work overtime. We have an obligation to take care of our patients whether we like it or not. Unfortunately, on a couple of those 20-hour days the traumas just kept coming one right after another and it meant I'd be working through the night. There was no break, no opportunity for me to go home. We tried to call people in but most people were sleeping.

Administrator–Clinician Disconnect

I think there are areas in which administrators and clinicians differ as to what each thinks of as problems. Most administrators are far removed from the front-line caregivers and I don't think they always see eye to eye about what is important. For example, making sure we have the equipment and supplies we need to do our jobs; having a flexible schedule so we can have work–life balance; dealing with unacceptable behaviors, including bullying, from surgeons and even from our colleagues in lateral roles.

My whole career has been in the OR so I can't speak to what happens outside the OR, but I think the OR attracts certain types of personalities, very strong personalities. And this is across the board—surgeons, anesthesiologists, everyone. I think over a period of time people get used to that challenging, tough environment. New people coming into that environment are kind of, I don't want to say "eaten up," but it can be difficult; there are expectations to be met, patients to be taken care of, and mentoring to be done. You know, you show someone something once and it might be expected that they should understand and be able to do it. And when they're not, you know, people can be unkind in what they say and what they do. No one wants to work in a culture like that and so people will leave. And they have left.

Fixing the Problems

Recognizing the Importance of Work–Life Balance

Over the years management and administration have realized that work–life balance is very important to healthcare professionals. They have worked to put out a schedule in a timely manner. In the past, when I'd receive my schedule would depend. Ideally, they like the schedule to be out eight weeks at a time so that people can make plans—you know, to make doctor appointments and so forth. However, things like staff shortages and unexpected resignations throw a monkey wrench into getting the schedule out in a timely manner. So sometimes people have only one or two weeks notice about what their next schedule will be.

The administration has really begun to listen to feedback from the staff over the last few years, particularly when people are leaving to go elsewhere. They have tried to make people happy by allowing them to have more control and more flexibility over their schedules. The work–life balance that enables is probably key to retention, along with fair compensation for one's work.

Addressing Surgeons' Behavior

Although for a long time surgeons' bad behavior appeared to be acceptable—remember, it is the surgeons, their patients, and the case volume they bring in that generates revenue for the operating room and for the hospital as a whole—as time has gone the administration has been more likely to address such behavior because it borders on abusive. Sometimes the resulting changes in behavior have been permanent; other times they've been only temporary. Although we're nurses and not at a high enough level to be privy to that sort of information, I do believe that if surgeons' abusive behavior is ongoing and consistent these surgeons have moved on, either by their own choice or because their contracts haven't been renewed.

I've seen a positive change over the last few years, and I've seen a decline in the number of resignations. When staff feel supported and respected by managers, administrators, surgeons, and colleagues, I think that helps with retention and recruitment.

Reflections

I think surgeons were actually worse in the community hospital than they are here. I don't know why; maybe because they were in private practice. There, the egos just seemed to be a lot bigger. Here, the doctors have roles within the hospital as well as in the school of medicine, and many of them are world-renowned for performing certain operations. Some of the most talented doctors I've worked with here are some of the most humble doctors I've ever worked with.

My job has been quite fulfilling. But because this is such a fast-paced, demanding, high-pressure environment, I think I would have suffered from burnout if I hadn't been able to move into a different role. After about 20 years as an OR nurse I needed to find a different career path, which is when I became an educator.

For the most part, although I find my job extremely rewarding, sometimes dealing with hospital administration, workplace politics, and a lack of respect from doctors and managers take their toll. For example, if we have a legitimate concern and verbalize it we don't really feel we're being listened to or heard. We don't feel supported. That can take away from the satisfaction of doing our jobs. When problems accumulate over a period of time, people leave. Difficult doctors are in the minority and, overall, most are terrific to work with. But the ones who show a lack of respect for what we do make some people choose to leave their jobs.

Advice

The only advice that I have for my superiors is to listen to the feedback from the people who report to you and take it seriously. Within reason, I think attempts should be made to try to implement processes, whatever they may be, to improve staff job satisfaction.

As for my colleagues, we need to be kind to each other. We're all in the same boat. Be kind to one another, help one another, work as a team, support one another, and offer our resources to one another. I may have strengths and skills in certain areas and someone else may have complementary skills and knowledge in other areas. If we put all our skills together, we could be dynamic. This does happen. It's just that people get so wrapped up in their own little worlds that they forget.

63. *Vivian G., PhD, Psychotherapist in Private Practice*

Vivian G., PhD, has had her own private psychotherapy practice for 30 years and has been a practicing psychotherapist for 40 years. She is also an adjunct clinical assistant professor who spends part of her time supervising graduate students, consulting with other therapists, speaking at conferences, and writing. For Vivian, joy comes from having autonomy and control over her work; feeling a deep connection to her purpose; pursuing her academic interests; and being able to balance work and fun.

I didn't really choose to go into healthcare or psychotherapy. It was not a direct path. I started out wanting to be in academics and had no interest in doing counseling. My master's is in social psychology; I envisioned myself working in a junior college teaching psychology and doing research. When I went to get my doctorate, I applied to two programs in social psychology. Then, almost by accident, I saw a program in counseling psychology at another university. I thought this was something I could do, so I applied and went there for my PhD.

I came out of graduate school with my PhD in counseling psychology still thinking I wanted to be an academic. I had my first child, I taught a few courses here and there, and then I tried to get licensed. After I taught six courses, I thought I had fulfilled my obligation in my first postdoctoral year to get licensed, but I was told I hadn't. By then I wanted to get some clinical experience, so I started working at a university counseling center and discovered how much I enjoyed it.

In the practice I started 30 years ago I see adult patients—individuals and couples—and consult with other professionals, such as referring physicians. Occasionally I have to write reports for insurance. I'm also I'm on the board of my professional organization, teaching at local and annual conferences.

Most of my referrals come from physicians, other psychologists, and former patients. Nowadays many young psychologists create web pages and their referrals come from the worldwide web, so there are patients who come from the general public. They need to do a lot of screening in those situations. When you're known based on your expertise and your reputation the way I am, people tend to refer patients to you who almost fit the mold of who you are. It's as if I were having a dinner party and I invited you. I would invite others who I thought would mesh well with you, not those who wouldn't. What I say about my practice, and I don't know a lot of people who can say this, is if I had a party and invited all my patients and all my friends, you wouldn't know who my friends were and who my patients were. That either means I have pretty crazy friends or pretty sane patients. Most but not all of my patients have responsible jobs and are upstanding members of the community. That makes it very easy to come to work every day.

One of the joys in my life is understanding things. I am passionate about trying to understand what makes things work and what motivates people. For me, the best match occurs when patients share that interest. For example, they want to change their behavior, but they also want to understand what's going on. That helps build a strong working alliance.

I typically see 20–22 patients a week and I work mostly three days a week, from 7:30 a.m. to 5:00 p.m. Those hours are available, but I don't always see patients straight through. It varies from week to week. I prefer to work this way rather than to see patients five days a week for shorter days. I need a balance in my life. I really like knowing that today I'm in a work mode and tomorrow, I'm not. I'll go to the gym, I'll take a class, and I'll do other things that feed *me*.

On Joy in Work

When I think about joy in general—when I think about joyful moments—I think about being filled with delight and happiness, like in television commercials where people are jumping through the fields and the sun is shining. Or looking at your child's face, when everything comes into alignment. I think of joy as exuberance, exhilaration. When I think about joy in work, it's more like a deep feeling of meaning—like I'm doing the right thing—and I'm in the right place.

I would compare it to marriage. If you're married to the right person, there are those moments of joy where you're just feeling, *I'm so glad I found you* and everything is just right. But then there's, "Take out the garbage." So, day to day, you know you're in the right place but you're not walking around with the music playing in the background.

That's how I feel about work. I can't say I wake up on a Monday morning saying, "Yippee! I get to see patients today!" But I'm where I need to be. Things are aligned. I'm doing the right *kind* of work. Moments of joy come when I'm sitting with someone and I have a connection and I say the right thing and it triggers a lightbulb.

With this kind of work there's a quantitative tipping point—I love what I do but if I were to see more than a certain number of patients, I wouldn't love it at all. My patients are always amazed at how much I remember but remembering is much easier because I'm not overwhelmed with patients.

I don't take insurance and I haven't in so many years that I don't even remember. It gives me great joy to not to have to deal with the bureaucratic constraints of insurance. It gives me joy to not see patients in the evening.

The key word that gives me joy in my life, overall, is balance. I love having a balance between being serious and being playful; between having long-term relationships in therapy with people I know over years, and being able to see that I was able to help someone in three sessions do something they never thought they could do; or being able to help someone in eight sessions who could never get on a plane and who now can fly. I really like the balance of doing some of each.

I most enjoy knowing people and getting to know people. I love to talk to people. I love to understand people. What would I be doing if I weren't working for pay? I'd probably be hanging out with people and talking to them.

My joy comes from feeling that I'm using my gifts. And getting paid well for it. It's a tremendous honor that I'm given, to be allowed to have intimate relationships with so many people. Many people never get to know anyone intimately. They never even know themselves intimately. But most people know a few people. If you're in a good relationship maybe you know your spouse really, really well; maybe your children, or at least one of your children; perhaps a couple of friends. There may be a handful of people who you not only know, but you really, really know, because there are all kinds of barriers to that. There are reasons why we put up defenses, why we only show that part of ourselves. We all do it.

So, to be invited in to know somebody in a really deep way is an honor. It's an honor to be able to enter that space of their lives and to be able to make a difference. When somebody says, "You have made such a difference in my life. You're one of the most important people in my life in terms of the role that you've played," there's nothing better than that. I don't do it for that positive reinforcement, but I get a lot of that. It gives me such a sense of meaning that I'm doing something important in the world. To be able to do that *and* have the flexibility and be able to make a decent income from it, how great is that?

One thing that gives me joy and that brings things full circle is that I started out wanting to be an academician, and I have found a way to do that, too. I supervise students through the university, I consult with other therapists when they call me because they feel stuck on a case, and I teach. I've published papers and a chapter in a book. These things all give me great pleasure. For me, it's all about balancing my needs, the different things I like to do, and the different parts of my brain.

On Money and Joy

Sure, I think there's a relationship between money and joy. From the time my kids were little I knew that I wanted the time with my kids and it wasn't worth it to me to have the pressure of seeing more patients, even though I could have made more money doing that. I still feel that way about having time to do the things I want to do. Time is a precious commodity. They say that money doesn't buy you happiness; I say money doesn't buy you happiness, but it buys you options. Money, for me, is about options, not because I want the fanciest car or the biggest house, but it provides a kind of freedom. A freedom from having to worry so much. I have a lot less money than people who work a lot harder, but that has always been a conscious choice.

What Diminishes Joy

If I'm working with someone who's really difficult and who sets up obstacles, not only in their own life but in my trying to work with them, that diminishes my joy. For example, there are people who are very, very conflicted about getting close; and so, as I move closer to them, they push me away. Some people ask me, "How can you listen to people's problems all day?" There's a piece of that. Sometimes people come in and they're just complaining, are standing in their own way, keeping me at a distance, or thinking, *what am I doing here? I don't know where this is going.* But in the big picture, I feel I'm doing something meaningful.

There are times when I have a long day. Monday might be six patients and it might be nine patients. Sometimes at the end of a long day I just feel exhausted. Sometimes it's about the content of the work. People go through very difficult things that can be emotionally draining for me. It's difficult when someone is having a lot of loss in their life, sickness or imminent death for themselves or their family members. I don't work with populations with serious disturbances like schizophrenia or borderline personality disorder.

I never had a patient I was seeing commit suicide, although I learned that a former patient whom I had seen for just a few sessions committed suicide a year after she stopped coming. She was very high risk and had been deeply depressed, so I referred her elsewhere. That was a very troubling and uncomfortable situation for me. I did feel a certain measure of responsibility for the referral. Although it was a year later and I wasn't actually seeing her, to somehow be connected with all that was very painful.

Sometimes someone walks through the door and I feel I just don't want to work with that person. I can't explain it. It's the nature of relationships. People stop seeing me for all kinds of reasons. It's only a problem for me if I feel I may have done something wrong, or if I wonder whether I gave them optimal treatment.

Advice

My advice to people starting out in this field is, ask yourself why you're doing this. What is it about this that you really like? And be sure that whatever the external reasons—the money, the flexibility, all that—are really being driven by the internal reasons.

There are a lot of really good things in this field but it's getting harder. I'm a dinosaur in the sense that in the future, the field will be more and more insurance bound. Psychotherapists in the rest of the country can't work the way I work. The future is going to be in large practices where there's a high turnover rate and all those things I associate with burnout. I'm not sure that if I were working in an agency or seeing people every 30 minutes back to back, I would even want to do this kind of work.

What Diminishes Joy

Train people well enough so they can leave; treat them well enough so they don't want to.

Richard Branson

Introduction to Part 2

In this section you will meet people who have felt—and still feel, to some extent—joy in work, but whose joy has been diminished by multiple forces both within and outside their organizations.

Regardless of degree or specialty, the radiologist, technologists, environmental services associate, emergency medical technicians, physicians, nurse practitioners, nurses, residents, and social workers interviewed here say what diminishes their joy is pressure to see more patients, and do more work, in less time; being evaluated on the quantity, rather than on the quality, of their work; the conflict between their organizations' demands for speed, their desire for accuracy, and their fear of lawsuits; the electronic medical record that is time-sucking and largely irrelevant to their treatment of patients; the failure of bosses and administrators to listen to their concerns, take them seriously, and act on them; and disrespect from bosses and co-workers.

More than "pebbles in your shoes," these are widespread, systemic, serious problems in healthcare that emanate from the top down. They are more like boulders that fall on the shoulders of those who are working as hard as they can to deliver effective, safe, and compassionate patient care every day. These problems are organized in this section around three main themes: pressure, stress, and fatigue; administrator–clinician disconnect; and disrespect.

That the healthcare professionals whose stories appear here have managed to find joy in work when and where they can despite these negative—and, in some cases, crushing—forces is a tribute to their commitment and tenacity, if not to their organizations, then certainly to their chosen professions and to their own sense of what is right. Their life and work, especially this profoundly important work, is made even harder by forces beyond their control.

Pressure, Stress, and Fatigue

64.   Charles G., MD, Radiologist

Charles G., MD, began his career in internal medicine at one of the most prestigious medical schools in the country. Personal upheaval caused him to leave internal medicine and, eventually, switch to radiology for "the most unconventional reason." A naturally funny man, Charles rarely smiles as we talk about the subject of joy in work. He has spent the last four years as a staff radiologist working a grueling night schedule for a large conglomerate regional medical group. Today stress and fear are the emotions that dominate Charles' life.

As far as feeling joy in work, I don't think I'm there. I'm not doing what suits my skills and abilities the best. Otherwise I probably wouldn't be so miserable. I don't feel I'm doing what I'm meant to be doing in a way that makes me feel fulfilled. I'm just too busy to think about what else I could be doing that would make me happy. Even alternating nights with days off, it takes me at least three days to recover from working nights. And then for those other days, with everything else going on in my life, I have time but no time. I can't even begin to think about what to do. I have to pay for my house and, hopefully, I won't get fired for being too slow. That's my number one stressor: please don't fire me.

I decided I wanted to go into medicine after working as a summer intern doing HIV research and watching my mother practice clinical social work at a local hospital. I thought I'd like to interact with people and be of some use.

I did my internship in internal medicine at one of the top medical schools in the country. I liked it. But I left and moved to a different part of the country to pursue a romantic relationship that ended in disaster—and once I got there I really missed where I'd been. I kept asking myself why I left that program. Sure, I could attend a good program somewhere else, but it wouldn't be *as* good. It wouldn't be the best. I got really depressed and childishly thought, *Well, if I can't do internal medicine at the best medical school then I just won't do it at all.* I took some time off. I sat around thinking about what I could do. I felt stuck and a little lost for a while.

I chose radiology for the most unconventional reason. When you're an internal medicine intern you're constantly running around like a chicken with his head cut off. So, I thought, radiologists sit in one place. I liked that because I was feeling very low energy. How's that for a reason to choose a specialty? One day I went onto a radiology website. Some of the cases looked interesting. This looked like something I could do. I'd been feeling lost and, all of a sudden, I latched onto something—and once I did that, I got into it.

I did a four-year radiology residency starting at one of the best radiology training programs in the country. I was at the top of my game again. But I still missed medicine and didn't feel like I totally belonged in radiology. After all, the people I was training with really *wanted* to go into radiology.

After a year-long fellowship I took my first job. The way radiology works these days, you work for hospital systems or hospitals contract out to radiology networks, so you really have to be part of a big group. My skill set is really good for reading acute cases out of the emergency room (ER) or urgent care. I'm not interested in doing a lot of daytime hospital work, fielding consults all day and doing procedures, which I hate doing. I don't want to go to surgery conferences and present. There are things I want to avoid that are part of a "normal" job, and I can avoid those things by doing what I do now.

I work from my little office at home. I'm part of a team but I'm fairly isolated. There is one other radiologist who is on with me, also reading remotely. Every once in a while we'll bounce ideas off each other and ask questions but most of the time I have no contact.

I don't think my feelings about my work, either positive or negative, affect my job performance. The main thing that affects my job performance is being slow, my intrinsic need to be more detailed than necessary. That's an internal conflict. It's a battle. I believe really strongly in being professional and approaching every patient, regardless of the way I'm feeling, with the same care—whether I'm sick, well, busy, or slow. I try to be very professional about that. That's how I was trained, that's the way I was raised. These are the ethics I bring to my job.

On Joy in Work

Joy in work means a good fit—that I'm doing something that fits my personality and makes full use of my abilities and my talents. If something fits well, then it can make me happy. When you're an intern, "enjoying" is a little bit of a stretch—you're working 80+ hours a week—but I was good at it. I felt I belonged there and it worked well for me. So, even in the torment of that often horrible experience, there still was joy.

A little bit of joy comes from the camaraderie of being in the trenches with people. Or sometimes you'll end up doing something out of the ordinary for a patient that makes you feel really good: I know I've saved someone's life or saved a patient from being permanently disabled. Sometimes, if I talk to a young person who is thinking about going into medicine—or if I talk to a medical student or resident and I can engage them or teach them something—*that* is fun for me.

I really did enjoy teaching. When I was a resident I was heavily involved in teaching for the department of radiology, and that was really great. I loved doing that. A lot of people have told me I'm very good at it. But I don't do it now. It's not part of my job description. I'd think I'd like to do this if it's something I could incorporate into my work schedule.

Someone I work with—a really nice guy—is one of the fastest radiologists in our group. One day I was on the computer with him and we were having technical problems. We both got assigned the same two cases, which had never happened before. In both cases I had to call him and the emergency room because I'd made two diagnoses that he didn't see at all. They were both significant misses but one of them, an aneurysm repair endoleak, could have turned out very badly. This kind of thing happens to me all the time.

In another case a neuroradiologist missed the finding of blood in the central spinal canal on a cervical spine computed tomography (CT) scan. A bit of blood isn't a big deal, but in this case there was a lot of blood—enough to cause problems, possibly spinal cord damage that could lead to paralysis. I entered a preliminary read on the case because there was network downtime that prevented me from dictating a final report. The neuroradiologist came in the next day and dictated his report on the case but he failed to notice the large amount of blood. However, after noticing my preliminary read, he amended his report. I received a "thank you" email from him. There are so many smart radiologists like him, but I know there are some who would miss this finding solely because of the fast pace. It's not that I'm the world's greatest radiologist but I always take the time to check for this finding on every cervical spine CT. These extra checks add up to longer read times, but the trade-off is better patient care.

The night before last I was reading a neck CT for a swelling or tooth infection that had abscessed. I happened to notice that there was an 8-mm aneurysm in the patient's brain, which is a good size, something that would need to be treated. Eventually that would have ruptured and either killed or severely disabled him. A lot of people would have gone pretty quickly over a part that's not relevant to the study they're supposed to be looking at. But I take my time and feel happy I caught something a lot of people wouldn't have. That's what keeps me going.

I've been very fortunate to work with good bosses for the most part. But they just don't get the idea that we need to be doing better reads as a group. The speed is the problem—and that's private practice radiology in general, it's not unique to our workplace. In many instances my standards of accuracy are higher than theirs. They do monitor; they do some quality assurance on different people's reports so there are ways, in theory, to measure. But if your standard is what it is, then you can put a checkmark next to that and say you're doing a good job. I feel we can do better. For example, I have people, like my grandparents, who bring me their scans all the time. I'll do a read taking the amount of time *I* want to take and the amount of detail *I* want to go into, and my report is unrecognizable compared to what a patient in the hospital would get.

A positive relationship with a colleague is something that brings me joy. As a radiologist I have to call people, most often emergency room doctors. One who feels really comfortable with me will text to ask me questions because she knows I give good reads. When I have a positive relationship like that and feel I can contribute to a patient's care, that's a little piece of joy. In radiology I do kind of miss working with colleagues sometimes. But then every once in a while I'll have to go into the hospital because computers break down and I snap out of it really quickly. I do miss patient care a little bit.

We had a work dinner recently with people I never see in person—I just email or talk to them on the phone. There was one guy there whose name I see on reports all the time. He recognized my name and said, "I just want you to know I called our bosses to tell them that you saw some really hard-to-find fracture on this cervical spine CT, and I can't believe you saw that!" Then I realized *that* is also one of those sparks of joy: I'm not being criticized for being slow, I'm being recognized for being good.

What Diminishes Joy

I'm really not happy with my job because it's so busy—it seems that every year we acquire another hospital and more work gets dumped onto our work lists. In order to keep up with the list I need to go at about twice the speed I'm going now. But because I don't, things get backed up. It's hectic and distressing. If we had less to cover, or if we had more staff to split up that work list, I'd be a lot happier.

For me, it's just the speed of it and not being able to think and take my time; that makes me really miserable. Sometimes I have to go faster than I want to but most of the time I push back against that. It's not good. I get calls from my boss telling me I need to review more studies. I guess the way I work, I catch more problems than most people. I guess there's a happy medium between speed and accuracy. A couple of people are really good at both, but the majority of speedy people are not very good at accuracy. I think I err on the side I do because I care. A lot of people don't.

I don't talk to my boss about accuracy because I don't want to imply that people who are really fast are *not* accurate. It's easy for a metric to measure your productivity. It's hard for a metric to measure how *good* you are—the quality of your work. So, unfortunately, that works against me. People suggest I raise this idea with my boss—that it's not easy to measure quality—but I can't really say that.

When I feel the opposite of joy in work I want to sit in a corner and rock back and forth. I have a bizarre job and a bizarre schedule, alternating stretches of working nights and days off. I like the fact that I get chunks of time when I don't have to go to work—that's really important to me, it makes me happy—because I feel I can sequester myself from that work environment. I have a stretch of concentrated pain and I get through it. Sometimes I work late evening shifts, sometimes I work the deep nights. Last night I started at midnight.

If I could change anything about my job, it would be to take the time I need without feeling pressured from the outside. I also feel pressure about being sued. Most doctors get sued at some point. That causes me a lot of anxiety. I've met with lawyers to try to malpractice-proof my life as much as I can. Everything I own is also in my spouse's name. My major sources of stress are the pressure to increase my speed and the fear of being sued. If I could work more quickly and not miss something that would cause a lawsuit, that fear would go away. That would make me happy.

Advice

I didn't realize that in medicine you have to deal with a lot of horrible things. Horrible people (colleagues and patients), horrible situations, especially in training. A lot of surgeons are difficult to deal with. I was so naïve, telling myself, *Oh, I'm going to help people, I'm going to be so happy.* But don't expect gratitude from patients. People hate you and they just want to use you for your skills or to get pills that their insurance company will pay for. You have to look for the joy in it and find it where you can. And you're probably going to be miserable.

People who are applying to medical school or thinking about applying ask me for advice all the time. I was helping so many people with their essays and advising them that I thought, *I need to make money doing this.* A friend of my spouse started and runs a company that helps place students from abroad in U.S. colleges. Some of the students they've placed want to go on to medical school here. We're doing a trial right now and I'm working with one of these students. When I work with students, I have to be really positive about medicine and not dissuade them from going into it. But it's not genuine.

My honest advice for someone choosing to go into medicine is, run! Run as fast as you can! When I'm talking to someone I'm not in a business relationship with I'm very honest and ask, "Are you sure you want to do this? Why do you want to do it? There are so many other ways you can help people and be happy." Like a lot of things in life, you may think you know what it's like to go into medicine or be a doctor, but you don't know until you do it. It takes a lot to do it. I try to explain to people that medicine is about speed and doing as much work as you can. And that you're busy but maybe not in a way that you want to be. That's one thing I didn't realize—just how busy I would be from the perspective of speed and needing to rush.

It would be wonderful if we could put quality—preventing something bad from happening—on the same level as quantity. But in radiology, as in other specialties, quality is harder to measure.

65.   Jamie Cieplinski, RN, Clinical Unit Leader and Floor Nurse at a Community Hospital

Jamie Cieplinski, RN, was drawn to nursing by a love of science, her admiration for a labor and delivery nurse, and the untimely death of her mother. The dedicated, empathetic nurses who took care of her mother, and of her, left their mark. Determined to make a difference and to "pay it forward," Jamie became a registered nurse and has been a nurse for six years. At the time of this interview she was studying for her master's in nursing and was poised to take a new job in home healthcare.

When I was young, I met a labor and delivery nurse. She was so devoted to her job. She wore scrubs and I thought that was so cool. She became my role model of what a nurse should be. In school I loved science and was very interested in chemistry. When I was in college, I got a job as a technician in a chain-store supermarket pharmacy and I thought I'd go into pharmacy. My major was biology.

Then right after college—I was 22 and my brother was 12—my mom got unexpectedly sick with what seemed at first like an upper respiratory infection. We took her to the hospital and her condition deteriorated rapidly while they tried to diagnose what was wrong. They tested her for pneumonia, for Guillain-Barré syndrome, and for other things. All her tests came back normal. She was in critical care and did not improve. They think she developed acute disseminated encephalomyelitis, which is rapid swelling of the brain, and she died within a week. That was ten years ago.

The nurses in the hospital who took care of my mom were amazing. They also took care of me. They told me to go home and eat, take a shower, and they would take care of her. They reminded me all the time to take care of myself. They were just as worried about me as they were about my mom. I've always remembered that.

It took me awhile to figure out what I wanted to do with my life. My mom was my best friend. In my grief my brother made me realize that my mom wanted us to do something with our lives. That was the turning point for me, when I was able to push myself to move in the right direction. I decided I wanted to "pay it forward," got my associate's degree, and became a registered nurse. *This* was my mom's legacy. She had a daughter whom she left too early, but I was able to learn something from her death instead of just sitting in a corner and crying all day. Now I try to do for families what my mother's nurses did for her and for me. I try to forge as much of a relationship with my patients as I can, when I can. I went from thinking nursing was "cool" as a child, to realizing nursing can be rewarding, to knowing I can make a difference.

I've been a nurse for six years and have had three jobs so far. My first job was working in a long-term care facility for one year. My second job was in a skilled nursing facility; I stayed there for ten months while I was trying to get a job in a hospital. My current job is at a suburban community hospital. We have a comprehensive stroke unit and even though it's a community hospital it's state of the art. I've been here for over four years but I'm going to be leaving soon to work in home healthcare. This hospital is burning me out. I always leave the hospital knowing I made a difference somehow, but I need to make a change. I'm constantly being pulled in multiple directions and I don't have time for myself. Sometimes you forget as a nurse to take care of yourself. You're so busy taking care of other people.

Leaving the hospital is going against everything I thought nursing was, but I really like what I've seen of home healthcare. It's one-on-one, I won't be bothered by other people, I won't have to wait for the patient in 708 to get off the commode, I won't have to deal with a patient with alcohol withdrawal jumping out of bed. I'll just be focusing on one patient and establishing a relationship—that is what I've really been craving. I can decide when I'll go to see patient A and patient B. I'll know how long I have with each patient. I'll have more autonomy. In home healthcare there is more control. And this will definitely allow me a lot more time for myself.

It just depends on what you need. That's the beauty of nursing—that you *can* make changes. If I don't like it, I can always go back to the hospital or do something else. There are options.

My Nursing Journey

My stereotypical idea of a nurse was that a nurse works in a hospital—so that's what I assumed I would do. That was my original goal. But when I got out of nursing school the hospitals in my area weren't hiring new grads, so I got a job in long-term care. I wasn't very excited about it because I didn't think of that as nursing but, looking back now, I learned so much from that first job. It was very stressful, but I wouldn't take it back. I used a lot of my skills, learned a lot about time management, and learned how to build relationships with my patients.

I don't know what the standard nurse : patient ratio is in a long-term care setting but it's more than in an acute care setting. I started with 32 patients. Now, granted, they're not 32 acutely ill patients, but they're still 32 patients you have to go and see and give medication to. There are Joint Commission policies that you have to give medication in a certain amount of time, and because that's not always possible it can be stressful. Most people are living there and also need some kind of medical attention, need help getting dressed in the morning, and so on. It's a lot to do.

Working in that long-term care facility was so stressful that I cried a lot for the first couple of weeks. That's just the way it was. There was a learning curve. I laugh now that I cried but I understand why I did. I learned a lot from a licensed practical nurse (LPN) when I worked there. She is a smart, smart cookie. There's no comparison between what you learn in nursing school and what you learn in the field. You can learn only so much from a book. I felt after a year that I'd learned all I could there. I didn't enjoy coming to work anymore because it felt mundane.

Then I got a job at a skilled nursing facility across the street from a hospital. They get a lot of the hospital's patients. I had about 14 patients, so the ratio was better. These patients may have been hospitalized for surgery, a bad case of pneumonia, a stroke, or some other problem; and because they had a hard time walking after being in the hospital, they needed rehab. In this facility the nurses make sure the patients get the medications they need and that they're not seeing any acute problems that would send them back to the hospital, which happens more than you'd think. Falls happen a lot, unfortunately. That job can be stressful, too, when we have a good number of patients to look after and they are a little higher acuity. I didn't necessarily want that kind of job, but I used it as a bridge position, as a way to get into the hospital. I worked there for ten months. When a job opened up at the hospital, I was able to make the move I'd always wanted. I've been here for four years.

I work on a neuro-medical–surgical floor. We take neurological patients who have had a stroke, or a seizure, or multiple sclerosis. We also take patients who have pneumonia, pancreatitis, gastroenteritis—we take them all. We take dialysis patients, too. Our floor was designated as the floor for patients who are withdrawing from alcohol. We don't take post-surgical patients or post-orthopedic surgical patients—they go to specific floors.

I have two roles in my job now. When I started I was a floor nurse, I'd take a team of patients, usually four. A year or 18 months into my job I was asked to rotate into the charge nurse position, called the clinical unit leader (CUL). Every floor has one. On the days when I am the CUL the rule is I don't take a team. I assist all the other nurses with aspects of patient care, helping them with things they can't get to because they are so busy. For instance, nurses will call me to say they need an intravenous line (IV) in this room because they don't have time to put one in. When I'm not the CUL I'm a floor nurse.

Some days I prefer being a floor nurse, other days I prefer being the CUL. It depends on the crew I'm working with. On the days when I'm the CUL I get asked a lot of questions and get pulled in a lot of different directions; we have a lot of newer nurses on the floor so right now those are my least favorite days. It's hard when nurses ask me to take on tasks for their patients when they say they're busy doing something else. I make assignments as a CUL, but I don't make any more money for doing this.

On Joy in Work

Joy in work means coming home every day and knowing I made a difference. Even on bad days I remind myself that all jobs have their downsides but that in my job I know I can make a difference. Even if it's just making a patient smile. Or if they come back to me after they've had a stroke and say, "Look at me now." It gives me joy when I can impact a patient or members of their family in such a short period of time.

No matter how much I complain about my job, I do love my work and I wouldn't trade it. The bottom line every day is I do love being a nurse. Nothing stands in the way of my patient care. My work is about defending my license, about my patients' satisfaction. But my job sometimes diminishes my satisfaction.

What Diminishes Joy

The opposite of joy in work definitely is burnout. I'm feeling this right now. There are so many interruptions and I always have to go off on different tangents. Doctors put in so many orders, labs and other people are calling me, and combined with other things this is very stressful. In the hospital we don't have control over when things happen—when people have to go for tests, or when doctors come and put in orders. Before I know it, I'm asking, "Where did my day go?"

Right now, the administration at my hospital is not viewed very highly. There are lots of problems. No matter what we say our concerns are tossed aside. I don't know if that happens everywhere. Decisions are made that affect nurses, but nurses aren't involved in shaping these decisions. Sometimes nurses aren't told why particular decisions have been made and the administration won't answer when asked why.

Some of the doctors are *horrible* communicators. If we blink twice, we'll miss them. Part of the bad thing about nursing is we get all this—pardon my French—shit dumped on us because doctors don't always act responsibly. When we communicate something, we're supposed to go up the chain of command. I understand that. But I shouldn't have to do that all the time when I feel the need to express that something is unsafe. We're dealing with human beings. We're dealing with lives. So, when I say I don't feel comfortable taking a patient, I would like to talk to a doctor and let him or her give me a reason why I shouldn't feel that way. But nobody does that.

Instead we're told to write an occurrence report. If a death occurs, if a fall occurs (with or without injury), if there's an issue with a doctor, or with housekeeping, or if there was a delay in care, or we didn't get a medication we were supposed to get—there are so many problems we might have—we're supposed to write an occurrence report. I guarantee that people don't write them often enough. Writing these takes time and people who don't want to write them, don't. I don't write them as often as I should, and I've forgotten to write them occasionally. If I don't get around to doing something it's because I'm busy, not because I'm slacking. But because occurrence reports don't get written often enough, things that are problems can't be improved because that information isn't available. I don't know what's done with occurrence reports once they're sent in. As far as I know we haven't asked for follow-ups. Supposedly they collect data and use the data to make changes, but if changes are made as a result of occurrence reports they are temporary and don't last.

At one point there was an issue with stocking. They call it supply and distribution, which is stocking for all the floors. The person in charge of that was out so people were needed to stock supplies on mother-baby and labor and delivery. Our floor was overlooked. We were looking for our stock; I didn't have the proper materials, so I went to my manager to tell him we weren't stocked properly. He sent somebody up to stock. Then a couple of days later we're in the same boat. I found out that if the woman in charge of stocking isn't there, then things don't get done. That isn't right.

Advice

It's important for upper management to come down and meet the people working in the hospital. In the four years I've been here I've never met the chief nursing officer, which tells you something. People who go to stroke conferences have seen her and people working on improvement committees have seen her. Someone on the her management team comes to our floor and knows all our names. It always makes me feel good when she comes down. But it's not good enough that the chief nursing officer sends down other people. I want to see her face. In four years, I should have seen her *once*. Many other nurses feel the way I do. The administrator of the hospital has come around to say hello to the staff, to have some staff members have breakfast with him in the morning. I've appreciated that.

We need to change the way we communicate with doctors. In 2018 we have instant messaging and text messaging, so we shouldn't have to page doctors. Many doctors don't always get back to us. I know they're busy but some call back quickly and others don't. I have some doctors' cell phone numbers and I use them to get orders and so on. Or I'll say, "Call me at this number so I can talk to you about the patient in 709," and they'll call me back. Or I'll ask, "How quickly can we get orders on the floor?" It's not like the intensive care unit (ICU) where the doctor is always there. On our floor, doctors are not easily accessible. Our hospitalists are much easier to get hold of. I take it upon myself to build relationships with doctors and I ask for their cell phone numbers so I can resolve patient questions easily, but not all nurses do that.

The nurse : patient care technician ratio should be based on acuity and not on numbers. A nurse might have four patients who are alert and talking, but might have four other patients who need feeders, total changing, and so on. Patient techs do a lot of our dirty work and it's a lot to ask of them. They get overutilized, which is another issue. They don't get paid enough to do what they do.

66.   *Carrie L., MD, Emergency Medicine Physician*

Carrie L., MD, has been an emergency medicine attending physician for eight years. She finds peace, and moments of joy, in her work but is exhausted by the stress and continually fluctuating schedule of her job.

I work in the emergency department of a small suburban hospital. I'm not employed by the hospital; I'm employed by a small private group that contracts staff to work in the emergency room. I work full-time—three or four eight-hour shifts a week, for a total of 1,400 hours a year. I've always worked for a group; I've never been a hospital employee.

I chose to go into healthcare in college mostly because it's such a hands-on occupation and I like being with people. I liked everything in medical school—doing minor procedures, talking with patients. I liked pediatrics and geriatrics, I liked hearing stories every day, a little flavor of everything. It wasn't until my fourth year of medical school that I decided to go into emergency medicine. I liked the surprise of not knowing what you're going to get, which is especially true in emergency medicine. I also liked the idea of shift work at the time, so that was one of the things that drew me to the field.

I was pregnant going into my first year of residency. We knew we wanted a big family and we liked the idea of knowing what days I'd be home and what days I'd be at the hospital. It is harder to juggle than I thought it would be but compared to other physicians—who are on call for a whole week at a time, get phone calls in the middle of the night and during the day, and who work many more than 35 hours a week—shift work sounded good. When you're there you're on, and when you're home, you're completely off.

In the ER you have to know a little bit about a lot. Everything from diabetes to coughs and colds to stitching up cuts to kidney stones to surgical emergencies. We don't know a lot about any specialty other than life or death situations—these are our specialty.

Every doctor's job is completely different. Every specialty is different. But emergency medicine is unique because we're like a knot at the end of some people's ropes. Going to the ER, even for a minor injury or illness, is a big event in some of their lives. It's interesting to be part of that.

On Joy in Work

Saving someone's life brings me joy. Saving the life of a man who came into the ER with an ischemic stroke is one example. He came into the ER completely paralyzed on his left side. He said his symptoms had started 30 minutes before. When patients have an ischemic stroke, we sometimes give them tissue plasminogen activator (tPA). tPA is a "clot-busting" medication and is the only medication that can reverse a stroke. It is a life-changing medication—but because it can cause bleeding in the brain and some people can die from it, we give it only in certain circumstances—one of which is that the patient come in within three hours of having symptoms. We decided to give him tPA. He came back about a month later to thank us. He was walking and talking and completely fine. That's not always the case with tPA, but patients who have good outcomes with tPA are joyful. It's like a miracle. When we save a life it's a really big moment in the ER.

There is one story I will never forget. A 40-year-old man came in one Christmas day with abdominal pain. He had a CT scan to rule out appendicitis. On his way back from the CT scanner he had what looked like a seizure. He had no medical history. The nurse put him on the cardiac heart monitor, and he was found to have a rare, abnormal heart rhythm called Torsades de pointes. We ended up intubating him, sedating him, and giving him magnesium sulfate, which is the treatment for Torsades. His wife was distraught. Someone from cardiology came in to see him. It turned out that he also had appendicitis. So, he had all this stuff going on. He ended up getting a pacemaker in early January while he was still in the hospital, went home, and then three months later I got flowers and a thank-you note from him. He said, "You made my family feel at peace on Christmas day when I thought I was going to die." I kept the letter at home in my drawer. It was so wonderfully written and so thankful and gracious. His note said, "I know this is a hard profession. Anytime you think about how hard it is or you feel down about your position I just want you to think about me and how you changed my life and helped my family."

Seeing families come together in life-changing circumstances may not bring me happiness, but it brings me a sense of peace: for example, when helping a family decide on hospice or a nursing home or helping them understand a family member's illness—even something as simple as kidney stones—or setting them up with a new specialist. In the ER there's not a ton of pleasure. But there are a lot of peaceful times for me, where I feel I did the best I could and worked to the best of my ability. I helped make a patient's or family's experience as good as it could be.

Then there are times when I've experienced happiness—for example, solving a problem with a quick fix, like removing a foreign body from a patient's ear who had been experiencing dizziness. Going in to see patients and talking with them—the bread and butter of medicine—is the part I really enjoy. I like hearing a different patient's story every 15 minutes. I like that I never know what's coming; some problems are relatively minor; some are major life or death scenarios. It really is a remarkable role to play sometimes.

I get joy from my co-workers: nurses, techs, ancillary staff, and physicians; sometimes in the ER we go through chaotic and crazy situations together, so we bond. Everyone gets along really well.

What Diminishes Joy

I don't work fixed hours. Not at all. That's part of what makes it hard for me to be joyful in my job. It's the fatigue, because I work a lot of days, a lot of nights, a lot of weekends and holidays. The job fluctuates week by week. The shifts are always changing—yesterday I worked from 8:00 a.m. to 4:00 p.m. Tonight I work from 7:00 p.m. to 3:00 a.m. So, I'm going into work and I'll already be tired at 10:00 p.m. If I could change anything about my job it would be the hours, the shift work. I'd love to work from 8:00 a.m. to 4:00 p.m. every day but it doesn't work that way.

Between juggling sleep and my schedule and my four kids' schedules, it's pretty complicated and tiring. I find out at the beginning of the month what my work schedule is going to be. I have a little bit of control over my schedule. The scheduler is one of the female physicians in our group and she takes requests; she's pretty good about granting them. But everybody has to do their fair share. You can't say "I never want to work nights. I never want to work weekends."

Dealing with families is hard. And, honestly, we're always worrying about the legality of everything. People can be litigious and blame you for the tiniest thing if they don't have a good outcome. That's always in the back of my mind. It *has* to be at the back of your mind when you're working in medicine. That's a really stressful thing to deal with, too.

Stress

The stress of the job itself diminishes joy in work for me. You know, having multiple ill patients at once. Having unexpected turns in patients' cases. Sometimes patients and families want instant satisfaction. They don't understand why they might be put on the back burner—they're unaware of what's going on around them and they think, *I came in here two hours ago and I'm still not fixed.* The harder days are when there are ten plus patients in the waiting room; if I don't see them quickly enough, I feel the stress.

Burnout

The biggest periods of burnout for me—I've had two, and one was during residency—were probably the lowest points not just in my career but in my life. When I was a resident, I was working 80 hours a week and just found out I was pregnant with my second child. I had a 12-month old at home and my husband was working 100 hours a week. Everyone gets some burnout during residency because the hours are so hard, and the work is so stressful, but given my circumstances it was even worse. I was completely exhausted. Now there's a law that limits the number of hours residents can work each week.

Lawsuits

The second period of burnout was caused by a lawsuit that went on for three years of my life. It was soul-sucking, it really was. I tried to do everything I could for this patient. She died several years after she was released from the hospital with cancer. It was disheartening to know I truly did nothing wrong, but I had to go in front of the family and the judge. It's hard when families don't understand that and they fight this legal battle. It was really difficult to have people rip apart my charts and say, "Well, you wrote this, but this happened." I was told that I was at the bottom of the totem pole and I clearly didn't do anything wrong, but I still had to settle because otherwise they were going to go to trial and threatened to attack my assets. I'm early enough in my career that I know this can easily happen again. It's happened at least once to almost every ER physician I know. Sometimes to have peace I have to realize there is nothing else I could have done. I'm a religious person and I know some things are in God's hands. It gives me peace to know that.

Advice

My advice to those going into emergency medicine today is to look for a group that backs you up and supports you during tough times; not going with a big corporate group can increase your job satisfaction.

Make sure you're working for a hospital where the administration is supportive, there's plenty of staff, and things run seamlessly. That helps to improve job satisfaction, too. What makes a difference in a lot of ER doctors' job satisfaction is the kind of group they work for, whether they're an employee of the hospital, and what their insurance company is like (do they cover your medical malpractice and do they "have your back?"). When I was working for a big group I was out there on my own. In big groups there is nobody there to support you in difficult circumstances such as lawsuits. The big group I worked for before was in another part of the country and they didn't know me from Adam.

Now I'm in a small, private group and there are 20 of us who work together in this one hospital. There is much more support in this group. It's a much better atmosphere; they want to make sure everybody's happy, they want to make sure our requests are honored, that we're not burning out. We are required to take a two-week vacation each year to prevent burnout. My group has one director, who is wonderful, and if I have any issues I go to him; he goes to the hospital administration if something isn't being done properly in the ER, if we need more nurses or beds to open up, or anything else that is the hospital's responsibility. We have a board of seven—I'm on that board—so of the 20 of us, seven of us make the decisions, taking into account whether anyone else in the group needs to be involved in the decision-making.

Go into emergency medicine knowing it might not be what you expect—not just in terms of some horrible cases that could alter your thinking in life, but in terms of the hours, too. It may seem like shift work is glamorous because I only work 30 hours a week, but 30–35 hours a week is exhausting in the ER. I think people should know that before they choose this field. A career in emergency medicine is a pretty short-lived career. You already have to be thinking about what you're going to do when you're done. I don't know what the answer will be for me.

67. *Paul T., MD, Neurosurgery Resident*

> Paul T., MD, is a fourth-year neurosurgery resident who rotates at five different city hospitals. He says that while being a neurosurgery resident is interesting and rewarding, it also is so demanding and involves so much pain that he gives no thought to the subject of joy in work.

I was always interested in becoming a doctor. For a brief period, I was interested in going into finance, but then when I was a junior in college the financial markets were all collapsing, and it sounded pretty miserable. So, I figured I'd just go into medicine instead. I was 22 and didn't understand what it meant to be a doctor or what real responsibility was.

I went into neurosurgery because there's a lot of interesting research on the brain, there's a lot we still haven't figured out, there are still a lot of interesting questions to ask, it's an area of medicine that's very high impact.

People don't go to neurosurgeons because they're bored; they go to neurosurgeons because they have very serious problems. For example, we just took care of a 22-year-old girl who dove off a boat while drunk and fractured her cervical spine and was unable to move. We took her into the operating room and straightened out her spine. She's gone from being unable to move to being able to lower her legs off the bed. She will probably go from being entirely paralyzed to being able to walk over the course of the year. The ability to help a 22-year-old walk again is a special thing.

On Joy in Work

Neurosurgery is such an enormous amount of work, especially in residency, it's difficult to define what joy is. It's an interesting and satisfying job. I go into work every day and I do impactful things and I learn every day. But it's hard to define what joy means. Neurosurgery is just pain. It's a lot of work, it never ends, and it's an enormous amount of responsibility. Every single year in residency the responsibilities go up and the time I spend thinking about neurosurgery goes up. It has gotten nothing but harder and more time-consuming. Physically, even though I'm not in the hospital as many hours as I was when I was a first- or second-year resident, I still spend a lot of time thinking about neurosurgery.

I don't think I try to define joy in work. I don't approach medicine that way. I may have gone into medicine originally with very different ideas from the way I think about medicine now, but I'm not interested in pursuing joy in medicine. I'm not interested in pursuing whatever the opposite is of joy in medicine. To me, neurosurgery is what it is. It's a very hard job, it's a very demanding job.

I enjoy it, I like it. Is the cost–benefit worth it to me? I'm far enough along, I've made so much money, I would justify a positive answer no matter what because I've spent the last three and a half to four years of my life trying to become a neurosurgeon. It's such a valuable skill to have. The average neurosurgeon in America makes $500,000–600,000 a year, which is an enormous sum of money; it doesn't make sense for me to do anything besides finish neurosurgery residency and pursue this path at this point. I think that people justify major decisions that they've made retrospectively.

I don't have any control over how the team operates and I don't have any control over my schedule but I'm happy in my life. I get to do interesting things every day at work and I help people. I think residents who work in demanding fields, for the most part, separate themselves emotionally from administrative concerns or processes because if it's not something you can control it's not something you can change. The attendings manage people the way they want to manage them. You let them do whatever they want, you don't have control over the system. You're much more of a cog in a machine.

Reflections

A lot of fields in medicine have moved to shift work, and it's a lot harder as a surgeon to be a shift provider. In general surgery and trauma surgery it's a little bit easier to do that. Within neurosurgery there are very few places that have implemented a shift-type setup. My attendings are essentially expected to be available 24 hours a day, wherever they are. Every single morning when we round on patients, we call the attending at 7:00 a.m. It doesn't matter if they're on vacation with their families in California. They're expected to wake up hours earlier and hear about the patients.

It's hard within neurosurgery to pass the responsibility for taking care of patients to someone else. I don't know if anyone has effectively figured out how to do it, so it just ends up being a lot of responsibility, and thinking about patients at all times, if you're taking care of sicker patients. It defines who you are, I think, and defines who you become.

68. Leonard R., MD, Pediatric Radiology Resident

Leonard R., MD, a pediatric radiology resident at a large academic medical center, enjoys problem-solving and puzzling out the causes of patients' symptoms. He has completed two years of residency so far—one year of general medicine and one year of a four-year residency in pediatric radiology. "Going into radiology was a tough decision for me," he says, but he was drawn to the radiology resident's primary focus on learning broadly.

I like a field in which knowledge for the sake of knowledge is the primary pursuit. I went into healthcare because my parents are doctors and I've been exposed to medicine my whole life. My mom is a general internal medicine doctor and my dad is a general surgeon. They talked about the bad side of medicine because it was always being romanticized on television. I got mixed impressions of medicine from my parents. My dad absolutely loved his job. He had to retire early because of health problems but he talks about going back. My mom is one of the disillusioned doctors who was kind of burned out. She liked medicine initially but tried to discourage me because of the way things have been going.

Science was my favorite subject in college. Medicine is nice because it allows you to work in science but also to work directly with people and try to help them. I liked the subject matter and wanted to do something I could feel good about, something that would give me a sense of meaning at the end of the day.

One thing I like about medicine is the problem-solving and puzzle-like aspects of it. I'll get patients who won't know what's going wrong: something is bothering them, they have certain symptoms, and I'm looking at their case like a puzzle to try to figure out what it could be. We have to know how to figure out what's going on in a wide range of specialties.

The nature of medicine has changed a lot over the last several decades; the days when the physician could sit down with a patient for half an hour and go over all their symptoms and do an exhaustive physical exam are gone in some ways. Now specialists tend to do that diagnostic problem-solving. In radiology that's pretty much all we do—try to make diagnoses for patients. It's a very visually oriented field, which appeals to people like me who look at a lot of pictures and try to make diagnoses based on those.

Because a radiologist is a consultant to specialists, we don't deal with the social aspects that come into other fields of medicine. If you're working directly with patients you're dealing with issues like insurance and fighting with people who don't want to cover procedures or pay for patients; that in itself can be frustrating. As radiologists we're somewhat insulated from the administrative side of medicine.

My hours vary from week to week. Since I'm a resident, things depend on my attending to some degree. I work in a patient-based system so I'm at work until the work gets done. I have a relatively fixed schedule compared to most residents. Theoretically, I work 75% of the time from 8:00 a.m. to 5:00 p.m., although I may work a little later if I'm finishing something up. But when I take call, I might be here from one to three hours later. As residencies go it's a fairly benign work schedule compared to medicine or surgery, where there is much less predictability.

On Joy in Work

For me, joy is the culmination of everything I've been learning—being able to apply everything I've learned to help solve a problem for a clinician or a patient, to find something that can send the patient down the right path for treatment. Probably the best feeling is when I figure out something that people have been puzzling over. That's a big part of my job.

The other thing that appeals to me is teaching. We work with a lot of medical students and we get other clinicians who read their own films, read their own x-rays, but who don't know the nuances and come to us to try to learn a little bit. It can be really rewarding to try to help people find a new way to look at things, to look more systematically, and to give them some tips. Clinicians usually are pretty thankful for that help. I find that really rewarding.

I also teach medical students and radiology technology students. I give lectures to them and now I have junior residents who I'm teaching as well. Teaching is one of my favorite parts of this job.

What Diminishes Joy

What diminishes joy in work for me is anything that isn't directed toward patient care—which is the reason I went into medicine to begin with.

Fear-Based Documentation

We do a lot of medical-legal administrative work to protect ourselves if something were to go wrong in the future. It's gone off the rails, to be honest. There's an inherent air of distrust among doctors. If I tell people what I see on an x-ray, they'll go and write it down. Not because they won't remember, but because in case I'm wrong they want to document that I was the one who was wrong. This weird feeling of inherent distrust makes people think they have to record everything that everyone else is saying. My colleagues and I talk about this informally all the time.

Inaccurate Documentation

We don't write a ton of notes in the medical record. We upload an x-ray to the electronic medical record (EMR). We don't have to document as much as others do, although that may change. We just report what we see on the studies. When I was a medical intern we didn't have to document; instead, the attendings would write, "I spent 45 minutes with this patient," or "I spent half an hour with this patient." But it's not necessarily all true.

I think it's become rote, with everyone writing down an arbitrary number. It's inherently inaccurate because people just put down what sounds like whatever should be right. They just cross their "t"s and dot their "i"s to make sure they meet the standard. We're spared a lot of documentation in radiology, but we do read clinicians' notes in the chart—we want to know what's going on with the patient and what clinicians are looking for. Those notes have become unreliable. It bothers me.

Unnecessary Testing

We do a lot of unnecessary testing "just because." I've literally heard people ask for studies, for tests that aren't necessary, saying, "I don't think this patient has this disease but if I'm wrong, I could lose my job." So, people ask us to do a lot of work that isn't really helping patients but makes doctors feel a little safer.

People look at how much medicine costs in the U.S. and estimates for defensive medicine—what we do when we're trying to avoid being sued—is 10%. But I think that's an underestimate because practicing defensive medicine is so pervasive.

Fear of Lawsuits

I'm absolutely afraid of being sued. Some people fear this more than others. You'll see some people take it to an extreme, where they'll look at an x-ray and mention everything, like a piece of clothing. They'll mention it just in case they look at this clinically and want to make sure it's not something bad. That's an extreme but everyone has lawsuits on their mind. There are residents who have been sued. It's fairly uncommon but it does happen. I'm certainly afraid of that as I become a senior resident. I'll be responsible for making calls semi-independently. I may say something looks okay on a CT scan but then my attending won't have time to look at it until several hours later. When you're reading so fast and attendings are so overloaded they can't get to a CT scan within a couple of hours that can be a problem. Not too long ago a senior resident on a busy night of call missed a really subtle finding on a CT scan and the patient ended up having a bad outcome.

Dread

I guess dread is the opposite of joy in work. I dread just how busy we can get sometimes, and the business environment of healthcare contributes to it. Hospital systems are becoming monopolies and are buying up other hospitals. Radiology is particularly affected because our attendings will read x-rays not only for our hospital, but also for any other hospital the system buys up. When one hospital buys another, a lot of radiologists lose their contracts. It's like big business mergers where they get rid of redundant personnel. Then the workload goes way up for the remaining staff.

I also dread seeing more tests and consults being ordered for patients who really don't need them—they're not medically necessary but they make clinicians feel they've done what's needed to protect themselves legally. This results in a ton of extra unnecessary work for us. We don't have the option to triage patients based on whether we think the patient's needs are real or whether we think clinicians are just covering themselves.

Everyone in the healthcare field feels pressure due to the volume of work. We spend a lot of time around our attending physicians and they're feeling overwhelmed. Probably what I dread most is the sense that my job is going to be completely overwhelming and I'm not going to be able to give the kind of care that I would if I had time to take things slowly. Everyone is trying to do more with less. Doctors who saw maybe half as many patients ten years ago are trying to see twice as many patients today in the same amount of time. We work on trying to get faster but there's an inherent inaccuracy that comes with trying to go really fast. We're maximizing what we can do safely with the number of attendings we have.

Fear of Burnout

What can lead to burnout is the ever-increasing workload that results in feeling overwhelmed and feeling that we're delivering substandard care. What definitely leads to burnout is feeling we're not really helping patients and that we've become depersonalized—like we're just a cog in a big machine that's not contributing much. Burnout happens when we feel we don't have much self-efficacy—when we're dictating reports so fast but don't have confidence we're seeing everything we need to see, we're not sure we're doing our jobs well, and we feel we're making more mistakes. There's pressure to be lean—a big buzzword in medicine—trying to do more with less. Trying to get the maximum efficiency out of any given physician. I think we're now at the opposite end of the scale.

Repaying Loans

The cost of training is a big problem facing doctors today. The average physicians I've talked to are $150,000–$300,000 in debt after medical school. The cost has become so high that we're kind of forced into these jobs. No one can afford to work part-time. Everyone is looking at getting a full-time job because we have massive loan debts to pay off, and full-time work involves being extremely busy. I like family medicine, but I can't afford to do that with my debt. If someone pays for your medical school and you have no debt, then that's an option. And there are some loan repayment options. I really admire the people who go into family medicine or pediatrics—they take low-paying jobs and they do it because they like it.

Negative Organizational Culture

I've been trying to figure out how to make morale a little better because we do have a morale problem. I'd advise my bosses and colleagues to celebrate the little victories: 80% of your day may be spent doing things you don't particularly enjoy, but there are times when you make a real impact on patients or help someone solve a problem; it's important to have time to dwell on those and, ideally, to have time to celebrate other people in the department. Some radiology departments have done things like celebrate great catches, or great diagnoses, and point to people who have done great things. We don't do much of that where we are. We just go on with our work and only scold each other when we do bad things. You just have to live in the moment and take note of the things you've done right and enjoy those. Because if you focus on every mistake you make, and you will make them, then you're going to be unhappy.

Reflections

Our attendings have inflexible schedules and have no control over them. They're scheduled for things without being told, and their schedules are shifted around and they're given extra shifts without being told. When I finish residency, I'll be lucky to find a job where I have any control over my schedule, partly because many hospitals are buying up small clinics and practices and their administrative burden has become so high. Insurance companies and hospitals have armies of administrators to fight over payments and it's really hard for small clinics to compete; they can't afford to hire the kind of staff to fight insurance claims and deal with the overhead. So, I'm afraid I'll end up working for a big practice and then I'll lose a lot of say in how much I work. I'll be subject to forces in which hospitals acquire new hospitals or new businesses, and I'll have to cover more and more practices. It's really hard to practice independently.

Yet, I look forward to going into practice as a pediatric radiologist. Nothing I know now has diminished my enthusiasm for that. I'm terrified but I'm also really excited. I still really like what I do at the end of the day and I still enjoy talking about it. I think it's stimulating, and it makes me feel like I'm doing something good with my life. Forty years from now I want to look back and feel that I did something I can be proud of.

69.   Ruby A., MSN, Pediatric Nurse Practitioner at a Federally Qualified Health Center

In her first job after graduating from nursing school, Ruby A., MSN, is a pediatric nurse practitioner at a federally qualified health center (FQHC). In this job she is expected to see at least 21 patients a day, Monday to Friday, and her productivity is measured solely by the number of patients she sees each day. Because her patients and their parents are primarily immigrants who are unfamiliar with the healthcare system or how to navigate it, and there is only one social worker at her FQHC, Ruby provides the needed medical treatment, education, and care coordination—all in the space of 15-minute appointments.

I am a pediatric nurse practitioner. I chose to go into healthcare for a couple of reasons. My dad died when I was a child and my mom went into healthcare. I think the combination of seeing the impact that healthcare providers can have on families and seeing the difference my mom made on her patients impressed me. And my sister is a doctor. So, the three of us are in healthcare. No one else in our extended family is in healthcare.

It was important to me to work with underserved patients. Before nursing school, I was a doula, someone who coaches and educates women about labor and delivery, breastfeeding, and postpartum care. I got the most out of it when I was working with teenage moms and immigrant moms. That's what got me interested in working with the populations I focus on now, primarily uninsured or underinsured Spanish-speaking immigrants. I found my niche.

I really enjoyed working with this population, but I wanted to do more. I felt limited by my role as a doula, and I wanted an advanced degree. I knew, at the end of the day, that I wanted to be a pediatric primary care provider. The question was, did I want to become a pediatrician, or did I want to become a pediatric nurse practitioner? For the role I'm in now as a primary care provider, the scope of my practice wouldn't have changed; but I would have had twice as much debt if I'd chosen the pediatrician route.

I work at an FQHC. FQHCs are health centers for underserved, high-risk populations and are sustained by federal funds. All patients are accepted here, and we take many types of insurance, but we serve primarily a Medicaid population.

Getting funding as an FQHC means there are some rules: providers are required to have a very high patient load; we have no cancellation policy; and we can't collect any money—we can't even charge $5 to someone who is a frequent no-show. We are overbooked to make sure we're seeing the minimum number of patients every day. If we have a lot of no-shows even more patients are added onto our schedules. There are five clinics here. I work in the clinic that has the highest percentage of uninsured patients. My patient population are primarily undocumented, recent immigrants from Honduras, El Salvador, and Guatemala. I speak only Spanish at work. I speak English at work only once or twice a day.

As a pediatric primary care provider, I see newborns, infants and children, and adolescents for well visits and sick visits. Depending on the season, my days are split roughly 50–50 between seeing children for well and sick visits. In the summer there are more well visits and in the winter there are more sick visits.

I also coordinate the care of patients with complex conditions. I work mostly on weekdays. My first patient is scheduled at 8:30 a.m.; my last patient at 4:00 p.m. My goal is to leave the clinic by 5:00 p.m. I usually do one and a half to two hours of work at home each evening.

Aside from scheduling a few 30-minute appointments each day when a child's healthcare needs are complex—for example, if a child has epilepsy or another syndrome that requires a lot of care—I am scheduled to see patients every 15 minutes. Those 15-minute slots apply whether the patient is a newborn, a teenager, someone coming in for an intrauterine device, or something else. And that's hard. That is certainly not enough time and patients feel rushed

For most of these visits I have to speak with the patient, examine the patient, treat the patient, and then document it all. Then I have to bill for it appropriately and update the medical history, which takes extra time for each patient I see. Patients call and leave messages, so I have to go through those. I also have incoming faxes and telephone encounters, which are virtual visits that we don't bill for. I spend a lot of time on these virtual visits when I'm not actually with a patient. I'm interpreting their lab results, prescribing their medication, telling them when I want to see them again, what needs to change, what specialists they need to see before they see me again, etc. And then I also get an influx of new referrals who are coming in.

To maintain what's referred to as my "productivity" I'm supposed to see between 21 and 22 patients a day. [Since the time Ruby and I talked, she says that number has increased by an additional two to four patients a day. ES] My goal is to try to see 21 patients by the end of the day. When I come in in the morning, I have 26 patients on my schedule, sometimes 28. When it's raining I have more no-shows. On a nice day when school's out people come more often. The weather matters a lot. Where my patient population comes from, which includes a lot of immigrants, they don't leave the house when it rains. It's something of a shock when I call them and say, "Where were you today?" and they say, "It's raining." When you're 23 and have multiple children under the age of eight and you don't have a car, there's not a lot of motivation to show up and hear about your kids' illnesses. Appointments with our nutritionist have a very high no-show rate.

I've been here for a year and a half now. I'm unable to have the kind of visits I was trained to have in school and that I anticipated doing in 15 minutes. So, what I'm learning to do is prioritize and bring people back. When a patient comes in and says, "I have headaches and I want birth control pills and I also get these abdominal cramps and sometimes when I'm typing my pinky hurts," I have to ask them what their priorities are because theirs may be different from mine. Sometimes I have patients who are not getting their asthma controller medications and are having exacerbations. In those cases, I try to squeeze two things into one visit.

A lot of what's involved in helping parents is to bring them back again and again. I'll say to a parent, for example, "Today is Tuesday. I'm going to check on how your child is breathing, and I want you to meet a social worker. And then I'm going to see you next Tuesday. And then we're going to check how he's breathing again. And then I want you to meet with an insurance navigator." So, I make sure there's care coordination, make sure parents have lots and lots of follow-up appointments so they can physically be in the clinic. When they're in the clinic they can see a variety of providers. However, because of the way patients are overbooked there often isn't time in my schedule to be seen for weeks or even months.

This is my first job after nursing school. I think as long as I'm in this area I'd like to stay here. The mission of the organization is well aligned with my personal career mission, which is to serve the underserved and to provide excellent care regardless of a patient's ability to pay.

I also teach nursing students once a week. That's been really great and has been bringing me a lot of joy. I'm able to give students a taste of the non-textbook healthcare world.

My career dominates my life but I'm trying to find work–life balance. Right now, my full identity is as a nurse practitioner. It's not as a girlfriend or a sister. I'm trying to figure out how to keep my professional identity and still maintain a healthy romantic relationship and familial relationships.

On Joy in Work

I've been thinking a lot about joy. I feel joy in my job when I hear a patient say, "Thank you!" Or when I can see the lightbulb go off for a newborn's mother, who says, "Oh, *that's* the breastfeeding latch! That no longer hurts me." Or when a parent says, "I totally understand why you used this medication—and you're right, because my son *has* only gone to the hospital one time in the last six months, that's awesome!"

Work–Life Balance

At the end of the day I think what brings me joy—not just at work but in my career—is finding work–life balance. I am very happy when I go to work. I see my patients on time, I'm able to give my patients what they need. When my patients don't have health insurance and they need to see a specialist and that's not an option for them it's frustrating. When I have a good day and I'm able to give my patients what they need, when I'm able to go home and finish my notes in a timely fashion and then go to yoga, run an errand, or walk the dog *that's* when I feel joy. I say, "Okay, I've done what I needed to do for my patients, *and* I've taken care of me." I feel this about once a week.

On Money and Joy

I do think there's a relationship between money and joy. I read some research recently showing that nurse practitioners at my clinic are paid well below market value for this area, which made me feel unappreciated. I expect, where I work, to get paid at the bottom of the spectrum. But we are paid *below* the bottom of the spectrum. I wrote an email and we did get a raise. It's hard to feel joy when you don't feel appreciated.

People leave because they're not making enough. There's a very high rate of burnout and people leave for economic reasons. You can make at least 25% more, if not 30% more, if you go into private practice.

What Diminishes Joy

"Productivity"-Based Evaluation

What diminishes joy in work for me is the way providers are evaluated based solely on the number of patients we see. It doesn't matter if I saw six patients just for flu shots and didn't even have to look at them, or whether I saw six patients for 30-minute visits to coordinate very complex care that kept them out of the emergency room. It doesn't matter. We're evaluated purely on the number of encounters. My "productivity" is measured in terms of the number of patients I'm supposed to be seeing and the percentage of patients I am seeing.

Our clinic determines the number of patients we need to see based on what we have to bill to sustain the clinic. I think all the staff is extremely frustrated that this is the way we're being evaluated. We have every single room occupied all the time. One thing I love about my clinic is that we have a health promotion team, we have nutritionists, we have all these great resources. But resources don't bill; it's up to us, the primary care providers, to bill. How we bill and the grants we get are what keep the whole clinic afloat. So, at the end of the day, they want numbers. When a provider at our clinic has under 95% productivity, four hours of administrative, or leave, time is taken away.

Stress

I feel tension between meeting my patients' needs, the administration's needs, and my own needs when my boss tells me I'm "only" at 94% productivity. Isn't it more important that I'm doing an excellent job for my patients? That's very frustrating. My boss is very flexible and says, "I don't care. I just want you to know that your productivity is technically low."

I think the greater point of tension comes from trying to meet my patients' needs and my own needs. I'm technically on paid time off this week. I'm not seeing patients but I'm still checking my labs every day, I have all these calls coming in—and I'm trying to help my sister breastfeed, to help my sister learn to be a mom, and literally I'm getting messages from patients and saying, "Aaaaah!"

My stress level at work goes up and down. There are always hours each day when my heart is beating very fast and I'm thinking, *how am I doing this?* and I look at my watch and see my heart rate and I am shocked. That's why I'm trying to work on mindfulness, do more yoga, be more self-aware. But it goes in phases—on some days I'll have two no-shows in a row. Or my referrals have gone though and everyone's labs are normal. And that's great. So, my stress level really fluctuates from day to day. On Mondays, everyone always comes to their appointments because they've been waiting through the weekend— so on a stress scale of 1 to 10 with 10 being the most stressful, Mondays are 8s and 9s. And sometimes on a Wednesday I can get it down to a 5 or 7.

None of the upper management works in the clinic so they don't get it. The CEO was in the clinic a few weeks ago and it was one of those days when I was at a two or a three and I thought, *oh, are you kidding me? He caught me sitting down at my desk. I never sit down at my desk!* I've seen the CEO in the clinic once in a year and a half.

Reflections

There is something upper management of the clinic could do to enhance my joy in work. They could reduce the patient load so we would have more time with our patients. That's the most important thing. More than a pay raise, more than anything. Everyone consistently raises this with administration and it's never even an option. They shut us down. They say the clinic can't function if we don't meet our productivity goals. The whole organization's budget is based on the assumption that all the providers are going to make 100% productivity. That's how people burn out and are miserable.

I think upper management acknowledges our problems, but they acknowledge these problems only because we complain about them. They see our problems as fires they have to put out, not as ongoing deficiencies that are reducing our sustainability. They don't want to make changes to make this a safe working environment because they see the need, but because the providers, primarily physicians and nurse practitioners, complain.

A lot of my families come from environments where they've never had access to consistent healthcare, so care coordination with specialists isn't always intuitive. I tell them, for example, "You have to see an endocrinologist for the thyroid issue but you have to see a neurologist for the seizures." Managing all that is really difficult. I think all of my patients would benefit from seeing a social worker, but we only have one social worker at each clinic because social work doesn't bring in money. And one social worker is not enough.

These families don't understand the system. The parents of my patients who are eligible for Medicaid haven't been educated about how to renew their insurance. How to keep their insurance from lapsing. How to take advantage of their insurance so they can go to the dentist. Many, many of my parents have first- and second-grade educations and can't read or write. So, my population needs more social work interventions.

Advice

My advice to my bosses is, ask for feedback. When upper management makes decisions, they make decisions based on what they think makes sense without checking with providers whose jobs are going to be impacted. Asking us for and listening to our feedback, even if they don't act on it, would make us feel listened to and appreciated.

My advice to colleagues is, stand up for yourself. For example, I didn't like the way school forms were being handled so I spoke up and they changed the process. I am a bit of a squeaky wheel. And being a squeaky wheel works. It gives you good outcomes. If you don't bring up a problem it will continue.

The federal government should provide healthy school lunches and universal pre-K. If the government could do these two things, children would be healthier, and I'd be able to see fewer patients. I'd say, "Wooo-hooo!" How am I supposed to manage all my four-year-old patients with obesity who weigh 60 pounds, when they're going to go to kindergarten and get fast food twice a day, every day? They eat breakfast and lunch in school and get junk food for both meals.

70. Raymond J., MS, Emergency Medical Technician, Director of Operations for an Ambulance Transportation Company, and Captain for an Emergency Medical Services Provider

Raymond J., MS, is an emergency medical technician (EMT) and director of operations for an ambulance transportation company in a multi-ethnic, working class city with a population of about 280,000. The median household income in this city is low and the rate of poverty, high. He works 24/7 to keep his company afloat, provide for the needs of his staff, and respond to emergencies. In a job with constant stressors, Raymond works hard to recognize his joy while wondering whether the rewards are worth the cost.

Medicine was something I always wanted to do. I knew people were always going to get sick and would need someone to take care of them. The prestige of "Oh, you're a doctor. We have a doctor in the family," and my parents pushing me because they wanted me to be the best I could be, pointed me in that direction.

I'd always been very good at school. I had just finished high school and my plan was to go to medical school. I was working at a retail location in town when I saw ads for volunteer EMTs. The next weekend I took a cardiopulmonary resuscitation (CPR) class because when I called, someone said I needed to have that basic skill first. I did that on a Friday. The following Saturday I started working in healthcare and never looked back.

My very first time out—I worked late Saturday overnight—the ambulance was dispatched to a motor vehicle crash on a small residential street that I had been on many times. When we arrived, a car was rolled over, flipped upside down, and I was hooked right then and there. This is a gritty city, one of the largest areas for emergency medical services (EMS) in the country and is busy with all types of calls. As a kid, I was never one of those people out on the street. I went to school, came home, did my homework, and played in the backyard. When I went to sleep at night, I figured most the world went to sleep as well. This experience opened my eyes to so many things—the world does not go to sleep as I so naively thought!

I don't think I ever really decided not to go to medical school. It just evolved that way. Good schools are very, very competitive. I had the opportunity to go to medical school offshore but at the time, I didn't want to leave home. I had never really been away on my own. I lived at home until I was married at thirty something. It's just our culture—we don't "kick" the kids out at 18. Even now that I'm married with kids, my parents would still love for all of us to live together. I never really wanted to go away and leave everybody and everything. I took the MCATs a couple of times, but my scores were not high enough to get into a competitive program at a home-based school—144 open spots for 2,200 applicants is extremely tough. I did a dual degree and got my graduate and undergraduate degrees in four and a half years, so I figured I was still ahead of everybody else.

When I worked on becoming an EMT in 2001 I was enrolled in the summer accelerated program. It was four months of school, a total of about 200 plus hours of training. I was in the classroom, went to lectures, did the hands-on practicums. I started this when I was a freshman in college. I've been an EMT since 2001. In my first job I started off as a volunteer, working my way up to sergeant, lieutenant, and then captain.

I've been in my current job since late 2005. When I started here, we only had two ambulances. Now we have ten and have the capability of providing specialized services.

We didn't have any contracts or accounts, basically the two ambulances were parked in a garage. All the things we've built and accomplished, we've built since I've been here. I often say, "It isn't my company as I am not the owner nor did I put down the money to start the company, but in every other way—it's my company." I've always felt, *keep it moving forward-forward-forward.* The clock keeps on tickin'—then I look back 15 years later and realize how much I've accomplished for this company.

As I get older, I sporadically find myself wondering if I've been wasting my life or just going through the motions. I never really decided that this is what I wanted to do, and still today, I don't really know if this is what I want to do for the rest of my life.

What My Job Entails

Our company is capable but does not provide "street" EMS. At companies that provide street EMS, people call the 9-1-1 system, the police or a regional dispatch center, and EMS will go out. People will call for anything traumatic or medical—it could be a traffic accident, shooting, stabbing, abdominal pain, or even a headache—anything at all. At our company, because we're a private service, we have contracts with certain facilities so most of our 9-1-1 calls are from those facilities.

My primary function is as an EMT, responding to emergency and nonemergency calls for medical transports. In my position as director of operations I of course have administrative duties, and I do some work in human resources, scheduling, recruiting, inventory, quality assurance, dispatching, and maintenance. I wear many hats. I manage as well as respond.

My hours are every single day all day long. Monday-Friday I'm here every day. Saturdays and Sundays, I don't come to the building unless something unexpected happens. If I don't have to be on a truck or out in the field, I don't necessarily have a set shift start time, but that doesn't mean I'm not working. Some guys think I get to come in as late as I please and I get to leave early. But they conveniently seem to forget that if I'm not here, the phone is attached to me at the hip as if it were an extra appendage. I carry two cell phones with me wherever I go. I get so many calls and emails, although nowadays it is more texting than anything. I take care of so many things at random hours of the day that sometimes I think I should be the definition of multitasking. Part of this is my fault, maybe even a little obsessive-compulsive on my part, but you know what they say, too many chiefs, not enough Indians? Here it's one chief.

Whether it's an issue of restocking, defective equipment, an accident involving the vehicle or crew, a problem with a patient, staff member, or anything else, the phone is always on. I'm on call every night, too. I get calls all the time. I've been doing it for such a long time that it has just become the norm. The only difference is now that my wife and I have young kids at home, I put the phone on vibrate. But I still hear it. I am always available. I always pick up the phone. If someone's calling me at 2:00 a.m. or 3:00 a.m. they're not calling to shoot the breeze. So, I'll answer the phone. I'm really always on.

We take patients to hospitals, nursing homes, doctors' appointments, dialysis centers, etc. But we're not constrained to one specific location. We cover multiple counties throughout the state and have even transported a couple of patients to neighboring states. It's nice to be able to get outdoors and interact with different people. That's what the guys and I like best. It's easy to get complacent when you're always going to the same place, seeing the same nurses, the same doctors. It's nice to build rapport with them but it's also very beneficial for one's personal growth to see how different people in different areas do things.

There are a lot of private companies in this area that do what we do or offer similar services, so sometimes finding good employees can be challenging. You have to look at the environment, the equipment, the relationships, and the interactions you have with your bosses. To some people you're just a number. Here, everybody has a name. I consider us a little family. I think it's a great benefit to be able to make an employee feel like a person and not just a number or name on a schedule. As much time as I spend here, I think of our building as my home more than my house is my home. I try to be friendly and make everybody feel welcome. It is human nature to want to do better for ourselves. Inevitably throughout the years people have left to go to other places where they perhaps made a little more money. Some have never returned, some went in different directions completely leaving the field, but many have returned. In fact, about half of our current work force has been with me since 2007. I think that says a lot about a place and the people who make it run.

On Joy in Work

Sometimes I do feel joy in work. I was once called to a home where a three-day-old baby had stopped breathing and became unconscious. The parents were obviously frantic. We immediately began treating the infant and rushed the baby to the hospital where he was breathing and alert by the time we got there. We made the front page of the paper. That was very rewarding. Not because we made the front page of the paper, but because we saved a three-day-old baby.

Sometimes we have patients who have certain medical conditions or present as very lethargic and so unresponsive we can't even rouse them. Then we do something simple like administer oxygen and a couple of other things, and by the time we get to the hospital they're alert and talking when they weren't responsive ten minutes prior to those interactions. Things like that are rewarding because I know I did something positive; it's the fast-paced, quick-thinking interactions that keep me going. We often see people at their worst moments. Knowing that we had a positive outcome is a rush.

I went out on one of my very first calls as an EMT when I was 17. The older guys on the truck didn't want me to see it. An 80-year-old man had stabbed himself and was lying in a basement in a pool of blood with the knife still stuck in his chest. The only time I'd ever seen anything like that was in the movies. It really does happen and look like that. But not every call is like that. It may be that a car has rolled over so many times to the point where you can't recognize the car, and they have to cut the car apart to get the person out. It may be that a guy has had half his head blown off from a gunshot (yes, I've encountered that as well). It may even be a simple cardiac arrest or a drug overdose. It's an adrenaline overload when we get those patients to the hospital alive.

Sometimes I feel we don't really save people, we simply prolong death; and while on some level this is true, knowing that we were able to transfer the patient to a higher or definitive level of care while they were still technically alive (due to our intervention) is amazing. That's the rewarding part. I feel that I've made a difference.

Sometimes people are very thankful. Sometimes people are upset or angry. Sometimes we do CPR and we "hurt" someone—when we're doing chest compressions, we can crack a patient's ribs, possibly causing further complications. Family members get upset because in the process of saving their loved ones we potentially introduced a new injury. Similarly, when CPR is performed correctly, it needs to be done on a hard or rigid surface. If the patient is on the bed or on the couch or whatever the case may be, the first thing we do is pull them onto the floor or another hard surface to avoid chest recoil while rendering care and providing optimal compressions. Someone will ask, "Why are you putting my mother on the floor?" In that moment of emotional distress, they don't know what's going on and on TV they don't see it like that. Sometimes things of that nature are frustrating because the average layperson doesn't understand, but it's nice when we get saves.

Sometimes I feel joy sitting in the office and doing office work. I mean, it needs to get done so I may as well enjoy it. After so many hours on a truck day after day, it is nice to have a day where you push papers around instead of a stretcher. Like everything else, that feeling is often short-lived, especially when the weather outside is nice. I love not being tied down to a desk every day and being able to roll down the windows and be out on the road, driving around, interacting with people. We go to so many different hospitals and facilities that we're not stuck in a single location. Being mobile has always been an appeal of the job.

On balance, weighing the positives and the negatives, I'd say I'm happy in what I do. I'll go a couple of days in the office doing all of the administrative tasks, often getting really frustrated due to the sheer amount of behind-the-scenes work that needs to be done to make the place run. Then one day I'll jump on the truck and be one of the guys. I tell the guys, "When I'm on the truck, I'm not your boss. You and I are just two co-workers." And we have a great day. We laugh and joke around. Some of our patients are regulars so they're kind of like family. They're stable enough and we'll have these conversations with them. If I haven't seen them in a few weeks they'll ask me, "How's your family?" Because they remember. That makes up for some of the bad times. On top of everything, this job affords us the ability to make lifelong friendships. When you're stuck in an ambulance with someone for 10–12 hours a day, you're bound to bond over something. Some of my closest friends have turned out to be some of my co-workers.

On Money and Joy

I know money is not happiness, but I look at it in terms of before the kids and before the family. Kids are really expensive. I start looking at what used to be enough and now realize I need to make a little bit more. But the job I have doesn't necessarily have to give me more. The pay rate is what the pay rate is. I can ask, but I feel badly when I ask and I'm told no for whatever reasons, especially when I'm on both sides of the fence, as a manager and an employee. I sometimes feel I'm worth more than I'm valued. Why should I have to ask for more money? Doesn't my work speak for itself? I hate relating appreciation to money, money doesn't make everything better. It doesn't make up for all the late nights at work, the constant phone calls, the stress and headaches of running a company, but it does on some level afford me the confidence of knowing I can one day put my kids through college.

Sometimes I wonder, *to get paid what I get paid now—and not have to deal with all the headaches and all the behind-the-scenes stuff and have more free time—would it be worth it?* Sometimes I really think it would be. My wife and family push me to go somewhere else and be happy. What if I were to go somewhere else, knowing that when I leave at 5:00 p.m. I'd have no responsibilities until 9:00 the next morning, the phones wouldn't ring, and I wouldn't have to rush in on a weekend, for the same amount of money? Money doesn't buy happiness, but free time does.

I go home many times and sit down at the computer at night just to try to catch up on some of the charts. And that's when I think, *Really? This is what it's like, and for what? How much am I bringing home at the end of the week? How much personal or family time did I actually lose—because even though on paper I look like a 40-hour-a-week guy, I'm not.*

What Diminishes Joy

I sometimes feel an overwhelming sense of frustration because there are so many things that my particular job entails. I live with a lot of sticky notes. I make lists and everything gets done and gets done well. Sometimes, I feel I can't give everything 100%, but I know I can't afford not to give it my full attention and I find myself staying later and later trying to get things done. I'd expend more energy having to go back and correct something I'd already done than if I'd spent the time to do it right in the first place.

Lack of Time

Sometimes I get frustrated because I have so much going on at the same time and I don't have enough hours in a day. A regular employee might come in at 9:00 a.m. and go home at 7:00 p.m. They might have a couple of extra jobs to do but there's no more responsibility. That's it. I have to make sure that all happens, and that the employees still have a job to come back to the next day. That there's a schedule made, equipment available, etc. Things don't magically happen on their own, showing up for work and having everything ready for you. I often wonder what it would be like to just be one of the regular guys. No responsibilities. Tell me when to start, tell me when to go home, and that's it.

When there so many things going on, everyone is pulling me in different directions, and I don't have five minutes to breathe, that is my definition of hell. I can't catch up fast enough. People look at me and depend on me and are standing there asking, "What's next? What do you want us to do?" Somebody has to dispatch them, somebody has to make sure the trucks are repaired and stocked, the insurances are paid, so many different things. I can't slack off.

When I first started back in 2001, I was at the volunteer squad for maybe six months. And in those six months I had a position as an officer right away. Obviously, I was doing something right, excelled, and rose quickly. I've always gravitated toward leadership. I didn't look for it, but it was placed in my lap. If I were to leave here and go somewhere else, it probably would only be a matter of time before I would be managing or had extra responsibilities again.

Lack of Appreciation

I go through periods when I don't feel appreciated. I don't always need a thank you. But understand that when you come to work and things are ready for you and there are no problems, that takes a lot of time and effort on my part. Yes, it's my job. But acknowledgment would be nice from time to time.

Loss of Family Time

What takes away from the joy is sometimes losing out on my family time and personal life. For example, if I were a regular guy who just came in from 9:00 a.m. to 5:00 p.m., I could schedule my family events around those hours. But when there's a bad snowstorm and everybody's home from work, police, fire, and EMS still have to work. It doesn't matter if it's a holiday, we work. And because I wear so many hats, even though I may not be on the ambulance doing patient care that day, I still have to manage the company. I still have to be around. I still have to be available. So sometimes I lose out on things like family gatherings or events because of work duties. That takes away from the joy of it.

Hospital Interactions

We let dispatch know that we're coming to the hospital with the patient and provide whatever treatment we can in the ambulance. When we get to the hospital, we go to the front desk and usually a charge nurse is there. She's going to take the information:

"Who are you bringing me?"

"A 70-year-old male, cardiac arrest."

She puts that information into the computer, assigns a nurse and an available room. When we get into that room and transfer the patient over, we can give a little bit more detail about the patient: what we found, what the complaints were, what we did, any intervention we provided, and whether the patient responded negatively or positively to it. Over the years, with increasing familiarity, they ask those questions not in a second-guessing sort of way, but as if they value what we're telling them; we've earned their respect and they feel we know what we're doing.

But, here's the flip side, which happens often: We're supposed to take vitals on every patient who comes into the ambulance. How else would we know if they're stable? When we get to the hospital, we give them the patient's vitals, then they start doing their hospital assessment. If they get vitals or assessments that are totally different from what we gave them, they'll ask, "What happened to the patient? You told me he had normal blood pressure; we took his blood pressure and it is really high. What happened in that 10- or 15-minute ambulance ride to spike the patient's blood pressure?" Things happen but if that happens a couple of times, they will start losing faith in us or trusting us. When we bring a patient to the hospital, they're going to make sure they double-check everything before they let us leave because we've given the impression of not being very good at our job.

The patient's condition can change quickly depending on what their situation is. But usually it won't be that big of a change. If the person's blood pressure is high, and I give the hospital a high number and they get a similar number, that's one thing. But if I tell them the patient is stable with a normal or low blood pressure and then for whatever reason the blood pressure takes off, that creates the impression that my partner and I didn't provide good patient care. The hospital staff jumps to that conclusion, asking "How did you not see that this patient was visibly having these problems?"

I was once with a patient on the ambulance; I spoke to her the whole time and gave what I thought was good patient care. I asked her all the right questions and she said she was in no pain. We got to the hospital, and the doctor was there. The doctor specifically asked the patient, "Are you having any chest pain?" And she said, "Yeah, my chest hurts a little bit." Now, mind you, we asked because it was a cardiac call. When we asked her the question, the woman mentioned no chest pain. As soon as the doctor asked her, she said, "Chest pain." The doctor gave me a look that said, "Really?" Implying that I had missed something. This doesn't happen with doctors who know me well. Over the years I've built that relationship and that level of trust. They know I do the proper thing. If I go to the same hospital but there are new doctors there, they may roll their eyes, but at least the nurses know me.

Going through experiences like that has made me a better EMT because I have learned to ask the patient specific questions and to keep asking. At the time, did I think my partner or I did anything wrong? There are always two of us on the ambulance. If I have a problem my partner can give a suggestion. We both agreed on the care we provided in that case and we know we did the right thing. But to the doctor who doesn't know—he hasn't spent the last 20 minutes with this patient, he has no idea—he just asked, "Chest pain?" She said, "Yeah," that changes the whole dynamic and the scenario that follows.

Condescension and Disrespect

On the hierarchy, paramedics are above EMTs. EMTs are the first responders. Anything happens, we're the first ones on the scene to render medical aid. We can't give medications and we can't start IVs in my state. So, we call paramedics who are a bit above us, and they can give certain medications and provide advanced life support. If we get to the call and it's a patient who is bleeding severely or we can't control their breathing, for example, we'll call the paramedics and they'll be able to give patients certain treatments or medications prior to getting to the hospital. Things are evolving in the field of EMS and what EMTS can do in the field—but for now, we still rely on the paramedics for more advanced treatments.

Sometimes we call paramedics and because of their demeanor we feel we're bothering them, but they have to come out—that is their role in EMS. If we call them and they say the patient can go with us (basic life support) and doesn't need the higher level of care (advanced life support), some of them look at us smugly and ask, "Why are you wasting our time?" That's their job. Needless to say, we get that reaction more often than not.

Before someone is a paramedic, they have to be an EMT. For example, someone could have been an EMT for ten years and took a couple of classes and then became a paramedic. Now they're too good for everybody else. They forgot where they came from. People do that all the time. Even some people who were EMTs and went to nursing school and who are now nurses. Sometimes it's as if they're saying, "Oh, well, you're just a dumb EMT." As a regular EMT, they were doing what I do until they went to school; they've done well for themselves. They became a nurse, that's great. But they shouldn't forget where they came from. Some people are perfectly content with what they have chosen to do and shouldn't be looked upon with disdain for their choices.

EMTs in our state are all state certified. We take the same test; we wear the same patches wherever we go. The norm is to have a company patch on the left shoulder and a state patch on the right shoulder. No matter what agency we work for, whether it's as a volunteer in a small town, a public municipal setting, corporate hospital, or the fire department, we all wear the same EMT patch. But EMTs themselves look down on other EMTS depending on what agency they work for. So, for example, an EMT who works for the town or city may think he is better than an EMT who works at a transport service or for a local squad. They all have the same patches and basic life support certification, so what's the difference? We went to the same schools; we had the same training. The only difference is that I can say I've done 1,000 calls and you've only done 300 calls, so I have more experience than you. But at the end of the day that basic training is exactly the same. The certification is the same. There's a lot of competition among EMTs. And we're at the bottom of the healthcare totem pole.

Going up the healthcare ladder, we have issues when we work with certain nurses when we go to nursing homes. First, there are registered nurses (RNs) and LPNs. The LPNs are lower than the RNs. And within that dynamic there is a constant need to prove one's status. We bump heads all the time. We ask them what's going on with the patient and they don't want to tell us anything: "You're just here to transport. Just do your job." Or "What's with all the questions, are you a doctor?" This patient is going to the emergency room and when we get to the emergency room, I have to tell the receiving nurse what's going on with this patient. So, often, we have to read all paperwork and try to figure out what's going on with the patient because the LPNs feel they are superior and don't want to give us information.

Everybody wants to think they're more than they are. At the end of the day we're just here to make sure this patient receives proper care in the prehospital setting until we are able to transfer care to the emergency department. I can't count the number of times a hospital nurse mocked a nursing home nurse or a doctor's office nurse. It's the same thing wherever we go, regardless of the profession. I've even heard of doctors mocking other physicians because some are MDs while others are doctors of osteopathy.

Costs

I'm part of management. When someone first starts doing this kind of work it's always about the patient and patient care. But whenever they move away from hands-on and start moving to higher positions, whether it's as a supervisor or manager or whatever it is, it's about efficiency and turnover because now they have different people to respond to. The most important thing is saving a patient's life, no question, no matter what equipment we have to use and no matter what it costs. A regular employee may get a "win" call—the patient did well, and the employee can go home. But managers have an operating budget. Money has to come from somewhere.

We do a chart for every patient we see here. There are several hundred charts on hold because the patients have no insurance—this has to do with the demographics of our city. So, even though we just responded to several hundred calls, these were basically several hundred free jobs. We wasted fuel, equipment. It's tough. At the end of the day healthcare is a business. At entry level, people don't see it that way. But as soon as someone like me moves up, there is all this added stress of making sure not that people are happy, but that the lights stay on. An ambulance running all day long, how much fuel do we waste, how much wear and tear? What do we do? We try to take it day by day. We've tried to restructure, and we do what we can to cut costs. But there's really little to no profit. We basically keep afloat and hope for better days when reimbursement rates increase, a day that never seems to arrive.

Advice

My advice to my bosses and colleagues is, take it one day at a time. That's one of the luxuries I don't have. I have to think and plan at least three or four days in advance. Today's Monday? I'm already thinking ahead to Friday and Saturday. Those who can live in the moment might be happier.

Don't forget your roots. Remember where you came from. Most of us started off as volunteers. Some people who today are doctors, firefighters, police officers, medics, and professional EMTs who work in this city all started volunteering like many of us. But the minute they were hired elsewhere, they were talking badly about the organization and making fun of the people who are still here, forgetting that the organization and its leadership were the ones who afforded them the experiences that brought them to where they are now.

Don't denigrate the people who are under you, who may not have had the opportunities you did. When you're condescending to them it makes them second-guess themselves. Yes, you went to school to be a paramedic. You had approximately 1,200–1,500 hours of training versus my 200 hours, of course you're going to know more about certain aspects of patient care. Same as the doctor knows more than a nurse. But don't make me seem insignificant and second-guess what I'm doing. That's a problem we encounter all the time. Condescension builds animosity, makes us feel insignificant and unsure of ourselves and the care we intend to provide. In this job, because we can literally be sent to any type of emergency one can think of, we cannot afford to be hesitant or unsure in our actions. In the prehospital setting, a team approach between EMTs, paramedics, police, fire, and other first responders always works best for the communities and residents we serve. Work is paved with stepping-stones. Everybody starts somewhere.

71. *Wayne K., MPH, Part-Time Volunteer Emergency Medical Services Technician*

Wayne K., MPH, has been a part-time volunteer emergency medical services technician for ten years, since he was in high school. He has a BS in microbiology, an MPH
in infectious diseases, and is studying for his PhD in public health. Throughout high
school, college, and in the course of his healthcare career, he has volunteered as an
EMT. Burnout is common for career EMTs, Wayne explains—burnout resulting from
a combination of low pay, the need to work too many hours to make ends meet and
witnessing unspeakable trauma.

I got a BS in microbiology. My father is a physician. One of my brothers became a physician
and I was thinking I'd go the premedicine route and become a medical doctor. But after
doing some research into this while I was in college, I thought it wouldn't necessarily be
the lifestyle I would have enjoyed.

I remember having a conversation with my 65-year-old father. He told me if he were
my age, and in my shoes, with the state of the medical field being what it is today, he
would not go into medicine. He said he loves his job but considering the competition with
other physicians, the amount of debt involved in becoming a doctor, and the way the profession has changed in terms of work hours, he wouldn't do it now. That was a big factor
in helping me decide what I wanted to do career-wise. I eventually decided I wanted to go
into public health.

My EMS Journey

I was in high school when I decided I wanted to be an EMT. I have two brothers two years
older than me, and they thought they might want to go into medicine. Their high school
advisors told them to take this EMT course—they said it was a good way to get introduced
to the medical field, a good way to get experience. My parents signed them up and asked
me, "Why don't you take it, too?"

So, I just happened to be introduced to the class between my junior and senior year of
high school. It wasn't my active choice to look into it, but at the time I thought it was worth
seeing whether it was a route into medicine I'd want to take. At first, I was apathetic about
it and felt that I was just doing this because it was something to do in the summer. But over
the course of the class my feelings changed.

Storytelling is a big part of EMS and all of healthcare. Our instructor was a 30+ year
veteran of EMS and had seen the whole range of calls, all the different types. When you
work with EMS providers, no matter where you go, everyone likes to tell stories. Stories of
bad calls, stories of good calls. But over the course of the class, learning about the things
our instructor and his co-workers had seen piqued my interest—not only in pre-hospital
care but also in the medical field in general.

I got my EMT basic certification in 2008. Wherever I've worked as an EMT I've done so
as a volunteer, which is what I prefer. Everywhere I've been, whether in college or at home,
I've volunteered as an EMT. I still volunteer regularly as an EMT during the evenings and
overnight. I go to school part-time for my doctorate, I work full-time, and I work part-time
volunteering as an EMT. I've been an EMT for ten years now.

I used to volunteer a lot more before I was married. Right now, I work every Tuesday evening starting at 5:00 p.m. and then overnight and into the morning. At that time if we don't have any calls I can sleep, which I do, obviously, because I work a nine to five job. Before I got married, I volunteered a lot more hours and overnights. That has since decreased so I can stay sane. My wife and I met working as EMTs. We still work together on the ambulance on Tuesday nights.

One of the areas I work in is the neighborhood where I grew up. I don't live there anymore, but I like to be able to see the people I know who still live there. Sounds cheesy, but that's why I still do it. Being able to help other people occasionally, on a Tuesday evening, is satisfying.

The people I've met over time volunteering are truly lifelong friends. You see some of the worst things you've ever witnessed with them and it really makes you close. When you get to that level of seeing not-so-great things with other people, you share a different kind of bond. You know you're going to be friends with them forever. I met my wife there, so it turned out well. The man I consider my best friend is someone I met through that service. He was in my wedding party and I still eat lunch with him every other week. There are countless people I've met through EMS who I consider friends to this day.

How EMS Works

EMS is the name of the field—emergency medical services. When people use the term "EMT" they're talking about emergency medical technicians who practice EMT basics, which is what I do. Being an EMT requires taking a three- to four-month class to learn the general skills. There's a different level called "paramedics," which is usually a course of about a year or so; that is a bit more rigorous, allowing them to deliver more advanced levels of care. Paramedics and other EMTs work together in the general realm of EMS.

Say, for example, someone is in a restaurant and starts to have chest pains or what they think is a heart attack and calls 9-1-1. This is the general way things work: there's a dispatch center within our local area that will take our call. The operators take the information: what's going on and where we are. They pass that along to someone else in that center who will relay that information to our station, to a police station if they need it, and to a fire station if they need it to say, "At this restaurant there's an 80-year-old man complaining of chest pain." From there, I and whoever I'm working with get into the ambulance, start driving to wherever the call is, and when we get there do our medical assessment. Usually we do an initial assessment wherever the person is, if it's appropriate. If not, we do it on the way to the hospital.

This initial assessment entails getting an overall impression of the patient, seeing what their vital signs look like, what their symptoms are, and getting the story of what happened. Then, based on those vital signs and other information obtained by paramedics, we and the paramedics can give certain types of medications or start an intervention that may help that person before they even get to the hospital for more advanced care. Vital signs we look for include blood pressure, heart rate, and glucose levels. Paramedics look at the electrocardiogram (EKG), which gives an overall impression of how to treat and go about stabilizing the patient.

When we get a good idea of what's happening with the patient there's a standard protocol for calling the hospital emergency room. We can either call a certain number, or we can radio them to give them a general idea of what's going on and what we've done so far. That way they can prep the emergency room for a smooth transition to take over the patient's care. Where we take the patient depends on where our station is and on how critical the patient is. Some hospitals are better for trauma, some are better for burns, some are better for bone fractures. It really depends on what the situation is.

Whenever we walk into the emergency department we're directed to a room. If it's a critical patient the paramedic will give a report either to the nurse or to the physician as we're transferring the patient over. We organize what is otherwise a scattered story into a streamlined report—with only the relevant information the hospital staff needs to hear—and present it to hospital staff; this includes the interventions we provided and any changes that have occurred since we gave those interventions. From there, care is transferred, and we leave the hospital.

When we get to the hospital the hand-off can be both verbal and written, but most of the time it is verbal. There's a moment when the physician and the nurse are all ears, listening to the story in detail. If they have questions they'll ask. If we did anything like an EKG, we'll give them a copy and go over it with them. What happens at the hospital is really situation dependent.

After a while, running the same shifts over and over, bringing patients mainly to the same hospitals, we get to know the people in the hospital who are on the same shift as we are. I know the majority of the nurses who I give handover care to and usually the docs. This is especially true of the career EMS providers. For me, as a volunteer, this doesn't happen as often but if this is your everyday job you definitely see the same people over and over. After awhile, just as when working with your EMS partners, you get a flow with the hospital clinicians and you can develop understanding and trust.

In EMS there's always a ranking to determine who outranks who. There's always a chief, a deputy chief, and from there, there are crew chiefs, more senior EMS providers, and from there seniority essentially is based on the years one's been working in EMS. Everyone I've worked with really respects rank. So, if you ask them to do something, or tell them to do something, they respect that. People definitely feel comfortable voicing any concerns they have with superiors.

On Joy in Work

Joy in work means you're happy to show up at your job, you feel like you're making a change in whatever it is that you're doing, and that you enjoy the company of the people you work with. If I have those things together, that triad, then I'm happy with my job. These are aspects of my job right now.

On Money, Joy, and Burnout

I think there is a relationship between money and joy. I've done my own research into this relationship and what I've learned is this: you get to a certain level of income and then, at a certain point, increased money won't actually increase your joy. But working in EMS, I'm pretty sure 90% of EMS providers aren't volunteers—and they will tell you EMS providers are underpaid. As a volunteer I can't really speak to that, I'm doing it for free. Most basic EMTs start out at something like $10–12 an hour. Paramedics start out at $18 an hour, so it's not a very well-paid field considering the stress of calls and the things an EMT has to go through. Not to get political, but a lot of people say the minimum wage should be $15 an hour. The EMTs are saying, "We don't even make close to $15," so it's difficult.

There are a lot of burned-out people who feel overworked—they need to work more because they're not making enough money. And then they get exposed to and see some terrible things. You add the stress of not having enough money on top of the stress of the job, and I've seen a lot of burned-out people over time.

I'm sort of an anomaly when it comes to EMS. I'm a volunteer, I have a steady job, and I have a wife who also has a great job. Career EMS providers who work at that job every day suffer the stresses of EMS. Their life could be enhanced by better work hours, better shift schedules, and increased pay. It's those EMS providers who really do struggle.

What Diminishes Joy

In EMS there are sometimes difficult calls where the patient doesn't live through the call; in reality, you know there's nothing you could have done. But telling yourself that and really believing it are two different things. It's one thing to tell yourself, "There's nothing I could have done. This person was going to die regardless." But believing that is a whole other step.

Conflict among co-workers is always difficult. Dealing with co-workers who don't like to work with each other is a downer on the job. In my personal experience it's rare. I pride myself in saying I could get along with a rock. I've had people who have disagreed with decisions I've made, but on a professional level we still work together well. I've worked with people whose personal and political views I don't agree with, but I'm able to put those aside and work with them professionally. I don't think I've ever come across a person I can't work with. It's witnessing other co-workers who don't work well together—and in the majority of healthcare you work as a team—that happens sometimes. And if you're not working well with others then the care you provide doesn't work well, either.

Sometimes we see EMS success stories—we help people in need of medical aid, bring them to the hospital, and we're able to follow up with the hospital and see that they were discharged. But often we have people we call "frequent fliers." In EMS terms, this means we get the same patients over and over and over, week after week, with the same issue. We bring them to the hospital, they get the same care, the hospital sends them home, and that issue arises again.

There are different kinds of frequent fliers. There are the people who fall, who really just need assisted living or someone at home to help them and they don't have that. Nowadays there are people who are overdosing on drugs and opioids. I still remember a few years back, the same woman would call every single Sunday because she took too many drugs or was drug-seeking because she ran out of drugs. It was every Sunday on the dot. We knew exactly who it was, and we would go through the same process. Then one Sunday she didn't call, and two or three weeks later I found out she had overdosed and died.

As EMS providers we do what we're trained to do, which is to help people as best we can and get them to the hospital where, we hope, they can be treated. But there are people much smarter than me who study the failings of medical care post-hospital discharge; too often people don't have access to home healthcare or better skilled nursing facilities, and the same thing keeps happening over and over and over again. That's the point at which we sometimes feel we're not making a change.

Reflections

On Stress

All EMS providers are well aware of the stresses we go through. As someone who volunteers once a week, I feel out of place advising others on what to do because they are very well aware of the problems and how to fix them. It goes back to being overworked and underpaid.

What some people are good at doing and some people are not good at doing is forgetting and letting go of the very bad calls that we see, whether sad emotional calls or gruesome calls. Some people are better than others at letting these go and not bringing them home. For example, there was an emotional call where a child died unexpectedly and we were there, trying to console the family. We just witnessed a kid die. It's a lot to take in. Things like that are what I mean by bad calls and they can get emotional for the provider. And then we wonder if we said the right thing or realize we didn't know what to say.

On Debriefing to Reduce Stress

A good EMS partner will debrief with their partner after a hard call to talk about it. And there are people who are trained and certified to hold debriefing sessions. For a very bad traffic accident, for example, when a whole family is killed, most good EMS stations and good fire stations—because on these calls it's not just us, but firefighters and police officers who are there—provide certified people, usually social workers, to hold debriefing sessions the very next day. Everyone will be there and we'll talk about it, we'll get things off our chest, and we're allowed to say whatever we want. And it's good to have that, to talk with other people at our station and other people who were on the call. Research has shown that if you do that, and if you have partners who will do that with you, people don't hold onto those calls. They don't let it affect their lives as much. I've been lucky to work with my friends and with my wife. We've seen some bad calls and we're able to talk about it. I believe that has helped me and others I've worked with.

On Respect

I've only been a part-time EMT for the past ten years. There are people who dedicate their whole careers to EMS and to being paramedics. Working with those people as a volunteer, and working with police and firefighters, has given me the utmost respect for them. Because of what I've seen just as a part-time, casual volunteer EMT, I can only imagine what the career people who see it every day go through, and I wonder how they handle it. I have so much respect for those people and always will.

72.   *Anthony F., MD, Internist, Associate Medical Director for the Insurance
      Division of an Integrated Health System and Adjunct Associate
      Professor of Medicine*

Anthony F., MD, knew he wanted to be a doctor in second grade. He is passionate about internal medicine and working in partnership with patients to improve their health. Yet, as the effects of time pressure, economic pressure, the explosion of medical information, and other stressors cause medical students to choose more lucrative specialties, Anthony worries about the future of his field.

Let me give you a heads-up on my work ethic. My parents were born in 1914 and 1918. My mother was Russian, my father was pure Italian. I was born in 1955. My dad was a tool dye worker. My mother worked before we were born and then came the devotion of being a mother. Later she went back to work as a secretary in a private school.

They lived through the depression. You do not borrow money. You work hard, achieve the best you can, and run with it. And, by the way, your education is on us. You don't worry about it. The motto was, when you leave home, you do the best you can; be the best you can be in whatever you do.

This mentoring didn't come from parents who were professionals. They were low-middle class. Their priority was their kids. My sister and I did very well with their love and their emphasis on education, and their saying, "We want you to get ahead. We're not going to be lavish, we're not going to take a lot of vacations—we're going to save our money and have you get the education you need to get ahead." We saw that they were hard-working, determined individuals and my sister and I have carried this through. She's as hard a worker as I am. The emphasis was, again, be the best you can be. Don't settle for second. If you have that opportunity, go for it.

Why did I become a doctor? Believe it or not, I was in second grade when we were told to write our autobiography. I can still remember the yellow folder where I wrote, "I want to be a doctor." Now I look back and ask why. My parents just said to work hard. They would have supported me in whatever I decided to do.

My father's parents emigrated in 1902 from a gorgeous hill town between Bologna and Florence. My mother emigrated from outside of Kiev, also around 1902, and both families finally settled in the same city in America. My paternal and maternal grandparents spoke minimal English. But, fortunately, my father's cousin went to school to become a doctor of osteopathy and got ahead. This cousin, Dr. L., was made to feel like the idol of the family. Here's a doctor! Everyone else had barely enough money to get through high school before they had to go to work. I thought my father was very bright, but his father looked at him and said, "You're not going anywhere. You're going to work."

Knowing Dr. L.—how he treated everybody well, and the respect he had for people—probably made me want to be a doctor, made me feel that was the career path for me. Heck, I was only seven or eight years old.

I can look back on this now and see that the decision to become a doctor blended three qualities I think I have: first, I love science—I love always thinking there's more to learn; second, I like caring for people. I mean, when I'm in a relationship with anyone it's always, "What can I do for you?" And third is being fair and communicating well: explaining things, having rapport, and not thinking that because I have an MD I'm above other people.

My Professional Journey

Going to one of the top ten medical schools in the country changed my life. Seeing people who were disciplined and influential puts a little boost into things. You're saying, "I want to be the best" because these are people who have achieved and done well. I graduated from medical school in '81.

I got through with med school in '81, came out here, did my residency, spent a year teaching at the university, and then faced the dilemma of whether to go into a specialty. The university was suggesting I do a geriatric fellowship—they needed a geriatrician—so I went and looked at several programs but thought, *I just cannot be a geriatrician. I'm going to see enough old people being an internist and I need to have a little spark in my life.*

As soon as I decided not to do that, I got a phone call from someone who said, "Listen. We're a nine-person group, why don't you come and take a look at us?" I thought it was a good fit for me because in 1985, people who lived on the west side of this city had poor care. The hospital here was nicknamed "Death Valley." And I had this ambition, as a young doc coming out into this community, to improve care. At the same time, this area was low-middle class. And I thought, *this fits my roots.* I've also always had this idea that my hard-working parents also deserved the best healthcare available. It doesn't matter about your income, it doesn't matter about your skin color, everyone deserves the same care.

So, I joined this practice, which started in the '50s with one or two family practice docs. I became the 11th doc and then it grew to 40, 50 docs and over the past five years we've grown to 180 docs. We have multiple satellites throughout the area. There have been good times and bad times throughout all that, but I have a comfortable life.

What My Job Entails

I am an internist in private practice, a dying breed. I'm an associate medical director for the insurance division of an integrated health system. I've been doing this for about 14 years. I'm also adjunct associate professor of medicine at the local university.

As associate medical director in this organization I wear multiple hats. I've been part of utilization review and quality programs (especially for oncology); I sit on the pharmacy and therapeutics committee, both for the insurance division and the health system; I am the medical liaison for the insurance division reaching out to our providers in pathology, genetics, and oncology; and I'm also the developer of medical policies for the insurance division.

I still see patients in my office 80% of the time; being the associate medical director of the insurance division, believe it or not, is my part-time job. This speaks to the joy of being a physician *or*, how I try to maintain the joy in my work. I do this to fulfill the ideological dream I had when I was in training that has since been replaced by something else.

To fulfill my current obligation with quality compliance documentation, on Mondays and Fridays when I'm in the clinic alone, I'm in my office at 6:20 a.m. every morning. I spend more than an hour finishing dictation and doing paperwork until 7:30 a.m., when I start to see patients. Lunch for me is either in my car or 15 minutes at my desk as I develop aspiration because I'm eating too quickly. I'm back in my office from 1:00 until 5:00 p.m., and even on a Friday night I don't finish dictations until 6:30 p.m.

On Tuesdays, Wednesdays, and Thursdays I work the same schedule—6:30 a.m. until, typically, 12:30 or 1:00 p.m.; then I go to the insurance side and work typically from 1:00

until 7:00 p.m. Tomorrow I'll be working on policy development and so forth. Now, that's a lot. This is not what a typical doctor is going to do.

I do feel a tension between meeting my patients' needs, my own needs, the needs of my bosses and administrators, and the government. What do I do about it? I ride my bike a lot. My wife and I decided years ago not to have kids. That's why I'm in the office on Saturday and Sunday. But I still feel the expectations and burdens and need a way to relieve some of that stress.

I've learned I need to take blocks of time off in order to just escape. And you know what? I can come back in and feel that need for caring is resorbed back in me. I typically go away for two weeks but I've started to realize that maybe every three months I just need to take a three-day weekend. I'm trying to take four or five weeks off a year. Luckily for me, financially I'm fine.

On Joy in Work

Joy in work means fulfilling your own needs. My needs are to care for patients and to learn about both life and the body—which is, to me, absolutely amazing. How could I satisfy both of those needs any better than by being a physician?

You can toss into that I make a respectable income. Being an MD, you can choose whatever you want to do. That MD degree is your ticket to endless opportunity. You can do research, you can do clinical work, you can do administrative work. You could go into business. I chose all of those areas. I had the opportunity to be good at clinical work, to be an administrator, and also, possibly, to change the dynamics of healthcare not only for my patients but for my community. I work for the largest insurer in the state and sit on quality, pharmacy, and therapeutics committees, and write medical policies to determine appropriate care for one million people.

There are some docs now who limit their time with patients. The patient walks into the room and they ask, "What is the *one problem* that we have to deal with today?" I don't do that. I have a lot of years of experience, I try to show that I'm caring, but I also try to show patients that I'm complete. I want to know not only the patient's health history, but I want to make sure all their problems are addressed during that visit and recap. Internists take care of sick people. They take care of the worst diabetics, the heart failure—I don't turn anyone away. I tell my medical students that part of the excitement of the day is, I never know what's behind that door. A patient may be in for a routine follow-up on a blood pressure drug that I changed, but I still don't know what's behind that door. They may spring something on me, and I'll say, "I'm not sure." But you never know. Which is part of the excitement, and should be, instead of the doldrums.

My patient visit is a minimum of 20 minutes. "You have a sore toenail. But you know what? You're here for that toenail but I've got you here. Let's go over your screening, your meds, and let's get this going. Let's make sure we capture these important things." The docs who only schedule ten-minute appointments are not able to do that. They're in and out, there's a lack of caring, and they're doing that partly because they need to make the money. I tell people, "Listen. I should be able to take care of 90% of your problems. I'm not good at everything. I know when I need to send a patient to a specialist. I don't do that procedure. But overall, I should be able to handle most of your depression. Control your blood pressure. Manage your diabetes. Deal with your sore throat."

On the Art of Caring in Medicine

Take care of people the way you want to be treated. I recently had a hip replacement. Being in pain, being limited, and seeing how the provider I went to handled that experience was very good for me; now I can better appreciate what people who have an orthopedic procedure go through and I can give them advice.

The doctor I saw is an orthopedist, a very good doc. When I was in the room, his approach was, "Let's deal with you." It was not a rush. I was impressed that either he or his close assistant called me for four days after I left the hospital, every day. Now, when I make a subtle change during a patient's office visit, I have my medical assistant call and ask, within a week, "Was that change good for you?" That phone call makes such a difference to the patient who knows you care about them. That art, that caring of medicine, is being eroded because of the limited time and the focus on money, rather than the interest of the patient. I'm a pretty passionate doc and I see that this is just going to go away.

In medicine we are not treating people the way we want to be treated. That art, that caring, is being lost. In the past three or four years I've even stepped back and asked myself, *how am I communicating? How am I being energized? Do I feel this is a penalty or a burden in the office?* Patients are here to see me. I didn't make the appointment, *they* made the appointment. There's a reason why they're here—they're here because they want my help. Help or reassurance or confirmation. Patients are saying, in essence, "We trust you to help guide us on the path to a better life."

But docs are cutting back their time. Instead of a 20-minute appointment it's a 15-minute appointment or a 10-minute appointment. One cannot be complete, compassionate, and caring in ten minutes. It takes three or four minutes to warm up to somebody. You may only have this opportunity once a year to reach out to somebody and grab 'em. You may tell them, "Well, you're here for a cough or a problem with pain." You could regroup with them in three or four months and say, "We need to spend more time," but that patient may not do that. You need to get as much in as you can.

We hear the adages all the time, "What's the most important thing in your life, your money or your health?" It should be your health, right? Here, physicians are a conduit for people to achieve that. I have a cardiology buddy who always says, "It's an honor for us to have patients come and let us lead them." I think it's not only to lead them, but to be part of a team together. For example, what I do more lately in the office with patients who are, say, morbidly obese, is to sit down with them and say, "Here's my suggestion. What can we do?" I look at them and say, 'You know, we're a team. You're the athlete and I'm the coach. Now I can give you suggestions. I can set a plan for you but you're the one who has to do it. We're going to work on this together." And besides the caring, the trust, is taking that extra five minutes to look at them, sit next to them, touch them, and say, "This is important for you and for me."

I take care of and I'm also friends with a world-renowned liver specialist. I met him about five years ago when he was in town. Everybody knows him. We're driving to go fishing and he's answering his phone.

I say, "What are you doing?"

He says, "Well, I give all my patients my cell phone number."

I say again, "What are you doing? You have no life."

But then I realize that the number of patients who call him are few. He's not taking care of the urinary tract infection, the pneumonia, the cough. He's taking care of *you had a liver transplant and it was just done.* Now, the severity of the problem can be high, which is part of why he wants to deal with it; but it's not the volume of calls a family practice doc might get. If you're a family practice doc and you do this, I'm astonished.

What Diminishes Joy

What diminishes joy in work is the burden of being a doctor. The overwhelming responsibility, the feeling that people can call you up at any time and interrupt your life. As a doctor caring for people, I almost feel the need to let them do that or I'm going to feel guilty. There is a balance between being responsible and being burdened. I think the Internet's going to kill us. The notion of, "Email me anytime…." What's going on here? Twenty years ago, that didn't happen. Except for things I impose on myself, what's going to stop me from being happy is that I have no time.

There is so much interference with the medical professional now—from the government, other entities, patients' expectations, your quality rating, your economic piece, balancing time between family and work—something has to give.

Information Explosion

I'm thinking, while I'm driving to my office, *how much did I have to know in '81?* They say medical knowledge doubles every 7–10 years. When I look at what third- and fourth-year medical students who come to work with me have to learn, and what I try to teach, I think, *not only do I have to teach them the basics, but there is so much more they have to know today.* And then you realize why people go into specialties. Look at what docs in primary care are being asked to do now. One of the reasons people are not putting the effort into being a general internist anymore is that they are overwhelmed by the amount of information they need to know. Now we can also talk about economics or other reasons why these changes have occurred.

Physicians who lack confidence or experience could be intimidated by their patients now because a patient may have spent three hours looking up on the Internet one specific topic of concern to them. A doc who walks into that room is now in a little jeopardy because the patient may think the doc is not knowledgeable enough to make a determination about his or her medical issue. That's the time when the doc should say, "You know, I'm not sure about this, so we're going to have make a choice here. Either I'm going to get back with you on this because I want to confirm my thoughts, or I'm going to send you to the specialist." And I'm going to tell you what happens for family practice docs: for those docs who don't have the interest in science—and if you don't have the time or the determination to pursue learning because it interests you—you're going to make that a shorter appointment, you're going to feel, *I don't have the time to do this,* and you're going to send them to the specialist. And the patient is going to think, *boy, that interaction didn't go too well.*

There is something I'll call the umbrella rule—meaning, everything that happens to a patient, I should know about. But a lot of docs, whether because of money issues or family issues, don't want to be the umbrella anymore. They just want to be a spot for that patient. Maybe they want to be that hub, but then they just want to send people out along the spokes to get their care. And, therefore, you have patient dissatisfaction.

Government Interference

The Electronic Medical Record   Sixty percent of the reason physicians don't like what they do anymore is the EMR. Here's the Center for Medicare and Medicaid Services (CMS) saying, "Documentation is key to reimbursement." You don't know how many clicks and boxes I have to check in order to make sure that my note is complete enough to get reimbursed. That's why the docs are staring at the screen—to make sure that things are documented. And not only that, but did you do this with your diabetic patient? Is her blood pressure under control? Did you do the albumin to creatinine ratio? Did you check the A1C level? Did you do the eye exam? Did you examine their feet? You have to do this on every patient with diabetes or you're going to be dinged in your quality award. And you have all these alerts on your EMR that come up to ask, did you do this? That's just for your diabetic patients.

What about your Patient Health Questionnaire-9 (PHq9) or Phq2 for your depressive patients? Did you go over their family history? Did you document their alcohol and smoking? The documentation is driving docs away from caring because they have to do all this. And if they have to do all this, do they really have time to hold the patient's hand? And to say, "I'm listening to you and I care about you?"

Interference with Prescribing

Other frustrations caused by government interference mean I almost can't be a doc anymore. I wrote a prescription for narcotics and the pharmacist said, "I'm not going to fill it." The patient is telling me this. I looked at the patient and said, "They had no right to do that. I can tell you legally they had no right to do that. They should have called me, and they didn't call me." Now, they may have a directive from their national pharmacy director, but if they have a problem with the prescription that's between me and the patient. Your job as a pharmacist is to be a conduit and to fill it. And if you have a problem you should call me. Physicians need to be part of solutions. Having administration or the government just dictate decisions and not involve us will create further disappointment in our jobs.

Quality Metrics

What takes away from joy, in addition to how much you have to be available, is the quality survey. What I'm seeing is the government reducing reimbursement for primary care, saying we now have to meet certain quality metrics. Quality metrics are blood pressure, A1C, and are you giving patients their cholesterol medication? Now it's important how the patient scores you. The health plan asks, "Did you have to wait more than 15 minutes for your appointment?" I don't like to get a bad comment and I want to make sure patients have access to appointments with me. But think about 25 patients a day, and that I have to have them in the room and see them within 15 minutes of their appointment. That's an enormous burden that takes away the time and the caring. What the health plan *should* ask is, "Did the doc help me?" "Did the doc make the right diagnosis?" Between patients' expectations of me and those of the government, it's a balancing act.

Money in Medicine

When I went into medicine people would ask us, "What's your interest? What do you like doing?" I would think that over 60–70% of med students now are thinking, *is this job or career going to earn me the income I want?* So, their choice is not being driven by their love, it's being driven by economic factors, their financial needs, and the expectations of their families. With the costs of post-graduate education, joining a practice, the mortgage on the house, many say, "I can't do this on a general internist's salary."

I'm a strong believer that the government needs to pay for the majority of medical school costs, with a two-year commitment that the doc goes anywhere in the country where the government tells them to go, to care for the needs of the underserved—and there's no way of buying it out and no way of making excuses because that experience is going to change your life no matter where you go. We helped you out from a financial point of view, therefore you have a greater opportunity of choosing a career you want because you don't have that financial obligation. It's like the armed forces paying for medical education. The armed forces say, "We'll take care of you. But you're going to serve. And no matter where you serve, you're going to learn and grow."

When I went to med school there was no emphasis on money. Nothing, alright? And I think this is one of the huge, huge issues in medicine right now that relates to happiness. I dove into it because I like people. And I think that the burden on docs—their mortgages, their kids, their expectations—is what's destroying medicine right now. The disparity in incomes in medicine is so big, the burden on the primary care provider is so big, that nobody is going to go into this.

To the medical students I see and take care of, I say, "If you're thinking about being an internist, you're going to do another rotation with me." I want to make sure that being an internist will meet their needs and make them happy by seeing what I do and trying to be as competent as I can be. This has to be something they want because they are never going to achieve the income typical of the specialists, the orthopedists, the anesthesiologists, or the pain specialists. And if their family needs cannot be met because of their income they're going to take shortcuts. Eventually it will catch up with them, leading to job dissatisfaction either because they weren't able to achieve what they wanted to early in their careers, or because their economic needs were too great and they had to make changes in their practice.

Even though I work for the insurance division of a health plan as an associate medical director, my clinic is a private clinic. I'm not on salary. Most docs are going to be compensated based on production, whether it's relative value units (RVUs) or some other measure. Even at the health plan you have to have a certain number of RVUs to achieve a certain income. That's why medical students say, "I want to know a narrow slit of medicine. I want to be a specialist. I want to get reimbursed because I'm a proceduralist." And if they have all the usual economic pressures they're going to go in that direction. And I don't blame them. How many times do you see an orthopedist now who says, "Sorry, I only deal with the shoulder. You have a sore knee? Sorry, I only take care of shoulders."

Accessibility

I get comments on my office email because you have to have a portal. You have to have a means for people to communicate besides leaving messages on the phone or calling your medical assistant. Now, people communicate by email and I'm thinking, *Okay, so now I have to address all the pharmacy calls, all the lab results, tell them about the radiology report—and now, besides an appointment, they get to access me and ask my opinion anytime?* Think about lawyers. If clients did this to lawyers, they'd be charging them. In medicine, we don't do that, do we? That's where telehealth can work: if you have a problem and you want me to talk to you, it's five minutes. But you know what? I'm going to charge you. That could actually be helpful for better care and also for de-burdening the doc. And, therefore, one of the things that actually may save docs from being as burdened is that patients will think, *well I'm not going to call because he's going to charge me.*

Advice

You should not go into medicine if you want to be in business. If your priority is to be in business and make money, go get your MBA. Because even if you think you're caring, if money is going to be your driving force, choose something different. You're not going to be showing the care, the understanding to your patients, if all of your focus is on money.

On Allied Health Professionals

We need to use our allied health professionals in the appropriate way so that all patients have access to care. At the same time, we cannot allow allied health professionals to destroy our profession. If you want to be an MD, get an MD. If you want to have the ultimate responsibility and act like a doc, get the MD. You're a nurse practitioner. You have two years of training versus my five. How do you even think you have as much knowledge as I do? Or want to be paid as much? Or want to have that responsibility? You know what? You're going to turn the patient back to me and I'm the one who's going to have to make the ultimate decision. Don't act like a doc if you cannot solve the problem.

Physician Excellence Project

There is something called the Physician Excellence Project. They are developing modules to try to restore that feeling of being a caring doc again. The premise is, as a doc, you have a problem. Participating docs will say, "Why don't you listen to five modules? Then let's meet. Maybe I'll be a coach for you in the practice. I'll watch you with some patients. How did you interface with the patients? Were you abrupt? Did you spend all your time looking squarely at the computer screen, not even looking at the patient?" This project helped me open my eyes a bit.

The Physician Excellence Project advises docs to reach out. Take care of that patient the way you'd want to be treated. The doc is so concerned about the money, the documentation. Step back. I think that concept of finding docs who are deficient and not penalizing them but helping them to be better docs is right: Show them modules, restore some of their faith in why they went into medicine originally, give them tools for how to improve their EMR, show them how to space their time and how to deal with a difficult patient. Then they can say, 'When this comes up again, this is how I'm going to manage it.'

Even with all I've talked about, my job has been the fulfillment of my dreams of going into medicine. Between my personality and my love of learning, there is nothing out there that could beat this. There is nothing better than having that patient look at you and say, "You saved my life."

73. Margaret E., LCSW/PAC, Physician Assistant for an Integrated Health System

As a physician assistant, Margaret E., LCSW/PAC, is a primary care provider with her own panel of patients in a not-for-profit integrated health system. She finds joy helping underserved patients with a complex combination of serious mental health problems and social needs in an organization that shares her values. She works in a supportive environment where she feels listened to and respected. Nevertheless, Margaret feels a low level of dissatisfaction most of the time due to a combination of long hours, a difficult caseload, and too much time spent with the EMR, paperwork, and patient emails.

My father was a social worker who became an attorney. He worked in poverty and disability and asylum law. He was a clinical law professor. He was passionate about serving the underserved. I became a social worker, and my sister has a master's degree in public health and works in community health center administration. I come from a family where going into business was not an option. You work to help others. That's the ethos of my family. I don't think I had a choice. I first went into healthcare as a clinical social worker. People had helped me in my life in some very profound ways and I wanted to be able to do the same for others.

When I was in my early 30s, I was already a social worker but thought I might rather be a psychiatrist because I get great satisfaction from working with people who have severe and persistent mental illness. I started taking some prerequisites for medical school but, as a single mom with a young child, that was not going to work for me. I worked as a social worker for 20 years and then I reached a point in my early 40s when I couldn't see working in this field for another 25 years because resources continue to shrink.

Part of my social work career was spent in an outpatient mental health emergency unit taking care of people who were in acute psychiatric crisis. But we had fewer and fewer resources—fewer places where we could refer them for mental health services, for healthcare, and for housing. Housing waiting lists were three years long. Emergency shelter waiting lists were three months long. Public sector funding for mental health services had really dried up, and this state had the best outpatient public mental health system in the country. We had been a model, but we were not a model anymore. Money dried up because of a lack of political will. This problem is nationwide.

While I still wanted to fight for my clients, I felt I was banging my head against a wall. With 20 years of experience and what I think was a high level of skill, I was making, in a managerial position, $45,000 a year. I had a child to put through college and I had to think about retirement. A friend of mine, who was also a social worker, felt the same way. I was thinking about either becoming a nurse practitioner or a physician assistant. She was going to school to become a physician assistant and talked me into it. So, at the age of 40-something, I got into the physician assistant program the first time I applied.

The reason I chose to become a physician assistant was that the path to become a nurse practitioner was much longer. I calculated that the amount of time it would have taken me to become a nurse practitioner would have been seven years. Becoming a physician assistant would take two years with more than 2,000 hours of clinical rotations, so that is what I did. I've been a physician assistant for four and a half years.

I work as a primary care provider for an integrated health system. I work with patients who are homeless, who need mental health treatment, and who have complex psycho-social situations. Although I'm not employed as a social worker, I draw heavily on my social work background in my work.

My official hours are Tuesday to Friday. On Tuesdays, Wednesdays, and Fridays I work, generally, about ten-hour days. I start at 8:00 a.m. I'm done seeing patients, tech-nically, at 4:00 p.m. I have an extra half-hour tacked on for administrative tasks. I have to write notes, so typically I get out at 6:00 or 6:30 p.m. On Thursdays, I start with administra-tive work at 8:00 a.m. and then see patients from 2:00 p.m. until 7:00 p.m. I'm usually here until about 8:00 p.m. I'm often up at 5:30 a.m. at home so I can be on the computer for half an hour or 45 minutes to catch up on work, and then I do that for at least an hour or two on weekends. This extra time is almost all time spent with the EMR, with a little bit of email. And I don't even work full-time. I'm 94% of a full-time equivalent (FTE).

In this integrated health system, physician assistants and nurse practitioners, who are advanced practice providers, have their own panels of patients. We serve as primary care providers in the same way that medical doctors and doctors of osteopathic medi-cine (DO) do. For some patients we may say, "I really think you need to have an MD or a DO as your primary care provider because things are just too complicated." But we all take care of some very complex patients. We all do basically the same thing: we conduct physicals and acute care visits, prescribe medications, order diagnostic tests, and make diagnoses. I do this in collaboration with a physician and I get advice from my physician colleagues as I feel I need to. I also get advice from my nurse practitioner and physician assistant colleagues, and physicians also come to me for advice, so it's very collegial. At other healthcare organizations in our region, physician assistants and nurse practitioners don't have their own panels of patients. They still evaluate, diagnose, and treat, but they are seeing only their supervising physicians' patients and serve as physician extenders. Here, we have a little more autonomy.

On Joy in Work

For me, joy in work means wanting to go to work even after a really long day or a long week. At the end of an exhausting day, joy means feeling I've connected with somebody, helped somebody, or figured out a problem. Even if I've given somebody bad news, I get satisfaction from making a diagnosis that needed to be made and untangling a knotty problem that we couldn't figure out before.

Many of my patients have had really difficult lives: they have severe mental illness, or they've been homeless, or they've had extreme trauma. They connect with me, I think, because I'm good at being non-judgmental and, quite frankly, because I'm not a physician. I come off as real and approachable. A lot of them trust me when they've never trusted a healthcare provider before. My joy in practice comes from working with them and being a witness to their journey toward stability.

Because we're a self-contained health system with an insurance side and a clinical side, I almost never have had a hard time getting medications or procedures approved if patients really need them. I also have some flexibility in scheduling patients, which I know is unusual. That's why work here and that's why I intend to retire from here. I'm very happy in that way. There is a balance, and that does contribute to my joy in practice. I am able to do what I have to do to provide appropriate care for patients.

I feel safe in expressing any dissatisfactions or problems; I feel listened to; and I feel most people are open to employee feedback. The values of the organization closely mirror my own. We're focused on providing excellent primary care, and we focus a lot of our resources on diversity and inclusion and equity—healthcare equity, serving underserved populations. We take care of all the undocumented children in our school district free of charge and we deliver care to refugees. These things align with my beliefs about what's important and how I want to practice.

Overall, the organization I work for is probably better than average in terms of supporting us and wanting us to have a work–life balance. The number of patients we're expected to see is reasonable and we just decided to decrease the number of contact hours for the advanced practice providers from 35 hours to 33 hours per week for full-time providers. They're paying us the same amount of money to work two hours less per week, which is huge, because people spoke up and they listened, which is amazing.

When a provider makes an error, the organization is generally very supportive. If there's a complaint or a significant error, that goes to the clinical review committee, and they look at our notes, they look at what the patient said, they look at the outcome, and they either find that we were deficient in some way or that we weren't. If they find we were deficient, they don't generally punish us but might recommend additional education or supervision.

On Money and Joy

I don't think I'd have more joy in practice if I got a $20,000 raise, although I wouldn't object. I know I could make more money working for other organizations, but I choose not to because of all the other things that make my job what it is. I don't think I'm underpaid; I think I'm paid on the lower end of the spectrum but not grossly underpaid. If I were grossly underpaid then, yes, that would affect my joy in practice.

What Diminishes Joy

I feel dissatisfaction, probably all the time, on a minimal basis. I have moments of burnout, but I think there is a difference between dissatisfaction and burnout. Dissatisfaction is momentary; burnout is more permanent or long term. Burnout affects the way we feel about our patients and the way we interact with them, whereas, hopefully, dissatisfaction doesn't. There's always more work piling on, piling on, piling on, and my job impacts my personal life in a negative way because this job is not easy.

The long hours don't help. I don't have a heck of a lot of control over my time. I guess I could ask to have my hours cut, but I work until the job is done and it takes a certain amount of time to work through my in-basket. Paperwork, dealing with insurance companies, having to get prior authorizations, arguing about whether a patient needs something, takes probably only 5–10% of my time, but it's just not what I want to do. It's a burden and that's not why I went into healthcare. The nurse I work with does a lot of that for me, but there are certain things that she can't do, so I have to do them. I'm 50, so I started using the Internet when it was introduced. Using the computer in practice itself doesn't bother me at all. I'm computer literate and comfortable.

The dashboard on our EMR reports everybody's metrics in terms of how many of our patients' A1C is controlled, how many are on a statin, and other metrics. This dashboard, which shows all the primary care providers, is updated quarterly. It always feels great if I'm in the top 10%. But if I'm at the bottom on some metric, which I have been and everybody has been, that feels very shaming. I'm not crazy about that at all. I don't think people who aren't doing as well should be shamed.

We do a lot of work with patients who send us direct messages over our secure Web portal. Nursing staff handles some of these, but many are outside their scope of practice, so they come to us. I can sometimes spend 30 or 40 minutes a day addressing patient issues this way. While administration sees this as providing good patient care, meeting patients' needs, contributing to patient satisfaction, and they appreciate our work, it's like having an extra hour of appointments that doesn't show up in our productivity. I think this is one of the things that's driving burnout for a lot of people.

Advice

My advice for my bosses, who have done a god job of hearing us and hearing our concerns, is to continue to listen and not lose sight of our experience. We're an excellent healthcare organization. The reason we're so good, in part, is that people love their jobs. And they love their jobs for all the reasons I love my job. Administration must keep listening to us and keep joy in practice as a priority, regardless of competing priorities.

I have the same advice for my colleagues as I have for myself but don't take: take care of yourselves. Some days your notes aren't going to be done but you need to walk away, go home and have dinner with your family, or go to the gym.

74. Melanie C., MD, Pediatrician in Private Practice

> Calling herself a "late bloomer," Melanie C., MD, has been a pediatrician for 24 years after having started her career as a nurse. She is a partner in a four-practice "super-group" that shares resources and expertise while maintaining the individual identities of each practice. While taking care of children brings her deep satisfaction—"What other job is there where people come in and hug your knees?"—the hours required to document each visit in the EMR; make phone calls; complete paperwork; handle referrals; and complete other tasks at the end of packed days delivering patient care has led, Melanie admits, to some degree of burnout.

I never grew up wanting to be a nurse. I went to a very small Catholic high school and graduated in 1977. At the time, the nuns would meet with us and we were geared to be either teachers or nurses. I wanted to do something with people, and I was bright, so they said I should go into nursing. I got a nursing scholarship and my mother said, "Your cousin's a nurse and she does well," so that was it.

I went to college for nursing and then moved to a city where I worked in labor and delivery at one of the hospitals. At that time, midwives were in the hospital delivering babies and I became friends with them. I decided I was going to be a midwife. Then one night, one of the midwives told me if she could have done it over again, she would have gone to medical school. "Why don't you try it?" she asked.

I had to take premed classes, so I thought I'd take one class at a time. I took one class, and then I took another class, and that took a couple of years. When I had all the premed requirements, I thought I'd apply. I was accepted and went to medical school with the intention of specializing in obstetrics.

When I went through obstetrics, I didn't like it. It was very different from the midwifery model. Midwives are much more holistic and they're much more patient than obstetricians. Midwifery is not as clinical as obstetrics. And, unfortunately, I think my instructor wasn't great and wasn't very inspiring. And I didn't like gynecology. A midwife can just deliver babies and take care of pregnant moms, but an obstetrician/gynecologist (OB/GYN) cannot sustain that. One would have to do both. I then tried pediatrics and loved it.

I am a pediatrician in a medium-sized private practice. Two years ago, we formed a "super-group," so to speak, with three other pediatric practices. We were in the planning stages for five years. Essentially, we are four practices in one. The super-group model allows us to maintain the culture of each group. The managing partner of each group makes her own day-to-day decisions, sets her group's schedules, and determines her group's salaries. We don't have to be the same across the board. But, in a super-group, the practices have the same tax identification number, bill under the same number, and share the services of a medical service organization, which then allows us to share risk. We have a CEO with an MBA degree that each of our groups probably couldn't have afforded individually. The merger has enabled us to share his services, gain from his expertise, and split the cost.

Each practice has good medical leadership, I would say, but with physicians in private practice there's a gap in business experience in terms of strategic questions such as, how can we enhance our revenue? How can we control costs? We're learning best practices from each other: group A made one small change and it helped them, so let's move that across the board. This super-group is physician-led by a board of physician-managers. The CEO takes direction from and answers to the board. I am a partner.

Our pediatric practice super-group has about 51 providers, including physicians and physician assistants, covering about 48,000 lives among the four groups. In my individual group there are four partner-owners and two employed docs, three nurse practitioners, one physician assistant, and one mental health counselor. The mental health counselor can't bill directly but she has taken some of the counseling load off me. For instance, if I'm seeing a ten-year-old and the mom has concerns—maybe attention or some regression or not fitting in—I can I finish up and say, "I'm going to go grab Jane and let's have her talk to you for a couple of minutes," so I can keep going and Jane can see that child and mom. If I need to talk to a counselor at school about a child, Jane will make the phone call. That's really taken the burden off some of the physicians for psychosocial work, and she probably does it better than we do. I think sometimes to invest in a team can really help and be worth its weight in gold.

What My Job Entails

My job is more business-focused now that it was before the merger. I typically don't see patients on Monday mornings. Before, Monday was my day off, and now I work on the business on Mondays. In the short-term my job has changed somewhat, but my long-term plan is to diminish my business hours. What I mean by "business" is meeting with the CEO and having committee meetings. We go over how each committee is doing and how we're moving forward. Today I'm going to meet with our accountant about a new tax framework. I don't mind. It's fun and we've come a long way, so the benefits clearly outweigh anything else. I see patients 100% of my time on the other days. My main job is seeing patients.

My hours vary. Monday is my lightest day because it's non-clinical. And then Tuesdays I work from 7:00 a.m. to 3:00 or 3:30 p.m.; Wednesdays I work from 1:00 p.m. to 8:00 p.m.; and Thursdays and Fridays I work from 7:00 a.m. to 5:00 p.m. On Wednesday mornings I do rounds at the hospital, which are easier now because we partner with the hospitalist. That really helps because each hospital has a different EMR system. I work every sixth weekend.

My clinical hours are fine, but that doesn't mean I leave at 5:00 p.m. Monday afternoons, for instance, I spend time making phone calls, reviewing documents from specialists, and closing out lab work. And then on my busy shifts, Tuesdays to Fridays, very often I can't finish my charting in real time. So, I finish seeing patients, get my coffee, and sit at my desk for an hour or two. I probably add six hours a week for charting, easily, to my patient hours. I went in this past Saturday when I wasn't on call to do charting. We also have forms to fill out and referrals. I don't work from home although other people in my practice do. We can log on remotely, but I made the conscious decision not to, deciding to do work at work. This is good for me. My son has baseball practice on Saturday mornings, so I drive him to baseball, I sit at my desk while he's at practice, and then I pick him up. I get a lot done. Other people log on from home. They get in their pajamas and stay up late working. That's very common.

Sometimes the schedule can be very tight. Even in pediatrics, and I'm sure with adults, it's different from what it was 24 years ago. It was much simpler when I started. People were simpler. I don't know. I think there's a lot of anxiety now, and a lot of mental health issues, and families are different. There are a lot of blended families and separated families, and at least a couple of times a week I see a kid with the mom. And then the dad calls, he wants to talk to me, too. With the electronics, and trying to talk to people, it just seems different.

On Joy in Work

I admit there is some burnout, but I still love my job. I get up and look forward to going to work. I tell my kids, "You have to like what you do, do what you like, because you get up every day and you have to go in and if you don't like it, it will kill you."

My deep satisfaction in my work comes from the kids. Pediatrics is, 90% of the time, very fun. When you meet a medical challenge, it feels good to figure it out and help that patient. We get a lot of positive feedback, I think, because in pediatrics, by nature, people send thank-you cards. It's just really a fun job. And kids are so cute. What other job is there where people come in and hug your knees? You can't beat that.

For me, feeling joy is very much about trying to embrace the little things. I do that with my patients and with staff. For instance, we got a therapy dog at work. One of our nurse practitioners' families used therapy dogs, so she presented a model to me and asked if she could try it. It was an investment because when she's handling the dog at the office, she's not seeing patients. But we did it. It ended up working out well for the patients as much as it did for the staff because when Daisy the dog is here, you can just feel everyone relax.

What Diminishes Joy

The Electronic Medical Record

The degree of documentation that is placed upon us for reimbursement with the EMR is just incredible. Under the payment model we have to document and click boxes in order to be paid. Before, we could write, "Healthy baby" with two lines about development and sign off.

The notes I have to write in the EMR are pretty detailed. There are certain things I have to address and identify. During well visits I have to address nutrition with every child, their BMI with every child, and I have to address counseling codes. Everything has to be precise so it can be pulled by the payers. I have to do it right so they can pull it, because if there's a blank space, if they can't pull it or read my record correctly, I'm not going to get the points. This is simplifying it a bit, but there are demands to document everything, most of which come from the payers.

I never was taught keyboarding. I never learned how to type. To take someone my age and say, "You can't write anymore, you have to type everything," has been really hard. I always document because I have to document what I do. But it's become much more complicated. I have to check more boxes. The notes have gone from one page to three pages. There are certain measures that as a practice or a practitioner we're assessed on, like quality metrics. So, if we document asthma in this manner and BMIs in this manner and nutrition in this manner and it's captured at the claims end, and we're showing that we're managing our population's health, we receive better payment. The idea is good. The problem is all this takes time. I don't do any of this while my patients are in the room. I'm the only one in my practice who doesn't.

What makes me the most tired at the end of the day or week is—I finish, I had a good session, I saw some cute kids, I did everything and then I think, *out of the 14 kids I saw this afternoon, I only did seven of the charts.* And then I have to sit there and finish. And it's unreimbursed time. I want to go home and make dinner and I want to have a life. In a business model, every time we're sitting at our desk making a call, filling out a form, or finishing a chart we're not getting paid.

Work Overload

I feel overloaded by work sometimes. Anyone does who has a really busy day. I always say, "I don't mind seeing the patient, it's the documentation." On Friday, I had a really busy day and I hadn't finished 80% of my clinic notes on the EMR. I got to my desk and there were five phone calls I had to make. I had a child in the hospital. Sometimes I get to the point where I just have to make sure I cover all the critical tasks—mission critical, and I don't let anything sit that's important. But for things like the charting I have to do, it's not going to hurt anybody to wait and I just have to go home. I have to walk away, close my computer. That's what I did Friday. I went in on Saturday morning and I felt much better, refreshed.

I can control when I come and go in terms of the days of the week I work and my hours, but I can't say, "Don't give me any more patients because I'm behind in my notes." In that sense I don't feel I have too much control. To some degree I can control how much time I spend with each patient. We try to give a patient extra time if it's someone with many needs, and that will be built into the computer. But if someone comes in and adds things on—for example, if I'm seeing a ten-year-old for a well visit and then the mom says, "I think he has attention problems, can we talk about it now?" I might say, "You'd be better served if you were to come back for more information."

I've learned to do that more over the years because not doing that is unfair to the people downstream. I could spend 45 minutes with that mom who was only scheduled for 20 minutes, but then everyone after her would have to wait and I'd be way behind. It's very hard to wait with little kids. I'm very conscious of that. I have to be polite and say it the right way so that person doesn't feel I'm invalidating their concern, but in the back of my mind I'm thinking, *there are two more people waiting after you* and I know how this is going to affect them. If a sick child comes in, I have to attend to her, I stop what I'm doing and finish up with the sick child. That's different. And then I have the staff apologize and tell people, "She's running behind because of an emergency," and people are usually very understanding. It depends on the patient and the situation.

75.   Victoria N., DNP, MSN, FNP, Nurse Practitioner and Director of a University Health Clinic

Victoria N., DNP, MSN, FNP, has spent her career, beginning in 2003, working with children—first as a nurse in a pediatric intensive care unit, then as a nurse practitioner in a school clinic with middle- and high-school students and, now, as a nurse practitioner and director of a university health clinic. Victoria finds joy in work despite pressures and stress by embracing change and being a lifelong learner.

I wear many different hats in my current job. I'm the main administrator for the university clinic. I have supervisory responsibilities over the nursing staff, including the administrative assistant and medical assistant. I don't supervise them medically but in all other ways the nurse practitioners and nurses report to me. Our collaborating physician reviews our charts and provides medical oversight. I see patients one or two days a week during the school year. In the summer, when my primary nurse practitioner is out, I see patients more often. I'm also on the faculty of the school of nursing.

I originally wanted to be a marine mammal veterinarian and went to veterinary school. I decided I wanted to study small animals but while I was there, I wasn't so sure. A classmate of mine was in pre-nursing and told me the courses she'd taken were all the same courses I'd taken. She asked, "Why don't you switch to nursing?"

I knew a nurse practitioner when I was growing up. She was one of the first nurse practitioners in my town; she worked in an allergy and immunology office and was one of my providers. I thought then it might be really cool to do something like that one day. So, when my friend suggested I switch to nursing, I thought that sounded great. I love medicine, I love helping people. Going into nursing would be a way to translate my desire to be in medicine but with people instead of animals. It seemed like a cavalier decision at the time, but I knew there would be flexibility in nursing; there are so many options in this profession. I knew that if I wanted to work as a nurse in a hospital or be a nurse practitioner one day, I could. I could morph into many different roles and responsibilities, and I liked the idea of being able to work in different areas and have different work schedules. Nursing isn't a traditional 8:00 a.m. to 5:00 p.m. kind of job for the most part, and that was really appealing to me.

Although I've had different stressors in my career, I feel so fortunate. I've never left a job because I didn't like it. I've always left because something else was the right next opportunity—a job I thought would fulfill me as much as the one I was leaving.

On Joy in Work

Joy in work means fulfillment, feeling valued and valuable. Joy in work means making things just a little easier for anybody who comes your way. Joy in work means to support, to encourage, to solve problems. I want to feel like I've done something at the end of the day. I also think that joy translates into a constant state of learning. I always say I'm going to be done with school and then I find something else I want to do to advance my skills. It's never-ending. And that's one of the things about nursing I really love—that I can learn so many different things in different ways and continue to grow professionally. I think I grow from that learning personally, too. That brings me a lot of joy.

People always ask me about pediatric intensive care because most people find that a really difficult area to work in. But I saw more miracles there than anywhere else in the hospital. Most people don't get to see the kinds of things I got to see. Kids are so resilient. Seeing kids who had suffered trauma or faced other serious challenges and then regain their functioning was inspiring.

I feel passionately about meeting the needs of a population I want to empower. Adolescents, in general, whether they're college-age or otherwise, are at a pivotal time in assuming responsibility for their own health. Understanding their bodies, how they work the way they do, why they work the way they do, and how it can be dangerous to abuse their bodies is crucial in the transition into adulthood. Students stand at a great precipice at this age, where they can make lifelong changes that will benefit their health for the rest of their lives. That's why nutritional education, sexual health education, or awareness of addictions is so important. This job gives me the opportunity and the forum to not only treat patients when they need it, but to educate them.

A Supportive Supervisor

I'm in the top level of clinic administration; I have a supervisor who also happens to be a nurse practitioner. I'm fortunate that she is even-tempered. Things don't rattle her. She has a good perspective on the gravity of a given issue. She has a good way of de-escalating a situation and looking at it differently, which she also helps me to do.

For example, I supervise a critical employee who is leaving unexpectedly for personal reasons. Now I'm asking, do we replace her with someone who will fill her exact role, or is this an opportunity to look at our broader vision for the functioning of the clinic and move in the direction we've been talking about? Do we want to restructure some of my responsibilities and some that had been hers? I was able to go to the executive director and, together, look at different staffing models for the clinic, asking where would different staff fit best? How many hours are they needed? It's like moving pieces on a chess board.

It's really valuable to have someone I can bounce ideas off of because I don't have an assistant or associate director here. So, going to her—and feeling comfortable going to her—is really great. She wants to have weekly meetings with me so I can talk things over with her and feel supported. From day one she's reminded me that I'm never alone. She's in another building across campus but she's only a phone call away. She's very supportive and very practical.

It's also important to me that my staff feels supported, encouraged, and heard. When they're doing a really stand-up job on something, or when they're doing something that's above and beyond, I tell them how much I appreciate their work. They are working so hard, especially this summer with so many new initiatives. They are saying they want to get trained to help, they have some time today, they have time this summer, and they're asking how they can be helpful. I love to see them use their skills and come together as a team. I want my staff to feel fulfilled because there are always new challenges. It's important to keep people interested in the positions they're in, and I like being able to foster that.

Aligned Visions

My vision for the clinic, thankfully, aligns with the vision of those who hired me. For example, they were looking for someone who would evaluate care from the patient's perspective and who would work to simplify things for patients. Many believed we needed to look broadly at *why* we do things the way we do them, not do them just because they've always been done that way. The staff were all ready for change and have been amenable to it.

Relationships

I had an opportunity to forge many great relationships from the get-go. When I started here as a clinician my intention was just to see patients one day a week with no additional responsibilities. Some of the staff knew who I was because I had been working here on and off, and because I have relationships in the community. They were really excited about me being a clinician here. It was great to come on in that role; they understood that I love patient care and that I love college health. I think I garnered a level of respect because I wasn't coming in fresh off the street; they knew who I was.

Fixing Problems

When I started as director, staff had been frustrated with the way patients were being scheduled. Part of the problem was that there weren't enough providers in the clinic, especially during the summer; another was that the decisions about scheduling appointments were being made by nonclinical staff. They didn't have the medical knowledge to prioritize patients who needed to be seen that day, those who could wait until the next day, or which type of provider a patient should be given an appointment with. We solved that problem by having them consult with a nurse or a nurse practitioner before making those kinds of decisions.

When I got here the front desk staff responsible for scheduling could feel tension and frustration from the nursing staff, and they felt the pressure of being on the front line of care in our office. They're the ones dealing with the phone calls and with patients standing in the window who are upset because they can't be seen that day. I want them to feel equipped. Now, if there are three to five appointments left at the end of the day, the staff has to consult with a clinician before scheduling any of these remaining appointments— maybe some people don't really need to be seen today and can come in tomorrow. But the responsibility for making those kinds of decisions should rest with clinical staff, not with the schedulers.

We've set up a form in our EMR where the appointment schedulers document any instance in which a patient is turned away for any reason, and who they consulted before turning them away. By tracking this information, we can be sure we're either turning patients away for the right reasons or sending them in the direction they really need to go. For example, was a patient turned away because they needed a service we don't offer? Is it because they were referred to us but really need to go to counseling? Is it a problem that was triaged to nursing but the patient can really wait until tomorrow to be seen? Or is there a service we're missing that we need to be offering? Seeing the big picture helps us to figure out whether what we're doing makes sense, and whether we're achieving the desired results.

What Diminishes Joy

Stress diminishes joy in work for me. Added levels of responsibility contribute to stress. I have a strong desire for perfection, so the idea of mistakes really scares me. In the medical field you make a mistake and it's potentially life or death. And mistakes definitely happen, we're all human. We're in this profession of liability and risk. I wish this weren't the case, but it's part of being in the business we're in. The level of risk is daunting at times because there's no room for error; it's a lot of pressure.

The fear of mistakes, combined with the stress of my additional responsibilities supervising clinicians—not their actual clinical work but making sure they have the resources they need, that they feel supported, and that they have the most up-to-date education—can kill my joy if I'm not careful. It's difficult to provide all that and still maintain my role as a practitioner, because I still have to support myself, make sure I'm focused on my patients, and that I'm able to care for them the way I want to and the way I think they deserve. There's a lot of anxiety. Being a nurse can lead to burnout. Even when we really care about what we do, the system can be exhausting to deal with. Caring for others can be exhausting.

Advice

It's important for people to understand that being stagnant in healthcare is dangerous. If you remain stagnant, no matter what your role is, you don't push to do better because you're not motivated for change. It's easy to get stuck in a rut because you don't want to try something new, because doing something new is kind of scary. But I wish more people would do something new because they could find new joy in it, and it can lead to better quality of care for patients.

I think people really need to love what they do, and not just stay in a job because they've always been there, or to continue to do what they do because they've always done it that way. What you do must make sense and must make care better for your patients.

Administrator–Clinician Disconnect

76.   Stephan D., MSW, Senior Therapist, City Department of Health and Community Services

> Stephan D., MSW, has been a clinical social worker in the public mental health system since 2013. He is deeply committed to providing the underserved with the best possible mental health and substance abuse treatment—but bureaucratic obstacles, combined with few opportunities for advancement, led him to change jobs two months after this interview. Stephan now works as a counselor in a public high school with a large immigrant population.

I always wanted to be in some sort of service profession. My mother is a teacher, so I grew up with that experience. I had a number of family members who struggled with addiction and mental health diagnoses. I think that's why I leaned toward mental health and psychology in college. I got a BA in psychology and much later in life got a master's in social work.

I am a public mental health therapist delivering individual therapy, family therapy, and group therapy in a city with a population of about 145,000. I also serve as a mental health case manager linking clients and their families to different resources and services in the community. I conduct risk assessments for suicidality and for symptoms of psychosis; I administer mental health evaluations, needs assessments, a little bit of everything. Before this I worked in a group home setting in another state serving individuals who have the dual diagnoses of mental health problems and substance abuse. There are a lot of disenfranchised individuals whose only option for help is a public mental health setting.

I don't work fixed hours. My contract is to work 80 hours per pay period, which is every two weeks, but I rarely come in at 80 hours. It's usually way more. My program and the interventions I provide are custom fit to clients so sometimes I work until late in the evening, sometimes I'm done at 5:00 p.m., sometimes I'm in early and out early; it varies. Working Monday to Friday is definitely the most fixed part of my schedule because we're part of the city government and the public health system. My being on call is uncommon and situational because there is an emergency services division to handle emergencies 24/7; but when a client is getting out of the hospital I may put myself on call so there is some continuity of care during the transition to home.

On Joy in Work

For me, joy in work means being an element of positive change in a person's life. That's what keeps me involved. Sometimes we don't experience it in the public mental health sphere because we have so many people dealing with generational poverty, addiction, mental health diagnoses, and homelessness. But having some part in the small wins my clients experience brings me joy and has kept me going in the field for this long.

What Diminishes Joy

Bureaucratic and administrative policies related to immigration status that interfere with successful treatment diminish my joy in work. Immigrants don't have a choice of psychiatric medications. They don't have insurance. They aren't able to get disability. They end up having to take older medications that have more side effects than newer ones. Someone who has full citizenship—a "red-blooded American"—is able to get selective serotonin reuptake inhibitors, Medicaid, and would have access to the most effective medications the psychiatrist can prescribe.

Administrator–Clinician Disconnect

A problem in the public mental health system is that people who aren't clinicians in the field are making decisions for those of us who are—those of us who have face-to-face contact with clients every day. People in administration and consultants come in and try to evaluate the most effective way to minimize costs or employee hours. They come up with algorithms that say, "For this size population you only need this many FTEs." As a team we're saying, "Absolutely not. We're at that level now and things are falling through the cracks." The consultants respond, "Well, that's not what the numbers say." These decisions are often made by people who are on the administrative/statistics side and not by clinicians who see clients and who know that an appointment scheduled for 30 minutes can easily turn into 90 minutes because somebody comes in with a crisis—and, of course, we're going to deal with the crisis. Somebody may be coming in for the usual weekly session and you planned to talk about coping strategies, but then they bring up some sort of trauma or relapse that changes everything.

There is pressure from the administration when I say my client needs more time or a different medication. The pressure comes down from the state capital, since the state has certain requirements for this position, and there is pressure from the federal government that comes all the way down to me. Even though that pressure is there I just don't fold to it. I push back and do what I need to do for my clients. Not that I want to lose a job. But I will lose this job doing what is best for my clients. In the end it's my professional license, it's got my name on it, so I'm going to provide the highest level of service I can provide. I've been blessed that for the most part, in the 13 years I've been working with the government, I've been able to put the clients' needs first and still meet the different data points I'm supposed to meet.

Indirect pressure is applied when it comes time for my performance reviews, which focus on the quantity of care rather than the quality by highlighting statistics like, "You've had x number of contact hours" or "You saw x number of clients during x amount of time." Most of my supervisors, though not all, have had the experience of being direct staff. Some haven't sat with a client in many years, but they do remember what it felt like to be a clinician. Most of my direct supervisors and those above them have been supportive and understanding. The higher up it goes, the less supportive the administration is.

The administration sees the big picture. What they don't see are the details—the nitty-gritty of the problems, the needs, and the objectives of the clients. Being a social worker, I take a client-centered approach to treatment. For example, we have a client who has schizophrenia and is marijuana-dependent, which continues to jeopardize his stability. The administration says he needs to continue to go to a substance abuse program for detox. As a clinician who has a relationship with him, I know that's not what he wants. I have to advocate for him and say, "You're right, he does need detox, but this is not what his recovery journey is. He wants to address his schizophrenia, not his marijuana use." They see problem–solution, problem–solution, very black and white, whereas we work almost exclusively in the gray. This is where the disconnect between clinicians and administrators becomes really apparent. This is when I say, "You guys haven't been on the ground for ten years—five positions ago."

Organizational Hierarchy

A title hierarchy in the organization does exist. I work with psychiatrists, and often it is the person with the MD whose advice supersedes that of a social worker. I've worked in two settings during my 13 years as a clinical social worker and this has always been the case. I work with young people with first-episode psychosis, and supervisors and administrators always side with the psychiatrist. I know it's purely because of the MD. I appreciate working with psychiatrists and the complexity of the field, and how difficult it is to make these sorts of medical decisions; that said, psychiatrists can come in and disrupt the course of treatment I've mapped out with my clients. This happens to me maybe three to four times a year. People above me don't want to go completely against what an MD says.

Lack of Upward Mobility

Another thing that takes away joy for me—and I've been working almost exclusively in the public mental health world—is that there aren't many career ladders in the system. When you have younger clinicians, younger treatment staff who want to get more education, there is a ceiling; when you hit it, you can't progress any further professionally. Usually, because there's someone sitting in the spot above you, you have to wait until that person moves out for you to take that spot, or wait for someone to retire or get promoted for you to take another step up. I've definitely encountered this. It doesn't take away the joy I have in working with clients but this obstacle to advancement does take the wind out of my sails sometimes.

Advice

Administrators should be required to have face-to-face contact with clients and do clinical work, to be "in the trenches" for at least part of their week, so they will remember that these are people with stories, with complexities; that's where the quality of work comes from—from understanding the complexities of the people we work with.

Administrators should recognize talent and ambition and structure career ladders to keep skilled staff on board, so that the public mental health system will have clinicians who are just as good as those in the private sector.

I think change really comes from the culture. The organizational culture in the public sector should be that we value each other regardless of our degree. If someone doesn't have a degree but has struggled with addiction and has been in and out of the hospital five times, that person brings equal value to the team. We tend to forget that. To change the culture, there is no head of the table. It is a round table, and we are all responsible for our own piece. No one's piece is more important than another's. That's the kind of culture we need in our medical services.

Future Plans

I think I'm going to move around in the public world. I recently accepted a position as a counselor in the school system, so I'm taking a side-step but into a lane where I see much more growth. The school that hired me wants to provide more intensive, purposeful interventions for their English language learner population because they're getting a lot of people who are crossing the border and being reunited with their family members. This has been happening for years but there has been a huge influx of immigrants in this city over the last two or three years.

There are a large number of adolescents who have had family reunification issues, assimilation issues, and acculturation issues. The vast majority are Spanish-speaking kids from Central America, many of whom were heavily involved in gangs and cartels in their countries and communities. Their parents have brought them here to try to escape that. The schools are encountering these kids, who also have trauma and undiagnosed learning disabilities. Their grandparents may have pulled them out of school for the last few years because they were afraid for their grandchildren's lives. They come here, are 17 years old, and are told they need to go to school. Putting them in school here creates all sorts of other problems.

77.   Alice H., MSN, Nurse and Surgical Services Educator

Alice H., MSN, has been a nurse for 19 years and a surgical services educator for the last one and a half years at a large academic medical center. After a time on the medical–surgical floor she transitioned to the operating room where she worked for ten years, got her master's degree, and then started teaching. Alice recalls, "When I finished my master's degree, I was ready to change the world. I had these rose-colored glasses and thought, *I can make things so much better. Let me in there!*"

I knew from the time I was nine years old that I wanted to be a nurse. I became a nurse because I just wanted to take care of people. I had an aunt who was a nurse. When I went to school, I had this idea—and maybe I was naïve—that I would sit with patients and talk to them and rub their shoulders and get to know their families. I went through my clinical training and thought, *Well, I may have a little time to do this but not as much as I thought I would.*

When I started to work on the floor, I didn't have time to do that. I'd have eight patients, the family would be there, the surgeon would put in new orders, I'd be called by somebody. I was disheartened that I couldn't give the care that I wanted to give, to spend as much time as I wanted to. I would always be on the floor late, charting, because I would take that extra time. That's when we used paper charts. I worked with nurses who had their routines down pat, but they weren't very compassionate. It was like, "You're breathing, okay, here's your medication, I'll see you later." I always liked to talk and get to know patients and make them feel safe, make them feel cared for.

My Professional Journey

I moved away from patient care at this academic medical center because I had my master's degree and got a lot of flak with people telling me, "You're wasting your degree just being a staff nurse." But I really didn't feel that way. I felt being a staff nurse made me well-rounded and better able to handle situations than if I'd just had classroom training. Deep down, though, I knew I wanted to use my degree, which was in education and leadership. The leadership part I tried, and it wasn't for me; education was.

Because burnout happens a lot, I thought I'd take a job as a supervisor in the operating room (OR) of a pediatric hospital. It was a sort of assistant director role. I didn't like it at all. Why? The place was great, the people were great, there was great satisfaction helping children in this role, but I saw the number of hours my boss worked—60 hours a week in-house and then she was at the beck and call of anybody who would need her on her off hours—and I said that's not the kind of life I want. I want balance in my life. And I realized then—maybe I was a little naïve—that being in leadership is a big financial responsibility. You have to be fiscally smart to have that job and I'm more patient- and people-focused.

So, I came back to the hospital where I was before and worked as a charge nurse on night shift and in the rooms for about three years when this job as a surgical services educator became available. I was encouraged to apply. I do miss patient care, but I think it's a good fit. I'm a people person. I want to see people grow, I want to see people learn, I want to see people do the right thing. That's what drew me to this job.

I've been doing this job for about a year and a half now. As a surgical services educator I'm bringing new folks into the department, learning about policies and procedures, managing the new orientees, guiding them through their training, and whatever else I'm asked to do. I make sure everybody is up to date with their mandatory education, their tests, etc. I also do clinical work wherever I'm needed. I teach new folks, who are unfamiliar with this facility, what we do here. We do trauma care, we're a transplant center, and so many patients get transferred here. It's an acute patient population. Often, I'm proud to say, this is the last stop for patients. We have the sickest of the sick patients and if they can't be fixed here, they can't be fixed.

On Joy in Work

What's most important to me is working the hardest I can to the best of my ability, knowing I did everything I could to do the right thing. That's what brings me joy. When I worked in the OR consistently, I loved to go home tired. I loved to go home with my feet hurting from running around because I felt satisfied, like I did the best job that I could do. That would give me great satisfaction and joy. To save a patient, to be part of a team that saves a patient who never should have walked out of that OR alive, would bring me joy.

I liked the chaos of the OR and not knowing what's going to be next, not doing the same thing day in and day out. It was always exciting. Honestly, anything could come through the door—you'd have to be ready at any moment to shift gears and change your plans. I'm not a fan of routine. In the OR we would see some really unusual circumstances that someone in a community hospital would never see. It's fast-paced, ever-changing—and I think that's why I like the off-shifts, meaning evenings and nights. What was working in the OR like? Working in the OR was crazy. That's what I loved about it.

In my current job as a nurse educator I want to teach, I want to pass things along, and I want to see people succeed. These are the folks who are going to be taking care of *me* someday. I don't want a slacker. I don't want poor care when I'm older. I straddle these two worlds by filling in when I'm needed. That satisfies me. There are times when I'll go and walk the halls of the OR just to round and check on people, make myself visible. I get my fill that way.

I get joy from seeing folks succeed, knowing that my guidance helps them. They do most of the work, but I want to feel that things like my impromptu meetings, or a kind ear, help them hang in there when they don't really want to continue. I give them the confidence they need to keep going. That gives me joy.

What Diminishes Joy

Power struggles between surgeons and the staff, sexism and disrespect, the combination of negativity and gossip, tolerance for bad behavior, dealing with difficult families, and disappointment diminish joy in work for me.

Power Struggles

The surgeons tend to dictate what happens around here because they'll reference the fact that it's a business. I understand that to a degree. But maybe some folks are kept overtime so surgeons can start their cases when it may not be warranted. Just because it's convenient for him or her, then things have to happen lickety-split, on the spot, let's go! Because the squeaky wheel gets the oil. I feel the thoughts and opinions of the surgeons are valued by administrators more than those of the frontline staff because the surgeons make the money for the hospital.

I don't feel demeaned by this because I've learned to thicken my skin, but there are a lot of people who do, especially those in the charge nurse role. Charge nurses feel undermined by surgeons regarding the decisions they were going to make. If the doctor comes in and you, as charge nurse, say, "No, I can't take your case right now," well then the surgeon goes into the other room and calls the bigwigs. And you get a call from the director, who says to make sure that case happens. So, after you've said no, you're undermined by the management, and they tell you, "Yes, you have to do it." So, I do feel a bit disrespected. But I've learned after 17½ years in the OR not to take anything personally. The worst thing you can do is to take something personally.

Sexism and Disrespect

I have witnessed sexism and disrespect. We're a teaching hospital so we have a lot of folks who are not from this country. Maybe in their homeland women are supposed to be barefoot and pregnant and their opinions don't matter, but I've seen male doctors treat female nurses dismissively if they say, "Doctor, I'm noticing this patient's urine is red" or "Doctor, these are the only sutures I have that you're requesting." Doctors might not really value what they're saying because they're women. But we really try to promote patient safety and encourage everyone to speak up for the patient, so I don't think nurses are intimidated into staying silent when patient safety is at stake.

I've seen a lot of female residents—and it doesn't matter what their nationality is, they're playing in "a man's world"—come off as really aggressive. I think maybe they're trying to match the guys in that respect. A lot of specialties are male dominated, like neurosurgery and orthopedic surgery, and I've noticed some of the women can really be standoffish because they're trying to prove themselves. I just look at them and say, 'You know, you don't have to be that way.'

Years back, probably 15 years ago, I saw a surgeon throw a piece of instrumentation across the OR—he was frustrated because it didn't work. It wasn't against me or the scrub tech. There are some divas for sure. I've heard stories about physical altercations between staff and doctors, but I never witnessed that. I've heard about the threat of choking. But that was a long time ago, before I started here, so I don't know if it's urban legend.

I've read that the culture needs to change. I often wonder if it's just here. Does this happen somewhere else? I wonder if this happens in any other professional setting. If I worked in a law office, would this behavior be tolerated?

Negativity and Gossip

Another thing that diminishes joy in work for me is negativity by co-workers. I could come in and be in the best mood, I'm having a really great morning—I have every green light on the way to work and I have a date with my husband later—and I come to work and the first thing I hear before I can even change in the locker room is a coworker saying, "This place is the worst." And gossip is another one—negative gossip. That can change my mood in an instant. I can be having the best day ever and it turns around in an instant.

People have their own perception of what's important to them and their perception is reality. One might say, "If I don't get my schedule it's going to make me very angry," while I couldn't care less. Or they complain they have to work a weekend and I love working weekends. Some people seem to thrive on drama and negativity.

Tolerance for Bad Behavior

The facility as a whole, maybe under different managers, have promoted bad behavior for so long that people think it's the norm and they can get away with anything: "They're going to kiss my butt because they don't want me to quit, so I can do or say whatever I want." The OR staff does this and the doctors do, too.

The administrators promote this behavior because the OR is the cash cow for the hospital, for any hospital. But as far as our OR staff, bad behaviors were ignored for so long because we were always so short-staffed. We were so desperate to keep somebody that we'd say, "Oh, well, you took off seven out of eight days without an excuse, just don't let it happen again." It was like a slap on the wrist instead of holding folks accountable. And now when you try to hold people accountable, they almost laugh at you, as if to say, "You're not going to do anything to me."

Difficult Families

I felt a tension on the floor between meeting the family's needs and the patient's needs. There were some very difficult families, very demanding. No matter what I'd do they'd want more, whether they were calling on the phone wanting an update or if they were physically in the building. They would want me to explain why was doing what I was doing. The patient was perfectly capable of asking me these questions. I may have had a conversation with the patient, saying, "I'm going to change your dressing," and explain the procedure—and then the family would come in and ask, "Why did you do this? Why did you do that?" as if they were questioning my plan of care for the day. That was really the biggest thing for me. I liked to joke that my patients in the OR can't talk.

Disappointment

I'd say what also diminishes joy is disappointment: disappointment that co-workers, doctors, or any of the other healthcare providers don't want to do the right thing. The right thing would be to do things by policy, taking the time to go through each step of a process instead of cutting corners. Say there's an emergency and someone thinks there might be time to perform an instrument count. But they're too lazy and say, "You know what, we'll just get an x-ray at the end." It's as if they're shirking their duties because they just don't feel like doing it. They think, "That will be the next person's problem." It doesn't happen too often. Some people do it more consistently than others. It's frustrating and disappointing. If we worked in a factory making neckties it wouldn't matter. But our commodity is human lives. I think people should give all they can.

In a trauma situation, the staff knows we write an incident report. They know there are circumstances when maybe the patient comes with their chest already open and the surgeon is performing cardiac massage. Or the EMTs don't call to say they're coming and show up on your doorstep with somebody's brain hanging out of their head. In those circumstances you just have to jump into action and get ready and you don't have the luxury of time to get neatly set up. But if you have the time to do it, just because it's a trauma doesn't mean you don't have time. It's not always crash and burn through the door. There are some controlled traumas that you can do the right thing for.

Fixing the Problems

In the last couple of years there has been an awareness that the staff was getting a little restless, a little unhappy with the way things were working. I have taken potential candidates on tours and someone asked me last week, "What's the biggest dissatisfier for nurses here?" I said, "It's really different for every person. You can interview ten people and get ten different answers." Being undermined is what's bothered me and what I've experienced. Some folks say it's schedules. With all the buildup of different issues the management is taking notice of how unhappy the staff is and they're really working on making changes.

The changes they made were better staffing so folks weren't getting forced to stay overtime; hiring more people for the later shifts; and putting the schedule out on time. Now that never affected me because I had a steady schedule. But a lot of folks need to plan their life around the schedule. You know, it's Thursday and I don't have my schedule for Sunday. So, they know they need to put the schedule out ahead of time so people can have a work–life balance.

Administration is doing a really good job now compared to the past when there were struggles to get what we needed. I don't know why things changed. We've had the same CEO. I've seen a steady improvement over the last four plus years. Our facility does an employee survey every year or every other year and these results are fed back anonymously to the management. Maybe they're told from higher-ups that they need to make changes if the scores are bad.

There is a connection now between what the staff thinks of as problems and what the administration thinks. In the past there was a big disconnection but now everybody is on the same page. I don't think the administration listened to the staff's concerns back then. Whatever the administration did, I've seen a change in staffing, listening, an open-door policy, and they're available when we need them. They really do make it easy for us to have everything we need at our fingertips to take care of a patient.

In terms of what the doctors do, I think that's gotten a little better. We have some new players in the ranks who are saying we're not going to tolerate any disrespect and we want to work as a collaborative team, not against each other. A code of professionalism was just introduced to the staff, which I think is slowly starting to pick up steam and be recognized.

We had a lot of folks leave but we've been steady on in the one and a half to two years since they started to make these changes. People who are leaving now are going because their spouse is moving to another state for a job—you know, those types of things, not because of dissatisfaction.

Reflections

If I could change anything about my job it would be accountability. Not just management holding staff accountable for the things they do, but even peer-to-peer accountability would be welcome. I wish folks would talk more—have an adult conversation—instead of going to the manager or to their friend in the break room and say, "that so-and-so, she's such a jerk, she did this, that, and the other thing." Joe Schmo in the break room can't make any of the changes. But if you come to me, we can talk about our differences and maybe work it out. There are no forums for doing that in this hospital.

In my role as a nurse educator, in conjunction with our unit director, we have a monthly meeting with our lead surgical technologist, and these are some of the things I preach to them when I make my little PowerPoint presentation. I ask, "How do you handle conflict? What's your teaching style? How do you think you come off to other people as far as your personality?" These are ideas that, little by little, we're trying to plant in them. Maybe they'll think about them and soften the way they do things, and maybe these things will catch on.

When people get discouraged and say, "That doctor was so mean to me," or "I don't like them, they're so mean," I tell them, "You have to make the best of your situation. Some folks just thrive on negativity." I did that early in my career. I was one of those people who would sit and complain and not have any solution to the problem. But now I try to just stay positive. I try to pass that along to the folks I'm working with: "Your situation is what you make of it. If you want to be miserable you will be, but if you want to be satisfied you will be."

I would like administration to take what staff says as truth instead of believing the doctors over us. Listening to the staff when we say we're tired. Listening to the staff when we say we need more equipment to take care of patients.

My job has not been the fulfillment of my dreams of going into nursing. I was the one who wanted to make changes, to make a difference, and be that nurse who would sit at the bedside and listen to you and spend time. That was my idea of what a nurse is. I soon learned this isn't a realistic dream. I do have a positive attitude about what my job actually is. I have to. I'm not saying I'm perfect all the time and there are days when I get frustrated. But my philosophy is you have to go into it with a positive attitude. You reap what you sow.

78. Craig M., Registered Polysomnography Technologist and Manager of a Pediatric Hospital Sleep Laboratory

Craig M., registered polysomnography technologist (RPSGT), has been working in the field of sleep technology for almost 20 years. As manager of a sleep laboratory in a pediatric hospital, he is rewarded by helping children and families, and by helping his staff to become a cohesive team of outstanding sleep technologists. Yet, Craig faces entrenched cultural and institutional barriers to making the sleep lab a "world class" facility, in the form of uncooperative doctors, big egos, failure to act on staff concerns, and a lack of leadership.

I've always liked helping people. When I was a kid, I would help my dad work on our cars. He was able to tell me what every part did, how the car worked, and what we needed to do to fix it. But when I would get sick and ask, "Dad, what's going on with *me*?" he'd say, "I don't know, son." I thought that wasn't how it should be. I thought, it's my body, I should know how it works and when something goes wrong, I should know the parts that need to be replaced. I remember that was my line of thinking when I was a kid: *we really need to figure this body out because nobody seems to know.*

In high school I took advanced classes in anatomy and physiology to try to get a jump on medical school, and I became certified as an EMT. But then as I got more into it, I realized that being a doctor meant a lot of other things, too, which I knew I would not enjoy. Part of that was deferring happiness. I knew it was going to be a long road. I knew it was going to be really hard. And I knew becoming a doctor would require me to put on hold many things I like to do, such as hiking and traveling. I knew I wouldn't be able to do those things while training to be a doctor. I'd really have to buckle down. But I know my personality and knew I couldn't wait until I was all done to feel rewarded. I wanted to do those things now. I'm 37 years old. Many of my friends continued on the medical path, and my best friend from high school just finished his fellowship two years ago. He's only had a real job for two years. He didn't get to travel. I've been all over the world. I've climbed a number of mountains and lived in different places.

I started working as a sleep technologist in college. I did the actual sleep studies overnight. This was a good job to have in college because I could work around my school schedule. I was good at it, and because I was excelling in this work, I embraced it and transitioned it into a career. I've been doing this for almost 20 years now. I worked for a couple of small, private labs in another part of the country where I got my first training. Then I moved to a university, which is where I worked before coming here. In that academic setting, I was able to do research and participate in some interesting studies. I was published a couple of times, which is what ultimately led me to be recruited by this pediatric hospital. I've been here, first as a sleep technologist and then as manager of the sleep lab, for 11 years. I am really interested in research and patient care.

Being a registered polysomnography technologist is the highest technical standard there is in the field of sleep medicine. As an RPSGT I'm proficient in all aspects of monitoring, recording, and analyzing data on sleep. Most of our studies are clinical studies. Our sleep studies involve a lot of biological metrics and patient care. Children are referred here because there is something wrong with their sleep. Sometimes the problem, like a breathing problem, is obvious. Sometimes the problem is less obvious. The purpose of most of our studies, which we run all night, is to rule things out so we can begin to target ways to improve the sleep of a one-day-old up to a 30-year-old. I don't do the sleep studies myself now, but I manage a staff of technologists who do.

My job has developed in a way that was a little beyond my control. When I first arrived, I spent half my time analyzing the sleep studies. This entails looking through them in a process called "scoring." This means going through the study, which takes hours, looking at every little thing—brain waves, respiratory signals, CO_2 levels. Leads on the arms and legs allow us to look at muscle movements. There are also video and audio recordings that go along with all this. These studies cover the entire body to reveal anything that could be going on during sleep. I go through the studies and stage the sleep (there are four stages of sleep), looking for any abnormalities. Then I give the doctor a fast and clear picture of what's going on.

Things have changed a lot. Now 70% of my time is spent administratively, managing my staff. This includes going to meetings, handling human relations issues, hiring, firing, quality assurance issues, and making the schedule. The other 30% of my time is spent staging the studies, which is something I enjoy. The administrative part of it is not something I enjoy and not something I planned to do in life, but I do think I make a good leader, which may be why I've ended up here.

At my last annual review, I was encouraged to take more business classes, more administrative classes, and then become more focused on that part of the job. I still wanted to be able to be involved in patient care and data collection and stay hands-on, but I did take all the classes. I know if I need help with something like handling employees who have difficult interpersonal issues, there are classes I can take to help me deal with those situations better. So, I find those classes and take them.

In the morning I come in between 8:00 and 9:00 and work until 6:00 or 7:00 in the evening. My hours depend on what's going on in the lab. If the techs need me, I stay later, or if a patient wants to talk to me, I stay for that. I'm on call evenings and weekends. If things happen at night, because studies are collected at night, staff members reach out and call me. I do not feel overloaded by work, but I think that's my personality. I'm the kind of person who can compartmentalize. I don't take my job home with me unless I'm on call and I have to, and then I don't let it take away from my family time.

On Joy in Work

I like my job. I feel happy at work. A lot of people, when it comes to Monday morning, think, "Ugh, I've got to go to work." I never feel like that. Sometimes, if it's a beautiful day, I'm not really excited to come to work, but I don't mind it. The reason I don't mind it is I know I'm delivering good care. I'm helping kids. I've seen it. I've seen a change in kids. The work I do can be life changing. Not only can it change kids' lives and help them develop and become better versions of themselves, but the whole family changes when I help their child sleep better. And that's rewarding to me.

I like helping my staff accomplish their goals so they can feel good about their jobs and feel rewarded. I like to stand up and advocate for them because I know what it's like to work in a place where a boss doesn't have your back. I know if I'm an advocate for them and I constantly coach them to help them be the best versions of themselves while they're here, their entire lives will be better.

When I first started here, the department director was of a different generation. She was a micromanager who did not trust the staff and tried to create distrust among us. I was always on edge. About six years ago my direct supervisor was fired, and I was given an ultimatum, essentially, to replace her. I was thrust into this job, but I wasn't overwhelmed or unprepared since I already knew how things worked. For me, it turned out to be a great job once I embraced it and did it for a while. It's opened doors for me and has allowed me to do many things I wouldn't have done otherwise. And now, of course, I have a skill set that I can use to work anywhere.

When I do reviews with my staff, I always start by asking, "Do you like your job? What can we do to make it better for you?" They all say, "I like helping the kids." The other thing I hear often is, "I like my co-workers." I am judicious when I hire staff; I don't take just any-body. I have a staff of 18. It's probably far too many for one person, but I think I do a good job. I always say I want to coach all the best technologists in the area, so I have recruited the most talented. I've tried to do that. And because of that, a lot of the techs say they've never worked on such a good team and they like each other. If you have a job like that, that's joy, right? When you come to work and you're with your co-workers giving patients care all night, and you find that comfortable, you want to stay.

On Money and Joy

Is there a relationship between money and joy? Not for me, but for a lot of people there is. I was raised poor, so I found other ways of finding joy when I was a kid. I have six brothers and sisters, so money was tight, but I didn't realize until much later in life that we were poor. I commend my parents for that. I always had what I needed, and I knew I wasn't going to get anything extra. But I thought that was how everyone was. We did fun things. But fun things for us were, my dad would take the TV outside and we would watch a movie on the trampoline. That didn't cost anything and that was great. So, because of the way I was raised, I can find joy in anything. I like to be secure and pay my bills, but I don't need much more than that. I don't need a big expensive thing.

That was part of my decision, too, when I decided not to go to medical school. Part of my thinking was, *it would be great if I made all this money and being a doctor is really pres-tigious. But you know what? I don't need all of that. If my real goal is to help people, I can do that today. Or tomorrow. I can start right now.* So, money is not as much of a motivator for me as it is for other people. I've been offered jobs in other countries where I'd make a lot more money, but I knew I wouldn't like the lifestyle, so I passed. I'm young, I have a kid. I live in an expensive place. So, obviously, more money would be better. But that's not primary to me.

What Diminishes Joy

Failure to Collaborate

Many people here have very big egos, and egos can make work difficult, especially in our department. Our sleep lab is shared between two other departments whose doctors don't get along very well. Each department wants ownership of the lab, but neither wants to put in the work that would be required to own it. Because the doctors in these two departments don't get along with each other, they don't come into the lab and don't interact with my staff to provide feedback. If they did, everyone would do their jobs better and the quality of their work would be better. But nobody will do this.

These departments are tied organizationally and financially to the sleep lab, but they don't want to interact with each other. I don't think they have a problem with the technologists. They like the techs and they like me. They just don't like each other, so they won't come into the lab. No one wants to do anything extra to have a presence in the sleep lab or to work on improvements. We have staff meetings, and they don't want to come to those because they don't want to see each other. We've tried multiple times in the last couple of years to have all-hands-on-deck retreats where we get together to talk about problems and make plans to resolve them, but these doctors don't attend. I'm there, my boss is there, but the doctors who are supposedly our leaders don't show up. If nobody is steering the ship, then we can't go anywhere. If we don't have a strong leader who's getting things done, then we're drifting.

Sleep Tech Appreciation Week is at the end of this month. I've been working for a month to get the doctors to participate. And they say, "Oh, yeah, let's get donuts." I say, "Donuts are great. But you know what would really matter? If you came into the lab for just 15 minutes and just met everybody. There are people you haven't met yet. Fifteen minutes, that's it, then you can walk out. You don't have to give them a donut. That's what would matter."

Each of these doctors will communicate with me, which they are required to do. I have a good rapport with them all. If someone in the group is trying to get information from a particular doctor who won't respond, they will respond to me. But, if I'm looking at a study and I think a tech could have done something differently that might have changed the outcome, I have to solicit this from the doctors, saying, "Tell me what you think of X so that I can tell the techs how they can be better at their jobs." We get really complex situations that are not textbook and that can be very ambiguous. Sometimes it's hard to know, which is why I want different opinions. But if I didn't ask, then they wouldn't tell me. I have to seek out their opinions on my own and sometimes I have to ask doctors more than once. If there were more camaraderie, I think our lab would be even better.

Lack of Leadership

I wish we had a stronger leadership structure in my department. I wish that our directors were really directing things, boots on the ground. Directors should *be in the lab*. We have an outlined leadership structure on paper, but they don't do what their jobs require them to do. If we had a really strong leader who was able to get these doctors to be accountable and to participate, that would trickle down and we would improve more quickly. And everyone's morale would rise.

Failure to Communicate

My staff definitely feel like their own islands. We tried to have a summer party this year as a way to reward the staff and do something fun. It was going to be a day outdoors and we were going to get good food. But none of my staff would attend because they had no desire to socialize with the doctors. They told me straight out, "The doctors didn't take time to meet me. They don't even know my name. So why would I spend my day off to go hang out with them when they can't even give me the time of day at work?" The techs all hang out with each other. They go to each other's birthday parties, so they would do that anyway.

Some of the doctors have not been in the sleep lab for years. So, while the staff may know a doctor's name, they have never seen his face. There's a doctor who is supposedly part of our center, maybe even one of the leaders of our center, who hasn't set foot in the lab for many years and has never met the techs. So, the techs feel disrespected in that way. There are some techs who have been here for a long time and have never met the laboratory director. That said, the doctors don't look down on the techs in the lab—not at all. The doctors all really respect and appreciate the techs' work, they know it's important, but the techs don't feel that directly.

Financial Inequity

I recently did a market analysis for equity and every one of my staff got a raise because of that. One tech got a 33% raise. After five years of trying, I finally got a raise and a title change that more accurately reflects the managerial work I do. This hospital only gives a 2.5% raise each year, which means they reward our loyalty by holding our salary below market value. At every other hospital, salaries go up and up and up. But the longer we stay here, the farther away we get from our market value.

Part of the problem is that while my staff gets a 2.5% raise a year, our CEO got a $1.5 million bonus last year. And the staff knows that. The staff no longer get bonuses. And here the administration tells us things like, "There's a hiring freeze. You can't hire any more people." Or they say there's no money for a new lab when I tell them we need one. Well, I know where they can find a million dollars.

The Organizational Culture

I always think about this place as a dysfunctional family—but they're only dysfunctional at the dinner table. When guests come over everybody's got their smile on and it's like, "Everything's great!" That's how it feels sometimes. I go to some meetings and I just think, *Wow. This is broken.* Everyone recognizes the dysfunction, but no one is motivated to change or to compromise.

I do think there needs to be a change in the organizational culture to improve joy in work, but people are reluctant to change. For example, we should be paperless by now, but we still have paper charts. We have paper charts *and* the EMR. We have both because some doctors are so reluctant to change that we have to have both. It's so hard to get people to change their day-to-day operations. There's so much pushback that change is almost impossible. I think the bigger the organization the harder it is.

Administration doesn't listen to the staff, but I find they will listen to families. If people go into patient relations, they're going to listen to that. If my staff were to say every day for a year, "This light above my head is broken, I can't see," nobody would care. But if a family were to come in and say, "Hey, this light should work," usually that gets a better response. If I want to get their attention, I have to use hot-button words like "patient experience." I can't just say, "The sink's broken, I need somebody to come and fix it."

When all is said and done, I know a lot of people respect me, and I feel respected by the people who matter to me. I like this hospital. It's true to its mission of helping children. The politics is all backstage.

Advice

To my bosses: Be more engaged with the lab and that will lead to better outcomes for your patients. Be specific about what you want from the staff. On any given day don't just say, "Try a therapy," but instead give us instructions for this patient. You know this patient better than we do. What do you want? What is your goal for this study? If you do that, then you're going to have a better outcome. It would be even better if you call the tech assigned to do the study and say, "Here's what I want to do." It will take three minutes of your time, and your patient is going to have a better experience and a better outcome. Some doctors do this sometimes, others never.

And forget the donuts. Just show up.

79. *Lawrence W., MD, Retired Obstetrician/Gynecologist and Professor of Obstetrics/Gynecology in an Academic Medical Center*

Lawrence W., MD, is contemplative yet reticent as he recalls his career as a professor of obstetrics/gynecology and as a practicing OB/GYN at an academic medical center. His soft southern drawl evokes a bygone era, a slower time. He graduated from medical school in 1968, was on active duty in the army for two years, did his internship and residency, and worked at the same institution for 42 years. Fearful of providing details of his organization's dysfunctional leadership even now, in retirement, Lawrence suggests that entrenched, unsupportive leaders engender fear and sap joy among even the most dedicated professionals. He spoke only on the condition of complete anonymity. Since retiring he has "taken on some part-time gigs in maternal and fetal medicine," consulting in areas of the country he enjoys.

As a child I was always thinking, what do I want to do? I spent a great deal of my childhood doing sequential elimination of multiple possibilities. I wanted to be a paleontologist, I wanted to be a missionary, I wanted to be a minister, I wanted to be a mechanical engineer, an architect. There were a lot of things along the way. For me, the choice to be a doctor was just a winnowing down of possibilities. I would go to places like summer camps where I would work for the surveyor. Another summer I worked in a factory making furnaces. I tried different things until I found something I thought I could do, and that I liked doing.

Within medicine, it was also a process of serial elimination. I had been a psychology major in college and so I was grappling with whether to get a PhD in psychology or to become a psychiatrist or a neurosurgeon working on the brain. I spent a few summers doing neurosurgical research on cats. That meant operating on the cats, dividing their brains up, putting electrodes in their brains—actual scientific stuff. The epiphany for turning away from that and heading into obstetrics came when a cat I was going to sacrifice in an experiment delivered kittens in her cage just before she was due to be sacrificed. I said, "Nuts to this. You and the kittens are going back." Some weeks later I adopted one of those surviving kittens and had him as a pet for 16 years. It was one little thing in that birth experience that pointed me in the direction of obstetrics. If you believe in signs in life, if you believe a robin is a sign of spring, if you think those things are omens, then that could have been part of what put me on this path.

On Joy in Work

I have felt joy in work from the very beginning. The excitement of doing obstetrics, particularly high-risk obstetrics, things that can involve some danger, is very intense. And although you feel the highs and the lows—the high of success and the low if things don't work out—for me, the highs make the lows something to watch out for, like you watch out for poison ivy. You don't want to have a negative experience—but I feel that obstetrics was something I was meant to do. That I was skilled at. It was rewarding to have success.

My skills away from obstetrics deal with mechanical things. Things like architecture and geometry. The inner geometry and spatial relationships of the pelvis and the neuromusculature related to the pelvis and uterus have always fascinated me. This was an interest I sustained consistently since my work with animals.

When I was recruiting residents I would always say, "This business of obstetrics is a calling. You should do it if it's what really makes you feel good and makes your life fulfilling. But if it's drudgery or if you find it distressing, don't do it." For me, it's very sustaining. Happy colleagues who create a team spirit of, "We can do this!" is wonderful. For the last ten years of my career I became involved in training midwives. That was just a wonderful, joy-enhancing experience. I believe in the positive power of team spirit.

Overcoming Obstacles to Joy

The original university model for the hospital got to be clunky and expensive. The hospital was old, and management of the hospital was entrenched. You know how bureaucracies can get, where you have to do things a certain way and you keep doing them that way because that's the way they've always been done? Time goes by and costs go up and if you stubbornly keep doing things the same way and the costs keep going up and revenue doesn't go up, you are in big trouble. That's what was happening at my institution.

So we got a partial divorce from the university. The board of trustees decided the university should just be the university and taught the physicians how to build a firewall of sorts between us. We got a commercial firm to run the hospital and they turned things around and made a profit. Instead of going bankrupt the doctors in the practice plan, who were now centralized and organized, created a viable structure. It felt good to succeed. Dealing with the negatives of being unwanted were keenly felt, but the positives of overcoming and improving negative expectations felt pretty good.

Positive feedback is great. Negative feedback kind of stinks, although it's important. I think to achieve really big, important things you need to have a big problem in the first place; you have to define the problem; and then you have to come up with a plan to change whatever it is you're dealing with so you change the world a little bit.

Advice

My advice to leaders today is to have good core values. You have a clear purpose—you're trying to make sick people well. You're trying to successfully and optimally treat disease. So, keep that as your target and keep trying different ways to do it better. Instead, people tend to get together and have big meetings. They'll write everything down and make a codified book of rules. But those who do that had better expect to review that book of rules honestly once a year, and change that plan and those rules, not just put it on the shelf and keep doing it according to the method they decided on—because the method will become outdated, suddenly, before they know it.

Continuous quality improvement's a great idea. This whole thing of top down—finding someone who's made a mistake and blaming the individual and then casting them out of the group—is a terribly destructive thing to do. That's the real truth. It was done at my institution plenty of times. It's done everywhere. It's a universal tendency for people to do it.

An organization's leaders have to be insightful and to have learned the Deming method—what is now called lean or Six Sigma—and use it, keep their wits about them, and not blame everything that goes wrong on the failure of one person—with the exception, let's say, of the person who is a complete drunkard on the job and has willfully done harmful things. But most things where human error occurs, rather than jumping on the person, it's important to restudy the process and find safer ways of doing things. That was a regular part of administration at my institution when everybody was feeling sane.

When people don't feel supported, they're afraid to be imaginative. And when they shut off their imaginations that's another way to doom the organization because they stay rigid. The rules are considered so strong that it's like a hot electrical fence. We don't dare touch it. And so, we're very fearful and we stay within the fence because the punishment for not doing so is great. We don't have enough imagination, freedom, or confidence to say, 'I think I've got a very good reason to reach over beyond the fence to do something.' So creativity gets stifled. A system of punishment takes over. I've seen that, I've suffered from that.

There still is a considerable culture of secrecy, negative top-down authoritarianism that's practiced in the name of policy. This has nothing to do with continuous quality improvement.

80.   Lisa W., MSN, Family Nurse Practitioner in a Small Internal Medicine Group Practice

Lisa W., MSN, is a family nurse practitioner who has worked for 12 years in an internal medicine group practice affiliated with a small teaching hospital. Her joy in work comes from feeling useful; but for the last seven years Lisa has felt underutilized, apart from her community of practice, disturbed by the lack of leadership, and is pondering her future.

I graduated from college in 1998. I got my undergraduate degree in human biology, which was like "biology lite," because I didn't want to take organic chemistry. I was always interested in medicine, but I was not particularly happy in college and could not see myself continuing for four more years of medical school and then residency, and then a potential fellowship, all in a row. So, I put any thought of medicine away for a few years. I worked at jobs unrelated to medicine after graduating from college.

In 2002 I decided to think about what I wanted to do next and started looking into medical schools. That was all I knew and what I assumed I was going to do. I talked to a few family friends at the time. One, who wasn't an MD—he had worked as an assistant to the dean of a medical school for many, many years—asked me what I envisioned in wanting to be a doctor. I said I envisioned taking care of people, probably in some rural place, and really being with my patients.

He said, "Well, I think you should look into becoming a nurse practitioner," which was a field I didn't know existed. He described physicians' administrative burden and lack of time with patients, and he thought being a nurse practitioner would be a good fit for me. The other variable was that by then I was 25 and felt I had already lost time. The way the math worked out, if I'd gone on to become a doctor, I probably would have gone into practice around the age of 37.

I'm not good at multitasking. I didn't like the idea of being a parent, which I knew I wanted to be, and becoming a doctor. A lot of people do it, but I knew that just wasn't for me. It was a lucky thing that this person came along and gave me a different idea. So, I started interviewing people I knew who had become nurse practitioners, and that's how I decided. I went to nursing school in the fall of 2003.

Today there are many of what are called "direct entry" graduate nursing programs, but at the time I think there were only about ten in the country. I got into one of these programs to do an intensive nurse practitioner training. My program was three years long and I did about 18 months of undergraduate nursing training. I didn't get a diploma, I didn't get an associate's degree, I didn't get a bachelor's. I got a certificate from the school to show that I completed that training and then took the registered nursing boards. Then I became an RN.

I couldn't have quit my program to get hired as a registered nurse because no one would hire someone without, at the very least, an associate's degree; and now, a lot of hospitals will only hire someone with a bachelor's degree. I had to keep going for another 18 months or so of master's-level training. Once I got my RN I got into my specialty, and there was another 18 months of training for that. I have a master of science in nursing, which allows me to be an advanced practice registered nurse.

If you think about it, a medical degree requires four years of undergraduate school, four years of medical school, and at least three years of residency. And my training only required three years. In my college it was only 18 months. Someone could go in with no knowledge of science and become a nurse practitioner in 18 months. I think this is dangerous, regulation-wise. Looking back on it now, I'm not surprised that this field has become popular, that people would want to train in a relatively short amount of time to make a good income. But I'm kind of shocked that it's been allowed. I guess it means that, luckily, there haven't been a lot of medical errors by undertrained nurse practitioners. But the short amount of training is definitely a concern to me. In terms of the intensity of training it's definitely rigorous, and then you finish and take the boards to become a nurse practitioner. There's no residency.

I graduated from nursing school in 2006 as a family nurse practitioner and went to work for the same federally qualified community health center where I had been a student. That was my first job. It was quite large, with many practitioners, nurse practitioners, and physician assistants. Each had his or her own panel of patients; they were the primary care providers for those patients. I worked there for about eight months before coming to this practice; I've been working here for 12 years.

The adult internal medicine practice where I work now is very different from that federally funded community health center. I'm the only nurse practitioner in this practice. I am not employed by the hospital; I am employed by the owner of the practice, a woman I'll call Jennifer. She is the founder of the practice, which just celebrated its 30th year. This has functioned for many years as a small group, even though the four doctors I work with are employed by the hospital. I am actually Jennifer's only clinician employee.

I do not have my own panel of patients here. I'm not considered a primary care provider. This really does function as a group practice, but Jennifer and the four other doctors are not in business together—they are not partners in that sense. She runs the business and reaps whatever benefits there are. She doesn't pay them; the hospital pays them. But in terms of the culture of the practice, and sharing call for patients, and covering each other's patients when they're in the hospital, they function very much like any other small practice. But I answer only to Jennifer.

I work five days a week from 8:30 a.m. to 2:30 p.m., and during that time my day is broken up into 15-minute slots. I am basically the "overflow valve" for the practice. Patients might call in for a sick visit and their primary care provider doesn't have a slot in their schedule, so I see them. A provider may be out this week, so patients need to reschedule an annual physical with me. Often for things like suture removal or blood pressure checks, the primary care provider will ask the patient to schedule those appointments with me. Also, I've been certified as a medical examiner for the state department of transportation. A medical examiner has to go through 40 hours of online training and pass an exam to be able to take a history and do a physical for commercial drivers. Every few years commercial drivers have to pass a medical exam saying they're fit to drive. I probably do two of those a month.

Jennifer and I are trying to get the physicians to be more organized about telling patients they should schedule routine follow-up appointments, like diabetes follow-ups, with me. It's a little hard to get everybody to agree to a workflow and stick to it since they're not business partners and my boss isn't their boss. We've all said it would make sense if I were to see patients for follow-ups: for example, if a patient has started on a new blood pressure medication, they need to come back in six weeks to have their blood work done and their blood pressure re-checked. I can do more than that, and the doctor can also do that, but it makes more sense for me to see those patients because the doctors' schedules are almost always full. It really needs to come from the physicians who their patients should follow-up with. It is unclear how this might be resolved.

What's my day like? As I said, I work from 8:30 a.m. to 2:30 p.m. I don't take a lunch. All the doctors take lunches, so I'm someone who can see people from 11:30 a.m. to 1:00 p.m. when most people are eating their lunches. Some days my schedule is full; if I were to see a patient every 15 minutes, the way my schedule is set up I could see 17 or 18 patients. But I rarely see more than 10 or 12. So I'm not fully utilized. I tend to have clusters of patients in the morning so they can go to work. I can have seven patients, one after the other, every 15 minutes, for a couple of hours. I can't spend more time with those patients necessarily, but then if it's quieter after that I'll have time to finish my notes before I leave for the day.

I am very lucky not to be in the situation of being paid based on productivity—or of having someone breathing down my neck about productivity. I would say we're on the other end of it. We should be doing a better job of making sure that my schedule is filled. But I feel very lucky and sheltered from that reality. Not only do I get paid no matter what, but I don't have anybody telling me that I need to boost my productivity. They say we as a group need to do this, but they're not pointing a finger at me. The physicians do get paid on productivity.

On Joy in Work

For me, joy in work is very much wrapped up with being useful. Am I being allowed by the system around me to be useful to patients in terms of my own knowledge? Am I as good a nurse practitioner as I can be? And is the necessary bureaucracy around me allowing me to do the best I can? I would say I'm lucky because in this position I've felt that most of the time. I've been the nurse practitioner I wanted to be, I've had the time I want to spend with my patients, and there haven't been any hindrances to that from the outside.

In the past three or four years as I've become more experienced, how I can be more useful has become more of a question to me. At this point I feel I'm not being used as completely as I should be, so that takes away from the joy. I haven't figured out what to do about that yet. I've been seeing if I can expand my role within this job by working with my boss to see how we can get the physicians to siphon some of their patients to me.

Barring that, I've always assumed I would work in community health, which I feel is a natural place for me. Being a student, and then working those first eight months practicing in community health, confirmed that. In the next year or two if I don't feel I've filled out my role in this position that will be my next job.

I made the decision that I didn't want to work 50 hours a week. I want time to be with my children. I could certainly have a much bigger job than I have, but my husband and I feel very strongly that there would be no point in having kids if we couldn't be with them.

If I were to move to the administrative or managerial ladder as some people suggest that would bring the opposite of joy to me. It's just that simple. I understand that going into administration or teaching is the next step in mastery, but neither of those things would bring me any joy. In fact, they would suck the joy out of work for me.

On Fairness to Individuals and Groups

Among the physicians in this small practice, I would say the work environment is absolutely fair to individuals and groups; there's a real feeling for how important fairness is. Three of them are gay or lesbian and one is Indian. Four are female. The three physicians who are gay came through the '80s with the AIDS crisis, they lost many friends, and they had to figure out how to be gay medical doctors when that was a new thing to be talking about. They're very, very aware and fair in that sense.

On Money and Joy

I don't think there's a relationship between money and joy. For me there isn't. But it does bother me immensely that my colleagues, who are some of the most brilliant, dedicated people I know, are paid at the bottom of physician incomes. Not just at my institution. But as primary care providers, as generalists, they are paid at the bottom. We have a friend who's an orthopedic surgeon in our town and he makes $1 million a year. And you cannot tell me that his placing of a knee joint is more important than what my colleagues do in caring for the *entire body* of a person for 30 years. I think about the disparity in pay in medicine a lot. And if I were a physician in general practice, I can imagine that would sap my joy because I'd feel I was literally being undervalued.

This doesn't affect me; I'm paid hourly. And I really like that. I like the direct relationship between the number of hours I work and the amount of money I make. What brings me satisfaction is that I get paid fairly for the work I do. I wouldn't say it leads to joy, but it doesn't take joy away. I wouldn't feel more joy if you paid me more.

What Diminishes Joy

Not a whole lot diminishes joy in work for me. I feel extremely lucky in my position, with the exception of feeling underutilized. I see people who do huge jobs, see patients, and still have kids. I'm still struggling with the reality of who I am. I don't have a whole lot of energy. I do need to sleep quite a few hours a night. I'm not good at multitasking. So that's guided a lot of choices in my life. It's an ongoing heartache to feel a little anemic in terms of my contribution as a medical provider. And I haven't figured out how to push that boundary yet.

Not Feeling Challenged

In my first five years of practice all my attention went into learning, which gave me a tremendous amount of joy. The doctors here are all incredible teachers and incredible doctors. For the first five years I was working for them I felt completely full because when I wasn't seeing patients, I was learning from the doctors. But now that I have the basics of learning under my belt, I have to figure out how I'm going to feel more fulfilled. Maybe it's time to hand off my position to an amazing nurse practitioner who can learn from these doctors, and then find another place where I can grow.

Inadequate Office Management

We do not have an effective office manager and haven't had one since I've been here. So, we have nobody who is good at hiring. The office managers we've had in the past didn't have the personality that an office manager or an HR manager should have. They weren't leaders and they had no ability to corral people in a positive way. They had no ability to make people feel they're part of a team or that they're supported. Or to make people feel appreciated. They also had no project management skills. They didn't know how to take an idea from a meeting and make it real. They hired ineffective people. There's very high turnover. And patients sometimes are not happy.

Problems often arise around prescriptions. If it's a prescription for a controlled substance, the prescription has to be mailed to the person's house or the patient has to come in to pick it up. They'll be some sort of, not miscommunication, but lapse in the front desk's transferring of that message to the provider. Things like that. I'd bet not a high number of those things happen, but I can't say the patients are always happy.

Although the physicians are fair to individuals and groups, the practice itself is not well managed that way; I think this is because the owner, Jennifer, hasn't been willing or able to—and again, I don't envy her this responsibility, I don't know how I would do it better—find and pay for an excellent office manager in at least a decade since I've been here. We have a diverse staff racially and ethnically. We have equal numbers of White, Hispanic, Indian, and African American staff, but if you don't have an effective leader it's like *Lord of the Flies*. It's cannibalism. Front office staff and medical assistants are getting into fights. One doesn't do her work because someone else isn't doing hers. The office manager comes into my office and rolls her eyes about my boss. It can be very, very petty and entirely inefficient.

This affects me more as a human being than as a nurse practitioner. I'm not trying to crank through 30 cases in a day. It's a bummer. Morale is low. The practice owner, my boss, is very dismissive of these problems when I talk to her about them. She says everyone should just buck up and do their work. She could enhance my joy in work by taking the time and spending the money to find a really good office manager. There is no resolution as things stand. But this makes only a small dent in my enjoyment of the job.

The Electronic Medical Record

We changed our EMR in 2017 from what we'd been using to Epic. These are totally different computer programs; from an information technology standpoint, the change-over was a huge amount of work for the hospital and the practice. Everything had to be abstracted into the new program and everybody had to learn how to use it. It's sort of like going from Microsoft Word to Google Docs times 50. I was learning a new computer program, but I was also dealing with how to get access to my patients' information without it taking me an hour. And figuring out how to get back into the old record because they didn't abstract every single thing. It's been very difficult for the entire system.

Having to deal with the EMR does sort of diminish my joy. But having chosen not to become a physician takes an enormous amount of that away. The burden would be much, much, much worse if I were a physician. Working with a computer program is not my favorite thing but that's just the way it is now. I didn't particularly love writing long-hand chart notes either. And I like writing. So, I don't mind the writing part. Most of the physicians dictate into a voice-recognition computer program but I type. I'm a good typist and I really like writing so that part doesn't bother me. In fact, I enjoy it sometimes. What I think would really sap joy for me is if I were inundated with paperwork. And that just doesn't happen because I'm nobody's primary care provider. If I were to go back to work at a community health center and I were a primary care provider, I would see more paperwork, though still not at the level physicians deal with. There are several things that only MDs can do so they're stuck with it. I have very little burden when it comes to paperwork.

Feeling Outside the Community of Practice

My supervisor is not the demonstrative sort, but my physician colleagues may tell their patients to come in and see me for their next appointment. They'll give me compliments, telling patients I'm their fabulous nurse practitioner. But in my position, I'm not part of a community. The doctors are very much woven into the fabric of the hospital where we work, a lovely, small teaching hospital. The hospital has been acquired by a bigger group and will be changing a lot. But until now it's been a true community of providers. I don't get to participate in that because my office is physically separate, three miles down the road. I'm very much siloed in my practice. In terms not of being rewarded and not being recognized as a provider, that sense of community is missing to some extent. I feel a little like a figment of the doctors' imaginations, I guess. But that's a function of the way my practice is organized.

It's going to be an ongoing question as to where people in professions like physician assistants and nurse practitioners fit. And how they regard themselves. For me, part of joy in work is feeling recognized, trusted. If you're a medical doctor you get to be highly regarded. Or if you're an electrician, nobody can take that from you. But with nurse practitioners and physician assistants it's more wishy-washy. Even registered nurses are a very proud group with a very well-defined position. They're often unionized and they're very good at making a bigger community. Whereas with mid-level providers that hasn't happened, and it certainly isn't part of my professional life. I think that's an interesting thing to consider.

Advice

In terms of advice, I think about what I'd say in an exit interview if and when I move on. What would I say that would be helpful if my boss were willing to hear it?

I don't think anything is insurmountable. I think more time and money needs to be spent to hire good, professional staff, including an office manager. And if we don't feel we're able to manage that ourselves, we should hire someone to find those people. I think we need to invest in that process. The amount of time and money wasted on hiring and training people only to have them quit, only to have them be fired, never mind the expense to morale when you work in an office where people are constantly leaving, is enormous. I know it would be an expensive process, but I also think it would pay dividends.

Disrespect

81.   Tina J., Radiographer and Assistant Director of Radiology at an Academic Medical Center

Tina J. has been an x-ray technologist for more than 22 years. As assistant director of radiology at a large academic medical center, she not only supervises x-ray techs but works "in the trenches" beside them. Tina describes how it feels to work in an organization where arrogance, non-inclusion, disrespect, and blame make people feel as if they're coming to work "with a gun to their heads."

I'm an x-ray technologist. I have a certificate in radiologic technology. I was aware of x-ray technology because my sister did it and I thought it was interesting. I always liked science, and you get to apply science in x-ray. I've always been a bit of a nurturer/carer but I didn't want to go into nursing. I thought that would mean becoming too attached to the patient. I thought that x-ray, and radiology in general, would mean I'd make you laugh, I'd make you comfortable, I'd give you love, and then you'd be gone.

When I first got out of school I worked in a walk-in medical center for a month or two. Then I was in an orthopedic office and was working per diem in another hospital. After that I assumed a job as a full-time x-ray tech here. I've been here for 21 years now. Altogether, I've been an x-ray tech for over 22 years.

I manage the radiology department of a large academic medical center from 4:00 p.m. to midnight. This is my normal, regular schedule. I can count on it. I've never worked a schedule that wasn't predictable here.

The radiology department is vast. There's x-ray, CT scan, magnetic resonance imaging (MRI), nuclear medicine, and ultrasound. I supervise the technologists in x-ray. I plug them directly into areas where they're needed, which happens at a moment's notice. I do their schedules, evaluations, and so on. It's my decision as to who goes where once a doctor has ordered an x-ray.

I don't staff the modalities outside of x-ray, but because I have the title of assistant director and there's no supervisor on between four p.m. and midnight in those areas, they call me when something goes wrong and they don't know what to do. There are CT scan techs on, of course, from 4:00 p.m. to midnight but I don't supervise them. x-ray is much busier than other imaging departments—we have higher volume—because x-ray is relatively quick compared to other kinds of imaging. We may do 40 x-rays in the time it takes to do one MRI. That's why, in x-ray, we have many more employees on from 4:00 p.m. to midnight than other areas of radiology do.

In this major medical center, I have to send techs to the OR, the ER, and up to the floor, and I have to keep techs in the radiology department to do procedures on patients who come down here. My job is a lot like playing a shell game—move three techs over here, pull one from the ER and have her go to the neonatal intensive care unit, send her back to the ER, have one go to the OR—just to keep areas that are always busy adequately staffed. That means I have to know what's going on in the hospital.

All different kind of codes are called, and I have to respond to them: a code T is a trauma and I have to make sure someone is in the ER waiting for the helicopter to land. I'm no physician but I can assess immediately whether I need to send an x-ray tech to the OR. I'll tell the techs they'd better go to dinner now because I'll be calling for them in about an hour.

I'm also in the trenches performing x-rays myself. I prefer it that way so I can keep an eye on my techs, see what they're doing, what they don't know, and guide them since it is a teaching hospital. I also feel I can give better evaluations to staff members if I'm working beside them. Up on the floors, I don't know what they're doing.

On Joy in Work

I think joy in work is getting something back, not just giving all of your soul without reciprocity. Joy used to come from the respect I'd feel from physicians and nurses, and from having teamwork. Now, we're treated like lower-level employees. There's never a "Thank you, good job," pat on the back.

I used to feel joy in work. In the beginning, even with technology, when I started we had a darkroom. I was literally in the darkroom developing films. And in developing films there is a lot of control. We really were photographers. And the process separated the men from the boys, so to speak, because if you were a good tech and you knew your numbers and your techniques and all the other things you had to know, you got a little more respect—not just from your coworkers but from your supervisors, the radiologists. A radiologist might walk in in the morning and read everything that was done in the ER the night before. And if she were handed poor films, she wouldn't be happy because her name would be on the line: is it pneumonia, or is it not? I felt joy in the beginning because I felt satisfaction in doing my artwork; I felt a sense of accomplishment. I really wanted to problem-solve. I also wanted to cross-check and know I had the correct result.

We are advocates for our patients and our patients love us. When we give to someone in time of need, it touches our soul and we get back. But when we're no longer thanked and there's no reciprocity for what we do, that takes away the joy.

On Money and Joy

No one wants to work with a coworker who complains all day. That used to be the minority and now it's almost the majority. A lot of this has to do with money. No one has gotten a raise in years. We can't make enough money to live where we need to. When they hire people who are making more than I am, I think, *What? I know more than they do. I do more than they do. I'm teaching them. How come I'm not getting a raise?'*

Hospital mergers are causing people to leave because people can make more money elsewhere. This affects radiology as well as nursing. People come in, they get a year's worth of experience, they throw on their resume "I'm a trauma tech," and they can get a job anywhere. There is a lot of dissatisfaction among the people who have decided to remain. We're at a crisis right now.

People are unhappy and it really is about the money, not because they're too busy at work. There's toxic negativity right now. There's less laughter. There's less ability to enjoy our jobs. Being immersed in such a negative environment has taken away the joy. Back in the day, as busy as we were, we always still managed to laugh and help each other out.

What Diminishes Joy

I can recall the day we ripped out our darkroom and got a computerized system. x-rays I'd been taking for seven years, I couldn't get to come out. I lost control. I lost the art form. I lost the ability to assess a patient by looking at her and thinking, *okay, she is older. She's going to have less bone density so I'm going to alter my numbers—because if I use strong numbers it will shoot right through her bones and "burn them out"*, as we say. Now, the computer doesn't want to know the age of the patient. This is supposed to be an ankle x-ray so it averages all the pixels. Back in the day I could make the x-ray look a lot prettier. The radiologist appreciated that. And so did the ER docs.

Now I feel my joy in work is gone—when it comes out of my mouth it sounds terrible. There have been a lot of changes. Twenty years ago, despite being busy and short-staffed, my co-workers and I had more fun at work. I'm not quite sure why. Maybe some of it is that healthcare has changed so much. It's a combination of things. And then came the computer revolution, which neutered what doctors think the average x-ray should look like.

All the x-rays come out the same now. Everything is computerized and that's all the techs are learning. We need to think about differentiation when we're "shooting" the patient. Their status. Many factors. In the past, people were more appreciative of a good tech because they had beautiful films to read. "Good job! These are gorgeous. I'm confident now in saying what we found." That was the pat on the back I got. Now, I have to send out reports that are wishy-washy, saying, "XYZ cannot be entirely ruled out." There is more mediocrity today than there used to be. There are only one or two pediatric radiologists here who look at an X-ray and ask, "Who shot this? This is a gorgeous film." And they're old-school. They're really collegial, knowing we get things the newbies don't.

Inefficient Processes

Administration wanted to find a way for patients to be seen in the ER more quickly; the building had simply run out of space, which meant patients could be waiting in the ER to see a doctor for two to three hours from the time they checked in. They did a root cause analysis to look into this problem. They decided that a patient will check into the ER and then see a nurse practitioner right away. This nurse practitioner will take a set of vitals and get a quick history, then order some simple tests like blood work and x-rays. Then orders are printed onto a list: for example, Mary Smith needs an x-ray.

At that point the patient is sent to a hallway. In the hallway there is an electronic tracking board showing where patients are waiting. We go to the hallway to look for Mary Smith, but we can't find her. She isn't there. So, a nurse has to go and find her. We spend all this time running around looking for the patient. At times we have aides getting patients for us, but at times we also look for patients ourselves. It varies. But it's a waste of time.

We can't find patients because people in the department keep moving them. They move them and move them and move them. I have a work list on my wristwatch. They think the tracking information on my watch is in real time, but by the time I get there they've moved them again. They funnel people to different areas in the hallway and move them in different directions. Trying to find patients has become a joke. We've been told, "You're not looking hard enough" for patients and "You can't just yell down the hallway and then walk away." My response has been, "How much time do you want me to spend looking for patients?"

Disrespect

Administration pretends to involve me in their decisions. They invite me to a meeting and then just tell me what to do. They don't listen to my point of view based on experience. The ER becomes tyrannical and they do what they want.

As a student in this field I rotated through radiology departments in various hospitals. There, I always felt radiology had a backbone. We could say, "No, you can't do this study in that order because it's going to compromise the second study. You have to do it in this order." The physicians who were ordering x-rays would say, "Okay, change this." Whereas here—I don't know if it's a teaching hospital thing or what—I've always felt there's no backbone in my department. There's no foundation. There's no respect for our point of view. If a radiologist says something is not an appropriate exam, the physician who's ordering it says, "I don't care; do it anyway."

We like to be patient advocates. We're treated like dummies who don't know what we're doing and who don't get the whole scope of things. We don't want to be treated that way. The signal we get from doctors and nurses is that, as x-ray techs, we're not the loving and caring people that nurses are. But I'm not lazy. I think, *I'm telling you this, I'm giving you friction, because I'm advocating for the patient and what you're telling us to do isn't right.* And they say, "Just do it."

Punitive Response to Errors and Inequity

There are computer glitches by which something might go wrong. There are rare glitches when something gets erased. In the past, if somebody fogged the film by opening the door to the darkroom—because you're never supposed to have light in the darkroom—the film might be ruined, the image would just disappear. Things went wrong then and they go wrong now. There's always the possibility of having to repeat an x-ray. Today, shooting the wrong body part by accident is considered an unprescribed dose of radiation; the response to events like this is more stringent and punitive than it used to be and has involved both changes in hospital policies and fines.

The administration implemented new policies to ensure patients would be double-verified and maybe have a second x-ray tech in the room to see that errors like shooting the wrong body part would never happen again. Our mistakes have decreased significantly since they put the new policies into practice, but they haven't stopped altogether. I tell new hires, "There's a reason you have to do these 97 steps. Every time a mistake happens, they look into why it happened, and we try to correct that problem."

Several years ago, the administration slapped people with exorbitant fines for shooting the wrong body part. To slap huge fines on employees is wrong. This went on for a period of time and everyone was in an uproar. These are technologists who makes $60,000 a year. Some people got lawyers. Those fines haven't been paid, and they are still hovering over us, years later. I've heard it said many times, "I feel like I'm walking into work with a gun to my head." What kind of a way to work is this?

Today, the fines have gone away, but now when mistakes happen, they take vacation days away from techs—but that is inconsistent. Sometimes they do, sometimes they don't. There is no rhyme or reason to what happens. One person has the fine hanging over his head because he was unfortunate enough to make a mistake three years ago; now if someone makes a mistake, they are threatened with having their vacation days taken away. Multiple people have been threatened that way and only certain people have actually had those days taken. We don't really know what goes on or why.

A new director came into our department at the height of the fines. He had all of these meetings and had a big whiteboard where he would write down everyone's thoughts and suggestions. Nothing happened at the end of that. People were hopeful that maybe change would come. But then, again, people were afraid to be 100% honest at those meetings.

The Business of Healthcare

What I don't like is that healthcare is more of a business nowadays. It's turned into volume, volume, volume, volume. These are *people*. This is your *grandmother*. And the physicians are treated that way, as well. I see it. It's one thing that you want me to pump out more x-rays in an hour. But you want to rush the radiologists now, too? If they rush a read, they're going to miss something. And they are pressured. The business aspect has no place in medicine. This isn't Wall Street. Stop trying to make this Wall Street. There is a conflict of interest in healthcare.

82. Helen H., Environmental Services Associate for an Academic Medical Center

Helen H. has been a working housekeeping supervisor in two hospitals within one large academic medical center for a total of almost eight years. She oversees and works alongside three housekeepers to turn over operating rooms quickly and efficiently. Helen takes pride in her work but her disrespectful treatment by doctors and nurse anesthetists, in particular, diminishes her joy and is a source of tension.

I have worked as an environmental services associate in two different hospitals, part of the same large academic medical center, for a total of almost eight years. I worked at the first hospital for almost seven and a half years and recently moved to the one I work for now. I started here as a manager.

Before this I worked in commercial cleaning, cleaning offices. To be honest, the office building that I was cleaning was sold and they were bringing in their own cleaning crew. I thought there would always be an opportunity at a hospital because there's a need to keep hospitals clean. I decided to give it a try. I applied and have been doing this ever since. I do like it.

I have an eight-hour shift but I'm usually here at least nine hours a day. I have the same schedule every week. I like the early shift. I'm usually here around 5:40 in the morning because surgery starts early, and I want to make sure everything is good to go before they start. The first thing I look at when I come in is the floor. I don't want to see debris on the floor. Appearance is everything.

We turn over operating rooms, so we have to be fast. We don't have a checklist, we just know what we're supposed to do. Everyone has a task. We have a 30-minute window, wheels in to wheels out, as they say. On my turnover team there are three people plus me. It's not just the four of us who clean the ORs, but it's the whole, larger turnover team. Sometimes multiple operating rooms need cleaning at the same time, so we split up.

The first thing we do when we clean the OR is to take out the dirty trash, which is usually linen and biological waste. Next, we take out the clear trash. Then we start our wipe-down—we wipe all the tables, the lights, the OR bed itself from top to bottom, and then we mop the floor and we're out. That's called an in-between case turnover.

We do a terminal clean at the end of the day when the ORs are closed. We move all the furniture to the middle of the room and pick up things left from anesthesia, like dropped caps and tiny things that get kicked under furniture. With such a quick turnover time between cases, those things get pushed to the back; we clean everything up at night. A lot is entailed in a terminal clean, such as high dusting, washing the walls, things we don't do in between cases. The instrumentation goes to surgical processing.

How Problems Are Communicated

Infection prevention specialists round in our areas and I round with them. They point out things that need to be addressed. If someone thinks there is a problem with the way the OR has been cleaned, that person goes to the director of the OR and the director comes to me. The director of the OR also communicates that problem to the director of environmental services.

Surgeons don't come to me to tell me something isn't good, they don't have time. They pass the little things on to someone else to let us know. If, for whatever reason, something big is not cleaned to their satisfaction, surgeons do say something directly. For example, before I came here there were some high dusting issues with the overhead lights, the ones with those arms that come down. One of the surgeons pulled the light down and dust came off. That's a big, big no-no. I got things back in order when I came here.

For the most part, the administration knows and respects what I do. Administration at the higher levels doesn't really have anything to do with what I do. We don't usually hear about anything unless there's a problem.

On Joy in Work

I'm a pleaser. I try to please everybody. I try to make everything the way it needs to be and to make everything flow correctly. That's my joy. I feel it most days. Every day is not going to be the same, but I do feel it a lot.

Compliments enhance my joy in work, just hearing nice things from the OR staff. I hear compliments quite often. They say things like, "Ever since you came here things are so much better."

I've grown to really enjoy working in a hospital. I meet so many nice people, both patients and co-workers. When I'm passing in the hall, I always speak to everybody. People get lost, I take them to where they need to go. Things like that. I do enjoy my job.

On Money and Joy

I think there is a relationship between money and joy. Some of my co-workers feel they don't get paid enough for what they do. I get paid a little more than they do, and since I'm a working supervisor I see both sides. Sometimes, with what we go through, I think, *wow, we really do deserve a little more*. If I could change anything about my job it would probably be the money. I love my hours. I wouldn't change that for anything. I'm not greedy—I would just ask for a little more money.

What Diminishes Joy

What diminishes my joy in work? Sometimes people in anesthesia or within the OR area are snooty and don't even want to talk to me. Then there are nurses who don't get patient rooms ready to be cleaned and I end up doing that.

Disrespect

I say good morning to everybody, I don't care who you are. But when people just look at me and don't even respond—that, right there—it's like, "Ugh. Housekeeper. Can't talk to her." I don't like that.

I think it's getting a little better. But quite a few of them still walk right past me, especially doctors and nurse anesthetists. That was true at both hospitals where I've worked. I don't know if that attitude goes with the job—it's not everybody and it's not all the time—but there are certain people who look down their noses at me.

One of the things I don't like is when doctors or nurses just throw their gloves and their masks on the OR floor wherever they happen to be. And there are garbage cans everywhere in the OR and at every scrub sink! They're everywhere. That's rude. I don't know why they do it but it's horrible. This has been true at both hospitals where I've worked. If they drop something, they don't pick it up. Ever.

Doing Someone Else's Job

My direct manager sticks up for housekeeping and is very supportive. Sometimes I'll raise with her that some nurses aren't doing what they're supposed to be doing. For example, they are supposed to have the beds stripped and certain things picked up off the floor, but sometimes they just walk away without doing that. When we're paged that the room is ready to be cleaned, we'll find that the bed hasn't been stripped and the nurses are nowhere to be found. Sometimes I will do it because they've got to get the next patient into the room. Sometimes there's a good reason why the nurses didn't do it—maybe they had to help transport the patient—but if they're just standing in the hall playing on their phone or something like that, I'll make a comment or I'll tell my manager.

I work hard. I feel I am undervalued financially, and the way some people treat me makes me feel undervalued personally.

Advice

My advice for bosses and colleagues is: communicate. People at my last hospital were terrible communicators. For instance, if we had to go into a room where a patient had an isolation order, sometimes they would forget to tell us. I guess it's because HIPAA (the Health Insurance Portability and Accountability Act) laws throw a monkey wrench into so many things. I can't tell you how many times we've cleaned a room and then have been told, halfway through, "Oh by the way, that patient has HIV." This would happen a couple of times a month. It's a good thing we wear our proper protective equipment at all times.

I'm working with one of the nurses right now to get a small committee together to work on communicating things like that because we want to keep everybody safe. At my last hospital we had something simple in place: it was a sign on the door that alerted us to the fact that a patient had *Clostridium difficile* or something else we needed to know about. But they don't do that here.

I think healthcare professionals should treat housekeepers more like equals, and then housekeepers might get more respect from everyone else. And doctors' and nurses' disrespectful behavior, like throwing things on the floor, creates tension.

As my mentor has always said, "It all starts with housekeeping. Because if you don't get the rooms clean, then we can't do our jobs."

83. *Judith S., MSW, Retired Clinical Social Worker*

> Judith S., MSW, is a retired clinical social worker who has worked with adolescent boys
> and adults in some of the poorest, most isolated areas of the country—sometimes in
> facilities that can best be described as physically and emotionally harsh. Soft-spoken,
> strong, kind, and empathetic, her social work path was plotted more by life's twists
> and turns than by design. In this interview, my old friend Judith told me, "I really
> think you make your own joy. I am a resilient person. I knew how to pick the joy out
> of the day."

As an undergraduate I majored in biology but switched to psychology, which I'd always
been interested in, probably because my younger sister had a mental illness. At 15 she
was committed to a state hospital because of a suicide attempt. I became interested in that
and how it affected my family. So, I majored in psychology with minors in sociology and
social work, graduated, and got a job with the state where I worked for two years doing
social work.

I loved that social work job. We went to people's houses and made sure they had what
they needed. It was a federal program that helped women find jobs, get ready for work,
and find all the social services they needed to support their being able to work. I liked
helping people. I liked going out to their homes. I had a rural caseload, going out in the
county and talking to these women, learning about them. It was a different world then. It
was not dangerous. I wouldn't do that here anymore.

I decided I wanted to go to graduate school. If you promised to work for the state for
two years, then the state would pay for your graduate work. I had not worked for quite
two years, so the state paid for one year and I paid the rest from my savings. That meant
I owed the state one year. I worked in protective services, which is what the state wanted
me to do. Then a county director of social services retired and wanted me to apply for that
job. I got that job, worked there for a year, then married a psychiatrist, dropped everything
to work for him, and let my social work license lapse.

My Professional Journey

Residential Treatment Facility Counselor

I eventually left my husband and wanted to get my social work license back so I could
get a job. I hadn't taken an exam since I'd finished graduate school 28 years before and
I was terrified. I contacted a friend who was the clinical director of a residential treatment
facility for adolescent boys in a very poor, rural area of the country. This was a fairly newly
established private residential facility for boys ages 10–18 who had psychiatric diagnoses
and substance abuse. She asked me if I wanted to come and work for her. She hired me,
helped me get my license, and I became a counselor.

I worked there for three and a half years. There were about 50 boys when I was there.
The facility was supposed to take in non-violent and non-criminal boys who were primarily wards of the state, who had acted out to the point where their parents or guardians
could not take care of them. None of the boys had been adjudicated as criminal, although
they had been adjudicated as juvenile delinquent because they were not 21. The worst
thing some of them had done was to get busted at school for smoking pot. We were not

supposed to take boys who had intellectual disabilities but there were some who were borderline.

There was a school at the facility. A psychiatrist came in twice a month to see the boys. We had social workers and counselors. And then there were lower-level staff who just had high school degrees. They did not live there but stayed overnight as behavioral aides.

I was a social worker, so I had a caseload of ten boys to start with. Some of them I saw daily and some of them I saw two or three times a week for counseling sessions. I'd also go down to the cottages to check in with them. Before I left, I became the social services supervisor, which meant supervising the other counselors. I was not in charge of the aides or the people who provided direct care for the boys. I provided counseling, mostly behavioral counseling to a group of boys once a week.

I enjoyed working with the boys, and I found that I was particularly good at working with boys who had serious mental illness—not so much those who were juvenile delinquent or oppositional, but those with schizophrenia, bipolar disorder, and depression. I just seemed to have a gut feeling for how to work with these boys. And these were the boys who became my caseload when I got to choose my own caseload as supervisor.

I left that facility after three and a half years because the clinical director who had hired me was moving up and I didn't like the direction the facility was moving in—taking in more boys who were adjudicated juvenile delinquent and fewer who were mentally ill. When I told the clinical director I was leaving, she just looked at me and said, "I don't blame you. I think you'll be happier."

Brief Transition to Human Resources

Next, I took a job in the state department of human resources, which included child protection, adult protection, food stamps, all of that. At that point I was 56 years old and had to take turns being on call for child protection out in this rural county. There were nights when I got called to pick up a child at the jail because his mother had been jailed, and that just wasn't for me anymore.

Mental Health Center Clinical Director

I left that job, got my clinical social work license, and got a job at the local mental health center as their clinical director. I was there from 2006 to 2013. As the mental health center clinical director, I supervised all the staff. I had a caseload of about 200, maybe more. It was a ridiculous caseload. In addition to that caseload, I supervised one counselor, a secretary, an office manager, two case managers, two van drivers who were also aides in the day treatment program, and the bachelor's-level person who ran the day treatment program. I had the adult caseload and the other therapist had the children's and adolescents' caseload. I probably spent only about 5% of my time managing staff. I was, absolutely, doing hands-on clinical work. The culture of this place was collegial and supportive.

A patient there did not have to have a diagnosis of serious mental illness. Someone could come in for depression, or for an intake to get diagnosed and see the psychiatrist. We had a really good psychiatrist who came in once a week but because he was on staff, he was available to us every day; this was wonderful for a rural mental health center. I worked closely with him and we had a good relationship. The office manager had been there for 25 years when they hired me. She knew all the current clients, she knew their families, she knew everything. I always joked that I worked for her because she was so good. She was the office manager, but she helped me learn the ropes there. I loved it. That was my favorite job. I have some regrets that I left, but things work out.

I was more comfortable working with adults than with children. My favorite people to work with were those diagnosed with schizophrenia and bipolar disorder. I just seem to have a knack for that. In very rural areas we had case managers who would go out, check on patients, make sure they took their medicines properly, and they would notice when people were just not doing well, when things were not going well. They would bring those patients in for me to see and talk to so we could get them in to see the psychiatrist if need be. We would get them into the hospital if they had to go.

A lot of people decompensated over and over and over again for all sorts of reasons. A *lot* of our population lived in substandard housing. The families were very poorly educated. There is a lot of mental illness down there. Little pockets of the county are cut off by the river so that transportation has been a problem for the last 200 years. Case managers provided transportation and mostly, patients would come to me. Occasionally, if somebody would just not leave home, I would go out with the case manager. There were times when a person had decompensated so badly and wouldn't leave their home that I would have to determine whether they needed to go to the hospital. We tried to keep people from getting to that point, but when it became obvious that they were going to hurt themselves or die or hurt somebody else, then we would have to go through probate court and have them sent to the mental hospital. When they would leave the hospital, we would send the case manager out, sometimes daily, to make sure they were doing alright.

Teaching Respect   I found that I had to do some re-education of the case managers and office staff in terms of giving people their dignity, which I found lacking when I came. When I got there, for one, I thought that my case managers had become rather jaded working with people with serious illness. There were times when I felt they were really talking down to our clients and to their families. And that is a way of life in this rural, poor county, with people who have become educated and successful. When they've made it, they're not as nice to the people who have not made it. There were times when I thought some of the staff were harsher with patients than they should have been. I'd just have to speak to them. I wasn't a really assertive supervisor. I don't like supervising, I really don't, I'd rather work for somebody. But that was the job and it paid more money, so I was the supervisor. I got a good response from most of my staff, and they did change their behavior. They became kinder, more compassionate.

My management style is fairly subtle and suggestive. You know, you catch more flies with honey than you do with vinegar. I can do it, but I don't do assertive very well. More often than not, I was able to help the staff see. I'd sometimes say, "Do you really under-stand what it's like to hallucinate all the time? Do you really understand how it feels to be paranoid?" We would have staff meetings and talk about this sort of thing. And even though these women had been working with people with serious mental illness for 15, 20, 25 years, nobody had ever tried to help them see the other side and how it really felt. And how people just really couldn't help being this way or acting this way.

I'd say, about the families, "How would you feel if you had to live with so-and-so all the time? You'd be mean to them, too. You'd get frustrated. And you might even beat them if you were not very well educated and didn't know any better." We had cases of adult abuse because it's very hard to live with someone who is mentally ill when you don't have support. I just tried to educate my staff that way and I found that they responded. I don't believe in humiliating and shaming. I'd had enough of that in my career. I never did that.

Residential Treatment Facility Counselor 2.0

In 2013, the residential facility offered me the moon to come back, so I did. It turned out to be a bad decision. By the time I came back the problems there were even worse. At this point they were taking in boys from state-run facilities, serious juvenile delinquents, who had failed in those facilities and had failed when they went back into the community. These were seriously disruptive children. Lower-level staff were getting hurt by boys who were combative. I stayed this time for less than a year.

On Joy in Work

Being the mental health center director was the job where I found the joy, because I measured my personal success and the success of the whole operation by how many people got well or better: if a person started coming in looking just a little cleaner every time; seeing how much more often they smiled; when they reported having better sleep; or when they had fewer hallucinations. We'd finally get to the point where we could just look at somebody in the waiting room and think, *Oh my God, she's better today.*

I define joy in work by feeling good at the end of the day. Maybe there was some really hard case, and maybe I didn't get anywhere with that person, but then somebody else came in and they were better. Establishing relationships with people is really important.

I decided when I took the mental health center job that I would leave work at the office. I almost didn't take it because, having worked in my ex-husband's psychiatry office all those years, I saw how he took it all home. He worried about people all day and all night and ruminated over whether he had done the right thing for his patients. The very few suicides we had over the years were devastating. Absolutely devastating. Not just to him, but to our whole family. I decided to take the job after talking to a former colleague, but I really lived in fear of a suicide. I was blessed because in all the years I was there we didn't have a suicide. That was not because of me, it was just one of those things. It was a relief for me to leave there without having to endure a suicide.

Joy in work is the feeling of having interacted well with people and, at the end of the session, being able to wrap up with something positive for them to take home to work on. That was just my style. And feeling that when I wrote that case note, things were wrapped up, at least for that day.

The mental health center was a good place to work and I was doing something I felt I was good at. When I worked at the boys' facility, even though the work was absolutely new to me, by the time I left I felt good about my work most days.

On Money and Joy

Is there a relationship between money and joy? That's a hard question to answer. I'm not sure because the job where I found the most joy didn't pay a lot, although I was able to get them to pay me more than they first offered. I was satisfied with my salary. My colleagues were not paid as well and there was a lot of grumbling and dissatisfaction. Personally, I don't think there's a relationship between money and joy.

What Diminishes Joy

Disrespect

What diminishes joy in work for me is bad staff, bad people to work with. By the time I went back to work at the residential facility the clientele had changed, and many of the staff were terrible from the top down. This time, I had to work directly under the man who owned the facility, and he was a tyrant. One moment you were wonderful, and the next moment he was yelling at you and everybody else. He mistreated staff. He expected miracles out of all the staff. He was constantly trying to add to his program. He was not a clinician, but he considered himself an expert in everything.

For a while the owner treated me well because I was in the upper echelon of staff. He treated everybody under that like garbage, and six therapists left during the six months I was there because of the way he treated them. We're talking about master's level social workers and therapists. He had no respect for them whatsoever. He wouldn't speak to them. He wouldn't even pay them very much. If one of the social workers, say, made a mistake, he would bark, "Fire 'em." He never tried to find out what happened or why it happened. Never. You never knew from day to day who this man was going to attack and blow up on. One day he verbally attacked me in a meeting. I resigned the next day.

Nothing diminished my joy when I was at the mental health center. I just loved my job.

Reflections

I'd never given joy in the workplace or in mental health services much thought before now. I really think you make your own joy. You're either a person who can be joyful with whatever life gives you, or you're a person who does not know how to do that. I don't think my work made me joyful. I knew how to pick the joy out of the day. I am a resilient person. I don't know if that has to do with joy or not. I think you have to be pretty resilient to work successfully in healthcare services because it's hard. It's hard from nurses' aides on up to your uber doctors. It's emotionally hard, physically hard, and financially hard. So, I think it takes a certain resilience to stay in those professions.

Many of these poor rural counties have lost their hospitals. We're just lucky to have one. We have very few doctors here. It's hard to entice healthcare professionals to this area. As far as mental healthcare, our only resource is this little rural mental health center. We don't have group homes, we don't have any hospital beds for the mentally ill, we don't have any resources. It's very hard and it's very frustrating for medical people. We have a nursing home. I'm sure it's hard to keep it staffed with competent people because our educational system is broken here. The whole system is broken.

84.   *Bonnie M., RN, Hospital Neonatal Intensive Care Bedside Nurse*

Bonnie M., RN, has worked as a neonatal intensive care (NICU) bedside nurse for 40 years, caring for the most seriously ill patients. Her joy emanates from a deep, spiritual well that enables her to help new parents adjust to their roles, calm their fears, and provide comfort in the face of loss. Yet, with a combination of anger, humor, and hesitation, she describes a hospital culture in which leaders are more focused on business than on caring for patients and families. In her institution, joy comes from the bottom up while being compromised from the top down. Nevertheless, she says, "I want you to know I have loved my job." This speaks to the power of personal passion, integrity, and resilience to overcome even the most entrenched obstacles to joy.

I knew when I was very young that I might want to go into nursing, but I'm not quite sure why. There were no nurses in my family, but I always knew nursing would be an interest. When I was 14 or 15, I was a hospital "candy striper." There were all sorts of weird things about that role I liked. I loved the uniform. It was walking distance to my house. It was the hospital I had been born in. I don't remember distinctly what I did, but I enjoyed that experience. I felt useful. There was something structured about the role. It wasn't that it was task-oriented, but there was a pretty quick feedback loop—I'd do something and would right away feel a sense of accomplishment. I could tell whether something I did was helpful or not. I liked being part of a team and working with a group. My mother remembers me telling her when I came home from candy striping that I liked the smell of the hospital. It was somewhere I felt I belonged. It just felt right to me.

The next thing I did solidified my professional choice of nursing and healthcare. During a couple of years in high school, I worked for three hours a day after school in the cafeteria of that same hospital. It was a paying job. I delivered the dinner trays to all the nurses in the ICU and the cardiac care unit, and I developed relationships with the six or seven nurses who worked evenings. It wasn't a very big hospital, but they treated me as an equal and they were very open to talking about what kind of patients they had and what was going on. I saw a lot.

In high school I didn't love chemistry, but I *loved* biology. When I was a sophomore I excelled in biology and loved it to the point of ridiculousness. I was also talking to the ICU nurses at the time and saw such a connection between science and a nurse's role in the ICU; that, as much as anything, made me sure I wanted to go to nursing school. I continue to marvel at the fact that I made the decision to be a nurse as a 17-year-old and still have this career 40 years later.

I got my RN degree in 1978. I've worked in the neonatal intensive care units of several hospitals over the course of my career, and I've been at this one for 32 years. I work at the bedside and take care of one or two critically ill, complex patients on my 12-hour shifts. I'm responsible for all their care, all their medication, the care of the family, and parental education and support. I have no management responsibility.

Nursing is easy to blend in with having a family. When I leave work, I pretty much leave work. I work from 7:00 a.m. to 7:00 p.m. That's the official line but it's not what I actually work. I'm lucky if I get out of here by 8:00 p.m. It certainly varies from day to day, but the expectation is that we're responsible for getting our work done and our charting done and all the other things that need to happen. Usually what I'm told is, "If you were more organized, if you were more this, if you were more that, then you'd be done earlier." On the whole, it doesn't matter to management whether we're here late or not.

On most days, most of us don't eat lunch before 2:00 or 3:00 in the afternoon and bathroom breaks are few. If we don't get lunch, we're told it's our own fault because we didn't coordinate with our fellow staff. It's up to us. It's our professional duty to get our own lunch. I'm left with four patients since I'm covering somebody else's two patients. Somehow, between the two of us, we're supposed to figure out how we're going to get out for lunch.

On Joy in Work

Planting Seeds

One of my greatest joys is to literally watch a family begin. I get to see that very first planting—yes, they knew they were pregnant, they knew they were going to have a child—but I get to see their reactions to this miraculous, spiritual, moment when I ask, "Okay, who wants to hold first, Mom or Dad?"

That is sometimes the first naming of their roles. I like to help them explore that, even in the midst of a NICU experience they didn't plan or want. Even in the midst of their sadness and grief and worry and anxiety, to be able to tell them, "You were a couple up until yesterday. But look how things have changed in 24 hours! Can you imagine your life without this other person?" To try to help them put their experience into words and to honor that is really joyful for me.

Then I point out that their relationship is also totally changed because, yes, they love each other—but nowhere near as much as they each love this same tiny being. Then to watch their fear or hesitation or timidity at taking on these roles build into what some people might call bossiness, or protectiveness, I love to see. Everyone says, "You love the difficult families." I love it when, all of a sudden, that seed sprouts roots. And they start displaying parental behaviors. It may not be pretty, it may not be socially acceptable to some, but I love to see that and support it.

If I have to prioritize between getting paperwork done and spending time with a family—and of course families come in between 5:00 and 7:00 in the evening—being with families is where I get my joy. I get out of work late because I'd just as soon sit with them for a few minutes and help plant that seed. Or help calm that fear. Or reassure a mother that there's not a woman in the world who gives birth for the first time who feels she's a confident mother. We were all beginners and I felt no different. I'm not afraid of that level of emotion and that gives me great joy.

I love problem-solving, having to be creative and think outside the box. I like to have to figure out how to do something, all of a sudden, for which there are no directions. I like the global creative problem-solving that goes on—whether it's something special that a child needs or the dynamics of the parents as they try to cope. My joy in work comes from seeing in this huge, global, empathetic, touchy-feely, spiritual world intersecting with this incredibly complex, technical, scientific, critical situation. I love both sides of it.

I also get tremendous satisfaction from helping walk a family through a loss. And respecting this baby, and respecting and honoring both life and death, and all that goes into that. I often work with the chaplaincy office and the palliative care people, who I've always felt were kindred spirits. Walking into sacred spaces is where my joy is.

Teamwork

I feel a sense of recognition and gratitude from my peers. There's a sense of companionship and being in a canoe without a paddle. On the best and craziest days, the things we can pull off are amazing. For example, a patient might be admitted who I know is going to need a great many resources. Because I know who is on staff with me, I can handpick people for their specific skill sets and coordinate a miraculous response.

Everything works so smoothly because people jump in and help. The ability to see what's needed and respond quickly is powerful. And for all of us, there is a sense of joy and accomplishment at the end of the day. We do what we do seamlessly. We have the right doctors, the right pharmacists, the right resources. The personalities are a good mix. People trust each other and don't judge. No one has a problem with my saying, "I'm not the best at starting IVs in babies" and asking someone else, who could put an IV into a rock, to do it. I am with a group of people to whom I can be honest and who know my strengths and my weaknesses. Those are the days we have joy—when we work together as a team, without that expectation of having to be perfect or having to do it all. The days when people get most stressed are the days when they feel they have to do it all because there are fewer peers and resources to support them.

On Money and Joy

Money doesn't provide joy, but it certainly helps to be living without significant financial concerns. I get paid well and I have a decent benefit package, even part-time, a fact that was often used against me by some managers during the recession. If we ever said anything about staffing, they'd say, "Be glad you have a job." That, I thought, was threatening.

I have ten weeks of vacation time in my vacation bank. I cannot take it. I have to cash it out. At my age, I could give a flying bleep about money. I want to be able to take a two-week vacation. I can't do it. I am still working Christmas. I am still working New Year's Eve. I have a friend at another hospital who told me that no one with my seniority would be working Christmas. But I'm working it here. When I once complained about this, I was asked, "When are you planning to retire?" That's not a legally allowed question, but message received, loud and clear.

What Diminishes Joy

What diminishes joy in work for me is lack of time. Lack of staffing. Lack of ability to sit with parents. Lack of ability to be present because I've got so many damned tasks to do. When the problems are so acute and there just aren't enough resources. By resources I mean staffing. Even though the patient doesn't look particularly sick, their care is complex, and the families are understandably needy. Often, I'll end up with what other people call difficult parents. The babies may not be as complex as other patients on our unit, but the parents may need much more support. In other words, they take up a lot of time. It takes time to develop relationships. It takes time to listen. It takes time just to be present. And the way staffing models work, and the way healthcare works today, time isn't something that's built in. I can't say that it was ever a lot better, but I think particularly in the last 15–20 years—and I don't think this is exclusive to this hospital—there has certainly been a push for the business model.

I have no control over which two patients are assigned to me when I come in to work. There is some fluidity built into our ability to move nurses or patients around a little or to change things, but not always. Things can get crazy if one patient gets particularly ill and we have to go from two patients per nurse to one patient per nurse. If somebody calls in sick, very often there isn't anybody to replace that nurse. Lack of staff, lack of resources, is probably the biggest consistent complaint in hospitals across the country.

Failure to Act on Staff Concerns

In our roles, there is the expectation of exceptional service, exceptional care, patient safety, and patient satisfaction. The rule is, "If you see something, say something"—but if I say something, I get pushback from managers. For example, if I tell my nurse manager, "This assignment is crazy. This is just undoable. Unsustainable." In the end I have to do it, but I end up doing what I call the bare, safe minimum. I may tell a nurse manager, "I did it. But not without an emotional cost and exhaustion. I'm angry. I don't feel that I did a good job. I'm going home feeling crappy."

I am really worried about the future of nursing. Because as much as I love families, my other joy in the last 20 years has been mentoring young people. I have a loose mentoring relationship with many 22–30-year-olds. If I'm struggling with an assignment, I have to report that to a 26-year-old in our nursing hand-off. And while I'm telling her what's going on with the patients, I'm trying to build her up and make her feel that she can deal with whatever is going on. Of course, I know there's not an inch of my face that isn't giving away this feeling that the situation is crappy. When I go into my nurse manager and say, "I worry about these young people, this is going to burn them out. We're going to lose them. Staff turnover is going to be high. They're not going to stay in nursing. It's just not fair to them, it's not fair to the patients, it's not fair to the parents," their response is mixed: "Oh, Bonnie [sigh]. You know we all have to do this." Or, "We appreciate that you're worried about the younger staff but they're resilient, they're doing fine." I never get an adequate response.

Moral Distress

We can never use the word "unsafe." If I come in and say something is unsafe, then I'm told, 1) You never say that; 2) That's not really true; and 3) Did you use all the resources that were available? It's always put back on us. What happens now is that no one says anything.

The director of all the ICUs and all the nurse managers run in this little circle thinking things are wonderful. What I know *for sure* is that there's an incredible mismatch between what the management wants to believe is happening and what the nursing staff are experiencing in all of our ICUs. This creates moral distress. For me, moral distress is a disharmony between one's personal value system and the value system in which you find yourself working.

Within the last two years there have been more shifts when I ask myself, *what am I doing?* More and more, I think I'm complicit in care that does not improve patients' outcome. Sometimes, the feeling that I'm doing more harm than good ties into my sense of moral distress. Sometimes, when I feel I'm providing care that may be painful or life-sustaining but not life-saving, I feel I'm doing a disservice to the patient and the family. The cumulative wear and tear of that is there. Sometimes I'm really terrified that either I'll make a mistake, or I'll really hate my job. I want to leave before either of those things happens.

On paper, there are employee support groups, an office of clinician support that provides one-on-one counseling and help, and a staff support person who comes every month to talk to us about what's going on and provide time to talk. But if you ask people on our units whether they use these services, they just start laughing. It all looks good on paper, there are supports in place, but no one has time to use them. I don't think that's just at this hospital. It goes back to what I said about what diminishes joy in work in general—it's lack of time.

Staff Shortages

A huge number of nurses have left because they're feeling overloaded. Turnover has been as high as 20% on some units. This has been going on more in the last 10–15 years than it had in the past. We never used to hire new grads. And then, at one point during the recession a few years ago, they started hiring new grads. At one point about 50% of the nurses in all the ICUs here were new grads. They were under 25 with less than two years' experience. A lot of new grads are starting out at 40 hours a week, which is just brutal. I don't know why management doesn't seem to care. They stopped doing exit interviews. They don't want to hear it.

Nurse managers I've had in the past would jump into the fray and lend a hand when needed. Many come from the units and from the bedside. These days, they are psychologically and physically far removed from this work. When we say we have no resources, they'll ask, "Well, why didn't you call me?" "Well," we say, "we did call. But you were in a meeting, or you didn't answer your phone." When the nurse manager walks in for multidisciplinary rounds, it's supposed to be a time when we can speak up about safety issues. But no one ever says anything. The charge nurse might say the staffing is really tight today, but that's where it begins and ends.

A long time ago, when the unit was smaller, a nurse manager used to work one day a month for a whole shift, and it did help her to see the problems and challenges we face. We had staff meetings, we had discussions. And disagreements. And decisions were made. The whole administration and decision-making policy used to be from the bedside up. Now it's from the top down.

Contributors to Burnout

Stress contributes to burnout. I also think moral distress contributes to burnout. Burnout also is related to inadequate staffing, organizational culture, lack of vacation time, lack of benefits, lack of control over schedules, not being heard or supported—lots of different things. All of these contributors to burnout are connected.

On paper, all the things that need to get done, get done. All the safety work gets done. Meds are given. So, on paper, it doesn't look like a bad day. The fact is that at 10:00 in the morning people are talking about the color wine they're going to drink when they get home that night, how they're going "deal with the day." We all laugh about it because the truth is, by the time we get home we're too tired to even pour a glass of wine.

Why I Stay

I stay because, on balance, I get more joy than I get heartache. When I had my second child, I reduced my hours. I'm here a lot but not too much. I was able to balance my work life while honoring my role as a mother.

The other reason I stay is, of the days I work, at least half have miraculous little windows of great professional satisfaction where I know I've made a huge difference.

I also stay because my gifts are good for mentoring staff who get younger and younger. Whether it's what to expect when admitting a child with a complex diagnosis, how to get car insurance, how to cook a chicken when some boyfriend is coming over, how to run through an epidural line, or how to talk to a family, I like mentoring these young nurses. I find that very satisfying. I have a new crop of nurses to grow. Nurturing in a professional way helps me to fill my empty nest—and I do it all in one breath, in the space of one 12-hour shift.

In thinking about retirement, I'm worried about not being with the young ones because it's a two-way street. They give as much as they get. I love their vitality and I love the way they care more about the patients and less about the hospital. They don't feel much guilt about calling in sick. And because they're from a different generation, they have no sense of long-term corporate allegiance or the workplace expectations I struggled with at times.

Advice

My advice to my bosses is, if you ask the question, "What do you need?" listen to the answer before you say anything. Don't assume, don't judge. I struggle so hard with the fact that I'm still not comfortable walking into my nurse manager and telling her that her emails are both sappy and condescending at the same time: "If you think we're the most wonderful staff in the world, why won't you listen to us?" It's frustrating for me when people say, "We want to make you the best staff possible." But when we tell them what we need, they somehow turn it around on us.

part 3

What Destroys Joy

The world breaks everyone, and afterward, some are strong at the broken places.

Ernest Hemingway

Introduction to Part 3

This section presented my biggest challenge in organizing this book. Other people whose stories appear throughout this book have talked about the same subjects as those whose stories appear here do: the lack of autonomy and control, lawsuits, experiences of moral distress, and their cumulative effects. But, on some deep level, the experiences described in this section just feel worse. As if they run deeper. Are more pervasive. More devastating. More destructive. With greater power to crush the spirit and to destroy joy. These are not your run-of-the-mill challenges; these challenges have required soul-searching, courage, strength, support, and sometimes, a leap of faith to overcome.

Remarkably, most of the healthcare professionals who stories appear here say they still feel joy in work, but they have taken heroic measures to recapture and protect that feeling in the face of the challenges they describe: By rebelling against the forces of government; seeking help to triumph over painful circumstances that made them feel diminished; finding new ways to help others in similar circumstances; leaving their organizations for new ones, for independent practice, or for retirement; or pondering a different future.

The most painful and destructive of these challenges is moral distress—the collision between one's deeply held, core, personal values with the demands and expectations of the organization—inevitable when the organization puts its interests, financial or otherwise, above what is best for both clinicians and their patients. Those whose interviews appear in this section found it both painful and cathartic to talk to me. In the interests of full disclosure, some, like internal medicine physician Rose S., cut substantial portions of her interview for publication—a testament to just how deep the fear of being identified and retaliated against runs, even after having left the organization she describes. On the other hand, former clinical social work student Sophia L. describes her experiences and the feelings they engendered in detail, with unvarnished honesty. She, especially, felt compelled to share her story so others, who are also struggling with a similar existential dilemma, might learn something about the need for moral clarity, courage, and action in the interests of self-preservation and, ultimately, a return to joy. In the immortal words of Rabbi Hillel, "If I am not for myself, who will be for me? If I am not for others, what am I? And if not now, when?"

There are important lessons here for all of us. I am humbled to present these heroes to you now.

Lack of Autonomy and Control

85.   Diane L., MD, Rheumatologist in Solo Private Practice

> Diane L., MD, has been a rheumatologist for 23 years and loves her work. As a solo
> practitioner, she has the freedom to set her own schedule and to run her practice the
> way she wants to. Despite this freedom, she nevertheless lacks autonomy: Insurance
> companies, big pharma, and the government restrict her ability to prescribe the
> medications of her choice, and require her to spend far too much time getting pre-
> authorizations and precertifications for the drugs, tests, and procedures her patients
> need. If Diane is not burned out she has clearly become disillusioned, essentially
> asking the question, what has the practice of medicine become?

My wanting to be a doctor goes back a long time. First, I've always loved science. I went
to college as a music major and figured out right away that wasn't for me. I wasn't good
enough to perform and I didn't want to teach. What that left were things like music therapy,
which I tried out along with some other things. Then I went the nutritional route. I got a
master's degree in nutrition and became a dietitian. I did a dietetic internship for a year
after college and would go on rounds with the doctors and interns and residents. I was
fascinated. It was inspirational. I thought, *this is so cool.* That's when I said, I think I want to
go to medical school. I worked as a dietitian for a while and thought, *No, I've got this bug
now and I'm going to medical school.*

My Professional Journey

I had to go back to college and take so many different courses—the things I hadn't taken
before—so I could take the MCATs and apply. And that's what I did. When I went to medical school, I was 31. I graduated from medical school in 1985. Then there were three years
of internal medicine residency, which I did in the armed forces, and I paid them back by
working for three years as an internist in the military. After that I did a two-year rheumatology fellowship.

I picked the field of rheumatology for a few reasons. It's a fascinating area of medicine;
the diseases are interesting and that was obviously a very important thing. I thought I'd
also have a much better lifestyle with rheumatology than with any of the other specialties
like cardiology, gastroenterology, or other internal medicine subspecialties.

I had a wonderful mentor while I was in my internal medicine residency. The truth
is, he probably taught me all the basics of rheumatology that I needed to know. He was a
wonderful human being. I also had some other very good mentors. At one point I had a
bit of a struggle with one of my attendings, who was really trying to put me down. I think
she was insecure herself and so that's what she did. I'd gotten so disgusted in my training
at that point that I just thought, *fine, I'll quit this program, I'll do something else. I'll do dermatology.* There was an opportunity to go into a dermatology residency. I will never forget one
of the pulmonary attendings coming along and saying, "If you go into dermatology you
are never going to use your stethoscope again." And that line just hit me. Because, to me,
medicine was all about *medicine.* You use your stethoscope, you analyze data. So, I decided
to stick it out.

I was all done in 1994, and that's when I went out and got my first real job as an
internist/rheumatologist with a multispecialty group. I was there for 13 years. I decided

to leave that practice in 1997 and go out on my own. Multiple things happened, a perfect storm developed, to make me decide to leave. First, the commute had become horrendous. When I first started, I could easily do the commute in 27 minutes, door to door. By the time I left there were days it took an hour or more to get home at night. I thought, *I'm not spending an hour to get home.* One of my kids was still in high school at the time. She played basketball and I wanted to be at her games.

Second, the partners in my practice were beginning to move in a direction I wasn't thrilled with. We could see the writing on the wall in terms of declining reimbursements, so we talked about what we were going to do. They thought we needed to do more things in the office that would be reimbursable, saying, "Let's start doing echocardiograms" and "let's start a sleep lab." That was all well and good, but then with every patient my partners saw they would hear a murmur and send them for an echo. The sleep center idea led to partners saying, "Oh, if you have fatigue, you need a sleep study." I had a problem ethically. Things came to a head and I decided I was going to go out on my own.

On Joy in Work

I have a lot of joy in my work. By joy I mean helping people who need help. The relationships. All of that. Having them come back and say they feel better. Or when they don't come back because I did something curative, which doesn't happen as often because rheumatic diseases are chronic. My job is more about helping the patient deal with a chronic disease.

I run an office that's unique. I am a solo practitioner. In fact, I don't have anybody working for me. I outsource my billing but otherwise I run everything myself. My published hours are Monday to Thursday, 8:00 a.m. to 4:00 p.m. and Friday, 8:00 a.m. to 12 noon. I do my own scheduling and make the schedule I want.

On Money and Joy

Money doesn't define joy. The state where I practice happens to be one of the worst for doctors because the reimbursement rate is controlled by the insurers, and mine is one of the worst-paying states for doctors in the entire United States. So why would anybody practice here? I don't know. We ended up here and things went from being very nice when we started to being really problematic in terms of reimbursements. But that's the way it is.

What Diminishes Joy

The downside of solo practice is that I have to do all my own administrative work, like taking care of all the prescription refills and filing them. And requesting, receiving, and filing x-ray reports. And calling people on the phone.

I do whatever I can do to meet the needs of my patients. That takes a toll, though. Sometimes I feel I can't do any more because of the constraints I'm under. And then I try to make the best of it. Here's an example: When a patient with significant rheumatoid arthritis had commercial insurance prior to going on Medicare, a new wonder drug, a biologic, was available to him. He had been doing really well on a regimen of a number of drugs, including some biologics, when he retired and switched to Medicare. I warned him, "You're not going to be able to get this once you go on Medicare."

Sure enough, he went through all the drug Part D programs and found these drugs were not available. I had to adjust his drug regimen, which is suboptimal compared with what he'd been getting before, because he could no longer afford those powerful, revolutionary biologics. Now he's on a regimen of three other kinds of drugs that are approved by Medicare but aren't biologic; he's managing okay, maybe has to use a little prednisone now and then, but it's not optimal. He doesn't have an extra $25,000 a year, or any thousand dollars a year, to pay for a drug if he were to fall through the "donut-hole." We don't even have time to talk about *that*. So, we're doing the best we can. Am I meeting his needs? Am I being constrained? I'm doing the best I can within the constraints I have.

If you ask me what the answer is, I think we have to go to a single payer. When that's going to happen, I don't know; but given the mess we're in and the power that the insurance lobby and pharma have with Congress, it's going to be a long time.

What Destroys Joy and Leads to Burnout

Getting prior authorization is the bane of most doctors' existence today, certainly in rheumatology and other specialties that use the new, higher-priced, revolutionary drugs to treat various diseases. These drugs are not even in the same ballpark as the "standard" drugs because of their cost. Doctors also have to get precertifications for procedures such as magnetic resonance imaging (MRI). Getting prior authorizations and precertifications are time-consuming, highly frustrating processes that destroy doctors' autonomy and lead to burnout. I would include electronic medical record (EMR) in this category but I have chosen not to use it.

Prior Authorizations

Prior authorization for a drug means if I have a patient who has rheumatoid arthritis, for example, we go through an evaluation process. There is sort of a hierarchy of medications, but the bottom line is we get to one of these new, revolutionary drugs that we want to use. Wonder drugs, if you will.

I have to go through a process of getting this approved for the patient; this can involve anywhere from pages of paperwork to 30 minutes on the phone, depending on the insurer. These drugs cost money. They cost in the ballpark of $25,000 a year, retail. That's not what the insurers pay.

The pharmaceutical companies strike deals with the insurers: if drug company X makes a deal with insurance company Y, I know that drug Z is going to be their preferred drug. Even if I don't think drug Z is the best drug for that patient, I know if I want a TNFL inhibitor I'm going to have to choose drug Z first. Because the insurers make deals with pharma, they want to steer you toward certain drugs and away from others—they drive our choices. Wait a minute, I'm the doctor, I'm supposed to be making the choice about what's the best drug for the patient!

Here's another example: in order to get drug A to treat rheumatoid arthritis it is a *standard* guideline recommendation that patients be checked for their tuberculosis (TB) status and hepatitis profile. If a patient is on Medicare, Medicare will not pay for the hepatitis profile. The labs that we order for a patient all go into Medicare under a code. And that code, or codes, has to cover the test. So rheumatoid arthritis has a code, MO5.79, and then if we're giving the patient a drug with a high risk of toxicity, we also code Z79.99.

Those two codes, one would assume, would cover that TB test and the hepatitis profile because they're standard, published guidelines for receiving the drug. But Medicare will not cover a hepatitis profile under those two codes. So, what do we do? Well, we fudge. We ask, what *are* the codes that Medicare will cover a hepatitis profile for? We look to see, did the patient ever have one liver enzyme that was elevated? If they did—boom!—we can use the code for an elevated liver test. If they haven't, now what? Oh, let's see. "Have you ever been fatigued, Ms. Jones? Yes? Oh, fatigue! We'll cover it!" Stupid, right? This is just one example of what we live with every day.

The insurers can deny approval for any drug; they can say whatever they want, that this is their policy. As a physician, I have no recourse. This makes me feel used. And powerless. And angry that I have to go through this mountain of effort, be it paperwork or time or whatever, to get a drug approved.

Now someone might say, "Doctor, you're running your own practice. Why don't you just hire somebody to do that for you?" Well, sure I could hire somebody to that for me. But I'd have to pay them to do it. Our state agency is now taking this issue on to try to help, as is the American College of Rheumatology, because this is something we have spoken out about that is absolutely ridiculous. They're trying to see what they can do to make this is a less onerous process. Patients have no idea this is going on. Even if they knew, they wouldn't be able to do anything about it because they're beholden to their insurers.

Precertification

Precertification from insurers applies to procedures. Say I want to get an MRI: I can't just order an MRI; I first have to go through a precertification process. Radiology groups have teams of people whose job it is to get precertifications. They're also there to make sure precertification happens because if precertification doesn't happen, radiology groups don't get paid. These are all independent radiology groups that perform various kinds of studies: x-rays, ultrasound, MRIs, etc.

I don't just order an MRI for patients, particularly a more advanced kind of MRI, like a contrast MRI, which often is needed. Those are never, ever approved right off the bat. So, depending on the insurer, I may have to submit chart notes to show why I want this. Sometimes I have to go head-to-head with the medical director—I've done that *numerous* times. Insurers have doctors who are beholden to their company, not to the physician or to the patient. And I can tell you this: I've never lost when I went head-to-head with a medical director. I have to make the argument to the medical director that this is an important study and explain why. Now, if my argument is full of holes, anyone would be able to see right through it. But the point is, there is a *reason* I'm ordering this. I wouldn't order something that wouldn't provide a necessary piece of information. But their job is to save money for their insurance company.

When I've presented my case I've never lost—except once. I lost on a plain MRI, not a contrast MRI. I lost because the patient had not had six weeks of conservative medical management before going to get the MRI. Medical management often will alleviate the symptoms of a simple musculoskeletal problem. But you're walking around with a torn meniscus, I'll just have to treat you with physical therapy and an inflammatory, and in six weeks we'll see where we are, and then the insurance company will approve the MRI.

Electronic Medical Record

I still use paper charts. I get dinged by Medicare. They're the only ones dinging for not having electronic medical records, for not having data that can be submitted by EMR. So, yes, I get paid by Medicare 1% or 2% less than anybody else. I made a conscious decision that I was going to take the hit. Because taking the hit wouldn't be as onerous as buying a whole EMR system or even using some of those free ones and then trying to use it. It was just too much, it wasn't worth it to me.

On Burnout

I *love* what I do! Every patient is different and that has fascinated me for the 23 years I've been a physician. Each and every patient is here for a reason, it's up to me to help them, I'm privileged to be a part of their life, and I'm honored they're coming to me for help—this is what keeps me here. But the need for preauthorizations, precertifications, and the lack of autonomy in practice have me feeling burned out—not in the sense that I can't see one more osteoarthritis patient today—but feeling exhausted, demoralized, angry, and powerless. This is not what medicine was 20 years ago.

Reflections

There are pluses and minuses to being in a solo practice but, for me, the pluses outweigh the minuses. The pluses of being on my own are that I'm on my own! I'm my own boss, I don't have to answer to anybody, I can set my own schedule, and I can do things the way I want to do them. I can see as many or as few patients as I want to, for as long as I want to.

The minuses are that I don't have, for example, bargaining power with the insurers or the reimbursement rates I would have in a big group. I don't have economies of scale for things I would have in a big group. I can ask for higher reimbursement rates, as I recently did with one insurer, and get them. They know I deliver quality, efficient, and good care. Of course, the implication is, if you don't increase my rates I'm going to go out of network. I try not to take that threatening stance unless it really comes down to the bottom line because that's all I've got.

I feel strongly that we need to look at how kids are being selected for medical school. In academia, they're in their ivory towers. They don't know what it's like to be in the 'doctor trenches' every day. Medical schools are choosing kids who are bright—no doubt about it, they're making the best scores, they've done all these extracurricular things, volunteering in Zimbabwe, whatever—and these are the kids they're picking. But these are not the kids who will necessarily make the best doctors. And that's a real problem. There was an article in the newspaper by an ophthalmology resident about how medical schools need to start fixing the way they are picking these kids. Besides IQ they should measure EQ: their *emotional* intelligence quotient. Even for residency, they're just picking kids with the best grades. These kids are the ones who can do the research to support their institutions, who will make their institutions look good, but they won't necessarily be the best *doctors*.

86. *Michael V., MD, Endocrinologist, Professor of Medicine, and Senior Staff Physician at an Integrated Health System*

Michael V., MD, is an endocrinologist with a master's degree in biomedical research. He is a professor of medicine, a researcher, and a senior staff physician employed by a large integrated health system. He is deeply committed to improving access to care and creating conditions that promote optimal care and joy in medicine. In this interview, Michael, who loves his work, reflects on the conditions that can and do destroy joy in work and lead to burnout.

I'm originally from South America; that's where I did my medical training. There, you decide to go into your profession as you're finishing high school. I finished high school at 16 and when I turned 17, I was in medical school. I think I decided to go to medical school because I was fascinated by the brain. I realized that in order to study the brain you had to be a neurologist or a neuroscientist. And to be a neurologist or a neuroscientist you had to study medicine. I didn't have one of those epiphanies where I wanted to change the world. It was more about what I'd have to go through to get to the good stuff. It was an eight-year journey, so by the time I was done I had seen a lot and matured a lot.

I went to medical school in the mid-late 1980s, when my country started having major problems in its economy and with violence and terrorism. 1987 marked a low point that went on for about five years, which essentially was for most of my training. There was an underinvestment in healthcare and violence was rampant. A lot of my training was in hospitals that were severely underfunded and understaffed, with patients who were in desperate situations. So whatever interests I had in research or the brain were swallowed by the terrible nature of that reality. I came here for additional training in internal medicine and endocrinology from 1996 to 2002, then conducted research in Canada for two years. I've been employed by this integrated health system since 2004.

How my experiences seeing the underserved in my country have informed my path is something I continue to discover. There, patients had to stand in line just to get on the queue for appointments of the day. Some people would show up at 4:00 a.m. to get on that line, and the line was already filled with people selling their spots. When they'd get to the front of the line, they'd get a ticket to get on the *real* line for that day's appointments. Some would have to go several mornings to potentially get in—and of course they were sick or injured.

Maybe that's what happens in a system that's very poor. But how do we justify problems with access in a system that is so rich, like ours? I began to recognize that what underfunds the system in my country—corruption, incompetence, violence, and poverty—is different from what underfunds the system here, which is mostly the extraction of value through greed and profit. But the end result is the same: People are not getting the care they need.

There are other contrasts between that system and ours. There, many of us were trained to be real Robin Hoods, collecting resources from patients who could afford to give some and then using them for patients who couldn't, even though the whole system was supposed to be free. Here, clinicians are basically accountable to the payers for what they're doing instead of being accountable to their patients. There, care was the end result of everything we did. Here, care is the means by which we develop our businesses and our healthcare enterprises. These contrasts have, I think, become obvious to me in part, though not entirely, from the experiences I went through in my home country.

I spend about 20% of my time seeing patients directly; half of that time is as their diabetes doctor and half is supervising trainees learning to take care of patients with diabetes. I spend the other 80% of my time conducting research on the way we take care of patients. This involves quite a bit of either direct observation or video recording of healthcare interactions, studying the effects of healthcare interactions, summarizing research, and so forth.

I come in around 7:00, 7:30 a.m. and I leave around 6:00, 6:30 p.m. I work maybe 12 hours plus a day, five days a week. I don't do any clinical work on the weekends and I try to minimize my research work as well. I'm extremely lucky.

I haven't looked back at my time with patients to see what my actual average is. I'm scheduled for 45 minutes for new patients. For returning patient consults I'm scheduled somewhere between 25 and 30 minutes. I think it's not enough. I rarely finish before the allotted time and I most often run about 15 minutes late. For my 5:00 or 4:45 p.m. patient, it's not terribly unusual for me to be 20–30 minutes late. I frequently go out to the waiting room and find those patients as I am moving from one patient to another to tell them I'm running late.

On Joy in Work

How do I define joy in work? Those are the days I come home energized, I come home telling stories, I come home smiling from a day at work. Those days are the days when everything clicks: the ability to collaborate with my colleagues, to reflect on a difficult case, to crack a case by using our collective insight that leads to our being able to uncover, finally, what is the problem, or what's in the way, of our ability to diagnose and treat a patient—and then being able to figure out what might make a difference.

When a patient comes back and is better and expresses gratitude or, expresses gratitude even when they're not better because they know we're working together to try to make things as good as they can be—that is joyful.

Because I spend about 20% of my time taking care of patients, I've been given the great gift of having some control over my time; this means I don't usually find myself in a hurry. So, for instance, yesterday was a holiday. Most of my clinic days are on Mondays. On a Monday holiday my patients are spread through the week. This afternoon I have two patients and I know I'm going to be able to give them the time they need without feeling too pressed. That's a luxury.

Some people actually derive a lot of joy from taking care of folks, and I would sign up to that list. For me, coming to work is not a pain. I enjoy coming to work. I enjoy seeing my patients, I enjoy teaching, I enjoy doing my research.

On Money and Joy

I work in a salaried environment. All of our doctors are salaried and everybody who does the same job gets the same salary. There is no gender gap in terms of income here. All the endocrinologists get paid the same whether they're boys or girls. It doesn't' matter. That, I think, prevents us from competing on salary internally. It's not as if I see more patients, I'll make more money. Or if our surgeons operate more, they're going to get more money. That doesn't happen here.

The money is sufficient—and, I would say, more than sufficient—to satisfy all our needs plus all the luxuries that people in the same positions elsewhere have. "Keeping up with the Joneses," which might drive someone to do crazy things, is not an issue here.

Many of my colleagues have gone to 80% time; they're reducing their full-time employment to try to cope with the demands of work as the demands have gone up. I think people recognize that they're overpaid and they let go a little bit of their full-time equivalent just to try to keep a better balance with their family life and other things. Some people just can't wait to get out of the clinic so they can go and enjoy what they really like to do. And some of the things they like to do take money, so the money helps them with that.

There are people who work beyond where it's fun, just so they can make adequate retirement, pay their bills, take care of kids in college, and so forth. There are people who practice beyond when they should have retired because they simply have to make their retirement targets.

I think physicians are overpaid and they've been overpaid for a long time, at least since Medicare came in. In the past we used to get paid with chickens or whatever. Once payers became formalized income became normalized.

What Diminishes Joy

I'm not joyful when I'm cutting corners. When I know that the best way to do something is A but I do B because it's expeditious for me—because it will allow me to finish up on time, to see the next person without making them wait too long, because I know they will otherwise be angry at me. But now I've taken a shortcut on the patient in front of me and wondering if that shortcut is going to have consequences. When I'm second-guessing whether I'm doing the best for my patients or just getting through the day, those days are terrible.

And sometimes the joyful and the not-joyful days are combined. Sometimes I spend a lot of time with patient A because that patient needs it and giving them that time makes a difference, leads to some breakthrough. But now I'm behind for the rest of the afternoon. I'm apologizing to everyone and everybody's upset with me because I've made them wait. And maybe my last patient decides not to wait any longer and just leaves. Then I feel guilty that I didn't get to them. I know that patient has wasted the afternoon and I wasn't able to contribute to her health. So, all this could be happening on the same day. But a day in which I experience most of the cruelty and none of the upsides of the system are the days in which joy is hard to find.

As I talk to my colleagues, those who have their calendars filled with the most difficult patients—meaning those to whom we cannot readily explain why they feel poorly, or to whom we must explain that we don't have a good treatment—struggle mightily to find meaning in their day.

What Can Destroy Joy

The Business of Medicine

Once you're in an administrative position in the current environment you figure out very quickly that your job is to satisfy the requirements of those who are paying the bills. And those who are paying the bills are not usually in the same building as those who are treating patients. Those paying the bills are insurers or health plans, and they've contracted with you not only for services in terms of the number of patient visits, but for measures of quality and performance that you have to meet. Unfortunately, most of those metrics and most of those contracts require you to think of your patients as a mass, not as individual patients. So, when those requirements come down to the front-line clinicians, they land in a way that feels completely out of place. And people either put up or suffer. They know their integrity is being stretched.

For example, in one of my visits to the clinical site of a different organization, I saw a sign in the waiting room that said, "75% of our patients with diabetes are currently taking statins. Help us get to 100%." I'm completely comfortable that whoever put the sign up was thinking about the well-being of their patients with diabetes and how cholesterol medicines might be good, on average, for most, if not all of them. But the way it was framed clarifies the problem: the clinic is asking the people in the waiting area to help the clinic get to 100% coverage of statins in patients with diabetes.

The job of the people in the clinic is to help the patients in the waiting room, not for the patients in the waiting room to help the people in the clinic. The inversion makes each and every one of those patients—and, by the way, each and every one of those clinicians—like workers on the factory floor. They're told by payers when to show up, what to do, and what outcomes to pursue as a group. And that's not the job. When that happens to me, on a personal level, I don't accept it. I ignore it.

When it comes to these recommendations, obligations, or target measures I try not to make them part of how I make decisions or how I engage with patients. I get no pushback from administrators. Why? I think I contribute very little to the bottom line by only spending one-fifth of my time seeing patients. I can be ignored. But I'm not the only one. There is a large group of clinicians who simply try their best. And their best, actually, is not that different from what the targets are—but they just don't focus on them as targets. But I have seen people deal with this conflict by complying. And it's *extremely* ugly.

I'd say that a lot of the attention right now is in meeting the demands of the payers, the contracts the administration has, and so forth. The front line is basically seen as a place where the "factory work" takes place. And the demands of the factory workers are not as loud as the demands of the payers. So, while we still have patients knocking on the door and clinicians showing up to work, to the extent that we can always see more patients in less time, the administration thinks we don't have a problem. I think there is a connection between what physicians think of as problems and what the administration thinks of as problems, but there is a difference in where attention is focused.

Clinicians are experiencing increasing levels of suicide and marital discord and so forth. But none of that is bubbling up to the level of concern for, say, how do we pay the bills this month? How do we maintain all these large buildings? How do we keep up with all the fixed costs? The only way we seem to know how to do that is by increasing the volume and output. I think care is no longer the primary goal of the system. The primary goal of the system is to make each of these business goals—and patient care is the means by which we accomplish that. I don't think that's good. I think that needs to change. I think it's a corruption of mission.

Conflicts of Interest

Here's an example of compliance by clinicians that, essentially, represents a conflict of interest. I don't do this, I don't have to do it, but if there were pressure to do this I would leave: Some clinicians are told to give a statin to their patients. So, when they see that a patient is coming in, they write a prescription ahead of the visit.

When the patient comes in, they say, "You should take a statin."

The patient says, "I'm not sure I should take it, I don't like it, I've seen the ads on TV, I think that there are side effects."

The physician says, "Well, here's a prescription. Think about it. If you decide to take it, go ahead and fill it. If you don't, that's okay."

The clinician gets the credit for having prescribed a statin so they don't get pressure for not doing it, and the patient is the one who is labeled noncompliant.

The Depersonalization of Patients

I saw a version of this attitude toward patients in my home country when the patients were making a beeline to get into the emergency room and the emergency room was filled with people. It doesn't take much for clinicians in the emergency room to begin to feel that these people are the enemy, that these patients are out to get them. And because clinicians need to get rid of them, they depersonalize them.

The depersonalization of patients is one of the strategies we have to cope with demands that don't make sense. If we start thinking of patients as members of our family or our friends, then we have to choose sides. And if we choose sides against our employer then that can make us miserable in other ways.

Reflections

On the Need for Conversation and Communication

At this institution, clinicians get together at lunchtime to talk about the challenges we face in practice. The institution pays for these lunches. And to me that's interesting, because what they're doing is creating a space for those conversations between colleagues to occur regularly, but they're doing it at lunchtime, so they won't affect the productivity of the place.

In the old days, these kinds of conversations occurred *all the time*. As a matter of course. As a matter of seeing patients, people would have discussions with colleagues. That's how we learned from senior colleagues how to do things, that's how we gained from colleagues that energy, that understanding, that commiseration--it came from the collegiality of those conversations. That's how we picked up whether one of our colleagues was in trouble—if they were depressed or needed help—because in those interactions we would notice and not have to wait for the monthly lunch.

On Creating Conditions That Promote Joy

As a matter of philosophy, I would ask my colleagues and those in leadership to focus primarily on care. I know that when my colleagues need a boost they go on medical missions. They go to Haiti or Africa or who knows where to take care of people who are indigent. They take a vacation to do the same thing they are supposed to be doing here. I think they do that because they get an emotional and spiritual kick from taking care of people *really*. Which suggests to me that doing what they're doing here every day is not that.

If we could create the conditions for which care is primary—that is, if we could match our language and our policies with our work and focus narrowly on caring for people—then I think our patients would notice. And we would experience, as a result, something similar to the experience of receiving love. I think that's what happens when you go on a medical mission—when someone who is quite desperate gets something that makes them better. And they smile back at you.

Somehow, we've lost the opportunities to feel the warmth of those smiles when we help someone. Because medicine has become such an industrial process—we're checking boxes, moving on, dealing with the computer when we should be having face-to-face interaction. By the time the patient is gone we've missed the "thank you," we've missed the smile, we've missed that moment of gratitude and satisfaction because we're ready to see the next person.

If we were to very narrowly focus everything in the organization on creating deep moments of human connection and caring with each one of our patients, then everything else should follow. And if it doesn't follow—that is, if the money doesn't follow to keep the doors open and the lights on—I am willing to bet that any of my colleagues would be willing to lower their salaries just to be able have those moments.

We need to stop building big buildings and stop building the third or fourth cancer center in the region and spending a lot of money on competing with each other, and move to a more collaborative approach where we don't have to outbid or outsmart, economically, the other hospital or clinic. But, rather, collaborate to be able to serve everyone who needs care. There is a lot of business to go around. I think it's essential that we focus on the mission of caring. That should carry everything else.

I suspect we'd have more joy in our practice if we also had an opportunity to take a breath and take stock of some of the magic that actually happens when we are with patients. I think some of that gets lost because we just don't have the time to take that breath and take stock of that. It's an incredible privilege to be at the bedside with these people and to hear their most intimate fears and to be there as a healing presence. It's an *incredible privilege*. It's so sad that for some people, it just feels like a job. They come in, check in, check out, and they don't get to experience the incredible position they are in. One of the reasons we may not have enough satisfaction or joy in our practice is that those moments are no longer apparent to us.

On the Need for Time

If you go to any website where patients are discussing the care of diabetes you will see that we endocrinologists don't do very well. The reason is that diabetes is a disease that affects all of a person's life. The only way we can get through consultations with patients with diabetes is by focusing on the biological aspects of the disease. Yet, if you don't look at the biology at the same time as the biography of the patient, you miss the heavy work of making the two fit together. If you want to pay attention to that, you need time. There's just no way of doing it quickly. Or you need home visits, which we stopped doing 30 years ago.

Advice

I advise administrators to ask themselves, is it really helpful to pile up patients in our schedules as happens now, leaving us no opportunity for moments of reflection and interaction? Or would we be better clinicians if we had those moments of reflection and interaction, even if it comes at an apparent loss in productivity? I would ask them to run that experiment and see what they learn.

87.   Natalie B., MD, Obstetrician/Gynecologist

Natalie B., MD, has been obstetrician/gynecologist for four years and feels fulfilled by delivering babies. Yet, this young physician who grew up using computers—and who is relatively new to practice—has had her joy in work diminished by the meaningless requirements of the EMR; the need to use an EMR that is inferior to the one she used in residency; and by patient satisfaction surveys, the Internet, and the ever-present fear of lawsuits.

My earliest memory of wanting to go into healthcare was when I was five. My mother asked me what I wanted to be when I grew up and I said, "I want to be a banker in the morning, a doctor in the afternoon, and a flutist in an orchestra on the weekends." My great-grandmother watched us a lot when I was little. We played doctor and we played banker, we'd make all this fake money, and she'd come and put in a deposit. She taught me how to make change. She helped me get my first white coat and let me give her fake shots. She was a great lady. The doctor is the only thing that stuck. I've always been more science-oriented than anything else. That's how it started, and over the years I wanted to go into medicine. I'm the first in my family to become a doctor. One of my distant cousins is a doctor but I didn't know her growing up.

I always used to tell my mom I was going to be a pediatrician. I've always loved kids. I started babysitting when I was about eight years old. I can't even believe someone let me do that. But right before medical school I was watching some television program about maternity care and I thought, that really looks like fun. And the more I thought about it, the more I realized how much I enjoyed talking about childbirth, birth control, and other things related to obstetrics and gynecology. I did my pediatric rotation and I hated it. Then I did my obstetrics rotation and loved it.

I'm an obstetrician/gynecologist (OB/GYN). I just passed my four-year mark in private practice. Before this I was in residency for four years. I work for a large multidisciplinary group that has 1,000 physicians under one umbrella, which gives us a lot of bargaining power with insurance companies. But I practice essentially as a community doctor in a small group practice of four OB/GYNs. The umbrella company gives us plenty of flexibility in terms of our work hours. If I were forced into a schedule, I'd probably be less happy. I'm an employee of the company so I don't have any ownership over the practice.

My office is in the suburb of a big city. I see patients in my office and deliver babies. I see patients in the clinic five days a week from 9:00 a.m. to 4:00 p.m., give or take, and from there come the deliveries and surgeries. I often have to round in the morning before work and I'm always in the office a lot later than 4:00 p.m. because of the electronic medical record documentation and paperwork I have to do. There are a lot of before and after work activities that don't include my office hours, and sometimes patients will come in at 4:00 p.m. I'm also on call every fourth day and every fourth weekend. Weekend call starts for me on Friday at 8:30 a.m. and goes until Monday at 8:30 a.m. Weekday call is just 24 hours, say from Monday morning until Tuesday morning.

I do feel as though I have control over my work environment and my workload most of the time. My practice set-up is pretty amazing. We cap our new patients at four a day, although sometimes I'll see six or seven new patients in a day, which is hard.

My patients are mostly young and healthy. If they have serious medical problems, they're seeing someone else, like their internist. I do have patients with high blood pressure, diabetes, and other illnesses who also need birth control, so I have to decide on the most appropriate birth control options for them.

I do feel overloaded by work on some days. Obstetrics patients are pretty fast and easy to see. But there are some days when I have patients who are more complex, who have more steps I have to follow-up on—labs and medications, for example—and on days when I see those patients I leave feeling drained because I've been documenting and ordering so much.

On Joy in Work

I define joy in work as liking what I do. Sometimes I feel it would be easier to be a barista at Starbucks and work from nine to five and get all the holidays and all the weekends off, but that wouldn't be fulfilling. I'd get bored. I feel I make a difference in people's lives. Years later, my patients say, "Thank you so much for delivering my baby." I had a patient the other day from residency. I delivered her baby eight years ago and she said, "You probably don't remember me, but I still remember you." Having those kinds of experiences make it all worthwhile. If I didn't have those, this job would be too hard.

On Money and Joy

To a certain extent I think there's a relationship between money and joy. Yes, we do this job for reasons that have nothing to do with money. I don't do this for the money. But we have to support ourselves. Getting appropriately compensated for the work is a reasonable expectation. I knew I was never going to make a million dollars like the old-school docs. I just want to make enough money to go on a couple of nice vacations a year, to put a roof over my head, and to have a car. I can't see myself doing anything else. I do love it.

What Diminishes Joy

The Electronic Medical Record

What diminishes joy in work for me is the paperwork. Oh my God. It's not even paperwork anymore. It's the EMR and other things. Medicare and Medicaid require that we document all this information in our notes. If we don't, we don't get paid. It also matters *how* we document them. If I enter information but don't click specific buttons to make it easy for the EMR system to accumulate the data, then I don't get credit for it. And people want us to measure useless things to see whether I'm a good doctor. I'm supposed to ask patients things like, "Today are you having any vomiting?" It's supposed to be there to make sure I'm not missing something, right? I always ask the questions that are pertinent to my patients and their situations. I don't always need to ask a patient if they're having chest pain because people always complain about chest pain if they're having it. Or they go to the emergency room for that.

Medicare and Medicaid have the Meaningful Use incentive program to encourage physicians to use the EMR. For example, we have to update patients' medications every time. That is important, I agree. But if we don't push the specific buttons that say we addressed their medications, then we don't get paid. Or we get penalized and have to pay the government back money. That drives me up the wall.

It's hard to quantify how much of my time using the EMR takes every day. If I had a really good, really easy EMR system that requires just a few clicks it would probably add about ten minutes a day. But since I have an EMR that takes forever and a day to figure out—I can spend, especially for my older patients who have many, many medications and I have to verify each one—20–30 minutes for *one patient*, just to go through them all and get it all right in the system. That's nuts.

Some EMRs are easier to use than others. In residency we used Epic. I think it's the best of all EMRs. They do everything they can to minimize what we call "physician clicks," which means the number of times a physician has to click to get the information into the EMR. They've done some innovative things to make it easy. But in private practice I switched to something else, which is horrible. The office has made some improvements, but to write up an easy patient note—even an easy 21-year-old new patient note—probably takes me, minimum, five to eight minutes. For other patients it can take me 10–15 minutes to write a note. Whether I write the note when the patient is in my office or later depends on my day. If at all possible, I try to get it done in the office, but I can't always do that.

In terms of the EMR, I'm adaptable, I'm young. I think some of my older colleagues have a harder time of it because they're not as technologically advanced. I've used better EMR systems than what I'm using now, which is part of what frustrates me. I have no control over the product I use. That is determined by the large medical group I work for. But what bothers me much more are the bogus requirements.

Yes, the EMR is government-mandated, which is why I think voting is so important. Because if we're going to try to make healthcare better, we need people at the top who know how to make it better. That requires not putting so many onerous requirements on doctors that go way beyond patient care.

Patient Satisfaction Surveys

Hospitals receive money from Medicare, which requires patients to fill out patient satisfaction surveys. These surveys ask patients to report their pain scores and ask whether their pain has been adequately treated in the hospital. Patients assign arbitrary scores and then hospitals are paid based on what patients report. There's a big push to make sure patients are satisfied when they leave the hospital, and making money quickly is a lot of what drives that.

Studies have shown that patients with higher satisfaction scores often have worse outcomes than patients with lower scores. Hospitals say, "Let's ask the patients how they feel about their care and get paid based on that." But that's not good medicine. Just because there is legislation or requirements for patient satisfaction doesn't mean better care is being provided. I find that really frustrating.

Pain Medication Seekers and the Internet

I've had some nasty reviews online from patients who were pain medication seekers. They can go online and say whatever they want—that I was horrible, I didn't treat their pain adequately, etc. And I don't have any recourse. I can't say anything because that would be a HIPAA violation. I can't say, "Remember, we had that pain contract? And you've gone to too many doctors for pain medication?" I can't say that. I find that incredibly frustrating.

Bad Outcomes

My job is awesome 95% of the time, but 5% of the time it's the worst thing that ever happened to anybody, for example when there is a fetal demise or a miscarriage at some point in the pregnancy. Miscarriages are obviously bad at any time but are particularly horrible in the third trimester.

When something goes wrong, in the case of an error or an adverse event, I'd say I'm more supported than blamed. Hopefully, God forbid, I never make a medical error. There are systems in place, not only through my employer but through the hospital—like a peer review committee—to examine medical errors. The majority of the most difficult outcomes, like fetal demise, we don't have any control over. Such cases will still go to peer review to make sure we didn't do anything to contribute to those outcomes. There's also a debrief after really, really bad situations, not so much at my hospital but at other hospitals I've worked, where the doctors, the nurses, and the neonatal intensive care unit (NICU) doctors and nurses will ask, "What happened? Could we have done anything better? Did we do everything right?" so we're all on the same page. Having processes like that in place are very helpful.

It can be pretty scary in obstetrics. First of all, I think if anything bad happens, I'm going to get sued. The worst part of my job is the constant fear of being sued and feeling there's nothing I can do about it. Just this thought—that I'm doing the best I can and then at any moment I can be sued—is frightening.

I did have a pretty bad outcome the other day and my hospital department chair called me and said, "How are you doing? Are you doing okay? Do you need to take a couple of days off?" That really shocked me because I've never had that kind of outcome before and I wasn't expecting it. She just reached out after hearing from risk management and said, "We have these services if you need them." I thought it was nice that someone out there thought of us.

There's a lot of talk, especially in obstetrics but not only in obstetrics, about the fact that when the patient has a bad outcome—when a terrible thing has happened—the team taking care of them goes through it, too. They grieve, too. It's called secondary trauma. That can also be pretty horrible. These things happen very rarely. If that weren't the case, I don't see how anyone could do this. It's amazing to me how many thousands of things can go wrong with a pregnancy, and most of them are totally fine.

Advice

My only advice is for hospital administrators: Ask doctors who do this work what they need. People who think they know what doctors need have no idea.

88. *Harold J., MD, Surgeon in Urology*

Harold, J., MD, a surgeon in urology who had been in independent practice for 20 years, became a salaried hospital employee a few months before this interview. Here, he explains the pluses and minuses of this move from the perspective of someone who has not fully adjusted to this recent change. Relieved of the business side of practice, this self-described type A personality now sees more patients, spends more time documenting in the EMR, has less time off, is feeling greater levels of stress, and has less fun at work than he did in independent practice. But Harold recognizes the jury is still out and sees this change as "a work in progress."

I always liked science. I always liked biology. I actually thought I was going to be a vet when I started, and my interest morphed into medicine. I fell into a study group of biology majors, and many of them were becoming premed or thinking about medical school. I started thinking about it, too, and then dove into it.

I did my rotations in medical school for the first two years. I always liked surgery. I always liked being in the operating room, but I didn't like the lifestyle of general surgeons or cardiothoracic surgeons who have to work a lot of late hours and take emergencies. In urology there is a nice mix but not a lot of clinical crises, middle-of-the-night emergencies. There are a lot of curable cancers, really cool surgeries, and a lot of variety. That's what I like about it.

Before a few months ago I'd been in an independent urology practice for almost 20 years, right out of residency. That was the only place I'd ever worked. My partners and I were our own bosses. We basically did what we wanted and made the schedules. But we decided to forego our independence and become hospital employees because we'd been struggling for many years. It just got to be more and more difficult dealing with insurance companies and bottom lines and fighting with all sorts of payers—it just became an onerous task. We decided this was the right time. Most practices were going this way. We felt we were one of the dinosaurs.

The administration at the hospital is familiar with us because we had our own practice for 20 years. They realize we know how to run a practice. They've pretty much left us to run our own practice as we always have, which is why there's been no stress about that. And they've been helpful; if we need something, they'll take care of it for us. The major benefit of being employed by the hospital is that we don't have to worry about the bottom line, lines of credit, making payroll, or who's going to pay the rent for the office. All those things that we don't have a lot of training for or time for, we don't have to worry about anymore. As long as we're making the bottom line and beating expectations for their quota, I don't think they're going to give us a hard time. We're busier than the hospital expected us to be. We've always been busy and have always prided ourselves on being busy. My partners and I are type A people, anyway.

This is a whole new system for us and it's all about relative value units (RVUs). Depending on the level of the visit and what we do, we put a value on it and calculate them all at the end of each quarter. If, at the end of a quarter we surpass our RVU quota for that quarter, we get paid per RVU. It feels funny. The busier I am, the more money I'm going to make. But it's kind of an odd feeling. It feels a lot different being a hospital employee than being part of an independent practice, but it's still a work in progress.

The hospital pays me a salary. They don't tell me how many patients I need to see in a day, but they do incentivize me. It's productivity-based, so the more I work, the more I make, and I get bonuses for productivity. When I was in private practice, my practice colleagues and I saw as many patients as we could and everybody basically worked the same amount, it all came out in the wash, and we split everything evenly.

It might be a figment of my imagination, but I think I have some say in how busy I want to be. There are so many people who need to be seen that I feel an obligation to try to see those folks. It's hard when someone calls up and says she needs an appointment and you tell her she can't come in until weeks later. But she has a kidney stone so she can't wait. I have some control, but crises do come up. The pressure doesn't come from the hospital administrators, it comes from my patients and from me. It's just a feeling that we have to take care of these people. They're part of our community.

I've been seeing, on average, about 30 patients a day. Some patients are complex. There are biopsies to review, complex surgeries to talk about, so it's a lot. Then I have all the notes, the EMR, for 30 patients a day. I think the sweet spot is about 22–25 patients. It's manageable—but when it gets to be 30 and above, it becomes stressful. The number of patients I see in a day increased once we started working for the hospital.

To start my day, I do rounds at the hospital so if there are any inpatients on our service, I see them. I get up very early to do that. And then I start my day seeing patients in the office at 8:00 a.m. and work until about 4:30 p.m. I usually make rounds after that. My actual hours are a lot longer than that. There are always emergencies, people who show up with a crisis and we have to squeeze them in somewhere, so we end up pushing people out a little bit. I finish seeing my last patient by about 5:00 p.m., usually. I do surgeries two days a week, rotating between two hospitals. I also rotate office hours between these two locations. I generally allow 15 minutes for an office visit per patient, and this was true in my private practice, too.

On Joy in Work

I get a lot of satisfaction out of helping people; that's always been a very powerful motivator for me. There are a lot of terrible cancers, a lot of things you can help people with, so I was drawn to that.

On Money and Joy

I don't really do this for the money, although we've never been paid all that much when you look at the national average. I have friends in other states who have always made a lot more than I do, but quality of life for me is very important. We didn't have a relaxing schedule when we were in private practice, but we always had a day off a week. So, one day a week we could catch up on our families, get a haircut, all these things that we never really think about. We don't have that anymore. Money's not a very important thing for me. I'd always like to make more, everybody does, but I don't think I'd be happier if I did. Balance is what matters.

A lot of people are retiring, a lot of doctors are leaving the state. This state is a tough place to work from a reimbursement standpoint. Doctors are not very well reimbursed by insurance companies. Our state has one of the lowest reimbursement rates in the country, so doctors tend not to stick around. They can make a lot more money 20 minutes down the road in another state. So, there's a lot of turnover, and as a result there are a lot of patients who need to be seen. It's always been that way, whether in private practice or as a hospital employee.

What Diminishes Joy

The Electronic Medical Record

The EMR is the most onerous part of my job. I used to have a lot more fun in the office. Now it's kind of a race to get all the data entered, so it's a bitter pill. I try to do a lot of this while I'm there, during my lunch. I take a half hour for lunch and I try to put the data into the EMR for some of the more complex patients so I don't forget what I was doing. And then at the end of the day I end up taking quite a bit of it home so I can see my family. I do a couple of hours of data entry when I get home. I know how to type and I'm a very fast typist. We have new voice recognition software in the office that's really, really good. It's come a long way. We've just started using that and it saves a lot of time. But we don't have that at home, so I don't have it for the work I take home.

Most of the dissatisfaction from my standpoint comes from the EMR. I think as doctors we let it go a little too far. I don't think it's helpful for the patient, I don't think it's helpful for the doctors, I don't know who it's helping. It's good to have centralized information, I understand that, but it's a little too much. It's onerous for me and the patients don't like it. They have to come in and redo all the paperwork and answer all of these questions. You know, they've been coming to my practice for 20 years and now they have to do all this new stuff. It's onerous for everybody and it slows down the flow.

Work Overload

I've never felt overloaded by work until probably this year. Maybe not exactly overloaded, but it's definitely a lot more work, a lot more stress. For me, it's the data entry—the race to get all this stuff into the computer. Because if I don't do it, the next day I have all my new patients to put in, and then I have all the ones I didn't do, and it's like dominos.

Overloaded schedules diminish joy in work for me. When we started there were five doctors in our practice. We had five for a long time, then one of them left so we were down to four. And then one retired and we were down to three, which was tough because that meant there was one more weekend call and one more during-the-week call. Then we hired two more doctors, so we were back up to five, which has helped with calls. When there were three of us, I was on call every third weekend. Now that there are five of us, I'm on call every fifth weekend, from Friday night to Monday morning. And that's for calls and emergencies—we don't have to stay at the hospital. But we're on call so we can't go very far, we can't drink or anything like that.

Adjusting to Change

I used to have a lot more fun in the office even one or two years ago, and certainly five years ago. And that's diminished. The morale in the office is down a bit because everybody's got more work and a different job to do. Part of that is due to growing pains. We have a new computer system, we have a new way of registering people, we have new phones, so it's been a little stressful. But it's a bit early in the game. I'm hoping when this all works its way out it will be better.

We've had some turnover. A lot of people who had been working with us for a long time left. They said they weren't going to keep doing this because the change was just overwhelming for them. We had some older folk in their 60s who enjoyed the practice, enjoyed helping people, but it became a bit more than they could handle because of the computer system and learning a new EMR and all that. Some of them were close to retirement age, anyway, so that was the straw.

We used to be a lot more personable. Now you call our office and get the automated, "Hit 1 for this, hit 2 for that…" There used to be a person answering the phone. It ruins a little bit not to have the personality there.

Stress

At what point does stress become burnout? That remains to be seen. I have a good support structure at home, which is very important. My wife is very supportive. So that helps me. I've been doing this for a long time. I've got to find a pattern and find a little bit of time to relax.

As I said, I've never really felt the stress as much as I do this year. I now work five days instead of four days, but everybody works five days, so we were a bit of an anomaly. But it's different. I don't feel I can catch up on my chores and life and everything yet. If I feel I'm getting burned out I go to bed a little earlier than I used to because I'm so tired. So, we'll see how it goes. I'm in it for the long haul. We signed a contract for three years and I suppose if it doesn't work out, we can always go back. But I'm looking at it long-term.

89.   *Charlotte J., MD, Internist in Private Practice*

Charlotte J., MD, is a long-time internist in a small group internal medicine private practice. After having first agreed to talk to me for this book, she later had second thoughts, realizing she had much less to say about joy in practice than about what saps her joy every day. Although she declined to be interviewed, Charlotte granted permission to publish the following comments, which she shared with me through email, about an example of aspects of her profession that have become not only onerous, but joy destroying.

Although I initially agreed to talk to you for this book, I soon realized I am not a good source for this topic. I love my patients and enjoy all the professional aspects of caring for them. That's why I stay in practice at an age when most of my colleagues have retired.

But the "joy" of medicine has been destroyed—corporate takeovers of hospitals and many practices, requirements to use electronic records that contribute little to patient care, interference in treatment decisions by insurers—the list continues. I'm not surprised that you are getting so many similar complaints about the state of medicine. Probably more in primary care (family practice, internal medicine, pediatrics, geriatrics) than in procedural specialties.

Everyone complains about the EMR, but the "grunt" work of prior authorizations, disability papers, etc. is dumped on the primary care people. Just recently, I had a request from one of my patients to try to get an expensive orthopedic consultation covered. She chose a specialist not in her network but was told by her insurance she only needed a referral from me to get partial coverage of the visit. I sent a referral note to the orthopedic office.

Now, a few months later, insurance is refusing to pay. She was told, "Your primary care physician just has to call the insurance company and talk to us." They even gave her a reference number (probably made up on the spot). I refused initially, because I told her the comment, "just call us" is a ruse to get rid of her call, it will take forever, and it will result in non-payment in any case.

Then I relented at the end of the day and tried. With a reference number and a phone number, I spent *one half hour* trying. The phone, of course, led to a robot answering, and the phone triage did not include any choices that fit our situation. The robot would ask for my tax ID number, then tell me I wasn't registered in their system and would disconnect. Then I would try again. On three separate calls I got a human, who would say, "wrong department," insisted on transferring me rather than give me an extension number, and this would either go to disconnect or back to the original robot loop.

For amusement I logged the transaction with my notes and sent them to the patient with the suggestion she contact the state insurance commissioner. This also will result in no changes, but at least the insurance company will be forced to waste their time replying to the commissioner's office.

Feel free to use my comment. I'll be eager to see the book.

Lawsuits

90.   Jacqueline M., MD, Internist, Attending Physician, and Assistant Professor of Medicine

Jacqueline M., MD, has been a practicing physician for 30 years. She is a primary care doctor in a group practice, an attending physician, and an assistant professor of medicine. Over the course of her career Jacqueline has worked in urgent care, at a university health center, in a large academic medical center, and has been in her current practice for the last three years. The biggest challenge to her joy has been the four lawsuits she has endured over the course of her career.

I've wanted to help people since I was a little girl and being in healthcare seemed like a good way to do that. For as long as I can remember I wanted to be a candy striper—a volunteer in a hospital. I volunteered in pediatric art therapy as a teenager. There, at the team meeting every day before work, I always heard, "The doctor will decide." And I thought, *I want to be in that deciding position.* I read the book, *The Making of a Surgeon,*[1] as a young teen, which inspired me to think about becoming a doctor. My experiences in research were terrible, but my experiences with patient care were great, so that reinforced my choice.

I chose internal medicine because I liked the continuity of it, the breadth of it. I liked the fact that I would deal with things ranging from not very serious to life and death. I didn't always want to be faced with life and death, but I didn't want to do things that didn't feel important, either. I wanted to care for a variety of people for long periods of time who had a range of illnesses and illness severity.

My biggest career dilemma was deciding between internal medicine and psychiatry. I sought out extra experiences in each of these areas but ultimately felt that internal medicine was a better fit. I like working with my hands, sometimes having a quick fix. Psychiatry was a little too cerebral for me. The kind of psychiatry I was most interested in was for people who probably wouldn't go to a psychiatrist but who might talk to their internists about their problems. That turned out to be a good career choice for me because right around the time I finished residency, psychiatrists were almost entirely constrained to treating patients with medication and doing very little psychotherapy.

I work four days a week and see patients in my office on each of these days. On three of these days I start a little before 9:00 a.m. and leave around 6:00 or 6:30 p.m. One day a week I start at 8:00 a.m. If I have to, I can leave the office earlier but then I'll have more hours of work to do later on. On average, I probably spend at least three or four hours a week writing notes from home. Some nights I might be doing this for two and a half hours on just one night; usually that will go fairly late, until 10:00 or 11:00 p.m. If I have a patient in the hospital, then everything gets backed up by at least an hour. When my patients are in the hospital, unless they are there for surgery, I am in charge of their care.

I precept residents who work in our practice part-time. I also teach medical students one afternoon a month. My job is considered a 75% job—and in that job, I spend 50% of my time on patient care and 25% teaching.

I work fixed hours as far as appointments go, but the work involved to take care of patients extends far beyond those hours. I haven't done the calculation in a while, but for every hour I see patients in the office it takes one more hour beyond that to write the notes from that visit and to keep up with all the other communications for those patients during the course of the year: answering questions, coordinating care, communicating with specialists, getting test results back, and more.

I feel a tension between meeting my patients' needs, my own needs, and the needs of my administrators. A late-in-the-day phone call when I'm trying to get out because I've got to be somewhere is stressful. I would say I felt that more frequently earlier in my career when we had kids at home who needed to be picked up. I have fewer days now when it would be a problem if I had to stay for an extra half hour; but I've tried to be aware of the fact that those other responsibilities were also healthy constraints on my work life so that work couldn't expand to fill all the crevices. I don't get calls on the weekends. I don't give out my cell phone number so I don't get contacted by patients outside of work.

Record-keeping has gotten slower through the use of electronic medical records. You can't just dictate a note straight out anymore. Everything has to go into different sections, there's a lot of clicking involved, and there are more requirements as to what we document—it's just slower. Everything is more precise with more complex electronic records but also more time-intensive after the visit.

On the other hand, in this practice I have a little more support in some of the record-keeping: medication lists are entered and updated by my medical assistant and I only have to review it and catch what was missed rather than do everything myself. I can also ask the medical assistant at the end of the visit, "Can you send this prescription to this pharmacy for this amount?" That saves quite a bit of time, which adds up.

There are five, soon to be six, physicians in my practice. I think there are enough support staff for what we ask of them. We don't have scribes. I know people who use scribes often say they're fabulous, but that hasn't really been an option, so I haven't allowed myself to think about it too much. I have a feeling there would be both gain and loss with using scribes. I've always felt my time in the room with the patient is precious, and that the other person in the room would likely make the patient a little more guarded; but I've heard people say they quickly forget the scribe is there.

When I was deciding about the kind of work I wanted to do I thought it would be hard enough just to be a doctor—I didn't feel I had the energy or time to devote to running a practice, too. So, I've had to accept that a lot of decisions are made that I don't have a say in. I've chosen to be a salaried doctor rather than an entrepreneur or an administrator. For the most part that was the right call for me because it has allowed me to have a very full life outside of work. Despite working many hours, I would work insane hours if I didn't work a three-quarter time job. Since having children I've always worked anywhere from 70% to 80%. I wish more people could do that.

On Joy in Work

Joy in work means I'm helping people by using my mind and my heart to my fullest potential. Joy in work means looking forward to seeing the people on my schedule. I was going to say that with joy in work time flies, but time flies for me no matter what, whether I'm happy at work or not. I have experienced joy in practice and have had periods of time when I've had much less. I do feel joy in work, but it varies. It doesn't take too many negative interactions to poison the way I feel for a while. I work on trying to give the positive interactions more weight so that the negatives ones don't feel overpowering.

Patient Feedback

There are some things that make me feel great. A new patient, a woman, came to me because she was having a back problem. She'd been talking to a woman in the bank who said she liked her primary care doctor. At that, another woman said, "Well, I *love* mine," which is why this new patient came to me.

Another new patient told me, "You're just what I've been looking for. My husband has to see you, too." Those interactions feel wonderful.

When I take care of somebody who's dying and afterward the family says, "What you said and what you did really meant a lot," this is deeply meaningful to me. I try to visit people who are dying at home once during the course of their illness, and that's always satisfying for me, as well as for patients and their families. These visits allow me to connect with them in a way that's more personal than is possible in the office or the hospital.

I was once at an event with my husband and a friend when a patient came up to us and said, "I've been a patient of hers for 30 years. She's a real gift." She's a patient who has followed me to all three practices. That was a great feeling and a great thing for her to say. Taking care of her for the past 30 years has been so meaningful to me.

When I left my practice, many patients didn't follow me because I moved somewhere different geographically, but they wrote me some really nice notes that made me feel joyful.

Having a patient come back after I made an intervention to say it helped and to say thank you brings me joy.

Hospital Culture

The ethos of this hospital, the spirit of the hospital, is collaboration, communication, and support, which are all sources of joy. I've had radiologists call me and be proactive, suggesting things or telling me what they're worried about before they finish writing a report that I'll eventually see.

When something goes wrong, my current hospital is more supportive than my prior hospital. There is more conversation here. We have mortality and morbidity rounds and Schwartz Center rounds, both of which help us to talk about the challenges of caring for people—that adverse outcomes occur even if things are done right; that errors occur because we are human; that we need to figure out what we can learn from errors without being afraid to explore them; and that we should be able to talk about these things without fear of negative consequences.

On Money and Joy

There's got to be some connection between money and joy. I wouldn't do this for free. But there's a volunteer job I do that's not medical that I get tremendous joy from. It's an antidote to the downsides of medicine, and people are so positive about and grateful for my work. I've asked myself why I like doing this volunteer job so much, and I think it's because what's required of me is to be very positive; there's nothing scary that I'm worried about missing.

If I were suddenly told "You're going to get 1.5 times what you're earning now," it would be a lovely piece of news, but I don't think it would actually make me happier. I feel I'm fairly compensated for what I do. There are some types of specialties where I wonder if they should be paid *that* much more than we generalists are, but I don't spend a lot of time thinking about that. I tend to think about the people in the world who earn a lot less than I do and have very hard lives rather than about people who earn more than I do and have easier lives.

What Diminishes Joy

Negative Interactions

Negative interactions with patients diminish my joy. Here's one example: I saw a new patient who was concerned about several different problems. She came in because she wanted me to renew her psychiatric medications after having moved from out of state many months ago. She'd seen a doctor she didn't like and after a while saw me. I expressed hesitation and concern. Several weeks later I happened to look at my online reviews, which I do from time to time, and saw that she had written an absolutely scathing review of me on two different sites. That was disturbing. I felt terrible. It was very public, or potentially public—I don't know how many people look at those reviews—but this is a pretty awful thing. She never talked to me about her complaints directly. She just took off. There were things she wrote that were not true, things that were distortions. But there was really nothing I could do about that. It's just out there. That's a pretty bad feeling.

Having patients leave over disagreements in care over time may be natural, but I take them to heart. Some are harder than others. I don't just brush it off. I think about whether it's an appropriate parting of the ways or whether I should have done something different.

Lawsuits

Lawsuits challenge my joy; I've been in practice since 1987 and four lawsuits have been brought to me since then. Three of those were dismissed and one is in progress. One went on for about seven years, another for six. One was dropped within the first year. The current lawsuit has been in progress for two years and I don't know when it will finish.

Each of these lawsuits has been different and very difficult. The first one was filed about six years into practice and was brought to my attention a year after the events occurred, when I was already at my second practice. That shook me. Though I didn't feel I did anything wrong it was still a difficult year, and my work was under tremendous scrutiny. There's a lot of shame. You're not supposed to talk about the details of a lawsuit with anybody. You have to report that it's happening every time you are asked to renew your license or your hospital affiliation, so every year or two you have to go into some detail about it; yet you can't talk about it enough to get much closure while it's going on.

The next lawsuit was about ten years later. That was similar. Then the last two, one of which was dropped immediately, happened right around the same time. And at that point I asked, "Am I a bad doctor? Am I terribly unlucky? Or am I going about handling bad outcomes in some kind of bad way?" I called it "the bads." I was tormented by this set of questions. At that point I decided to work with a therapist for the first time in my life and I found it really helpful. Her assessment was that it's largely bad luck, but she has also helped me to work on some of the feelings that are specific to being sued.

When I've had to talk to people in the administration about a lawsuit, they've all been very good but I've always dreaded it. Two lawsuits pertained to my second practice but arose only when I had started in my third practice. Then after a year and a half of being at this new practice, I had to let people know that this was going on. It was a very tough thing to do. I didn't need to let people know about it right away, I needed to let them know a year later when I was being re-credentialed. And I dreaded doing it. People were incredibly supportive and said, "There are people I respect tremendously who've been through this," and my department chair was extremely supportive. There was dread on my part that was not validated—instead I was met with a compassionate, kind response.

The fact that one can't talk about the details of a lawsuit at all is hard and this is still true. But what I've figured out is that one *can* talk to people and say, "I'm being sued and it's really stressful and here's how it makes me feel." I've done more of that with each successive experience, and that's been good. I talk to friends who are doctors and to friends who are not doctors.

Pressure

I'm scheduled to see new patients for 40 minutes, physical exams for 40 minutes, and other patients for 20 minutes. It seems like a luxury compared to some but it's barely adequate for me. I'm thorough. And, of course, I don't get my notes done in that time.

There are people who say, "Why aren't you seeing more patients?" and "Why aren't you admitting more patients to the hospital?" These are interesting questions. There are financial pressures to provide more care, and financial pressures to avoid unnecessary care. Practicing while feeling both pressures is referred to as "having a foot in two canoes." As far as I'm concerned, I'm going to give the right care at the right time to the person.

For the most part, I ignore the requests to see more patients than I feel I have time to see. Nothing has happened yet as a result and I've been here for three and a half years. I've had a lot of terrible things happen to me in the last few years—a parent died, then I injured my knee, so I was out for surgery—so there have been valid reasons for lower productivity. I also came here as a new doctor, so although I brought between 100 and 200 patients with me, I had lots of empty slots in the beginning. I'm much closer to being fully scheduled now but there are days that are not full. That's just the way it is.

The head of my small group has recently been saying, "When somebody needs to have their thyroid dose retested after you've adjusted their dose, you need to schedule them for a return visit. Because that's what other people do, and it will earn revenue for the practice." I feel no, that really isn't what I should do, but I'm in a bit of a dilemma on that one.

The Business of Medicine

Telemedicine is not compensated for us. There are practices that do bill for it. I would be afraid if we were to bill for phone calls, we would make people less likely to call when they need guidance.

I understand that patients might prefer to deal with something over the phone—but if I can do a more thorough job in person, I'm going to try to encourage them to come in. When patients come in, I can bill for my time and I don't look as un-busy to an administrator as I would if I were talking to the patients on the phone. In reality, of course, I'd be equally busy either way, but since I'm doing the work it should look like I'm doing the work. There is a bit of a disincentive to manage patient care extensively by phone.

I don't like to email back and forth with patients because I think it's problematic. As a doc I like to ask questions, get answers, and ask more questions depending on what I hear. Not only is email inefficient for that, it's not nuanced. We have secure email so it's not about security. Email is an emotionless communication that also allows people to expect a lot. I currently have several emails, each of which I've looked at and won't respond to right away because they're going to take thought and time.

I moved to this practice because it's a small practice that's relatively well-run. And it's well-run because my boss pays attention to whether we sink or float. I think it's been harder and harder for him to manage. I think he has managed longer than many practices that have become parts of big, big conglomerates. Part of how he's done that is by thinking about and paying a lot of attention to the bottom line.

Reflections on Promoting Joy in Work

In terms of promoting joy in work, I think systemic improvements would help a lot. Scheduling the time for the work we need to do, including note-writing; the fact that most physicians don't get their documentation done during the time they're scheduled means we should probably be scheduled less tightly.

Documentation should be easier—it should be designed for ease of entry of information by the people who are doing it and not for other purposes.

I think we should always have a support person, like a medical assistant, one-on-one with us when we're working. I have that in my practice now. I didn't in my prior one and that's why I moved. Someone who goes over medications, enters basic data about family history, social history, smoking, alcohol use, and who does a lot of the things that would otherwise require us to check off in the time-consuming electronic medical record. As long as we're constrained to using records like this, having somebody who can help us with that is really key.

Having secretarial staff who take good messages, and who figure out where the messages need to go so that we only have to see messages that need our input, is another very helpful thing.

I sometimes get feedback from administration that people are disappointed that I'm not seeing more patients and I say, "I'm doing what I can." I feel that I'm working about as hard as I can, acknowledging that I'm working 75% of the time. When I applied for this job, they really wanted me to work full time, but I said I can't; I have other interests and things I care about beyond work and that this works for me. And they hired me.

As far as what the administration could do to improve my joy in work, I'd like it if I were scheduled even less frequently, which sounds luxurious. Specialists have more time per patient and they're focusing on just one area. The constant stress of not wanting to run behind—and feeling that things are undone and need to be done later—is really tough, so I actually think more time with patients would make a difference.

I once I had this idea of a "snow day" in medicine. Earlier in my career we would have to show up, even in the worst weather. We would have days when only one or two patients would show up. And then I'd see somebody for 45 minutes who I'd normally see for 20 minutes, just because I could. I remember one man who said, "This is terrific! I should always come in on days like this." So, I think that time pressure does affect a lot. We can do a better job with more time. Time really is the currency for us.

I don't think support, or yoga, or stress management classes are the most helpful interventions. I do think there are ways to reduce the stress of being a doctor by improving our support and not having ridiculous time constraints. I think the expectation that primary care doctors see 20 patients a day, every day, is not right. I don't know what the right number is for what I do, but that's not right.

Some of the things my administration does are good, such as being open about the importance of talking when things go wrong and making us feel safe in doing it. And holding up as examples the great work of primary care doctors and finding ways to show appreciation for what we do in a genuine, sincere way.

Working less than full time—having that day a week to do things with my children and for the household—really was important when my children were younger. That made it possible for me to be involved in their lives while still being involved in and committed to my work.

Advice

My advice to colleagues is, set limits. Learn to say no when people are asking you to do something you feel you can't, whether it's about a patient or a new responsibility you are being asked to take on. It's okay to say no. If you say no to one thing, you'll be free to say yes to something else.

We need to cut ourselves some slack. We tend to be very hard on ourselves when things do go wrong. There are bad outcomes despite the right care. At the same time, we need to be open to acknowledging when we've made a mistake and feel safe talking to somebody about it.

Note

1 By William A Nolan (Random House, 1970).

91. *Gregory C., MD, Vice Chief of Staff of a Large Suburban Community Medical Center, Hospital Informaticist, and Director of Provider Relations*

Gregory C., MD, has been an emergency medicine physician, administrator, informaticist, and legislative advocate for 13 years. He is an optimistic, joyful, passionate man who cares deeply about patient equity, fostering a culture of safety, and working in an environment where there is support, collegiality, and love. Gregory's joy in work has been dimmed by lawsuits, diminished by misguided legislation, and challenged by exhaustion, but, he says, "I cherish the good parts of being a doctor."

I've been surrounded by healthcare since the moment of my birth. Everyone in my family is in healthcare, so it was probably conditioning that led me to become a doctor.

Probably my greatest personality flaw is that I have need to be liked, to be needed, and to feel valued. Maybe everybody feels that way if they're honest. Practicing medicine really does make me feel needed, especially emergency medicine, where people come in at their worst or their most fearful or when they're in pain, and I have the ability to take that away—whether it's their anxiety or their pain, I have the ability to make a diagnosis or fix their wound or reset their bones. If you're having a medical emergency on an airplane, you want an emergency medicine doc to be on that plane with you. And I love the feeling of knowing that no matter what comes through the door of the emergency department, I can help.

During my residency I worked in the EDs of six hospitals in the area. When I was in training I would moonlight in an emergency room so I could earn money to pay my student loans, pay for my car, and so I could move at the end of residency to a city where I would be in the right place to work in healthcare advocacy. I wanted to be able to attend meetings and meet decision-makers in order to have a more meaningful impact.

One of my passions is expanding access to healthcare to those who otherwise wouldn't have it, which is one of the reasons why I'm an ED doctor. Emergency physicians see anyone who presents for care, regardless of their insurance or lack of insurance. Access to care is also one of the reasons I felt driven to work in the policy arena.

How I Spend My Time

I spend about 80% of my time in clinical care, 30% in administrative work for my medical group, and about 20% in administrate work for the hospital. I do a lot of volunteer work as well. All of these commitments mean that I work about 1.7 full-time equivalents so I'm pretty stretched. I'm also treasurer for the medical staff.

As a clinician my job entails the rapid diagnosis and treatment of people who present to the ED with potentially emergent medical conditions. A full-time emergency physician works 16 shifts a month. I work about 13–14. I also spend anywhere from two to four hours a day on administrative work for my medical group, doing medical contracting negotiations, working with the payers to resolve disputes, and so on. My role as hospital informaticist takes about one hour a day on average—sometimes I don't spend any time on this and sometimes I'll spend four to five hours in a day.

I'm a physician first and a reluctant administrator. In my role as vice chief of staff I serve as chair of the peer review committee, which is where we review cases that did not have optimal outcomes or that had complaints from patients or other physicians or staff members. We review the events for themes; we make sure that the physicians are practicing competently; and when there is concern regarding the quality of care, we interview those involved and try to implement process improvements. My role as vice chief of staff takes about 30 hours a month—about an hour a day or an hour and a half a day.

One of the downsides of my job is I don't have set hours so it's hard for me to have a social life. That, and I take on too many things. But I work nights, so my shifts usually start at 10:00 p.m. and they go until 6:00 a.m. I have to get to work two hours early to get my charts and email done, so I usually get to the hospital at 8:00 or 8:15 p.m. Because I have administrative roles at the hospital I am fortunate to have my own office, which enables me to sequester myself so I can get my work done.

My shifts are scattered because I have all these other administrative roles. There are some nights I can't work because I have morning meetings. I have to admit that not having a routine makes it difficult. Many of my meetings have to conform to day-shift work, which makes calendaring difficult. Although the hospital is a 24-hour operation, administrators and staff generally work from 9:00 a.m. to 5:00 p.m., which means that I sometimes have to interrupt my sleep cycle in order to attend meetings. This can be frustrating; however, because scheduling usually supports the schedules of the majority, I'm generally outnumbered. It would be more humane if we could schedule more of our meetings at 4:00 in the afternoon or 8:00 in the morning so that I could maintain a regular sleep cycle.

Ultimately, my heart is one of a clinician, and I will not sacrifice safe patient care by skimping on sleep—that would increase the risk of errors. I never want to wonder if a mistake was the result of my exhaustion. I refuse to do that to anybody, including myself.

Working Toward a Culture of Safety

I am the peer review chair. We have worked very hard to establish a just culture. We're trying to establish a culture of safety and I think we've come a long way. But I think culture is something that is developed over long periods of time. I think that in my profession there has been a tradition of blame, which leads to defensiveness and interferes with identifying potential areas for improvement. I think it takes time and trust to reprogram that kind of thinking.

I think you reprogram thinking by setting examples. So, for instance, when cases are brought before the peer review committee, more often than not practitioners are defensive about the process. Even though we are working to adopt a just culture and a culture of safety, when clinicians find there are opportunities for improvement in either their care or comportment, they get what we call "dings," or strikes against them. If you get more than five strikes against you in a credentialing period, you risk not being re-credentialed at the hospital. This, understandably, leads to anxiety and defensiveness. A strike against you doesn't necessarily mean you've done something egregious; it just means you've done something that may have been within the standard of care but perhaps was not *optimal* care.

In addition, the system doesn't take into account whether you are a consultant or a hospitalist or an ED doctor. If you take a step back and think about it, an ED doctor takes care of about 3,000 patients a year. A hospitalist takes care of about one-fifth as many, maybe 800 patients a year. A specialist takes care of about one-quarter as many. So, the denominator changes. The numerator threshold is the same for everybody. I can understand why a hospitalist or an ED doctor might be defensive, because they have 3,000 opportunities to get a strike against them in a year. But when we invite people to come before the peer review committee it is to present opportunities for improvement and education.

None of us can be expected to know everything. The hospital and the medical staff may have adopted policies for different kinds of clinical situations that someone has never seen in her career. Many of these learning opportunities could have happened to anybody. The fact that she doesn't know about that policy doesn't mean she's a bad clinician; it just means she didn't know about that policy. We take that on as a means to educate everybody. We'll say, "Take this back to your departments to make sure people know about this policy."

Some people are happy to have these opportunities and some people grumble about them. Often their reaction depends on the personality of the clinician, how they are approached, and whether they feel they've been heard and understood. I think generally physicians are harder on each other than anybody else is. With respect to clinical care, that is definitely true. We are trained to scrutinize care.

Serving as Hospital Informaticist

As an informaticist, I'm responsible for overseeing and trialing new technologies at the hospital and then engaging physicians and medical staff to adopt them. I think I show my medical staff, in my role with the EMR, how they're supported more than anything else. If a clinician has a problem with technology, for example with our EMR, they will raise it with their department chair and the department chair will raise it with me. I work to get the system improved. Then I will make that clinician aware of our progress, even though it may take a year to be resolved. I want to let them know the problem is being worked on.

There is a voice-to-text dictation system, so clinicians don't have to type their records in the system. The hospital rolled that out initially only for the ED docs, but I thought anyone who's completing lots of charts should have the opportunity to use that technology. I was able to show the hospital how they would save money on their dictation services if they would pay for the other physicians' licenses for this technology, and then it was rolled out to everybody.

On Joy in Work

My greatest joy is impacting peoples' lives, helping them when they're in pain, alleviating their fears. I really like being able to teach the nurses and the patients and medical students, as well as the nursing students and paramedic students. I like being a bedside instructor and I also like being able to manage a stressful situation and bring order to it. I view teaching as part of what I do as a clinician. I'm teaching a patient, I'm teaching the nurses. My teaching is hands-on, at the time of clinical care. I like to give some clinical pearls. I feel that for the nurses, the sharper their skills, the better we're going to work as a team and our patients will receive better care. They'll grab me when they see something concerning and they'll be able to help educate the patients. The more they know, the more satisfaction they get from their jobs, too. When nurses have questions about the care they're expected to ask; it's not as if they need to tiptoe around and wonder whether they can. The nurses teach me as well—this is one of the joys of working in the ED, the teamwork.

I work at this hospital because, even though the remuneration is higher at other locations, when I walk through the door I'm greeted with affection from my co-workers. I love it. And I think it puts patients at ease and they often give hugs too. I think the ED can be a very intimidating environment and I think it's very important to consciously try to take the fear-factor out of it. I do that by joking around, by putting my hand on someone's shoulder; when I have a patient who's nervous, I just hold their hand or sit on the edge of their bed. I'm a pretty tall guy so I try not to hover over people so as not to appear intimidating. I view myself as the leader of the team, so I feel that if I'm not conscious about the tone I'm setting when I walk through the door, it can ruin people's day or cause anxiety. I try my absolute best to not do that.

There are definitely a few people who, when I'm having an anxious moment, will tap me on the shoulder and say, "What's going on?" or put their arm around me, which helps me regain my equilibrium. Because none of us is always at our best. That is what I like. I want the staff to know that this is the environment we all work in—we're all friends, we're all colleagues, we respect one another.

I like working in the hospital at night because I like feeling that the community's well-being rests on our shoulders. I'm the only doctor in the ED at night. Sometimes there are two of us. There's an obstetrician in the hospital and a trauma surgeon and an anesthesiologist, and, together with the nurses and ancillary staff, we are responsible for the health of our community at night.

Working in the ED is supremely gratifying—at the end of the day, when I go home and look at myself in the mirror, I know I've alleviated pain, quelled anxieties, and sometimes even saved a life; I can't imagine anything more fulfilling than being an ED physician.

I feel both joy and burnout. Honestly, I'm exhausted. I am so tired. But I still love my job. I love what I do. I wouldn't have done it differently. You know, when I put that white coat on, I just feel a little taller. I feel I'm talented at medicine, I feel I know what I'm doing. I had great training and amazing mentors; and I still have great mentors. Almost every day I'm learning something new, even after 13 years.

Being happy is a choice. I feel lucky to have the problems I have. I went onto the World Health Organization website one day and read that one out of every 15 people in this world don't know whether they're going to eat today--which makes my concern about not getting enough sleep or not having meetings conveniently scheduled seem very unimportant. If I take a step back, I realize that my problems are very, very minor.

I sometimes comment to our staff, when they're feeling tired or burned out or cranky, "Just remember, you feel better than everyone you've taken care of today." It's true, and I love what I do because it also helps me to maintain perspective.

On Money and Joy
I definitely think there's a relationship between money and joy. I love what I do but I get joy from who I do it with. I think if I had the same team and we had the same amount of fun, I could probably do almost anything. If I laughed as much as I do and got as many hugs as I do and I felt valued for what I do and I got paid what I do, then yes. However, if I weren't as intellectually challenged as I am now, I'd get bored. I'm never bored now. It's always a challenge.

I work at the hospital, but I don't work for the hospital when it comes to working in the ED. I work for a large multi-specialty group with about 2,000 doctors nationwide. I'm essentially a contractor who goes into the hospital to staff the ED. I get paid from the insurance companies, which is why it's so difficult. We get money from Medicare, Medicaid, insurance companies, and we get money from patients when they pay their co-pays. On average we collect a little less than half of patients' co-pays. When a patient doesn't have insurance or their insurance company doesn't want to pay, the physicians don't get any compensation. This destabilizes access to emergency departments for everyone.

What Can Destroy Joy

Lawsuits

I've been sued twice. Once I was sued by someone whose life I actually saved. Let me tell you, that process is brutal. Maybe people don't really understand how personally devastating this process is for physicians. Being sued for some other infraction generally isn't personal: if you sue because a wall was built over a property line, it might be irritating but it's not as though the dispute strikes at the core of someone's identity. Being a physician is integral to a clinician's identity; this makes medical liability lawsuits personal.

In my case, each case took over two years to resolve—they were both dismissed. Even though an observer might consider this a "win," it still felt like a loss—even talking about it now raises my anxiety level. I lost sleep, lost confidence, and lost the joy of caring for patients as the constant fear of the next suit lingered in my mind. I can't imagine how deeply this must impact other physicians. When it happens to you it's immensely upsetting. When one of the suits was dismissed, the plaintiffs vindictively reported me to the medical board of my state, which they then had to investigate. It took another six to eight months before that case was also dismissed. It just dragged it on; it felt as if the system was being used as a sword instead of for righting a wrong and ensuring safe care.

The lawsuits definitely affected my ability to practice. I lost confidence, I second-guessed myself all the time. I had a very difficult time sleeping. I was perseverating on cases. I had to focus on my coping skills. I listened to YouTube videos on meditation. During that process you're not allowed to talk to anybody about it aside from your attorney. You are literally suffering in silence. It was an excruciating time.

It is hard not to look at patients differently now. During that time, one of my partners said, "You're not seeing as many patients as you normally do. You don't seem to be working as hard as you normally do." I think he was right. I was so preoccupied with the next plaintiff instead of the next patient that it really took away from my experience. I took it particularly personally because the reason I went into emergency medicine was because we're the only specialty that takes care of everybody no matter who they are, no matter how much money they have in their pockets. I always worked so hard to make sure people have access to healthcare. To be sued at my job by a patient I have devoted my career to protect, was just devastating.

The effects of the lawsuits are still there. I think the last one was dismissed about a year ago without payment. It still does impact me. I chart differently, I probably over-order tests. If someone is insisting on an x-ray when they don't need it, they're going to get it as long as what they are asking for won't harm them; my barrier to "yes" is much lower even if the test is not necessary. I have seen this reflected in the literature as well: for example, we're not supposed to prescribe antibiotics to patients to treat the common cold, but I just read an article saying that doctors who do prescribe them have better patient satisfaction scores than those who don't. After these experiences, that article rings true. However, I still feel my calling is to protect the patients even if that means protecting them from occasional ill-conceived expectations.

Probably seven years ago now, a patient came in by ambulance after his foot was allegedly run over by an automobile. He received 10 mg of morphine in the ambulance on his way to the hospital. That's a generous dose. He came in and still reported pain. I looked at his foot and I didn't see any deformity, I didn't see any bruising, I didn't any abrasion, I didn't see anything. His foot looked like a soiled version of my foot. I needed to get the x-ray because he was in pain. I gave him 0.5 mg of Dilaudid®, which is equivalent to five more milligrams of morphine. He got his x-ray, he came back, and, as with the exam, the x-ray showed no injury. I gave him some Motrin® and sent him home. I wasn't aware of this at the time but apparently he yelled at the nurse when he was being discharged, "How dare you not give me Norco® to go home? I'm in so much pain." The nurse said, "You don't need it, there's no problem." And he said, "If you don't give me Norco here, I'm going to go to another hospital, and they'll give it to me there." Fortunately, the nurse documented this interaction.

About four months after this encounter I received a letter from the medical board—the medical board! That man had complained because, apparently, I did not treat his pain. I asked my attorney to respond to the medical board on my behalf. Of course, that lingered over me because the medical board took four months to get back to me. That may not sound like a big deal, but it would be like the Department of Motor Vehicles sending a warning to a truck driver telling them that they may not have a drivers' license anymore. I felt I was in danger of losing my license. And here we are in the middle of an opioid epidemic. Fortunately, the nurse had documented what happened, my attorney wrote a letter, and four months later the complaint was dismissed. But I had to hire a lawyer and sit with that hanging over my head for four anxiety-provoking months.

Misguided Legislation

The system is broken, and doctors too often are blamed. I like to work in advocacy to try and improve the system. Often misguided policies are enacted, sometimes because the legislature, administrators, journalists, etc. think they understand the practice of medicine. But without the education, many misguided notions find their way into policy or are served up by the media for public consumption. One example of this is the requirement to document pain and the notion that pain is as severe as whatever the patient asserts, regardless of their presentation. So, if a patient were to report having 9 out of 10 on a pain scale, if you don't address it that's grounds for medical liability. In the '90s and early 2000s, doctors were getting sued for not adequately controlling patients' pain. As physicians, we were told that if someone says they have level 9 pain on a 10-point scale, we had to treat it like 9 out of 10 pain. We were prescribing narcotics like Vicodin® and Norco. Well now, 25 years later, we're facing an opioid epidemic.

Now regulators and legislators are turning to the same tools that created the problem in an attempt to find a remedy. Physicians must check the state-run database on prescriptions to see what our patients have already been prescribed. We can't prescribe more than a certain amount, and on and on. So now the government is telling us what *not* to prescribe—and I heard on the news recently that the heroin epidemic is getting out of control. Well, why do you think that is? We've created all these addicts over the last 25 years and now the doctors are afraid of prescribing pain medication. Patients with chronic pain or addiction have nowhere to turn but to find an alternative narcotic, and they're buying heroin. With too few addiction recovery programs, I am convinced that we are on the cusp of a rise in HIV and hepatitis as patients turn to IV drugs.

It's one thing to say let's pull back on prescribing—but you can't pull back on prescribing if you don't increase resources for drug rehabilitation and mental health services. You can't just wish addiction away. But the physician voice is often lost in policy making. Rather, it is more common that policy is made in response to a sad story and a legislator, who is well meaning, and who wants to do something to address whatever the sad story is—and then you have a bad policy. There's a mantra in policy that "bad facts make bad policy." That's what happens. It drives me crazy. I went to school for a very long time and I worked very hard to protect and promote health to become a doctor. Before policymakers introduce legislation, it makes sense to me to ask a practicing physician first.

Work Overload

I feel constantly overloaded by work. I've asked a couple of my mentors what they do when they feel overloaded by work because it often does feel overwhelming. One strategy that I haven't been able to successfully implement yet is to disconnect for a day, or even an afternoon, and make myself unavailable. One of the reasons I work at night is that I won't have to do administrative work while I'm taking care of patients. But then I feel I'm working all the time. I do travel and take a week off in the summer. I choose to work on holidays because that way I won't have to balance meetings with patient care. For me, working on holidays is almost like a gift. To work the week of Thanksgiving is beautiful because all I have to do is see patients.

Insurance Companies

The insurance industry is frustrating beyond belief and I think that's true for both patients and clinicians. I do not work in an integrated health system. Working outside of an integrated health system is frustrating because the insurance companies will find any excuse not to pay us. The insurance companies know that whether they contract with you or not, you have to take care of their patients when they come to the ED. For me, as an ED doctor, the patient arrives unannounced, there's no preauthorization, they're not necessarily in network, and they get their care the same as anybody else would. Then I submit a bill to the insurance company. If I'm contracted with the patient's insurance company they'll pay according to the contract, hopefully. If I'm not, they will pay whatever they unilaterally feel is fair and either leave the patient "holding the bag" or leave the physician with uncollectable accounts receivable. This, in effect, pulls the rug out from under the emergency safety net and destabilizes access to care for everyone.

Reflections on Paternalism

When I was in training in the late 1990s and early 2000s, the idea of paternalism in medicine was frowned upon. I think the loss of paternalism has been damaging to patients and to doctors. I think medicine should reconsider paternalism, and this is why: when I take my car to the mechanic, I do exactly what the mechanic tells me to do because I don't want to have my brakes fail, or I don't want to get stranded—I don't have time for that. I need my car to work well and reliably. The mechanic knows my car much better than I do. Back in the day, when a doctor would give the patient a recommendation, the patient would generally follow it.

Now, we discuss care with patients and provide recommendations. Sometimes they follow our recommendation and sometimes they don't. I think what's happened is physicians don't take ownership of their patients' care and health because they don't feel that they own the decisions. This is what we've been told when we talk to patients: we're supposed to give patients the options and the patients are supposed to decide what they want to do. But how is the patient supposed to decide what they want to do? When I go through these exercises with patients, they say, "Well, what would you do, doc?" Why would I give you the best option and then the second-best option? Why don't I tell you what the best option is? I still tell the people I mentor that you are responsible for your patients' care. You've got to own what you do to them; you've got to own their care. But doctors today view themselves as consultants. They're consulting a patient. They're giving them advice. And if patients take their advice, great. if they don't, that's fine, too. I'm not sure that this is always good for patient care.

Advice

My advice to administrators is, let people practice at their highest level of competence. If you're an administrator, be a damned good administrator, but don't try to be a doctor and don't try to be a lawyer. If you have doctors, let them be doctors. Why would I do work that someone else would be able to do? Why should I be a data entry clerk? Let me practice at my highest level of competence. Let me do the most good with that and you either avoid my area of competence or try to facilitate it. At the end of the day I'm not going to tell a hospital administrator how to be a hospital administrator. That's not my field of expertise. I don't think people have that same respect for doctors anymore.

My other piece of advice is, show your residents you value them. Even small gestures like providing lunch goes a long way. Some residency programs do this, but many do not. If residents are going to be working long and stressful hours and are going to be exhausted—and they'll only have time to go home and shower—wouldn't it be nice, wouldn't it show you care about them, to just give them a sandwich every once in a while? When I first arrived at this hospital, they didn't provide food at all. In my early years there were some serious morale problems. I and other members of the staff suggested they provide food. When they started providing it there was now a venue for the staff to come together and break bread—it definitely helped morale. I know that it sounds rudimentary but being fed is a daily reminder that someone cares about you.

92. *William C., MD, Neurologist in Private Practice*

William C., MD, is a neurologist who has worked in a large group single-specialty private practice for 32 years. Some changes in healthcare over the course of his career—like having hospitalists in charge of patients' hospital care, which have made nights and weekends his own for the first time in 20 years—have made his life more manageable, more predictable, and less stressful. But the advent of the time-wasting EMR and his fear of making honest mistakes, along with his fear of lawsuits, have become new sources of worry and ever-present stress that have diminished William's joy in work.

I took a meandering path into healthcare. I had planned to go into the scientific domain of neuroscience, which was very young at the time. My professors were neuroscientists and neurologists, and I found what the neurologists had to say, and what they were studying, to be very interesting. I decided after a couple of years in the neuroscientific program that I would be happier on the medical side. Instead of completing that program and getting a PhD, I diverted and went to medical school and got an MD degree, then pursued a career practicing neurology.

It was the clinical side of things that interested me. So much of what we learned in neuroscience was basic science, like how cells work in the visual system. But the neurologists were coming in and talking about these different syndromes in people, and I found that very interesting. Fascinating. It just intrinsically appealed to me.

I wasn't motivated to help people, as most of medical school applicants say they are. Not that I didn't want to help people, but I wasn't coming along to save the world. It wasn't a calling in that sense, although I was familiar with the concept. My father was a physician, so I grew up aware of that, certainly. It was my interest in scientific neurology that drew me to the field.

I work in a large urban single-specialty group practice, a collection of people who are neurologists and work in allied fields, like neuropsychology. There are 18 neurologists in my practice. It's not the biggest practice but it's big. We're spread out in six or seven offices around the area. We have regular meetings and communicate with each other through an intranet as a group immediately, at any time. We have a separate committee of physicians who manage the practice. We also have an administrative structure: A CEO, a human resources officer, a comptroller, all those things. They do most of the day-to-day running of the practice and operate the business side. I focus on medicine, with limited management responsibilities. I'm the physician in charge of my office, which has only three doctors, and we meet to manage our practice as a group.

These days, I probably work about eight to ten hours a day, five days a week. I don't have call. There are two things that have changed in the past few years that have made my life different: one is that last year, when I reached age 65, I no longer was on call. Giving up call isn't mandatory, it's just our group policy. Many groups do that, although not all. This policy is in deference to our aging and the fact that we don't do as well with lack of sleep as we used to.

I did hospital work for more than 20 years—consultations in the hospital in addition to outpatient work in my office. During that time I'd see patients during the bulk of the day, I'd do all my paperwork, and then I'd go to the hospital where I'd see patients who were often sicker, and whose problems were more complex, than those I'd seen in my office. But because of changes in the way medicine is practiced we gradually reduced our involvement in the hospital. For the last several years we haven't gone to the hospital at all. This has increased my feeling of control and enjoyment in my work.

I didn't like not going to the hospital at first because I felt that seeing hospitalized patients was part of the practice: if I had patients and my patients got sick and went into the hospital, I went to see them. And when they came out of the hospital, I continued to follow them. That was good continuity of care. When I was on call back in the day I might see, over a weekend, as many as ten or 12 patients in as many as five or six different hospitals. I'd be out all day long and get calls at night. It was very busy and very intense. That lasted for over 20 years. I always got calls from the hospitals, which might be for new patients. A new patient might come in with a stroke and the hospital would need a neurologist to come in and see him. And off I would go. Now hospitalists see those patients, which is what changed all this. As things began to change, the hospital would call me only for my patients' problems and prescription refills, things like that. This has allowed me to increase my presence in the office.

Doing less and less hospital work was gradual; it happened slowly. This meant that the phone calls got to be fewer and fewer, and then probably within the last two to three years the number of hospitals I would go to became smaller and smaller. And then the only calls I was taking were outpatient calls from my own patients. That made both call and my life a lot easier because my day ended in the office at 5:00 p.m. Before, sometimes I would go to the hospital and see three or four patients and get home at 8:00 p.m. Now I would just go home. The people taking call in our practice now still have to answer the phone for our patients, but I don't even have to do that.

On Joy in Work

Joy in work is a sense of satisfaction at having utilized my knowledge and experience in a way that is beneficial to the patient. I do feel it.

I maintain my joy by not seeing as many patients as some. I have the ability to control how many patients I see in a day. Of course, that's going to affect things like income. But I don't have any kids to put through college now, I don't have any expensive weddings to pay for, bar mitzvahs, and the like. And we get to a certain age where we've built up some assets and I have an employed spouse, so these things allow me that luxury. If I were to add three or four more patients a day and just whip them through, I could increase my income. But if I did that it would stress me terribly. I would have no joy in work. Other people, I don't know how they get their joy, but without the opportunity to interact with and connect to people, I wouldn't have joy.

After you've done something for 30 years or more—putting in your 10,000 hours— you're practicing your craft. That's one of the nice things about medicine, certainly neurology, because when you've done it for this long the various classes of disorders organize themselves. You recognize them. You learn what the stories are and what they're going to tell you and what those things mean. And what's serious and what isn't serious. After a while you can just sort of divine that. You get this sixth sense. It takes a long time and a lot of experience. That's what the whole process of medical education is. You start off and you don't have a clue about how to do this. You can't learn this from reading books. You just need the experience. There's no other way to do it.

I derive a lot of satisfaction because people come in and they're often very worried about things. Especially with the Internet. They come in utterly panic-stricken about various disorders they've read about online that they don't have, usually. One of the most rewarding things for me is to see what the issue is and to be able to *confidently* tell a person, "You don't have this." Someone comes in with a little bit of a headache and they're worried they have an aneurysm. I can tell that person, "Here is why you don't have an aneurysm." And by giving them the reasons why, I'm gradually able to persuade patients that they don't have that. And they're so relieved. They'll say, "My goodness, I have a little tremor, but I don't have Parkinson's disease. I was so worried about that. All the people at work were telling me I had Parkinson's disease." Well those people at work aren't doctors, they don't understand about tremor, and they don't know what they're talking about. The capacity to do that—to see the weight being lifted from their shoulders—gives me deep satisfaction.

What Can Destroy Joy

All kinds of factors diminish joy in work. They include the tremendous burdens being placed on us by the need for documentation—meaning we have to fill out all our reports and acquire all kinds of information from our patients, much of which is irrelevant to our management of them. Most of this is Medicare driven.

The Electronic Medical Record

Medicare requires that we ask our patients certain questions, and to collect certain information about them, that isn't essential to their neurological diagnosis or management. But we're required to ask. The insurance companies have all followed suit. We have to document all sorts of information to send in a completed bill—and if we don't do that, they're forever looking over our shoulders. And if we haven't done that properly, these agencies are waiting to swoop down and accuse us of fraud and make our lives absolutely miserable. We operate under a certain level of fear that if we don't do it right according to a set of rules that get changed every year, with new requirements being added, then we're going to be in big trouble.

It's almost as though there are forces out there trying to trip us up. I've never been accused of fraud. But the point is, if we don't properly complete this documentation, then the government regards it as fraud. We may not have any intent to deceive in our hearts, nor are we engaged in any fraudulent activity, but the government has the potential to claim that we have defrauded them. And there are penalties that come with fraud, which is a felony. It's very scary. If we don't dot all the "i"s and cross all the "t"s in the proper fashion, the penalties are huge.

Then there are people incentivized to find the mistakes that we make. And in any system as complicated as the one we work in mistakes are going to get made. They're innocent, by and large, but the financial penalties for making them are huge. Beyond a certain point, if there are significant abuses, we're talking about legal penalties like loss of license, jail time. We go to extraordinary lengths in our practice to put safeguards into place in terms of reviewing charts and meeting regularly to discuss our documentation and to educate ourselves. We do this so that if anyone ever were to bring a case against us, we would be well prepared to show that if a mistake were made it would be a *mistake* and not an act of fraud.

It's hard to estimate how much time this takes, but it's every day, for every patient. I usually see 12–15 patients a day. I have to note that all the required information is documented for each patient; and if a patient doesn't provide some piece of information on the intake sheet, I have to get it. For example, I have to get a history of alcohol use for every patient I see. Admittedly, that's important, but it may have nothing to do with the patient's case. And I have to enter that information every time I see the patient. There are many things like that.

We converted to the EMR about five years ago. Converting to the EMR is a traumatic thing to do, so we did it one office at a time. Since one of the younger doctors in my office is sort of a computer whiz, we decided that my office would be the first one to do this. But when we did it, all the doctors in the office had to do it. The third doctor in the office at the time was getting ready to retire and he was on vacation a lot, and he wasn't really interested. I was basically the number two person in the organization to convert to the EMR. People were very interested in how I was doing; they didn't have too many doubts that the other guy would do well because he's a computer wunderkind. I did okay.

Pressure

I feel overloaded by work quite frequently. I've learned what I have to do, and I get it done. But I can't see as many patients as some of the younger doctors do, first because I have to get all this documentation done. But, second, I'm a little bit from the old school. I'm a schmoozer. And I just have a need—I really do—to sit there and talk to people, answer their questions, reassure them, and that's what doctoring is really about. Or so we were trained. The younger doctors are much more about, get 'em in, get 'em out. They get patients in there, they get all their requirements done, and have very limited interaction with their patients—just move 'em out and see them back for follow-up once they've had testing done or whatever. That's what these forces are doing to people. They're changing the nature of the doctor-patient interaction.

The time that used to go toward empathizing and talking and reassuring is now, instead, devoted to collecting all this useless information we have to acquire. And the younger people who grow up this way, that's what they know and that's what they do. That's what they think is normal. But economics drive all of us. I have one colleague with eight children. And those children are all going to have to go to college. And all the younger doctors have all the financial responsibilities I used to have. They're saving for college, they have a mortgage, they have medical school loans to pay off.

Disgruntled Patients

If a patient is upset about something that happened in our care, we have staff who will contact them and bend over backward to try to address their concerns. They certainly keep the doctors involved because, ultimately, the buck stops with us. If something goes wrong—like an adverse reaction to a medication or a misdiagnosis—we try to open lines of communication with the patent. It's the physician's responsibility to do that. And that's where a relationship with the patient comes in. Every year our malpractice insurance company requires us to take a course in things we can do to reduce the risk of being sued. And what always leads the list is, talk to the people; explain things to them. People who sue say, "Something happened to me and I called, and no one would talk to me." And they get pissed off and they call a lawyer.

I do a nerve and muscle test called electromyography, or EMG. It involves sticking a needle into the patient's muscles. And occasionally you get a little bruising. I've been doing this for 30 years and never had any complications. It's not a complication-causing test as a rule. But one of my patients called up and said she had a lot of bruising and was very concerned about it. Where you'd get into trouble in a situation like that is by not doing anything. You don't call back; or you call back and say "Well, come back and see me in a month;" or you just turn a cold shoulder toward them. Instead, I had her come right in. She came in, I saw her, and I didn't charge her for the visit. And I saw there was quite extensive bruising. I made sure there was no obvious reason for it, I'd never seen anything like that before. I sent some blood tests to the lab to see whether she had a clotting disorder. When they came back normal, I called her up, spoke to her every couple of days, and she told me things were getting better. And then after a few weeks everything was fine. That's the sort of thing I mean. It took some extra time but that was a situation where my response was motivated by genuine concern; also, in the back of my mind, what I was doing was deciding to lower the risk of a malpractice claim or something like that. I always have that in mind, the threat is always there. This example would not have resulted in such a claim because there was no harm done to the patient, but I didn't know that at the beginning.

Lawsuits

I have been sued in a case that went to trial. The whole process took many, many months. There were many months of preparation and deposition and getting ready for it, and then the trial went on for more than a week. It was a verdict for the defense, which means we won. It was a really awful experience. And it is for most doctors who go through it. It was my own patient who sued me. When people sue, they feel they've been harmed and they want recognition that they've been harmed, with financial compensation. When this was going on, I felt sure I hadn't done anything wrong. My self-confidence was not shaken. But because I saw the way the legal system works, that wasn't enough to guarantee that things were going to go my way.

The legal system is fraught with devious means of distorting the picture to try to persuade a jury that I *was* at fault. There is a tremendous amount of distortion. It's not about finding the truth. When this happens to you and you go in and see how it works, you realize that the truth is whatever someone can persuade someone else it is. The attorneys for the plaintiffs usually are just plain whores. Unfortunately. That's one of the eye-opening things about the legal system. They go from case to case to case and they just destroy information and say anything that the plaintiffs want them to say. It's just mind boggling. And they make a lot of money—hundreds of thousands of dollars.

During the suit the doctors in the group were very sympathetic. Probably the biggest tangible form of support is that we have our own internal rule in place that when a doctor is being sued—because we may spend one, two, or even three weeks in court and aren't working during that time, we're not seeing patients—we guarantee to continue to pay each other a certain baseline amount. That money comes from income earned by other doctors seeing patients. That means when I was sitting there in court, I was continuing to get paid a certain minimum and when other doctors have been sued, I've returned the favor and supported them.

Most malpractice suits aren't malpractice, they're bad outcomes. And bad outcomes are, unfortunately, what happens in medicine no matter what you do. But some people say, "Well, this person was 45, he shouldn't have died." Well, unfortunately, some 45-year-old people do die. No matter what happens and despite excellent medicine, they still die. But the bad outcome cases are the ones that result in lawsuits. So, some doctors come in and do defense work. They don't make a lot of money, but they're educating juries about what really happened. And they're usually fair-minded and honest. There were a couple of good doctors in my case who came in and testified for the defense on my behalf. They got paid well for it, but nowhere near what the plaintiff attorney's witnesses were getting paid.

After I got through that experience the lawyer who defended me asked whether I'd like to start educating juries for the defense, and I said yes. I've been cutting back, but I've been doing it for the last ten years. I can't call myself an expert witness but that's how the court would designate me. In the rare case where I think real malpractice has occurred,

I tell them I can't help them defend it; it was a mistake. I've got to tell the truth. The vast majority of these cases are bad outcomes but they're not malpractice.

Giving Patients Bad News

When you have to tell someone who is unconcerned about something that it is bad news, the one thing I've learned is to be honest. People appreciate that no matter how difficult the news is. You don't sugar coat it. You do have to tell people. You try to find ways where there's optimism to try to mitigate the blow. But you do have to tell the truth.

Moral Distress

93. *Sydney G., MD, MPH, Retired Critical Care Pediatrician*

> As a critical care pediatrician, Sydney G., MD, MPH, was—and continues to be—passionate about improving patient safety. She acknowledges that process improvement alone is not enough. To improve patient safety, she says, organizations must promote improvements in culture by creating environments where professionals feel safe in questioning existing processes without fear of blame or reprisal, feel able to express their doubts and vulnerabilities, and show up as full human beings in environments where they are too often expected to leave their emotions at the door.
>
> Sydney has asked me to make clear that the material we discussed during this interview was not rehearsed (which is true of all the interviews in this book), and that she has gently edited it to provide context and corrections where needed.

Medicine was one of the few professions that was modeled for me when I was little. We lived a rather isolated life where it felt as if adhering to others' expectations was key, rigidity ruled, shame was everyday, and nurturing was sparse. My mom was a homemaker. I had a parochial education. So, beyond the nuns and my mom, I really didn't have any female role models. My dad was a physician, an internal medicine doc, and my two uncles and my grandfather on my mom's side were physicians. That's all I knew growing up. On the surface this played an important part in my decision to become a doctor, although there were deeper emotional factors that I'm still working to understand.

In my family, emotions were absolutely not allowed to be a part of anything in life. Basically, bottom line, I experienced emotional abandonment. It was not okay for my own emotions to be evident to anyone. In fact, I didn't even know I had them, that I was an emotional being. Part of my reason for wanting to go into medicine was that it felt okay, and was expected, for me to care for others, but I had no idea who I was or how to care for myself.

A lot of us come to healthcare as injured beings in one way or another. Healthcare provides a setting that is satisfying for us in some way. I thought working in an emotion-free environment might be okay. What I *didn't* realize was that I was *not* an emotion-free being and, in fact, healthcare is *not* actually an emotion-free environment.

We go into this field *because* we relate to the humanity of our patients. We understand on an emotional level how important that is. I was okay, and still am, in the presence of patients who are hurting on a physical and emotional level. But being able to relate to the emotions of others—asking questions and being curious about their experiences and actually responding to them—didn't mean I could relate to my own emotions.

Having chosen to be a physician, I decided on pediatric critical care because kids are resilient. During residency I thought it was wonderful to experience families coming together around kids in a way I hadn't experienced before. But I didn't like kids dying on me and not knowing what to do, which was one of my two reasons for choosing critical care. The other reason was, if I'd been in private practice and kids were getting sicker, I did not want to give up my responsibility and relationship with those children and those families and refer them to someone else. I wanted to be able to take care of them at their sickest. And although in the emergency room I didn't see them before they came in and oftentimes didn't see them after they left, I didn't want to be in a primary care practice where I referred them out when they were at their most vulnerable. I didn't want to give up that relationship or that responsibility.

On Joy in Work

I'm not sure I thought about joy in work while I was a practicing physician. I *loved* my job—helping kids get better. One thing that occupied me and probably occupies most people in training and in the early years of practice is simply doing the work. I worked to gain a set of skills to support people, kids in this case, in getting better; and especially when they responded to my treatment and did get better, that felt pretty good.

I'm not sure I had a sense of joy, but I truly had a sense of meaning and satisfaction. Part of that came from working with my professional colleagues doing what needed to be done, being able to count on them for their skills and expertise and knowing we would have the important conversations we needed to have about patient care.

What Can Destroy Joy

Two sets of circumstances diminished whatever sense of satisfaction and certainly joy I may have had in my work. First, pain and suffering in children is very hard to experience and if they didn't get better and died, those times were always very difficult. Even if we knew we did all we could for patients and families in those situations, knowing that did not make the experiences any easier.

Second is the "organizational culture" that makes acknowledging the myriad reasons for medical errors--let alone learning from them—difficult, if not impossible. I have thought a lot about this and have a lot to say.

Medical Errors

As individuals—humans—we make errors. These are not planned and are more appropriately called "unplanned events." Some unplanned events are detected and averted, some not; some are small, some large; and these are generally determined by patient outcome. Staff on the forefront of care ("sharp end of care") are usually the ones who detect the patient deterioration and are often the ones held responsible, shamed, and potentially fired when complex systemic processes—possibly involving top levels of administration ("blunt end of care")—share responsibility for inadequate processes of care and for detecting and averting an event.

Here's the rub: when an organization interprets a process or a systems failure as the personal or moral failure of an individual, learning and needed change become impossible.

Lack of a Safe Culture: How Do Organizations Learn?

On an organizational level—and this happens in many, many organizations and certainly happened in my organization—there is little to no sense of how to learn from errors/ unplanned outcomes. My organization had no interest in truly learning: favorable data, yes; true organizational learning, no. I have limited confidence in organizational learning because for organizational learning to take place there needs to be an environment—that is, an intentional and consistent set of conditions throughout the organization—where individuals feel safe in being vulnerable, in being human. And we don't promote vulnerability in healthcare. In all my years in healthcare, it was never okay for professionals to be vulnerable. I felt this in every organization in which I worked. The organizational leaders were most concerned about getting the work done. Period.

The resignation to what was, and the lack of curiosity about what could be, were discouraging to me, a pediatric intensive care unit attending physician on the receiving end of many unplanned outcomes. I found the healthcare environment to be one where productivity was more valued than understanding what actually influences it. Joy and meaning were to be left at the door, along with our humanity.

We were cogs in a wheel. In my case and, I think, in many, many cases, burnout, fatigue, whatever you want to call it, *has nothing to do with the work*. It has to do with organizational culture.

Contributors to Burnout

I worked for 30 years in the healthcare system, and 28 years into it I felt as though I didn't belong. Shouldn't an organization be the *least* bit interested that someone who has been there for 28 years feels like she doesn't belong? I felt dead. I could not get myself off my family room couch.

If we do not feel safe enough to talk about and express our vulnerability and emotions, we will feel alienated in our environments and cannot feel that we belong. I don't know how we can feel joy and meaning in such a context. Yes, working with patients, one-on-one, is satisfying. But we all work in a context, an organizational climate of intentional or unintentional conditions, that influences how we feel about ourselves, our work and our behavior—the organizational culture of what we do. And the cultures where I worked were dehumanizing.

What is *really* important and is totally invisible in the healthcare system is not what we do but *who we are*. And *that* topic and *those* questions are never asked in healthcare and are actually actively avoided. What brings us to this profession? For me, the answer to this question goes way deeper than who my role models were and is more complicated. The key to answering this question is understanding *who we are* as individuals—as emotional, human beings coming to this work. We are human beings, not human doings. We are interested in our patients as human beings, yet we cannot show up as human beings professionally. This needs to change.

Blinders to Patient Safety

I recall a hospital-wide staff meeting that was called only once in my career following a tragic and unplanned (and maybe quite public) death in the emergency department. To the full auditorium of staff, the CEO referred to our work as "sloppy, sloppy, sloppy," and implied that if we would just clean up our act and be more careful, unexpected events in our highly coupled, complex system wouldn't happen. There was no visible reaction to that assessment in the audience. I was livid. Down the hall afterward I got no satisfaction from the CEO about his assessment.

Getting no satisfaction over the years, I decided to complete a patient safety leadership fellowship, and my teammates and I had to present a final project. We decided to put together a curriculum for our board of directors to inform them about, and learn what they thought of, safety in the organization. This was in the mid-2000s or so. And, astonishingly, this board of directors thought we were perfectly fine! There were no safety problems, they were convinced—our organization was special, patient safety was everybody else's problem but not ours. I had been living in this universe and I was aghast. I thought maybe we'd made some inroads because now, on the board of directors, were patient safety people. But as an early adopter of patient safety evaluation and data I was never comfortable there. Or welcomed. I just went totally against the grain

That took the heart right out of me. No one had the skills, including myself, at either the personal or the organizational level, to have the needed conversations about patient safety. My colleagues' approach to safety was, "If the nurses would just do what I said we'd be fine." Literally. Plus, a common opinion was that work hours were for getting patient care done, not spending time figuring out how to make that care better and safer.

Prerequisites for Patient Safety

Patient safety depends on acknowledging the many aspects of who we are as human beings and recognizing that imperfection and error in the workplace is part of *who we are*. This should be our starting point in addressing the problem—the eventuality—of unplanned medical events. We can't pretend. Medical care is extremely complex. Yet, *organizational* errors were *never* acknowledged in my facility; the individual was always blamed.

Related to my own experiences, I'm skeptical about root cause analyses (RCAs), just one method of organizational learning, because of the way they were conducted in my previous organization. Among the patients I cared for directly, two underwent RCAs after unfortunate and unplanned events led to death, and both RCAs occurred without my being informed and without my being in the room. In fact, for at least one, and maybe both, I was never informed of what that the discussions were about. In a casual conversation two years after one of these deaths, I learned that an RCA was done for that case; I sought out the results and learned that a clinical decision I had been held responsible for was never raised or discussed with me. Joy? Meaning?

Improving Patient Safety

Kids are admitted to pediatric intensive care units (PICUs) for a large variety of life-threatening diagnoses. In the early 1990s I recognized that a number of kids were unexpectedly ending up in the PICU while being cared for in the hospital; their conditions were related to unexpected medication reactions, unrecognized shock, airway or respiratory difficulties, or to the inherent risks of moving ill children for care. I'm not saying I'm perfect by any means, but these kids would come to me and after awhile I'd think, *we should be doing something different here to prevent recurrence*. And we did a lot of good things around education, monitoring, soft stops (options given), hard stops (process stops for reevaluation), redesigning processes between departments, etc.

Broadening Our Perspective

In the early 2000s I had a nagging feeling and I went back and looked at what we had accomplished in terms of patient safety over the previous 10+ years. I wondered, *have we made anything better here?* I really wasn't sure how much better we had made things. I was disappointed in the results. We had had quite a few conversations and committee meetings and then I began to ask, "How do we think about error? How *do* we begin to think about error and adverse events?"

And then I read my first book by Sidney Dekker, about event evaluation. It's a pretty simple book but wonderful. It made me realize that the way I'd been thinking about error was not as broad as it needs to be. I began to understand that it's not only what *I* think about a process that's important, what's important is how *every individual* involved in that process thinks about it. The question is not so much, "What went wrong and why?" but "Why did something seem like the right decision in the moment to the many professionals involved in those complicated processes but, in retrospect, was wrong?"

We don't come to work every day to make mistakes. We are there and we are functioning second-to-second doing what seems like the right thing. And yet, unplanned events happen. When unplanned events happen and a day later, a week later, or six months later—when people say, "You should have done X, Y, or Z and, by the way, if you had just done X, Y, or Z, that wouldn't have happened"—that's oversimplifying layers of factors around complicated processes. We don't have much curiosity about complicated processes in our organizational environments.

Organizational processes are very, very easy to hold up as the answer to improving safety. The problem is: 1) These processes don't always work; and 2) Denying flaws in the process and casting blame and shame for errors on individuals is disheartening to professionals who are on the front lines every single day.

The Importance of Questioning

Everything comes back to the question, why are we here to start with? My personal background, my emotional background, practically, from the day I was born, was *don't question; don't look at*. So, actually, until very, very recently, I didn't understand why I accepted the organization's message of individual responsibility for errors. In healthcare, we show up as people who are taught never to ask questions, not to rock the boat, and not to challenge the status quo. But if we don't question—or if we feel uncomfortable challenging processes and leaders' attitudes toward those processes— we cannot expect different results.

A few years ago, after I retired, I met with a radiation oncologist and a small group of other doctors and the discussion was about his brand new cancer inpatient facility. The group was talking about how nice the place was, its beautiful lobby, that it was airy and had lots of light, and had pleasing artwork inside. The leader of this facility said he'd been frustrated, though, because he wanted the staff to leave their emotional selves at the door and just do the work. A cancer center! "Don't bring your emotional selves into the room or into the workplace. Everything would be better if staff left their emotions at the door." I was appalled. But then again, I realized I was on the other end of the learning curve about the importance of emotions in healthcare.

94.   Rose S., MD, Internal Medicine Physician and Medical Director of a Subacute Rehabilitation/Skilled Nursing Facility

Rose S., MD, an internal medicine physician for 14 years, was medical director of a subacute rehabilitation center/skilled nursing facility at the time of our interview in 2018. Previously, she had been medical director of a community health center. For more than two hours in 2018, Rose detailed how it felt to work in organizations that put profits before patients—and expected her to do the same—and devalued and disrespected women. The moral distress she experienced at one organization after the other propelled her to go into private solo practice shortly after this interview, where she hoped she would finally be able to put patients first.

I grew up on a Caribbean island and my mother was a nurse. She once had to take me to work with her. As the head nurse, my mother managed the nurses with an iron hand. As I was watching her run the ward, the doctor came. He was male. Everything was hushed. He told her, "Do this, do that," and then he left. I asked my mother, "Who was that?" because I thought the nurses were really running things. She said, "That was the doctor. He gives the orders. He tells us what is really wrong." And I thought, *Okay*. It's not that I made up my mind then, but every time someone asks me why I wanted to become a doctor, that image, that dynamic, always comes back into my head.

I think that incident was my earliest conscious realization of who physicians were and what they did. When I got older, we immigrated to the United States. For people from where I come from, it was always about education and doing what you had to do—and no matter how you got it done, you just did. For my mom it was always, "Yes, I'm a nurse but you have to do better." Every generation has to do better than the one before. So even when I vacillated about pursuing medicine, my mother was always quietly supporting me.

As a female physician, I would feel real gratification when I'd walk into a room to see a female patient and she would express relief that a female doctor would be treating her. As a resident I once had a patient who spoke Russian. We did not speak the same language, but we would sign to each other. She was grateful that I was taking the time to understand her. We had interns and interpreters who spoke Russian, but she always asked to see me. That has always been the biggest thing for me: regardless of what is going on, I'm able to connect with my patient and get a good history. This enables me to help them. This has become the cornerstone of my approach to patient care and it still drives how I practice medicine today.

This is my one-year anniversary as medical director of this skilled nursing facility. Before this role, I was the medical director of a community outpatient primary care facility. I did that for almost five years, but I just couldn't do it anymore. I had to commute at least 45 minutes each way to work, and I had two young children and working there was starting to become life-impacting for me.

What My Job at the Community Healthcare Facility Entailed

The community healthcare center is a government funded facility authorized to provide healthcare to underserved communities—the underinsured or uninsured.

We used a hybrid team-based approach to deliver patient care. The team was usually led by a physician and supported by an array of providers—a nurse, a pharmacist, a nurse practitioner, community health workers, and behavioral health specialists, as needed. Primary care providers were often overwhelmed by the social barriers to providing care, many of which they were unaware such as patients' excessive drinking that masked anxiety or mental illness; their lack of access to nutritious food; their inability to afford their medications; their low literacy or illiteracy, which made following the doctor's instructions difficult. Pulling community health workers into patient visits helped to break down some of these barriers and increase doctors' awareness of them.

As a medical director at the community facility my role was more administrative than clinical. I saw patients only twice a week and my panel of patients diminished significantly from what it had been when I was a full-time clinician. While, as medical director, I did not have to face the grind of daily patients, I still had to spend time with patients. This provided insights that helped to inform policy decisions regarding clinical care.

Working in community health provided an opportunity to identify the various barriers to care that exist in our communities and develop ways to solve or eliminate them. We spent a lot of time in meetings discussing what was best for the "patient" without genuine patient feedback. We developed campaigns built around quality metrics and outcomes. While this was good for measuring a patient's risk for disease it often overlooked the individual. Somewhere in the process the patient and the individual were separated, all for the goal of meeting quality metrics or outcomes.

Establishing Trust

There is a lot of mistrust of healthcare in the underserved community. Older minorities in particular are very suspicious of healthcare providers and with getting involved in any healthcare initiative or program. They didn't want to be part of "your experiment." I had to learn to understand this perspective.

Before working at the community clinic, I had been in private practice with a lot of retirees as patients and it was a very different lifestyle. For some, going to the doctor was almost a social visit. Here, it was the complete opposite. I had to learn how to: 1) Cultivate the trust of my patients so they would open up to me and let me know about their personal situations; and 2) Convince them that when I'd say, "Go get your mammogram," I mean: Go and get your mammogram! Or when I'd say, "Come back in three months," they should actually come back in three months. If I give the patient a prescription, I want them to be honest and say, "I won't be able to afford it until the 15th, which is two weeks from now.' For a patient to be able to confide in this way takes trust. But when they do, I would have to have a solution for them. Because if I didn't, they won't bother saying anything to me again. Why would they?

Establishing trust in the doctor-patient relationship is truly an art. It has a lot to do with who's sitting in front of me. There's no cookie-cutter approach to that. One thing I've always made sure to do is introduce myself to the patient, make eye contact and engage with active listening. I always like to get a sense of the patient and pay attention to who I'm dealing with. If I think someone may have a lower level of education, I'm not going to speak to them in words they can't understand. And if I think someone has a higher level of education, I won't assume they don't need me to explain things. I always feel that I'm cultivating trust. It's as though I have a little garden and I'm going to plant a seed and see how it responds.

Being a primary care provider in that setting was a balancing act. I was managing patients' medical issues and spending half the time trying to figure out what their barriers were—*Why can't I get her A1C down? I keep adding medicine and she's not budging. She says she's taking the medicine. "You could die if you don't take this medicine."* But I'd have to listen to the perspective of the patient and not just sit there in judgment. If people are working two jobs, they're running back and forth, balancing all their other responsibilities, and sticking themselves twice a day is hard. Fitting in particularly well-balanced nutritious meals is very difficult for them, especially when they live in a food desert. If you're a truck driver, for instance, and you have hypertension or diabetes and you're on the road, it's hard to eat properly. So those are the kinds of things that, as a doctor, I need to know and understand. And until I understand them and let them know I understand, I really can't help them. But first, they have to trust me enough to tell me the truth.

The Barrier of the Electronic Medical Record

The standard in primary care is 15 minutes on average with each patient. There are also metrics that have to be achieved. At each visit we have to check all these boxes and ask certain things. We need to screen for smoking or for alcohol use, for example. I remember during the Ebola outbreak—everyone had to embed in their EMR system these screening questions—and this had to be done on every visit. So, all of these "click-click-clicks" in the EMR system that we have to do with every patient at every visit start to become, them-selves, a barrier to interacting with the patient.

Many times, when my patients would go to see a specialist, I'd ask what he said. They'd say, "I don't know, he spent the whole time looking at his computer. He was talking to me, but he didn't even look at me." And I understand that, because as far as that physician is concerned, his performance is based upon checking those boxes. These are the administrative tasks we're being held accountable for, and that our managed care organization and insurance company is basing our reimbursement on. Sometimes our compensation is based upon our performance. and the insurance companies hold us accountable. But the patient is sitting there looking at us and thinking, *he's not even hearing what I'm saying.* But the EMR is a fact of life and we have to check off metrics to be reimbursed by insurance companies or by the Center for Medicare and Medicaid Services, which is one reason why doctors in some areas and in some practices have stopped accepting insurance.

What Can Destroy Joy

I struggle right now because burnout is real. As a resident you know you just have to suck it up, you just have to put in the hours. But you know that has an end. And then when that's over, you're a doctor. You're an attending. And you can decide how you want to manage your patients. There is this light at the end of the tunnel. Then you get out here, you're doing what you want, based on your training, and things just start to change. The reality however is that medicine is a for-profit industry and the physician is stuck between the patients' needs, productivity metrics, and the insurance company guidelines. These elements contribute to the loss of passion for medicine.

Devaluation and Disrespect

One of the biggest struggles we have as female physicians is that we don't feel valued by patients, by people on the administrative side, or by the people who are driving the bus—the insurance companies. And we're spread so thin. Our families don't understand how stressful it is to be here all day and absorb everybody else's issues and try to solve them, putting aside personal issues.

It's harder because I'm a woman. As women, we tend to be more empathetic when it comes to patients and their care. But beyond that, we are also mothers. We are caregivers to our patients, to our families and our children. It's tough as women because we're expected to perform at the same level as a man but on many more planes. Yet, I feel that we're invisible. We are not compensated equally as our male counterparts across the board.

As women we're definitely not as respected as men. We may say something in meetings and the reaction is, "Yeah, right." This implied disrespect comes collectively from men, but even women sometimes don't respect women doctors. We know how hard we work, so one would guess we'd respect each other. But there will be an administrator who's a woman—a business-person, not a doctor—and she will take what the male doctors say as having greater validity. It can't be because we tend to not speak with authority, or that we tend to alter our opinions in deference. I have seen very good female speakers who are articulate and express themselves well, and they're not always well received.

Not being valued diminishes joy in work for me. Not being valued comes through, especially for women providers, in not having flexibility in our schedules while getting less compensation even with the demands on our time. On average, most primary care providers are expected to see 22 patients a day. To me, that, in and of itself, shows a true lack of value. It is disrespectful. And that's what you're measured by in most organizations: How many patients do you see a day?

In any organization I've worked in, the provider who is most valued, who is most rewarded, who is known by all the administrators and even the CEO, is often the provider who sees the most patients in a day. He may see a high number of patients or have high numbers checked off for his quality metrics, but he's not necessarily the one who provides the best care. The doctor who will sit with someone, let's say an elderly patient, who comes in and brings all her prescriptions in a plastic bag, and she's trusting that doctor to go through it and tell her what to do, is a different kind of doctor. This is the kind of doctor patients need because they still see their doctors in a paternalistic way. Just checking the box and telling them to stop their meds and start doing this or that doesn't work for them. They get angry and frustrated.

But the doctors who spend time with patients are the ones who run behind. We feel overwhelmed because we feel the pressure of not being able to see more than 16 patients a day and think, *what am I supposed to do, it's 1:00 p.m*? And then we get feedback. We're hearing it, and sometimes it gets to the point where we *don't* want to see the patient. We start to resent the patient, who now becomes this entity that we're being measured by. We're expected to somehow do very well—this is what we're trained for—but somehow it starts to become something else. It's sort of amorphous. We're not able to quite get our heads around it but we know what we feel. It's a struggle, it really is. It sounds like burnout.

What I've found when I sit down and talk to my girlfriends about our daily struggles and why we don't want to do this anymore, it always surprises me that some of them say, "I don't mind if I don't see another patient. I just can't make the living I do now, so that's why I still do it. If I find something else that would let me live and pay my bills, I would do it." I say, "No, I want to see patients how *I* want to see patients. I don't want someone telling me how to see patients. I would love to be able to make my schedule and have time to see my patients and do all those things that are expected for health maintenance, but not have this thing hanging over me of having to use particular vehicles and metrics and everything else in order to be compensated."

When I finished residency and moved to a different part of the country, I had a male patient who was 98 or 99 at the time. The first time I saw him I introduced myself, and he looked at me and said, "You're the first n***** I've ever let touch me." And I was stunned.

I could feel his wife implode. I first felt a tension in my body, but I paused, then just looked at him, smiled, put my hand on his thigh, relaxed, and said, "Well, congratulations." That's the only thing I could think to say. I didn't know what else to say and that just came out of my mouth. He just sat there, and a sound came out of his mouth. He became very quiet. Before he left, he turned and said, "You're a good doctor." His wife came back and apologized for him and I told her that wasn't necessary. I wouldn't let that stop me from being his doctor. But after that, I thought, *I'm fine.*

My current role as medical director in the subacute rehab facility is more like a figurehead than a leader. Medical directors in this organization have no real say in what decisions are made. Here the decision is made from corporate, and that's it. I'm expected to just carry out what they decide. Decisions are handed down to the administrator, and we are told about them. There is an administrator at each facility. They are not doctors. There is a nursing administrator who oversees the nurses. The medical directors are completely out of decision-making in this arena. We're only listened to when we stomp our feet because we have an example of a bad patient outcome. We shouldn't have to do that.

If I could change anything about my current job, it's that I would like to have a say. And a valued one. I'd like to have a say in how we do things clinically in our centers and how we engage externally, as well, with other hospitals. I would like to have a say in how we're valued, how we're regarded as doctors, and to have our opinions matter.

Moral Distress

I've been in situations where I was expected to put the financial needs of organizations ahead of what was in the best interests of patients. This created direct conflicts for me and made me feel terrible. I won't go into details, but in one instance this involved persuading patients who came to see us for one reason that they should seek an additional type of treatment they hadn't sought, didn't want, didn't need, and couldn't afford, in another facility. In the past I'd dealt with things that impacted the people I cared for, but now I had to deal with things that directly impacted me. The only way I could deal with it was to compartmentalize what was going on. As doctors we have a well-developed ability to compartmentalize our feelings in order to navigate patient care, and I had to use this ability to cope with a practice I found unethical, at best, and fraudulent, at worst.

With money at stake on both sides, hospitals pressure rehabilitation facilities to walk an awful tightrope; the ones who are in danger of falling off are the patients. Hospitals sometimes release patients before they're quite ready to be released, sending them to a subacute rehab facility—but the rehab facility isn't equipped to take care of these patients adequately. That notwithstanding, the hospitals do not want us to send these patients back—and if we do, our facility is penalized. Everyone loses sight of the patient. It's not about the patient, it's about the numbers. Hitting those numbers. Everyone is making decisions for patients, the outcomes of which can be fatal. This is not why I went into medicine.

What's Next

Right now, I'm putting myself in a position to go into private solo practice for myself. I know it's counterintuitive at a time when everyone is going into group practices. But I need a space where I am in charge. I'm the doctor and I can connect with the patient the way I want to and collaborate with my patients to make decisions that are in their best interests.

95.   Theresa E., Licensed Physical Therapist for a Large Integrated Health System

Theresa E. has been a physical therapist for 30 years. She has worked in outpatient orthopedics in a physician's office, in hospitals, and has worked for a large integrated health system for seven years. Having worked in a private practice where she was respected and her work was valued, Theresa knows that joy in work is possible. But joy is not possible in her current organization, where her opinions are disrespected, her work is not valued, and the conflict between the organization's interests and the patient's interests puts her squarely in the middle and continually stressed.

My grandmother was a nurse. She wanted someone in the family to be a nurse. My older sister started out in nursing and then changed her mind. When I was in high school we had what was called Career Day of the Week, when we could pick different fields we thought we might be interested in, then go to a facility to observe whatever we thought we wanted to do in actual practice. When I saw physical therapy it automatically clicked. I thought, *I want to help people in this way to get better.* I didn't want to do it in a nursing way, I felt that physical therapy would be more restorative. You can see the start and you can see the finish and see the gains made in between. That was really eye-opening for me. It was an instant grab. I decided this is what I want to do. From there it was just a process of going in that direction and staying on that path.

I work from 6:30 a.m. until, supposedly, 2:40 p.m. But my actual hours are closer to between ten and twelve hours a day. This has always been the case here. In my previous settings I worked more of an eight-hour day. I get to work at 6:30 a.m. because I start at 7:00 a.m. Just to get set up, get organized, make sure everything's in place. My last patient is scheduled at 2:40 p.m. I'll usually finish with them at about 3:30 p.m. but then I have to do any paperwork I wasn't able to finish during the day or during my lunch—usually I work through lunch to get some of this done. It's not exactly a free lunch; it's a working lunch so I can try to get more work done.

I always see a variety of patients. Patients are based on referrals, but often what the doctor may send the patient in for is different from what I actually see. My job includes starting with an initial, detailed assessment of the patient based upon the referral. Part of the reason for a detailed assessment is that the doctor may say, "Patient has leg pain," but may not be any more specific than that; for example, they don't indicate whether the pain is related to the hip, the knee, the foot, or the back. We have to be detailed enough in our assessment to figure out what it is causing the pain and how we're going to treat it. I evaluate the areas I suspect need treatment, which could be done with a combination of exercise, flexibility, manual skills, and modalities (using equipment to help relieve pain) to restore function.

On Joy in Work

I get joy in work from seeing patients get better. That is what gives me the most joy. When I see a person come in a certain way or have a certain problem and it gets better or it resolves, that is the icing on the cake for me.

The job I had before this one, I really enjoyed. I worked closely with the physicians. The physician would come and say, "Can you look at this MRI, I want to show you this."

We had this wonderful back and forth. He'd say, "I think this patient has a secondary infection from the surgery, I want you to come look."

We had this nice working relationship. The staff was great. The practice closed. He sold the physical therapy department and that was the end of it. I was there for five years until it closed. But I really loved the working relationship. It was casual but professional. He was the kind of physician who would tell me I'd worked long enough: "Go home," he'd say. When I protested he'd say, "No, go home, you can do that tomorrow." On the eve of a holiday he'd say, "I want everyone to be done by 12 noon. Everybody, wrap your patients up, we're going home early." There was mutual respect. He'd say, "You did a really nice job with this patient today. You did well. Thank you."

That was a wonderful experience. These were good physicians. Their surgeries went well. They had good relationships with their patients. There was joking and laughing, and really it was just the way you'd want things to be. I know enough now to know joy can exist. It was ideal, it was respectful, it was everything you could dream of and want in a job. And the patients were so happy that you could see them.

What Can Destroy Joy

I'm not paid for more than eight hours. The work I have to do afterward—whether it's checking emails, sending doctor-patient messages, documenting my notes, or attending compliance trainings—is all on my time and I've got to figure out a way to do it.

Lack of Time

Every year we are required to have different types of training. We have to show what we are doing to be safe; there are certain standards we have to follow pertaining to things like needle sticks, using sharps, and how to transfer patients. They're good things to know but I'm not sure exactly why we do it. They're the kind of things we've always known, but we have to certify that we've done this training every year. Each one of these can take 30–45 minutes to do and we have a deadline to do it. They say our next training is due in two months; I'll have to work that in somehow to get it done. It's on our time. Perhaps if a patient cancels, I can start it and try to finish it the next time another patient cancels. Otherwise, I'll either have to come in early or stay late to get it done.

These things diminish joy in work for me because I feel I'm on a deadline to get things done. There is pressure to make sure I complete my work every day. And that takes away my freedom to walk out the door at a certain time and think, *okay, my day begins after I finish.* I'm either tied to the computer at work or I bring the work home and do it. Which interferes with family life or family time.

Being Devalued and Disrespected

Another thing that robs joy is that we don't have a lot of freedom in decision-making. We have to do what is delegated to us. We can't push back too much. For example, if I say in a meeting—even if I broach it in a diplomatic way—"I'm not sure why X is done this way but I think it creates more stress," or "Really, this is not fair to the patients," or "It's more benchmarks for the therapists," the response I've gotten is, "If you don't like it, leave." Really. They shut me down. So, I don't have a lot of flexibility to implement change or to make suggestions for things that might work better. What we're told is, "Do what we say and if you don't like it, leave." The administration is pretty cavalier in telling us if we don't like something we can leave. They don't care about us. I'm pretty certain that if I were to leave, they would just say, "Okay, let's start advertising and get somebody else in there."

My hands are tied in terms of making change or being a part of change, or for taking something beyond my supervisor, who I think also has limitations as to what she can say or do. I'm a professional but I'm not being treated as one. I'm not an individual in this organization, I'm an item that needs to perform a task. If I were going to leave, they'd say, "Okay, when? When's your last day so we can start looking?" They wouldn't say, "Will you consider this? Can you stay?" It would be, "Just go so we can get somebody else in here." We're not valued.

Our point of view is not respected. And we are not heard. We have asked, "Can we meet with senior level management and let them know our concerns?" The answer from our supervisor has been, "That wouldn't be wise because they would be quick to fire you if they didn't like what you said." So, openness is discouraged.

I push only so far, then I back off. Because I know that if I go too far, then they'll say, "Okay, you need to be quiet and stop complaining." I think, *no, I'm trying to advocate for the patient. Patients are the ones we are treating. That's what we're supposed to be doing.* I'm always thinking about what angle to use to approach the problem. But it still goes back to, "We don't want to hear it." I'm kind of persistent but I'm not persistent to the point where I'll hear, "If you don't like it, leave" again. Because that, to me, is total disrespect. I still try to challenge it when I can; when I see an opportunity to sneak it in, I will.

I've always been driven to help the patient and I've never been driven by the business end. I feel that we're transitioning more to business from patient care. It's almost a 60:40 ratio. I feel that's the opposite of what we should be doing. That's my struggle. If I'm in a meeting and I can bring it up, I try to be as politically correct and diplomatic as I can. What I'm trying to say is, "This is not what our patients need. This is what they are complaining about. When I hear a complaint from the patient, this is what they're saying. And this needs to go to a position where somebody's going to hear it and it's not going to be dismissed."

Every once in a while I have a patient who is an employee somewhere else in the organization. And they tell me how stressed they are. Someone once came in and said, "You know, even when I was pregnant, I wasn't supposed to sit. I was exhausted but they wouldn't allow me to sit down." She was in tears and I was almost in tears for her. Because I'm thinking, if you're a professional, you're pregnant, you need to take a break. Well, they said you're not allowed to sit down. Sometimes she said her knees hurt. But they don't want you to sit at all except during your lunch. And she said, "I may be on my feet seven hours of the day without a break and it's really difficult." I don't know if this is just my organization. I don't know if this is the future of medicine.

I've met only two doctors since I've been in this organization. I don't know who the doctors are. I've never seen them, they've never seen me. The administrators never come to the physical therapy department. I believe in the past they've been invited to shadow just to see what we're doing but they declined.

Juggling to See Patients

What is most difficult are times when a patient is unhappy about not being able to get back into the office as often as they need to, which we also want for them. The patient may sometimes call a supervisor to complain. We're told to try to work them in as best we can, to try to get creative in our schedules to accommodate them. The problem is that this happens more often than not, so we're constantly juggling to try to get people in.

Management can't get more staff into our department because there's limited space. We can only get so many therapists into rooms where they can see patients and treat them. The organization is looking at other locations so they can get a larger department to accommodate more therapists. But even in another of our facilities that's much larger, with a larger physical therapy staff, some of this problem still exists. In each facility there are more patients who need to be seen than there are therapists. Patients will come in for a problem with their neck, for example, and then need physical therapy for their back. So, we may keep those patients for a while. Some patients have fractures or injuries. We can't control that. In the wintertime there may be more injuries because of ice and snow.

Initially our schedule was fixed—there were five consults with new patients in a day, and then that went down to three consults with new patients so we could spend more time treating returning patients. That was better. But then administration just opened it up, saying, "If you have an opening, we're going to put a new patient in there." For those of us who sometimes have six, seven, or eight new patients a day, not only do we have less time to treat returning patients, but our documentation time continues to increase. So again, we may be working for 12 hours. That's not uncommon.

I have 45 minutes to spend with each new patient. But because returning patients who need treatment are being squeezed out in favor of new patients, I try to do as much as I can in the first visit because I know I may not see that new patient again for a while. I'm going to try to treat them and maximize the treatment as much as I can. When I was in private practice outpatient therapy, I was seeing my patients two or three times a week. If I didn't get to everything in the first visit, I knew they'd be coming back to see me on Wednesday or Friday so I'd think, *okay, I can finish then.* But here, because I know patients are having pain and I know they're not going to come back for a while, I'm striving to do as much as I can to maximize that visit. And I feel badly about that.

The Stress of Conflicting Needs

I want to meet my patients' needs. They want to get back to what they were doing before. They're in pain. A lot of my patients are very active, even at older ages. They want to get back to their yoga, their swimming, their tennis, their jogging. This is stressful because I know what they need to do but I know I can't give it all to them at one time. Or I can't see them often enough to help them progress as quickly as they want. Their therapy may drag out longer than either of us would like. So, instead of being able to get them better within a month, it may take me four or five months to give them everything they need. And that is stressful.

The needs of my supervisors conflict with the needs of my patients. I feel the stress of wanting to get my patients better but not being able to see them often enough to do that quickly, combined with the stress of being told "You're not meeting our goals." They measure how many consults we're seeing. Are we keeping up with them? Are we losing patients because we couldn't get them in? At staff meetings they give us our stats and say, "This is what you need to improve on. This is what you can still do." So, we're working on those goals plus we're trying to treat our patients.

My stress level rises when I think *I've gotta do this and I've gotta do that and I've gotta get these things done.* All of that together is very stressful. And as I said, some things I take home because I'm trying to get this done—because if I don't, I'll get a little email that says "You've got to get this done," or "You need to do this."

There are two different types of stress. One is the enjoyable stress of working with patients to get them better. That's different from someone saying, "You still didn't do this right. You need more of this. You need less of that." I'm criticized because I spend too much time with my patients. In my mind I say—I don't say it out loud—*I'm sorry but that's too bad because that's what I'm here to do.*

My supervisor might say, "You spend all of your time with patients. You spend the whole 45 minutes."

And I say, "I need every second of that to do what I need to do."

She'll say, "Well, your colleague spends only 30 minutes."

And I say, "I don't know what he's doing. I know what I need to do."

I can't wrestle with that. I think, *I hear what you're saying but that's one thing I can't change.* And I won't change that. I'm sorry. That's what I went to school to do. That's what I'm here to do. That line doesn't budge. I pay them lip service and say, "Okay, yup yup yup," but then I do what I need to do. It's not right. It's not right by the patient. And I'm not going to compromise that.

Reflections

There is a disconnection between the way administration sees problems and the way I see problems. For them, the problem is we're not seeing enough patients. I have to believe that there's a number they're looking at and they want us to meet that goal. It's not about anything more than the numbers. For me, the problem is I don't have enough control over my schedule, and I don't have time to treat all the patients who need treatment. I've been in my current job for seven years. I'm not sure whether I'm going to stay. Part of it depends on what happens here in the near future.

On Patient Safety

They're talking about making things more challenging than they are now—double-booking patients—seeing two patients at the same time, trying to be more accommodating. In certain ways they want us to do even more. And I don't know how that would play out. For example, they might say, "You're going to see two patients at the same time." And I'm thinking, *how would I treat two people together? And go back and forth to see them both?* I have concerns about safety. I have patients who have a high fall risk, they walk with walkers, I can't do both and say that I'm being cautious at the same time. Things like that make me think I can't compromise the patient. I can't compromise my life.

On Longevity

The turnover rate here is fairly low. Let me see if I can explain it this way. Right now, our organization is hiring new grads to fill in. For example, we had a new grad who stayed a year and left. They are just now hiring another new grad. The problem is a lot of therapists who are seasoned or experienced know that the consult rate—the number of new patients we see—is not reasonable or normal and they won't come to work here. This came to me from a former supervisor who used to work in the physical therapy department who now works at an administrative level. The problem with hiring new people is that anybody who's been out in the field for a while knows that this organization pushes and drives you a bit harder. So, they go after new grads because they don't know. And sometimes the new grad can become overwhelmed and say, "This is way too much, I'm still on the learning curve from having graduated." It's too much and they may not stay.

One of the other therapists has been here five years, I've been here seven, and there are two other therapists, one who is going into her second year and the other who has been here maybe three or four years. So, they've come and gone but it's not a fast turnover. I will say this: At a certain point people are vested benefit-wise and then they're hooked. That's when they'll say, "I'd like to go, but at this point I don't want to lose my 401K." So, while they may be stressed, they say, "I can't really leave now because I'm vested."

On the Downside of Private Practice

One of the great things about working in private practice is there is so much freedom and flexibility, but I had no benefits. I didn't have healthcare. I didn't have 401K. I didn't have anything except leave. That is good if you can afford to get something on your own, but it's not good in terms of retirement or other benefits you would ordinarily get from an employer. That's why some people go to a larger institution because in private practice, although it's great—it's flexible, the stress level is much lower—you don't get anything for it.

On Work–Life Balance

I don't have much work–life balance. I work the time, I go home, I get ready for work. I may sneak in going to the gym a couple of times a week if I can get home on time and get to the gym on time and get into bed on time. I've got to be in bed by 10:30 p.m. so I can get up at 4:30 a.m. to get ready for work. I need my sleep. I need the gym, but I need my sleep, too. It's a tradeoff. I have to pick and choose my battles. When I started here my daughter was in high school. It was her idea to do her homework on the floor while I was on the computer finishing up my work so we could spend some time together. We did that until she went to college.

Advice

To enhance my joy in work the administration should lessen the number of new patients I have to see. Because so many slots are taken by new patients, we don't have enough slots for the returning patients. If they would do that, it would mean that I could see my patients more often, they would get better faster, they would be happy, and, as I said, that's my joy: seeing them get better.

If this organization would tell me they'd pay me $10,000 less but give me more flexibility and freedom and time to do what I need to do, I would take it. I would take it in a minute without hesitation. Sometimes people tell me, "If you do this or that we'll give you a bonus." I may not take that if it means you're compromising more of my time. It's just not worth it to me. I need my time more than I need that money.

I would like to feel appreciated and respected by the company. I get that from patients, but we are just numbers to administrators. We're not even significant. I don't feel valued or appreciated. They're telling us to just be quiet and work. I would like to feel that I'm acknowledged for the work I'm putting in, for the extra hours I work that go unnoticed.

96.   Daniel M., MD, Psychiatrist in a Private Solo Practice

Daniel M., MD, board certified in psychiatry, has been a psychiatrist since 1991. A self-described "dinosaur" who maintains a private solo practice, he began his career when health maintenance organizations, insurance company behavioral health "carve-outs," and managed care companies were coming of age. The abuses perpetrated by those organizations caused Daniel such moral distress that he severed ties with them all and focused on treating patients in his solo practice, where he has worked for more than 25 years with autonomy, integrity, and joy.

I can't give you a clear idea of why I went into healthcare; I can't say that the clouds parted. I'm a nice Jewish boy and my family expected me to go off to college and become a lawyer or a doctor. I didn't have any interest at all in the law. I went away to college, started taking the premed courses, and got turned off by how cut-throat, how competitive, it was. Somebody stole the organic chemistry final. I just got turned off to it and was much more interested in literature and philosophy. At some point I dropped being a premed and just studied literature and philosophy, which I enjoyed. My image of the doctor was very much inspired by reading literature: I had this image of the heroic doctor who goes out to make house calls and rides in a buggy, basically family practice or internal medicine.

As I got to the end of my undergraduate degree, I realized I really didn't want to go to grad school and become somebody who sits in a cubby in a library writing articles no one would ever read. At that point it was sort of a practical decision. I wondered, *what can I do to make a living that I could justify that seems morally okay?* I went back to thinking about medicine. Then somebody told me about these postgraduate premed programs that had just started up, where you could take all the premed courses you needed, and that's what I did.

I didn't get into medical school right away because I was a nontraditional applicant, which counted against me. So, I ended up spending three years doing bench research in a medical university setting, which was very interesting. I was doing research in molecular immunology. It turned out that a lot of issues I was looking at in the immune system were important in neurotransmitter systems—the same ligand receptor ideas were being teased out. So that knowledge stood me in good stead down the road.

Eventually I got into a very good medical school and had a great education there. I enjoyed every aspect of what I studied. Although, oddly enough, the thing I found the most difficult in the early years was neuroanatomy, because that depended on memorizing all these anatomic locations, and I was used to learning things by system and by mechanism. And this was just completely visual. I had to memorize all the holes in the head and what nerves came out of them. I found it quite daunting. On the other hand, my favorite course before I finished medical school was neuropathology, which was taught by an old "cracker" who many people found frightening, but who I thought was a wonderful teacher.

The first time I knew I was interested in psychiatry was when I did my third-year psychiatry rotation. I was interested in the storytelling aspect of psychiatry and I probably still get the most pleasure from figuring out people's stories. I think of psychotherapy as a form of extended literary criticism. I think it works pretty well that way. You can apply theoretical ideas but at some point, you have to drop theory and just listen. I've always enjoyed that. Ever since I was a teenager, people have always wanted to tell me their stories. I never thought back then of being a psychiatrist. I just thought I was being a listener. Professionally, it was a natural fit.

I had the research background in molecular cell biology of looking at receptors, and then I found myself on a research psychiatry unit in medical school seeing people who were given medicines designed to go after certain neurotransmitters, and they were getting better. I saw people who had severe depression or psychoses or mania and they actually were getting better with these medicines—I thought that was magic. And then translating what was going on at the molecular level to what could be done with medicine was fabulous. Now, it turns out, that was a rather naïve point of view.

I told myself that's what propelled me in the direction of psychiatry. But the truth is, and what I blocked out of my awareness but that undoubtedly was important, was that I have a sister with schizophrenia. She had her first psychotic break toward the end of my undergraduate degree. Before I moved to go to medical school, she was hospitalized and ended up living with me for six months. She was three years younger than me, was very smart, was a normal kid growing up, and had friends and intellectual interests. That was all wiped out. That showed me what could happen if someone has a disorder of the mind. It was clear to me that this was not something that was going to be treated with psycho-analysis, even though I was interested in psychoanalytic thought and Jungian thought and I had those interests before. So, all these things came together for me. I loved my psychiatry residency.

Personal and Historical Context

I have worked on a hospital staff—not as an employee, but as an attending physician. I haven't done that for many years. I stopped doing that because managed care made it odious.

I started in practice right out of residency in 1991. I'm five years older than my cohort because I didn't go straight into medicine. When I first got out into practice, there were the first glimmers of health maintenance organizations (HMOs) coming in to take over the economics of healthcare—and, within two years, there were not just HMOs but behavioral health management companies.

Large healthcare systems were just developing then, and they contracted out their psychiatric services to behavioral health carve-outs. The insurance companies and HMOs contracted utilization review services out to behavioral health management companies. Some of these management companies were owned by psychiatrists, who abandoned their identities and missions as doctors to become profit-takers and owners. Instead of delivering the care patients needed, these psychiatrists were looking out for the fiscal interests of their insurance companies. They ran utilization review on behalf of the insurance companies and these intermediaries were particularly incentivized to deny care. They thought, *this money is going into doctors' pockets and it could be going into our pockets, too*. The carve-outs were also being run by MBA-types, for the most part, who thought of their companies as saleable entities. They often hired under-skilled workers and offered meager services, counting eventually on selling their ginned-up businesses. The sole benefit was to the owners and investors. The employees and patients more often than not got screwed. As physicians in the hospital we were seeing, ostensibly, these very sick people and trying to help them. However, the flip side of that was there had been a lot of abuse, which is why managed care came in. It was a war between greedy psychiatrists and hospital administrators and greedy insurance companies and behavioral health carve-outs. That's my reductionist analysis of the situation.

Here's some additional background: Back in the 1980s, the first attempt to rein in healthcare costs led to the development of diagnostic-related groups (DRGs). DRGs were established by Medicare to determine reimbursement rates for hospital services, and insurance companies followed suit and developed algorithms for DRGs—so as soon as a patient hit the hospital they would be given one or two diagnoses, which would determine the per diem that the hospital would be paid and how many days they'd be given to treat this patient, based on the algorithm. This was pretty tough for hospitals to deal with because it's a guessing game as to what you're going to find when somebody hits the door.

The DRG system couldn't figure out what to do with psychiatry—the field just didn't have the algorithms. So, they made psychiatry DRG-exempt. This had a remarkable effect on the field because, all of a sudden, psychiatry became a profit center: there were no limits on your reasons for putting somebody in the hospital, how long you could keep them there, or how much you could charge. All of a sudden, every hospital had an inpatient psych unit and a bunch of for-profit psychiatric hospital chains sprang up. They were making millions and millions of dollars. They were just sucking the insurers dry. A lot of immoral, if not downright illegal, activities were going on. For-profit psychiatric hospital chains were making many people very wealthy. Of course, this spawned a reaction. That's when the insurance companies started tightening the purse strings. At least one, a national chain which owned the hospital where I admitted patients for a year and a half, was shut down by the Department of Justice.

Moral Distress

So here I am, a green, freshly minted psychiatrist, and I come to town needing to hit the ground running. The flagship hospital of a national chain offers me an income guarantee for my first year of private practice, which basically is a no-interest loan with no strings attached. What was in it for them? They figured I'd be more likely to admit my patients there. There's no requirement because that would be illegal. I checked with them, and if I wanted to admit somebody to another hospital I could, but it's really inconvenient to have to travel around to multiple hospitals; plus, I was new so I didn't have a stable of patients to draw on.

I was on the medical staff as a self-employed psychiatrist admitting patients there, which seemed fine initially. But then I began to discover all these scams going on. And then I found out, after I'd been there for a little while, that the entire chain was under investigation by the Justice Department. Little by little I found out what was being done and I saw some of it—it was hair-raising. It definitely took the joy out of the practice of psychiatry when I discovered I was in the midst of a den of sociopaths. And they were. I'm not exaggerating. These people were recycling their patients and keeping them until their insurance ran out. The most common thing they did was upcoding—they would bill for a much higher level of service than they delivered, including no service at all. It was fraud. And they got busted.

A locally founded behavioral health management company that covered a lot of the patients admitted to the hospital where I was working was created to serve the insurance industry. A psychiatrist started this particularly big one. I still have this memory of him, the owner of the company, the profit-taker and not an employee, getting on the phone with me. Here's what happened:

> In the early 1990s, I had a patient who had just been admitted, a woman
> who had tried to commit suicide by jumping out of a moving truck. She

> *sustained a head injury. We had a neurologist look at her to make sure she was okay from a neurologic perspective and then we were trying to figure out why she tried to kill herself. Within 24 hours of her getting to the hospital I get a call from the owner of the company telling me, literally, "I want that patient out of there. I don't want any fucking psychoanalysis." That's what the guy said. And here I am, fresh out of training, and I thought, is this for real? He said, "I want her in a day treatment program." I already knew that her insurance didn't pay for day treatment, so I said, "That's an interesting idea but it's not possible." Besides, it would have been an unethical thing to do with somebody who was acutely suicidal. I was on the phone every day with the guy to justify the admission. That was my introduction to psychiatric practice. I severed my connection with the hospital about a year and a half later. It took me awhile to discover what was going on and figure out how to make it on my own.*

Other than the fact that he was the owner of the company, that wasn't so atypical. As doctors we had to constantly—daily—justify admissions. Now, of course, that evolved based in part on the physician abuses that had happened before. But I was spending way too much of my time on administrative tasks like that. For the most part I didn't have to follow suit with the hospital's pressure. It wasn't that they were forcing *me* to do anything unethical. In fact, there was one instance when they admitted a patient to me who I judged didn't need to be in the hospital, so I discharged her to my outpatient practice. In fact, she's still my patient. But it was just unpleasant to be in that atmosphere.

There were some decent people there. I met some excellent therapists but shortly after I got there, they fired all the more highly trained therapists and hired all newly minted master's-level therapists to take their places because that was cheaper. I left and I was able to devote myself full time to the office-based practice I had already started. I had already paid back my loan to that hospital, which was just for the first year of practice. I didn't feel any sense of loyalty toward them, knowing what they were like. A lot of the guys who were involved in this are dead. They were older at the time.

Private Solo Psychiatric Practice

A number of insurance companies then formed managed care plans that allowed patients to see only doctors who were in their plans. Each managed care plan contracted with psychiatrists who were qualified to see their patients, which meant, basically, that we would be in-plan providers for insurance companies. When that happened, which was shortly after I went into practice, there was a big scare in the whole psychiatric community that if we were not on managed care panels we were not going to get any patients, which definitely would have negatively impacted my joy in work.

Suddenly these managed care plans were taking over the market, and everybody I knew was signing up for these panels. Also, if we were doing hospital work, we had to be on the plan. So, I signed up to be on all these plans. Every single one that came in front of me, I signed up for. Then, as I was doing outpatient work, I discovered these were terrible deals. One plan would pay me $35 for a patient. These plans also wanted us to do 10–15-minute medication checks, which is where that started. The whole concept of a 10–15-minute med check started with managed care. These companies figured, *if we pay psychiatrists $35, that will motivate them to squeeze more patients into the hour. So, if the* *psychiatrists are going to make money, they're going to have to see a lot of patients, and that's going to be good for us.*

Well, it was terrible. I actually talked to one of these people from the managed care company. I said, "I don't see patients for 15 minutes, I think that's fraud; you can't do anything in 15 minutes. Even if I'm not doing psychotherapy, I need to know what's going on with the patient. I need at least half an hour." And he said "Well, you can take half an hour. But we'll still pay you $35."

One of the things that gave me joy back then was, one by one, resigning from each of those managed care companies. I started with the most abusive one first. I think within a year or so I was off all of them. My practice was robust enough that I didn't need it. That was joyful. I decided I didn't want to screw the people I was already seeing. If they wanted to keep seeing me, I would still see them. It would cost them a little more, but they wouldn't have to pay my full fee. That was my compromise. A lot of people stayed with me even though their insurance wasn't paying for it.

Other than the first year and a half, the bulk of my job is seeing outpatients, one at a time, in my office. The number of patients I see in a day varies—anywhere from eight to sixteen, depending on the day. A lot of these are half-hour sessions because they're people I'm seeing only for medication. Most of my patients come from therapists who send them to me for medication. Some come from physicians, and some by word-of-mouth. I think I've gotten one or two from a local magazine that rates area doctors, although that's rare.

I start my office hours late, anywhere from 9:30 a.m. to 11:00 a.m. and I work until 7:00 p.m., five days a week. On Fridays I cut out early. I probably have around 40 hours a week of face-to-face patient time, which is a lot less than I used to do. This is the way I want it at this point in my life. When I first started and I was doing both hospital and office work, I was working about 100 hours a week, and I got burned out pretty quickly doing that.

On Joy in Work

One major source of joy is to see people getting better. And there are different types of people getting better. I can think of at least three categories. There's the person who has a subacute illness—I'm thinking, in particular, of one young man who was a schoolteacher. His depression was so bad that he had lost his ability to teach. He was married. He was looking at disability. He was being treated by another psychiatrist who had not changed his medicine for a year while watching this kid go downhill. It just boggled my mind. What was interesting in this case was I discovered he was vitamin B_{12} deficient—that's part of what I had learned how to recognize as a resident. (It's interesting, when I moved here, I got comments from internal medicine docs when I would ask for this kind of bloodwork, like, "What does a psychiatrist care about B_{12}?" They were pissed off. They thought I was treading on their turf. Now there's a whole field of people who do even more detailed research to find the causes of symptoms—more refined than anything I do.)

Anyway, I discovered this guy did have B_{12} deficiency. It was cool to be able to figure out what was wrong with him and to start him on B_{12}. Then I ended up needing to put him on a rather unusual combination of three medications, which I was attempting to tweak. As it turned out, he stayed on these three medicines and he completely revived. All of a sudden, it was as if his brain turned back on. His wife was thrilled, and his parents were thrilled. They said, "You brought our son back." That was so exciting. He didn't go on disability. He and his wife bought a house, he got a job in a different school district, and for reasons of convenience he got his primary care doc to continue prescribing for him. But he kept up with me and told me when he had a child. That was really exciting.

That's one category of people. Then there are people who may have some medication-related issues. I'm thinking about an older guy who was a Vietnam veteran, a very smart guy who had post-traumatic stress disorder. Initially I gave him some medicine for that. But we also did weekly therapy together and discovered a whole host of issues that knocked the hell out of his ability to maintain relationships and jobs. He was extremely motivated. As a soldier he had performed exceptionally well, and he took that same ethos and applied it to doing psychotherapy. It was a long process. He learned how to tell the truth, which was a big thing, and it changed his relationship with his wife, it changed his relationships in business, and he's doing great. He has two kids who just graduated from college who sound terrific, and they're going off to do great things in life. So that was another very joyful thing.

Yet another category is the people who are severely, chronically mentally ill who I might think, *nothing good is ever going to happen here*. To be able to make a difference there feels really good. I have a patient who comes to me from another state. She has been coming to me for many years. She has chronic psychotic symptoms that she has insight into. When I first saw her, she was practically mute. She crouched at the far end of my office, unable to even look at me. That was quite a few years ago so this has been a slow, slow process. Part of it was just getting her to trust me. I tried probably dozens of medicines with her that either hadn't worked or gave her terrible side effects and finally, finally—recently—I'm working with her internist and I've got her on medicines and dealing with the side effects and for the first time, her psychosis is receding, and she's doing artwork. She's become a painter. Her painting is so vivid and moving. So that's exciting. The thing is, seeing her the bulk of the time she wasn't doing so well. And it's just heartbreaking. It's hard to even say what kept me hooked. I just felt this sense of, there's got to be something I can do here. And maybe, in the back of my mind, it's my sister. I'm not consciously aware of that, but it could be there. This patient also tries very hard in spite of how symptomatic she is. She's raised two boys herself.

People getting well, that's certainly a source of joy. There's also a more subtle source of joy, which is seeing this constant parade of humanity coming through my office—seeing and hearing every possible story imaginable and getting a ringside seat to seeing the whole variety of human experience and to understanding it. There are a lot of deeply spiritual experiences.

What Diminishes Joy

What diminishes joy in work for me is mostly bureaucracy. In the beginning, as I said, managed care and hospitals definitely diminished joy. Then there was a period when we needed prior authorizations for *all* psychiatric treatment—for how many therapy sessions, and whether the person could be in treatment at all. That was definitely joy diminishing. Ever since the Mental Health Parity and Addiction Equity Act passed in 2008, insurance companies can't do that anymore. That was a good thing. Now, instead, the insurance companies—particularly the pharmacy benefits plans—are asking for prior authorization for every medicine and it takes a lot of paperwork just to get the damn medicine for the person to take. That's a major problem for every doctor I know, having to do all this prior authorization. And the thing is, it's geared toward large, corporate-style practices that have nurse practitioners whom they pay to do this. This certainly puts an undue burden on a solo practitioner like me.

The other thing that diminishes joy are patients who don't really want to take on their own care. It's as though going to the psychiatrist is like going to the nail salon. Once in a while I do get patients like that. I try to hang in there with them hoping they'll eventually see that nothing's going to happen if they don't take it on themselves. And some of them do change. Some of them do begin to do things for themselves. It's kind of cool when that happens, but sometimes they wear me out before that ever happens. In those cases, I mostly just keep going. In the 27 years I've been in practice I may have "fired" two or three patients. When I really feel that the person's goal is to remain sick, and I've tried and tried and tried and tried—maybe for years—I'll just tell them, "I don't think I'm helping you. I think you need to try with somebody else." And sometimes getting a new doctor really is the change they need.

97. *Sophia L., MSW, Clinical Social Work Student*

Sophia L., MSW, was as a graduate school intern in an urban comprehensive social services agency working with the most vulnerable clients. The moral distress she experienced, first at the hands of the agency's manager and then at the hands of her own school of social work, taught her about organizational dysfunction and taught her the most important lesson of her graduate school career: it is vital to recognize when organizations, including healthcare and educational institutions, prioritize their own needs over the needs of their staff, their students, and, most tragically, their patients. As Sophia learned, it takes all one's strength, tenacity, self-awareness, and self-assurance to stand up to injustice and do the right thing for yourself and, by extension, for your clients.

Organizational Dysfunction

As social work students, we spend a lot of time reading literature and having classroom discussions on organizational function and dysfunction. Because social work is explicitly focused on vulnerable people and institutional trends that lead to marginalization, social workers sign up to be at the front lines of moral conflict. That's basically the nature of social justice work: it's our job to support and advocate for the people with the least power in society. This means we are often working against the tide every day.

At my university, our curriculum included a lot of theory on how "organizational agendas" tend to collide with the needs of clients. This is true of course in any healthcare institution. Social work education is unique in the degree to which it accepts this as the basis of the profession. The distinctive role of the social worker is to have eyes wide open about when they are being asked to do something that serves the agency they work for, or a funder, or any agenda that is not centered on the client. Before we even leave the classroom, we are asked to think about how we are going to handle these inevitable situations, and how those issues are influenced by race, gender, setting, etc. In the abstract, social workers are expected to navigate organizational pressures and to stand up for their clients. This isn't positioned as a circumstantial skill on top of a core role. It is the core role.

That moral code gets tested almost immediately when social-workers-in-training step into an actual workplace. Many social services agencies are stressful places grappling with society's most damaging and emotionally draining problems: addiction, homelessness, crime, abandonment, abuse, displacement, loss.

As a social work student, I was an intern in an agency where I worked with extremely vulnerable people who had lived through major traumas, and incarceration, and had serious daily risks in their lives. It was a phenomenal experience. I was so humbled by the resilience and persistence of these clients. It was very much the kind of work I had entered into social work hoping to do. And the placement had many characteristics that make this kind of hard work enjoyable—talented and friendly colleagues, productive daily challenges, the opportunity to seek advice and learn. I loved it. It inspired me to pursue a future in criminal justice and social work.

Shortly after my internship began, my supervisor left and a different person in the agency stepped in to oversee my internship. Until that point, I'd had a really nice relationship with the person who took over my supervision, and I was delighted that she would be my mentor. But once she became my supervisor, it was soon clear that her responsiveness to me was mostly being dictated by a manager higher up in the agency. That person, let's call her the manager, was in an administrative role and looked after multiple programs. She was not particularly connected to clients and had no clinical training or formal social work background. So, her perspective on my work was completely removed from the orientation I was being taught from a theoretical standpoint at school.

What I'm about to describe wasn't a personal situation—my co-workers and I were all in the same position, except that they had employee status and rights, at least. I observed these dynamics carefully. I watched how people around me were treated, how this manager placed obstacles in the path of clinicians that made it difficult for them to do their jobs properly, how she unexpectedly shifted goals, issued edicts, and shamed people.

Bluntly speaking, this manager was widely known in the agency for being fickle, verbally abusive, callous toward clients, and disorganized. She was the kind of boss who would neglect something and then would show up later and ask, "Why did everybody mess this up?" For example, a new therapist was hired into our program. She was Hispanic, and the manager, who was white—and I say that because it feels relevant in this situation—walked in and started screaming at her one day in her cubicle. In our office environment, everybody could hear everything. The manager's complaint was that the new therapist was entering things wrong in our database, which had not been properly taught to her yet; it was also a complex system that took all of us time to pick up. That was the kind of thing that was typical of the manager.

So just to emphasize the archetypal conflict I've set up here: I'm a student intern working with very vulnerable clients—people who had been victims of violent crime, who had been incarcerated, who had experienced multiple traumas throughout their lives, who are dealing with substance abuse, homelessness, and separation from children, and who have the Department of Children and Family Services going through their business. Many are mandated clients, which means they are required by the court to attend our programs and meet certain requirements, and we have to report to their parole officers about their attendance, which can influence their incarceration status or ability to live with their kids. And my direct supervisor is aligned with a person in authority above her, the manager, who is known for being out of touch with the experiences of clients but who perceives herself as being very knowledgeable about them.

Luckily, for the most part, I was okay. I was able to focus on working with fantastic people around me and on the rewarding daily interaction with our clients. I spent about seven months in this internship and throughout that process got overall positive feedback, including from my direct supervisor, my peers, and even accolades from the famous manager herself. But even though all the feedback was that I was doing a good job, I felt vulnerable. I was always worried that the unpredictable manager would surprise me with something one day, as I saw her regularly doing to others. I was so concerned that I called my university advisor pre-emptively to discuss it, and then I emailed her after our phone call with words I would read over and over in the next year: "Although it's going well enough, if there's any issue down the road I just want to have checked in with you ahead of time."

On the last day of my internship, I finished with my last client. I had exceeded my university requirements for hours, staying more days than needed because I was enjoying the work so much. All that was left was for me to write up my notes and come in the next day for a goodbye party, where I'd planned on teaching my co-workers an art therapy project I'd designed. Saying goodbye to my last client was terribly bittersweet. When she closed the door behind her, I felt sad and full at the same time. It's hard to describe, but I think many healthcare providers and particularly those who work with clients over longer periods of time will know what I mean. You grow to feel very invested in people and deeply honored to have been privy to their lives. In a therapy setting, when someone leaves on that last day, you will probably never see them again.

I went to my desk to write up my final notes. When I sat down, I had an email calling me in to a meeting with my direct supervisor and the manager. I walked into her office, and with nothing left of my internship but a farewell party, the manager fired me from the internship. She did the same thing I'd watched happen to other people: faulted me for things that had never been explained, retold past events in a warped and inaccurate way, and made up new policies on the spot that had never existed. I had to watch my direct supervisor, whom I had once admired, align herself with these narratives in order to protect her job. I'm hardly the only person who's experienced something like this at work. It's a terrible feeling, like an alternate dimension where all the facts are changed and trees are blue, and worst of all, where people you trusted look you in the eye and say, "Yes, trees are blue, and therefore you have failed."

The manager reported me to my university. And this where I think my experience says something important about education in healthcare services. My advisor, whom I had called months earlier in anticipation of something like this, didn't contact me or ask me what happened. Instead she directly turned me over to an academic disciplinary proceeding that lasted for four months. I was a straight A student. I received three letters of recommendation from people I'd worked with in my field placements. Nobody ever contacted them.

All that talk of agency agendas had failed to include the agendas of educational institutions. What I learned that summer and fall was that, if left to choose between priorities, the university was not there to protect me or ensure I developed skills as a client advocate within the complexities of social services agencies. The university was there to protect itself.

Educational Dysfunction

The academic disciplinary process consisted mainly of a hearing in front of a faculty panel. But my university was so disorganized that I didn't receive any notice of this process until the end of the summer. So, you can imagine how that felt, after such an upsetting termination from my field placement, to be left dangling and uncertain of what was going to happen next for two months. And only to have it end with a stern letter calling me in to a hearing.

During those two months, I actually thought all I needed to do was show what had happened, and the whole thing would be realized as a big mistake. I tried everything I could think of. I met with the director of the program. I wrote down a timeline of events. I got letters of recommendation from other supervisors at the agency. I forwarded old emails. These efforts produced no results at all.

When the fall semester began, my university decided to delay the start of my second-year internship while they completed the disciplinary process that had been on hold all summer. Until that point, the new agency didn't know that the disciplinary process was underway, but once the school contacted them to say I was being held back from beginning my internship there, that confidentiality was effectively ruined. I had signed a contract with the new agency five months earlier, and my professional standing there was immediately thrown into question.

I remember sitting in the office of the dean in tears that day. I wanted to know why I was being pre-emptively punished, why nobody would call my professional references, why the documentation I had made no difference, why the amount of bad or incomplete information was accumulating, why the advisor who had recommended me for disciplinary action had left the school and was nowhere to be found, or how any of this was proportional to anything I could be criticized for doing when I had received positive feedback over the entire course of my internship. My pleas fell flat, and I was dismissed.

That was the point at which I finally called a lawyer. I had to pay a few hundred dollars for legal counsel to call the university before the school relented and let me start my final year internship as planned. Meantime, I had paid my full tuition and had course requirements whose completion depended on being in a field placement.

It was calling the lawyer that really started fanning my moral fire. I was very conflicted about it because I knew that most students at my university wouldn't be able to take advantage of legal counsel. It was a huge privilege that I had the resources, experience, and support to be able to take that step. I was infuriated that other students in my position would have been left waiting helplessly while the university undermined their relationships in their immediate professional community. Which of course was also happening.

No sooner was I told to begin my new field placement than my new boss called to say my position was staying on hold. Very appropriately, she wanted me to come in and explain what was going on so she could re-evaluate whether I was a trustworthy person to have working with clients. So I had to sit down with my new boss and find a dignified, clear way of revealing all of these experiences—the haphazard manager, the events of the spring and summer, the administrative dysfunction at my school—without appearing defensive or problematic. Luckily, this new boss was all business and a person of high integrity and clarity, and I came out of that conversation with my field placement back intact. I've often looked back on that day and that boss's actions as a reference point that I want to model when I am a supervisor. But I also walked out of that meeting thinking, again, how unreasonable this might have been had I been younger, or if English were my second language, or if I hadn't been raised in a family of professionals with higher degrees. It made me furious.

The academic hearing finally came at the end of September. The purpose of the hearing was to review the events at hand and issue a decision as to whether I should be expelled. I sat around a conference room table looking at eight faculty members. Eight! One was there as my support person, but she was not given any meaningful space to say much in my support. Now, I'm relatively self-assured, but any student in a room of eight faculty is going to feel a little outnumbered. And just as in the agency setting, in the university setting I was looking at a circle of faces I had both trusted and admired. Faculty I had taken classes with and been inspired by, who had encouraged me. It was so disheartening.

In the hearing, there was no review of the information I had spent the summer compiling and submitted weeks ahead of time. Still nobody had spoken with my references. The advisor who had reported me didn't attend the hearing. The tone of the hearing was succinct: I was expected to accept full responsibility for the still-unidentified issue that the hearing was about.

I'm a bit sheepish to admit that even then, I was unprepared for the fact that we weren't going to talk through any of the real issues. Such as, that the education of social work students inevitably involves major ethical binds in field practice, just as the work will when students later become employed professionals. Or that I had reported these issues early on to my advisor and they were later handled poorly. Or that the university had inadequately managed its relationship with the agency and its responsibility for my educational outcomes.

In retrospect, my greatest regret is that I didn't thank everyone and simply leave the hearing. Instead I tried to engage these issues, to reference my documentation, to correct falsities. But that wasn't really the purpose of the hearing. And even though I also didn't play the repentant role I was expected to, three weeks later I received a letter saying I could continue my education, as long as I didn't break any rules. "Nice to have you back," the director told me as she handed me this letter. She was such a nice person. But she had also led these events.

I remember that I couldn't come up with a proper response. Where had I gone?

Moral Distress

Educational institutions in a lot of ways are extremely bureaucratic, and what I realized at some point was that once the disciplinary process was launched, it had to be carried through. No new evidence or perspective I brought up midway could deter it. And by the same token, once it was over, it was over and everything was supposed to go back to normal.

But I was left steaming. I felt that hearing itself, as well as the process before and after it, had been abusive. I use that word intentionally. Because I'd watched an administrator at the agency where I worked create ripple effects of abuse that fell on the heads of clients, and when that administrator turned on me, her behavior was transferred over to my educational institution. Then I observed educators—people I admired and respected—repeat the same outrageous accusations that had been created by this other person. So, by extension, the indignation I felt on behalf of clients at the agency, I came to feel toward the school. In both cases, the lesson I was taught was, *fall in line and do not ruffle feathers under any circumstances.* It was definitely not, "Be attuned to the forces around you and stand up for those with no influence," which is supposed to be the basic grounding of a social worker.

During and after the academic disciplinary process, I reflected deeply on the education we were being given upon entering this field. We were being taught to value what's convenient for agency or a university or whatever hierarchical structure we happen to be in, versus to value what's good for the clients who we entered into the profession to serve. Of course, we can't always *do* the best thing for our patients or clients. But I felt I was being taught to erase my discernment, my integrity, my sense of what being a good therapist and social worker even means.

It felt as if the experience had exposed a seed of the same conflict that plays out over the course of a lifetime in a profession in social services. In the classroom we were diving into literature and theory on social change and social justice and institutional bias and structural violence. We were explicitly being taught principles of advocacy; we were being lectured to about aligning ourselves with moral codes of conduct that are guaranteed to be challenged by competing agendas in the workplace. And yet, when this happened in the real workplace during my student internship, I saw my university's responsibility to me, and to these values, fold like a house of cards.

I also understood that the whole thing wasn't really about me. I just happened to be the person in the crosshairs. The next student would come along, and the same thing would happen again by way of a sort of automated bureaucratic march. That person, and the next one, might not have the family supports that I have, or the background or resources or risk tolerance to weather it without simply playing along. I felt I had a bird's-eye view of how this process was rigged to educate social workers to conform in unhealthy ways before they even graduated from training. I didn't want that for myself.

There was a moment of clarity when I decided that I was going to use this experience to challenge myself in a deeper way by filing a complaint. If I wasn't going to do it, who would? People die for important causes, and I had very little at stake, other than fear. Fear of disapproval from a university bureaucracy is definitely not fear for your life, but it can make you sweat when you're a lowly student. I specifically made a decision to confront the discomfort of standing out, of being disliked by a system that had lost my respect but from which I still preferred approval anyway. Because if I couldn't stand up for the right thing in school, my future as an advocate was hopeless—what would I do in the real world when the stakes were absolutely guaranteed to be higher?

Part of my thought process was that I imagined a worst-case scenario (which I knew was probably impossible) of getting kicked out of school. Right then my choice was clear. Because what it came down to was that I did not want a diploma that was an achievement in fear. I didn't come to social work school to learn submission. It was actually more important to me to be a person of integrity than a person with a diploma. I decided I would be a social worker either way.

I had advantages in life that made that calculation easier for me than it might be for the next person, and that influenced my thinking too. I had no excuse to not be accountable. As soon as I realized this, the fear evaporated. The need for approval revealed itself as a hallucination once I accepted it as a trade for the exhilaration of standing up for what I felt was right.

My Response: Organizing and Speaking Up

The first thing I did was approach offices higher up in the university, above the school of social work. I had meticulously organized a file of documentation and when I shared it, I was told I probably didn't even need to file a complaint. Instead, they suggested I write a letter to the dean asking for a revision of academic disciplinary rules.

Well, I decided that instead of writing a letter myself, I'd go to the graduate student organization and ask them to make the request on behalf of the entire student body. So at the moment when the disciplinary process usually concludes and things go back to status quo, I mobilized the graduate student organization to demand that the school create a committee to review whether their policies and procedures were in line with the rest of the university and whether they protected the rights of students. That committee was formed. It included both student representatives and someone from a supervising body at the university outside the school of social work. For six months, the committee poured through and reviewed the procedures that were used to bring me into that academic hearing. And by the end of the school year, those procedures were adjusted and made significantly fairer to students.

During those six months, I reached out to other offices at the university, such as the ones that deal with racial and gender equity. It was my opinion not only that my treatment had been extremely sexist, but that I'd benefited significantly by being a native English speaker from a highly educated family and by being white. So, I engaged every system I could find to pressure for changes to the policy that would protect minority students and low-income students who found themselves in vulnerable field placement conditions or under academic review. Being protected from preemptive punishment shouldn't require a lawyer.

I also wanted to make sure the committee couldn't meet for show and make superficial policy adjustments that didn't really change the school's accountability for student rights. So, in February, some other students and I circulated a petition that talked about common problems that a lot of students faced in field placements. It's the kind of stuff that students talk about all the time with each other, but that the school administration tends to dismiss easily—which may be similar to the way clinicians frequently talk to each other about problems they face in their workplace, but that administrators and the powers that be either are not confronted with or likewise dismiss. Our petition said, basically, "These are issues many of us face in field settings, but when we bring them back to our advisors and supervisors, we're not well supported. We're blamed for problems inherent in these settings. You're telling us, in theory, we need to be able to fight for clients and stand up for the values that brought us into this profession, but when we do, we don't get the support we need." More than half the school of social work—150 students—signed the petition.

I sent the petition to the dean of our school, the dean of the whole university, the ombudsman, and the university offices that deal with diversity and inclusion. Then I made sure students had contact information for the ombudsman's office, and people started calling him to share personal experiences related to the problems we described.

Finally, at the very end of the year, after those rule changes were basically in place, I filed an official complaint on my own behalf for violation of university standards such as creating a hostile environment, interference and intimidation, and poor application of policies. I submitted 70 pages of emails and documents. That led to another hearing, but this time I was the one bringing the complaints. A senior representative from the school of social work and I came together in front of a panel of faculty from the other professional schools. And, finally, I laid out my case. All the things I didn't get to say when I was the target of the hearing, all the documentation nobody read, and all the recommendations that nobody followed up on, I brought before this new committee in a systematic and organized way. It was very empowering.

The result of my complaint hearing was a "recommendation"—which I'd learned in bureaucracy-speak is the strongest statement one can get to an admission of wrongdoing—that the school needed to improve their training of advisors. Over the course of the year, I'd become much more knowledgeable about the coded ways that big institutions make changes while protecting themselves from possible lawsuits and liability. I wasn't awarded any damages, lawyer fees, or anything like that. But my case left a pretty strong paper trail behind. Part of the reason I'd had no leverage during my academic disciplinary proceeding was that my school could always claim it was following its own rules. Now, if another student were treated the same way I was, they would have a clear-cut case that they were being mistreated as per school policy, and in violation of the recommendations of the university at large.

Lessons Learned

In the bigger picture I was floored—*floored*—at how shamelessly this educational system was set up to teach me to be complicit in making clients the last priority. The most viable scapegoats. The least important people in the system. To teach me that I'm not only going to be ineffective, but that actually I'm a bad person if I speak up about that or if I disagree with that or if I seek to change any of that or conduct myself in a different way. That speaking up so I can do better for clients is a character flaw. That it's arrogance. That it means I don't respect authority. Or that I'm not interested in learning. That I don't listen. Being told you are this way or that way, and taking a step back, talking with people you trust, and then straightening your shoulders and saying, "Actually, that's not who I am, I know myself better than that," is a huge opportunity. It's how we grow and become strong in our personal and professional identities.

I was very grateful for this experience in the end, because I mostly come from a background where I *do* have a say. And being a student in the school and having all that rain down on me gave me, in certain ways, a new kind of empathy for the clients I was working with.

Coming up hard against the pressure to conform while I was still a student was the most useful part of my social work training *by far*. That was the part of my education that made me uncomfortable, that made me afraid, that made me angry, that was diminishing, that left me disoriented. That made me look at myself and make some decisions about who I want to be and how I want to be. I came to the realization that no one at the school cared about what had happened in my field placement, or with my advisor, or anything. It was just about me being put in my place. So, either I would have to accept that place, or I'd have to accept that there would be a reaction if I refuse to claim that place. That's life, man.

So, what I learned from this was how to have the courage to tolerate the discomfort of being looked at as an agitator and to put up with that, because even though it's uncomfortable I know it's the right thing to do. And if I can't do that in school then good luck in the world. This experience taught me so much about how people are fed into this system. I had a very acute experience of it, but on some level everybody in that program is learning something about negotiating those tensions and leaving with a template for negotiating moral conflict.

I learned from this experience that you have to know your own truth. That's not the same thing as thinking you're right all the time. But if the organization you are in is telling you to believe something you know is not true, that's how you know you're in a place you can't be. Otherwise you will have completely lost yourself. And you are the most important thing that you bring to healthcare and healing. If you can't stand up for yourself, how are you going to stand up for your clients or patients or anyone else? Where is your compass? What will ground you when things get crazy?

The other thing I learned has to do with the process of education and the educational experience: that countless people have implicitly learned that their truth is not the most important thing, that it's more important to conform. I had to ask myself, "Is it more important for me to graduate with this degree or is it more important to use this confrontation as my sharpening stone? To become the instrument that I want to be in the world?" Having the time and space to consider that, come to a decision, and have people who championed me in that decision has been a huge gift.

Advice

Listen, you aren't right all the time and all of us have blind spots, weaknesses, and bad days. But where the rubber meets the road, trust yourself. You're where you are because you care about people. A lot of what gets lost in the firestorm of making a healthcare facility function, in mechanical issues like money and insurance, are people. Just being a human being. That thing that you have on your first day, where you're fresh and you're excited and you have your first patient, that kind of gets squashed out of you. During that squashing, maybe the message is that if you're responsible and you understand the system, you'll get more realistic about things like that. Don't get realistic about things like that! What's real are people. Everybody's had the experience as a patient where we walk in and there's that person in the healthcare facility who sees us as a human being. That's incredibly healing for people. It's why you're there.

part 4

What the Experts Have to Say

Expertise is the mantra of modern medicine.

Atul Gawande

Introduction to Part 4

During the course of my interviews for this book, at least for the first six to nine months, I questioned what I was finding. After reading so much about burnout and physician suicide, the last thing I expected to find was a population of healthcare professionals of all kinds who said they felt joy in work—if not because of their organizations, then in spite of them. Where was all the burnout? The depression? The disillusionment?

I am grateful to the three experts in the field of coaching physicians and healthcare organizations who agreed to talk to me for this book. Paul DeChant, MD, was the first to allay my fears and explain why I wasn't finding more burnout—and that it wasn't because I wasn't asking the right questions. Bridget Duffy, MD, confirmed what I was learning while shining a light on what is possible. And Allan Frankel, MD, provided an elegant, thoughtful, master class on burnout and joy that mirrored what all the healthcare professionals I interviewed had to say. It is to these generous experts that I give the last word and convey my thanks.

Lessons From the Field

98.   Paul DeChant, MD, MBA, Author, Speaker, and Coach in Reducing Physician Burnout

When I interviewed Paul DeChant, MD, I was puzzled by what I'd found in my research for this book up to that point: Why had only one healthcare professional admitted to burnout? What was I missing or not understanding? Was I asking the "wrong questions" of the "wrong" people? I thank Paul for helping me to understand and for putting my findings into context—and especially for helping me to reaffirm my focus on joy in work and understanding what it takes to achieve it on the part of individuals and organizations.

One's personal mission—the reason why someone goes into healthcare to begin with—is the strongest contributor to resilience and the ability to find meaning in work. Meaningful work is the antidote to burnout. We go into healthcare to experience a deep human relationship with patients; that's what gives us professional fulfillment. If we can just have that relationship with our patients that enables us to keep going, that can help us to maintain joy. Another of the rewards is collegiality with our fellow clinicians. When people don't get these at all, they'll surely burn out. In radiology that's happening intensively now. But most people still get that.

So, if you're talking to people about what gives them joy in their work, they're going to focus on relationships—with patients and with colleagues. That's what gets people through their day. And it is those personal relationships with patients, knowing one has made a difference in patients' lives, that are really powerful. Probably the people who are beyond joy are those you're not connecting with.

I think the other thing that may be happening is that people are getting so used to the dysfunctional workplaces that exist now in healthcare that we don't even see it. So, if people are telling you they're not burned out but just deal with their "pajama time," they don't even see how they've lost work–life balance. It's just become "normal" to not have full time and attention with your family and loved ones during evenings and weekends.

We've become so accustomed to doing data entry ourselves, to spending half our time with patients with our eyes on the computer screen. Each one of the challenges to our day, like the electronic medical record (EMR), the *International Classification of Diseases*, Tenth Revision, etc., has been added one by one over time and we've just adapted to them slowly. Each of these negative things are like straws on a camel's back. We've now added the last straw, and people are breaking.

Organizations today require physicians to be hypervigilant and focused in order to be able to deliver care well and not let things fall through the cracks. We can be vigilant and focused for short periods of time and it's really exciting. And it *is* really fulfilling to do what we feel we were meant to do. But to do this without recovery periods, where it's continuous, is not sustainable.

Can you have joy and have burnout to relative degrees? Manifestations of burnout are defined as exhaustion, depersonalization, cynicism, and lack of self-efficacy. People who are feeling joy are feeling as though they are making a difference. But if people are working too much, they could be experiencing exhaustion—and there's a whole spectrum of that. Exhaustion generally comes from having too much work to do. And depersonalization or cynicism comes from being in a toxic work environment where you don't feel that you have control, or you don't feel that you're aligned with your organization or your boss does not respect you. That's when people tend to get more cynical, either protecting themselves from their patients or protecting themselves from their organizations.

The key is to enable people to focus as much of their time as possible on what's truly meaningful for them. Doing data entry isn't meaningful. If we could minimize or eliminate data entry, then that would free physicians up to spend more time with patients.

Some doctors cope by cutting their hours. Many are working "part time" simply because there are not enough hours in the day to see as many patients as doctors could see 15 years ago, before the EMR and regulatory burdens.

Healthcare leaders have an important role to play in reducing burnout. One challenge some face is that they don't have a clinical background. Some feel intimidated by what clinicians do and don't understand it, so they are hesitant to go into the clinical environments where the work gets done. And if they see dysfunctional work activity, they may feel they want to fix it, but they don't know what to do. So, there's risk for them spending time in the clinical world. They can have a very positive impact when coached through the process, which is what I do: www.pauldechantmd.com/

99.   Bridget Duffy, MD, Chief Medical Officer, Vocera Communications, Inc.

Bridget Duffy, MD, Chief Medical Officer at Vocera Communications, Inc., helps to design the next generation of healthcare innovations and works with organizational leaders to bridge communication gaps, improve team collaboration, and enhance clinician connectedness to improve clinician effectiveness, well-being, and enhance joy in work.

We measure our joy by how we prioritize our time and how we spend our lives. The absence of joy is causing doctors and nurses to leave the profession earlier than they intended. Medicine is one of the greatest professions on earth. To witness what I call "wounded warriors" in the trenches in hospitals and clinics is heartbreaking. Most clinicians won't recommend the profession to their children.

The cause of a demoralized workforce in healthcare is too much administrative bureaucracy and too many antiquated processes and technologies that create more hassles. There is the assault of the electronic medical record on individuals' lives; taking them away from direct patient care and time with their loved ones at home because they are spending hours typing data into a computer. William Edwards Deming, said, "the problems in any organization are system problems, not people problems." The broken systems in healthcare have contributed to a lack of joy.

When I became the nation's first chief experience officer in 2006 at the Cleveland Clinic, I spent 30 days, in my scrubs, walking in the shoes of staff members, including valet parking attendants, cafeteria workers, nurses, laboratory technologists, doctors, and more. After observing the frontlines, I came back into the boardroom and said, "I cannot focus on the patient experience until we first focus on the staff experience." Initially, some scoffed at me, saying, "People should manage their own work-life balance before they walk in the door here." What I witnessed were people checking their souls at the door [read Sydney G., MD's, experiences in her interview in the section "Moral Distress" in Part 3 (interview 93). ES]. They were putting on a brave face and just getting through the day, and then going home to their families on an empty tank.

Doctors, nurses and front-line staff entered the profession because of a higher purpose. We are all accustomed to working hard and working long hours, but we want to work in smart, efficient, and meaningful ways. There is a difference between working hard and going home at night feeling a good tired versus a bad tired. We all know what that feels like. The bad tired is pervasive and it is stripping away the joy in healthcare.

Is there a role for technology in restoring joy? I know there is technology that has helped take it away—the electronic medical record (EMR). I believe healthcare needs an EMR as a repository for clinical, regulatory, and financial data, but it should not be the main interface between the sacred relationship that a doctor or a nurse has with a patient. To truly understand a patient's story and build trust, doctors and nurses must look their patients in the eyes, spend time at the bedside—not looking at a computer screen.

Too many doctors and nurses don't have trusted relationships with each other because they have become data entry clerks rather that team members. We have lost the narrative, we have lost the patient's story, and we have lost the valuable connection to our colleagues. Before the EMR, I would go up on a floor, talk to the nurse and say, "I just admitted Ms. Smith. These are the things I've ordered. I'm really worried about X. Would you watch for this throughout the night, and keep me posted?" Some healthcare technology can enable these relationships and promote such knowledge exchange. People can be virtually connected to other human beings by video, they can connect by text, and they can connect by voice instead of sitting and typing into a computer. We have created a "checklist of always events" to ensure that any technology chosen in healthcare values the impact on both the patient and the care team.

At Vocera we design technology that improves communication and saves valuable time, helping return clinicians back to the bedside and to purpose. There is a role for technology in restoring joy in healthcare if that technology can enable human-to-human interactions and instant connectivity to human beings. Restoring the voice of patients and care teams can help heal healthcare. Listening to the patient's story and looking in their eyes builds trust, which increases compliance, improves outcomes, and reconnects us to why we entered the profession in the first place.

At a recent Grand Rounds, an orthopedic surgeon asked me, "Is there a metric for joy or humanity?" The Vocera Experience Innovation Network is developing a metric for humanity. It will measure baseline scores for well-being and can be used before and after the deployment of technology to see whether we have enhanced or destroyed joy. If we had used this metric with the EMR, we would have done things much differently.

On Joy in Work

What gives me joy is helping lead a movement through the Vocera Experience Innovation Network to humanize the way we deliver healthcare technology.

What else gives me joy? When I get a call, as I did last week, from a woman who had just been diagnosed with cancer. I picked up the phone, navigated and advocated for her and, within 24 hours, had her tucked into the place she needed to be. It gives me a sense of pride, a sense of joy that I can help ease the suffering of somebody else. What keeps me going is that I realized that if you don't "know someone," you can't navigate or access the complex healthcare system. I wake up every day worrying about those individuals who have no one to advocate for them.

When I can bring all of my gifts to bear to enhance the well-being of another human being, that is what joy means to me. Serving those most in need and focusing on under-served and diverse populations is where I like to spend my time. My husband once asked me why I was happier practicing medicine in India than at home in U.S., and I realized what gave me joy in India came from three things: 1) A sense of human-to-human connection with my colleagues. In India we had breakfast, lunch, and dinner together, talking about what we could do for patients; 2) I had a relationship with patients—I knew every single thing about them and their lives; and 3) In India, spirituality is at the core of healing.

What Diminishes Joy

What diminishes joy in healthcare organizations are rules for rules' sake, hierarchical culture, and competing priorities. We need more leaders who will take a human-centered approach to leadership and who will make investing in their people a top strategic priority. The most important investment leaders can make is in a strategy that empowers and supports staff. An engaged and joyful workforce will foster an ideal working and healing environment, which leads to higher quality of care, safer care, market differentiation, and loyalty.

The absence of well-being and joy are directly related to quality care and patient safety. When clinicians experience cognitive overload or compassion fatigue, it directly impacts the care they deliver. It is important for healthcare system leaders to understand that addressing staff experience and joy is as important as quality, safety, and operational efficiency. There are established metrics for quality, safety, and productivity. They alone are not enough. It's time to implement a metric for joy and humanity.

100. Allan Frankel, MD, Managing Partner of Safe and Reliable Care

> Allan Frankel, MD, is a managing partner of Safe and Reliable Care, a company
> he and his partners founded in 2011 to survey people in healthcare organizations
> about culture, engagement, burnout, and resilience, and to run interventions to facili-
> tate improvement. Their most recent survey had one million respondents. Over the
> course of his career, Allan has moved from practicing anesthesiology to administra-
> tion to advising organizations about how to improve their culture, which underpins
> joy in work and the delivery of safe, reliable patient care.

My dad was a physician. When I was in college, I couldn't quite figure out what I wanted
to do. I thought for a while I'd be a writer. And before that I actually thought I might be
a pretty good dancer, and that if I trained hard enough, I could join one of the troupes in
New York. No one thought the dance idea was a very good idea. No one could figure out
how I'd make a living doing it, so I didn't get much approval for that. At the time they
had something called the MMPI, the Minnesota Multiphasic Personality Inventory. I took
the MMPI and it came back saying, no great surprise, "Gee, you really think like a physician." Not only was my dad a physician, but most of the people I knew were physicians,
so I thought, *alright, I'll apply to medical school.* And lo and behold, here I am.

I became an anesthesiologist. Why anesthesiology? What I discovered I *loved* in medical school was physiology and pharmacology. And the beauty of anesthesia is that it's
applied physiology and applied pharmacology. And you have to be really good with your
hands, which I am. I was a sculptor for many years. So, when you put it all together,
I ended up in anesthesia because it is hands-on and you get to spend all this time thinking
about cardiac, respiratory, and vascular physiology, and tinker with all these drugs. Oh,
what fun.

I finished my training in 1985. I was an academic anesthesiologist doing cardiac and
acute care work, I did some pediatrics until 1991, and then I went into private practice in
a community hospital. We were the only anesthesia group in that hospital, but we were
independent physicians. I did that from 1991 to 2006, although more and more of my work
was administrative and less and less was anesthesia. It was something like 60% anesthesia,
then 40%, then 20%, and then I stopped. In 2007 I went out on my own and started Pascal
Metrics. We started Safe and Reliable Care, the company I'm in right now, in 2011. I basically moved from clinical care and administration to being a businessman.

I was thrust into this world in the late 1990s. I was chairman of the pharmacy and
therapeutics committee when there were two terrible deaths in the space of a week,
new moms, one of which was due to an overdose of narcotics. Neither of them was my
patient. I was one of the central figures in analyzing why those deaths occurred. Part of
the hospital's response to the investigatory and regulatory fever that resulted was to hire
me for, essentially, 40% of my time, to think about how to make administering medication
in the hospital safer. That was 1997. That launched me out of my clinical practice and by
1998 I was running collaborative studies. In 1998 I went to a drug event collaborative at the
Institute for Healthcare Improvement and in 1999 I co-chaired the next one. In 1999–2000
I went from doing clinical work to thinking about this world of safety and reliability. And
now, in 2018, the area that I choose to think about and that I enjoy thinking about concerns
the culture and the places where healthcare personnel live, and how that relates to their
ability to deliver safe and reliable care. That's what I've done for almost 20 years now.

Healthcare organizations hire my company, Safe and Reliable Care, to evaluate their culture, and that's Culture writ large—safety culture is included in that but so is burnout, resilience, and engagement. Organizations sometimes ask us for help in improving the safety and reliability of their care, so I go in and interview staff and help put together programs to train middle management and senior leadership to run their organizations more effectively. I work across the board with front-line clinicians as well as leadership. Sometimes organizations are interested in bringing in management systems to increase their effectiveness in ensuring both safety and joy in work.

I'm equally interested in the care patients receive—obviously that's the "holy grail"— but the fact is that patients receive what the people working in healthcare are able to deliver. If healthcare professionals have a great deal of joy in work, then the likelihood is they're going to deliver a better product for the patients.

Defining Culture

The first thing we need to do is to define what culture is. We have to define it before we can start to talk about how it changes. Colloquial descriptions of culture—"the way we do things around here"—is a nice little "button" statement but it isn't very helpful. When we look at the surveys we've gotten, what are we looking at? There's a panoply of things that, when you put them all together, paint a picture of something called "culture."

It is pretty clear, based on the decades of experience we've had in doing this work--and also from the literature, both inside and outside of healthcare—that there are certain types of environments people come away from saying, "This place is special." Over the years I've been doing this work, when I go into one of these environments people basically say the same thing. In probably the most common statement, or variations of it, people will say, "I can't imagine working anywhere else than right here, because nowhere else makes me feel as good about myself as here." Which, when you think about it, is an extraordinarily powerful statement.

If you tease that back and ask, "What is it about places where people would be inclined to make that statement?" the "elevator description" of what characterizes those places emerges. One of the big ones is: "My values and the values of the people who run this place, the senior leaders, are aligned. So, when I come in each day to do the work, I feel I'm doing work that is perceived as valuable by the organization and our interests are all aligned." Most people go into healthcare because they want to help people, so there's a sense that everyone is working in the same direction. That's hugely powerful. As people move up into the senior levels of administration, there is a tendency to pursue the wrong kind of metrics, especially financial ones, which are huge. These metrics are obviously needed, but they are secondary to the core values: that is, to take care of patients and deliver to them the best care. The way to do that is to be the best. The finances will stem from that, not the other way around. So that alignment is number one.

The other two characteristics of places where people feel good about working, which are massive, are, first, "I have voice. I have voice so I have the opportunity to speak up. I have an equal opportunity as everyone else to speak up, although not necessarily at the same time, and when I speak up, my voice leads to actions and changes around me so I can see that my voice influences my alignment." And, second, "I have a sense that the people around me care about me."

When you arrive in places where the perception is, we're all pulling oars in the same direction and our values are aligned; I have the opportunity to speak up and, when I do, changes occur that make things better or, at least, that my voice is responded to; and I have a sense that the people around me actually care about me, those are the places where people say, "You know, I can't imagine working any place else because there are so few places like this." We measure culture by asking questions that examine these attributes, or domains. When we ask such questions over time, we get a feel for how the culture is changing.

Two of the domains we measure are learning and local leadership. We ask: 1) To what degree are we capable of improvement? Do we look at ourselves, reflect, and take action when appropriate? 2) To what degree does local leadership support that process of self-reflection? 3) To what degree do I have a relationship with my manager, the person I report to, in which they coach and give me good feedback, taking time to pause and reflect on these issues? It turns out that one of the main, if not *the* main determinant of how long people stay in their jobs is the relationship they have with the person they report to. That is number one.

We measure the domains of teamwork and collaboration: 1) To what extent do we work together? 2) How difficult are the colleagues I work with? 3) How much psycho-logical safety is there? 4) How comfortable am I speaking up about a variety of issues? 5) How effective is communication in my unit and with other units?

We measure the safety domain, which looks similar to the teamwork domain, with subtle differences: 1) Do we learn from our errors? (which is really a management function); and 2) Would I feel safe being treated here as a patient? (which is a global statement about safety). Teamwork is multifactorial because it focuses on communication, difficult colleagues, psychological safety, and collaboration. The domains of learning, leadership, teamwork, and collaboration outlined so far relate to culture.

We measure burnout by asking another category of questions: 1) Do you feel emotion-ally exhausted, frustrated, burned out? and 2) How do you perceive the others around you? Do you perceive *them* as exhausted, frustrated, and burned out? Burnout is a spec-trum of mild to severe symptoms that begins with emotional exhaustion and frustra-tion, progresses to cynicism, then inefficacy and depersonalization, and then to complete burnout, at which point one has lost interest. The vast majority of physicians who, when we talk about burnout in healthcare and look at those studies, show signs of the earlier stages—emotional exhaustion and frustration. According to the most recent studies, 54% of physicians nationally are showing some signs of burnout. I think that has a lot to do with the emotional exhaustion/frustration stage, which is early on in the game—it's not that half of the physicians are actually cynical and depersonalizing patients, which is far into the spectrum. But burnout has certainly gotten worse because of the pressure physicians are under.

The concept of resilience has two parts and is the focus of another set of questions: 1) To what degree do I feel that I thrive in this environment? To thrive means, "At the end of the day I'm invigorated by the work I do." To thrive, there must be some element of what we call flow in the work one does. There's something special about the concentration and the sense of enjoyment one gets from the work itself. So thriving is obviously very special, and God only knows, it's rare. The other part of resilience is: 2) What is my capacity to recover when things go badly, or when things aren't great? One obviously wants to be able to recover quickly.

The third group of questions focuses on what we call engagement: 1) Do I earn a living wage? 2) Can I advance appropriately? 3) For the people who do advance around me, is that process is seen as fair? 4) Can I grow in this position and can the organization help me grow? And then a couple of questions address job certainty: 1) Do I think I'll be in this position in a year? and 2) Will I have the opportunity to leave this position?

In general, the higher you are in the hierarchy, the better it feels and the more glowing things appear to look. We certainly see that people who title themselves as administrators and managers tend to have the rosiest view of the world. The interesting thing about physicians is that their status has been changing over the last few decades. The perception of autonomy by physicians is really on the wane. When you think about what's happening, at least in the U.S., we are buying physicians' practices at a massive rate right now, putting them on salary, and, in a sense, bringing them into the hierarchy; when they were independent they could come in, ply their trade, and leave. They certainly felt very independent then and they perceived the world as more attractive than they do now. But now that they receive salaries and have been brought into the hierarchy, they increasingly find themselves subject to the demands of the organization. So, their level of satisfaction has been dropping—in part because of this change in status and in part because of the electronic medical record, which has been so destructive to culture. The electronic medical record makes life for physicians and nurses more complicated, not necessarily better.

What is certainly true is that the lower down you go in the hierarchy—for example, social workers, nurses, nursing assistants, and transportation folks—the lower are their perceptions of the world. And that then becomes *very* variable, depending on which unit or work setting they're in. So, the culture can look very different in different places. But if you just take the average across thousands of people, the world looks better the higher you are in the hierarchy.

On Joy in Work

How do I define joy in work? It's an interesting question. I know I've experienced it clinically and in the intervention work we do. Csikszentmihalyi talks about the concept of flow. You know, you come in to do something and it's so engrossing and so enjoyable that time passes so quickly you don't even notice it. I used to have days as an anesthesiologist when it was so satisfying to go in and meet people and put in anesthetic blocks and deal with problems. I loved that early in my career. I got tired of it after a while, which was perhaps why I ended up where I ended up. But I would say the same is true for the work I do now. My joy in work now is going into organizations and spending time teaching people how to think about the issues we're talking about; joy actually manifests itself when people come back to me and say, "Because of what I learned from you (or your group), what I do now, I can do better; and I like it more; and I think I deliver better care to patients." This occurs reasonably frequently I'm pleased to say. But it certainly is rare enough that when it does occur, I realize that's the reason I get up every day.

Joy in work is feeling capable in an environment where you have influence. I guess I can say, I have voice. I have a sense that the people around me care about me, both in my company and in the places where I go to work. And when I see all that come together and change the care of patients for the better, it's very powerful.

On Money and Joy

In terms of the relationship between money and joy, think about Maslow's hierarchy. You need to have enough money to have a roof over your head and to buy food. And then after that it's pretty clear to me that there is most certainly not a direct relationship between money and joy.

What Diminishes Joy

What diminishes joy in work for me? Oh God. In my space I manage people. Managing difficult people is just a royal pain in the neck. In our company we have about 20 people at this point. The work that characterizes us is that we're always on the edge of what we know how to do because our growth has been pretty explosive. That is tremendously exciting. But managing the people when they disagree with each other is not so exciting.

What we don't do very well in healthcare, for the most part, is leadership. Leaders have to set behavioral expectations and then be comfortable sticking to the line. People are like small children in grown-up bodies. It's just amazing how silly people can be in their behavior, so leaders have to state expectations for behavior in terms of being respectful and professional in the clinical environment. Leaders have to verbalize these expectations and be clear every single day. In the clinical environment, a big part of people loving or not loving what they do depends on how effectively the leaders around them have established these expectations and hold people to account. Because if leaders don't do that, then people misbehave. And when that happens, all those things that contribute to joy in work and achieving flow become harder to achieve. Managing is really hard. I'm doing it in my own company, but every time I walk into hospitals and look at what senior leaders are supposed to do, and what middle managers get hired to do, they are not taught to do what I'm describing. A few do it well. Some will never do it well. And then you've got this huge group in the middle who are well-meaning but who haven't been trained.

It can be very frustrating for me to go into organizations where leaders and staff are so misaligned that in order for me to do *my* work, senior leadership first has to do the work that needs to be done. If I haven't been brought in to realign the leadership but they're looking for results without the necessary alignment, it's difficult. Someone from a service might call me in, like the chief of surgery or the emergency room. I come in to look at the service and realize it is made up of the chief nursing officer and all the ancillary personnel, like respiratory and transportation. Then radiology is linked to the emergency room, so I'm very quickly back at the clinical leaders. And even when the clinical leaders—the chief medical officer and chief nursing officer—call me in to do the work but the people who pull the purse strings—the chief operating and the chief financial officer—aren't aligned in the direction the clinical leaders want the organization to go, and they very often are not aligned, then it means the board and CEO haven't figured out how to get anybody to pull the oars in the same direction. I go into one organization after another where the disagreements at the senior level are significant enough, or the activities are siloed enough, that there is little chance for the units of the organization to achieve what I think everyone wants them to achieve.

Here's an example. I go up to a nurse manager because nursing is such a key role at every level, both in acute care and out in the community. I ask a nurse, "How do you spend your time?" And I've had nurses tell me, "I spend 40% of my time on payroll and finances and 30% of my time on supply management." Well, they're supposed to be running a self-reflecting, improvement-capable unit. And 70% of their time is spent on tasks like payroll and making sure they have supplies. That's stupid. I ask, "Why 40% on payroll and finance?" The answer is, "Because payroll and finance is so disorganized that people can't figure out if their paychecks are right, and they're not getting their overtime worked out, and so my staff is complaining to me, and then I've to go and talk to payroll about it." I go back to the leadership and say, "You've got to be kidding me. You give these managers these clinical workloads and they have to spend half of their time figuring out paychecks? And you want them to make sure that the clinical operations are reliable?"

People have to be capable at what they're doing. An organization may have to hire more people. Maybe a finance/payroll system is so antiquated that it doesn't work, or maybe there is an ineffective person whose job it is to fix it. People in finance may think they are the most important in the organization because money drives everything. They set expectations for what's going on at the front lines because they want to make sure that every dollar is accounted for. Who's going to argue with that? I wouldn't argue with that, but what I would say is that if my clinical manager is spending 40% of his or her time trying to get that right, then the organization is absolutely looking at the wrong metrics of effectiveness and is pretty much guaranteed to be mediocre. I run into that all the time—all the time. It's about value alignment. It's catastrophic when values are not aligned.

Reflections

I genuinely believe people come in to do good work and that the mechanism to achieve what I want to achieve depends on seeing the good in people. And then it's necessary to negotiate and get people to collaborate. Collaboration means that when people have differences, they have to explore them, and inquire carefully and gently enough about them, to be able to see things differently, and in a bigger way, so they can come to an agreement. It's not always perfect, but the process leaves people feeling intact, like they've had a say, and that they're heading in the right direction. That is both challenging and satisfying.

The other thing I'd say is that the complexity of care, the complexity of patients, and the complexity of organizations—which have grown exponentially year by year—requires increasingly refined systems to deliver good care, certainly in terms of our ability to make and to treat diagnoses. There are more diagnoses to be made and more treatments to be delivered and delivered effectively. That's why a doctor's life has become much more complex.

What's also become more complex is that we've realized that care has to occur across the continuum. It's not just acute care; it is also the whole process that goes on in the community. Public health is becoming increasingly more integrated in the U.S.—but the integration of that activity is really complicated because now we're dealing with all the community services linked to hospitals and physician groups. And people are living longer with more comorbidities. This is more than anyone expected they'd have to manage. There are so many people to train. The National Health Service in England has done a much better job because they're further ahead as a national health system. This has hit us hard. And with all of that, we want people to have joy in work as they do this. So, leaders have a very tough job.

Index